+HD30.28 .S385 1990+

HD
30.28
S385
1990

Selected cases in
strategic
management

DATE DUE

MAR 7 1996

7/17, 2003

2/26/04

COLLEGE FOR HUMAN SERVICES
LIBRARY
845 HUDSON STREET
NEW YORK, N.Y. 10014

McGraw-Hill Series in Management
Fred Luthans and Keith Davis, Consulting Editors

Arnold and Feldman: Organizational Behavior
Cascio: Managing Human Resources: Productivity, Quality of Work Life, Profits
Certo and Peter: Selected Cases in Strategic Management
Certo and Peter: Strategic Management: A Focus on Process
Certo and Peter: Strategic Management: Concepts and Applications
Daughtrey and Ricks: Contemporary Supervision: Managing People and Technology
Davis and Newstrom: Human Behavior at Work: Organizational Behavior
Dobler, Lee, and Burt: Purchasing and Materials Management: Text and Cases
Dunn and Rachel: Wage and Salary Administration: Total Compensation Systems
Feldman and Arnold: Managing Individual and Group Behavior in Organizations
Frederick, Davis, Post: Business and Society: Management, Public Policy, Ethics
Gerloff: Organizational Theory and Design: A Strategic Approach for Management
Hampton: Management
Hampton: Inside Management: Readings from *Business Week*
Hodgetts: Effective Supervision: A Practical Approach
Jauch and Glueck: Business Policy and Strategic Management
Jauch and Glueck: Strategic Management and Business Policy
Jauch and Townsend: Cases in Strategic Management and Business Policy
Karlins: The Human Use of Human Resources
Kast and Rosenzweig: Experiential Exercises and Cases in Management
Knudson, Woodworth, and Bell: Management: An Experiential Approach
Koontz and Weihrich: Essentials of Management
Koontz and Weihrich: Management
Kopelman: Managing Productivity in Organizations: A Practical, People-Oriented Perspective

Levin, Rubin, Stinson, and Gardner: Quantitative Approaches to Management
Luthans: Organizational Behavior
Luthans and Thompson: Contemporary Readings in Organizational Behavior
Miles: Theories of Management: Implications for Organizational Behavior and Development
Miles and Snow: Organizational Strategy, Structure, and Process
Mills: Labor-Management Relations
Mitchell and Larson: People in Organizations: An Introduction to Organizational Behavior
Molander: Responsive Capitalism: Case Studies in Corporate Social Conduct
Monks: Operations Management: Theory and Problems
Newstrom and Davis: Organizational Behavior: Readings and Exercises
Pearce and Robinson: Corporate Strategies: Readings from *Business Week*
Porter and McKibbin: Management Education and Development: Drift or Thrust into the 21st Century?
Prasow and Peters: Arbitration and Collective Bargaining: Conflict Resolution in Labor Relations
Quick and Quick: Organizational Stress and Preventive Management
Rue and Holland: Strategic Management: Concepts and Experiences
Rugman, Lecraw, and Booth: International Business: Firm and Environment
Sayles: Leadership: Managing in Real Organizations
Schlesinger, Eccles, and Gabarro: Managing Behavior in Organizations: Text, Cases and Readings
Schroeder: Operations Management: Decision Making in the Operations Function
Sharplin: Strategic Management
Steers and Porter: Motivation and Work Behavior
Steinhoff and Burgess: Small Business Management Fundamentals
Sutermeister: People and Productivity
Walker: Human Resource Planning
Weihrich: Management Excellence: Productivity through MBO
Werther and Davis: Human Resources and Personnel Management
Wofford, Gerloff, and Cummins: Organizational Communications: The Keystone to Managerial Effectiveness

SELECTED CASES IN STRATEGIC MANAGEMENT

SAMUEL C. CERTO
Roy E. Crummer Graduate School of Business
Rollins College

J. PAUL PETER
University of Wisconsin—Madison

McGraw-Hill Publishing Company

New York St. Louis San Francisco Auckland Bogotá
Caracas Hamburg Lisbon London Madrid Mexico
Milan Montreal New Delhi Oklahoma City Paris
San Juan São Paulo Singapore Sydney Tokyo Toronto

SELECTED CASES IN STRATEGIC MANAGEMENT

Copyright © 1990 by McGraw-Hill, Inc.

All rights reserved. Portions of this book have been taken from *Strategic Management: Concepts and Applications*. Copyright © 1988 by Random House, Inc. All rights reserved. Printed in the United States of America. Except as permitted under the United States Copyright Act of 1976, no part of this publication may be reproduced or distributed in any form or by any means, or stored in a data base or retrieval system, without the prior written permission of the publisher.

2 3 4 5 6 7 8 9 0 DOC DOC 9 4 3 2 1 0

ISBN 0-07-010448-4

This book was set in Veljovic Book by Monotype Composition Company.
The editors were Kathleen L. Loy and Peggy C. Rehberger;
the production supervisor was Louise A. Karam.
The cover was designed by Rafael Hernandez.
R. R. Donnelley & Sons Company was printer and binder.

Library of Congress Cataloging-in-Publication Data

Selected cases in strategic management/Samuel C. Certo, J. Paul Peter.
   p.   cm.—(McGraw-Hill series in management)
  ISBN 0-07-010448-4
   1. Strategic planning—Case studies.   I. Certo, Samuel C.
II. Peter, J. Paul.   III. Series.
HD30.28.S385   1990
  658.4'012—dc20   89-7999

CONTENTS

Preface xi

SECTION ONE OVERVIEW OF STRATEGIC MANAGEMENT 1

CASE 1 TSR Hobbies, Inc. / Margaret Friedman 3
   INDUSTRIAL HIGHLIGHT ■ TOYS AND GAMES INDUSTRY 10

CASE 2 Kitchen Made Pies / James J. Chrisman and Fred L. Fry 12
   INDUSTRIAL HIGHLIGHT ■ PROCESSED FOODS AND BEVERAGES INDUSTRY 24

CASE 3 **Classic Case:** Wall Drug Store / James D. Taylor, Robert L. Johnson, and Gene B. Iverson 29
   INDUSTRIAL HIGHLIGHT ■ DRUG STORE SEGMENT OF THE RETAIL TRADE INDUSTRY 47

SECTION TWO ENVIRONMENTAL ANALYSIS AND ORGANIZATIONAL DIRECTION 51

CASE 4 Federal Express: Is There Any "Zip" Left in Zapmail? / Per V. Jenster 53
   INDUSTRIAL HIGHLIGHT ■ TRANSPORTATION SERVICES INDUSTRY 65

CONTENTS

CASE 5   Caterpillar Tractor Company / Donald W. Eckrich   71
INDUSTRIAL HIGHLIGHT ■ CONSTRUCTION MACHINERY INDUSTRY   82

CASE 6   Kellogg Company and the Ready-to-Eat Cereal Industry / Joseph A. Schenk, Dan S. Prickett, and Stanley J. Stough   85
INDUSTRIAL HIGHLIGHT ■ CONFECTIONERY AND BAKED GOODS INDUSTRY   113

CASE 7   **Classic Case:** The Southland Corporation / J. W. Brown   117
INDUSTRIAL HIGHLIGHT ■ FOOD RETAILING SEGMENT OF THE RETAIL TRADE INDUSTRY   136

SECTION THREE   STRATEGY FORMULATION   143

CASE 8   Midstate Dental Lab, Inc. / Lynda L. Goulet and Peter G. Goulet   145
INDUSTRIAL HIGHLIGHT ■ MEDICAL AND DENTAL INSTRUMENTS AND SUPPLIES INDUSTRY   156

CASE 9   Toys 'R' Us / Caron St. John   159
INDUSTRIAL HIGHLIGHT ■ DOLLS, TOYS, GAMES, AND CHILDREN'S VEHICLES INDUSTRIES   171

CASE 10   Turner Broadcasting Systems, Inc. / William H. Davidson and G. Robert Joseph   174
INDUSTRIAL HIGHLIGHT ■ BROADCASTING INDUSTRY   192

CASE 11   Pontiac Division of General Motors / Peter Langenhorst and William E. Fulmer   196
INDUSTRIAL HIGHLIGHT ■ MOTOR VEHICLES INDUSTRY   222

CASE 12   K Mart Stores: Where America Shops and Saves / John L. Little and Larry D. Alexander   227
INDUSTRIAL HIGHLIGHT ■ RETAIL TRADE INDUSTRY   248

CASE 13   Hershey Foods / Richard T. Hise   251
INDUSTRIAL HIGHLIGHT ■ CONFECTIONERY PRODUCTS INDUSTRY   274

CASE 14   **Classic Case:** Anheuser-Busch Companies, Inc. / Douglas J. Workman et al.   277
INDUSTRIAL HIGHLIGHT ■ ALCOHOLIC BEVERAGES INDUSTRY   300

SECTION FOUR   STRATEGY IMPLEMENTATION AND CONTROL   305

CASE 15   Lema Supply Company / Mary Couter and Charles Boyd   307
   INDUSTRIAL HIGHLIGHT ■ GENERAL COMPONENTS INDUSTRY   316

CASE 16   Nike, Inc. / Robert G. Wirthlin and Anthony P. Schlichte   318
   INDUSTRIAL HIGHLIGHT ■ SPORTING AND ATHLETIC GOODS INDUSTRY   328

CASE 17   The Lincoln Electric Company, 1989 / Arthur Sharplin   332
   INDUSTRIAL HIGHLIGHT ■ METALWORKING EQUIPMENT INDUSTRY   355

CASE 18   Polaroid Corporation/Inner City, Inc. / John A. Seeger and Marie Rock   357
   INDUSTRIAL HIGHLIGHT ■ PHOTOGRAPHIC EQUIPMENT AND SUPPLIES INDUSTRY   375

CASE 19   Mary Kay Cosmetics, Inc. / Phyllis G. Holland   381
   INDUSTRIAL HIGHLIGHT ■ COSMETICS INDUSTRY   399

CASE 20   Hines Industries, Inc. / Robert P. Crowner   405
   INDUSTRIAL HIGHLIGHT ■ PUMPS AND COMPRESSORS INDUSTRY   426

CASE 21   **Classic Case:** Marion Laboratories, Inc. / Marilyn L. Taylor and Kenneth Beck   429
   INDUSTRIAL HIGHLIGHT ■ DRUGS AND COSMETICS INDUSTRY   450

SECTION FIVE   SPECIAL ISSUES IN STRATEGIC MANAGEMENT   455

CASE 22   Tylenol's Capsule Crisis: Part I / Yaakov Weber   457
   INDUSTRIAL HIGHLIGHT ■ DRUG INDUSTRY   474

CASE 23   Tylenol's Capsule Crisis: Part II / Yaakov Weber   477
   INDUSTRIAL HIGHLIGHT ■ DRUG INDUSTRY   487

CONTENTS

CASE 24   Coca-Cola Company / Lincoln W. Deihl and
          Thomas C. Neil   489
              INDUSTRIAL HIGHLIGHT ■ BOTTLED AND CANNED SOFT DRINK
              INDUSTRY   515

CASE 25   Ford of Europe / H. Landis Gabel and Anthony E. Hall   520
              INDUSTRIAL HIGHLIGHT ■ MOTOR VEHICLES INDUSTRY   545

CASE 26   **Classic Case:** Fourwinds Marina / W. Harvey Hegarty and
          Harry Kelsey, Jr.   552
              INDUSTRIAL HIGHLIGHT ■ HOTELS AND MOTELS INDUSTRY   565

SECTION SIX   A COMPREHENSIVE APPROACH TO
ANALYZING STRATEGIC PROBLEMS AND CASES   569

APPENDIX   SELECTED SOURCES OF SECONDARY
             INFORMATION   589

PREFACE

Selected Cases in Strategic Management is designed for both undergraduate and graduate courses in strategic management or business policy that emphasize learning through the case method. It can be used as the sole text in the course or in conjunction with other texts or methods including the authors' *Strategic Management: A Focus on Process,* which contains an exposition of strategic management theory.

The cases in this book are divided into five sections which include (1) Overview of Strategic Management, (2) Environmental Analysis and Organizational Direction, (3) Strategy Formulation, (4) Strategy Implementation and Control, and (5) Special Issues in Strategic Management. In addition, each section ends with a classic case. A classic case is a case which has been successfully used in strategic management education for a number of years and is viewed by both instructors and students as an excellent learning device.

It cannot be overemphasized, however, that all the cases in this book are multidimensional and contain a number of different issues for analysis. The cases are included in each section because an important *part* of their analysis involves issues suggested by the section heading, not because they deal only with these issues. For example, a special feature of this book is that each case concludes with an *Industrial Highlight* that gives an overview of the industry at the approximate time of the case. These highlights may contain useful information for analysis independent of the section the case is listed in. Thus, while case analysts should be mindful of the issues involved in each case section, they should not overlook other important areas of strategic management analysis.

The final section of the book offers a comprehensive approach to analyzing strategic management problems and cases. We believe that this section is useful for developing strategic management case analysis skills. It is placed at the end of the book for convenient reference should the instructor choose to emphasize this approach.

INSTRUCTOR'S RESOURCE PACKAGE

Selected Cases in Strategic Management is supported by a comprehensive Instructor's Resource Package. The package consists of the following items:

- *Case Enrichment Portfolio.* This innovative supplement features detailed support materials for each of the cases. It includes transparency masters, teaching notes, current company issues, case analysis visuals, industry highlight notes, in-class exercises, and supplemental discussion questions.
- *Computer Software Package.* In recognition of the growing popularity of microcomputer use in case analysis, a software package has been developed for use with a number of the cases in this book. *Decision-Making Toolkit for Strategic Management* by Joseph A. Russo, Jr. and Melvyn Fisher, both of Pace University, can be used in conjunction with Lotus 1-2-3 or STARCALC spreadsheet packages. This software allows students to use personal computers effectively in strategic management analysis.

ACKNOWLEDGMENTS

There are many people to whom we offer our sincerest thanks. First, of course, are the authors who contributed the outstanding cases that make up the body of this book. These authors include:

Larry D. Alexander, *Virginia Polytechnic Institute and State University*
Kenneth Beck, *University of Kansas*
Rich Bonaventura, *University of Virginia*
J. W. Brown, *University of Tennessee*
Charles Boyd, *Southwest Missouri State University*
John Cary, *University of Virginia*
James J. Chrisman, *University of South Carolina*
Karen Cook, *University of Virginia*
Mary Couter, *Southwest Missouri State University*
Robert P. Crowner, *Eastern Michigan University*
William H. Davidson, *University of Southern California*
Lincoln W. Deihl, *Kansas State University*
Donald W. Eckrich, *Ithaca College*
Margaret Friedman, *University of Wisconsin*
Fred L. Fry, *Bradley University*
William E. Fulmer, *University of Virginia*
H. Landis Gabel, *INSEAD*
Lynda L. Goulet, *University of Northern Iowa*
Peter G. Goulet, *University of Northern Iowa*
Anthony E. Hall, *INSEAD*

W. Harvey Hegarty, *Indiana University*
Richard T. Hise, *Texas A & M University*
Phyllis G. Holland, *Valdosta State College*
Gene B. Iverson, *University of South Dakota*
Per V. Jenster, *University of Virginia*
Robert L. Johnson, *University of South Dakota*
G. Robert Joseph
Harry Kelsey, Jr., *California State College*
Peter Langenhorst, *University of Virginia*
John L. Little, *University of North Carolina, Greensboro*
Scott McMasters, *University of Virginia*
Thomas C. Neil, *Atlanta University*
Dan S. Prickett, *Bell South*
Marie Rock, *Data General Corp.*
Joseph A. Schenk, *University of Dayton*
Anthony P. Schlichte, *Butler University*
John A. Seeger, *Bentley College*
Arthur Sharplin, *Northeast Louisiana University*
Neil H. Snyder, *University of Virginia*
Stanley J. Stough, *Southeast Missouri State University*
Caron St. John, *Georgia State University*
James D. Taylor, *University of South Dakota*
Marilyn L. Taylor, *University of Kansas*
Yaakov Weber, *University of Kentucky*
Robert G. Wirthlin, *Butler University*
Douglas J. Workman, *University of Virginia*

Second, we are grateful to the members of the case advisory board for their hard work and recommendations of outstanding cases. These educators include:

Phil Fisher, *University of South Dakota*
C. Kendrick Gibson, *Hope College*
Barry Gilmore, *Memphis State University*
Robert Goldberg, *Northeastern University*
Rose Knotts, *North Texas State University*
Dan Kopp, *Southwest Missouri State University*
Charles Schilling, *University of Wisconsin—Platteville*
James R. Sowers, *University of Houston*
Irv Summers, *Avila College*
R. W. Swisher, *Troy State University*
Marilyn Taylor, *University of Kansas*
Charles E. Watson, *Miami University*

Finally, we extend thanks to our colleagues, students and the many other strategic management educators who provided inputs into our thinking about this project. We acknowledge the support of Dean Martin Schatz of the Crummer Graduate School, Rollins College, and Dean James Hickman of the School of Business, University of Wisconsin—Madison, who have supported our efforts. We also thank June Smith and her staff at McGraw-Hill who made this project a reality. Of course, we thank our families and friends for their encouragement and tolerance during the preparation of this book.

Samuel C. Certo
J. Paul Peter

SELECTED CASES IN STRATEGIC MANAGEMENT

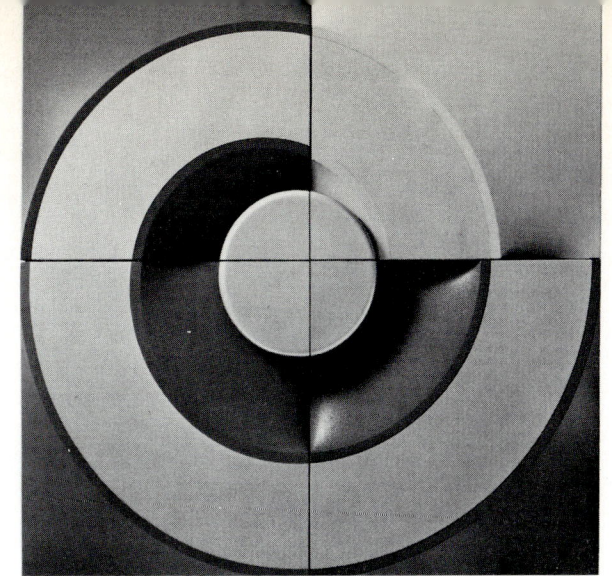

SECTION ONE

Overview of Strategic Management

CASE 1

TSR Hobbies, Inc.

MARGARET L. FRIEDMAN
University of Wisconsin–Whitewater

TSR (Tactical Studies Rules) Hobbies, Inc., had grown rapidly since its start in 1973 to sales of $27 million in fiscal 1983. TSR's star product responsible for this rapid growth was "Dungeons and Dragons," a unique fantasy/adventure game. The game was unique because it happened largely in the minds of its players. Its emphasis on cooperation among players and dependence upon their imaginative powers set it apart from traditional board games.

OVERVIEW

Company History

TSR Hobbies, Inc. was founded by E. Gary Gygax in a small Wisconsin resort town. Gygax never graduated from high school, but pursued his passion for fantasy in the forms of war games and science fiction books. When Gygax lost his job as an insurance underwriter in 1970, he started developing fantasy games almost full-time, while supporting his family with a shoe repair business in his basement. In 1973 Gygax persuaded a boyhood friend and fellow war game enthusiast, Donald Kaye, to borrow $1,000 against his life insurance and TSR Hobbies, Inc. was founded.

The two gamers published a popular set of war game rules for lead miniatures called "Cavaliers and Roundheads." In January of 1974 another inveterate gamer friend, Brian Blume, invested $2,000 in the company, and the three partners printed the first set of rules for "Dungeons and Dragons." The game was assembled in the Gygax home and was sold through an established network of professional gamers. In 1974, 1,000 sets of the "Dungeons and Dragons" game were sold. Eight years later it was selling at the rate of 750,000 per year. The sales history for the company is shown in Exhibit 1.

The rapid growth of TSR was not necessarily a reflection of keen and experienced management skill. The three top officers in the company all lacked formal management training, but felt they could remedy this deficiency by taking management courses and seminars. Although TSR wanted to attract

---

This case was prepared by Margaret L. Friedman, Assistant Professor, School of Business, University of Wisconsin–Whitewater. Reprinted by permission of the author.

OVERVIEW OF STRATEGIC MANAGEMENT

EXHIBIT 1 TSR Hobbies Sales

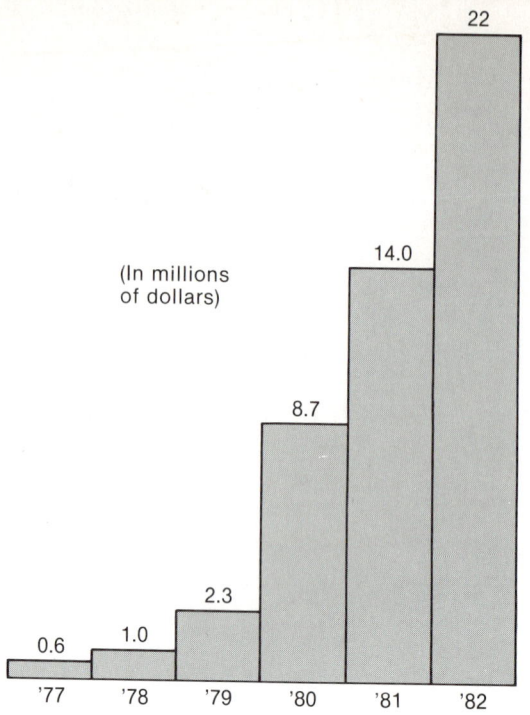

Source: Adapted from *The Wall Street Journal*, January 7, 1983.

older, experienced toy and game managers to their ranks, most of their recruits came from outside the toy/game/hobby industry.

Between 1977 and 1982 the TSR work force grew from 12 to more than 250 employees. Gygax's original partner, Donald Kaye, died of a heart attack in 1975, and so the partnership was assumed by Gygax and brothers Brian and Kevin Blume. Gygax was president of TSR, Kevin was chief executive, and Brian was executive vice president. All company decisions were directed through Kevin Blume, from major decisions down to authorization for a $12 desk calendar for a secretary. There was some personnel turnover and evidence of employee dissatisfaction due to nepotism in the company's hiring policies. It was reported that between 10 and 20 of Brian Blume's relatives were on the company's payroll.

The "Dungeons and Dragons" Game

"Dungeons and Dragons" represented a significant innovation in the game and hobby industry. A basic set for a "Dungeons and Dragons" game consisted of a lengthy instruction book, dice, and a wax pencil, all of which sold for $12.

The game begins when each player generates a mythical character with a roll of the dice. The personality profile for each character is determined according to rigorous guidelines given in the instruction booklet. For example, there is a Dungeon Master role in each game. It is the Dungeon Master who develops a map of the dungeon layout as there is no game board. Each character has particular spells and powers which are critical in negotiating the game's adventure. The goal is to navigate through a treacherous dungeon, arrive at a particular destination, and depart alive with the treasure. The combination of mythical characters and adventure is why "Dungeons and Dragons" is called a role-playing/fantasy/adventure game. No two "Dungeons and Dragons" games are alike since the way the game unfolds depends upon the players' imaginations.

To survive, players must work together, rather than against one another, winding their way through a dangerous path to the treasure. Players are confronted with conquest after conquest involving ghouls, monsters, dragons, and other obstacles to finding the treasure and escaping with it. The instruction booklet describes the various powers and spells available to the different characters and general rules for behaving in the dungeon. The crayon is used to keep track of pathways taken and used-up spells. The game can last from two hours to weeks on end—it is all up to the imaginative powers of the players.

MARKETING STRATEGY

TSR's goal was to double sales every year. The strategy used to achieve this goal was based heavily on target market expansion, product line expansion, expansion of promotional activities, and more intensive distribution.

Expansion of Target Market

When "Dungeons and Dragons" was first introduced, it was targeted solely to experienced gamers. The first edition of the game came in a plain brown bag and the rules were so complex that only experienced gamers could decipher them. Word of the game spread to college campuses with the help of publicity involving a Michigan State University student who was rumored to be lost in the steam tunnels under the campus while playing a "live" "Dungeons and Dragons" game. This potentially negative publicity for "Dungeons and Dragons" turned into an advantage for the company since it created word-of-mouth advertising and interest among college students.

As the product matured, the median age of new buyers dropped from college age to the 10–14-year-old bracket. Typically, these consumers were boys described as introverted, intelligent, nonathletic, and very imaginative. The game provided an outlet for such boys to join in a group activity and helped bring them out of their shells. In fact, educators noted that "Dungeons and Dragons" welds a group of players into an ongoing joint project that teaches participation, assertiveness, and cooperation.

To further increase sales of the product, TSR targeted the product to new consumer groups. For example, at one point, women made up only 12 percent of the total number of purchasers. TSR conducted consumer research and found that women felt the game was created as a release for "macho" fantasies. Many women also stated that the lengthy instruction manual (63 pages) would take too long to read and be wasteful of their time. In response to such perceptions, TSR (1) publicized the fact that the game is not cutthroat and competitive, (2) reduced the length of the instruction manual, and (3) created a game which can be played in a limited amount of time. TSR also targeted downward to the younger children's market with a product that transferred the "Dungeons and Dragons" theme to a more conventional board game called "Dungeons!"

Expansion of Product Lines

Initially, the basic "Dungeons and Dragons" set was marketed as a hobby, rather than as a game. A hobby involves a starter toy which is enhanced with a myriad of add-ons. For example, a miniature train is considered a hobby since the engine and track form the basis for building an entire railroad system, including special cars, track, scenery, stations, and so on over time. Similarly, for each $12 basic "Dungeons and Dragons" set sold, retailers could expect an additional $150 in satellite or captive product purchases in the form of modules that provide supplemental adventures of varying complexity. There were at least 50 such satellite products on the market.

Since TSR management recognized that their short product line was vulnerable to competition from such toy and game giants as Mattel, Parker Brothers, Milton Bradley, and Ideal, several other new products were introduced to extend the line. Most of these new introductions followed the role-playing, fantasy theme. For example, since each fantasy world in a "Dungeons and Dragons" game has its own set of characters and monsters, a line of miniature lead figurines of these creatures was introduced. These included miniature dragons, wizards, and dwarves. Although these figurines are not necessary to play the game, it was hoped that a market of figurine collectors would develop.

TSR also marketed a number of other role-playing games, including "Top Secret," a spy adventure game; "Boot Hill," a western adventure game; "Gamma World," a futuristic game; and "Star Frontiers," a science fiction game, all of which were quite successful. Somewhat less successful have been TSR's other board game entrants, "Snit's Revenge," "The Awful Green Things from Outer Space," "Escape from New York," and "Dungeons!" These more conventional board games were intended to change the company's image from that of a producer of complex, esoteric games to a producer of a broader range of game products.

TSR also added new lines to their product mix. For example, they produced a feature-length film using a "Dungeons and Dragons" theme, as well as a successful Saturday morning cartoon program for children and an hour-long pilot for a radio-theater program.

TSR's other ventures included purchase of *Amazing* magazine, the oldest science fiction magazine on the market (since 1926) and publishing *Dragon* magazine which was begun in 1976 and obtained a circulation of over 70,000 copies per issue. The Dragon Publishing division of TSR also produced calendars and anthologies of fiction, nonfiction, and humor. TSR's most popular publications included *Endless Quest* books. Young readers determine the plot of these stories by making choices for the main character. Depending on the choices made, the reader is directed to different pages in the book. Therefore, each book contains a number of different adventure stories. TSR also developed a line of books called *Heart Quest*, which are romance novels for teenagers in this same create-your-own-plot format. TSR had performed consulting services for a failing needlework company owned by a friend of Gygax. To further its diversification efforts TSR acquired this company briefly, realizing soon, however, that it was a poor investment.

TSR found licensing to be a profitable form of product line expansion. Arrangements were made to permit 14 companies to market products that displayed the TSR and "Dungeons and Dragons" name. For example, Mattel, Inc. was sold a license for an electronic version of "Dungeons and Dragons" and St. Regis Paper Company was sold a license for a line of notebooks and school supplies.

Expansion of Promotional Activities

In the beginning, TSR relied on word-of-mouth advertising among gamers to sell the "Dungeons and Dragons" game. As their markets expanded, TSR employed other promotional methods, including television commercials and four-color magazine ads. TSR's ad budget in 1981 was $1,194,879 which was divided as follows: 13 percent on trade magazines, 28 percent on consumer magazines, and 59 percent on spot television. During the Christmas season of 1982, $1 million was spent on a television campaign for the "Dungeon!" board game.

The company's logo and accompanying slogan were updated in 1982. Formerly, the logo showed a wizard next to the letters TSR and the slogan "The Game Wizards." The updated logo included a stylized version of the letters "TSR" and the slogan "Products of the Imagination." This updated logo and slogan were designed to convey an image with broader market appeal.

TSR sponsored an annual gamers convention which attracted dozens of manufacturers and thousands of attendees to Kenosha, Wisconsin. This became the largest role-playing convention in the world which included four days of movies, demonstrations, tournaments, seminars, and manufacturers' exhibits. The company also sponsored the Role Playing Game Association. This association offered newsletters and informational services and was responsible for calculating international scoring points to rate players in official tournaments. It also provided a gift catalog of premiums available only to RPGA members.

In the beginning, the printing and artwork needed for the "Dungeons and Dragons" instruction booklet were contracted with suppliers outside of TSR.

The company has since engaged in backward vertical integration into the manufacturing process by hiring a staff of artists and purchasing its own printing facility.

Expansion of Distribution Channels

Retail distribution was originally concentrated in hobby stores, but expanded rapidly into department stores and bookstores, although some mass market retailers such as Sears, Penneys, and K mart were reluctant to stock all of the satellite products generated by the basic "Dungeons and Dragons" set. This evolution from exclusive distribution through hobby stores to intensive distribution followed naturally from the concomitant expansion of target markets and product lines.

Over time TSR employed as many as 15 manufacturers' representatives who marketed the product through independent wholesalers in nine territories. One problem with this distribution system was that the company did not have close contact with its wholesalers, and hence, was not able to offer much merchandising assistance.

TSR opened its own retail hobby shop for a brief period. However, this outlet attracted a lot of mail order business, creating channel conflict among other retail hobby outlets, and the shop was closed in 1984.

EXPANSION PROBLEMS

TSR obviously grew quickly and expanded in many different directions which caused several problems. For example, TSR announced it would hire over 100 new employees and 50 new hires were actually made in June of 1983. However, by April of 1984, over 230 employees were laid off. The rapid loss of personnel resulted in coordination problems. For example, two different products were packaged in boxes with identical graphics on the covers. The layoffs also created morale problems.

In an effort to "tighten the reigns," Kevin Blume eliminated half of the company's 12 divisions to streamline accounting, reporting, and general decision making. TSR was then divided into four separate companies: TSR Inc. for publishing games and books, TSR Ventures Inc. for supervising trademark licensing, TSR Worldwide Ltd. for managing international sales, and Dungeons and Dragons Entertainment Corporation for producing cartoons. Each company functioned independently of the others, with its own stock and board of directors. Still, the three partners sat on all four boards in order to maintain tight control over the company.

TSR's full-fledged entry into the mass market also drained their cash reserves, creating cash flow problems for the company. Business practices in the mass market were different than what TSR was accustomed to in the specialized hobby market. For example, it is common to cater to mass retailers by allowing six months payment whereas 30 days or less is more usual for small hobby shops. Also, demand is relatively smooth in the hobby market unlike the mass market which experiences a Christmas buying rush. Thus, TSR was not prepared for the retail Christmas buying rush and many items ordered were out-of-stock.

TSR also faced an image problem in the mass market, illustrated in the positioning map shown in Exhibit 2. The early success of "Dungeons and Dragons" depended largely upon its image as a mysterious hobby that was not for just anyone, but only for an elite few. Because of this image, many consumers in the mass market were convinced that the "Dungeons and Dragons" game was "bad for the mind" because it involved hours and hours of make-believe. Dr. Joyce Brothers was engaged to endorse the product and to legitimize its role-playing format. In supporting the product she pointed to research results illustrating that children who played "Dungeons and Dragons" developed better reading skills, math skills, and basic logic and problem solving skills.

TSR faced formidable competition in the mass market. Large companies such as Milton Bradley, Mattel, and Parker Brothers spent more on advertising each year than TSR earned in profits. However, TSR's fantasy/role-playing concept was unique. Only Mattel's "He Man" and "Masters of the Universe" could be remotely compared to TSR's product concept. While the other traditional toy and game giants had no comparable fantasy/role-playing games, they dominated the northwest quadrant of the map in Exhibit 2, the market TSR wanted to enter. Though TSR was a market leader in fantasy/role-playing games in the hobby market, it remained to be seen whether this type of product could gain a respectable share of the mass market.

EXHIBIT 2 Positioning Map

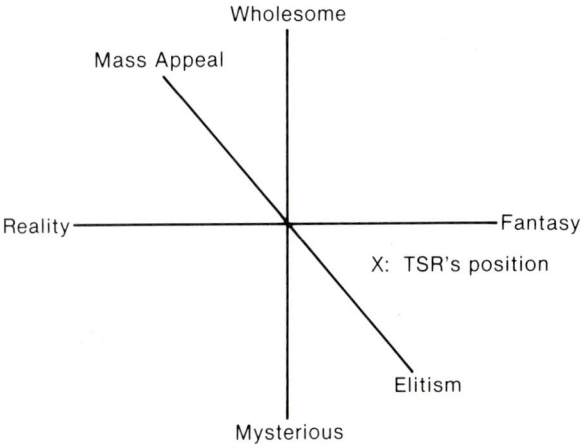

INDUSTRIAL HIGHLIGHT

Toys and Games Industry

Below is a capsule summary of the dolls, toys, games, and children's vehicles industry, of which TSR Hobbies, Inc., is a part. Information in this highlight was compiled by the U.S. Department of Commerce and focuses on this industry during the approximate period of time covered in the case. Keep in mind that industrial highlights contained in this text are not intended as a complete synopsis of an industry but as a profile of certain issues that can be relevant to a case situation.

CURRENT SITUATION

The current-dollar value of shipments of dolls, toys, games, and children's vehicles rose to an estimated $4.96 billion in 1983—adjusted for inflation, an increase of only 0.3 percent. This slow rise reflects a sharp decline in video game shipments, which severely constrained total industry shipments.

In 1983, shipments of video games, not including game cartridges, declined about 10 percent, in current dollars, to $1.6 billion, while shipments of dolls and traditional toys rose an estimated 7.7 percent to $3.36 billion. The traditional toy category was led by shipments of preschool toys, which increased an estimated 15 percent.

Price increases in the industry were moderate in 1983, so most of the change in current-dollar shipments was real and not the result of inflation. Through the first 6 months of 1983, producer prices for dolls rose at an annual rate of less than 1 percent and prices for traditional toys, 3 to 5 percent.

The changes in shipments represent dramatic shifts in the demand for toys in 1983. The decline in video game shipments follows a sharp rise in previous years, from $0.25 billion in 1979 to $1.76 billion in 1982. Conversely, the 1983 increase in shipments of traditional toys, excluding dolls, follows a decline from $2.77 billion in 1979 to $2.62 billion in 1982. Dolls shipments have risen steadily since 1980.

Employment in the industry rose slightly in 1983 after a 1982 decline. The number of production workers rose by an estimated 1,500, after falling 3,000

Source: U.S. Industrial Outlook, Department of Commerce, 1984, pp. 44-9–44-11.

in 1982. Nonproduction worker employment remained unchanged in 1983. Video game production workers were subject to layoffs, some permanent, in 1983 as shipments fell and production began to move offshore.

The current-dollar value of traditional toy shipments rose an estimated 8.0 percent in 1983. These shipments comprise toys, games, and children's vehicles, except video games. The growth was led by shipments of preschool toys, which increased an estimated 15 percent. Growth in domestic production of traditional toys has been very weak in the past decade, due in part to imports from the Far East. Imports of traditional toys rose from $188.5 million in 1972 to $1,011.0 million in 1982. Based on data for 6 months, 1983 imports of traditional toys and games will total $900 million. Exports of traditional toys declined 25 percent in 1983 to an estimated $115 million.

Dolls shipments rose an estimated 6 percent in 1983 to $520 million, while imports of dolls and parts rose 10 percent to $350 million. Exports of dolls and accessories, while only $15.8 million in 1983, were 21 percent above the depressed levels of 1982.

LONG-TERM PROSPECTS

Constant dollar shipments of dolls, toys, games, and children's vehicles are expected to increase at a compound annual rate of 1.0 percent through 1988. The decline of video games overshadows the long-term prospects of the industry. Many analysts, including some major producers, think the low-priced home computer will take the place of the video game console. Because of this shift, constant-dollar shipments of video games will decline an estimated 7.2 percent compounded annually during the 5-year period ending in 1988.

Shipments of dolls and traditional toys and games should do well in the 1983–1988 period. These items are primarily purchased for children from birth to 9, particularly the 5- to 9-year age group. The number of 5- to 9-year olds is expected to grow 2.5 percent annually to 1988, increasing by more than 2 million children, while the total population under 10 will grow by 3.2 million children. This increase comes after the number of these children declined every year from the mid-1960's until 1981.

Continued improvement in incomes and the increased number of children indicate doll shipments, adjusted for inflation, may rise 1.9 percent annually during the forecast period. Constant-dollar shipments of traditional toys are expected to increase 4.5 percent annually in the same period.

Imports continue to pose a problem for the domestic industry. Employment in the labor-intensive industries, such as dolls and traditional toys, could continue to decline as manufacturers shift production to the lower cost Far East.

CASE 2

Kitchen Made Pies

JAMES J. CHRISMAN
University of South Carolina

FRED L. FRY
Bradley University

As 1982 approached, Paul Dubicki, owner and president of Kitchen Made Pies, realized something needed to be done to strengthen his company's competitive market position. Company sales had stagnated since 1975, and the firm was about to suffer its fourth straight year of losses. Competitive forces were strong, the local economy was in bad shape, and Kitchen Made was experiencing a number of difficulties with a big customer and with its bank financing. To further compound things, the firm's financial condition had deteriorated to the point where options for turning the situation around were limited. Nonetheless, Mr. Dubicki was dedicated to returning his business to profitability and, in fact, was confident that the task could be accomplished if he could only get enough relief from the press of day-to-day decision making to attend to the company's future direction and strategy.

In commenting on the current situation at Kitchen Made, Mr. Dubicki emphasized volume as the key to the company's success: "We must increase our customer base, and we must somehow encourage our present distributors to provide the promotional support retailers need to sell our products. One well-publicized special can sell more pies in one day than can be sold in a normal week without one. That's what I'd like to concentrate on, but every day something else comes up around here."

COMPANY HISTORY

Kitchen Made Pies produced a wide variety of pies and other bakery products for distribution in the Midwest. Its offices and baking facilities were all located at a single site in Peoria, Illinois. The firm was founded in the 1950s by Frank Dubicki, Paul's father, and was run like most family businesses.

As a youngster, Paul Dubicki often worked at odd jobs in the plant, but he was not really very interested in the family's baking enterprise. After leaving the business for a while to pursue other activities, Paul returned to the company in 1968 and later became, along with David Dubicki, a minority stockholder. During this time, he often found himself frustrated by the never-ending details associated with the operational and administrative aspects of the business. In 1981, however, Paul became owner-manager of the business. Earlier that year,

This case was prepared by James J. Chrisman, University of South Carolina, and Fred L. Fry, Bradley University. Reprinted by permission of the authors.

the elder Dubicki had been persuaded to sell out, though he did retain ownership of the company's land and facilities. The sale took the form of a redemption of Frank Dubicki's stock by the corporation and an elimination of his debt to the corporation. During the same period, David exited from the business leaving Paul as the sole owner.

Upon assuming control, Paul immediately set about changing and updating the firm's operations and, for the first time in the firm's recent history, made a commitment to devote top-management time (mainly his) to charting a course and strategy for the company. Unfortunately, at the same time, problems building up over a long period of time began to surface, and Paul's commitment to his role as chief entrepreneur took a backseat to wrestling with daily operations.

PRODUCT LINE

Kitchen Made Pies makes a full line of pies, some on a regular basis, some seasonally, and a much more limited variety of cakes. Exhibit 1 lists all major sizes and flavors of pies currently produced by Kitchen Made, as well as the cake products which the firm makes.

Kitchen Made sells both fresh and frozen pies, though the former is preferred due to better turnover and more predictable ordering on the part of the customers. Another problem restricting frozen pie sales is limited freezer space. Kitchen Made can currently freeze and store only 3,500 pies per day.

EXHIBIT 1 Pie Categories at Kitchen Made Pies

4-INCH	8-INCH	9-INCH	OTHER
Apple	Apple	Apple	Shortcake
Pineapple	Applecrumb	Applecrumb	10-inch cakes
Cherry	Peach	Peach	
Blackberry	Pineapple	Pineapple	8-inch cakes
Lemon	Lemon	Blackberry	Sheet cakes
Coconut	Coconut	Black Raspberry	
Chocolate	Chocolate	Walnut	
Peach	Black Raspberry	Cherry	
	Pumpkin	Lemon Meringue	
	Cherry	Coconut Meringue	
	High-Top Meringues	Chocolate Meringue	
	Regular Meringues	Banana Meringue	
		Pumpkin	
		Chocolate Boston	
		Boston	
		Lemon Whip	
		Coconut Whip	
		Chocolate Whip	
		Banana Whip	
		Pumpkin Whip	

Kitchen Made takes pride in its long-standing use of only the highest-quality ingredients in its products. Many customers have reported that Kitchen Made pies are better than competitors' products. However, Kitchen Made's emphasis on quality results in its pies being priced above the competitors' products. Mr. Dubicki views the quality of Kitchen Made's pies as a major strength, especially to maintain repeat business. Still, he concedes that many buyers are price conscious and select lower-priced pies over Kitchen Made's products. On balance, though, Mr. Dubicki believes quality counts for more than lower price insofar as his company's business is concerned.

MARKETS/CUSTOMERS

The majority of Kitchen Made's sales are to food bakery distributors who basically supply two major market segments. The first is the institutional segment which consists of restaurants, as well as university, hospital, corporate, and government cafeterias. The second is the retail segment which includes supermarkets and convenience food store outlets. The institutional segment accounts for the majority of Kitchen Made's cake and 9-inch pie sales, while sales to the retail segment are mainly comprised of 4-inch and 8-inch pies. Most distributors concentrate on one market segment or the other, thus determining the type of products they buy. Buying motives for both markets vary depending upon the customer and market area involved. Kitchen Made's distributors report that some of their institutional customers are very price conscious in their selection among pies and brands. However, restaurant users are usually quality conscious, and many grocers, while price and quality conscious, are quite concerned about having strong promotional support for the brands they choose to stock (to help achieve high turnover and shelf space productivity).

Most of Kitchen Made's products are sold in the Peoria and St. Louis areas, but the firm also serves customers in other parts of Missouri and Illinois, as well as in Iowa and Wisconsin. Major distributors of Kitchen Made products, as well as their served markets, are included in Exhibit 2.

Besides the differences in buying motives and the type of products purchased by the two end markets, there are several other distinguishing features which differentiate them from each other. Institutional users frequently prefer frozen pies, partly because of their tendency to buy supplies on a monthly basis and partly because of the lower risk of spoilage. On the other hand, in the grocery business, where purchases are made weekly or bi-monthly, the economics favor fresh pies because they can be put directly on the shelf, they do not require more expensive freezer storage, and handling costs are lower—although there is greater risk that the products will lose their freshness before they are sold to shoppers. Generally, fresh pies sell best in those supermarkets with in-store bakeries because of the "freshness" connotation perceived by shoppers.

Unlike institutional users, grocery retailers depend heavily upon promo-

EXHIBIT 2 Distributors of Kitchen Made Pies

DISTRIBUTOR	TYPE OF SEGMENT SERVED	PERCENT OF KITCHEN MADE'S SALES
Dean's Distributing	Institutional Retail	40%
McCormick Distributing	Institutional	10
Lowenberg	Retail	11
Eisner's	Retail	8
Master Snack & New Process	Retail	13
Edward's	Retail	4
Other (including Schnuck's)	Retail	16

tional assistance for sales. One reason Dean's Distributing has become a less important customer for Kitchen Made is because of its policy of not offering grocers promotional support. As a result, Dean's and Kitchen Made (as Dean's supplier) have lost much of the retail grocer business in recent years in the Peoria area. Today, most of Dean's pie distribution business done in the Peoria vicinity, as well as in other markets, is institutional.

Some distributors sell to grocers on a guaranteed basis, with unsold products returned to the dealer at no charge. Others sell products unguaranteed, where grocers take full responsibility for all products they buy. Naturally, profit margins for the methods differ. Grocers usually make about 23 to 25 percent on guaranteed sales, while unguaranteed sales yield margins of approximately 35 to 40 percent. However, because of the inherent risks involved in unguaranteed purchases, most grocers prefer the lower-but-safer profit margins of guaranteed arrangements when dealing with "door-to-store" distributors such as Dean's. Nonguaranteed sales work well through efficient drop shipment techniques customarily used by bread bakers.

Door-to-store distributors accumulate individual orders on a daily basis, pick up what they need from the pie baker, and deliver merchandise direct from the pie baker to the grocer. On the other hand, drop shipment distributors order large supplies of pies from the pie baker, take them to warehouses, and fill individual customer orders from their warehouse inventories. In some cases, drop shipment distributors, such as Eisner's, sell direct to their own or an affiliated grocery chain and, thus, enjoy profits on both the wholesale and retail end. This can be an important competitive advantage since 40 to 50 percent of the product cost is in distribution.

Mr. Dubicki has expressed a desire to expand Kitchen Made's sales to drop shipment distributors because they operate on a lower margin of markup than door-to-store distributors, thus helping to hold down the prices retailers charge for Kitchen Made pies. This, he feels, could help circumvent the higher prices Kitchen Made charges distributors. Furthermore, since drop shippers order larger quantities, longer production runs and, therefore, lower pie-baking costs are possible.

In addition to sales to bakery wholesalers, Kitchen Made also operates its own delivery truck to handle specialty or rush orders. No plans have been made to expand this portion of Kitchen Made's operations.

THE BAKING INDUSTRY

Though the outlook for the baking industry has been helped by scalebacks in flour and sugar prices, overall prospects have been unfavorable and should continue to be so until economic conditions pick up. The baking industry, and particularly the pie and cake segment, is more susceptible to cyclical economic variabilities than other foodstuffs due to the discretionary nature of purchases. Pies and cakes are more or less luxury foods and are readily cut from household shopping lists when times are hard.

Further dampening the outlook for the industry is the national swing toward nutrition. Sweets and sugar intake have decreased because too much is considered unhealthy, besides, of course, being very fattening. Additionally, because of demographic changes, the average age of the population is higher. Historically, younger individuals account for a large portion of the consumption of pies, cakes, and other desserts.

The frozen segment of the bakery industry currently is in even worse condition, owing to the higher prices of frozen food items, including pies. Frozen food items, given the effects of recession and consumer budget tightening, are not expected to assume a bigger role in grocery budgets until shoppers are in a mood to spend more money on more expensive types of food items.

In addition to the conditions previously cited, other developments were changing in the industry's makeup. Between 1972 and 1977 the number of firms included under SIC code 2051 (Bread, Cake, and Related Products) dropped from 3,323 to 3,062, but at the same time, the number of establishments employing less than 20 workers increased. A major contributor to this trend was the economic impact of higher gasoline prices; the industry's transportation costs, already high due to the perishable nature of bakery products, became a big distribution factor. The transportation cost advantage went to the large-volume, national-brand firms with internal delivery capabilities and to the smaller firms which emphasized local business. Medium-sized firms which did not have the volume to support their own delivery function and which depended on a more diffuse range of customers were hurt most by rising distribution and shipping costs.

Other factors likely to affect the performance of the industry in the future were recent trends toward eating out and the emerging popularity of pre-prepared foods. With more women in the work force and more working couples, the food away from home segment was expected to grow. Dessert sales to restaurants and fast food outlets were viewed as having growth potential. However, many fast food chains had a policy of using standard desserts, supplied from central sources rather than each unit making its selections and purchases from local dessert manufacturers. As of yet, Mr. Dubicki had not investigated the opportunities of Kitchen Made making desserts to meet the specifications of area fast food chains.

Overall, the bakery industry was giving every sign of being very mature. There had been little real growth in sales over the past few years. However, prices and costs had risen substantially, reflecting inflationary conditions and shortages of certain ingredients. Since ingredient costs represented a major expense (approximately 50 percent of the manufacturer's selling price), recent declines in the prices of baking ingredients (e.g., sugar prices fell from $.55 per pound in November 1980 to $.26 per pound in October 1981) had given bakers the opportunity to improve profit margins. Changes in cereal and bakery prices, both wholesale and retail, as well as the consumer price index for the past six years, are provided in Exhibit 3.

THE LOCAL ECONOMY

Changes in the local retail market, prompted by changing demographics and a fluctuating economy, were threatening to have a dramatic effect on Kitchen Made's pie sales. Even though the Peoria area, like most midwestern cities, had shown little or no population growth in the past decade, the economy in Peoria had traditionally been solid due to the dominant impact of Caterpillar Tractor Co., a Pabst Brewing plant, a Hiram-Walker distillery, a number of other medium-sized manufacturing facilities, and a host of small plants—many of which are suppliers of Caterpillar. Peoria wage rates had consistently ranked in the top 20 cities in the nation, and local people were fond of saying, "Peoria doesn't have recessions." But this was changing rapidly.

Caterpillar endured a 12-week strike in the fall of 1979 that idled many of the 30,000 Peoria-area Caterpillar workers and did far more damage to the many suppliers and other businesses that depended either directly or indirectly on the firm. In addition, the Hiram-Walker plant closed in 1981, and the Pabst plant was scheduled to close in March 1982. Caterpillar, for the first time in 20 years, laid off substantial numbers of workers in 1981 and 1982. These

EXHIBIT 3 Comparative Changes In Price Levels of Cereal and Bakery Products

	1975	1976	1977	1978	1979	1980
Retail						
Cereal and bakery products	11.3%	−2.2%	1.6%	8.9%	10.1%	11.9%
All foods	8.5	3.1	6.3	10.0	10.9	8.6
Consumer price index	9.1	5.8	6.5	7.7	11.3	13.5
Wholesale						
Cereal and bakery products	4.0	3.3	0.1	9.8	10.5	12.2
All foods	6.7	3.8	4.4	10.5	9.6	8.2

Source: U.S. Department of Labor.

events posed a significant threat to the sale of pies and other desserts in the Peoria area. For instance, Caterpillar's cafeteria was now using less than half as many pies compared to 10 years ago.

COMPETITION

Kitchen Made was the only pie manufacturer located in the Peoria area, although it did face competition from food service firms which had their own in-house baking capabilities. The biggest competitors were other regional and national firms which sold their products in the same areas as did Kitchen Made (see Exhibit 4).

Some of Kitchen Made's rivals made a full line of pies, and several were diversified into breads and other bakery products. Some of the smaller rivals concentrated on specific sizes or types of pies to allow longer production runs, permit lower inventories, and help contain production costs. Mr. Dubicki felt, however, that Kitchen Made's full line of pies gave the firm an advantage over competitors in attracting new customers and protected sales from changes in customer taste.

PRODUCTION

Baking and production techniques at Kitchen Made are relatively simple, though not without their own special problems. In most instances, pie crusts and fillings are made via the assembly line method. One person operates the dough machine which flattens the dough and rolls enough out to make one crust. The dough is passed to a second person who places it into a pie pan. The machine then presses the dough into the pan. Afterward, the crust passes under a filling machine which is set according to the size of pie being made. After the crust is filled with the desired ingredients, the pie passes under another station where the top crust is molded onto the sides of the pie pan and the excess dough removed. This excess is transported by conveyor back to the dough machine. Once the pies are assembled, they are placed on racks

EXHIBIT 4 Kitchen Made's Major Rivals in the Peoria-St. Louis Market Area

COMPANY	HEADQUARTERS LOCATION	GEOGRAPHIC AREA SERVED	PRODUCT LINES	MARKET SEGMENTS SERVED
Lloyd Harris (Div. of Fasano)	Chicago	East of Rockies	Fresh 9-in pies	Institutional and retail
Chef Pierre		Nationwide	8-inch and 10-inch frozen	Institutional and retail
Mrs. Smith	Pottstown, PA	Nationwide	8-inch and 10-inch frozen	Institutional and retail
Bluebird Baking	Dayton	Midwest	4-inch and 8-inch fresh	Retail
Shenandoah Pie	St. Louis	St. Louis	Full line fresh	Institutional and retail

and wheeled over to the ovens for baking. All fresh pies are baked, frozen pies may or may not be baked, depending on the type of pie and filling.

A major problem associated with production is the frequent conversions required each time the size or the flavor is changed. It takes approximately 15 to 20 minutes to change over pie size and 4 to 5 minutes to change the type of ingredient. Size changes usually occur twice a day (from 4-inch to 8-inch to 9-inch), but ingredients must be changed from 20 to 25 times per day depending upon the production schedule.

All fruit pies are put together by the method described above, but currently cream pies are filled by hand. Mr. Dubicki intends to go to automated pie assembly for both fruit and cream pies in the near future. He is also studying the purchase of a more efficient pie machine: the drawbacks are the $150,000 purchase price and the long production runs needed to maintain peak efficiency with this type of machine.

One way to cut production costs is to limit the numbers of different types of pies made. Substantial savings in change-over time and production efficiency are available by limiting pie varieties. For example, with full crews, Kitchen Made currently bakes about $30,000 worth of pies and cakes per week. Yet, on those occasions where the firm has received a large order for one type of pie, a half crew has been able to produce $10,000 worth of pies on a single eight-hour shift. However, Mr. Dubicki is concerned that a move to fewer varieties could hurt sales since many retail and institutional buyers prefer to buy full lines of products from the same supplier.

Recently, Mr. Dubicki hired a production manager to allow him more time away from the pie assembly operation. The production manager is still in the process of learning all the requirements of the job and Mr. Dubicki has been spending a lot of time giving the new manager on-the-job training. Mr. Dubicki has so far been reluctant to delegate full authority to the new manager even though he is pleased with the progress she is making in taking over the supervision of pie making activities. The transfer of authority has been hindered by the fact that all aspects of the pie making operation have not been smoothly worked out and some are in the midst of being changed.

One positive development has been the progress made to reduce inventory. Though done as much out of necessity as out of design, the move has nonetheless helped in many respects. In the past, ingredients were often bought in six-month quantities. Today, the firm tries to buy only what it needs for one or two weeks, except in special cases when supplies are hard to find or favorable price breaks can be obtained.

FINANCIAL SITUATION

Mr. Dubicki believes that with Kitchen Made's current product mix, sales of approximately $35,000 per week ($1,820,000 per year) are needed to break even. Variable expenses are estimated to be about 85 percent of sales revenue. Exhibit 5 provides a breakdown of Kitchen Made's sales and gross profits by

EXHIBIT 5   Sales/Operating Profits by Product Lines, Last 12 Months

PRODUCT	SALES REVENUES Dollar	Percent of Total	GROSS PROFITS Dollars	Percent	GROSS PROFIT MARGIN
4-inch pie	$ 536,000	33.5%	$147,600	61.5%	27.5%
8-inch pie	296,000	18.5	24,700	10.3	8.3
9-inch pie	704,000	44.0	50,400	21.0	7.2
Cakes	64,000	4.0	17,300	7.2	27.0
Total	$1,600,000	100.0%	$240,000	100.0%	15.0%

product line in percentages and dollar amounts. Margins on the 4-inch pies and the cakes are the biggest, with margins on the 8-inch pie and 9-inch pie varieties substantially lower.

The prices of Kitchen Made's pie and cake products have not been changed for approximately 12 months. Exhibit 6 shows the prices for the various types of pies made by Kitchen Made.

Kitchen Made's management is particularly pleased with the company's high-top meringue pie. Because of its superior looks and acceptance by consumers, the high-top pies command a 50 cent premium over the price of regular meringue pies, yet they cost only a few pennies more to make.

Because of stagnant sales and rising costs over the past several years, the financial condition of Kitchen Made has deteriorated. Exhibit 7 provides condensed operating results for the years 1971 through 1981. Exhibit 8 shows a condensed balance sheet for 1981. Exhibit 9 presents the computable financial ratios for Kitchen Made as compared to industry averages for SIC code 2051 businesses (i.e., Bread, Cake, and Related Products) with sales of under $50 million.

The most immediate financial problem relates to the unsecured $70,000 bank note which has currently come due. Kitchen Made has had an agreement with a local financial institution which allowed the firm to borrow $70,000 on a program resembling revolving credit. Kitchen Made pays only interest on this loan, with the principal due in lump sum at the end of the borrowing period. One option Mr. Dubicki is considering involves trying to refinance the loan and get the borrowing period extended. But he is also considering whether

EXHIBIT 6   Wholesale Pie Prices for Kitchen Made Pies

4-inch pies	$.25	8-inch regular meringue	$.90	9-inch fruit pies	$1.30
		8-inch high-top meringue	$1.40	9-inch whips	$1.30
		8-inch fruit pies	$1.00	9-inch meringue	$1.25
				9-inch specialty	$1.60
				9-inch walnut	$2.00
				9-inch cherry	$2.25

EXHIBIT 7 Kitchen Made Pies' Condensed Operating Results, 1971–1980

	SALES	NET INCOME (LOSS)		COSTS AS A PERCENT OF SALES REVENUES[1]				
YEAR	REVENUES	Dollars	As a Percent of Sales	Materials	Labor	Selling	Administration	Facilities, Equipment, and Other
1971	$ 844,000	$14,000	1.7	51.2%	30.0%	2.9%	9.9%	7.6%
1972	955,000	8,000	.8	50.5	29.3	2.8	9.5	7.1
1973	1,246,000	24,000	1.9	52.7	24.6	2.8	9.2	8.9
1974	1,453,000	18,000	1.2	57.0	22.3	2.5	7.7	9.3
1975	1,604,000	110,000	6.9	53.9	20.7	2.2	6.9	9.4
1976	1,580,000	109,000	6.9	48.8	23.0	2.6	7.4	11.3
1977	1,642,000	7,000	.4	48.9	26.0	2.7	8.5	13.5
1978	1,608,000	−24,000	(1.5)	50.9	26.3	2.2	9.4	12.7
1979	1,601,000	−58,000	(3.6)	50.6	27.0	2.8	10.0	13.1
1980	1,506,000	−91,000	(6.0)	51.3	28.3	3.3	10.3	12.8
1981	1,635,000	−178,000	(10.9)	54.3	27.7	4.1	11.2	13.5

[1] All of the cost percentages are not completely comparable from year to year due to several changes in how costs were allocated between categories of expenses.

EXHIBIT 8 Kitchen Made Pies Balance Sheet 1981

ASSETS			LIABILITIES AND EQUITY	
Current assets			Current liabilities	
Cash	$ 2,000		Accounts payable	$291,000
Accounts receivable	163,000		Unsecured bank note	70,000
Inventory	137,000		Accrued payroll and taxes	25,000
Prepaid expenses	17,000		Note—F. Dubicki	8,000
Total current assets	319,000		Total—current liabilities	394,000
Fixed assets (after depreciation)			LONG-TERM LIABILITIES	
Leasehold improvements	1,000		Note on truck	15,000
Machinery and equipment	48,000		Note on equipment	12,000
Autos and trucks	28,000		Total long-term	27,000
Total fixed assets	77,000		Total liabilities	421,000
Total assets	$396,000		Owner's equity	(25,000)
			Total liabilities and equity	$396,000

EXHIBIT 9 Selected Company and Industry Financial Ratios, 1981

	INDUSTRY SIC CODE 2051	KITCHEN MADE PIES
Current ratio	.76	.81 (without Dean's .66)
Net profit/sales	3.8%	Negative
Net profit/total assets	6.5%	Negative
Net profit/equity	19.5%	Negative
Sales/equity	7.6x	Negative
Sales/total assets	2.5x	4.1x
Collection period	14 days	36 (without Dean's 23)
Sales/working capital	8.8x	Negative
Sales/inventory	53.3x	11.9x
Fixed assets/equity	131.6%	Negative
Total debt/equity	201.7%	Negative

Source: *Key Business Ratios 1981*, Dun & Bradstreet.

to switch his business to another bank. Mr. Dubicki feels that because Kitchen Made often has a $20,000 to $30,000 balance in its bank account, it is entitled to some relief on the interest rate being paid. Furthermore, in discussions with the bank's loan officers over the possibility of refinancing the loan, Mr. Dubicki has been informed that the bank will insist on a secured note. Since Mr. Dubicki's father holds title to Kitchen Made's property, the bank has mentioned the use of a second mortgage on Mr. Dubicki's personal home as possible security for the loan. This is not attractive to Mr. Dubicki, and he is hopeful that other Peoria banks will be interested in giving Kitchen Made an unsecured loan in the amount of $70,000. Mr. Dubicki is quite willing to establish a business relationship with a different bank in the event satisfactory terms can be worked out. If not, he sees little option but to agree to the second mortgage condition for a secured note at Kitchen Made's present bank.

Another problem causing concern is slow payments by some customers. While such customers as Lowenberg and Eisner's consistently take advantage of discounts for early payment (usual terms are 2%/10 days, net/30 days), Dean's Distributing currently owes over six months back payments amounting to $60,000. Mr. Dubicki feels most of this account is uncollectible but has not, as of yet, written the amount off as bad debt expense. Mr. Dubicki has expressed a desire to eliminate or substantially cut back on the business done with Dean's Distributing but in an effort to maintain sales levels has continued to supply its pies to Dean's on a strictly cash basis.

In spite of these financial difficulties, Kitchen Made has been able to generate enough cash flow to meet its current obligations and also to make small payments on the amounts owed to creditors of longer standing. Thus, while the situation is far from ideal and the firm is very vulnerable to unforeseen events, liquidity is probably not a life-or-death concern at the moment. However, Mr. Dubicki realizes that any further decline in sales and cash flows could be extremely hazardous and potentially fatal.

PERSONNEL

Most of the managerial activities at Kitchen Made Pies are handled directly by Mr. Dubicki. Besides the production manager, Ms. Barbara Britt, the only other management personnel are Ms. Charolette Watson, office manager, and Mr. Lonnie Beard, the sales promotion manager. Mr. Beard is responsible for making sure products are stocked and advertised properly at local retail outlets, which he visits periodically. Mr. Dubicki, besides being president and owner, acts as sales and distribution manager, prepares cash flow projections, searches for new accounts, and, of course, oversees all day-to-day activities. He also is really the only person who completely understands all aspects of the business. About the only activity he is not directly involved with is the actual assembly of the pies.

Kitchen Made currently employs about 30 production workers, 6 office workers, several maintenance workers, and a truck driver. The shop is unionized and pays wages comparable to other like-sized firms.

FUTURE PROSPECTS AND OUTLOOK

Though the current situation at Kitchen Made Pies is far from ideal, Mr. Dubicki believes the situation is not hopeless and that a turnaround in his company's fortunes is manageable. As he put it, "I'm optimistic about our future, but then again, isn't that the only way I can feel?" He thinks good progress is being made in solving internal operating problems, and he has established good rapport with his work force; he feels the latter will facilitate making many of the remaining internal changes he is considering. Yet, Mr. Dubicki recognizes the need to address several nagging issues:

- Would lengthening production runs reduce costs enough to justify a move to narrow Kitchen Made's product line?
- How important to Kitchen Made's competitive position is a broad product line? What product mix really makes the most sense?
- Would it be economical for Kitchen Made to purchase more equipment to automate its pie assembly operations, and how could such equipment be financed in the event it would improve Kitchen Made's efficiency?
- Should Kitchen Made continue to position itself at the high end of the price/quality range?

Mr. Dubicki also realizes that plain old hard work and dedication on his part, while helpful and necessary, will not be sufficient—improved operating results and a workable strategy are, of necessity, high on his agenda.

INDUSTRIAL HIGHLIGHT

Processed Foods and Beverages Industry

Below is a capsule summary of the bakery foods segment of the processed foods and beverages industry. Kitchen Made Pies is a part of this bakery foods segment. Information in this highlight was compiled by the U.S. Department of Commerce and focuses on this industry segment during the approximate period of time covered in the case. Keep in mind that industrial highlights contained in this text are not intended as a complete synopsis of an industry but as a profile of certain issues that can be relevant to a case situation. A list of additional references at the end of this highlight can be used for further industrial analysis.

BAKERY FOODS

Current Situation

In 1981, the value of industry shipments of bakery foods reached an estimated $18 billion, a 10-percent rise from 1980 levels. Representing about three-fourths of total industry shipments, the bread, cake, and related products sector shipped $13.8 billion worth of goods, an 11.1-percent increase from 1980. For the remainder of the industry, cookies and crackers, shipments rose 6.9 percent in current dollars.

Aggregate industry shipments in 1981 registered a 1.4-percent inflation-adjusted increase. The bread, cake, and related products industry shipments increased by 2.7 percent, after adjustment for inflation. The cookie and cracker segment of the industry experienced a 3.0-percent decline in the constant-dollar value of shipments.

Primary industry concerns in 1981 related to cost uncertainties and trends in consumer tastes. Input prices dominated the list of problems confronting manufacturers. When consumer tastes change, firms must adapt their product mixes rapidly. The diminishing number of bakeries producing bread, cake, and related items portends increasing concentration in this industry.

Source: U.S. Industrial Outlook, Department of Commerce, 1982, pp. 303–306.

Varieties Gain and White Bread Loses

White bread consumption has been declining since 1963. Between 1977 and 1982, it declined at an average rate 3.2 percent a year. Consumers perceive variety breads as more nutritious than white bread. Firms in the industry recognized this trend and launched a myriad of specialty breads, especially white hearth and wheat. To enhance sales of white bread, bakeries introduced variety white hearth breads with richer formulas and heavier crusts. Production of variety items frequently requires special pans, more expensive packaging, longer baking times, and shorter runs. Firms charge higher retail prices for these products, but consumers readily purchase them. Growth in consumption of variety breads will probably begin to wane, however, if their prices continue to rise without moderation.

Consumer Prices

From August 1980 to August 1981, retail prices of bakery products rose more than 8 percent. White bread prices increased 9.0 percent in the same 12-month interval, and prices for other bread rose 8.1 percent. Fresh cake and cupcake prices advanced 9.9 percent, between August 1980 and August 1981 while cookie prices rose 11.1 percent.

During the first 8 months of 1981, the price of bakery products increased 8.4 percent compared with a 9-percent increase for all food products. Prices of highly sugared goods—cakes, cupcakes, and cookies—rose at a faster rate than bread. Cake and cupcake prices increased 12.1 percent, while cookie prices rose about 12.0 percent. Bread manufacturers used high-fructose corn syrup as a sugar substitute to help maintain lower prices, but cake recipes require sugar exclusively. Companies producing cookies attempted to include less sugar in their items and promoted sales of crackers.

Distribution of Costs

During 1980, the wholesale price of ingredients used in the production of bakery products advanced considerably. The cost of sugar soared 66.0 percent, although the price of flour, the industry's major agricultural input, climbed only 8.0 percent. Hourly wages rose 11.4 percent in 1980.

According to a 1980 American Bakers Association (ABA) survey of 277 plants, ingredients accounted for about one-fourth of white bread's wholesale price. Flour in white bread represented almost two-thirds of ingredient costs, while sweeteners accounted for 10 percent.

The 1980 ABA white bread survey indicates that direct manufacturing labor expenses accounted for approximately 9 percent of total wholesale bread cost. Distribution expenditures, almost exclusively wages and benefits to route drivers, accounted for about 20 percent of the wholesale bread cost. Because of its 7-day maximum shelf life, fresh bread and cakes must be transported rapidly. Cookie and cracker producers must also maintain an extensive distribution network, but these products possess a longer shelf life, which varies from 2 months to 1 year, depending on the item. Advertising and other

EXHIBIT A Interest Rates (In Percent—Monthly Average)

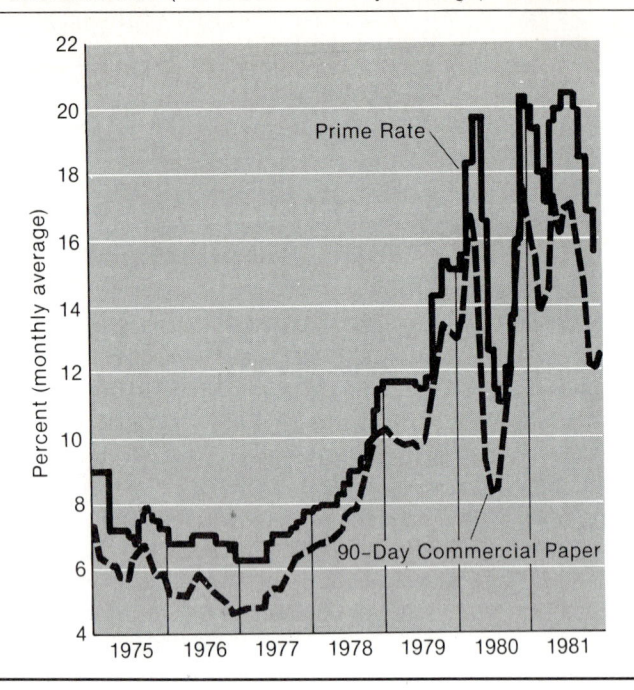

selling costs are about 20 percent of white bread's 1980 wholesale value. Bread companies may alter their mix of ingredients, but they cannot, in the short run, reduce manufacturing, distribution, and advertising expenses. Together, these expenses constitute more than 70 percent of producers' costs. Pretax profit margins remain low—about 3.6 percent of sales. One significant factor in keeping profits lower over the last few years is the escalation of interest rates, as shown in Exhibit A.

Sugar Prices and Industry Response

Reflecting the volatility of commodity markets, sugar prices plummeted 14.8 percent in the first 7 months of 1981. Bumper harvests in sugar-producing African and Caribbean countries contributed to lower world sugar prices, which in turn influenced domestic prices. The price of flour and flour-based mixes declined 1.5 percent during the same period.

To mitigate sugar price oscillations, baking companies joined a coalition of food processing firms, the Sugar Users Group, to monitor the gyrations of the international sugar market. The purpose of the organization is to promote stable sugar prices and encourage the use of less expensive sugar substitutes. Bakeries are expanding their use of sugar alternatives. During 1981, bakery firms used 748,000 tons of sweeteners other than sugar. The substitutes include all varieties of natural and artificial sweeteners, though corn-based products led the list.

Since 1975, high-fructose corn syrup (HFCS) has provided a consistently larger share of sweeteners for bread and roll producers. An estimated 20 percent of these firms use HFCS exclusively, because of its lower cost. Though sugar prices declined in the first 7 months of 1981, they remained higher than the price of HFCS.

Labor: Wages Up While Employment Declines

According to the Bureau of Labor Statistics, output per employee hour in the baking industry increased 1.5 percent annually from 1976 to 1980, reflecting larger plants and more sophisticated equipment. Because of the economic doldrums in 1981 and increased automation in new plants, the total number of production workers in the baking industry dropped 2.7 percent. Average wages, however, gained 10.2 percent in 1981. Production workers represented 58.5 percent of total employment; the balance were route salesmen and management.

During 1981, the bread, cake, and related products sector experienced a 4.4 percent decline in employment of production workers, while hourly wages increased 9.0 percent. In the same year, production workers in the cookie and cracker segment of the industry increased 1.6 percent, and their average hourly pay rose 11.4 percent.

In-Store Bakeries Soar

Between 1979 and 1981, the number of on-premise bakeries in supermarkets rose from 7,900 to 10,600. These units are of two types. Scratch operations combine basic ingredients into a final product. Bakeoff units use manufactured frozen dough as raw material and require less initial capital and fewer skilled workers. Two-thirds of the present in-store bakery units are in the bakeoff category.

School Lunches

Recent budget reductions for the Food and Nutrition Service (FNS) of the U.S. Department of Agriculture will affect school lunch programs at 94,120 schools. The bakery industry could benefit from this action if more students use bag lunches. In 1981, FNS food service units declined 3 percent, and the program experienced a 1-percent, inflation-adjusted drop in sales.

Long-Term Prospects

Expanding use of HFCS in the bread sector will probably continue for the remainder of the decade. The industry will seek to lessen the dependency of sweet goods production on sugar. Increased efficiency in distribution methods may lower costs for this energy- and labor-intensive aspect of the industry. Between 1981 and 1986, shipments of bakery foods are expected to decrease about 0.3 percent annually, in dollars adjusted for price changes.

ADDITIONAL REFERENCES

Bakery Production and Marketing, Gorman Publishing Company, 5725 East River Road, Chicago, IL 60631.

Bakery Products, SIC 2051 and 2052, *1977 Census of Manufactures,* Industry Series, Bureau of the Census, U.S. Department of Commerce, Washington, DC 20230.

Chain Store Age, Lebhar-Friedman, Inc., 2 Park Avenue, New York, NY 10016.

Employment and Earnings, Producers Price Index, Consumer Price Index, Bureau of Labor Statistics, U.S. Department of Labor, Washington, DC 20212.

Milling and Baking News, Sosland Publishing Company, 4800 Main Street, Kansas City, MO 64112.

Progressive Grocer, Progressive Grocer Company, 708 Third Avenue, New York, NY 10017.

"Sugar and Sweetener Report," Economics and Statistics Service, U.S. Department of Agriculture, Washington, DC 20250.

CASE 3

Wall Drug Store*

JAMES D. TAYLOR   ROBERT L. JOHNSON   GENE B. IVERSON
all of the University of South Dakota

Ted and Bill Hustead, primary owners and managers of Wall Drug Store, found themselves confronted with several key strategic issues in the winter of 1973. Should they invest aggressively in inventory for the tourist season of 1974, anticipating an increase in business, or should they buy conservatively? Should they continue to expand Wall Drug in the future, or should they seek out new business alternatives? Although Wall Drug had been an unqualified success for the last 27 years and had been written up in newspapers and magazines on numerous occasions, times suddenly seemed more precarious. Rising gasoline prices, the prospect of a long-term fuel crisis, confrontation with the American Indian Movement (AIM) at Wounded Knee, and the highway beautification laws governing the location of Wall Drug's famous roadside signs all combined to pose new threats to tourist travel in South Dakota and to Wall Drug in particular.

COMPANY BACKGROUND

Ted Hustead majored in pharmacy at the University of Nebraska and graduated in 1929 at the age of 27. Less than three years later, in December 1931, Ted and his wife Dorothy (who grew up in Colman, South Dakota) bought the drugstore in Wall, South Dakota, for $2,500. Dorothy and Ted, and their four-year-old son Bill, lived in the back 20 feet of the store for six years during the height of the Great Depression. Business was not good (the first month's gross revenue was $350), and Ted was not able to maintain a separate home and still keep the store going.

One writer described Wall in 1931 as follows:

> Wall, then: a huddle of poor wooden buildings, many unpainted, housing some 300 desperate souls; a 19th century depot and wooden water tank; dirt (or mud) streets; few trees; a stop on the railroad, it wasn't even that on the highway. US 16 and 14 went right on by, as did the tourists speeding between the Badlands and the Black Hills. There was nothing in Wall to stop for.[1]

---

* **This is a classic case in the strategic management literature.**

Prepared by Professors James D. Taylor, Robert L. Johnson, and Gene B. Iverson of the University of South Dakota. Reprinted by permission.

[1] Dana Close Jennings, *Free Ice Water: The Story of the Wall Drug* (Aberdeen, S.D.: North Plains Press, 1969), p. 26.

Neither the drugstore nor the town of Wall prospered until Dorothy Hustead conceived the idea of placing a sign beside the highway promising free ice water to anyone who would stop at their store. The sign read "Get a soda/Get a beer/Turn next corner/Just as near/To Highway 16 and 14/Free ice water/Wall Drug." Ted put the sign up on a blazing hot Sunday afternoon in the summer of 1936 and no sooner had he done so than the first cars started turning off the highway to go to Wall Drug. This seemingly simple advertising effort marked a turning point in the Wall Drug's business strategy—and in the success of the enterprise as well.

With the value of highway advertising thus made dramatically apparent, Ted began erecting novel signs along all the highways leading to Wall. One sign read "Slow down the old hack/Wall Drug Corner/Just across the railroad track." The distinctive, attention-catching signs were a boon to Wall Drug's business and the town of Wall prospered, too. In an article in *Good Housekeeping* in 1951, the Husteads' signs were called "the most ingenious and irresistible system of signs ever devised."[2]

Just after World War II, a friend traveling across Europe for the Red Cross got the notion of putting up Wall Drug signs overseas. The idea caught on and small Wall Drug plaques were subsequently carried all over the world by South Dakota GIs who were familiar with the store's advertising techniques. A number of servicemen even wrote the store requesting signs. One sign in Paris announced "Wall Drug Store 4,278 miles (6,951 kilometers)." Wall Drug signs have appeared in Shanghai, Amsterdam, the Paris and London subways, the 38th Parallel in Korea, the North and South Pole areas, and on Vietnam jungle trails. The Husteads sent more than 200 signs to servicemen in Vietnam. The worldwide distribution of Wall Drug signs led to news stories and publicity which further nurtured the unique image and reputation of the store.

In the late 1950s, *Redbook Magazine* carried a story about Wall Drug which was later picked up and condensed in *Reader's Digest.* Since then, the newspapers and magazines carrying feature stories or referring to Wall Drug have included:

National Enquirer, November 11, 1973.

Grit, October 28, 1973.

Las Vegas Review—Journal, September 22, 1973.

Senior Scholastic Magazine, October 4, 1973, p. 11.

Congressional Record, September 11, 1973, Si6269.

The Wall Street Journal, September 5, 1973.

Omaha World-Herald, May 15, 1972.

Elsevier (Dutch magazine), February 12, 1972.

Rapid City Journal, April 12, 1970.

A Cleveland daily paper, May 16, 1971.

The New York Times, Sunday, January 31, 1971.

Oshkosh, Wisconsin, *Daily Northwestern,* August 2, 1969.

[2] Ibid., p. 42.

Sunday Picture Magazine, Minneapolis Tribune, September 21, 1969.

American Illustrated, U.S. Information Agency in Poland and Russia, June 1969.

Ojai Valley News and Oaks Gazette, August 14, 1968.

Chicago Tribune, Norman Vincent Peale's syndicated column, "Confident Living," October 8, 1966.

Norman Vincent Peale's book, *You Can If You Think You Can,* p. 34.

San Francisco Examiner, February 12, 1966.

Women's Wear Daily, September 16, 1966.

Coronet Magazine, April, 1964.

Cleveland, Ohio, *The Plain Dealer,* date not known.

The June 1969 issue of *America Illustrated,* a U.S. Information Agency publication distributed in the Soviet Union and Poland, featured a story entitled "The Lure and Fascination of Seven Fabulous Stores," by Mal Oettinger. The seven stores were Macy's; Wall Drug Store; Rich's; L. L. Bean, Inc.; Neiman-Marcus; Gump's; and Brentano's.

GROWTH AND DEVELOPMENT OF WALL DRUG

The sales and square footage of Wall Drug have grown steadily since the 1940s. From 1931 to 1941, Wall Drug was located in a 24- by 40-foot rented building on the west side of Main Street. In 1941, an old lodge hall, which acted as the gymnasium in Wasta (15 miles west of Wall), was bought and moved to the east side of Main Street across from the original store. It then became the site of Wall Drug; the store now occupies over an acre, taking up the better part of one side of Wall's block-long business district.

When World War II ended, tourist travel to the Badlands and Black Hills picked up considerably, and Wall Drug's highway signs attracted so many people to the store that the Husteads claim they were embarrassed because the facilities were not large enough. There were no modern rest rooms even. Sales in the 1940s ranged from $150,000 to $200,000 per year.

In 1951, the Husteads' son Bill graduated from South Dakota State College at Brookings with a major in pharmacy and returned to Wall to join his father in managing Wall Drug. Ted and Bill proceeded to initiate a series of expansions in the business. In 1953, a storeroom on the south end of the building (see Exhibit 1) was remodeled and became the Western Clothing Room. The next year, a new area adjacent to the Western Clothing Room was added. Sales increased about 30 percent to around $300,000 per year as a result of these two expansions to the store. In 1956, a self-service cafe was installed on the north side of the premises. By the early 1960s, sales had climbed to $500,000.

In the early 1960s, Ted and his son Bill began seriously thinking of moving Wall Drug out to the highway. The original Highway 16 ran by the north side of Wall, about two blocks from the store. But later Highway 16 was rerouted to the south side of Wall, though still only two blocks away from the drugstore.

In the late 1950s and early 1960s, a new highway was built running by the south side of Wall paralleling the revised route. Ted and Bill Hustead were considering building an all new Wall Drug, along with a gasoline filling station, adjacent to the new highway just where the intersection to Wall was located.

They decided to build the gasoline station first, and did so, calling it Wall Auto Livery. But when the station was finished, they decided against moving the drugstore and, instead, elected to continue expanding the old store in downtown Wall. This proved fortunate, since soon after that a new interstate highway (I-90) replaced the new Highway 16 route and the new I-90 interchange ran right through the site of the proposed new Wall Drug.

Once the Husteads decided to keep the store in downtown Wall, expansion was continued. In 1963, a new fireproof construction coffee shop was installed where the present soda fountain is (see the store layout in Exhibit 1). In 1964, a new kitchen, again of fireproof construction, was added in back of the cafe and main store. In 1964 and 1965, offices and the new pharmacy were opened

EXHIBIT 1 Layout of Wall Drug

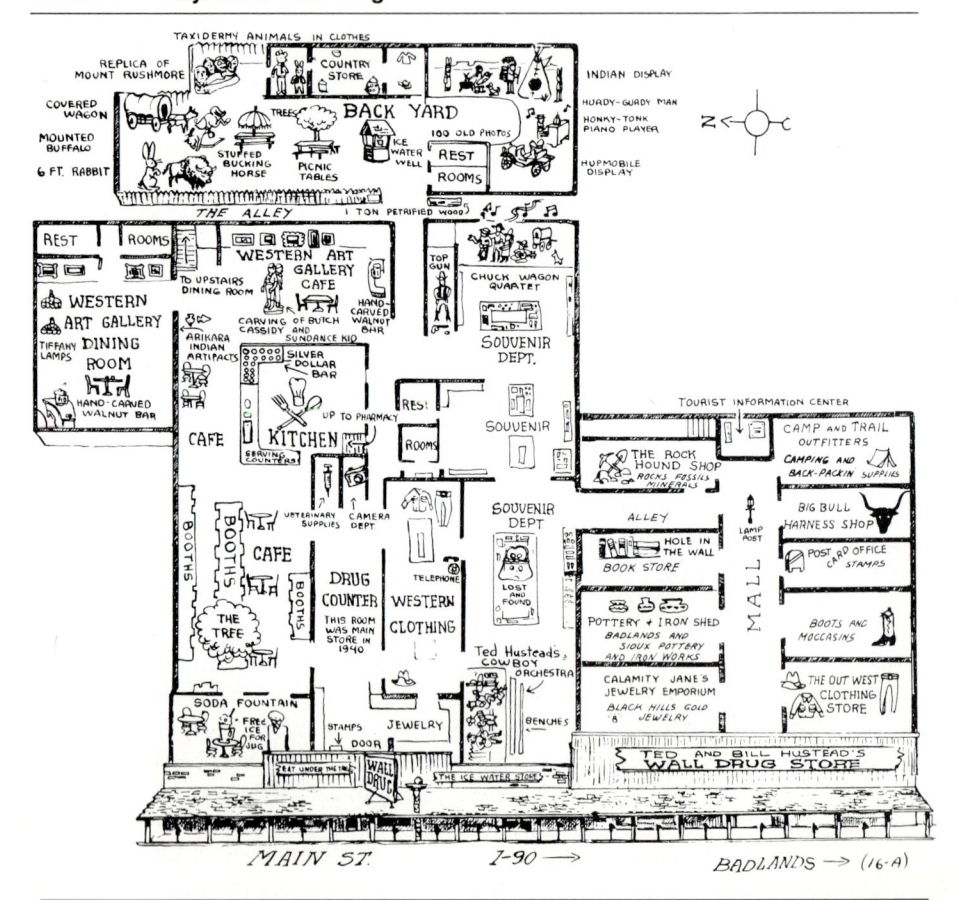

on the second floor over the kitchen. In 1968, the back dining room and backyard across the alley were added. This was followed in 1971 with the Western Art Gallery Dining Room. These expansions helped push annual sales volume to $1 million.

In 1971, the Husteads bought the theater that bordered Wall Drug on the south and continued to operate it as a theater through 1972. In early 1973, they closed the theater and began to convert the location into a new addition called the "Mall." By the summer of 1973, the north part of the Mall was open for business. The south side was unfinished. That year, Wall Drug grossed $1,600,000—an increase of about 20 percent over 1972. Bill attributed the increase to the new Mall addition. Currently, Wall Drug covers almost 32,000 square feet and is air-conditioned; the facility also contains 960 square feet of office space and almost 12,000 square feet of storage space.

THE MALL

For about five years prior to starting construction, Bill Hustead thought about and planned the concept of the Mall. The Mall was conceived as a town within a large room. The strolling mall was designed as a main street with two-story frontier Western stores on either side—in the fashion of a recreated Western town. The shop fronts were reproductions of building fronts found in old photos of western towns in the 1880s. On the inside, the stores were paneled with such woods as pine from Custer, South Dakota; American black walnut; gumwood; hackberry; cedar, maple; and oak. Many photos, paintings, and prints lined the walls. The shops stocked products that were more expensive than the souvenir merchandise carried in other parts of Wall Drug and, in many respects, were like Western boutiques. The northern half of the Mall opened for business in July 1973. But Bill was uncertain as to whether to go ahead with construction of the south side.

The construction of the Mall prompted a distinct change in the financing strategy of Wall Drug. All previous expansions had been funded out of retained earnings or with short-term loans. But the Husteads built the Mall by borrowing approximately $250,000 for 10 years. Part of this money was also used to erect 20 large new signs standing 660 feet from the interstate highway.

THE DRAWING POWER OF WALL DRUG

The Husteads operated Wall Drug and Wall Auto Livery as two separate corporations. Both businesses were heavily dependent on tourist travel, and in 1973 the sales of each was at an all-time high. The economic base of Wall (1970 population, 786) consisted of 11 motels and a number of service stations—all keyed to the tourist traffic drawn by Wall Drug. The town's business district was one block long. Nearly a third of the labor force worked at Wall Drug. The president of the Chamber of Commerce once observed that without Wall Drug the town would dry up and blow away.

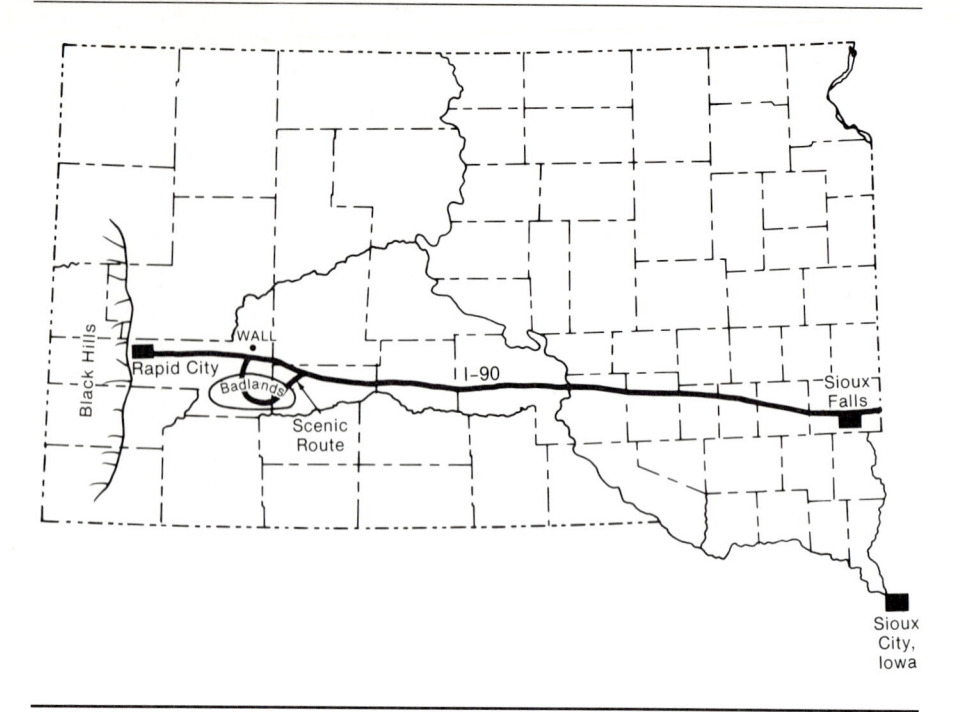

EXHIBIT 2 South Dakota: Location of Wall in Relation to the Black Hills, Badlands, Interstate 90, Rapid City, and Sioux Falls

Wall is situated right on the edge of the Badlands (see Exhibit 2) and is 52 miles east of Rapid City, South Dakota's second largest city (1970 population, 43,836). For miles in either direction, travelers are teased and tantalized by Wall Drug signs. Along one 45-mile stretch of interstate highway leading to Wall, travelers encounter 53 Wall Drug signs. As tourists approach the town (those westbound usually after driving 40 miles or more through the Badlands), they are greeted by a large Wall Drug sign on the interchange and an 80-foot high, 50-ton statue of a dinosaur (see Exhibit 3).

As many as 10,000 people might stream through Wall Drug on a busy day. In the summer of 1963, a traffic count made on the highway going by Wall showed that 46 percent of the cars were eastbound and 54 percent were westbound. Of the eastbound traffic, 43 percent turned off at Wall. Of the westbound traffic, 44 percent turned off at Wall. On another occasion, a survey of state licenses of autos and campers parked in front of Wall Drug and in the camper and trailer park one block from Wall Drug between 8 A.M. and 10 A.M. on Wednesday, June 4, resulted in the following percentages:

Neighboring states and South Dakota (nonlocal)	37%
South Dakota, local county	32
Balance of states and Canada	31

EXHIBIT 3　The Wall Drug Dinosaur

THE MAIN ATTRACTION

The Husteads have made Wall Drug a place of amusement and family entertainment, a gallery of the West, a cultural display of South Dakota history, and a reflection of the heritage of the West. Some even say Wall Drug has become a South Dakota institution. Nostalgia addicts have a "field day" in the store, and children delight in animated, life-size singing cowboys, a tableau of an Indian camp, a stuffed bucking horse, a six-foot rabbit, a stuffed buffalo, old 10-cent slot machines that pay out a souvenir coin, statues of cowboys, a coin-operated quick-draw game, and souvenirs by the roomful.

Free ice water is still one of Wall Drug's biggest attractions. Ted Hustead, in his 70s but still on the job every day, estimated that the store gives out 5,000 glasses of water a day, plus filling and icing water jugs free of charge. The store has $30,000 worth of ice-making equipment with a capacity of one and one half tons of ice per day—a far cry from earlier years when Ted cut winter ice from nearby farm ponds and stored it for summer use. Another of the store's traditions is a nickel cup of coffee and a breakfast of two eggs and a slice of toast for 25 cents. However, rising costs have since upped the price of the breakfast to 49 cents (as of 1973). On a busy day, patrons consume 250 dozen eggs and 6,000 homemade donuts.

The dining rooms are decorated with wood paneling and paintings of Western art; diners are entertained with Western music. Patrons can select from a moderately priced menu that includes buffalo burgers, roast beef, steak, and select wine, beer or a "Jack Daniels" at a rustic, American walnut bar. The original soda fountain has been expanded into a 475-seat cafe built around a huge cottonwood tree growing up through the roof.

STORE OPERATIONS

Wall Drug does most of its business during the summer months. In 1973, sales for June were $258,000; July, $423,000; and August, $414,500. April sales totaled about $40,000 and in May were $100,000. Late tourists and hunters traveling through typically generate a modest volume of business in September and October. About one fourth of Wall Drug's sales consists of food; beverages and soda fountain sales account for another 5 percent to 10 percent (although these percentages do vary with the weather). The remaining portion of sales revenue is distributed among jewelry items (10–15 percent), clothing and hats (15 percent), souvenirs (35–40 percent), and drug sundries and prescriptions (5–10 percent). Both Ted and Bill are registered pharmacists, and they fill at least 20 prescriptions a day.

During the summer the store is staffed by a crew of about 150 people, working seven days a week in two shifts from 5 A.M. to 10 P.M. About 40 to 50 percent of the employees are college students recruited especially for the summer months. The students are housed in 10 homes that over the years have been bought and converted into dormitory apartments. The students pay $8 per week rent, but if they stay through Labor Day, they get a $5 per week refund as an incentive to stay the full summer. There is a modern swimming pool for their use. The Husteads set curfews of 11:30 P.M. on weekdays and 1:30 A.M. on weekends for their student residents; according to Bill, now the general manager, "It's hard work, and we feel they need a full night's sleep to do a good job. Besides, auto accidents can happen late at night, and we want to send our kids back home in one piece."[3] About half of the student workers return each year for another season.

When the student employees arrive at the beginning of a new summer season, they are given a cram course in the history of the Badlands and the Black Hills and are told to memorize the mileage from Wall Drug to other tourist attractions such as Mount Rushmore. Then, to make sure the information has been learned, the students are given a quiz. According to Ted Hustead such procedures are used because "If tourists remember Wall Drug, it won't be because we have such a great store but because of the people who waited on them. We want them to be cheerful and helpful."[4]

MERCHANDISE ORDERING

The inventory in Wall Drug varies from around $300,000 in the summer to a low of around $80,000 in the off-season. Ordering for the following summer season begins the preceding fall. Orders begin arriving in December, but most of the merchandise arrives in January, February, March, and April. Many large souvenir companies postdate their invoices until July and August. Each year brings new offerings from souvenir companies and other suppliers. Wall Drug generally buys its souvenir merchandise directly from the producers or importers. The same is true of photo supplies and clothing. Most of the purchasing is done by Bill and Ted, who admit they rely on trusted salesmen of their suppliers to advise them on merchandise purchases. Many of these companies have supplied Wall Drug for 20 years or so. In addition, the Husteads rely on their department managers for buying help. The manager of jewelry, for instance, will recommend on the basis of last year's orders and experience with customer reaction how much to order for the next season. All ordering is approved by Bill and Ted.

Years ago, much of what Wall Drug bought and sold was imported or made by manufacturers in the eastern United States. In recent years much more of the merchandise has been made locally and regionally. Nearby Indian reservations now have small production firms and individuals that supply handcrafted items to Wall Drug. For example, Wall Drug stocked items made by Sioux Pottery, Sioux Moccasin, and Milk Camp Industries.

The merchandise carried ranges from the usual drugstore items to steer skulls, cowboy boots, snakebite serum, lariats, Levis, leather chaps, as well as tourist souvenirs. One of the best-selling items was a snake ashtray made from plaster of paris and painted to resemble a rattlesnake; these were obtained from a resident of the Black Hills who used live rattlers to make the molds for casting the ashtrays. Another feature item was jack-a-lopes (stuffed jackrabbits sporting antelope horns), made by a local taxidermist.

---

[3] As quoted in *The Wall Street Journal,* September 5, 1973, p. 12.
[4] Ibid.

PROMOTION

As indicated earlier, Wall Drug relied heavily on roadside signs to bring people to the store. By 1968 there were about 3,000 signs displayed along highways and roads in all 50 states. The company utilized a truck and two men working nine months a year to maintain the store's signs in South Dakota and adjoining states; however, many signs were put up by volunteers. The store gives away approximately 14,000 6-by-8-inch signs and 3,000 8-by-22-inch signs a year to people who request them. The signs are plastic and weather resistant. Many people have sent in photographs and snapshots showing a Wall Drug sign displayed in some unusual place; these are prominently posted in the store for visitors to see. Making new signs keeps two professional sign painters busy; in 1973 Wall Drug had a $100,000 budget for new signs.

In the mid-1960s, the Highway Beautification Act was passed by Congress and signed into law by President Johnson. The act regulated the use of outdoor billboards along interstate highways and posed a threat to the Husteads' continued reliance upon extensive highway advertising. However, Bill and Ted believed that the media publicity about Wall Drug, together with their sign giveaway program, would help offset the possible reduction in highway signs. Nonetheless, the Husteads felt that it was very important for Wall Drug to gain as much attention and publicity as possible. Subsequently, small ads were placed in New York City's Greenwich Village publication *The Village Voice* advertising 5 cent coffee, 49 cent breakfasts, and animal health remedies at Wall Drug. These ads resulted in a telephone call, several letter inquiries, an article about Wall Drug in *The Village Voice,* and some attention from other media sources. An article in *The New York Times* and some other publicity led to Bill Hustead's appearance on Garry Moore's television program "To Tell the Truth." Wall Drug's posters in the London subway produced a 20-minute, taped telephone interview with Ted by the British Broadcasting Company. Shortly thereafter, several British newspapers carried stories about Wall Drug because of the signs on the London Underground trains. Posters and signs were also erected in the Paris Metro subway (in the English language) and on the dock in Amsterdam in full view of people boarding sight-seeing boats.

Recently, the Husteads began printing two brochures: (1) *Motel Guide for South Dakota,* and (2) *South Dakota Campground Directory of Privately Owned and Operated Campgrounds and Trailer Parks.* Over 200,000 of these guides were given away to Wall Drug visitors each summer. The Husteads hoped that each of the motels and campgrounds in the brochure would reciprocate by displaying a Wall Drug sign on their premises, if asked to do so. This "we'll promote you if you promote us" approach, however, was in the initial stages and its success undetermined. Bill and Ted had plans for erecting Wall Drug signs which could be seen when travelers turned off the interstate at exits on either side of Wall; such signs on roads leading off the interstate, if appropriately located, were not under jurisdiction of the Highway Beautification Act.

FINANCE

Until December 1973, all of Wall Drug's expansion programs were financed with internally generated funds, supplemented with short-term borrowing. In effect, each addition was paid for as it was built (or soon thereafter). However, to fund construction of the Mall, a 10-year, $250,000 loan in the form of a real estate mortgage was negotiated. Payments on this loan, including 8 percent interest, were $34,000 in 1974 and $37,000 annually from 1975 through 1983.

The company generally financed inventory purchases for the upcoming season with short-term loans if internal funds were inadequate. However, seasonal billings by a number of suppliers obviated the need for heavy financing of inventories. Of course, the company was vulnerable to a cash squeeze if a large inventory was left unsold at the end of any tourist season. This potentiality was aggravated by the fixed annual repayments on the long-term loan.

Exhibits 4 through 10 present the financial condition of both Wall Drug and Wall Auto Livery.

EXHIBIT 4 Wall Drug Store, Inc. Balance Sheets As of December 31

ASSETS	1973	1972
Current assets:		
Cash on hand	$ 1,037	$ 946
Cash in bank	2,450	138
Investment in commercial paper, at cost	70,000	—
Accounts receivable—trade	12,121	7,183
Accounts receivable—officers and employees	4,300	3,323
Accounts receivable—income tax refund	—	19,824
Inventories	144,013	86,890
Accrued interest receivable	463	—
Prepaid insurance	9,455	9,068
Total current assets	243,839	127,372
Investment and other assets:		
Bonds, at cost	$ 1,675	$ 1,675
Organization cost, at cost	972	972
Total investments and other assets	2,647	2,647
Property, plant, and equipment, at cost:		
Land	70,454	50,079
Buildings, building improvements, and parking lot improvements	692,488	527,456
Equipment, furniture, and fixtures	366,651	303,108
	1,129,593	880,643
Less: Accumulated depreciation	427,866	369,743
Depreciated cost of fixed assets	701,727	510,900
Goodwill, at cost	31,386	31,386
Total assets	$ 979,599	$672,305

(Continues)

EXHIBIT 4 (Continued)

LIABILITIES AND STOCKHOLDERS' EQUITY	1973	1972
Current liabilities:		
Notes payable—Wall Auto Livery, Inc.	$ 20,000	$ 50,000
Notes payable—bank	—	20,000
Current maturities of long-term debt	20,058	—
Accounts payable—trade	22,709	30,979
Income taxes payable	11,161	—
Accrued taxes payable	25,880	18,457
Profit sharing contribution payable	30,542	18,231
Accrued payroll and bonuses	40,073	28,559
Accrued interest payable	2,573	255
Total current liabilities	172,996	166,481
Long-term debt:		
Real estate mortgage payable	232,742	—
Contract for deed payable	11,200	—
Total long-term debt	243,942	—
Stockholders' equity:		
Preferred stock, $100 par value, 4%, cumulative, nonvoting, 1,000 shares authorized, 300 shares outstanding	30,000	30,000
Common stock, $100 par value, Class A, 500 shares authorized, 480 shares outstanding	48,000	48,000
Common stock, $100 par value, Class B, nonvoting, 4,500 shares authorized, 400 shares outstanding	40,000	40,000
Retained earnings	444,661	387,824
Total stockholders' equity	562,661	505,824
Total liabilities and stockholders' equity	$ 979,599	$672,305

The accompanying notes (Exhibit 7) are an integral part of these financial statements.

**EXHIBIT 5 Wall Drug Store, Inc. Statements of Income and Retained Earnings
Years Ended December 31**

	1973	1972
Net sales	$1,606,648	$1,335,932
Cost of goods sold	805,827	687,613
Gross profit	800,821	648,319
General and administrative expenses	690,461	577,767
Income from operations	110,360	70,552
Interest income	2,946	188
Rental income	3,647	4,248
Trailer park income	6,020	4,600
Theater income	—	5,197
Gain on sale of assets	176	4,286
Other income	747	902
	123,896	89,973
Other deductions:		
Interest	19,735	4,072
Theater expense	—	2,689
Trailer park expense	4,223	3,433
Loss on sale of assets	—	1,674
Loss on demolition of theater building	—	13,860
	23,958	25,728
Income before income taxes	99,938	64,245
Provision for income tax—current year	40,701	20,176
Net income	59,237	44,069
Retained earnings:		
Beginning	387,824	343,755
	447,061	387,824
Dividends paid	2,400	—
Ending	$ 444,661	$ 387,824
Earnings per share	$ 65.95	$ 48.71

The accompanying notes (Exhibit 7) are an integral part of these financial statements.

EXHIBIT 6 Wall Drug Store, Inc. Statements of Changes in Financial Position Years Ended December 31

	1973	1972
Financial resources were provided by:		
Net income	$ 59,237	$ 44,069
Add income charges not affecting working capital in the period:		
Depreciation	58,723	43,862
Demolition loss on theater building	—	13,860
Working capital provided by operations	117,960	101,791
Proceeds from borrowings	264,000	—
Basis of property and equipment sold	625	2,750
Total resources provided	382,585	104,541
Financial resources were used for:		
Acquisition of land	21,000	5,799
Acquisition of building	165,031	149,924
Acquisition of equipment and signs	64,144	50,636
Reduction in long-term debt	20,058	—
Dividends paid	2,400	—
Total resources used	272,633	206,359
Increase (decrease) in working capital	$109,952	$(101,818)
Working capital:		
Beginning	(39,109)	62,709
Ending	70,843	(39,109)
Increase (decrease) in components of working capital:		
Current assets:		
Cash	2,403	(1,850)
Investment in commercial paper	70,000	—
Marketable securities	—	(59,375)
Accounts receivable—trade and other	(13,909)	684
Inventories	57,123	7,204
Other current assets—net	850	(3,650)
Total assets	116,467	(56,987)
Current liabilities:		
Note payable—banks and others	(50,000)	70,000
Current maturities of long-term debt	20,058	—
Accounts payable—trade	(8,270)	12,891
Income tax payable	11,161	(32,272)
Other current and accrued liabilities—net	33,566	(5,788)
Total liabilities	6,515	44,831
Increase (decrease) in working capital	$109,952	$(101,818)

The accompanying notes (Exhibit 7) are an integral part of these financial statements.

EXHIBIT 7 Notes to Financial Statements

Note 1. Summary of Accounting Policies

Accounting Method. The corporation uses the accrual method of accounting for income tax and financial statement purposes.

Inventories. Inventories are generally valued at the lower of cost or market on a first-in, first-out basis computed under retail method.

Fixed Assets. Fixed assets are stated at cost. Depreciation is calculated under the straight-line method, 150 percent declining-balance method and 200 percent declining-balance method. The same depreciation methods are used for financial and tax purposes. The useful lives selected for the assets are as follows: Buildings and building improvements, 15 to 40 years; parking lot, 8 years; and furniture, fixtures and equipment, 5 to 10 years. The provision for depreciation for 1973 of $58,723 and 1972 of $43,862 was charged to operations.

Repairs and maintenance costs are generally charged to expense at the time the expenditure is incurred. When an asset is sold or retired, its cost and related depreciation are removed from the accounts and a gain or loss is recognized on the difference between the proceeds of disposition and the undepreciated cost as the case may be. When an asset is traded in a like exchange, the cost and related depreciation are removed from the accounts and the undepreciated cost is capitalized as a part of the cost of the asset acquired.

Income Taxes. The provision for income taxes is based on the elements of income and expense, as reported in the statement of income. Investment tax credits are accounted for on the "flow-through" method, which recognizes the benefits in the year in which the assets which give rise to the credit are placed in service.

Note 2. Long-Term Debt

The real estate mortgage is an 8 percent mortgage dated December 3, 1973, and due October 1, 1983. The mortgage is to be paid in annual installments of principal and interest as follows:

10-1-74	$34,035.28
10-1-75 and thereafter	$37,257.50

The Drug Store in downtown Wall is pledged as security on this real estate mortgage.

The contract for deed payable is a 7 percent contract for deed, dated January 16, 1973, and is due January 16, 1978. The contract is to be paid in annual installments of $2,800 plus interest. This contract is for the purchase of approximately 202 acres of land which is the security for the contract for deed.

Note 3. Profit Sharing Plan

The company has a profit sharing plan for all full-time employees who meet the qualification requirements. The company contributed $30,542 in 1973 and $18,231 in 1972 to the profit sharing trust.

EXHIBIT 8 Wall Auto Livery, Inc. Balance Sheets As of December 31

ASSETS	1973	1972
Current assets:		
Cash on hand	$ 100	$ 100
Cash in bank	14,590	19,916
Marketable securities, at cost	58,715	—
Notes receivable—Wall Drug Store, Inc.	20,000	50,000
Accounts receivable—trade	1,967	8,205
Credit cards	2,010	—
Miscellaneous receivables	—	75
Inventory, at lower of cost (FIFO) or market	8,462	9,261
Prepaid insurance	1,557	1,469
Accrued interest receivable	729	247
Total current assets	108,130	89,273
Property and equipment:		
Land	7,367	7,367
Buildings	103,133	103,133
Equipment	26,297	26,076
	136,797	136,576
Less: Accumulated depreciation	57,685	52,548
Depreciation cost of fixed assets	79,112	84,028
Total assets	$187,242	$173,301

LIABILITIES AND STOCKHOLDERS' EQUITY	1973	1974
Current liabilities:		
Current maturity of long-term debt	$ 5,000	$ 5,000
Accounts payable—trade	754	5,696
Income taxes payable	7,286	2,774
Accrued profit sharing contribution	2,666	2,446
Accrued payroll and sales taxes	840	756
Accrued interest payable	125	250
Total current liabilities	16,671	16,922
Long-term debt:		
Note payable noninterest bearing contract payable to F. M. Cheny maturing March 1, 1976	5,000	5,000
Note payable—6 percent to Perpetual National Life Insurance Company maturing in annual installments of $5,000 plus interest	—	5,000
Total long-term debt	5,000	10,000
Stockholders' equity:		
Common stock, $100 par value, 2,000 shares authorized, 444 shares outstanding	44,400	44,400
Retained earnings	121,171	101,979
Total stockholders' equity	165,571	146,379
Total liabilities and stockholders' equity	$187,242	$173,301

The accompanying notes (Exhibit 7) are an integral part of these financial statements.

EXHIBIT 9 Wall Auto Livery, Inc. Statements of Income and Retained Earnings Years Ended December 31

	1973	1972
Net sales	$191,969	$172,195
Inventories—beginning of year	9,261	9,467
Purchases	132,698	124,399
Freight	35	—
	141,994	133,866
Inventories—end of year	8,462	9,261
Cost of goods sold	133,532	124,605
Gross profit	58,437	47,590
General and administrative expense	44,568	41,443
Income from operations	13,869	6,147
Interest income	5,441	2,436
Rental income	17,917	15,440
Miscellaneous income	—	1,434
	37,227	25,457
Other deductions:		
Interest expense	510	775
Rent expense—depreciation	3,005	3,128
	3,515	3,903
Income before federal income tax	33,712	21,554
Provision for income taxes	14,520	7,574
Net income	19,192	13,980
Retained earnings:		
Beginning	101,979	87,999
Ending	$121,171	$101,979
Earnings per share	$ 43.23	$ 31.49

The accompanying notes (Exhibit 7) are an integral part of these financial statements.

EXHIBIT 10 Wall Auto Livery, Inc. Statements of Changes in Financial Position Years Ended December 31

	1973	1972
Financial resources were provided by:		
Net income	$19,192	$13,980
Add income charges not affecting working capital in the period:		
Depreciation	5,137	5,390
Working capital provided by operators	24,329	$19,370
Financial resources were used for:		
Acquisition of equipment	221	3,310
Reduction of long-term debt	5,000	5,000
Total resources used	5,221	8,310
Increase in working capital	19,108	11,060
Working capital:		
Beginning of year	72,352	61,292
End of year	91,460	72,352
Increase (decrease) in components of working capital:		
Current assets:		
Cash	(5,326)	15,394
Marketable securities	58,715	(58,087)
Notes receivable	(30,000)	50,000
Accounts receivable	(6,238)	3,371
Credit cards	2,010	—
Miscellaneous receivables	(75)	(57)
Inventory	(799)	(206)
Prepaid insurance	88	73
Accrued interest receivable	482	40
Total assets	18,857	10,528
Current liabilities:		
Accounts payable—trade	(4,942)	1,064
Income taxes payable	4,512	(1,925)
Other current and accrued liabilities	179	329
Total liabilities	(251)	(532)
Increase in working capital	$19,108	$11,060

The accompanying notes (Exhibit 7) are an integral part of these financial statements.

INDUSTRIAL HIGHLIGHT

Drug Store Segment of the Retail Trade Industry

Below is a capsule summary of the drug store segment of the retail trade industry, of which Wall Drug is a part. Information in this highlight was compiled by the U.S. Department of Commerce and focuses on this industry during the approximate period of time covered in the case. Keep in mind that industrial highlights contained in this text are not intended as a complete synopsis of an industry but as a profile of certain issues that can be relevant to a case situation.

CURRENT SITUATION

Corporate management has found ownership of drug chains to provide increased profits as well as opportunities to maximize facilities and services provided by the parent organization. Recently, two large food store chains, a general merchandiser, a large discounter, and a conglomerate acquired substantial retail drug operations. In a move to broaden product lines, a food store chain and a drug chain agreed to develop food-drug units 75,000 to 80,000 square feet in size, to sell both food and drugs in one retailing operation.

Drug stores are facing increased competition from other retailers. Chain store managements are concentrating their efforts on constructing more of their own stores, increasing sales in existing stores and consolidating their penetration of existing markets.

During the past decade, the size of drug stores has continued to expand as management broadened the number and type of non-drug items offered for sale. Efforts are being directed toward utilizing existing selling space, with emphasis placed on high profit, nonprescription items. Drug store sales are expected to increase to a record $16.3 billion in 1974, a 6-percent increase over 1973.

Store Locations

Locations favored by drug chains are in "strip" and neighborhood developments rather than large regional centers or enclosed mall shopping areas. Sixty percent

Source: U.S. Industrial Outlook, Department of Commerce, 1973, pp. 400–401; 1974, p. 152.

EXHIBIT A   Prescriptions Increase Share of Drug Store Sales—1967–1973

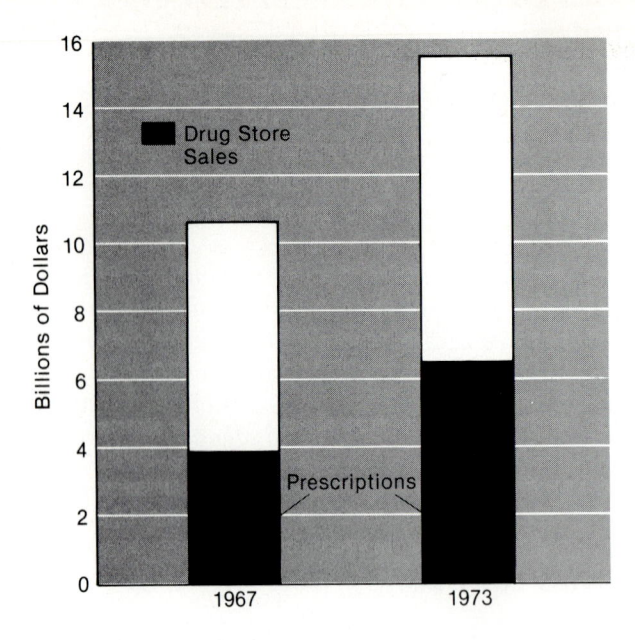

[Bar chart showing Billions of Dollars for Drug Store Sales and Prescriptions in 1967 (~4 prescriptions, ~10.7 total) and 1973 (~6.6 prescriptions, ~15.7 total)]

Source: Bureau of the Census and Bureau of Domestic Commerce.

of new chain stores were scheduled for "strip" locations, 15 percent in enclosed malls, and 25 percent on free standing sites elsewhere. A drug store of only 15,000 to 50,000 square feet qualifies for an anchor position in a smaller neighborhood but not in a larger center.

Third Party Prescriptions Rising

Third party prescriptions—private or public health insurance paid—accounted for 13 percent of chain store prescriptions written in 1971, compared with 5 percent in 1970 and only 2 percent in 1969. The average chain drug store filled almost 100 third party prescriptions each week in 1972, and the number of such prescriptions filled per store is expected to grow substantially in the years ahead as health insurance coverage for medicines expands.

Health Foods Spur Sales

Aided by the growing popularity of natural food products, drug store sales of organically grown health foods are increasing rapidly. Individual retail sales of $5 to $8 are typical and sales of $25 to $30 are fairly frequent. Natural vitamin supplements as well as foods containing vitamins are favored sellers along with such items as wheat germ, dolomite and shelled nuts and seeds. Additional receipts result from the sale of fruit juices, salads and health breads and health food luncheons at food counters.

LONG-TERM PROSPECTS

Industry sources estimate that about 6 percent of all chain drugstores rely on leased pharmacy departments to provide prescription services. Drug department leasing in department stores, grocery chains and general merchandise stores is expected to grow in the years ahead because of favorable profit margins on drug merchandise and the traffic drawing capacity of prescription departments.

SECTION TWO
Environmental Analysis and Organizational Direction

CASE 4

Federal Express: Is There Any "Zip" Left In ZapMail?

PER V. JENSTER
McIntire School of Commerce, University of Virginia

As the annual stockholders' meeting for Federal Express Corporation was approaching on September 29, 1986, increasing interest focused on chief executive officer Fred Smith's future plans to improve the profit performance of ZapMail and the company as a whole.

BACKGROUND

History

The birth of Federal Express Corporation in 1973 marked a virtual revolution in the air cargo industry. Initially conceived by company founder Fred Smith in an economics paper written while he was an undergraduate at Yale, the idea of an all-freight airline for small, time-sensitive packages ran counter to all the proven caveats of an established air freight industry. Smith proved to be a better predictor of market need than his professor, however. His economics paper received a C−, yet Federal Express is now a Fortune 500 company earning multi-million dollar profits annually.

Prior to Federal's market entry, the traditional air freight industry consisted of "freight forwarders," firms who sent packages as cargo on regular passenger airlines. Fred Smith contended that these companies were not in a position to provide adequate service to an ever-expanding, technologically-based economy.

The forwarders were restrained from providing rapid delivery by passenger airline schedules designed to meet the needs of travelers. Passenger flights ran primarily during the daytime with planes grounded at night. Able to move cargo for only twelve hours each day, it was virtually impossible for the forwarders to guarantee overnight delivery of packages. Passenger flight schedules also limited forwarders in the number of cities they could service. Above all, the freight forwarded provided airport-to-airport service only. Costs and inconvenience associated with transporting a package to and from the airport were left to the shipper and cosigner.

This case was written by Professor Per V. Jenster, McIntire School of Commerce, University of Virginia, with the assistance of Deborah Chevion, Joanne Gardner, and Deborah Rinehart, Dec. 22, 1986.

Given the seemingly obvious shortcomings of the existing air freight industry, Smith conceived the idea of an all-freight airline combined with a pick-up and delivery service. Packages would be picked up from shippers, flown to a central location during the night, sorted, and flown to their destination for delivery the next day. This "hub-and-spokes" concept was tailored specifically for shippers of priority materials for whom speed of delivery is more important than cost. As Smith himself observed in later years:

> America was spreading out technologically. . . . The efficacy of our society is to be smarter, not to work harder . . . that's what we (Federal Express) are all about—reacting to the needs of today's society, which wants things done fast, or I should say faster.

Upon returning from Vietnam in 1972, only six years after receiving the mediocre economics grade, Fred Smith began to put his air express idea into action and became the founding father of Federal Express Corporation: "A whole new airline for packages only."

The nature of the Federal Express concept required a tremendous capital outlay before Smith and his fledgling company could even begin operations. In addition to the normal start-up costs facing any entrepreneur, Smith needed to purchase entire fleets of airplanes and delivery vehicles, lease airport hangars and runway space, and finance the building of an air terminal. Never one to be daunted by seemingly insurmountable obstacles, however, Smith addressed these astronomical cash outflow requirements by embarking upon the largest venture capital campaign in American business history. Between 1972 and 1974, Smith managed to raise a staggering $40 million in equity capital as well as $50 million in loans.

In its first two years of operation Federal Express lost an average of $1 million each month. The effects of the 1973–74 fuel crisis and recession were felt strongly by the new company. Even as daily package counts increased, the company failed to gain ground in overcoming the immense start-up costs.

Undeterred, Fred Smith retained confidence in the soundness of the people and ideas behind Federal Express. The company finally broke even and realized its first profit in July of 1975. That same year overall revenues surpassed $1 million per week and package counts averaged 11,500 daily. Since 1975, Federal's revenues have more than doubled every two years.

The company, as of 1984, owned approximately 60 percent of the small package and document delivery market, in spite of several new firms which joined the market in the late 1970s and early 1980s. While these newcomers were struggling merely to establish themselves in the new industry, Federal was moving light years ahead in terms of technology, service, and organization.

Industry and Competitors

Federal Express competed in the small package/document market of the $6 billion air cargo industry. This market had been the fastest growing sector of the industry over the past six years, with 20 percent annual growth rates. The two major factors defining the express market were package size and delivery time-constraints.

Trends 1973–1982

After Federal Express' entry and cultivation of the new, express-mail market, many other courier companies saw the potential for increasing their market share of the air freight industry. Two new entrants were Emery Air Freight and Purolator. Competition in the new industry became heated. The race was on to establish networks and to gain market share. Many of these networks were based on the hub-and-spokes concept innovated by Federal Express. Expansions included huge asset acquisition of planes, trucks, and distribution centers.

Trends 1982–1985

The three-year period following the industry expansion was characterized by increasing competition for market share, which translated into fierce price wars. United Parcel Service, the largest privately owned U.S. package transporter, lowered the industry price floor for its Second-Day Air service in 1982. This price decrease forced Federal Express to emphasize its own two-day option, Standard Air, at a lower price.

The continuing competition brought new innovations into the industry (see Exhibit 1). In 1984, Federal Express introduced its Overnight Letter, proffering a 10:30 A.M., next day delivery service. Purolator responded to Federal Express' move by offering the Puroletter, while Emery offered the Urgent Letter and Urgent Pouch. In 1985 UPS introduced Next Day Air Letter. As the 1985 price war continued, Federal Express' revenue per package declined by 8.7 percent while Emery suffered a decrease of 26 percent per package. These shrinking margins placed a greater emphasis on cost-cutting and control.

Trends 1986

The industry began to look toward international service as the U.S. market appeared to become saturated. By 1986, Federal Express had achieved 95 percent coverage while UPS offered service to every address in the 48 continental states, Hawaii, and Puerto Rico. Additional pressures arose from the decline of U.S. industrial production, shrinking the demand by domestic business for overnight express.

This decline motivated the courier companies to look beyond the domestic market, focusing on ever-expanding international trade. As business itself

EXHIBIT 1

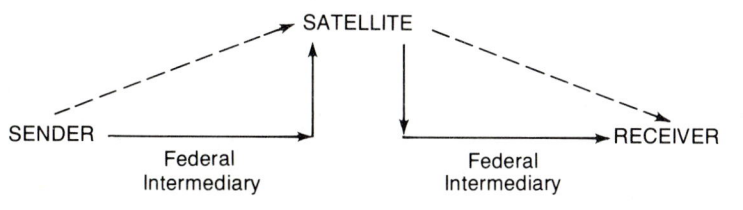

GROUND LINE RELIANCE

became more global in nature, demand for improved document transportation offered new opportunities for overnight express carriers overseas.

Fred Smith

The dramatic success of Federal Express Corporation can, without question, be attributed to aggressive, expertly designed marketing, management, and expansion strategies. It is equally indisputable that the main impetus for these strategies is Chairman Frederick W. Smith.

Remarkable ingenuity and foresight allowed Fred Smith to establish an industry-leading enterprise and, indeed, an entire industry in a remarkably short period of time. Organizationally speaking, the structure and corporate personality of Federal Express emanate entirely from its brash, outspoken founder. Smith's eclectic background (comprised of, among other things, an Ivy League education followed by two tours of duty in Vietnam) combined with his aggressive entrepreneurial spirit have given Federal Express and its employees a sense of commitment to excellence that has been the cornerstone of the firm's success.

Following Federal's emergence as one of the most profitable new ventures of the 1970s, Smith, himself, emerged as a symbol of glamour and entrepreneurial achievement in the corporate world. At its outset, the Federal Express concept was considered to be reckless, yet Smith's ingenuity and stubborn devotion to his brain-child convinced investors, and eventually the world, of the soundness of his air freight innovation.

Throughout Federal's history Smith has dominated the planning function. He has set goals and policy for all aspects of the company's operations, and has been the guiding force in the evolution of Federal's corporate image. Robert Sigafoos characterized Smith most effectively in the following manner in his book, *Absolutely Positively Overnight!*:

> Smith fits nicely into that special category of skillful, opportunistic, egotistical, strong-willed 'one man shows' heading successful ventures into contemporary corporate America . . . Fred Smith possesses the desire for power and achievement found in all great corporate leaders.

Simply put, Fred Smith is Federal Express. His dominance was strongly felt throughout the development and introductory stages of the company's newest service, ZapMail.

ZAPMAIL

The Opportunity

With the emergence of the high tech boom in the early 1980s, it became apparent that telecommunications technology was destined to make its mark on the document transfer industry. Fred Smith saw an opportunity, even a necessity for Federal Express to enter the market, and, with his customary drive and charisma, he committed a major portion of the company's resources to the development of ZapMail, an electronic mail facsimile transmission system.

The ZapMail system, catering to those times "when overnight just isn't enough," was developed as a combination of the courier service with a facsimile transmission network. The network was already an integral part of Federal's internal operations which enabled the company to track packages, couriers, and customer orders. ZapMail, in essence, expanded the use of the network from the transfer of information *about* customers' documents to the transfer of those documents themselves. The addition of facsimile technology to the network enabled Federal to use telephone lines (or satellites) to transmit an actual photographic image of a document from a transmitting to a receiving terminal.

The Concept

Conceptually, the ZapMail system was relatively simple to understand. Federal placed at least one facsimile machine in each of its 318 Business Service Centers located throughout the United States. Accommodating the needs of the customer, a Federal courier would pick up the customer's document and take it to the nearest Business Service Center. The document would then be transmitted by ground line and/or satellite to another machine in a Federal Express office near the destination (see Exhibit 1). A courier at that office would then deliver the transmitted copy to the addressee, hopefully not more than two hours later. Upon introduction in July of 1984, the new system had a few problems, but Federal was committed to providing complete customer satisfaction with ZapMail. Customers whose documents were not delivered within two hours were generally given refunds.

ZapMail service initially cost $35 for up to 10 pages with an additional charge of $1 for each page thereafter. The money-back guarantee on two-hour delivery applied only to documents of 10 pages or less. Because of the speed limitations of facsimile technology, Federal had to add an hour to delivery time for each additional 10-page increment after the initial one. The installation of high speed transmission lines by AT&T, though, enabled Federal to cut transmission time down to five seconds per page. Further technical improvements were to be expected after Federal launched satellites, further cutting transmission time and also limiting dependence on AT&T, a potential competitor in electronic data transfer. The price of ZapMail service was projected to decrease with increased sales volume and technical improvements. Amortization of the substantial system start-up costs would also result in lower prices. Soon after its introduction, ZapMail service was expanded, in response to consumer demand, to include the rental and installation of receiving terminals in customer's offices. "ZapMailers" rented for $525 per month plus $0.25 per page and a $10 delivery cost.

The Strategy

Federal Express was criticized for its use of facsimile machines rather than a computer-based system. Critics argued that facsimile machines were slow transmitters and produced low quality images. They also believed that since computers were destined to dominate the electronic data transfer market in the future, it was frivolous to implement a facsimile system in the present.

Due to the proliferation of computers in business offices, industry analysts estimated that the market for computer mailboxes would grow to more than $1 billion by 1990. Federal Express, however, was "wagering [that] the personal computer won't conquer offices as fast as some competitors think." The fact that neither sender nor receiver need own or operate a computer made facsimile transmission a very appealing short-term alternative for businesses.

As Fred Smith put it, ZapMail was based in "a medium which lends itself to the way people [now] work, with paper." Federal's strategy was to utilize proven facsimile technology in the present, while developing computer technology for introduction in the future, when the systems were more defined and the market more accepting. It was hoped that the eventual introduction of a complete Federal Express data transfer network would benefit from the early establishment of customer loyalty to the ZapMail service.

The Market's Response

The market did look promising. In 1984, 500,000 Zap terminals were installed with an additional 250,000 installations expected by the end of 1985. As of March 1985, 100,500 units had already been installed. The ZapMail concept was apparently right in line with the changing needs of business. There was a very real demand for two-hour document transmission. George M. Stamps, president of GMS Consulting, Westport, CT, predicted, "Shipments will soar and prices will drop by one third in the red-hot facsimile market this year [1985]." Although ZapMail was still a long way from breaking even, Stamps thought the service would succeed.

Federal Express, too, predicted enormous growth in the electronic mail/facsimile market and set investment projections at $1.2 billion for ZapMail. Satellite transmission would eventually supplant groundlines, and reliance on outside suppliers of telecommunications services such as AT&T would be reduced. Federal would use and install its own satellites, leading to a decrease in operating costs and steady improvement in bottom line profits for ZapMail.

The Industry and Competitors

Facsimile machine production was regulated by the Consultative Committee for International Telephone and Telegraph (CCITT) for intercompany compatibility.

By 1986, four categories of facsimile machines had been established. Group 1 standards set in 1974 produced a machine that could send a document in six minutes per page. By 1976, Group 2 machines could send documents in half the time. Groups 3's improvements not only cut the sending time down to one minute but included better quality of reproduction. The Group 4 standards had been set to produce machines that can send documents in one to five seconds per page. While these fourth generation machines existed, they were not widely available.

Trends

The major change in the facsimile industry during the preceeding 12 years had been improvement in machine efficiency, while prices dropped in 1986 to half the original 1974 prices. The four major advantages of facsimile transfer included:

- No special training required
- No typing time involved. The facsimile machine would transfer an image of the actual document
- Handles graphics, including signature reproductions
- Can operate unattended

Although these advantages and the price decreases might have indicated opportunities to improve document transfer for many businesses, the 500,000 facsimile machines installed as of 1984 represented only a fraction of the 25 million potential business users. Many of these machines were bought outright from original manufacturers such as Xerox, Sharp Electronics Corporation, Harris/3M, and Teleautograph. Not only did Federal Express have to contend with these purchases, but both Western Union and MCI Communications Corporation offered facsimile services, EasyLink and MCI Mail respectively.

The Problem

Unfortunately, this improvement in profits did not materialize on schedule (see Exhibits 2–5). ZapMail continued to lose money due to several factors. Users balked at the original $35 charge for 10 pages and were only partially appeased when the company exercised a $10 price cut. Technical bugs increased customer resistance. Messages were garbled and machines often broke down due to overloaded groundlines, an integral part of the data transmission.

EXHIBIT 2   Long Distance Courier Comparison Chart

	AREA SERVED	WEIGHT LIMITS	OVERNIGHT COSTS	DELIVERY TIME	REFUNDS
Airborne Freight	U.S. and 31 other	None	1 lb–$14 2 lb–$25	Noon	Yes
DHL	U.S. and 12 other	70 lb/box 210 lb/bill	5 ozs–$14 25 lb–$25	Varies	No
Emery Worldwide	Most of North America	None	8 ozs–$14 2 lb–$23	10:30 am	No
Federal Express	98% U.S. coverage and 81 other	None	½ lb–$14	10:30 am	Yes
Purolator	All of U.S.	125 lbs	2 lbs–$13.75	11:59 am	No
UPS	Any address in U.S. and P.R.	70 lbs	1 lb–$11.50 2 lbs–$12.50	Varies	No
U.S. Postal	All of U.S. and P.R.	70 lbs	2 lbs–$10.75	3:00 pm	Yes

EXHIBIT 3

SEGMENT INFORMATION IN THOUSANDS	EXPRESS DELIVERY	ZAPMAIL	CORPORATE	TOTAL
1986				
Revenues	$2,573,229	$ 32,981	$ 0	$2,606,210
Operating income	406,800	−131,880	−62,779	212,141
Identifiable assets	1,887,107	170,351	218,904	2,276,362
Depreciation	191,574	18,860	1,970	212,404
Capital expenditure	529,867	134,345	10,559	674,771
1985				
Revenues	$2,015,920	$ 14,741	$ 0	$2,030,661
Operating income	308,183	−121,894	−49,566	136,723
Identifiable assets	1,668,029	185,945	45,532	1,899,506
Depreciation	158,203	12,281	1,849	172,333
Capital expenditure	496,223	70,410	4,421	571,054

EXHIBIT 4 Federal Express Consolidated Income Statement (in thousands)

	1986	1985	1984
Revenues	$2,606,210	$2,030,661	$1,436,305
Operating expenses:			
Salaries	1,162,920	907,186	622,675
Equipment and facilities rental	214,372	146,389	87,572
Depreciation	212,404	172,333	111,956
Fuel	149,688	133,473	93,520
Maintenance and repairs	125,087	90,992	59,482
Other	529,598	443,565	295,892
Operating income	212,141	136,723	165,208
Other income:			
Interest capitalized	6,808	9,736	11,851
Interest income	10,908	9,209	13,166
Gain on disposition of Aircraft	11,877	8,499	2,463
Other expenses:			
Interest expense	65,505	72,329	36,350
Net other	12,024	8,460	4,078
Pretax income	164,205	83,378	152,260
Taxes	32,366	7,301	36,830
Net income	$ 131,839	$ 76,077	$ 115,430
EPS	2.64	1.61	2.52

Leasing fees coupled with the inability to handle the volume produced by NECs (Japanese manufacturer of the ZapMail hardware) high-speed machines, resulted in frequently faulty transmissions. Though rapid development of satellite capability could solve many of the problems stemming from overused ground lines, these prospects were dampened by the *Challenger* space shuttle disaster in March, 1986. Until NASA resumed the shuttle project (scheduled

EXHIBIT 5 Federal Express Consolidated Balance Sheet
(in thousands)

	1986	1985
Current assets:		
Cash	$ 185,036	$ 12,189
Net receivables	347,010	292,797
Spare parts	49,342	56,537
Tax refund	0	42,858
Prepaids	31,902	18,763
Total current assets	613,290	423,144
Property and equipment:		
Flight	841,410	774,114
Ground support	418,053	341,108
Computer	391,146	297,509
Other P and E	551,992	380,285
Total P and E	2,202,601	1,793,016
Less depreciation	650,756	446,993
Net P and E	1,551,845	1,346,023
Other assets	111,227	130,339
Total assets	2,276,362	1,899,506
Current liabilities:		
Current LT debt	72,979	44,730
Account payable	184,534	127,721
Accruals	174,397	144,427
Total current liabilities	431,910	316,878
Long-term debt	561,716	607,508
Deferred taxes	189,513	159,810
Other commitments	1,509	3,043
Total liabilities	1,184,648	1,087,239
Stockholders' equity:		
Common stock	5,081	4,703
Paid-in capital	530,618	340,753
Retained earnings	598,215	466,811
Less deferred compensation	42,200	0
Total equity	1,091,714	812,267
Total liabilities and equity	$2,276,362	$1,899,506

for 1988, at the earliest) there would be no means of launching commercial satellites.

Not to be defeated, Federal announced on March 20, 1986, a moratorium on new ZapMail installations "until the bugs were worked out." Despite hard-nosed efforts by management, costs continued to escalate. "The bugs" were proving quite expensive to repair. Federal was facing new competitors in its base business (overnight delivery) as well. It was becoming apparent that a substantial reinvestment of earnings in the overnight carrier business would be necessary in the near future.

Competition for market share was fierce, demanding ever increasing attention to cost and innovation. While Federal had shown overall profit gain of 42 percent to $131.8 million in the year ended May 31, 1986, ZapMail had lost $132 million on revenue of only $33 million.

Strategically, ZapMail seemed to make sense. It would surely take time for a whole new communications system to catch on, and Smith did not like the idea of doing away with ZapMail, which had, for all practical purposes, been his brainchild. He pointed to the birth of telephone technology as evidence that communication networks don't spring up "overnight." As with the telephone, consumers needed time to realize that the benefits of ZapMail are so essential to modern business that everyone must subscribe, thus making the network a success. Smith reasoned:

> We've had a few things over the years, small things mostly, that we've cut loose where we just couldn't do it—where we felt we didn't have the skills or where we hadn't thought about the business problem in sufficient detail. . . . But as to ZapMail, as best I can tell at the moment, there's no question it is going to work. We know we're headed in the right direction in terms of the market. The basic numbers are headed in the right direction. It's now just a matter of when.

But financial problems persisted and the question became, "Aren't we risking our stronghold in overnight mail? Can judgment be that easy?" Publicly Smith had argued that:

> Most innovation doesn't look like it makes much financial sense when you're right in the middle of battle—it looks like you never should have done it. It's only when it's been done and it's out there that everybody says, 'Oh, but of course, that was easy.' Then the money starts flowing in and you become a very big deal, and it all looks very logical.

Senior management wondered what lay ahead for ZapMail, and for Federal Express. The potential market existed and the Zap service seemed to be a sound concept, yet sales revenue had been disappointing. Something was very wrong, but what? Could ZapMail become a profitable service? If so, how? And if not, could Fred Smith be persuaded to see its shortcomings? Decisions and a plan for the immediate future of ZapMail had to be formulated for Smith to present to the stockholders.

Exhibits 6 through 8 present Federal Express revenues, net income, and operating income for the years 1982–1986.

EXHIBIT 6   Federal Express Revenues

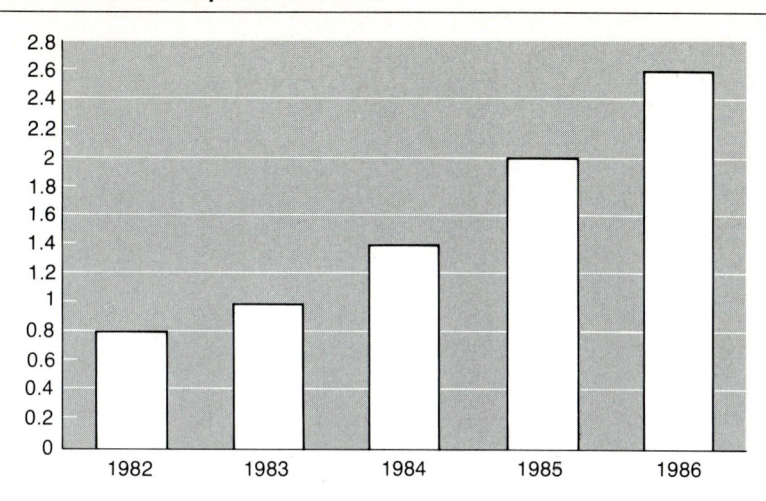

Year	Revenues
1982	0.8
1983	1.0
1984	1.4
1985	2.0
1986	2.6

EXHIBIT 7   Federal Express Net Income

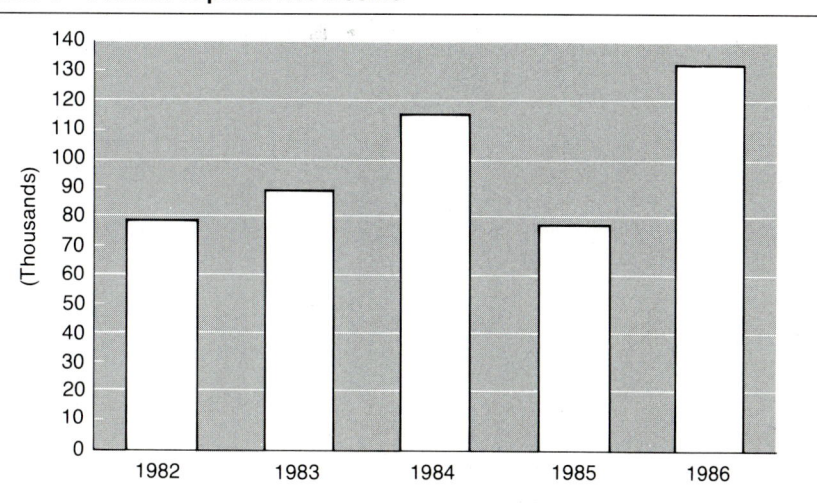

(Thousands)

Year	Net Income
1982	78
1983	88
1984	115
1985	76
1986	131

EXHIBIT 8 Federal Express Operating Income

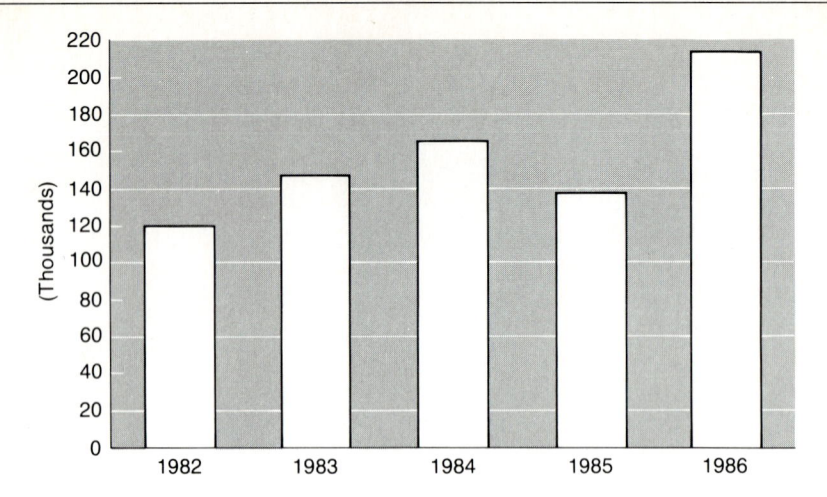

INDUSTRIAL HIGHLIGHT

Transportation Services Industry

Below is a capsule summary of the airlines segment of the transportation services industry, of which Federal Express is a part. Information in this highlight was compiled by the U.S. Department of Commerce and focuses on this industry during the approximate period of time covered in the case. Keep in mind that industrial highlights contained in this text are not intended as a complete synopsis of an industry but as a profile of certain issues that can be relevant to a case situation.

The U.S. airline industry consists of some 250 individual commercial air carriers operating over 4,200 aircraft. In 1984, these carriers logged 304.5 billion revenue passenger miles (RPMs)—equivalent to one paying passenger traveling 1 mile—up 8 percent from 1983. In addition, the industry recorded 8.2 billion cargo ton-miles. Total operating revenues for U.S. carriers in 1984 amounted to $43.8 billion, up from $39.0 billion the year before.

The industry is highly skewed with respect to airline size. Dominating industry output are the major airlines with annual operating revenues in excess of $1 billion each. Twelve majors—including giants such as Eastern, Pan American, United, and Trans World—captured 80 percent of the industry's revenues and 83 percent of the passenger traffic in 1984.

The next smaller group, the nationals, includes 16 carriers with annual operating revenues of $75 million to $1 billion each. Their market share is much smaller than that of the majors, but growing. For example, it rose to 14.1 percent of RPMs in the first 6 months of 1985 from 11.6 percent in the same period of 1984.

Next in size are the large regionals (annual revenues of $10–75 million) and the medium regionals (annual revenues of less than $10 million). The large and medium regionals total approximately 40 companies, including both scheduled airlines and operators providing primarily charter flights, but they have only about 3 percent of the passenger traffic. Finally, there are the smaller regional and commuter airlines, traditionally classified as "operating aircraft with no more than 60 seats." These carriers, numbering just over 200, recorded

Source: U.S. Industrial Outlook, Department of Commerce, 1956, p. 55-1 to 55-3.

4.1 billion RPMs in 1984—only 1.3 percent of the industry's total, but up a strong 29 percent from 1983.

CURRENT SITUATION

As 1985 drew to a close, it was clear that U.S. airlines were well on their way toward completing another year of sustained economic growth. With record numbers of passengers now taking to the airways, many airlines are recovering dramatically from the industry slump of 1979–82, although some carriers have experienced severe financial problems because of the intense competition.

At the nadir of the slump, in 1982, the industry suffered an operating loss of some $773 million. However, it rebounded in 1983 with a minor operating profit of $310 million, which then soared almost 700 percent to over $2.1 billion in 1984.

The industry's operating profit for the first 6 months of 1985, at $929 million, was only negligibly lower than the $959 million posted for the same period in 1984. Operating revenues for the first half of 1985 ($21.4 billion) exceeded the $20.0 billion received during the first 6 months of 1984, and they are forecast at $47.7 billion for the full year, 9 percent above 1984's. These figures are in spite of huge losses suffered in early 1985 by United and Pan Am due to strikes.

Revenues from air cargo represent a little more than 8 percent of the industry's total operating revenues ($3.5 billion in 1984). However, the fastest growing segment of the airline industry lies within the air cargo field—that of small package and express air freight. For the first 6 months of 1985, such shipments numbered 92.7 million (including the U.S. Postal Service's express mail), up 25.3 percent from the same period of 1984, and revenues from them rose 24.3 percent to just under $2 billion.

Economic Factors

A number of factors have contributed to the recent economic health of the industry. Most important among these has been the general growth of the U.S. economy. The real state of GNP growth for 1984, 6.8 percent, was almost twice that of the rate of growth for 1983, 3.7 percent. The rate of inflation for the past several years has averaged only 3–4 percent, far below the double-digit figures recorded in the late 1970s. The airline industry, which has consistently reacted sharply to macroeconomic developments, had enjoyed relative prosperity concomitant with these recent trends.

Another factor is fuel prices. Long an important element of the airlines' expenses, the cost of fuel has been steadily decreasing over the past 5 years. The average price per gallon of all aviation fuel in June 1985 stood at 80.3 cents, down 6.5 percent from June 1984. This was well below the rates in the slump year of 1981, when the price per gallon of domestic fuel averaged over a dollar.

A third factor is the stimulation of air travel through increased use of discount fares. Supported by the Airline Deregulation Act of 1978, established air carriers frequently have responded to market penetration by new entrants by discounting fares in order to retain their existing passenger clienteles. When the new entrant follows with like discounts, fare wars ensue. In 1984, these discounted tickets accounted for 81 percent of all domestic air travel and averaged 51 percent off from the full fare (up three percentage points from 1983). Some passengers previously inclined to travel by rail or automobile have been lured into air travel as a result of these fare wars.

A constraint on labor costs is a fourth factor contributing to the turnaround. Labor costs traditionally represent the single largest element (approximately 35 percent) of airlines' total operating expenses. In 1985, airline management, by and large, continued to receive concessions from labor. At least some of the motivation for these concessions seemed to arise from the financial hardship suffered by some of the carriers, both large and medium-sized. With some carriers teetering on the brink of bankruptcy, employees were inclined to take cutbacks (or at least demand no increases) in order to keep airlines out of the red.

International Aspects

International Air Traffic Summary

The importance of international operation to the airline industry vis-a-vis domestic operation varies with the quantitative measurement used. For example, international air transport accounts for less than 7 percent (22.0 million passengers out of a total of 343.3 million in 1984) of passengers carried by U.S. airlines. Its significance is markedly different, however, when measured by RPMs, since the average trip distance for international travel (2,600 miles) is almost three times greater than for domestic air travel (880 miles). Thus, for 1984, international air travel accounted for 21.5 percent of the industry's total performance (65.5 billion RPMs out of a total of 304.5 billion RPMs). When measured by revenues, a third value is produced since passenger yield (cents per passenger mile) is slightly lower, on average, for international traffic than it is for domestic traffic (12.1 cents versus 12.7 cents). Out of $36.9 billion in passenger revenues earned by the industry in 1984, $5.7 billion (15.4 percent) was from international operations.

Regardless of how the international component of air transport is viewed, it is clear that U.S. international air transport is growing. In 1984, 44.8 million passengers traveled by air between the United States and foreign points (excluding Canada). This is an increase of 11 percent from the 40.5 million international air travelers in 1983.

International charter service accounted for 7 percent of all U.S. international passenger traffic in both 1983 and 1984. For U.S. carriers, the 1984 charter volume dropped 5 percent from the 1983 traffic of 2.0 million passengers. However, traffic on foreign flag charters to and from the United States increased 63 percent to 1.3 million passengers.

Behind Canada, for which no statistics are collected, the top five country markets in 1984 for all U.S. international passenger travel (scheduled and charter) were, in order of descending volume, the United Kingdom, Mexico, Japan, West Germany, and the Bahamas. These five markets together comprise almost half of all international service. The early months of 1985 saw a slackening of the growth rate for international service, to 5 percent from 11 percent tallied for all of 1984.

Passenger Fares and the U.S. Balance-of-Payments

Spurred by the expanded buying power of an appreciating U.S. dollar, increased numbers of U.S. citizens have traveled abroad during the past few years. The strong dollar has simultaneously boosted the cost of travel to the United States from overseas, as well as the cost of tickets on U.S. carriers vis-a-vis foreign carriers. As a result, the passenger fare balance-of-payments for the United States reached a deficit of $2.5 billion in the first half of 1985 as U.S. citizens purchased some $4 billion of tickets from foreign carriers but non-U.S. citizens bought only $1.5 billion worth from U.S. carriers. This deficit was the same as that for all of 1983 and well ahead of the rate in 1984, when the full-year deficit reached $3.5 billion. (The 1984 passenger fare deficit represented almost 4 percent of the $90.1-billion deficit for all goods and services transacted in the U.S. balance-of-payments.)

In 1984, 63 percent of the passengers in international air travel were U.S. citizens, up from 60 percent in 1983. Yet U.S. airlines carried only 49 percent of this 1984 traffic compared with 51 percent in 1983, reflecting the competitive disadvantage of the strong U.S. dollar.

International Air Cargo

Prior to 1982, international air cargo generally offset passenger fare deficits by contributing surpluses to the U.S. balance-of-payments as U.S. receipts from air cargo services exceeded freight payments to foreign airlines by U.S. citizens. This trend was reversed in 1983, however, when the United States recorded an air cargo services balance-of-payments deficit of $446 million. This deficit continued to spiral upward in 1984, more than doubling to $956 million, and it totaled $470 million in the first half of 1985, with U.S. receipts at $345 million and U.S. payments at $815 million. The air cargo deficit in 1984 represented 45 percent of total air cargo revenues traded internationally that year ($2.2 billion), whereas the passenger fare deficit was only 37 percent of the $9.5 billion in passenger fares.

Air cargo's importance as a mode of transport for U.S. international merchandise trade has been steadily increasing. When measured by weight, air cargo accounts for less than 0.5 percent of all U.S. international trade. However, when measured by the value of these goods, air cargo is much more significant. In 1984, 26 percent of the goods moving to and from the United States were carried by air, up from 15 percent a decade earlier.

Air cargo's role is greater for U.S. exports than for imports. In 1984, $103.4 billion of U.S. exports were oceanborne and $51.9 billion were airborne, so that air cargo represented over 33 percent. U.S. imports that year totaled $245.3 billion, with $193.0 billion carried by vessels and $52.3 billion (or 21 percent of all imports) carried by aircraft.

OUTLOOK FOR 1986

The outlook for the airlines in 1986 is generally good, as the economy is expected to continue moderate growth, and fuel prices should remain stable or decrease slightly. Two factors, though, may bode ill for the industry.

The first factor is labor. As of the end of 1985, airline labor appeared to be less inclined to continue concessions to management. Part of this may be labor's perception of the performance of carriers thought to have been close to bankruptcy: some of these did not close their doors and others have actually prospered. Consequently, labor's demands may become stronger and more entrenched, whereas airline management seems more willing to resist labor demands. The industry, therefore, may experience an increase in strikes.

The second factor is fare wars. Competition among the carriers remains keen, with new airlines being formed and established airlines entering new markets. The trend toward discounted fares is expected to be evident again in 1986, although the overall effect may be somewhat mitigated by increased interlining arrangements where carriers agree to provide interconnecting services. These arrangements allow the larger carriers (the majors and nationals) to preserve market shares on well-traveled routes while providing established connections with the regionals and commuters to less frequented destinations.

LONG-TERM PROSPECTS

There are no indications now that the industry is headed for the kind of slump from which it just recently emerged. As long as the economy continues to exhibit a healthy performance, the airlines will prosper accordingly. Total annual operating revenues should now consistently exceed $40 billion, with RPMs approaching 400 billion by the end of this decade. The role of air cargo in U.S. international trade should continue to be important, especially for U.S. exports, since items in which the United States has an international comparative advantage (including electronics, computers, and other high-technology goods) are most likely to be air-transported.

ADDITIONAL REFERENCES

Air Transport 1985, The Annual Report of the U.S. Scheduled Airline Industry. Air Transport Association of America, 1709 New York Avenue, N.W., Washington, DC 20006.

FAA Aviation Forecasts. Fiscal years 1985–1966, February 1985, (FAA-APO-85-2), U.S. Department of Transportation, Federal Aviation Administration, Washington DC 20591.

U.S. Exports, FT 455/1984 December and Annual, Bureau of the Census, U.S. Department of Commerce, Washington, DC 20233.

U.S. General Imports, FT 150/1984 December and Annual, Bureau of the Census, U.S. Department of Commerce, Washington, DC 20233.

CASE 5

Caterpillar Tractor Company

DONALD W. ECKRICH
Ithaca College

INTRODUCTION

In January 1984, Caterpillar Tractor Co. Chairman Lee L. Morgan was actively involved in corporate-wide planning efforts. These efforts were directed at reestablishing Caterpillar's tradition of profitability and world leadership in the heavy equipment and machinery industry. Looking to the coming year, he reported:

> 1984 should be a markedly better year. The 1983 loss of $345 million reflected the deep recession in most of the world's economies. Current indicators suggest . . . strong sales increases for our kinds of products. Sales should be significantly higher in 1984, and we expect to be profitable.

By year end, it was anticipated, specific plans detailing actions on new business opportunities would be completed and long-term sales and profit strategies would be identified, effective through 1995.

HISTORY

Headquartered in Peoria, Illinois, and currently the largest multinational company which designs, manufactures, and markets construction equipment, machinery, engines and parts, Caterpillar's roots date back to the late 19th century and the evolution of mechanized agricultural equipment. In February 1889, Daniel Best introduced the first steam-powered harvester, replacing the 40-horse-drawn combine with an eight-man, 11-ton, self-propelled tractor using eight-foot wheels. Shortly thereafter, Benjamin Holt began field testing the first crawler-type equipment, built simply by replacing the wheels on existing equipment with new "track" structures—pairs of treads comprised of wooden slats linked loosely together.

Driven by increasing demand in agriculture, road building, military equipment, and industrial construction, the two companies prospered. The

---

This case was prepared by Donald W. Eckrich, Associate Professor and Chairman, Department of Marketing, Ithaca College, as the basis for class discussion rather than to illustrate either effective or ineffective handling of administrative situations and problems. A special thanks for her invaluable assistance throughout the preparation of this case is due Barbara A. Wright.

introduction of the internal combustion engine provided yet another boost for the evolving heavy equipment industry.

In 1925, the Holt and Best Companies merged to form Caterpillar Tractor Co., thereby setting the stage for several decades of dramatic and systematic growth through technological leadership and new applications in the emerging equipment and machinery industry. Agricultural applications quickly gave way to forestry opportunities, which in turn gave way to oil field and highway operations.

In 1931, the first Caterpillar Diesel Tractor was introduced. This product initiated an incredible six-year sales growth spurt from $13 million to $63 million and launched the track-type tractor into prominence as the single largest user of diesel power.

Caterpillar's growing reputation for industry leadership and technological superiority was further strengthened during World War II by U.S. government defense contracts. These contracts included demand for both existing equipment (e.g., bulldozers and graders) and special government requests for revolutionary and sophisticated equipment such as air-cooled diesel engines for advanced military operations.

Throughout the postwar years, the Korean conflict, and into the 1970s, Caterpillar generally concentrated on the development of large, industrial-sized machines and engines. In 1944, Caterpillar announced its plans to build a line of matched earthmoving equipment, and quickly found a receptive and profitable market. Later, in 1951, the Trackson Company of Milwaukee was purchased to produce hoists, pipe layers, and hydraulically operated tractor shovels for Caterpillar crawlers. In 1965, Towmotor Corporation was acquired, continuing the expansion into heavy equipment with forklift trucks and straddle carriers for a wide range of materials handling in industrial, shipping, warehousing, and other markets. Thus, by the early 1970s, Caterpillar had achieved at least foothold positions in a variety of heavy equipment product lines, with the objective of achieving industry leadership in each of the new areas.

In 1977, Caterpillar unveiled the single-largest, most technologically advanced tractor in the world—the D–10. Foremost among its advantages were (1) an elevated drive sprocket and (2) modular-designed major components. The elevation of the drive sprocket removed it from high-wear and shock-load areas, reduced overall stress on the undercarriage, and produced a smoother ride. The modular design of major components not only permitted faster and more efficient servicing, but also provided the opportunity to pretest components before final assembly. Modular designs thereby reduced repair and overall downtime in some cases by as much as 80 percent. Perhaps most significant regarding the D–10 and its modular-designed components was the extent to which they reflected the intense product quality and service orientations adhered to throughout Cat's history. It had long been assumed by management that industrial users' needs would best be served through the progress of technology, largely irrespective of the effects on pricing.

Only four years later, in 1981, several more years of research and development were capped off with the introduction of a 16-cylinder, 1,600 horsepower, 1200 kilowatt engine—also stressing modular design and repair convenience. In early 1982, a new D8L crawler tractor was introduced, the third in a series of crawler tractors to employ the elevated sprocket. Finally, several other technological advances previously introduced on smaller, track-type loaders were extended to larger models, thereby permitting the relocation of the engine to the rear and, correspondingly, improving balance, operator visibility, and serviceability.

Thus, over several decades, Caterpillar Tractor Co. managed to establish a pace-setting position in the heavy equipment industry by focusing directly on state-of-the-art technology and continuous product redesign. Specifically, concern for increased *user productivity* through greater equipment capacities, enhanced reliability, and quicker serviceability contributed most heavily to Cat's success and superior image. Maintenance of this leadership position across numerous product lines has also translated into the industry's highest prices.

MANUFACTURING AND WAREHOUSING

Caterpillar manufactures products in two principal categories: (1) machines and parts (M&Ps), which includes track-type machinery like bulldozers, tractors, rippers, and track-loaders, as well as several wheel-type machines such as motor graders, loaders, off-highway trucks, and tractor-scrapers; and (2) engines, used to power a variety of equipment for highway, marine, petroleum, agricultural, industrial, and electric power generation applications, ranging from diesel to natural gas and turbines. The category of M&Ps, it should be noted, includes all related parts and equipment for all of the machines. Exhibits 1, 2, 3, and 4 present sales, profit, and other financial data for the years 1979 to 1983.

EXHIBIT 1   Consolidated Sales and Profit Data from 1983 Caterpillar Tractor Co. Annual Report

	1983	1982	1981	1980	1979
Sales	$5,424	$6,469	$9,154	$8,598	$7,613
Profit (loss) for year—consolidated	$ (345)	$ (180)	$ 579	$ 565	$ 492
Profit (loss) per share of common stock	$ (3.74)	$ (2.04)	$ 6.64	$ 6.53	$ 5.69
Return on average common stock equity	(10.1)%	(4.9)%	15.9%	17.4%	16.9%
Dividends paid per share of common stock	$ 1.50	$ 2.40	$ 2.40	$2,325	$ 2.10
Current ratio at year-end	2.15 to 1	2.87 to 1	1.50 to 1	1.71 to 1	1.88 to 1
Total assets at year-end	$6,968	$7,201	$7,285	$6,098	$5,403
Long-term debt due after one year at year-end	$1,894	$2,389	$ 961	$ 932	$ 952
Capital expenditures for land, buildings, machinery, and equipment	$ 324	$ 534	$ 836	$ 749	$ 676
Depreciation and amortization	$ 506	$ 505	$ 448	$ 370	$ 312

EXHIBIT 2 Total Sales by Category (in billions $)

	1983	1982	1981	1980	1979
Inside the United States					
Machines and parts	$ 2.08	$ 1.84	$ 2.62	$ 2.84	N/A
Engines and parts	.85	.96	1.35	.85	N/A
Total inside	$ 2.93	$ 2.80	$ 3.97	$ 3.69	$ 3.51
Outside the United States					
Machines and parts	$ 2.08	$ 2.92	$ 4.48	$ 4.36	N/A
Engines and parts	.41	.75	.70	.55	N/A
Total outside	$ 2.49	$ 3.67	$ 5.18	$ 4.91	$ 4.10
By country (millions)					
Africa/Mid East	$ 680	$1,062	$1,886	$1,282	$ 960
Europe	771	927	993	1,267	1,153
Asia/Pacific	515	800	927	922	764
Latin America	266	637	903	879	716
Canada	262	239	472	563	505
Combined totals	$ 5.42	$ 6.47	$ 9.15	$ 8.60	$ 7.60

Manufacturing and warehousing activities take place worldwide through 22 plants in the United States and several wholly or partly owned subsidiaries located in Australia, Belgium, Brazil, Canada, France, Japan, India, Indonesia, Mexico, and the United Kingdom. Each international location has been carefully selected to provide significant cost advantages by reducing global transportation costs, eliminating duty applicable to U.S.-built machinery, and by capitalizing on the manufacturing cost advantage derived from lower foreign wage levels. Such trends, it should be noted, have not been without some repercussions. The United Automobile Workers, for instance, representing over 80 percent of Cat's stateside hourly employees, is ever alert to this threat to their jobs and has become vitally concerned and quite vocal regarding possible extensions of foreign plants.

In addition, major warehouses and emergency parts depots are strategically located throughout the world. As a result, these combined facilities form a worldwide organizational network which attempts to maximize Caterpillar's flexibility and customer responsiveness. All parts manufactured by any one

EXHIBIT 3 Research and Engineering Costs (in millions $)

	1983	1982	1981	1980	1979	1978
New product development and major project improvements	n.a.[1]	$230	$227	$200	$191	$160
Other—general	n.a.[1]	$146	$136	$126	$ 92	$ 96
Total	$340	$376	$363	$326	$283	$256
Percent of sales	6.3%	5.8%	3.9%	3.8%	3.7%	3.6%

[1] n.a. = not available

EXHIBIT 4 Heavy Equipment and Machinery Manufacturer Earnings (in millions $)

Caterpillar Tractor Co.	($ 345)	($ 180)	$ 579	$ 565	$ 492
International Harvester[1]	($ 539)	($1,738)	($ 393)	($ 397)	$ 369
Deere[1]	($.052)	($ .039)	$.250	$.228	$.310
Allis-Chalmers	($ 133)	($ 207)	($ 28)	$ 47	$ 81
Clark Equipment	($.012)	($ .155)	$.029	$.051	$.106

[1] Fiscal year ends October 31—latest year's figures are estimates. Losses indicated in ( ).

Source (in part): Harlan S. Byrne, "For Heavy Equipment Makers, Recovery To Be Delayed Another Year," *The Wall Street Journal*, November 3, 1982.

plant are completely interchangeable with the same parts manufactured by any other plant. Thus, replacement parts are generally available on extremely short notice wherever Caterpillar machines are deployed throughout the world. In short, all dealers and customers recognize Cat's parts and distribution as one of the two or three major advantages of owning Cat equipment. Heavy equipment purchasers widely acknowledge that no other firm in the industry can touch Cat in this category.

DEALERS

Recognized as the strongest in the industry, Caterpillar's dealer network handles all sales and service worldwide, with the exception of direct sales to the U.S. government, the Soviet Union, and the People's Republic of China which are handled by a subsidiary division of Cat known as CIPI (Caterpillar Industrial Products, Inc.). Comprised of 213 independent dealers (84 in the United States), Caterpillar dealers represent an enterprise almost as large as the company. They operate 1,050 sales, parts, and service outlets in more than 140 countries, employ about 75,000 people, and have a combined net worth of approximately $3.1 billion. A typical dealership sells and services Caterpillar equipment exclusively, represents an average net worth of approximately $12 million, and is likely in a second or third generation of affiliation. Industry estimates place the capitalization of Caterpillar's dealer network at 10 times that of any competitor.

With Caterpillar's sales and service activities outside the direct control of Caterpillar executives, increasing efforts have been directed at improving service to dealers and informing users of the advantages of Caterpillar products. In 1978, a computerized dealer terminal system was completed which linked dealers and Caterpillar facilities to the European parts distribution department in Belgium. Essentially it provided direct computer access for ordering and locating parts for dealers in Europe, Africa, and the Middle East. In 1979, more than 3,000 customers and dealer personnel attended Caterpillar-sponsored seminars, 47,000 visitors viewed Caterpillar products and manufacturing operations, and representatives from 26 countries attended a week-long International Agricultural Seminar.

Comparable levels of seminar and visitation activity can be noted throughout the past few years, further promoting selective demand to both engine and equipment users. In one instance, 400 representatives of energy-related mining operations attended a seminar held at a West Virginia coal mine which not only highlighted the use of Cat machines, but perhaps more importantly, the dealers' capabilities to support special needs of mine operators. In another instance, in order to demonstrate dealer commitment to servicing the on-highway truck industry, Cat cosponsored the National Fuel Economy Challenge, a competition open to owners of new trucks equipped with Caterpillar 3406 and 3408 Economy Engines. Results confirmed impressive fuel economy statistics for Caterpillar engines and provided hands-on exposure to dealer support facilities.

In what was called "targeted marketing" by Cat executives, the predominant dealer support theme during the past few years has begun to focus dealer efforts on special end-user groups. U.S. dealers brought over 1,000 owners of competitive equipment to Peoria to learn about Cat equipment, its advantages and capabilities, as well as to actually operate Cat equipment. In another program, "Build Your Future," small machine owners, unfamiliar with the differential advantages of Caterpillar equipment and dealer support capabilities, were instructed on various general business topics and specific Caterpillar operations capabilities including equipment maintenance. Factory tours and machine demonstrations were also provided.

In 1983, the continuing efforts to improve service to users and dealers achieved a milestone with a major restructuring of the company's marketing organizations in the United States and Far East. The changes generally consisted of moving from a centralized, functional organization to a geographically dispersed, marketing-oriented team structure. As a result, the new structure recognizes the growing diversity of competition and product applications and the need for more individually tailored programs. It is more responsive to dealer needs and opportunities, shortens the lines of communication, and speeds up vital decision-making processes. As a result, Caterpillar's dealer organization has become widely regarded and consistently mentioned by customers as a prime reason for purchasing Cat equipment and represents Cat's single largest advantage over all competitors, both in the United States and internationally.

RESEARCH AND ENGINEERING

Improving quality and technological leadership have long been key ingredients of Caterpillar's long-term growth strategy. In a 1983 statement to stockholders, Chairman Morgan asserted, "We will not allow our product leadership to be diminished." Expenditures for research and engineering (R&E) have consistently ranked number one in the industry, and have permitted Caterpillar to develop state-of-the-art products, manufacturing processors, and apparatus. In 1982, for example, expenditures for R&E reached a record $376 million (data on other recent research and engineerng expenditures appear in Exhibit 3). As a result, Caterpillar's product leadership is not only widely recognized, but manufacturing facilities, as well, are considered the most modern and best equipped in the industry.

A carryover of this commitment to product leadership is the general practice of passing along specific product advances as soon as reliably feasible rather than accumulating several modifications and incorporating them all simultaneously in periodic model changes. Not only would the latter fail to permit the entire line to be completely up-to-date at all times, but it would also fail to insure maximum sales opportunities for existing, but aging, products. As an example of the success of this market penetration strategy, a simple addition of rubber grousers on tractors used primarily for log skidding created 200 immediate new machine sales for other agricultural users.

COMPETITION

As a result of decades of domination of the heavy equipment and construction industry, Caterpillar has an estimated 45–50 percent share for earthmoving machinery in the U.S. market and roughly 30–35 percent of the market worldwide. Mr. Morgan readily admits the toughest competition facing Caterpillar is from Komatsu Ltd., of Tokyo, which has rapidly grown to second place in worldwide sales. In addition, considerable domestic competitive pressures come from J. I. Case, Inc. and Deere & Company, considered No. 2 and No. 3 respectively.

In 1981, the president of Komatsu Ltd. stated a goal of achieving 20 percent of the U.S. market within five years; the company has succeeded in boosting market share from approximately 2 percent in 1974 to 15 percent in 1983. Komatsu is gaining sales basically in selected markets such as specialty bulldozers (i.e., including amphibians and remote-controlled units especially for underground use), and in equipment larger than Caterpillar's largest. Number one in terms of the latter is Komatsu's 1,000 Hp. tractor bulldozer, which far surpasses Cat's biggest, the D-10 with only 700 Hp. In these specialty areas, Komatsu does particularly well. Projections are that Komatsu Ltd., as a result of aggressiveness, adaptability, and a number of complex economic factors, will continue to encroach into the U.S. market largely at the expense (or demise) of many smaller competitors. As one industry analyst put it, "When elephants fight, the grass dies."

Nevertheless, despite claims of durability and efficiency which rival Caterpillar, Komatsu probably will not match the current sales of Cat in the United States. With approximately 60 part-time dealerships in America (i.e. those who sell Komatsu and other manufacturer's equipment simultaneously), and several competitive handicaps in the United States, such as ocean freight costs and narrow product lines, Komatsu cannot compete head-to-head with Cat. Thus the company initially adopted a strategy of allying itself, through joint-venture subsidiaries, with International Harvester (IH) and Bucyrus-Erie (B-E) to manufacture wheeled vehicles and excavators. In 1980, Komatsu bought out B-E with financial assistance provided directly by Japan's Fair Trade Commission and, in 1982, IH's share of the joint venture was also purchased. Thus, domestic entrance for Komatsu has been achieved through limited and well-conceived flanking attacks providing American-based manufacturing facilities and distribution links.

The U.S. presence of Komatsu, however, is considered by industry analysts more a matter of competitive visibility than an operational threat to Caterpillar's leadership position. The most direct threats to Caterpillar's domestic markets are J. I. Case and John Deere & Co. J. I. Case has an estimated 35 percent share of the earthmoving equipment market and John Deere has an estimated 30 percent share of the farm-machinery market.

However, each of these organizations, as well as several others (Allis-Chalmers, Clark Equipment, Harnischfeger Corp., IH, and Massey-Ferguson), has been undergoing considerable upheaval as a result of the early 1980s worldwide recession (see Exhibit 4 for performance data from selected competitors). As one analyst put it:

> Producers of construction, farm, and other heavy equipment have been in varying degrees of recession ... and had expected recovery to start by now. Instead, widespread weakness is showing up, and companies are awash in red ink.
>
> Executives and analysts have been surprised by the depths and breadth of the slump. In past recessions, declines in some markets have been at least partly offset by strengths in others. Not so today. Practically all major markets are weak. For instance, the collapse of the oil and gas drilling boom and the financial problems of many countries weren't anticipated. And the farm depression has been deeper and more prolonged than machinery makers expected.[1]

Thus, although Caterpillar has probably fared better than the other firms, the most significant domestic problem for Caterpillar is the delay in the recovery of the market.

Internationally, and despite the worldwide slump, Komatsu Ltd. is Caterpillar's single-largest and growing competitor with 15 percent share of the world market (second only to Caterpillar), and 60 percent of the Japanese market. Cat accounts for roughly 50 percent of the world market but only 30 percent of the Japanese market (Caterpillar Mitsubishi).

Typical of many Japanese manufacturing firms, Komatsu's competitive thrust focuses directly on a long-term strategy to equal or exceed Caterpillar's position. Considering Cat vulnerable to superior managerial efficiency and operating flexibility, Komatsu's broad marketing strategy has emphasized expanding market share, largely on the basis of lower prices and efforts to match Caterpillar's follow-up service parts capabilities. The slogan "Maru-C" is widely acknowledged as one of Komatsu's greatest challenges—to "engulf Caterpillar." Komatsu offers customers prices up to 15 percent below Caterpillar and endeavors to accommodate every conceivable special heavy equipment need through continual adaptation of existing products. In one instance, special

---

[1] Harlan S. Bryne, *The Wall Street Journal,* November 3, 1982.

equipment was developed exclusively for the particular needs of Australian coal miners. In another instance, an electric-powered bulldozer was developed for a small number of contractors whose special needs required them to operate equipment within legal noise limits.

Determined to produce the world's best earthmoving equipment, Komatsu executives lay claim to offering superior equipment in terms of power, durability, and lower fuel consumption.[2] Indeed, considerable evidence is available to support such claims, and industrial customers have responded to Komatsu's discount pricing and manufacturing flexibility. In terms of follow-up support, Komatsu maintains a crew of salespeople (engineers), ready to fly anywhere in the world to solve Komatsu equipment problems. Within the United States, Komatsu maintains five regional centers to directly support dealer efforts.

OTHER PROBLEMS

The suddenness of Caterpillar's 1982 $180 million loss, the first in 50 years, found President Robert E. Gilmore and Chairman Lee Morgan stunned and hopeful of a quick return to profitability. In a 1983 joint address to stockholders they reported:

> We hope that the worldwide economic malaise is coming to an end, and that people will soon be able to return to more normal lives.
>
> The economy will recover, and the world will need capital goods of the kinds made by Caterpillar. Roads will be built . . . ore and coal will be mined . . . fields will be cleared and dams constructed . . . oil and gas will be produced. These and other applications for our products are essential to a growing world population.
>
> Our concern isn't whether demand will revive and grow. It will.

However, by early 1984 Caterpillar's troubles were beginning to prove far more pervasive and devastating than first thought.

In retrospect, several contributing factors began emerging as much as five years earlier, and not without Caterpillar's awareness. For instance, as the only manufacturer of pipelayers in the United States, Caterpillar was particularly hard hit by President Carter's 1979 "high tech" export control measures against the Soviet Union. Caterpillar was on the verge of a multimillion (perhaps billion) dollar contract with the Soviet Union for 2,000 heavy tractors at approximately $500,000 each and hundreds of pipelayers at $250,000 each. However, the export control measures ended this opportunity and the sale went to Komatsu.

Later in 1979, additional clouds surfaced. As a result of ever increasing oil prices, worldwide economic growth abruptly halted. Adding to the U.S. problems, the growing and unprecedented international trade deficits of the 1970s prompted ever higher interest rates and greater uncertainty regarding the future of the international trading system, and contributed significantly to

---

[2] Bernard Krisher, "Komatsu on the Track of Cat," *Fortune*, April 20, 1981, pp. 164–74.

inflation. The Consumer Price Index in 1979 was up 13 percent and Chairman Morgan noted, "inflation has become deeply embedded," and "solutions will neither be simple nor quick."

By 1981, effects of the world's economic recession began to appear at Caterpillar as physical sales volume declined "moderately"—as the company called it. Slowdowns in world markets, considered the most significant long-term growth opportunities for heavy construction equipment manufacturers, were particularly difficult to manage insofar as the U.S. competitive posture was slumping in general. Unlike the embargo against the Soviet Union, some developing world markets were being diminished by a variety of anti-U.S. export/import restrictions issued by developing countries themselves. Loss of accessibility to such markets, restricted information flows, and the growing trend in foreign government subsidies were leaving Caterpillar in a hopeful, but retrospective, position, as noted in a joint letter to stockholders by Chairman Morgan and President Gilmore:

> We have a competitive edge . . . Outside authorities frequently confirm that ours is the preferred product.
>
> Our very substantial capital investment and research and engineering programs . . . should help us maintain a technological lead . . .
>
> Toward that end, we seek the renewed commitment of Caterpillar people everywhere.

Unfortunately, throughout 1982, conditions continued to deteriorate. After the first quarter of operations, management began imposing numerous temporary plant shutdowns and indefinite layoffs. Domestic interest rates were sufficiently high to cause most U.S. capital spending to be abandoned. Worldwide, the previous decade of accelerated oil explorations and refinement had resulted in overproduction such that oil prices also began to slump, which further resulted in reduced energy development and construction. Facing the unprecedented reduction in practically all markets simultaneously, Caterpillar experienced a 29 percent sales decline, and reported the first loss in common stock prices in 50 years. Common stock prices plunged from $55–$60 per share in 1981 to $35 per share in 1982.

On October 1, 1982, the United Auto Workers Union struck (20,400 members or roughly 80 percent of Cat's active, U.S. hourly employees), seeking an extension of the existing contract. For almost 30 years, the UAW labor contract had established a pattern which provided workers with automatic, annual, 3 percent wage increases. Management now resisted these increases because the increase in labor costs would make it even more difficult to compete. Recent data, for instance, placed Cat's per capita U.S. labor costs at roughly twice those of Japanese firms.

Throughout 1983, even well after the labor settlement, ripple effects of the dispute continued to emerge. Inventory shortages of both parts and equipment resulted in lost sales, lost good will, and a considerable strain on efforts to return to profitability. These efforts included reductions in expenditures for perhaps Cat's most sacred budget item—research and engineering—as well as the second annual cut in the capital expenditures budget—from $836 million in 1981, down to $324 million in 1983. These cost-cutting efforts resulted in layoffs and plant closings leaving employment figures at the end of 1983 markedly reduced from previous years. Hourly employees, reduced in 1982 by 21,501 dropped another 624 in 1983, while the number of salaried employees was cut 3,077 and 2,585 in these two years.

The combination of a deteriorating worldwide economic climate and postsettlement reconstruction efforts required management to assume an adaptive posture while long-term solutions were worked out. Perhaps most noteworthy in this regard is the Cost Reduction Program (CRP), aimed at positioning Cat's 1986 cost levels more than 20 percent below those of 1981 (in constant dollars adjusted for volume). These cost reductions were intended to be permanent and included plant closings, new applications of computer and scientific technology, inventory reduction programs, and faster deliveries from suppliers. At the end of 1983 considerable efforts were being directed at achieving a scaled-down, more efficient organization.

The achievement of a long-term, strategic growth perspective has captured management's attention. Beginning in late 1982, management initiated efforts to focus planning specifically on future opportunities in diesel, natural gas, and turbine engines, and to review the basic role of the lift truck in Cat's product mix. In 1983, Caterpillar management held a Business Strategy Conference which developed specific objectives along with a timetable for activities through 1995. The plan involves what are designed to be the most productive means of "establishing, confirming, or modifying current strategies for . . . existing business; developing, evaluating, recommending, and selecting for implementation 'new' strategic growth opportunities; and developing corporate goals consistent with the findings and decisions produced by the conference."

Based on this planning, U.S. dealers recently launched a marketing program targeted at non-Caterpillar owners. Recognizing the strategic growth opportunities associated with market development, this program, called PLUS 3, provided a means for end users of competitors' equipment to gauge the superiority of Cat dealers in after-sales parts support and service. Specifically, the program guaranteed a 48-hour repair turnaround or the customer would be given a machine to use from the dealer's rental fleet, and a 48-hour parts delivery or the customer would receive the part free! It also included one of the most extensive power train warranties in the industry—36 months or 5,000 hours, whichever came first. Results of PLUS 3 were quite favorable, most notably among small- and medium-sized machine owners.

As a result of additional analyses regarding the role of the lift truck to Caterpillar, at least one U.S. plant was closed and management began labor negotiations with two non-U.S. production facilities. Indications were quite strong that more and more production throughout the product mix will be moved overseas in the future (e.g., lift trucks to Korea). Identifying future growth opportunities and detailing appropriate marketing strategies for the next decade were seen as becoming more critical as no significant upturn had been experienced through mid-1984, and the future seemed to be even more unstable and uncertain.

INDUSTRIAL HIGHLIGHT

Construction Machinery Industry

Below is a capsule summary of the construction machinery industry, of which Caterpillar Tractor Company is a part. Information in this highlight was compiled by the U.S. Department of Commerce and focuses on this industry during the approximate period of time covered in the case. Keep in mind that industrial highlights contained in this text are not intended as a complete synopsis of an industry but as a profile of certain issues that can be relevant to a case situation. A list of additional references at the end of this highlight can be used for further industrial analysis.

CURRENT SITUATION

Construction machinery is sold primarily for four purposes: building construction, 20 percent; public works (highways, airports, water and sewer projects), 20 percent; surface mining equipment, 20 percent; and exports, 40 percent. Sales of construction machinery remained at low levels in 1983, although some increases in sales of small machines used in the housing industry were recorded (see Exhibit A). U.S. construction contractors have large quantities of relatively new machinery—much of it idle—and therefore will need little new equipment in the immediate future.

Exports continue to decline drastically (see Exhibit B). After totaling more than $6.3 billion in 1981, exports dropped to less than $4.0 billion in 1982 and are estimated at $2.6 billion in 1983. This substantial drop was caused mainly by contraction of the world market rather than loss of U.S. competitiveness. The worldwide recession, cash flow problems within OPEC, and a sharp decline in bank loans to developing nations have contributed to the market shrinkage. The high value of the dollar in the face of strong Japanese and European competition is also a problem for U.S. producers.

Imports, which reached an all-time high of $887 million in 1981, dropped to $779 million in 1982 and to an estimated $580 million in 1983. The primary sources of imports are Japan (21 percent), Canada (20 percent), West Germany (18 percent), and the United Kingdom (10 percent).

Source: U.S. Industrial Outlook, Department of Commerce, 1984, pp. 22-1–22-4.

CATERPILLAR TRACTOR COMPANY

EXHIBIT A Construction Machinery Shipments

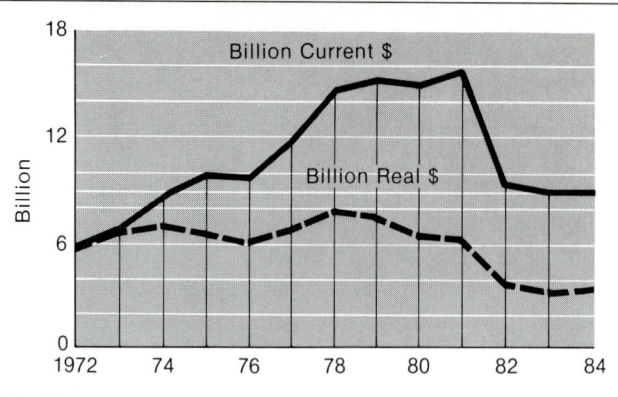

Source: Bureau of the Census.

Product shipments in 1983 are estimated to decline 8.7 percent in real terms from 1982.

LONG-TERM PROSPECTS

Substantial growth in domestic building construction, surface mining, and public works, as well as in levels of exports, must materialize if the construction machinery industry is to regain its former levels of production. Measured in 1972 dollars, product shipments declined about 48 percent from 1981 through 1983, while exports, measured in current dollars, dropped from over $6.3 billion in 1981 to an estimated $2.6 billion in 1983.

EXHIBIT B Construction Machinery Trade

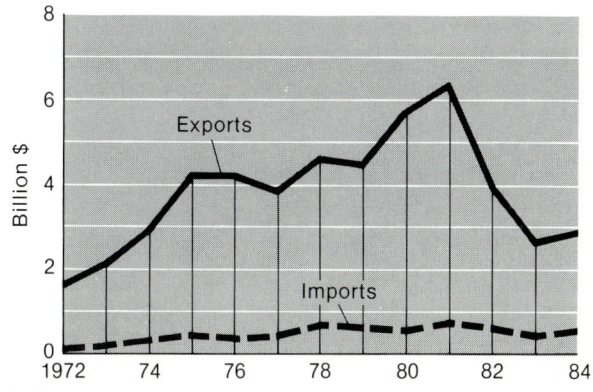

Source: Bureau of the Census.

Competition from Europe, Japan, and Brazil is rapidly increasing as foreign producers expand their product ranges and match many of our technologies. Foreign competitors—including subsidiaries of U.S. companies—are gaining increased shares of their own and Third World markets. This suggests that the strong export recovery necessary if this industry is to regain its previous vigor is unlikely to happen soon.

Repair of U.S. highways, bridges, and water and sewer systems over the next 5 to 10 years will require greatly increased spending for construction machinery. Hence, the long-range outlook for the industry in the domestic market is not as bleak as the outlook for the immediate future. Although foreign competition has increased, the U.S. industry should maintain its leadership through effective worldwide distribution and service, product improvements, and its reputation for quality products.

ADDITIONAL REFERENCES

Current Industrial Reports: Construction Machinery, Series MA-35D: Tractors, Except Garden Tractors, Series M-355, Bureau of the Census, U.S. Department of Commerce, Washington, DC 20233.

1077 Census of Manufactures, Bureau of the Census, U.S. Department of Commerce, Washington, DC 20233.

Construction Equipment, 270 St. Paul Street, Denver, CO 80206.

Highway & Heavy Construction, 666 Fifth Avenue, New York, NY 10103.

CASE 6

The Kellogg Company and the Ready-to-Eat Cereal Industry

JOSEPH A. SCHENK DAN S. PRICKETT
STANLEY J. STOUGH

You take care of the outside.
We'll help take care of the inside.

1985 AD FOR KELLOGG'S ALL BRAN

Advertising campaigns for Kellogg products in the 1980s stress the healthy, nutritious quality of cereal flakes—corn, bran, wheat, oats—a Kellogg theme that began almost a century ago. Dr. John H. Kellogg and W. K. Kellogg sought to develop a cereal that could replace meat in the diets of the patients at the Battle Creek sanitarium that the Kelloggs managed. The product of their efforts, Corn Flakes, became popular enough with the patients that the Kelloggs formed two companies that became the Kellogg Company in 1899.

Eighty-six years later Kellogg is one of the largest food companies in the world, with annual sales exceeding $2.5 billion and earnings greater than $250 million. Kellogg has established a position in the ready-to-eat (RTE) cereal market almost twice as large as either of the two nearest competitors, General Mills and General Foods. "Kellogg knows the cereal business better than anyone else" said William Wason of Brown Brothers Harriman & Co., "and the management has had the wisdom to stick with what they know." In December 1985, Kellogg was named one of the five best managed companies in the United States by *Dun's Business Month* (Dec. 1985). Kellogg won this acclaim because of its performance throughout the 1970s and early 1980s, the darkest time in the industry's history, and the progress Kellogg made in recovering during 1984 and 1985.

THE READY-TO-EAT CEREAL INDUSTRY

The RTE cereal industry is composed of firms that are engaged in the manufacture and sale of prepackaged, processed foodstuffs made primarily of grain products. The user does not have to prepare the product prior to use, and it can be eaten in dry form or with the addition of other substances, such as milk and sugar. Advantages of the products from a consumer perspective include convenience of use and easy satisfaction of nutritional requirements. Consumption of the product takes place primarily at breakfast, but they are

Address reprint requests to: Joseph A. Schenk, Management Department, University of Dayton, 300 College Park, Dayton, OH 45469-0001. Copyright © 1986 by Joseph A. Schenk.

EXHIBIT 1 The Ready-to-Eat Cereal Industry: Market Share Data[1]

Company	1976	1977	1978	1979	1980	1981	1982	1983	1984
Kellogg	42.6	42.5	42.0	41.5	40.9	39.3	38.5	38.5	40.3
General Mills	20.8	20.5	20.4	22.2	22.4	23.0	23.1	23.2	23.1
General Foods	15.7	16.8	16.0	15.4	15.0	15.0	16.0	16.1	13.3
Quaker Oats	8.9	8.9	8.7	8.6	8.6	8.6	8.9	8.9	8.6
Ralston Purina	4.9	3.4	5.7	5.6	6.2	6.1	5.6	6.1	6.3
Nabisco	4.0	4.2	4.2	4.1	3.8	3.9	3.8	3.8	4.2
All others	3.1	3.7	3.0	2.6	3.1	4.1	4.1	3.4	4.2

[1] All figures are percentages.

Source: *Advertising Age*, Aug. 5, 1985, p. 42; Jun. 14, 1982, p. 62; May 25, 1981, p. 62; Aug. 28, 1978, p. 217.

also used as between-meal snacks. The first products in the market were introduced by W. K. Kellogg, Wheat Flakes in 1894 and Corn Flakes in 1898.

The $4 billion RTE cereal industry is composed of several large companies that dominate the market. Led by Kellogg, the industry includes General Mills, General Foods, Quaker Oats, Ralston Purina, and Nabisco. Exhibit 1 lists the market share performance of the major competitors as of 1984.

The significance of cereals within the product lines of the competitors changes as a result of competition and developments within the companies themselves. Although cereals represent more than 75 percent of Kellogg sales, cereals are estimated to constitute no more than 13 percent of General Foods sales and 7 percent of General Mills sales. Kellogg sales and estimated operating profits by division are listed in Exhibit 2.

EXHIBIT 2 Kellogg Company: Operating Profit at Year End December Estimated by Division
($ millions)

	1982	1983	1984	1985	1986 (estimated)
Net sales	$2,367	$2,381	$2,602	$2,930	$3,250
Operating profits					
Domestic RTE Cereals	238.0	255.0	311.0	395.0	450.0
Mrs. Smith's	29.0	28.5	31.5	36.9	43.0
Salada	9.0	10.0	11.0	12.5	14.0
Fearn	13.8	15.5	17.0	19.0	21.0
International	107.9	105.4	96.7	95.0	110.0
Total operating income	397.7	414.4	467.2	558.4	638.0
Net income	227.8	242.7	250.5	281.3	320.5

Source: Prudential-Bache Securities, Inc., Apr. 2, 1986

EXHIBIT 3 Cold Cereal's Top Ten in Market Share[1]

	1983		1984	
Brand (company)	Pounds	Dollars	Pounds	Dollars
Corn Flakes (K)	6.8	4.7	6.8	4.7
Frosted Flakes (K)	5.2	4.8	5.6	5.2
Cheerios (GM)	5.5	5.8	5.2	5.5
Raisin Bran (K)	4.6	4.1	4.5	4.0
Chex (RP)	4.3	4.4	4.3	4.6
Shredded Wheat (N)	4.0	3.1	4.0	3.3
Rice Krispies (K)	3.6	3.9	3.5	3.8
Raisin Bran (GF)	3.0	2.5	2.7	2.1
Cap'n Crunch (Q)	2.9	3.5	2.7	3.2
Honey-Nut Cheerios (GM)	2.3	2.6	2.6	2.9
Total	42.2	39.4	41.9	39.3

[1] All figures are percentages.

Abbreviations: K = Kellogg; GM = General Mills; GF = General Foods; Q = Quaker Oats; N = Nabisco; RP = Ralston Purina.

Source: *Advertising Age*, Aug. 5, 1985, p. 42.

Vigorous competition in the RTE cereal industry requires intensive and decisive actions to expand investments in research, in the development of new products, and in marketing. Marketing plans generally center on facing the competition squarely and forcefully. Budgets for advertising and promotions have increased substantially in recent years, both to give additional support to established products and to successfully support new product introductions. Market shares for the top ten products in the industry are listed in Exhibit 3. Selected information regarding each major competitor is presented below.

General Mills

General Mills managed to increase its market share significantly during the 1976–1981 period. Since then market share has stabilized, and General Mills has been able to maintain a share position in the industry at about 23 percent. Recent new product activity included the national roll-out of E.T.s, which failed to produce significant sales, reflecting a decline of consumer interest in licensed properties. Cinnamon Toast Crunch, Fiber One, Bran Muffin Crunch, and S'More's Crunch are all expected to perform well after national roll-out in early 1986. General Mills' brands and the market share performance of each brand for the period 1982–1984 are shown in Exhibit 4.

General Mills has concentrated its efforts on its snack food, yogurt, and restaurant businesses. It has divested some toy operations and repurchased 7 million shares of its own stock (44 million shares outstanding). General Mills net sales and operating profit by segment are listed in Exhibit 5.

EXHIBIT 4 General Mills' Ready-to-Eat Cereals: Market Share Data[1]

	1982		1983		1984	
Brand	Pounds	Dollars	Pounds	Dollars	Pounds	Dollars
Cheerios	5.6	5.9	5.5	5.8	5.2	5.5
Honey Nut Cheerios	2.1	2.4	2.3	2.6	2.6	2.9
Total	1.7	2.4	1.9	2.6	2.1	2.8
Lucky Charms	1.7	2.2	1.6	2.1	1.7	2.1
Trix	1.5	1.9	1.5	1.9	1.5	1.9
Wheaties	2.5	1.9	2.3	1.7	2.0	1.4
Golden Grahams	1.3	1.3	1.3	1.3	1.3	1.3
Crispy Wheats 'n Raisins	1.1	1.3	1.1	1.3	1.0	1.1
Licensed Products	0.4	0.5	1.1	1.3	0.7	1.0
Monsters, etc.	0.7	1.0	0.6	0.9	0.5	0.8
Cinnamon Toast Crunch	—	—	—	—	0.6	0.7
Cocoa Puffs	0.7	1.8	0.7	0.8	0.6	0.7
Buc Wheats	0.5	0.6	0.4	0.5	0.3	0.4
Others	0.3	0.2	0.5	0.4	0.6	0.5
Total	20.7	23.1	20.8	23.2	20.7	23.1

[1] All figures are percentages.

Source: *Advertising Age*, Aug. 5, 1985, p. 42.

General Foods

Throughout the 1970s, General Foods relied on coffee—Maxwell House, Sanka, Yuban, and Brim—for approximately 40 percent of its total revenue (*New York Times*, Sep. 15, 1985). Since then, it has made major acquisitions. Currently, the company gets 40 percent of its revenues from packaged groceries, 28

EXHIBIT 5 General Mills: Operating Profit at Year End May, by Segment
($ millions)

	1983	1984	1985	1986 (estimated)
Net sales	$4,082	$4,118	$4,285	$4,550
Operating profits				
Consumer foods	269.4	275.3	265.6	300.0
Restaurants	80.0	70.0	91.5	97.0
Specialty retailing and other (loss)	10.4	19.8	(1.7)	23.0
Total operating profit	359.8	365.1	355.4	420.0
Net income (loss)	245.1	233.4	(72.9)	182.9

Source: Prudential-Bache Securities, Inc., Apr. 2, 1986.

EXHIBIT 6 General Foods' Ready-to-Eat Cereals: Market Share Data[1]

	1982		1983		1984	
Brand	Pounds	Dollars	Pounds	Dollars	Pounds	Dollars
Post Raisin Bran	3.1	2.8	3.0	2.5	2.7	2.1
Grape-Nuts	2.9	2.4	2.5	1.9	2.2	1.5
Super Sugar Crisp	1.4	1.6	1.5	1.6	1.4	1.4
Honeycombs	1.1	1.5	1.2	1.5	1.1	1.3
Post Fruit & Fibre	1.5	1.7	1.3	1.4	1.3	1.4
Pebbles	1.2	1.4	1.2	1.4	1.1	1.3
Smurf Berry Crunch	—	—	1.0	1.1	0.5	0.6
Post Toasties	1.3	0.9	1.2	0.9	1.0	0.8
Alpha-Bits	0.8	0.9	0.8	0.9	0.7	0.8
Bran Flakes	0.8	0.8	0.8	0.8	0.8	0.8
Honey-Nut Crunch Raisin Bran	0.3	0.3	0.7	0.7	0.2	0.2
Raisin Grape-Nuts	0.8	0.8	0.6	0.6	0.4	0.4
Fortified Oat Flakes	0.6	0.5	0.6	0.5	0.5	0.4
C.W. Post Hearty Granola	0.2	0.2	—	0.1	0.1	0.1
Others	0.4	0.2	0.1	0.2	0.3	0.2
Total	16.4	16.0	16.6	16.1	14.3	13.3

[1] All figures are percentages.
Source: *Advertising Age*, Aug. 5, 1985, p. 42.

percent from coffee products, and 18 percent from processed meats (*Economist,* 1985). Coffee is still General Foods' largest single product, and it holds a 38 percent share of the coffee market (Philip Morris, 1986). In fiscal year 1985, General Foods achieved total revenues of $9 billion and the RTE cereal sales accounted for $512 million of total sales (Drexel, Burnham, & Lambert, May 20, 1985).

Sales of Post Toasties and Grape Nuts are eroding. Raisin Bran and Honey Nut Crunch Raisin Bran are reported to be performing well in the health-conscious market segment (*New York Times,* Sep. 15, 1985). Exhibit 6 lists General Foods' RTE cereal products and market share performance for the 1982–1984 period.

Most of General Foods' development in the 1980s has consisted of creating or acquiring product lines to enter new markets, particularly convenience, low-calorie foods. Acquisitions include Oscar Meyer, Entenmann's bakery, Ronzoni, and Orowheat. New products developments include Crystal Light, Pudding Pops, Sun Apple, Lean Strips, and Crispy Cookin' French Fries, of which only Crystal Light and Pudding Pops had met with success as of the end of 1985.

Simultaneously, General Foods has divested its pet foods division and the Burger Chef restaurant chain and repurchased 11 percent of its stock. In 1985, Philip Morris acquired General Foods to integrate its food operations into the tobacco products company. General Foods sales and operating profits by segment are listed in Exhibit 7.

EXHIBIT 7 General Foods: Operating Profit at Year End March, by Segment
($ millions)

	1983	1984	1985	1986 (estimated)
Net sales	$8,256	$8,599	$9,022	$9,500
Operating profits				
Packaged groceries	427.8	470.5	419.3	451.0
Coffee	131.1	107.9	127.2	135.0
Processed meats	90.1	96.9	104.2	115.1
Food services and other	38.4	39.9	51.2	55.0
Total operating income	686.6	715.2	701.9	756.1
Net income	288.5	317.1	302.8	316.4

Source: Prudential-Bache Securities, Inc., Oct. 1, 1985.

Quaker Oats

In the 1960s, Quaker Oats acquired many diverse businesses. By the 1980s, Quaker Oats had divested its restaurants and chemical products units and was concentrating on acquiring packaged foods and specialty companies including Brookstone (tools), Jos. A. Bank (clothiers), Eyelab (eyeware retailing), and Stokely Van Camp (pork and beans, Gatorade). In addition, Quaker Oats repurchased 5 percent of its own shares in March 1985. The 1980s witnessed an aggressive Quaker Oats expanding its operations throughout its product lines.

Quaker Oats has bundled its product development (20 new products and line extensions since 1983) under the Quaker umbrella and has pushed those lines in which it has a leadership position: hot cereals, granola bars, and Gatorade. Spending $200 million in 1985 for advertising, Quaker Oats has shown a 16 percent growth in advertising expenditures and a 31 percent growth in merchandising expenditures since 1984.

As a result of this stategy and increasing new product development at Kellogg, General Mills, and Ralston Purina, Quaker Oats has allowed its share of the RTE cereal market to erode from 8.9 percent in 1983 to 8.6 percent in 1984. Halfsies and Cap'n Crunch have lost market share, whereas Life and 100% Natural have maintained their sales levels. Quaker Oats RTE cereal brands and market share performance are listed in Exhibit 8, and Quaker Oats net sales and operating profits by segment are shown in Exhibit 9.

Ralston Purina

Ralston Purina led the RTE cereal industry in restructuring through the use of share repurchase. Ralston Purina has acquired almost 40 million shares of its own stock, and, through divestiture of its Foodmaker division, can acquire more. Ralston Purina acquired Continental Baking in 1984, which added the Hostess brands to the Ralston Purina product lines.

EXHIBIT 8 Quaker Oats' Ready-to-Eat Cereals: Market Share Data[1]

	1982		1983		1984	
Brand	Pounds	Dollars	Pounds	Dollars	Pounds	Dollars
Cap'n Crunch	3.2	3.8	2.9	3.5	2.7	3.2
Life	2.5	2.3	2.4	2.2	2.4	2.2
100% Natural	1.6	1.5	1.6	1.5	1.5	1.4
Halfsies	—	—	0.7	0.7	0.2	0.3
Corn Bran	0.7	0.6	0.7	0.6	0.6	0.6
Others	0.9	0.7	0.6	0.4	0.9	0.9
Total	8.9	8.9	8.9	8.9	8.3	8.6

[1] All figures are percentages.
Source: *Advertising Age*, Aug. 5, 1985, p. 42.

Ralston Purina is expected to focus on its pet food operations and the Hostess lines for the foreseeable future. New product activity in 1985, greatest in company history, brought extension of the Chuck Wagon line with three new dog food products, expansion of the dog treats line with Waggles and T-Bonz, and new cat foods. New products in cereals include Sun Flakes, Rainbow Brite, and Cabbage Patch. Ralston Purina's RTE cereal products and market share performance for the 1982–1984 period are presented in Exhibit 10. Ralston Purina's net sales and operating profits by segment are listed in Exhibit 11.

Nabisco

Since 1983, Nabisco has introduced 140 new products and line extensions globally. This aggressive posture indicated a recognition by Nabisco of the

EXHIBIT 9 Quaker Oats: Operating Profit at Year End June, by Segment
($ millions)

	1983	1984	1985	1986 (estimated)
Net sales	$2,611	$3,344	$3,520	$3,650
Operating profits				
U.S. and Canadian grocery	193.8	219.5	250.0	272.0
International grocery	49.1	32.9	49.7	60.0
Fisher-Price	29.6	43.6	47.1	50.0
Specialty retailing	15.8	12.7	15.2	18.0
Total	288.3	308.7	362.0	400.0
Net income	119.3	138.7	156.6	174.2

Source: Prudential-Bache Securities, Inc., Apr. 2, 1986.

EXHIBIT 10 Ralston Purina's Ready-to-Eat Cereals: Market Share Data[1]

	1982		1983		1984	
Brand	Pounds	Dollars	Pounds	Dollars	Pounds	Dollars
Chex	4.2	4.0	4.3	4.4	4.3	4.6
Donkey Kong	—	—	0.7	0.7	0.6	0.6
Cookie Crisp	0.6	0.6	0.5	0.7	0.4	0.7
Others	0.3	0.2	0.3	0.2	0.6	0.4
Total	5.9	5.6	5.9	6.1	5.9	6.3

[1] All figures are percentages.
Source: *Advertising Age*, Aug. 5, 1985, p. 42.

importance of the international market, which accounts for 40 percent of its normalized operating income.

In 1985, Nabisco was acquired by R. J. Reynolds, a tobacco products company. The combined R. J. Reynolds and Nabisco advertising budget weighs in at $1 billion. This financial strength is to be applied, among other things, to joint product marketing. For example, Del Monte coupons may come with Shredded Wheat. It is hoped that this mixed marketing approach will boost sales of product lines throughout the combined companies.

Nabisco's major product in the RTE cereals market is Shredded Wheat. Shredded Wheat held a 3.3 percent dollar market share in 1984 (4.0 percent in pounds). All Nabisco RTE cereal products held a total market share of 4.2

EXHIBIT 11 Ralston Purina: Operating Profit at Year End September, by Segment ($ millions)

	1982	1983	1984	1985	1986 (estimated)
Net sales	$4,803	$4,872	$4,980	$5,864	$5,350
Operating profits					
Pet food	227.0	263.5	303.0	350.0	399.0
Seafood (loss)	(11.0)	14.5	9.5	10.0	11.5
Cereals	38.5	43.5	41.5	45.5	50.0
Continental baking	—	—	—	84.0	94.0
Other consumer goods	3.7	5.5	1.6	6.6	8.0
Agriculture	96.6	105.6	92.5	74.9	82.0
Restaurant	46.7	58.5	61.4	47.2	0.0
Diversified operations	27.1	33.6	35.9	24.2	30.0
Total operating income	428.6	524.7	545.4	642.4	674.5
Net income	69.1	256.0	242.7	256.4	371.0

Source: Prudential-Bache Securities, Inc., Apr. 2, 1986.

percent on a dollar basis (4.9 percent on a poundage basis) (*Advertising Age,* Aug. 5, 1985).

INDUSTRY CHALLENGES

The RTE cereal industry emerged from the 1970s facing continuing challenges from the Federal Trade Commission (FTC). Founded in 1914 to combat monopolies, the FTC is charged with preventing unfair methods of competition and unfair or deceptive acts or practices that affect commerce. For almost a decade, the FTC had pursued the RTE industry leaders on two issues: children's television programming and advertising, and the operation of an oligopolistic "shared monopoly."

Children's Television and Advertising

As early as 1970, consumer groups pressed for greater regulation of children's television and advertising. (*Federal Register,* vol. 49). A group called Action for Children's Television (ACT) prodded the FTC to establish minimum requirements for age-specific programming for children. In 1971, ACT petitioned the FTC to ban all vitamin advertising on programs intended for children. (One third of advertising on TV programs for children had been for vitamin products.) To avoid further pressure, the manufacturers voluntarily complied with the petition (Ward, 1978).

From 1971 through 1974, the Children's Television Task Force studied the state of children's television and recommended that licensees increase the amount of television programming created for children, particularly programs of educational and informational content. The task force recommended that selling, promotion, or endorsement of a product by the host of the program be prohibited, and that program content be clearly distinguished from commercial messages.

The ACT and other watchdog groups increased their efforts to influence the FTC in the late 1970s, with the result that the FTC introduced proposals for regulations to limit advertising on programs whose primary audience was children. Despite efforts toward self-regulation by industry groups such as the Children's Advertising Review unit of the National Council of Broadcasters and the Codes of the National Association of Broadcasters (Ward, 1978), the FTC banned all commercials on shows aimed at children of a very young age and commercials for highly sugared foods on programs directed at older children. The regulation also required advertisers to devote money to public service announcements to promote good dental and nutritional habits.

In 1980, Congress limited the scope of the FTC's attempts to regulate children's advertising to matters of deception and "unfair" or misleading advertising (Dewar, 1980). By October 1981, the FTC dropped its pursuit of the broadcasters and advertisers with respect to "Kid Vid" issues (*Federal Register,* vol. 46). The ACT continues to monitor television and file complaints to the FTC on those companies that ACT believes exploit the innocence of youth. The ACT has filed against Quaker Oats (1982), General Mills (1983), and General Foods (1983), charging unfair or deceptive advertising by each company (*Associated Press,* Jul. 18, 1983).

In 1983, Kellogg was brought to court in Canada to force the company to cease advertising to children. Kellogg claimed that such a ban would limit the company's ability to release new products and thus freeze competitors' present market shares. The availability of U.S. television in Canada obscures any verification of Kellogg's claim. However, Kellogg and other companies marketing products aimed at children, including games, toys, and foods, were restricted from advertising to children on Canadian television. The Canadian court stated that ads are presumed to be intended for children if they include "themes related to fantasy, magic, mystery, suspense or adventure," if they depict authority figures, role models, heroes, animals, or "imaginary or fanciful creatures," or if they rely on cartoons, children's music, or attention-getting technical devices (Lippman, 1983). Products of interest to children can be presented on Canadian television only if addressed to adults in a mature fashion.

Shared Monopoly

In the ten years that followed the FTC's initial complaint against Kellogg, General Mills, General Foods, and Quaker Oats, 243 days of testimony produced more than 36,000 pages of transcript and 60,000 pages of documents. The FTC charged the industry leaders with operating a "shared monopoly" that resulted not from conspiracy or collusion but from the collective power of the few firms (Kiechel, 1978).

The concept of shared monopoly arose from a study by a Massachusetts Institute of Technology economist, Richard L. Schmalensee. He argued that the cereal companies crowded the supermarket shelves with a large number of brands that left little space for new entrants. The flood of products into the market invited competition among those brands with similar characteristics—crunchiness, flavor, sweetness—but not competition between all brands on the market. The profusion of brands ensured that only existing firms could afford to compete; a new entrant would be required to invest $150 million in development with little assurance that it could gain the 3–5 percent share necessary to gain scale economy in production (Sebastian, 1979).

Specifically, the FTC charged the companies with the following practices (FTC vs Lonning & Kellogg).

> *Brand proliferation.* "The four companies introduce a profusion of ready-to-eat cereal brands into the market," that fill the "perceptual space" of the consumer with over 200 brands on the supermarket shelves.
>
> *Aggressive marketing.* "The brands are promoted by intensive advertising aimed primarily at children, which . . . conceals the true nature of these cereals." For example, Honey and Nut Corn Flakes implies significant sweetening by honey; in fact the flakes contain more brown sugar, white refined sugar, vegetable oil, salt, and malt flavoring than honey (Sebastian, 1979).

Product differentiation. The four companies produce "basically similar" ready-to-eat cereals that are artificially differentiated through trivial differences.

In addition to creating barriers to entry into the RTE cereal market, the companies were also accused of other unfair methods of competition in advertising and product promotion. The charges included:

1. Cereal advertising is false and misleading. This issue, also raised by ACT, pits the claims of nutrition and health against the high sugar content of many cereals. The sugar content has been blamed for health and dental problems.
2. Kellogg's program of shelf-space allocation, a program emulated by other cereal manufacturers, controls the exposure of breakfast food products. Kellogg records the sales of cereals in the supermarket and recommends brand selection and shelf-space allocation to the supermarket manager.
3. The companies made numerous acquisitions to eliminate competition in the RTE cereal market. These acquisitions have enhanced the shared monopoly structure of the industry.
4. The companies have exercised monopoly power by refusing to engage in price competition or other consumer-directed promotions.

The FTC claimed that the results of these acts were artificially inflated prices, excessive profits, and an absence of price competition. Government economists used the concept of shared monopoly to explain the reluctance of large consumer-products companies, such as Procter and Gamble, to enter the lucrative, albeit competitive, cereal market.

The FTC hoped to apply shared monopoly or oligopolistic behavior restrictions to other industries after establishing the validity of the concept in a landmark decision with references to the RTE cereals industry case. Any industry in which relatively few companies hold 90 percent market share (examples include telecommunications, oil, automobiles, and computers) would then be vulnerable to FTC action (Cowan, 1981; *Time,* Oct. 5, 1981).

Demographic Changes

Another basic challenge facing the industry has been a slowdown in the rate of growth of cereal consumption, brought about, in part, by the aging of the U.S. population. The U.S. median age is now 30 and is forecasted to reach 35 by the year 2000. The total population is expected to grow by less than 1 percent per year during the 1980s, primarily because of a slowdown in the U.S. birthrate.

Age-group populations do show different growth rates. Several changes expected in the 1980–1990 decade are listed below.

- The 15–24 year age group will decrease by 17 percent or 7.1 million.
- The 25–34 year age group will undergo a strong 14 percent increase.

EXHIBIT 12 Age Distribution Changes and Composite Percentage Change

Age (yr)	1970–1980	1980–1985	1985–1990 (estimated)
<5	−8.7	32.1	7.6
5–13	−16.3	1.2	25.6
14–17	2.3	−11.6	−11.3
18–21	16.6	−9.9	−6.1
22–24	21.6	2.3	−14.3
25–34	38.5	13.8	3.1
35–44	8.6	24.8	16.6
45–54	−1.5	−2.2	12.7
55–64	12.3	3.7	−4.4
65+	22.8	10.7	9.2
Total	8.1	7.4	6.6

Source: U.S. Bureau of Census.

- The 35–54 year age group will undergo the largest increase of all age groups, 25 percent.
- The 55–64 year age group will shrink by 2 percent.
- The over-65 age group will show the second largest increase, up by 20 percent (*Newsweek,* Jan. 17, 1983).

These demographic trends pose a threat to companies that sell a significant portion of their production to the youth market. The greatest consumers of RTE cereals are children under the age of 13. In the 1970s, the industry had experienced a decline in the population of this group. Exhibits 12–15 provide additional data on demographic changes facing the industry and on consumption of RTE cereal products.

Despite the challenges faced by the industry, the 1980s held some promise for the RTE cereal makers. Grain prices were weakening, with strong gains in

EXHIBIT 13 Ready-to-Eat Cereal Consumption: Percent of Total Consumption by Age Group

Age (yr)	1984	1983	1982	1981	1980	1979	1976	1972
<13	31.0	31.5	31.5	31.6	31.8	31.9	32.2	36.1
13–18	13.9	13.9	13.8	13.8	13.8	13.9	14.0	12.9
19–49	28.9	28.1	28.0	28.2	28.1	28.0	27.9	25.7
50+	26.2	26.5	26.7	26.4	26.3	26.2	25.9	25.3
Total	100	100	100	100	100	100	100	100

Source: Drexel, Burnham, & Lambert Brokerage House Report, "Kellogg Co.," Apr. 8, 1985.

EXHIBIT 14 Pounds Per Capita Ready-to-Eat Cereal Consumption by Age Group

Age (yr)	Pounds
<6	11.5
6–11	14.3
12–17	13.4
18–24	7.0
25–34	5.6
35–49	5.8
50–64	7.7
65+	11.3

Source: Kellogg Company publication.

production continuing through mid-decade. Moreover, cereal companies were able to levy 5 percent and 6 percent price increases while maintaining cereal at the lowest cost-per-serving of any breakfast food.

KELLOGG'S BUSINESS SITUATION

For Kellogg, the end of the 1970s and the beginning of the 1980s was an era of severe problems. The company retained its market leadership position, but their erosion of market share in the United States was a growing concern.

EXHIBIT 15 Ready-to-Eat Cereals: Consumption and Tonnage Shipped

Year	Pounds Consumed per Capita	Percent Change in Year-to-Year Tonnage
1971	6.76	3.00
1972	7.75	9.30
1973	8.30	15.20
1974	8.62	7.20
1975	9.03	5.40
1976	9.06	5.80
1977	8.89	1.00
1978	9.07	0.20
1979	9.07	1.30
1980	9.13	2.80
1981	9.26	2.40
1982	9.30	2.10
1983	9.41	2.30
1984	9.74	4.20

Source: Drexel, Burnham, & Lambert Brokerage House Report "Kellogg Co.," Apr. 8, 1985.

Domestic Sales

The introduction of generic and private-label brands contributed to a loss of Kellogg market share. Kellogg's position in the industry weakened as its market share dropped from a high of 43 percent in 1972 to a low of 38.5 percent in 1983. Consumers appeared to switch to the less-expensive generic brands as the rate of inflation grew to double digits in the 1970s. The cost of this share erosion was substantial: each percent of the RTE cereal market is valued at approximately $40 million.

Kellogg executive Arnold Langbo stated that Kellogg was particularly vulnerable to the generic and private-label inroads in the RTE cereal market. He observed, "The whole philosophy or principle of the private label is to copy the leading products in the market" (Johnson, 1983).

Kellogg fought the invasion of generic and private-label cereals with aggressive price decreases, recovering 1.8 percent of market share in 1984 as generic goods dropped 10 percent in tonnage shipped. Kellogg's two primary competitors held 36.4 percent of the market, considerably less than Kellogg's 40.3 percent share. In 1984, General Foods market share dropped 2.8 percent to 13.3 percent; General Mills held constant at a 23 percent share. Sales trends for several of Kellogg's products are presented in Exhibit 16. Market share performance of the Kellogg brands for the years 1982–1984 is presented in Exhibit 17.

Research and Development

In addition to price decreases, Kellogg increased its efforts in research and development (R & D) advertising, and new product introduction. With an R & D budget of $6.5 million in 1978, Kellogg began to develop cereals to appeal to different segments of the cereal market. By 1981, Kellogg was investing $20 million a year in research. Kellogg built two advanced research centers and acquired Agrigentics, a research company exploring improvements in grain development. Kellogg's efforts in research produced the first flaked cereal with no sugar or preservatives, Nutri Grain in 1981, the first cereal to combine two grains with identity separation, Crispix in 1983, and the first cereals to

EXHIBIT 16   Kellogg's Principal Products' Sales Trends ($ millions)

Product	1983	1984	Change (%)
Corn Flakes	$141.3	$162.5	15.0
Rice Krispies	144.1	141	−2.2
Raisin Bran	134.3	151.9	13.1
Special K	70.3	82.9	17.8
Fruit Loops	88.9	103.6	16.5
Frosted Flakes	188.8	217.9	15.4
Total	767.5	859.7	12.0

Source: Drexel, Burnham, & Lambert, Inc.

EXHIBIT 17 Kellogg's Ready-to-Eat Cereals: Market Share Data[1]

	1982		1983		1984	
Brand	Pounds	Dollars	Pounds	Dollars	Pounds	Dollars
Frosted Flakes	5.2	4.8	5.2	4.8	5.6	5.2
Corn Flakes	6.8	4.7	6.8	4.7	6.8	4.7
Raisin Bran	4.7	4.2	4.6	4.1	4.5	4.0
Rice Krispies	3.9	4.2	3.6	3.9	3.5	3.8
Fruit Loops	2.2	2.8	2.2	2.8	2.3	2.9
Special K	1.5	2.1	1.7	2.3	1.9	2.5
Bran Products	2.7	2.0	2.8	2.1	3.1	2.3
Frosted Mini-Wheats	1.8	1.8	1.8	1.8	1.9	1.9
Apple Jacks	1.0	1.5	1.0	1.5	1.0	1.5
Sugar Smacks	1.3	1.3	1.3	1.3	1.2	1.3
Sugar Pops	1.1	1.3	1.0	1.2	1.1	1.2
Product 19	0.8	1.1	0.8	1.1	0.9	1.1
Nutri-Grain	1.0	1.0	1.0	1.0	1.2	1.1
Crispex	—	—	0.7	0.7	0.5	0.5
Honey & Nut Corn Flakes	0.6	0.7	0.6	0.7	0.5	0.6
Marshmallow Krispies	0.5	0.7	0.5	0.7	0.4	0.6
Cocoa Krispies	0.5	0.7	0.5	0.7	0.6	0.8
Frosted Rice	0.6	0.8	0.5	0.6	0.4	0.4
Fruitful Bran	—	—	—	—	0.7	0.6
C-3PO	—	—	—	—	0.5	0.6
Apple Raisin Crisp	—	—	—	—	0.5	0.6
Raisin Squares	—	—	—	—	0.3	0.3
Most	0.3	0.4	0.3	0.4	0.2	0.3
Raisins Rice & Rye	0.5	0.6	0.3	0.4	0.1	0.1
Others	1.2	1.4	1.0	1.3	0.8	1.4
Total	38.5	38.5	38.5	38.5	40.5	40.3

[1] All figures are percentages.
Source: *Advertising Age*, Aug. 5, 1985, p. 42.

fully enrobe fruit, Raisin Squares and OJ's in 1984 (patent numbers: 4,178,392, 4,103,035, and 3,952,112).

Advertising

In 1984, Kellogg increased its advertising budget by 49 percent to $160 million, an aggressive move when compared to the 16 percent increase (to $52 million) of General Foods, and the 1 percent decrease in advertising by Post. As General Foods limited its primary advertising on its top five (of 14) leading brands, Kellogg was able to devote considerable push to its new products (*Forbes,* Oct. 7, 1985). Kellogg advertising themes for selected products are presented in Exhibit 18.

Kellogg was able to take advantage of reports connecting a high-fiber diet with a reduced risk of colon cancer and they positioned their new All Bran cereal as a cancer-preventive tool. Kellogg advertised, "At last, some news

EXHIBIT 18 Kellogg's Cereal: Products and Advertising Themes

Product	Themes
Special K	Thanks to the K, Staying in Shape Never Tasted so Good—Can't Pinch an Inch
Product 19	Flaky, Bumpy, Crispy, Crunchy *Vitamins*—100% of Your Daily Allowance of 10 Vitamins
Fruitful Bran	Bushels of Taste!—Fiber Rich
Nutri-Grain	Whole Grain Goodness . . . No Sugar Added—Dedicated to the Ones We Love
Apple Raisin Crisp	New Great Taste—New, Big, Juicy Chunks of Real Apple
Frosted Flakes	Gr-r-reat Taste—Tony the Tiger—The Taste Adults Have Grown to Love
Raisin Bran	Two Scoops of Raisins—Fiber Rich—Here is the Goodness of Fiber
All Bran	High Fiber—The Highest Fiber Cereal Ever
Rice Krispies	More Vitamin Nutrition than Old Fashioned Oatmeal—Snap! Crackle! and Pop!—The Talking Cereal Talks about Nutrition
Corn Flakes	The Original and Best—Provides 8 Essential Vitamins and Iron—How 'bout these Kellogg's Corn Flakes Now?—The Surprise is the People Who Eat Them
Just Right	High Nutrition . . . Uncompromising Taste—Kellogg's Just Right Cereal
Bran Flakes	Fiber-rich *Bran Flakes*—We'll Help Take Care of the Inside, You take Care of the Outside
Fruit Loops	Natural Fruit Flavors with 100% U.S. RDA of Vitamin C—All Natural Flavors: Orange, Lemon, Cherry—Delicious Natural Fruit Flavors with a Full Day's Supply of Vitamin C

Source: Kellogg advertisements.

about cancer you can live with." By the end of 1984, $250 million of Kellogg's sales came from bran cereals: All Bran, Bran Buds, Cracklin' Oat Bran, Fruitful Bran, Kellogg's Bran Flakes, Kellogg's Raisin Bran, and, in 1985, All Bran with Extra Fiber (Tracy, 1985).

The advertising campaign sparked controversy among industry, medical, and government groups. Officials at the FTC hailed the campaign as "the type of advertisement that we believe should be encouraged" (Kronhelm, 1985; Wollenberg, 1985). The Food and Drug Administration, however, protested that Kellogg was making medical claims for its product and considered seizing all boxes of All Bran from the shelves (Marwick, 1985). The National Food Processors Association petitioned the FDA to allow its member manufacturers to tout the health benefits of their products as long as the labeling was truthful and could be substantiated.

"Everyone has his opinions of advertising, but we didn't think anyone would misinterpret our commercials," explained Kellogg Vice President of Public Affairs, Peggy Wollerman. "Our goal is to communicate recommendations of the National Cancer Institute's findings that maintaining a high-fiber diet is a direct means of reducing the risk of cancer" (Rotenberk, 1984). The Kellogg advertisement had been cleared by Kellogg and National Cancer Institute scientists and lawyers for accuracy, and it had been passed by lawyers for the three television networks.

Until 1970, the FDA prohibited manufacturers from making any health claims on behalf of food products. In the following years, the FDA relaxed its standard for claims of "low calorie" and "low cholesterol." If a product is claimed to be useful in the treatment of a disease, it is considered a drug and the manufacturer must prove the efficacy of its claims (Cowart, 1985).

New Marketing Developments

Kellogg's move into the adult market in the late 1970s and early 1980s signaled a new direction for the cereal industry. Kellogg's strategy included promoting vitamin-enriched, whole grain, and sugarless cereals to the 25–49 year age group, high fiber to the 65+ age group, and C-3POs and OJs to the under-17 market (*Business Week,* Jan. 8, 1977).

Recognizing sociological changes in the United States, Kellogg introduced all-family cereals to enhance the convenience of shopping. Kellogg also introduced Smart Start, a cereal aimed at the working woman (*Business Week,* Nov. 26, 1979). Key to Kellogg's development and marketing were the themes of health, diet, convenience, and taste (Brody, 1985). Numerous surveys and surveying organizations, including the Bureau of Labor Statistics, have recorded significant social demographic changes in the last 15 years. A few of the changes that Kellogg and the other cereal companies had to address are listed below.

- In 1985, the numbers of families with school-age or preschool-age children increased by 460,000; the number of employed mothers increased by 765,000 to 18.2 million.
- In 1985, the median family wage and salary earnings increased 4.6 percent. Since 1982, the median family earnings increased 16 percent compared to a consumer price increase of 11 percent over the same period (*New York Times,* Feb. 19, 1986).

In the 1980s, breakfast has become a more significant part of the American diet, with 89 percent of the populace eating breakfast each day. Frozen breakfast foods were also becoming an important part of the breakfast food industry. In 1985, sales of all frozen foods totalled $849.3 million, 15 percent more than in 1984. In part, this increase was caused by the fact that more than 44 percent of American homes now had a microwave oven, making cooking at home easier. Sales of frozen breakfast entrees tripled from 1979 to 1985: sales of frozen pancakes increased 390 percent; frozen toaster items increased 1000 percent. Moreover, between 1978 and 1984, the number of Americans eating breakfast at a restaurant increased 45.7 percent compared to the overall restaurant increase of only 6.3 percent (Callahan, 1986).

Despite the decline in the population of children under 13 years of age, competition in breakfast food market segment continued without any slackening of intensity. As consumers of the greatest per capita amounts of cereal, children have long been the focus of cereal company advertising. Although Tony the Tiger has represented Kellogg's Sugar Frosted Flakes for many years, General Mills broke new ground in products for children with the first licensed character, Strawberry Shortcake. This was a move to link the cereal with other commercial media. Other RTE cereal companies followed quickly. The RTE cereal companies' licensed character products now include General Mills' ET, General Foods' Smurf Berry Crunch, Ralston Purina's Donkey Kong, Rainbow Brite, and Gremlins, and Kellogg's C-3POs.

The benefit of tying a cereal to an established figure from television, movies, comics, or toys (character licensing) is a quick gain in market share through exposure in a good trial period. Although traditional cereal products have existed for more than 30 years, the licensed-character cereal may have a life cycle of only 6–18 months. "The first licensed characters did well for about a year. Now their life span is about six months," said Nomi Ghez of Goldman Sachs & Co. (Spillman, 1985). The editor of *New Products News*, Martin Friedman, stated, "the characters that have been created by cereal companies go on forever, and the others don't" (Hollie, 1985). To seek a license for a character, Kellogg depended on assurances that the character would continue, that the character had personality and integrity, and that the character would not alienate adults.

By 1986, the cereal companies had less interest in developing licensed-character products because of a general decrease in the popularity of the characters with consumers (Friedman, 1986).

International Operations

By 1980, Kellogg measured sales in 130 countries from 19 manufacturing locations (Kellogg Annual Report, 1982). Kellogg International was divided into four divisions: Canada; United Kingdom and Europe; Latin America; and Africa, Australia, and Asia. International sales accounted for 30 percent of Kellogg's total sales. In France, Kellogg planned to target all segments of the population in hopes of replacing the croissant with cereal. In Japan, Kellogg has targeted children to establish the habit of eating cereal (*Dun's Business Month,* Dec., 1985). Financial results for several geographic operating segments are detailed in Exhibit 19.

Federal Trade Commission Case Revisited

In addition to the problems created by the introduction of generic and private-label brands, Kellogg management also attributed the previously mentioned loss of market share to the inability of top management to concentrate on operating the business. The Chairman of the Board, William E. Lamothe, estimated in 1982 that 40 percent of top management time had been spent on the FTC litigation (*Business Week,* Dec. 6, 1982).

For Kellogg, losing the FTC case would have significant effect. If the FTC had won the case, it would have divided Kellogg into five separate operating companies organized around its major product lines. Additionally, the FTC

EXHIBIT 19 Kellogg Company: Geographic Operating Segments ($ millions)

	1985	1984	1983	1982	1981
Sales					
United States	$2,074.9	$1,789.6	$1,560.0	$1,514.3	$1,454.0
Canada	177.6	178.9	176.0	169.0	170.2
Europe	474.9	425.9	437.8	453.0	435.9
Other	202.7	208.0	207.3	230.8	261.2
Total	2,930.1	2,602.4	2,381.1	2,367.1	2,321.3
Net Earnings					
United States	222.7	194.7	170.5	163.0	150.7
Canada	11.7	11.6	27.6	15.2	13.1
Europe	38.8	35.0	38.6	36.9	34.0
Other	7.9	9.2	6.0	12.7	7.6
Total	281.1	250.5	242.7	227.8	205.4
Assets					
United States	833.6	731.6	677.1	639.0	606.9
Canada	262.7	247.5	192.3	143.4	130.2
Europe	337.9	223.3	195.4	199.0	197.5
Other	158.9	148.6	139.8	153.7	178.0
Corporate	133.0	316.1	262.6	162.3	166.5
Total	1,726.1	1,667.1	1,467.2	1,297.4	1,279.11

Source: Kellogg Annual Reports.

would have required Kellogg to license its brands to smaller, regional manufacturers. Kellogg argued that such actions would place Kellogg at a competitive disadvantage in the RTE market and would produce inconsistent quality within Kellogg's brands.

As the trial entered the 1980s, Kellogg changed its passive strategy of litigation, becoming an aggressive champion of the industry's positions. Kellogg sponsored intense letter-writing campaigns to congressional representatives from districts in which Kellogg maintained facilities. As a result, the FTC received numerous inquiries from congressional representatives regarding the efficacy of continuing the case further (*Business Week,* Now. 26, 1979).

In 1981, Kellogg created Project Nutrition, a teaching unit for secondary grade school children, as well as nutrition inserts for children's television. Kellogg also provided cereals in 33,000 school breakfast programs. In 1982, Kellogg introduced Fitness Focus, a physical education program for high schools. Kellogg believed that the program would enhance its image as a producer of health-related foods, an image that could benefit Kellogg in its case against the FTC as well as in its position in the market.

Procedural errors in the handling of the case by the administrative judge and the FTC raised challenges from Kellogg and the other cereal companies.

Judge Harry R. Hinkes decided in 1978 to retire from the judiciary in order to gain full pension benefits, some of which he would lose if he postponed his retirement. The FTC, fearing a considerable delay and possible dismissal of the case, offered the judge a salary to stay on the case. The impropriety of such an arrangement, alleging a possible conflict of interest, was raised by Kellogg as grounds for dismissal. A new judge was appointed to continue the suit in 1981. Later, in 1982, the FTC dropped its suit (*Federal Register,* vol. 47).

Following the collapse of the FTC lawsuit against its four largest companies, the RTE industry witnessed increased competitive rivalry. This increased rivalry manifested itself in new product releases and advertising, and in corporate-development activities including acquisitions, divestitures, and share repurchases.

Diversification

The slowing growth rate in the cereal industry compelled Kellogg to look toward diversification for continued growth and comparable rates of returns for reinvestment of its retained earnings. In 1970, Kellogg entered the frozen food industry with the acquisition of Fearn International. In 1976, Kellogg acquired Mrs. Smith's Pie Co. and in 1977, it acquired Pure Packed Foods. Products such as Eggo waffles, salad dressings, LeGout soups, Salada Tea, Whitney Yogurt, Mrs. Smith's Pies, and pickles entered Kellogg's lines. Kellogg consolidated its frozen food operations under the Mrs. Smith's label in 1980 to gain greater efficiencies in manufacturing, warehousing, transportation, and marketing as well as a stronger product identity in the marketplace (Prokesch, 1985). By 1984, 25 percent of Kellogg's sales were noncereal (Blyskal, 1984). Exhibit 20 presents net income contributions of several elements of Kellogg, and Exhibit 21 presents sales and operating income for several segments of the company.

Despite LaMothe's declaration that Kellogg was "gung ho" on diversification, Kellogg lost in three attempts to acquire Tropicana and in attempts to

EXHIBIT 20   Kellogg Company: Net Income Contributions

Product/division	1981	1982	1983	1984	1985 (estimated)	1986 (estimated)
Domestic cereals	$121.0	$135.7	$138.0	$169.9	$206.0	$231.0
Canadian operation	11.0	13.0	13.8	9.4	10.0	12.0
Salada	12.1	13.0	14.0	15.0	16.0	18.0
Fearn International	9.0	9.5	10.5	11.6	12.0	14.0
Mrs. Smith's Pie Co.	8.7	7.0	8.0	8.9	10.0	11.0
Kellogg International	41.6	49.6	44.6	39.2	42.0	50.0
Total	203.4	227.8	228.9	254.0	296.0	336.0

Source: Drexel, Burnham, & Lambert, Inc., Oct. 7, 1985.

EXHIBIT 21 Kellogg Company: Estimated Sales and Operating Income
($ millions)

	1979	1980	1981	1982	1983	1984	1985
Sales							
RTE Cereals	$1,426	$1,687	$1,802	$1,792	$1,755	$2,000	$2,260
Salada	128	140	154	165	182	180	190
Fearn International	118	132	145	165	177	165	180
Mrs. Smith's Pie Co.	157	172	200	218	239	222	235
Other	18	19	20	27	50	35	35
Total	1,847	2,150	2,321	2,367	2,381	2,602	2,900
Operating income							
RTE Cereals	240	297	331	343.7	370	408.2	510
Salada	12	12	13	14	16	14	15
Fearn International	8	9	10	11	12.5	11.5	13
Mrs. Smith's Pie Co.	19	20	22	24	27.5	25	28
Other	2	2	2	3	4	4.5	5
Total	281	340	378	395.7	430	463.2	571

Source: Merrill, Lynch, Pearce, Fenner, & Smith brokerage house report: "Kellogg Co.," Oct. 31, 1985.

acquire Binney and Smith, manufacturers of Crayola crayons, and Seven-Up. Kellogg believed in each case that the price was too high for the company. "Today we are kind of glad we did [lose]," said LaMothe, "There is no embarrassment in losing. The big embarrassment is to win by paying too much and then never being able to make a return to your shareholders" (*Dun's Business Month,* Dec., 1985).

Capital Projects

Productivity improvements were made at many Kellogg manufacturing facilities in the late 1970s and 1980s, culminating in a $100 million expansion and improvement in the Battle Creek plant in 1985, the largest single capital expenditure in the company's history. Kellogg's ability to improve productivity is demonstrated by the 50 percent increase in revenues per employee that the company enjoyed between 1979 and 1985 (Drexel, Burnham, & Lambert, Oct 7, 1985). Early in 1986, Kellogg ended a long practice of public tours of the Battle Creek facility because of a desire to protect proprietary information. Several Kellogg capital projects for the years 1980–1983 are listed in Exhibit 22.

Preventing Takeover

Matching Kellogg's rates of return in an acquisition candidate is difficult. Moreover, the consumer-products companies such as Kellogg are attractive takeover targets themselves because of their high returns. To reduce the risk

EXHIBIT 22 Kellogg Company: Capital Projects

Year	Location	Project
1980	Rexdale, Ontario	Frozen food manufacturing facility
	Wrexham, England	Expanded capacity for Super Noodles
	Valls, Spain	New cereal plant
	Rooty Hill, Australia	Expansion of frozen food plant
	Queretro, Mexico	New corn milling operation
	Sao Paolo, Brazil	Expansion of cereal plant
	Maracay, Venezuela	New office building, processing, and packing
	Guatemala	Expansion of grain storage
	Arlington, TN	Pure Packed dry materials warehouse
	McMinnville, OR	Expansion of Mrs. Smith's plants
	San Jose, CA	Expansion of plant
	Blue Anchor, NJ	Mrs. Smith's facility
	Milpitas, CA	Eggo salad dressing plant
1981	Battle Creek, MI	Expanded for Nutri-Grain cereal
	Lancaster, PA	Increase capacity for cereal
	Battle Creek, MI	Advanced technology facility for research and development
	South Korea	New processing plants
	London, Ontario	Advanced technology center
	Manchester, England	Expansion of packing facility
	Bremen, West Germany	Purchased land
1982	London, Ontario	Expansion of plant
	Seoul, South Korea	Plant completed
	Manchester, England	Conversion of packing line
	Sao Paolo, Brazil	Expansion of facilities
1983	Pottstown, PA	Expansion of office space, storage Warehouse

Source: Kellogg Annual Reports.

of a takeover, Kellogg purchased 20 percent of its own stock in 1984, an "investment in our own business," said LaMothe. The effect of the stock repurchase added $500 million of debt to the Kellogg balance sheet. Before the transaction, Kellogg enjoyed only $19 million of debt against $1 billion in equity. The 20 percent block of stock had been held by the Kellogg Foundation. Any potential sale of the stock, said LaMothe, was a "cloud we didn't think was good to leave hanging out there in today's time" (Willoughby, 1985).

Kellogg's competitors employed a range of strategies in response to the same takeover challenge. Ralston Purina also acquired blocks of its own stock,

EXHIBIT 23 Recent Acquisitions of Established Brands

Buyer	Acquisition	Brands
Procter and Gamble	Richardson-Vicks	NyQuil, Vidal Sassoon, Clearasil
Philip Morris	General Foods	Jell-O, Maxwell House
Monsanto	G.D. Searle	Nutrasweet, Metamusil
Brown-Forman	California Cooler	California Cooler
Greyhound	Purex' Cleaning	Purex Bleach, Brillo
Sara Lee	Nicholas Kiwi	Kiwi shoe polish
Nestle'	Carnation	Carnation Milk, Friskies pet food
Ralston Purina	Continental Baking	Hostess Twinkies, Wonder Bread
	Nabisco Foods	Oreo cookies, Life Savers, Ritz Crackers, Shredded Wheat
Beatrice Foods	Esmark	Wesson Oil, Playtex
R.J. Reynolds	Canada Dry	Canada Dry soft drinks
Quaker Oats	Stokely-Van Camp	Gatorade, canned goods

Source: Brown (1985).

continuing this strategy through mid-decade. In 1985, R.J. Reynolds acquired Nabisco Brands, itself a result of a merger between Nabisco and Standard Brands. Philip Morris acquired General Foods. Exhibit 23 lists several recent acquisitions of established brands.

Some of the largest companies in the food industry have been built through a series of acquisitions: Beatrice and Sara Lee Corporation are both the products of acquisitions. Traditionally, regional brands were acquired to take advantage of a larger, national sales force, as well as the financial strength of the parent company. When product lines of the two companies overlapped, the strength of the broader product line commanded greater influence in attracting shelf space in the supermarket, and greater discounts in advertising rates (Brown, 1985).

For Reynolds and Philip Morris, acquisition of food products carried other benefits. Slower sales of cigarettes and pending lawsuits and legislation about smoking are expected to eventually erode profitability in the cigarette industry. The higher than average returns of the cereal and food companies, with a strong brand image of health and nutrition, is an attractive inducement for investment.

According to Marc C. Patricelli of Booz Allen & Hamilton Inc., 19 of 24 RTE cereal brands retained their leadership position from 1923 to 1983. "So if a company buys a leader, and if they run it correctly, they are buying an annuity, because brand leadership is sustainable" (Brown, 1985). Kellogg's financial performance and dominance in the cereal industry makes it an appealing target for merger or acquisition. Exhibits 24–26 give financial information on Kellogg.

EXHIBIT 24 Kellogg Company: Consolidated Balance Sheet ($ millions)

	1985	1984	1983	1982	1981
Current Assets					
Cash and temporary investments	$ 127.8	$ 308.9	$ 248.8	$ 159.8	$ 163.7
Accounts receivable	203.9	182.5	157.1	140.7	158.9
Inventory					
Raw materials	135.6	119.7	115.7	128.8	129.4
Finished goods and work in progress	110.3	101.4	101.1	98.9	101.8
Prepaid expenses	40.5	39.0	40.4	35.9	28.4
Total current assets	618.1	751.5	663.1	564.1	582.2
Property					
Land	25.6	25.6	26.3	25.1	24.0
Buildings	321.2	277.7	274.1	263.4	263.8
Machinery and equipment	903.2	762.4	692.7	677.6	620.6
Construction in progress	280.4	215.7	143.7	83.5	90.0
Total property	1,503.4	1,281.4	1,136.8	1,049.6	998.4
Less accumulated depreciation	494.5	425.4	393.6	367.4	340.0
Net property	1,035.9	856.0	743.2	682.2	658.4
Intangible assets	28.3	30.5	29.0	33.6	32.2
Other assets	43.8	29.1	31.9	17.5	6.3
Total assets	1,726.1	1,667.1	1,467.2	1,297.4	1,279.1
Current Liabilities					
Current maturities of debt	34.8	340.6	20.0	6.5	16.5
Accounts payable	189.7	127.4	116.8	99.1	104.5
Accrued liabilities					
Income tax	29.4	51.4	85.0	81.9	77.4
Salaries and wages	41.8	38.7	36.2	31.4	29.9
Promotion	71.3	60.2	66.4	45.0	30.9
Other	46.4	45.8	36.3	43.7	41.7
Total current liabilities	444.3	664.1	360.7	307.6	300.9
Long-term debt	392.6	364.1	18.6	11.8	88.2
Other liabilities	12.3	9.5	9.2	11.0	9.8
Deferred income tax	193.9	142.2	100.8	82.3	69.9
Shareholders' Equity					
Common stock	38.4	38.4	38.2	38.2	38.2
Capital in excess of par value	44.5	40.8	34.4	32.9	32.5
Retained earnings	1,288.5	1,118.4	991.5	872.8	761.6
Treasury stock	−576.8	−577.8			
Currency translation adjustment	−111.6	−132.6	−86.2	−59.2	−22.0
Total equity	683.0	487.2	977.9	884.7	810.3
Total liabilities and equity	1,726.1	1,667.1	1,467.2	1,297.4	1,279.1

Source: Kellogg Annual Reports.

EXHIBIT 25 Kellogg Company: Consolidated Earnings and Retained Earnings
($ millions)

	1985	1984	1983	1982	1981	1980
Net sales	2,930.1	2,602.4	2,381.1	2,367.1	2,331.3	2,150.9
Interest revenue	7.2	27.7	18.6	21.3	18.2	18.7
Other, net	−2.8	3.9	18.1	2.1	0.0	0.0
Total revenue	2,934.5	2,634.0	2,417.8	2,390.5	2,339.5	2,169.6
C.O.G.S.	1,605.0	1,488.4	1,412.3	1,442.2	1,447.8	1,385.2
S.G. & A exp.	766.7	650.8	554.4	529.2	501.1	435.7
Interest exp.	35.4	18.7	7.1	8.2	12.0	10.4
Total	2,407.1	2,157.9	1,973.8	1,979.6	1,960.9	1,831.3
EBT	527.4	476.1	444.0	410.0	378.6	338.3
Income taxes	246.3	225.6	201.3	183.1	173.2	154.3
Net earnings	281.1	250.5	242.7	227.8	205.4	184.0
Retained earnings, Jan. 1	1,118.4	991.5	872.8	761.6	665.1	583.5
Dividends	−111.0	−123.6	−124.0	−116.6	−108.9	−102.4
Retained earnings, Dec. 31	1,288.5	1,184.4	991.5	872.5	761.6	665.1

Source: Kellogg Annual Reports.

CONCLUSION

"The question is not whether this is a mature market," said LaMothe, "it's whether we can be inventive enough. . . . [Americans now have] the highest level of per capita [cereal] consumption in U.S. history. A lot of areas are close to 13 pounds. Why not make the whole country average 13?" (Willoughby, 1985). Kellogg's challenge is to increase the market for cereals, both domestic and foreign, by increasing consumption. In the United States, middle-aged and older Americans are the target segments. According to LaMothe (*Dun's Business Month,* Dec. 1985):

> Dr. Kellogg and Mr. Kellogg were going on either intuition or their basic beliefs coming out of a Seventh Day Adventist background, where they believed that meats were not healthful for the diet. . . . We think that it (cereal) has a tremendous future. . . . The whole grains . . . healthy lifestyle . . . avoidance of major disease in the Western World . . . more grains, fruit and vegetables. Where else can you get such nutrition for 20 cents a serving? There will be 6 billion people on the face of the earth by the year 2000 and grains will continue to be the most efficient way for most people to get their calories and nutrition. We are going to help feed them. That's what Kellogg is all about.

EXHIBIT 26 Kellogg Company: Changes in Consolidated Financial Position
($ millions)

	1985	1984	1983	1982	1981	1980
Source of funds						
Net earnings	281.1	250.5	242.7	227.7	205.4	184.0
Depreciation	75.4	63.9	62.8	55.9	49.1	44.7
Deferred tax/other	54.9	62.6	12.0	27.1	10.4	12.0
Total funds provided by operations	411.4	377.0	317.5	310.7	264.9	240.7
Changes in working capital components						
Accounts receivable	−21.4	−25.4	−16.4	18.2	−9.2	−17.0
Inventory	−24.8	−4.3	10.9	3.5	26.1	−19.2
Prepaid expenses	−1.5	1.4	−4.5	−7.5	−3.7	−7.1
Current debt maturity	−305.8	320.6	13.5	−10.0	−10.0	5.7
Accounts payable	62.3	10.6	17.7	−5.4	−1.5	−9.8
Accrued liability	23.7	−27.9	21.9	22.1	25.2	46.2
Net change	−267.5	275.1	43.1	20.9	26.9	−1.2
Funds provided by operations and changes in working capital	143.9	652.1	360.6	331.6	291.8	239.5
Long-term debt	31.5	348.1	1.5	0.0	7.9	0.4
Common stock	3.7	6.7	1.1	0.4	0.0	0.0
Property disposal	4.3	12.0	38.0	5.3	2.9	5.0
Tax-lease benefits	1.2	3.1	6.2	12.0	0.0	0.0
Other	7.9	0.9	0.5	3.1	0.5	1.4
Total source of funds	192.1	1,022.9	407.9	352.4	303.1	246.3
Use of funds						
Property	245.6	228.9	156.7	121.1	146.4	122.9
Cash dividends	111.0	123.6	124.0	116.6	108.9	102.4
Treasury stock purchases	0.0	577.9	0.0	0.0	0.0	
Investment in tax leases	0.0	0.0	11.6	14.2	0.0	0.0
Long-term debt reduction	2.8	2.7	3.6	75.7	0.4	2.8
Other	23.8	14.7	10.5	13.9	6.4	1.1
Total use of funds	383.2	947.7	306.4	341.5	262.1	229.2
Exchange rate effect on working capital	10.0	−15.1	−12.5	−14.9	−9.1	0.0
Increase in cash and temporary investments	−181.1	60.1	89.0	−4.0	31.9	17.1

Source: Kellogg Annual Reports.

REFERENCES

Advertising Age, Aug. 5, 1985. p. 42.

Associated Press, "FTC Accused of Sanctioning Bad Advertising Practice," Jul. 18, 1983.

Blyskal, Jeff (1984) "Branded Foods," *Forbes,* Jan. 2, p. 208.

Brody, Jane E. (1985) "America Leans to a Healthier Diet," *New York Times,* Oct. 13, p. 32, section 6.

Brown, Paul B., et al. (1985) "NEW? IMPROVED? The Brand Name Mergers," *Business Week,* Oct. 21, p. 108.

Business Week, Industrial Edition, Jan. 8, 1977, p. 46.

Business Week, Industrial Edition, Nov. 26, 1977, p. 80.

Business Week, "Too Many Cereals for the FTC," Mar. 20, 1978, p 166+.

Business Week, "Still the Cereal People," Nov. 26, 1979, p. 80+.

Business Week, "Kellogg Looks Beyond Breakfast," Dec. 6, 1982, p. 66+.

Callahan, Tom (1986) "What's New With Breakfast; Morning Meals, Fresh from the Freezer," *New York Times,* Feb. 16, p. 17, section 3.

Cowan, Edward (1981) "F.T.C. Staff is Rebuffed on Cereals," *New York Times,* Sep. 11, p. D1.

Cowart, V., (1985). "Keeping foods safe and labels honest; Food Safety and Applied Nutrition." *Journal of the American Medical Association,* 254, 2228-2229.

Dewar, Helen (1980) "FTC Curbs are Adopted by Senate," *Washington Post,* Feb. 8, p. A1.

Drexel, Burnham, & Lambert, Brokerage House Report, "Kellogg Co.", Apr. 8, 1985.

Drexel, Burnham, & Lambert, Brokerage House Report, "General Foods," May 20, 1985.

Drexel, Burnham, & Lambert, Kellogg Company, Research Abstracts; Food Processors, Oct. 7, 1985.

Dun's Business Month, "Kellogg: Snap, Crackle, Profits," Dec. 1985, p. 32+.

The Economist, "Philip Morris/General Foods: Chow Time for the Marlboro Cowboy," Oct. 5, 1985.

Federal Register, Federal Trade Commission, "Children's Advertising," 46 FR 48710.

Federal Register, "Childrens Television Programming and Advertising Practices," 49 FR 1704.

Federal Register, Federal Trade Commission, "Kellogg Company, et al; Prohibitive Trade Practices, and Affirmative Correction Actions," 47 FR 6817.

Federal Trade Commission v. J. E. Lonning, President, and Kellogg Company, a Corporation, Appellants, 539 F2nd 202.

Forbes, Oct. 7, 1985, p. 126.

Friedman, Martin (1986) "Cereal Bowls Spill Over with Nuttiness," *ADWEEK,* Feb. 10.

Hollie, Pamela G. (1985) "New Cereal Pitch at Children," *New York Times,* Mar. 27, p. D1.

Johnson, Greg (1983) "Who's Afraid of Generic Cereals?" *Industry Week,* May 16, p. 33.

Kellogg Company Annual Reports, 1981, 1982, 1983, 1984, 1985.

Kiechel, Walter III (1978) "The Soggy Case Against the Cereal Industry," *Fortune,* Apr. 10, p. 49.

Kornhelm, William (1985) "Should Food Labels Carry Health Claims, FDA's Policy Challenged," *Associated Press,* May 15.

Lippman, Thomas W. (1983) "Quebec's Ad Ban No Child's Game; Advertisers, TV Try to Adjust," *Washington Post,* Apr. 17, p. G1.

Marwick, C., (1985). "FDA prepares to meet regulatory challenges of 21st century," *Journal of the American Medical Association,* 254, 2189–2201.

Meadows, Edward (1981) "Bold Departures in Antitrust," *Fortune,* Oct. 5, p. 180.

Newsweek, "A Portrait of America," Jan. 17, 1983, pp. 20–33.

New York Times, Sep. 15, 1985, section 3, p. 1.

New York Times, "More Mothers are Working," Feb. 19, 1986, p. C4+.

Patent Number 3,952,112, "Method for treating dried fruits to improve softness retention characteristics," Fulger et al., April 20, 1976.

Patent Number 4,103,035, "Method for retaining softness in Raisins," Fulger et al., July 25, 1978.

Patent Number 4,178,392, "Method of Making a ready-to-eat breakfast cereal," Gobble et al., December 11, 1979.

Philip Morris Co., Press Release, Apr. 24, 1986.

Prokesch, Steven (1985) "Food Industry's Big Mergers," *New York Times,* Oct. 14, p. D1.

Prudential-Bache Securities, Inc., Oct. 1, 1985.

Prudential-Bache Securities, Inc., Apr. 1, 1986.

Rotenberk, Lori (1984) "Ad Exec Blasts JWT's All-Bran Ad," *ADWEEK* (Eastern edition), Oct. 29.

Sebastian, John V. (1979) "A Slight Taste of Honey," *Business Week,* Reader's Report, Dec. 17, p. 10.

Spillman, Susan (1985) "It's a Kid's Market," *USA Today,* Oct. 7.

Tracy, Eleanor Johnson (1985) "Madison Avenue's Cancer Sell Spreads," *Fortune,* Aug. 19, p. 77.

Ward, S., "Compromise in Commercials for Children," *Harvard Business Review,* Nov. 1978, p. 128+.

Willoughby, Jack (1985) "The Snap, Crackle, Pop Defense," *Forbes,* Mar. 25, p. 82.

Wollenberg, Skip (1985) "Reagan's Cancer Diagnosis Sparks Prevention Ads," *Associated Press,* Jul. 29.

INDUSTRIAL HIGHLIGHT

Confectionery and Baked Goods Industry

Below is a capsule summary of the cereal breakfast foods segment of the confectionery and baked goods industry, of which the Kellogg Company is a part. Information in this highlight was compiled by the U.S. Department of Commerce and focuses on this industry during the approximate period of time covered in the case. Keep in mind that industrial highlights contained in this text are not intended as a complete synopsis of an industry but as a profile of certain issues that can be relevant to a case situation.

CURRENT SITUATION

In 1984, the estimated value of shipments by the cereal breakfast food industry increased to $4.5 billion (current dollars). Adjusted for inflation, the value dropped 1.1 percent. Breakfast cereal, sold in many brands and package sizes, comes in two principal varieties—ready-to-eat and hot. Cold cereal generated about 90 percent of retail sales of cereal in supermarkets, with $2 million or more in annual sales, based on a 1983 survey. Hot cereal sales accounted for the remainder.

Changing population characteristics and consumer tastes both contribute to the demand for breakfast cereal. Historically, children aged 5 to 14 are the core consumers of presweetened cereals. Between 1979 and 1984, this group's population edged downward 0.6 percent annually. The population aged 20 to 49, important consumers of unsweetened cereal, rose 2.6 percent yearly during the same period. Recognizing this trend, cereal manufacturers have targeted more advertising toward an adult audience.

Convenience, nutrition, and parental concern about children's consumption of presweetened cereals are important factors affecting consumer purchases of cereals. Many consumers want cereals with convenient packaging and ease of preparation. Vitamin fortification, fiber, and bran in cereal also attract adult consumers.

Presweetened cereals account for about 30 percent of supermarket sales of cold cereals. In 1984, consumer advocacy groups continued their criticism

Source: U.S. Industrial Outlook, Department of Commerce, 1985, pp. 41-8 to 41-10.

of the nutritional value of presweetened cereals and the child-oriented advertising of these products. Complaining about child-oriented sweepstakes advertising on television, one group again requested the Federal Trade Commission (FTC) to prohibit cereal companies from using such advertising. The FTC denied this petition.

Other cold cereals include bran and wheat germ products (15 percent of ready-to-eat cereal sales), high-protein or fortified cereals (11 percent), and natural cereals (8 percent). Hot cereal products include oatmeal, wheat-based items, and hominy grits.

Brands: Generic and Private Label Retreat

To attract the loyalty of certain types of consumers, cereal firms market almost 300 distinct brands and package sizes. In an effort to supply every identifiable, viable market niche, manufacturers systematically launch new brands. From August 1983 to July 1984, they introduced at least 14 new brands of cold cereal, 10 of which were brought out by the five leading companies. Firms also marketed two new brands of cereal meal bar. Originally conceived as a breakfast product, certain varieties of chocolate-enrobed cereal meal bars now resemble confectionery products. Heavily advertised national brands of breakfast cereal recovered ground lost during the last recession. Never reaching more than 5 percent of sales, the sales share of generic and private label cereals contracted to less than 2 percent.

From 1972 to 1977, per capita consumption of breakfast cereal increased. Per-person use of wheat-based cereals rose markedly, while corn-based items experienced slower growth. Growth of rice breakfast foods ranged between corn-based and wheat-based products. During 1977–1982, however, per capita consumption of corn-based cereals edged up 2.1 percent a year, whereas per capita use of wheat-based products dipped 0.6 percent. In 1984, estimated consumption of corn-based items dropped an estimated 3.2 percent, while per capita use of wheat-based products advanced appreciably—9.7 percent.

In 1984, the four major companies of the breakfast cereal industry supplied an estimated 75 percent of the total market, slightly less than in 1983. Ranking first, Kellogg had 33 percent of total breakfast cereal sales. General Foods generated 21 percent of sales; Quaker Oats held an 11-percent market share; and General Mills produced 10 percent of all sales.

International Trade and Investment

The value of U.S. breakfast cereal exports has consistently surpassed imports. In 1984, exports reached $37.6 million but accounted for only 1.1 percent of new supply. During 1979–1983, the value of exports rose an average of 9.2 percent a year. In 1984, four countries purchased almost 80 percent of U.S. exports of breakfast cereal: Canada (62 percent), the Bahamas (10 percent), Japan (4.1 percent), and Saudi Arabia (3.4 percent).

U.S. imports were $10.7 million in 1984, or 0.3 percent of new supply. From 1979 to 1983, imports climbed 6.8 percent annually. More than 80 percent of the value of imports originated from four countries—Canada, Mexico, Switzerland, and Colombia.

U.S. breakfast cereal companies have invested abroad, particularly in Western Europe. Until recently, Kellogg and Quaker Oats have mainly fulfilled the French demand for cold cereal. In 1984, General Foods and Poulain Industries of France completed a plant under the auspices of a joint venture subsidiary, Eurocereales. The two companies seek to gain a 30-percent share of the French market.

Input Costs

In 1984, ingredient price changes ranged from a 12.6-percent rise for oats to a 3.7-percent decline for wheat. Packaging costs increased more rapidly than most ingredient costs. Prices of paperboard food packages jumped 7.4 percent. Used as a liner in cereal boxes, glassine experienced an 8.7-percent rise in price.

During 1977–1982, changing consumer preferences caused firms to alter their mix of ingredients. Sugar use dropped 0.4-percent yearly. To attract health-conscious, usually adult, consumers, companies increased their tonnage of dried and dehydrated fruit 15.5 percent annually.

Producer and Consumer Prices

The Bureau of Labor Statistics (BLS) reported that 1984 manufacturers' prices for cold cereals and hot cereals gained 3.7 percent and 2.1 percent, respectively. In comparison, producer prices of all foods increased 4.4 percent.

Changes in retail prices of breakfast cereal exceeded those in manufacturers' prices. According to BLS, consumer prices jumped 5.7 percent, while retail prices for all food consumed at home climbed only 3.5 percent.

OUTLOOK FOR 1985

In 1985, shipments by the cereal industry should rise 1.4 percent, adjusted for inflation. Changes in the prices of agricultural commodities, especially fruits, will likely have a greater impact on ingredient prices than in 1984. According to the Census Bureau, farm products as of 1982 represented 44.4 percent of the value of material used in breakfast cereal production, a rise from 38.0 percent in 1977.

Manufacturers will continue to emphasize high-protein, whole-grain, bran, and natural cereals for adults. The 20- to 49-year population group is expected to increase 1.8 percent in 1985, while the population category aged 5 to 14 will contract an estimated 0.3 percent, half the rate of decline in 1984. This population change for children may signal increased consumption of presweetened cereals.

LONG-TERM PROSPECTS

Adjusted for inflation, the value of industry shipments of cereals in the next 5 years should rise 0.9 percent annually, a rate equal to the total population increase. The number of children aged 5 to 14 in the population will increase 1.2 percent yearly between 1985 and 1990. This demographic phenomenon along with a product mix of breakfast cereals containing less sugar or sweetened with alternative sweeteners may portend significantly greater consumption of presweetened cereals. The population segment aged 20 to 49 will gain 1.3 percent annually so cereal companies also will probably continue marketing unsweetened, minimally processed, high-protein cold cereals targeted to the adult market.

Firms in the future may devote more resources to important markets for hot cereals. Between 1985 and 1990, the population aged 65 years and over will rise 2.1 percent yearly. Likewise, the population of children aged 5 years and under will increase 0.8 percent annually. Both these population groups groups are large consumers of hot cereal for reasons of taste, texture, nutritional value, and lower retail price.

ADDITIONAL REFERENCES

Advertising Age, Crain Communications, Inc., 740 Rush Street, Chicago, IL 60011.

1982 Census of Manufactures, Cereal Breakfast Foods, Series MC82-1-20D-2, Bureau of the Census, U.S. Department of Commerce, Washington, DC 20233.

Milling and Baking News, Sosland Publishing Co., 4800 Main Street, Kansas City, MO 64112.

Preserved Foods, Gorman Publishing Co., 5725 E. River Road., Chicago, Il 60631.

Progressive Grocer, Maclean Hunter Media, Inc., 1351 Washington Boulevard, Stanford, CT 06902.

Snack Food, Harcourt Brace Jovanovich, 1 E. First Street, Duluth, MN 55802.

CASE 7

The Southland Corporation*

J. W. BROWN
University of Tennessee

In 1978, the world's largest chain of convenience food stores was 7-Eleven markets, a division of the Southland Corporation. The 7-Eleven chain started from very humble beginnings in 1927 to surpass the $3 billion sales figure in 1978. Southland showed all indications of continuing its 15 percent annual growth rate and capitalizing on consumer acceptance of convenience shopping.

COMPANY HISTORY

In 1924, Jodie Thompson wanted to get married, but his $40-a-week salary from a Dallas ice-making firm was not enough to support a wife and family. From working on the ice docks and overseeing sales that summer, Thompson came upon the solution—chilled watermelons. No one had ever tried to sell chilled watermelons (or any other retail item for that matter) off the ice docks in Texas. Thompson's boss was initially very skeptical but finally gave approval to try the idea. The venture was a success, and, by the end of the summer, Thompson had made $2,300.

In the summer of 1927, one of the dock managers of the Southland Ice Co. found that he could do a much brisker business by staying open 16 hours a day, seven days a week. He also noted that late-hour ice customers often complained about there being no place to pick up a loaf of bread or a bottle of milk. The dock manager persuaded Mr. Thompson, who by then was secretary-treasurer and a director of Southland Ice Co., to finance an inventory of bread, milk, and eggs and stock them on the dock. The items sold well, and shortly thereafter, when Thompson became president, all the company's ice docks were stocked with grocery items and the enterprising dock manager was assigned the task of finding new store sites. At the advice of a local advertising agency, Thompson named the stores 7-Eleven because they were open from 7 A.M. to 11 P.M.

By the mid-1950s, Southland had expanded to about 300 stores, mostly in Texas and Florida. As the United States became more urbanized, with many people commuting to work from the suburbs, Thompson and his two oldest

---

* This is a classic case in the strategic management literature.

Prepared by J. W. Brown, M.B.A., 1979, at the University of Tennessee, under the direction of Prof. John Thiel. Reprinted by permission of the author.

sons believed that Southland could move into and redefine the niche once dominated by mom-and-pop corner grocery stores; they felt that selling customers convenience in the form of accessible hours, handy locations, big parking lots, and well-selected merchandise would translate into a competitive edge and accelerate a shift of buyer patronage from the rapidly failing corner groceries to Southland's convenience food store concept. Southland's store expansion program began in earnest about 1960.

SOUTHLAND'S CURRENT BUSINESS STRUCTURE

In 1978, Southland's business interests were organized into three major groups. The Stores Group was the world's largest operator and franchiser of convenience stores with 6,599 7-Eleven stores in 42 states, the District of Columbia, and 5 provinces of Canada. Its three distribution centers served 3,916 7-Eleven stores with approximately 50 percent of their merchandise needs. Food Centers, located at each distribution center, prepared a variety of sandwiches for distribution to 7-Eleven and other customers. Other retail operations included 109 Gristede's and Charles & Company food stores and sandwich shops in metropolitan New York, 383 R. S. McColl confectionery, tobacco, and news stores, and 7 7-Eleven units in the United Kingdom. Southland also had an equity interest in 5 Super Siete stores in Mexico and 23 Naroppet stores in Sweden. An additional 279 7-Eleven stores were operated by area licensees in the United States, 559 in Japan, 5 in Canada, and 12 in Australia.

The Dairies Group, another part of the Southland Corporation, was a major processor of dairy products which were distributed under 11 well-known regional brand names in 34 states and the District of Columbia.

The Special Operations Group included the Chemical division, Reddy Ice, Hudgins Truck Rental, and Tidel Systems which manufactured money handling devices for retail operations. In addition, Chief Auto Parts, a retail automobile supply chain of 119 stores in Southern California, was added to the Group in late 1978.

Exhibit 1 gives a breakout of the sales revenues and operating profits of these three groups. Exhibit 2 provides a corporatewide financial summary and Exhibit 3 is a condensed statement of consolidated earnings.

CUSTOMER PROFILE OF SOUTHLAND'S 7-ELEVEN STORES

Approximately 5.4 million people patronized 7-Eleven stores daily in 1978. Based on a study it conducted that year, Southland came up with a profile of its customers:

69.8 percent male
80.2 percent in 18–49 age group
80.9 percent live/work in area

EXHIBIT 1 Southland's Revenues and Operating Profits by Major Business Segment

(all dollar figures in millions)

	1974		1975		1976		1977		1978	
Revenues:										
Stores Group	$1,405.4	87%	$1,556.0	87%	$1,857.5	88%	$2,271.9	89%	$2,791.0	90%
Dairies Group	184.0	11	208.3	12	236.1	11	236.5	9	253.4	8
Special Operations Group	22.6	2	25.0	1	26.0	1	33.7	2	40.9	2
Corporate	2.2	—	1.5	—	2.4	—	3.3	—	4.8	—
Total	$1,614.2	100%	$1,790.8	100%	$2,122.0	100%	$2,545.4	100%	$3,090.1	100%
Operating profits:										
Stores Group	$ 68.5	85%	$ 80.8	88%	$ 92.3	86%	$ 115.7	90%	$ 142.7	92%
Dairies Group	8.1	10	10.1	11	8.6	8	6.0	5	6.7	4
Special Operations Group	4.0	5	.9	1	6.4	6	6.7	5	6.0	4
Total	$ 80.6	100%	$ 91.8	100%	$ 107.3	100%	$ 128.4	100%	$ 155.4	100%

Source: Company records.

4.3 average trips a week

30.1 percent shop weekends

50.2 percent shop 1 P.M. to 10 P.M.

$1.54 average purchase

822 customers daily per store

On the average, the typical customer spent less than $2—and three to four minutes—at the store, and often made at least one unplanned impulse purchase. Though these small unplanned purchases did not amount to much extra expense for the individual customer, they resulted in significant extra sales and profits to Southland, given that over five million customers a day were involved.

According to a reporter for *The Wall Street Journal*:

> Southland's 7-Elevens are successors of the old-fashioned mom-and-pop grocery, but they prosper by catering to the modern urge for instant gratification. Their customers fill their pantries at the supermarket but dash instead to the closest 7-Eleven to fill their latest desire for, say, cigarettes or cold beer. Indeed, well over half the goods a 7-Eleven sells are consumed within 30 minutes.[1]

The same article quoted a 7-Eleven customer who lived in Dallas: "I usually stop by on the way to work to get a roll, in the afternoon to pick up a TV dinner, and sometimes during the day to get a coke. I'm a bachelor and it's quick and convenient." This view reflected management's own perceptions that Southland was really in the convenience business rather than in the retail grocery business.

---

[1] Gerald F. Seib, "Despite High Prices and Sparse Selection, 7-Eleven Stores Thrive," *The Wall Street Journal*, May 1, 1979, p. 1.

EXHIBIT 2 Southland Corporation Financial Summary

	1974	1975	1976	1977	1978
Operations:[1]					
Total revenues (in 000s)	$1,614,188	$1,790,805	$2,122,023	$2,545,415	$3,090,094
Increase over prior year	15.47%	10.94%	18.50%	19.95%	21.40%
Net earnings (in 000s)	$27,167	$32,068	$37,849	$45,317	$57,097
Increase over prior years	25.85%	18.04%	18.03%	19.73%	25.99%
Per revenue dollar	1.68%	1.79%	1.78%	1.78%	1.85%
Return on beginning shareholders' equity	13.16%	13.72%	14.56%	15.62%	17.30%
Assets employed:[1]					
Working capital (in 000s)	$72,495	$80,196	$101,536	$136,693	$141,633
Current ratio	1.55	1.58	1.63	1.66	1.54
Property, plant, and equipment including capital leases (net) (in 000s)	$406,486	$447,392	$506,190	$567,442	$667,284
Depreciation and amortization (in 000s)	43,078	47,974	55,029	61,735	67,724
Total assets (in 000s)	639,599	696,107	799,261	942,531	1,134,476
Capitalization:[1]					
Long-term debt (in 000s)	$105,609	$119,911	$153,093	$195,520	$261,460
Capital lease obligations (in 000s)	155,918	163,380	178,556	192,547	211,342
Shareholders' equity (in 000s)	233,659	259,940	290,142	329,952	374,467
Total capitalization (in 000s)	495,186	543,231	621,791	718,019	847,269
Shareholders' equity to total capitalization	47.19%	47.85%	46.66%	45.95%	44.20%
Per share data:[1,2]					
Primary earnings	$1.42	$1.63	$1.92	$2.26	$2.83
Earnings assuming full dilution	1.35	1.58	1.85	2.19	2.74
Cash dividends	.30	.36	.44	.55	.68
Shareholders' equity	$12.21	$13.23	$14.68	$16.48	$18.55
Other data:					
Cash dividends (in 000s)	$5,834	$7,033	$8,660	$10,961	$13,627
Dividends as a percent of earnings[1]	21.47%	21.93%	22.88%	24.19%	23.87%
Stock dividends	3%	3%	3%	3%	3%
Average shares outstanding[3]	19,137,414	19,642,947	19,761,788	20,015,512	20,181,879
Average diluted shares[3]	20,854,737	20,883,719	20,911,047	21,028,143	21,129,981
Market price range[3]					
High	$18 7/8	$26 1/4	$26 1/8	$25 1/8	$33 3/4
Low	11 3/8	14	19 1/8	19 1/4	21 1/2
Year-end	14 1/4	20 3/8	25 1/2	24 5/8	26 3/4
Number of shareholders	9,351	9,093	8,881	8,764	8,627
Number of employees	28,200	28,600	31,000	34,000	37,000

[1] The years 1974 through 1977 have been restated for the change in the method of accounting for leases to comply with the provisions of *Statement of Financial Accounting Standards No. 13*, which was adopted early in accordance with the requirements of the Securities and Exchange Commission.
[2] Based on average shares outstanding adjusted for stock dividends.
[3] Adjusted for stock dividends.

Source: *1978 Annual Report.*

THE SOUTHLAND CORPORATION

EXHIBIT 3 Consolidated Statement of Earnings

	1974	1975	1976	1977	1978
Revenues:					
Net sales	$1,609,257	$1,787,928	$2,115,769	$2,536,109	$3,076,532
Other income	4,931	2,877	6,254	9,306	13,562
	$1,614,188	1,790,805	2,122,023	2,545,415	3,090,94
Cost of sales and expenses:					
Cost of goods sold, including buying and occupancy expenses	$1,184,835	1,323,799	1,577,141	1,903,791	2,311,024
Selling, general, and administrative expenses	348,797	374,234	435,687	510,337	619,519
Interest expense	8,674	7,936	9,707	13,540	15,804
Imputed interest expense on capital lease obligations	12,982	13,969	15,388	18,064	19,325
Contributions to employees savings and profit sharing plan	5,899	6,995	8,346	9,726	11,714
	$1,561,187	1,726,933	2,046,269	2,455,458	2,977,386
Earnings before income taxes	$ 53,001	63,872	75,754	89,957	112,708
Income taxes	25,834	31,804	37,905	44,640	55,611
Net earnings	$ 27,167	$ 32,068	$ 37,849	$ 45,317	$ 57,097
Per share					
Primary earnings	$1.42	$1.63	$1.92	$2.26	$2.83
Earnings assuming full dilution	$1.35	$1.58	$1.85	$2.19	$2.74

All figures are in thousands of dollars except the per share data.
Source: *1978 Annual Report.*

STORE GROWTH AND LOCATIONS

Southland's management looked upon convenience as "giving customers what they want, when they want it, where they want it." As a consequence, in 1978, 5,407 of Southland's 6,599 7-Elevens were open around the clock and 91 percent were open beyond the traditional 7 A.M. to 11 P.M. hours. Moreover, Southland emphasized easily accessible neighborhood locations and quick, friendly service: its product lines included popular fast foods selections and, at 30 percent of its locations, self-service gasoline.

In recent years Southland had opened about 500 new 7-Eleven stores per year. The net gain in stores was smaller, however, because population shifts, changes in traffic patterns, lease expirations, and relocations to newly available and more desirable sites resulted in some existing stores being closed. The number of store openings and closings since 1972 are shown in the table below:

	New Stores Opened	Existing Stores Closed	Total 7-Eleven Stores
1972	424	83	4,455
1973	426	80	4,801
1974	n.a.	n.a.	5,171
1975	566	158	5,579
1976	528	154	5,953
1977	658	254	6,357
1978	550	308	6,599

Southland used a meticulous store site selection system; the primary criteria included such factors as (1) the traffic count in front of the site, (2) the ease with which passing cars could enter and leave the site, (3) the site's visibility from the street or road, (4) the number of people living within a one-mile radius, (5) the site's proximity to apartments, subdivisions, and high-traffic commercial establishments, (6) the adequacy of parking space, and (7) whether the site was a "natural" stopping-off point in the traffic flow by the site. To make sure its small, 2,400-square-foot stores were readily seen from approaching traffic, they were carefully positioned in a heavy traffic area where they could be seen easily and were convenient to passers-by. Traffic patterns and flows were so crucial that stores had failed because a street was made one-way or because the opening of new streets and subdivisions had shifted traffic away from a site. Southland extensively studied potential sites and used a computer to estimate a proposed store's sales for its first five years.

John Thompson, Southland chairman, recently indicated that when a store starts looking like a loser, "We would rather close then and take our licks." The poor performers were identified by computerized analysis; by merely punching the store number into a computer terminal, executives could call up on a terminal display the store's current sales and earnings and tell how close it was to its budget. The company's management kept a close check on each store's operating performance.

In 1977, Southland started opening central-city stores. Located in high-density metropolitan residential areas, Southland saw them as filling a genuine need for walking customers. The company had central-city stores in Philadelphia, Boston, San Francisco, and New York City; more were planned. According to Thompson, the central-city stores "open up a whole new market area we haven't yet been able to serve. We will attempt to build and merchandise stores according to their neighborhoods."

PRODUCT LINES AND MERCHANDISING

Southland continually experimented with the product mix offered in the stores. Some products, like the frozen concoction, "Slurpee," became huge successes. Others, like 7-Eleven beer, turned out to be quiet flops.

One Southland executive stated, "There's little risk involved in experimenting. We have a built-in market base of 5 million customers a day. Things that don't work out we can throw out after a week or two. Things that catch on in one store we can try nationwide. Our computers in Dallas can tell us overnight about any new market trends."[2] 7-Eleven stores carried 3,000 different items, about 23 percent of them Southland's own house brands. The larger percentage of brands available in a 7-Eleven store were nationally recognized brands; however, each item was located in a space predetermined by a Southland computer in Dallas. One Southland executive indicated:

> There is no room to stock a lot of different brands of the same product. Our customers don't have time to make choices anyway. We usually put on our shelves only the top one or two sellers of every product line and we put them in the area of the store where we think the customer would like to find them. It's all been researched and market tested. I can walk into most stores blindfolded and find any item you want.[3]

Through 1977, Southland's biggest selling item was tobacco—cigarettes primarily—followed closely by groceries, beer and wine, soft drinks, nonfood items such as magazines and Kleenex, and dairy products (see Exhibit 4). However, tobacco products dropped from number one in 1978, the change primarily due to increased gasoline sales. 7-Elevens had at times sold shotgun shells, television tubes, watermelons, and cancer insurance. Among the stores' best selling items were fast-food sandwiches, disposable diapers, and *Playboy* magazines (of which 7-Elevens sold far more than any other retailer). In general, the items carried were products that would be needed on a fill-in basis or else bought on impulse.

By the end of 1978, self-service gasoline accounted for 60 percent of all gasoline sales in the United States and showed every indication of increasing beyond that figure, according to industry sources. In response to this demand, 7-Eleven provided self-service gasoline at 1,857 locations. A substantial increase

---

[2] "7-Eleven Creates a Mood of Convenience at a Price," *The Washington Star,* November 27, 1978.
[3] Ibid.

EXHIBIT 4 7-Eleven Store Sales by Principal Product Category[1]

	1974	1975	1976	1977	1978
Groceries	17.1%	15.3%	14.6%	14.0%	13.4%
Gasoline	2.7	3.9	6.8	9.8	13.4
Tobacco products	15.7	15.6	14.7	14.2	12.9
Beer/wine	14.1	14.8	14.4	13.7	12.9
Soft drinks	11.5	11.5	10.7	11.0	10.9
Nonfoods	9.3	9.5	10.2	9.9	9.4
Dairy products	10.5	9.5	9.6	9.3	8.9
Other food items	3.9	4.2	4.7	4.7	5.5
Candy	5.3	5.7	5.4	5.0	4.7
Baked goods	5.9	5.7	5.3	5.0	4.6
Health/beauty aids	4.0	3.9	3.6	3.4	3.4
Total	100.0%	100.0%	100.0%	100.0%	100.0%

[1] The Company does not record sales by product lines but estimates the percentage of convenience store sales by principal product category based on total store purchases.

Source: *1978 Annual Report.*

in volume at existing units, as well as the addition of gasoline at 284 stores during 1978, resulted in a 70 percent gasoline sales increase for the year. The availability of gasoline also led to the generation of additional sales, as more than 30 percent of 7-Eleven's gasoline customers in 1978 purchased other merchandise.

One merchandising trend of particular import was that of adding higher-margin items to each store's product line to try to boost store profitability. Fast-food items like sandwiches, pizza, soup, coffee, fruit punch, and draft soda (like "Slurpee") carried gross margins in the 40 percent range. Nonfood impulse items, which had margins in the 35 percent range, were also being added. Both compared favorably with Southland's recent storewide margins of 25 percent to 27 percent. Southland's fast food division, which in 1978 experienced a 30.5 percent sales gain, produced approximately 30 sandwiches marketed under the 7-Eleven and Landshire labels. These were distributed either fresh or flash-frozen for reheating in microwaves or infrared ovens. The division in 1978 sold approximately 80 million sandwiches to 7-Eleven stores, other retailers, and institutional customers; it also furnished 7-Eleven stores with more than 1 million gallons of Slurpee syrup.

Southland's management was optimistic about the potential for increasing its share of the food-away-from-home market. Projections called for this segment to increase its share of the consumer's total food dollar owing to greater numbers of women entering the work force, higher family incomes, smaller families, and more single people—all of which acted to reinforce the lifestyle where a higher percent of disposable personal income would be spent for food prepared outside the home.

PRICING

According to Southland's marketing research director, people just about everywhere are willing to pay a little extra for the convenience a 7-Eleven offers—especially when the consumer is hit by an urge to buy. Most of the items in a 7-Eleven are therefore priced some 10 to 15 percent above the levels in most supermarkets. But, as shown in Exhibit 5, a few items, like milk, are priced more competitively.

As one 7-Eleven customer put it: "There's a lot I don't like about 7-Eleven stores. They look tacky. They charge too much. They sell stuff that isn't good for you, and they always seem to be getting robbed. But yes, I do shop there.

EXHIBIT 5 Sample Comparisons of Prices at 7-Eleven Stores and Safeway Supermarkets in 1978

ITEM	7-ELEVEN	SAFEWAY
Cascade (20 oz.)	$ .98	$ .89
Shredded wheat (12 oz.)	.93	.75
Tuna (chunk light, 6 oz.)	1.19	.99
Campbell's chicken noodle soup	.36	.30
Jello instant pudding (4 oz.)	.40	.35
Log Cabin maple syrup (12 oz.)	1.15	.93
Hellmann's mayonnaise (16 oz.)	1.23	.99
Franco-American spaghetti (14 oz.)	.39	.34
Domino sugar (5 lbs.)	1.59	1.49
Wesson oil (16 oz.)	1.19	.99
V-8 juice (46 oz.)	1.09	.85
Maxwell House instant coffee (6 oz.)	4.29	3.79
Kellogg's corn flakes (12 oz.)	.85	.69
Hydrox cream-filled cookies	1.19	1.09
6-pack of Budweiser (12 oz.)	2.33	1.99
6-pack of Schlitz Light	2.34	1.99
Gallo burgundy wine	2.23	1.99
6-pack of Pepsi (16 oz.)	2.02	1.89
7Up (32 oz.)	.71	.63
Hostess cup cakes (2)	.35	.33
White bread (22 oz.)	.73	.40
Hostess powdered doughnuts (12)	.99	.99
Dozen eggs (grade A large)	.89	.79
Minute Maid orange juice (quart bottle)	.85	.75
Philadelphia cream cheese (3 oz.)	.43	.34
Salt (26 oz.)	.35	.30
Bayer aspirin (50 tablets)	1.19	.89
Heinz ketchup (14 oz.)	.79	.61
French's mustard (9 oz.)	.55	.43
Carton of Winston cigarettes	4.79	4.49
10 Briggs hot dogs	1.69	1.39
Half-gallon milk	.91	.91
Total (32 items)	$40.97	$35.55

Source: *The Washington Star*, November 26, 1978.

They're so convenient."[4] So far, though, no customer activist groups had targeted 7-Eleven for either its high prices or its line of merchandise.

Southland seemed to have discovered, and was helping perpetuate, its own market segment—a world of customers caught in a time crisis, willing to pay extra to save themselves a few seconds waiting in line. A Wall Street analyst said:

> It is perplexing to us why Southland's revenue growth has accelerated when rising prices have stretched the consumer's budget to a considerable extent. Perhaps it is time rather than money which is the precious commodity to most Americans at present. The appeal of convenience stores has nothing to do with price. It has to do with people's lifestyles and their constant need for fill-ins. The more tightly the pocketbook is pinched, the less frequently the housewife shops at her supermarket, and the more need she has for last minute fill-ins.[5]

FRANCHISE ACTIVITIES

Of the 6,599 7-Eleven stores operating at the end of 1978, 4,056 were company operated and 2,543 were franchised. The typical franchise agreement allowed for the company to lease the property and equipment to a franchisee in exchange for a fee of $10,000 plus roughly half the store's profits. Southland allowed new franchises a 120-day grace period to pull out of their contracts without losing their initial investments. Most of the franchisees were couples with children and the family typically worked in the store.

SOUTHLAND'S ADVERTISING FOR 7-ELEVEN

In January 1978, Southland introduced its first prime-time network 7-Eleven commercial to the largest audience in television history prior to Super Bowl XII. Product awareness messages featuring Hot-to-Go coffee, Egg Hamlette, Chili Dog, Slurpee, or sunglasses reached 58 million households each broadcast week. In addition to the network television commercials, advertisements were aired on approximately 500 radio stations and published in more than 200 newspapers nationwide.

During 1978, broadcasts remained the company's major advertising vehicle with spot radio getting 30 percent, network television 35 percent, spot television 25 percent, newspapers 4 percent, and outdoor advertising 6 percent. Total television advertising increased 22 percent during the first half of 1978, compared with the same period in 1977.

7-Eleven stores were decidedly male-oriented. However, due to the increased buying power of women in today's society, Southland's advertising had begun to be geared specifically toward women.

[4] Southland Is the Best Example I Know of Modern Capitalism," *The Washington Star,* November 26, 1978.
[5] "7-Eleven Creates a Mood of Convenience."

DISTRIBUTION CENTERS

Southland's 7-Eleven stores were served by distribution centers in Florida, Virginia, and Texas that were specifically designed to meet the needs of 7-Eleven for a reliable and efficient source of supply, frequent delivery, and a high in-stock position. The system also enabled the stores to have the flexibility to respond quickly to customer preferences and seasonal changes in demand, as well as to implement promotional programs and introduce new products. The centers serviced 3,916 7-Eleven stores at the end of 1978.

Store stock lists, compiled and updated monthly by computer, were tailored to the merchandise specifications of each store, enabling personnel to easily determine restocking needs. The store orders were then transmitted through a network of computer terminals located at 7-Eleven district offices and connected to the computer center in Dallas, which assimilated the orders and transmitted them to printing terminals at the appropriate distribution center. From these printed lists, the store orders were then "picked" and assembled for delivery. Custom-designed trucks with separate compartments for dry, chilled, and frozen merchandise followed computer-planned routes to achieve maximum savings of energy and time.

Southland's concept of delivering prepriced merchandise in less-than-case-quantities eliminated overstocking, assured fresh merchandise on the store shelves at all times, promoted more productive use of selling space, and improved store profitability. The importance of stores not having to order full cases of merchandise was highlighted by Southland's manager of information services: "Can you imagine how long it would take to sell 48 cans of tomato paste in a 7-Eleven? Now we can give them three cans and keep it fresh." During 1978, the computerized inventory control system enabled the stores to achieve an average inventory turnover of 23 times while maintaining a 99 percent order fill rate.

In many cases, store managers did not even bother to order groceries; that was done by warehouse employees whose only job was visiting each 7-Eleven twice a month to take inventory and order merchandise.[6] The computer then took over, sending hundreds of orders to a warehouse, deciding which orders to ship on what truck, and telling employees how to stack goods inside the truck to fill it to the brim. The trucks were able to begin delivering only hours after the warehouse got the order. Southland's computer also helped analyze the layout of merchandise in the store—by keeping track of what items sold well in which shelf locations.

FINANCING

The long-term policy of Southland was to finance expansion from retained earnings, although other methods of raising funds were used when necessary.

---

[6] Seib, "Despite High Prices."

In late 1978, the company offered $50 million of unsecured 9⅜ percent Sinking Fund Debentures, due December 15, 2003. These debentures, as well as a 1977 8⅜ percent issue, were rated A by both Moody's and Standard & Poor's and were listed on the New York Stock Exchange.

In April 1978, the annual cash dividend rate was increased 20 percent to 72 cents per share. Cash dividends had been paid each year since 1957, and the annual rate had been raised seven times in the last eight years, providing shareholders an average compound growth rate of 20.7 percent. In addition, for the 13th consecutive year, a 3 percent stock dividend was distributed.

In recent years, Southland had been forced to increase its debt burden to finance corporate expansion—especially the growth in the number of 7-Eleven stores. To open a new store, Southland had to invest more than $180,000. This included land costs of about $50,000, a store building costing an average of $70,000, equipment installation of $46,000, and initial inventory costs of $18,000 to $25,000. In the case of franchised stores, Southland advanced most of the up-front investment, with the exception of the $10,000 franchise fee.

The capital costs of financing 400–500 new stores per year had exceeded Southland's retained earnings and internal cash flow capabilities during recent years; the resulting debt increases were in such an amount as to cause a steady decline in Southland's equity capitalization percentage (see Exhibit 2).

Although a 41-year-old Southland official expressed the view that the company would be adding a net of 300–400 stores per year for the rest of his lifetime, it was not clear that Southland could continue to finance such an ambitious store expansion program without adversely affecting earnings. Higher site and construction costs and higher interest rates were becoming significant factors; so was the move to increase store size from 2,400 square feet to the 2,700 to 3,000 square feet range. In 1977, Southland spent an estimated $75.3 million to open 658 stores; in 1978, the figure exceeded $95 million for 550 new stores.

Nor was it clear that such a rate of expansion was consistent with market opportunities. Already there were over 33,000 convenience food stores in the United States—approximately one for every 6,600 persons. Prime sites were becoming hard to find and were increasingly expensive. According to one industry trade publication, several factors were at work:

> Munford executives, like most in the business, have set their sights on prime corner locations with high visibility and heavy traffic counts. Because Munford is selecting former gas station sites for its new units, traffic counts have replaced household density, once the sacred cow of the industry's site selection procedure.
>
> In fact, one Majik Market is making $7,000 per week in food sales—the industry average is $5,257—without a house within a five-mile radius of the store.
>
> Secondary sites, mainly at the mouths of suburban subdivisions and in shopping malls, are a thing of the past. "The suburban, residential convenience store is doomed," explains Tom Ewens, vice president of real estate for Houston-based National Convenience Stores Inc., "because the sales volume that those units produce simply can't keep pace with the costs of land, construction and operation."
>
> But the recently sought-after, first-rate corner spots are getting harder for

convenience store chains to find due, in part, to increased competition from other retailers for the same locations. As store sizes creep up to the 3,000-square-foot mark, the lot sizes expand to allow for increased gas and parking facilities, convenience stores are looking for roughly the same size lot that a fast-food unit, drug store, bank or gas station might want. This means that the sector's traditional strength of flexibility in site selection is being somewhat impaired.

What's happening is that convenience stores are pinning their hopes for higher sales volumes and profits on primary locations, while coping with higher real estate and operations costs than they faced at former sites.

This means that convenience stores' profit and loss statements will likely get tighter and tighter, the line between a winning and losing location more thinly drawn.[7]

Exhibits 6 and 7 contain additional financial data on Southland.

RECENT TRENDS IN THE CONVENIENCE FOOD INDUSTRY

In 1957, the industry consisted of 500 stores with an annual volume of $75 million. Ten years later, there were 8,000 convenience stores with combined sales of $1.3 billion. In 1978, the corresponding figures were some 33,000 stores and an annual sales volume of $8.7 billion. Average annual sales growth during the last five years was about 17 percent. Sales volumes in convenience food stores were approaching 5 percent of total U.S. grocery sales, up from 1.7 percent in 1967. Many industry sources predicted favorable sales growth for convenience food stores for the years ahead. Sales revenues were projected to increase at a 15 percent annual rate and volume was expected to reach 8 percent of total grocery sales by 1980.

For the extra convenience and service they offered, convenience food stores took higher mark-ups on the items they sold. Whereas conventional supermarkets had an average gross margin of 22.4 percent in 1978, the gross margins in convenience food stores were typically 28 to 30 percent. Exhibit 8 gives a breakdown of the 1976 gross margin, expenses, and net profits for the representative convenience food store.

Recently, industry observers had become concerned with the increased competition that supermarkets seemed to be initiating. Specifically, the trends of many supermarkets toward longer hours, Sunday openings, and express-lane checkouts had the potential of eroding the market shares of convenience food stores. In response, some convenience chains were keeping prices on selected high volume items as close to those of supermarkets as possible. Munford's Majik Market stores, Southland's biggest competitor, recently adjusted the prices of some 25 of its best-selling items to be competitive with supermarket prices.

In addition to competition from supermarkets, competition from other retail sectors was emerging. Fast-food chains, liquor-delis, gas stations carrying

[7] "What's Down the Road for Convenience Stores," *Chain Store Age Executive,* June 1979, pp. 23–24.

EXHIBIT 6   Consolidated Balance Sheets, Southland Corp., 1977 and 1978

ASSETS	DECEMBER 31, 1977	DECEMBER 31, 1978
Current assets:		
Cash and short-term investments	$ 65,903,801	$ 82,745,504
Accounts and notes receivable	75,171,378	78,968,103
Inventories	126,913,578	161,254,967
Deposits and prepaid expenses	21,436,624	26,777,392
Investment in properties	53,319,492	55,857,419
Total current assets	342,744,873	405,603,385
Investments in affiliates	26,717,136	27,364,352
Property, plant, and equipment	389,251,583	479,554,364
Capital leases	178,190,671	197,730,040
Other assets	5,627,054	24,223,652
Total assets	$942,531,317	$1,134,475,793

LIABILITIES AND SHAREHOLDERS' EQUITY	DECEMBER 31, 1977	DECEMBER 31, 1978
Current liabilities:		
Accounts payable and accrued expenses	$168,894,391	$ 211,920,848
Income taxes	15,481,417	18,636,987
Long-term debt due within one year	4,142,055	13,254,868
Capital lease obligations due within one year	17,533,856	20,157,217
Total current liabilities	206,051,719	263,696,920
Deferred credits	18,460,424	23,235,908
Long-term debt	195,520,000	261,460,472
Capital lease obligations	192,546,677	211,342,074
Common stock $1 par value, authorized 40 million shares, issued and outstanding 20,200,557 and 19,557,287 shares	195,573	202,006
Additional capital	223,499,143	242,339,822
Retained earnings	106,257,781	131,925,591
Total shareholders' equity	329,952,497	374,467,149
Total liabilities and shareholders' equity	$942,531,317	$1,134,475,793

Source: *1978 Annual Report.*

food items, and discount and drug outlets with newly added food items were a new competitive threat. These types of firms were expected to expand their convenience food lines and to begin to carry high-traffic nonfood items. Furthermore, many of the drug stores were staying open longer hours and opting for locations with many of the same features of convenience stores.

7-ELEVEN'S COMPETITORS IN CONVENIENCE FOODS

7-Eleven in 1978 was more than seven times the size of Munford, its nearest competitor. (Munford is the only other convenience chain listed on the New York Stock Exchange.) In recent years, while 7-Eleven had been booming,

EXHIBIT 7 Consolidated Statements of Changes in Financial Position, Southland Corp., 1977 and 1978

	1977	1978
Sources of working capital:		
From operations:		
Net earnings	$ 45,317,241	$ 57,097,109
Expenses charged to earnings which did not require outlay of working capital:		
Depreciation and amortization	41,991,861	46,839,875
Amortization of capital leases	19,743,097	20,884,330
Deferred income taxes and other credits	3,415,874	6,552,597
Working capital provided from operations	$110,468,073	$131,373,911
Long-term debt	61,534,160	70,658,506
Capital lease obligations	37,409,857	41,907,748
Retirements and sales of property	12,774,857	13,555,200
Retirements and sales of capital leases	6,191,948	1,397,049
Issuance of common stock		
Conversion of notes	2,690,000	—
Acquisitions	2,310,000	—
Key employees incentive plan	462,278	470,992
Employee stock options	97,343	704,463
Total sources of working capital	$233,938,516	$260,067,869
Uses of working capital:		
Property, plant, and equipment	$ 96,324,184	$141,438,084
Capital leases	37,409,857	41,907,748
Reduction of capital lease obligations	23,419,196	23,112,351
Payment of long-term debt	16,862,491	4,718,034
Cash dividends	10,960,976	13,627,443
Net noncurrent assets of businesses purchased for stock and cash	9,111,552	29,180,394
Retirement of long-term debt upon conversion of notes	2,690,000	—
Investments in affiliates	1,061,359	647,216
Other	836,640	366,089
Cash paid in lieu of fractional shares on stock dividends	105,267	130,199
Total uses of working capital	$198,781,522	$255,127,558
Increase in working capital	$35,156,994	$ 4,940,311
Changes in working capital:		
Increases in current assets:		
Cash and short-term investments	$ 39,504,544	$ 16,841,703
Accounts and notes receivable	7,788,618	3,796,725
Inventories	21,884,637	34,341,389
Deposits and prepaid expenses	1,482,830	5,340,768
Investment in properties	9,342,429	2,537,927
Total changes in working capital	$ 80,003,058	$ 62,858,512
Increases (decreases) in current liabilities:		
Accounts payable and accrued expenses	38,624,253	43,062,457
Income taxes	4,442,417	3,155,570
Long-term debt due within one year	(611,614)	9,112,813
Capital lease obligations due within one year	2,391,008	2,623,361
Total increases (decreases) in current liabilities	$ 44,846,064	$ 57,918,201
Increase in working capital	$ 35,156,994	$ 4,940,311

Source: *1978 Annual Report.*

EXHIBIT 8 Breakdown of 1976 Margins, Expenses, and Net Profit for the Representative Convenience Store*

Sales	100.0%
Cost of goods sold	71.2
Gross margin	28.8
Employee wages	10.6
Employee benefits	1.9
Advertising and promotion	0.7
Property rentals	3.3
Utility expenses	3.2
Other expenses	5.7
Total expenses	25.4
Net profit before taxes	3.4%

* Determined by trade sources from industrywide data.
Source: *Convenience Stores*, September–October 1977, p. 44.

Munford had been having more than its share of problems. While in the process of closing marginal and unprofitable units, earnings and sales for Munford suffered accordingly. In addition to their stores group, Munford experienced problems with Farmbest Foods, a dairy operation acquired in 1975. The Farmbest operation lost money in 1977 due to unsettled industry conditions in Florida and Alabama.

A new merchandising concept being tried by Munford, in order to catch up with the industry, was to join forces with major oil companies such as Texaco, Gulf, and Amoco by putting Munford's Majik Market convenience stores at existing gasoline station sites. The executives of Munford saw many advantages for this concept and were convinced that consumers were accepting the idea of buying gasoline at convenience stores very well.

Another competitive factor in the convenience store field was Circle K. For a period of four years through 1977, Circle K virtually halted its store expansion program in favor of remodeling and renovating older, existing stores. The Circle K chain, like Munford and others, entered the gasoline business, but with a basic difference from Munford. Circle K's strategy was to retain its recognition and image as convenience first and gasoline second. For this reason, Circle K chose to add gasoline pumps to their existing stores, not vice versa, as Munford did. Circle K planned to add 60 to 70 stores a year through the mid-1980s.

A third competitor of 7-Eleven was the National Convenience Stores chain. In 1976, a young, dynamic man named Pete Van Horn became president of National Convenience. Not being fettered by the bonds of tradition in the industry, Van Horn slashed the number of stores, lowered personnel turnover, increased sales in remaining stores and, in general, put National Convenience on a sound footing. Van Horn was anxious to try out his ideas about store

EXHIBIT 9 Sales and Earnings of Convenience Chains

	SALES ($000)			EARNINGS ($000)		
Company	1976	1977	1978	1976	1977	1978
Southland	$2,121,146	$2,544,414	$3,089,000	$40,277	$45,348	$57,000
Munford	334,770	340,174	378,950e	3,427	(770)	6,090
Circle K	262,362	302,603	363,783	5,122	6,912	8,196
National Convenience Stores	212,606	233,208	263,705	2,652	3,536	5,011
Utotem Group	192,499	206,041	221,423	8,822	8,788	9,658
Convenient Industries of America	123,368	146,598	177,732	857	896	1,148
Sunshine-Jr. Stores	68,899	81,225	93,553	1,387	1,432	1,622
Shop & Go	60,780	70,136	82,729	1,650	1,655	2,271
Hop-In Food Stores	14,077	22,739	31,714	280	392	658
Lil' Champ	18,807	21,006	22,727	592	647	778
Grand total	$3,409,314	$3,968,144	$4,725,316	$65,066	$68,836	$92,432

Note: Includes sales and earnings from operations other than convenience stores where applicable.
e Estimated.

Source: *Progressive Grocer*, April 1978.

EXHIBIT 10 Average Sales and Profit Statistics for Top Ten Publicly Held Convenience Food Store Chains

	1974	1975	1976	1977	1978
Yearly sales per store	$213,890	$232,140	$240,828	$263,895	$274,115
Weekly sales per store	$4,113	$4,452	$4,606	$5,061	$5,257
Profit on pre-tax sales	3.39%	3.32%	3.64%	3.48%	3.65%
Profit on after-tax sales	1.77%	1.71%	1.92%	1.8%	1.98%
Yearly pre-tax profit per store	$7,242	$7,723	$8,762	$9,194	$10,026
Yearly after-tax profit per store	$3,789	$3,978	$4,523	$4,752	$5,431

Source: "Eighth Annual Dollars-per-Day Survey of Small Food Store Industry," as published in *Chain Store Age Executive*, June 1979, p. 26.

layout, merchandising and expansion; his goal at the end of 1977 was to double earnings in the next four years.[8]

Exhibit 9 presents comparative sales and earnings for ten leading convenience food chains. Exhibit 10 contains per store sales and profit statistics for the 1974–1978 period.

SOUTHLAND'S DAIRIES AND SPECIAL OPERATIONS GROUPS

Initially, the Dairies and Special Operations groups were formed to vertically integrate their activities with 7-Eleven. The Dairies Group processed and distributed milk, ice cream, yogurt, juices, eggnog, dips, and toppings; in 1978, it served 5,295 of Southland's convenience stores and supplied 66 percent of

[8] "The Convenience Stores," *Financial World,* November 1, 1977.

all the dairy products sold in all 7-Eleven stores. The group included 28 processing plants and 86 distribution locations. However, more and more of the Dairies Group sales volume was coming from outside Southland. In 1978, 65 percent of the unit's $400 million sales revenues were to food retailers such as Denny's and Wendy's. The expansion of sales to outside companies was being pursued through the development of new high-margin novelty items such as sundae-style yogurts, cheeses, and frozen dairy items like Big Deal, Gram Daddy, and Big Wheel.

A similar trend was evident in the Special Operations Group. While this division supplied other Southland units with food ingredients, ice, Slurpee concentrate, preservatives, sanitizers, and cleaning agents, in 1978 a total of 72 percent of sales were to outside customers. In 1978, the chemicals unit was expanded by the acquisition of a New Jersey fine chemicals plant; this acquisition allowed Southland to market a broader line of products to customers in the agricultural and pharmaceutical industries. The division's Hudgins Truck Rental unit was expanding its efforts to provide full-maintenance truck leasing to national and regional customers, as well as to Southland operations; in 1978, its outside sales were up 10 percent and accounted for 68 percent of revenues. In 1978, a new unit called Tidel Systems was added to the Special Operations Group; it manufactured an innovative money-handling device designed to reduce losses from robberies and to increase store-site cash handling efficiency. While Southland planned to install the device at its 7-Eleven stores, there was an even greater potential for sales to other retailers and a nationwide sales and maintenance organization was being assembled.

THE ACQUISITION OF CHIEF AUTO PARTS

In December 1978, at a cost of $20 million, Southland acquired the assets of Chief Auto Parts, a chain of 119 retail automobile supply stores in southern California. A typical Chief store was 2,000 square feet in size, open seven days a week, and located in a neighborhood shopping center close to homes or businesses. The stores sold approximately 7,500 replacement parts and accessories and carried both national brands and private-label products. The average purchase was $5 and a large percentage of sales was on weekends when most do-it-yourselfers had time to service their cars. Chief also had a modern warehouse in Los Angeles, from which it supplied its stores.

There was some thought that the Chief acquisition signaled a move by Southland to diversify into small store retailing, particularly those kinds of retail businesses which had operating characteristics similar to those of 7-Eleven stores.

FUTURE OUTLOOK

Southland management's view of the future for its 7-Eleven stores was exemplified by John Thompson, chairman:

> We believe that the growth opportunity in the convenience store area is great. I'm very bullish on the future. There are many parts in the United States that are not saturated with convenience stores, and I would say that Texas and Florida are the two most saturated areas. Even in those states we can go 20 to 40 more stores a year, depending on housing. But in the rest of the United States, there is relatively must less saturation, so that as far as we're concerned we think we can build 500-plus stores a year for a long time. Why, the Northeast is a great area. We haven't really saturated that market at all. And the Midwest? Well, we've hardly gotten started there. And California? Well sure we have 900 stores in California, but you can build forever in that state. I guess you could say the future for us looks marvelous.[9]

However, in 1979, several industry observers were taking a more cautious stance and asking if the industry was not on the verge of maturity.

[9] "Southland Is the Best Example."

INDUSTRIAL HIGHLIGHT

Food Retailing Segment of the Retail Trade Industry

Below is a capsule summary of the food retailing segment of the retail trade industry, of which Southland Corporation is a part. Information in this highlight was compiled by the U.S. Department of Commerce and focuses on this industry during the approximate period of time covered in the case. Keep in mind that industrial highlights contained in this text are not intended as a complete synopsis of an industry but as a profile of certain issues that can be relevant to a case situation.

CURRENT SITUATION

Food retail stores in 1979 are expected to achieve only minimal real growth, continuing the trend of recent years. Current sales are estimated at $184 billion, an 8 percent increase over estimated 1978 sales of $170.4 billion. Sales growth in 1978 was less than the estimated rate of food inflation in that year—producing a decline in real growth.

Sales growth is projected to be minimal in real terms primarily because per capita food consumption is not expected to rise appreciably and food retailers face a market composed of nonfood store competitors—i.e., restaurants. The impact of food prices on consumption and shopping patterns also is a significant factor.

Problems that interfered with progress in 1978 are likely to continue this year. Although food price inflation, the major factor contributing to poor real growth, moderated somewhat in the second half of 1978, it is not expected to ease significantly in 1979.

Alternative approaches that food retailers undertook to improve profitability, expand sales, or reduce costs in a highly competitive market in 1978 will continue to be tested in 1979 and beyond. The use of generic products will become more widespread; different types of stores such as the warehouse and limited assortment will continue to appear; games, double couponing, and

Source: U.S. Industrial Outlook, Department of Commerce, 1979, pp. 469–474.

trading stamps will be more frequent. Stores will be larger, services expanded, and merchandise mix altered to include nonfood merchandise. Perhaps most significantly, the use of computerized checkout systems should continue to increase as more companies begin to test or permanently install this productivity-enhancing equipment.

Convenience store sales continued to significantly outpace sales of chains and independents, due primarily to new store growth. Chains (11 or more stores) and independents (10 or fewer stores) achieved growth of lower rates. This pattern is a reflection of past years; for example in 1977, an industry survey found that convenience stores' sales growth was 2.5 times that of chains and 2.6 times that of independents.

Food Prices Rise

Exceedingly cold or wet weather coincided with a biological cattle cycle to force prices of produce and beef up early in 1978. Food prices were rising at an annual rate of nearly 18 percent until farm prices began declining slightly in July 1978. Other factors besides weather and cattle cycles played a role in food price inflation. These included U.S. Government farm price support programs; strong agricultural export demand; and higher costs—especially in transportation, labor, energy and packaging.

Although prices rose more rapidly in 1978 than earlier in the 1970's, retailers were spared a repeat consumer boycott in reaction to high food prices. It is difficult to explain the different consumer behavior, but one apparent reason is that the industry, including its suppliers and manufacturers, made substantial efforts to educate consumers regarding the price surges. There were, for example, signs posted at produce and meat counters. However, the consumer did attempt to beat the prices through strategic shopping; the *Wall Street Journal* compared supermarket shopping to "guerrilla warfare" at the height of price rises. The weaponry used by the consumer included coupons, specials, quantity purchases, and altered consumption patterns.

Food prices should continue rising, but at a more moderate pace through most of 1979.

Indications were that summer and fall 1978 harvests and crops were good and that the 1978 winter effects were lessened; and cattle and other livestock prices had receded. In addition, the world harvest appeared to be good, a fact which lessens the upward pressure on prices through export demand.

Market Less Captive

The consumer's food budget is split between at-home and away-from-home consumption. Leaving aside the debatable inquiry as to whether "eating out" is more economical, studies show that between 1 in 3 and 1 in 4 dollars are spent away from home.

Certainly, the increases in personal disposable income, and the increasing number of working women, have contributed to the "eating out" trend, to the

EXHIBIT A 1978 Profile: Food Retailing

SIC Code: 54	
Value of sales ($ million)	170,400
Total employment (000)	2,180
Number of establishments (1972)	267,352
Number of companies (1972)	n.a.
Compound annual rate of change, 1973–78	
Value of sales[1]	10.0
Total employment	3.2

[1] Rates of change based on current dollars.

Source: Bureau of the Census; Bureau of Labor Statistics; Industry and Trade Administration (BDBD) estimates.

detriment of food stores. The proliferation of fast food restaurants which offer convenience and frequently economy also has been a major factor.

Many industry representatives no longer categorize expenditures away from home as a major threat. Conversely, fast food and other restaurants do not face a major threat from food retailers trying to recapture some of the food dollar through entrance into the field, although in certain regions, supermarkets are adding snack and coffee shops in reaction to a locally diminishing market share.

Also, many food retailers are guarding against further deterioration of their share of the food dollar by creation of delis, bakeries, and fresh seafood departments. Food retailers would probably also benefit from stressing convenience foods—since convenience is a major reason for the expenditures of food dollars away from home—as well as making shopping itself more convenient. This latter approach is being explored by the supermarkets' adding to nonfood merchandise inventory on the theory that a busy consumer is attracted by the promise of one-stop shopping.

Convenience stores are attempting to meet the competition from fast food establishments and restaurants. The chances of their success lie in similarities to fast food operations, specifically longer hours and one-stop shopping. According to a 1977 survey, 83 percent of convenience stores have initiated a fast food program, selling sandwiches, coffee, and, to a lesser extent, pizza and soup. These programs are clearly in response to the challenge posed by fast food establishments.

Labor and Productivity

Labor is a major cost factor to food retailers. Heavy bargaining occurred in 1978 and significant wage increases were negotiated. In addition, legislated minimum wage increases became effective January 1, 1978. Thus, both chains and independents were affected by labor increases in 1978. Although negotiated wage increases typically have the heaviest impact in the year negotiated, 1979 and 1980 also will be affected; in addition, the minimum wage will jump to $2.90 on January 1, 1979 and $3.10 on January 1, 1980.

Given these labor cost increases, productivity—the efficient use of labor—will continue to present a difficult problem in this labor-intensive industry. An average annual decline of over 1 percent in productivity between 1971 and 1976 was followed in 1977 by a slight gain of .8 percent. It is generally felt that the competitive requirements of food retailing—longer store hours, expanded weeks (i.e., Sunday shopping) and enhanced services in delis and bakeries—are a large factor contributing to lowered productivity since extra personnel are needed.

Retailers will continue to take different approaches to improving productivity. For example, retailers are trying "warehouse" or "limited assortment" stores. Typically, these stores—as their name suggests—offer only a bare minimum of services. In some areas of the country, these stores have been successful at improving productivity and generating respectable sales. However, 1978 was not a typical year and one would question whether food prices played a substantial role in generating sales.

Other food retailers have de-emphasized certain services by reducing staff—which in turn results in longer lines, more poorly stocked shelves, and less food variety. Some view this approach as risky, since supermarkets are built on services. When services are reduced, convenience is lessened, and the consumer goes elsewhere.

The greatest potential for a breakthrough in industry productivity lies in adoption of computerized checkout systems. Such systems employ scanners which read the Universal Product Code (UPC) symbols on items and print out a detailed itemized receipt much faster than a clerk could ring up groceries with a standard cash register. Cost savings from computer checkouts are of two types. "Hard savings" are largely quantifiable and refer to decreased unit labor requirements for checking, register balancing, and item price marking. Reduction of pricing errors (misrings) also is usually to the store's advantage. "Soft savings," while less quantifiable, are at least equally important and involve use of computer-generated data to improve personnel scheduling; analyze the impact of sales and promotional efforts; minimize "stockout" situations; eliminate or limit slow-moving items; improve inventory control (e.g., through automatic reordering), and generally better evaluate store management.

The end to item pricing has been opposed by labor groups concerned over potential job losses and consumer groups, which argue that it diminishes consumer price consciousness. As this resistance led seven states to legislatively mandate continued item pricing, most elements of the industry agreed to forgo this portion of potential cost savings, estimated to account for more than a quarter of total potential "hard savings." This has lessened opposition to computer systems but at the same time has hampered their adoption by smaller stores, which may find the reduced level of potential savings insufficient to pay off installation costs.

Installation costs, however, continued to decline in 1977, thereby adding to the incentive side of the balance sheet as more supermarkets appraised the cost/benefit aspects of scanning. The rate of installations accelerated, bringing the total to well over 400 by year's end, up from only 109 two years earlier. Further substantial growth is anticipated in 1979 and beyond, but the following also should be noted: the number of supermarkets that have adopted scanning still represents a small fraction of the industry; perceptions of cost/benefit relationships vary significantly; advantages of scanning will probably continue to be marginal at best for many small stores—especially with continued item pricing; and the large national chains generally have viewed computer systems more cautiously than certain regional chains.

Energy Costs Are Concern

Energy cost increases have been a major problem for food retailers. Some surveys indicate as much or more than a 30 percent increase since 1972–73. Energy costs are difficult to minimize beyond a certain point. The competitive need to stay open, to keep stores lit at least at a bare minimum, and the indispensable refrigeration requirements set floors which food retailers cannot easily go below. Nevertheless, rising energy costs have resulted in several conservation measures. One industry report for 1977 concluded that these measures slowed the rate of increase in energy costs. Important measures include cutting back heat or air conditioning; replacing or eliminating equipment; and reducing lighting levels.

There also are indirect energy consumption operations. Primary among such operations is packaging. One study concluded that packaging accounts for 12 percent of food costs. Most packaging materials are petroleum-based products (hence are energy intensive), and their prices have risen accordingly. One question that arises is whether packaging is excessive; that is, must a box containing plastic wrapped contents be wrapped in plastic—or is there a more energy-efficient method?

One trend, however, speaks against maximum energy conservation: larger stores. Many studies have noted that smaller stores are more energy responsible; however, food retail stores appear to be getting bigger. This trend can be seen as a tradeoff: the need to stay competitive encompasses the inevitability of higher energy costs.

Competition

Higher operating costs facing food retailers combined with a market characterized by intense competition are keeping profits down. Profit margins as a percent of net sales in food retailing averaged less than 1 percent in 1978.

Competition is heightened in this industry by what some view as rapidly approaching market saturation, when overbuilding of stores coincides with too little volume. There are segments of course which are further from saturation—such as convenience stores. Many industry executives feel this segment will not peak until the mid-1980's, if then.

Despite the already intense competition stemming in part from overbuilding of stores, most indications are that new store construction will continue at a good pace in 1979, as it did in 1978. However, renovation of existing structures and closings also will continue to occur. It is important to note that saturation is a regional problem; some areas lack a sufficient number of supermarkets. Other areas are serviced by old or unprofitable stores.

With many chains and independents finding themselves stabilizing, a major question arises as to the possibility of a merger wave. The summer of 1978 witnessed what many interpreted to be a harbinger of things to come with Grand Union Company's attempted merger with Colonial.

The size trend for these new stores is larger—25,000 square feet at minimum. One national chain planned expansion in 1978 with stores averaging 35,000 square feet in order to obtain potential economies of scale.

Retailers Seek Profitability Improvement

As is the case with combatting higher costs, food retailers are experimenting with a variety of old and new programs designed to improve profitability.

Generics are "no name," "no frills," lower-priced products that aren't advertised. Food as well as nonfood merchandise is included. Generics are estimated to cost as much as 35 percent less than brand names and as much as 15 percent less than private labels.

Generic products are becoming more prevalent, although two key questions associated with generics remain unanswered: (1) where are the sales coming from—private or brand labels; and (2) is consumer acceptance adequate? Random studies on the first question have proved inconclusive, although many feel that consumers naturally trade up or down only one level at a time and consequently believe that generics detract from private labels. The level of consumer acceptance is not yet known—although the fact that a major national chain entered the generic market in mid-1978 with a modified generic campaign provides partial evidence that the industry views the generic experiment as at least a preliminary success.

Barring any supply dislocations and consequent price increases of the standard grade—which is used to produce food generics—generic products should continue to stimulate sales. Sales will increase, it would appear, as long as food prices rise and the shopper is more price conscious than quality conscious.

Food retailers also are changing their merchandise mix to incorporate more nonfood merchandise. Nonfood merchandise—such as health and beauty aids and automotive supplies—not only allows a higher markup but its presence can promote the convenience of shopping for the working woman with limited shopping time.

LONG-TERM PROSPECTS

Real sales growth of food retailers will expand at a compound annual rate of approximately 1 percent between 1979 and 1983. Factors that will have an impact on and minimize growth in the longer term are similar to those affecting the near term: food prices, competition for the consumer's food dollar, and general inflation in operating costs.

Whether the decline in per capita food consumption that occurred in 1977 will provide the basis for a longer term trend is unclear; the 1977 decline followed a record high consumption in 1976. Per capita food consumption could very well either change patterns or decline due not only to price influence but also lifestyles and increasing concern in the public and private sectors over nutrition and the role that diet plays in health and disease prevention.

One of the major questions which will be confronting food retailers in the next 5 years is whether or not government regulation will increase the cost of food. The current emphasis in both the public sector and among consumer groups on the health and safety of food products will have an impact. Mechanically deboned meat, nutrition, labeling nitrites and other food additives, and open dating are examples of issues which, when resolved, will potentially raise the cost of food and indirectly, if not directly, involve food retailers. It is relatively clear that no party—industry, consumers, government—will be immune to the need to balance cost against safety and health when dealing with what will surely be sensitive issues.

SECTION THREE

Strategy Formulation

CASE 8

Midstate Dental Lab, Inc.

LYNDA L. GOULET   PETER G. GOULET
both of the University of Northern Iowa

Midstate Dental Lab is a dental laboratory founded in 1971, by Henry Lickert. The lab was soon supplying a full line of services to about two dozen dentists in a moderately-sized community in the Midwest. In late 1981, the founder sold the lab to a group of five local dentists, all of whom had been customers of the lab for many years. Since its purchase the lab has produced mixed results for its owners.

THE PURCHASE

During 1980, Mr. Lickert had moved the lab to the lower floor of an office building owned by three of the dentists who subsequently purchased Midstate. The move increased the space available to the lab to accommodate more dental technicians for the growing market in the area. By the end of 1981, financial statements prepared for the sale transaction showed record revenues of nearly $375,000, with after-tax profits of $12,000. Total assets were $107,500, including $38,200 in net fixed assets. Mr. Lickert's equity was $37,500.

For over a year prior to the sale of Midstate Dental Lab (MSDL) Mr. Lickert had been chronically ill. Sales growth was pressuring the owner-manager to spend more time overseeing the business, while he was becoming physically less able to do so. Earnings had declined in both 1980 and 1981, in spite of sales growth. Mr. Lickert's decision to sell the lab produced an immediate offer from Drs. James, Colworth, Halliard, Schiller, and Wentberg. Midstate was purchased at a price equal to five times its 1981 earnings, to be paid in cash to the owner, with the new owners assuming the firm's existing liabilities at the time of the sale. Only $5,000 of the purchase price was assigned as equity in the business with the rest of the purchase price being transferred to the firm as a debt to the owners. This debt, to be paid from the firm's earnings, was due in $5,000 annual installments at an interest rate of 18% per annum.

Subsequent to the purchase, Jim Franklin was appointed as manager of MSDL until his planned retirement in 1988. Mr. Franklin had been employed

---

This case was prepared by Lynda L. Goulet and Peter G. Goulet, of the University of Northern Iowa, Cedar Falls, Iowa 50614, and is intended to be used as a basis for class discussion. Presented and accepted by the refereed Midwest Case Writers Association Workshop, 1986. All rights reserved to the authors and the Midwest Case Writers Association. Copyrighted © 1986 by the authors.

by Mr. Lickert since 1971 and had been a dental technician for 30 years. Dr. James was named President and Chief Executive Officer of the new firm.

During the first year under the new ownership MSDL achieved both record sales and earnings. However, during the first quarter of 1983, the trend began to reverse, resulting in two years of losses. Financial statements for 1982 through 1985 appear in Exhibits 1 and 2.

NATURE OF THE BUSINESS AND LOCAL ENVIRONMENT

A dental laboratory is a service business which produces the more complex restorations and prostheses required by dentists for their patients. Historically this work was done by the dentists themselves, and in some cases, it still is. The major output of a full-service dental lab includes dentures, partial dentures,

EXHIBIT 1 Midstate Dental Lab, Inc. Income Statement

	\multicolumn{4}{c}{FOR YEARS ENDING DEC. 31}
	1982	1983	1984	1985
Sales:				
In-house work	$465,000	$310,000	$270,000	$268,500
Subcontracted				26,500
Total Sales	465,000	310,000	270,000	295,000
Cost of Sales:				
For subcontracts				23,000
Materials	133,200	81,000	68,200	68,000
Technicians	182,000	144,500	120,000	108,000
Total COGS	315,200	225,500	188,200	199,000
Gross Profit	149,800	84,500	81,800	96,000
Operating Costs:				
Salaries	54,000	40,300	38,800	37,800
Variable Lease	14,000	9,300	8,100	8,800
Fixed Lease	12,000	9,000	6,000	6,000
Auto Expense	6,200	4,800	5,800	5,700
Other Expenses	8,400	6,000	6,700	6,300
Depreciation and Amortization	9,500	9,200	9,000	8,800
Total Operations Expenses	104,100	78,600	74,400	73,400
Operating Profit	45,700	5,900	7,400	22,600
Interest	17,400	14,700	12,900	12,300
Earnings Before Tax	28,300	(8,800)	(5,500)	10,300
Taxes	6,000	0[1]	0[1]	0[1]
Net Income	$22,300	($8,800)	($5,500)	$10,300
Dividends	$15,000	$ 500	$ 1,000	$ 5,000
Number of Technicians	14	11	9	8

[1] Taxable income protected by tax loss carry forward

EXHIBIT 2 Midstate Dental Lab, Inc. Balance Sheet

FOR THE YEARS ENDING DEC. 31

	1982	1983	1984	1985
ASSETS				
Cash	$ 4,800	$ 3,200	$ 2,600	$ 3,800
Accounts Receivable	37,500	29,900	26,200	32,100
Inventory	62,100	52,200	43,800	52,300
Other Current Assets	1,000	1,300	1,800	2,600
Total Current Assets	105,400	86,600	74,400	90,800
Fixed Assets	68,500	65,300	63,100	66,400
Less Accumulated Depreciation	(35,300)	(40,000)	(44,500)	(48,800)
Intangibles	22,500	22,500	22,500	22,500
Less Accumulated Amortization	(4,500)	(9,000)	(13,500)	(18,000)
Total Fixed Assets	51,200	38,800	27,600	22,100
Total Assets	$156,600	$125,400	$102,000	$112,900
LIABILITIES				
Accounts Payable	$ 36,900	$ 32,900	$ 21,800	$ 23,400
Notes Payable[1]	42,600	30,800	32,800	40,100
Other Current Liabilities	14,800	13,700	10,900	12,600
Total Current Debt	94,300	77,400	65,500	76,100
Long Term Notes	50,000	45,000	40,000	35,000
Total Debt	144,300	122,400	105,500	111,100
OWNERS' EQUITY				
Capital Stock	5,000	5,000	5,000	5,000
Retained Earnings	7,300	(2,000)	(8,500)	(3,200)
Total Equity	12,300	3,000	(3,500)	1,800
Total Capital	$156,600	$125,400	$102,000	$112,900

[1] Includes current portion of long-term debt = $5,000

---

gold and porcelain crowns, bridgework, inlays and orthodontic appliances. The proportion of sales in each category has remained fairly stable for MSDL over the last few years.

A crown, covering the whole tooth, may be constructed of porcelain and platinum, gold, or porcelain fused to gold. The metal provides strength, while the porcelain replicates the color of the tooth. An inlay, by contrast, covers only one or two surfaces of a tooth and is made primarily of gold. Partial dentures are relatively more expensive than full dentures and typically replace five to eight teeth. Crowns are the most expensive product group and require the most technical skills to make. Crown and bridgework, together with inlays, constitute 40% of MSDL's sales. Full and partial dentures account for another 45% of sales. MSDL's other work includes primarily plastics work such as retainers and bite splints; porcelain jackets for cosmetic value; and orthodontic appliances. These items contribute only 5%, with repair work constituting the remaining 10%.

When a patient needs restorative work a dentist takes impressions of the patient's mouth and then instructs the lab as to what is needed. The technicians at the lab then make the item and return it to the dentist for fitting into the patient's mouth. If the technical work has been done properly the item should fit with only minor adjustments and need no further work in the lab. Since the dentist is the one who is responsible for any adjustments after the restoration is in place, high quality work is a necessity, regardless of which lab does the work. A dentist is not likely to use any lab that produces work that must constantly be reworked before it fits properly.

The work in dental labs is performed by technicians who are generally trained in technical schools. Dental technicians must have significant manual dexterity skills and require much on-the-job training once they are hired. Technicians specializing in porcelain and precious metals work are among the highest paid, generally earning up to 50% more than non-specialized workers. This wage differential reflects limited availability, as well as the advanced training and experience requirements for such specialized technicians. A dental technician training program is located within a three-hour drive of MSDL's market area, providing a ready source of labor and an opportunity for technicians to upgrade their skills. Typical wages for dental technicians range from $5 to $15 per hour nationally. Regional rates vary, with the South having the lowest rates and the coastal regions having the highest pay scales.

Most communities of even modest size have at least one dental lab. Dentists in small communities, however, may have access to a lab only through the mail, or must do their own work. In addition to the numerous small local labs there are a few very large, high volume labs that serve dentists in several states, principally by mail. These large labs, often located in the South, may charge lower prices than their local counterparts because of their volume and their overall productivity. These large labs often act as subcontractors for local labs who cannot justify adding a specialized technician for certain low volume tasks. For example, many labs subcontracted porcelain work in the early 1980's.

In addition to general service labs, both small and large, there are also laboratories which specialize in one or more product types. This is the case in Midstate's community. There are four other small competitors providing dental lab services in the city, one of which specializes in orthodontic appliances. Altogether, the five labs serve approximately 75 dentists in the city, as well as several others in the surrounding small communities. These outlying dentists are generally served by mail or U.P.S.

In the Fall of 1979, two of the area's largest employers instituted dental insurance plans as part of their union contracts. As a result, about one out of every three or four families began to take advantage of this fringe benefit to have expensive, previously-postponed dental work completed. It was this circumstance which prompted Mr. Lickert to expand MSDL in 1980. However, by the middle of 1982, the boom ended. Continuing economic pressures in the farm-related local industries prevented other businesses from following the trend of offering dental coverage, as had been otherwise anticipated. Further, many large employers had begun to lay off significant numbers of workers, resulting in an unemployment rate of 10% in the area by the end of 1984. In addition, between 1981 and 1985, the area's population had shrunk another 10% when many workers left the area to seek employment. However, by the end of 1985, the five owners of MSDL were once again beginning to experience an influx of patients as economic recovery began to have an effect.

MIDSTATE'S OPERATION

Customers

MSDL does approximately 45% of its business with the five dentists who form the owner group. The lab has 18 other regular customers among the remaining local dentists, though almost all of these use at least one other lab as well. Many of these customers prefer Midstate for their work in either dentures or crowns and inlays. Few customers, however, use the lab for all of these products. Only the owners patronize the lab for orthodontic work. Midstate has added only one new regular customer since 1982. However, the lab has not lost a regular customer in that period, and several dentists have recently begun to use the lab on a trial basis.

Historically, MSDL provided 30 day terms for payment. Recently, Mr. Franklin instituted a 3/10, net 30 policy for open credit. Experience with this new policy in the first three months of 1986 indicates that about three-fourths of the non-owner clients have begun to take advantage of the discount. These clients were generally already paying within the 30 day period.

Personnel

Midstate Lab currently employs eight technicians; Mr. Franklin at a salary of $24,000; a bookkeeper/receptionist at $10,000; and a part-time young woman who makes pick-ups and deliveries to the dentists. Mr. Franklin is not only the manager, but also inspects the work of the technicians and makes calls on all the customers at least once a month. The bookkeeper also makes a daily delivery/pick-up trip on her way home in the late afternoon to as many as a dozen customers whose offices are in the north end of the city. Of the eight technicians, two are highly skilled in gold and porcelain work, earning $18,000 annually. The other six people average $12,000 each. Wages are competitive with other area labs. By contrast, in 1982, MSDL had employed four specialty and ten other technicians.

Jim Franklin has a general rule of thumb which he uses to measure the productivity of his workers. Gold and porcelain specialists should be able to complete goods with a sales value between $50,000 and $55,000 if they are operating at reasonable efficiency. The sales value of the work completed by the general technicians should average about $25,000–$27,500. Franklin's assessments of worker productivity are used as a basis for layoff decisions.

Work schedules are as flexible as possible to accommodate the six women technicians at the lab. All employees who have been with MSDL for over two years have access to the lab upon request. This permits flexibility in working times, enabling early arrival or late departure, or weekend work. All the technicians have taken advantage of this policy with noticeable regularity. In 1984, a modification was made to the lab's flextime policy. Many dentists experience an early Monday "rush" of patients who suffer emergency problems on the weekend. To serve its customers better, MSDL now gives priority to rush work after the weekends, promising 24 hour maximum turnaround time on repair work. For that reason all technicians are expected to be in the lab the first thing in the morning on Mondays and Tuesdays.

MSDL also has a policy of providing continuing education for its technicians at the regional technical school. The lab will reimburse its employees up to $300 per year for fees spent on skills development. One week of paid leave is allowed for this purpose. Typically, one or two technicians take advantage of such benefits each year. One technician was recently denied this opportunity because her productivity was low. Mr. Franklin felt this performance was fostered by laziness, rather than a lack of skills.

Inventory Management

Most of the materials used in the lab are inexpensive, do not spoil, and are easily stored. These include such items as plaster of Paris, grinding and polishing compounds, wax, and the plastics and ceramics materials used in prostheses. Other items, such as artificial teeth, are more expensive and require the firm to maintain a selection of sizes and color shades. Porcelain compound is also expensive, as are the gold and platinum used. All these materials are purchased by mail from large dental supply firms annually, usually in June when MSDL's business is somewhat slack. When necessary, inventory purchases are financed by a short-term loan from the owners. This loan is usually repaid in gradual installments, and generally carries a rate comparable to the rate earned on the owners' personal investments, currently about 14%. Gold and platinum supplies are stored at a local bank, with a two or three day supply kept at the lab. Only Mr. Franklin has access to this material. Approximately one-tenth of an ounce of gold is used in an average crown. MSDL maintains an average inventory of precious metals totalling about 16 ounces, which is about a two month's supply.

There are over 500 manufacturers of dental supplies, with the 20 largest producers accounting for 70% of the industry's sales. Not all of the larger firms provide full lines of the equipment and supplies used by dental laboratories. Further, most of these larger firms also manufacture equipment and consumable supplies used by the dentists themselves. There are nearly 50,000 individual products produced by the industry. These products are almost entirely distributed to dentists and dental labs through a network of about 1,000 wholesalers, who also distribute the precious metals used in dentistry. One-third of the industry's sales are made by direct mail catalog. The remainder of the sales are made through sales representatives.

Product Prices

Mr. Franklin develops a price list for MSDL's products during the summer months. This is then distributed to the customer group by Labor Day. Prices are based on a standardized base cost for the materials and labor in the product, adjusted annually for cost increases and labor raises. The final price is derived by adding a markup to the total standard labor and material cost. These standard costs are based on data prepared in a study done in the mid-1970's by Mr. Lickert. Mr. Franklin's standard markups were 60% for crowns and bridges; 50% for dentures, partials, and miscellaneous work; and 30% for repair work. When a job is subcontracted to another lab the cost is marked up 15%. These markups placed MSDL's prices slightly above those of their competitors. However, recently Mr. Franklin noted that two competitors have raised prices, narrowing the gap.

Facilities and Equipment

During the summer of 1983, MSDL gave up half of its space on a five year sublease in response to economic trends. The remaining facilities, however, can still accommodate ten technicians comfortably; twelve is the absolute limit. All technicians have their own work stations, fully equipped with most of the instruments and equipment requisite to their work. Larger pieces of equipment and specialized machines, such as ovens for firing and curing and heating and cooling tanks, are shared. Except in unusual circumstances there are no significant delays involved in access to the shared equipment. Though MSDL's equipment is functional, most of it is over ten years old. New equipment is only purchased to replace existing equipment that can no longer be repaired. On numerous occasions technicians have been heard expressing a desire to have access to some of the newer kinds of equipment on which many of them received their training.

Quality and Service

Because high quality lab work is a necessity for dentists, Mr. Franklin and the owners committed MSDL to a campaign to produce the best quality work in the city. Quality was to be measured on the basis of the amount of rework needed. Mr. Franklin was to ensure this quality by careful inspection of the lab's work at each stage in the production process. To further assure quality levels it is also a policy of the lab to have only one employee work on each job from start to finish so that any recurring quality problems can be isolated. If illness or absence interrupts a job, Mr. Franklin finishes it himself.

High levels of service are provided by Midstate in two ways: having numerous deliveries and pickups each day, and having standard completion times for most work. MSDL owns one car for use by the delivery person to call on customers. Three regular deliveries are scheduled each day. All dentists who have work completed or require a pickup are covered in a given trip. It is not unusual for the car to be used in excess of 25,000 miles per year.

In 1985, Mr. Franklin put a stop to the common practice of having technicians deliver work on their way to or from the lab. While many of the customers appreciated having their work returned as soon as possible, Jim insisted on inspecting the final product, even if it meant a delivery delay until the next morning. Recently, a further conflict has developed over the lab's delivery policy because of abuses by the owner group which had begun to require as many as 15 "emergency" trips per day to their offices. The delivery difficulties became more complicated in February, 1986, when the delivery person quit. Finally, in addition to having to find a replacement for the delivery person, the car needs to be replaced as soon as possible.

In late 1985, Mr. Franklin, concerned about the cost of excessive delivery trips and increased inspections, suggested to Dr. James that product prices be raised and a delivery fee be assessed to cover extra out-of-pocket costs of deliveries. The owner group vigorously opposed both changes. They felt that as long as gasoline prices were falling the lab could afford to make extra trips. Further, Dr. Halliard insisted that markups should not be increased, in spite of quality improvements. He said, "Dentist-owners naturally insist on quality. But when it comes to asking customers to pay for that quality they may think we are trying to line our own pockets at their expense. Since our prices are already slightly above our competitors', we should leave well enough alone."

Work Scheduling

Besides frequent deliveries, the other way MSDL tries to ensure high service levels is through the scheduling of work. Each lab job is assigned a normal completion time, depending on the complexity of the job and the number of intermediate steps at which time materials must be given drying or hardening time, for example. If a technician falls behind in his or her work, s/he is expected to remain at work over lunch or after normal hours to complete the job. Excessive or frequent delays in job completion are grounds for termination, though no one has been terminated on this basis since the policy was instituted in 1983. One employee was fired, however, because completion deadlines caused him to cut corners and the quality of his work deteriorated as a result.

Having known completion times for lab work is beneficial to the dentists because it enables them to better schedule their patients for fitting the finished appliance. Late completions require the dentists to reschedule patients, causing the dentist and the patient significant inconvenience. Almost all of MSDL's work is completed in less than a week's time.

Work scheduling is one of the most harrowing, yet unavoidable, tasks for Mr. Franklin. Frequently the work mix is unbalanced. When too many jobs come in at once for the technicians to handle in the standard completion time, Mr. Franklin will either request that they work overtime or else he must call the customers and inform them of the expected delay. This problem happened with particular frequency with porcelain and gold work in 1985. Work schedules have often become unbalanced because Mr. Franklin tends to assign work only to technicians who excel at the particular tasks involved in a given job. Thus, daily demand patterns may leave some technicians with too much work and others with idle time.

There are also difficulties with the specialized technicians when their workload is slack. Mr. Franklin has no established policy for this situation. If a specialized technician is given ordinary lab work to occupy idle time and crown or inlay work is received, one of the jobs must be postponed or Franklin has to finish one of them himself. On the other hand, if the specialized technicians are not kept busy, the general technicians resent seeing the more highly paid specialists sitting idle while they have to work through lunch to meet completion deadlines.

OWNERS' PERSPECTIVE

When Dr. James and his colleagues purchased Midstate in December, 1981, they had two primary motivations. First, they were determined to ensure the quality of the lab work they received for their patients. Secondly, the rising demand for dental services at that time made the financial prospects for the lab very attractive. As their own practices became more profitable, they desired additional investments for their own personal cash flows. A dental lab seemed an ideal business to purchase because the dentists had a background in the technical aspects of the business.

According to census data from the Department of Commerce, in the late 1970's, 76 of the 9,138 operating dental labs had sales exceeding $1,000,000 and employed an average of 70 persons. The total payroll of these "superlabs" averaged 47.5% of sales. Labs with sales between $500,000 and $1,000,000 number 189, employed an average of 30 persons, and had a payroll of 51% of sales. When they purchased MSDL, all five owners envisioned continued expansion and the possibility of becoming such a large, regional, mail-order lab.

Dr. James, the oldest and perhaps the most conservative of the five owners, began to become extremely concerned in 1983 when revenues continued to plunge and the mid-year financial statements showed only a meager profit. He was concerned that not only was their original investment in jeopardy, but that the additional capital they contributed to finance seasonal inventory purchases was at risk as well. Further, their personal incomes from their dental practices were becoming systematically lower. This had constrained the dentists' personal cash flows sufficiently to make it difficult for them to put additional money into the lab should that become necessary. As a result of these circumstances Dr. James initiated two cost saving measures in late 1983: reducing the physical facilities and cutting back on the personnel.

In 1985, when sales had finally begun to rebound, Dr. James advocated the practice of subcontracting certain specialized work to a mail order lab rather than hire an additional full-time technician. This decision led to a division among the owners. Three of them felt strongly that both quality and service would suffer if their gold and porcelain work were subcontracted. Quality problems would require rework, causing even longer time delays from using mail service. In spite of these objections subcontracting was initiated on a trial basis.

By early 1986, noticeable quality deficiencies and service problems had led to some heated confrontations between Dr. James and several of the other owners. Further, several of the owners were now thoroughly displeased with their investment in the lab and wished to dispose of their interest in it. Drs. Colworth and Wentberg shared the feeling that running their own practices was sufficient effort. Worrying about the lab had turned out to be much more time consuming than they had originally imagined. Dr. Halliard believed that the lab required too much effort for the level of returns that could be expected, even in the best of times. All three agreed that they would not invest any more funds in Midstate.

Dr. James, however, wanted to retain his investment in the lab. As long as the lab continued to provide returns commensurate with his other portfolio holdings, he believed the effort required was justified by the control the lab provided over quality and service. Dr. Schiller, the eternal optimist and the most financially independent of the group, still believed the lab could become extremely profitable. Since other local labs were also financially stressed, Schiller believed that now was the time for MSDL to become more aggressive in the market.

Reluctantly, Colworth, Halliard, and Wentberg agreed to give the lab until year-end to prove itself. At that time James and Schiller could buy the interests of the other three or the remaining owners would vote to sell the lab for whatever it would bring—even to liquidate it if necessary to get out from under the pressure.

PLANS AND OBJECTIVES

By March, 1986, Drs. James and Schiller had developed plans and objectives for MSDL which they felt would "improve performance significantly" and position the lab as "the leading full-service dental lab in the community." Volume was projected to increase 10% on the existing customer base. This growth projection was based on growth in client traffic in the owner-dentists' own offices. Given increased sales activity, the hiring of one more general technician, and continuing control over expenses, Dr. James believed a 5% margin (net income/sales) would be a difficult, but obtainable goal. James said, "Even with a substantial dividend payment, such a margin would allow the lab's retained earnings to return to positive levels."

Both James and Schiller agreed that once MSDL reached the point where it was no longer technically insolvent it could become more aggressive. As a first step Dr. Schiller proposed that the lab should begin pick-up and delivery service to neighboring communities in a thirty mile radius of the lab. Currently such customers are served by local labs by mail. Three of the larger outlying towns have seven dentists that he thought could easily provide the lab with $100,000 of additional sales, helping push the lab to sales of $500,000 by the end of 1987. To attract the dentists in the outlying communities Shiller suggested placing local advertisements or using direct mailings, rather than relying solely on word-of-mouth to attract customers. Dr. James was especially interested in attracting high markup specialty work like crowns and gold work. Both James and Schiller agreed that some consideration should be given to hiring an assistant manager. Dr. James summed up his thoughts about MSDL as follows:

> If Midstate is to become a local leader, it will need much more emphasis on marketing and general management methods. For this reason we should probably try to hire an assistant manager with a degree in business. If we hire him next year he should be ready to take over when Jim retires. Both Mills Schiller and I are thoroughly committed to Midstate and confident we can turn it around within the year. If, as I projected, we can afford to double our dividend, our colleagues should come around to our way of thinking. I personally see no obstacles to becoming the large mail-order lab we all envisioned when we bought MSDL.

INDUSTRIAL HIGHLIGHT

Medical and Dental Instruments and Supplies Industry

Below is a capsule summary of the dental equipment and supplies segment of the medical and dental instruments and supplies industry. Information regarding this industry segment may be useful in managing the Midstate Dental Lab, Inc. Information in this highlight was compiled by the U.S. Department of Commerce and focuses on this industry during the approximate period of time covered in the case. Keep in mind that industrial highlights contained in this text are not intended as a complete synopsis of an industry but as a profile of certain issues that can be relevant to a case situation. A list of additional references at the end of this highlight can be used for further industrial analysis.

CURRENT SITUATION

Shipments by the dental equipment and supplies industry increased an estimated 0.4 percent in 1985 (in constant dollars). This follows a similar increase in the previous year and declines in 1982 and 1983. The industry is the smallest in the medical group, with only about 7 percent of its shipments.

The value of industry shipments of dental equipment and supplies is expected to increase by less than 1 percent in 1986 (in 1982 constant dollars).

Total employment is forecast to remain unchanged from the 1985 level. Production workers will account for 60 percent of the total.

Exports of dental equipment and supplies are expected to increase 7 percent in 1986, if the U.S. dollar continues to decline. Imports are expected to increase 8 percent.

General economic conditions have a greater impact on this industry than on the other industries in the medical and dental group. In recessionary periods, dental care is sometimes postponed, and even after recovery begins, demand may increase slowly.

Source: U.S. Industrial Outlook, Department of Commerce, 1986, pp. 34-1–34-9.

Industry Structure

Products of this industry include dental chairs, cabinets, and tables; dental laboratory equipment; dental instruments and hand pieces; dental sterilizers; precious and nonprecious dental metals and alloys; dental impression materials; and dentures and artificial teeth.

The industry's 485 manufacturing plants are mostly small, privately owned companies: about 73 percent of total plants have fewer than 20 employees. California has approximately one-quarter of the plants but only 17 percent of production, whereas New York—the largest producing State—accounts for roughly 20 percent of industry shipments.

Industry employment was about 14,500 in 1985, a 1.4 percent decrease from 1984 and 20 percent below the 1981 peak of 17,400. Production workers accounted for approximately 61 percent of all employees in this industry.

Technological developments in the dental equipment and supplies industry center on improving existing products, especially those with the greatest immediate market potential. New features in dental drilling, cleaning, and polishing instruments include faster, lighter designs for easier use and the addition of fiber-optic lighting accessories. Dental delivery systems using chemical solutions to soften decaying tooth material may in some cases eliminate the need for anesthesia and drilling during treatment of tooth decay. In addition, research and development activities are focusing on products similar to human tooth enamel for use in filling teeth.

Research and development expenditures average less than 2 percent of sales. The National Institute of Dental Research of the National Institutes of Health administers Federal support of dental research and development. Most of this research, however, relates to preventive dental care technology, rather than the development of new dental devices and equipment.

Foreign Trade

U.S. exports of dental equipment and supplies were $144 million in 1985, 4.5 percent above 1984, and accounted for about 12 percent of domestic shipments. Important export products were dental instruments and parts, dental hand pieces, artificial teeth and dentures, and dental cements and fillings.

U.S. imports increased 11.8 percent, reaching $74 million and accounting for about 7 percent of apparent consumption. Over one-half of the imports consisted of dental hand pieces, mostly from West Germany, Japan, and Switzerland. Also important were dental burs and other instruments and parts.

In 1984, the EC received 31 percent of U.S.-produced dental equipment and supplies and accounted for 40 percent of such U.S. imports.

LONG-TERM PROSPECTS

Dental equipment and supply industry shipments in the 5-year period ending in 1990 are projected to grow at a compound annual rate of 3.2 percent (in constant dollars). Despite increasing numbers of people covered by some form of dental insurance, growth in demand for dental products is expected to be very gradual during the next 5 years. Increased awareness regarding health and hygiene may boost demand for dental services and have a corresponding positive effect on the dental equipment and supplies industry.

ADDITIONAL REFERENCES

Miscellaneous Electrical Equipment and Supplies, SIC Industries 3691, 3692, 3693, 3694, 3699; 1982 Census of Manufacturers, Industry Series MC82-1-36F; Bureau of the Census, Washington, DC 20233.

Medical Instruments, Ophthalmic Goods, Photographic Equipment, Clocks, Watches and Watchcases, SIC Industries 3841, 3842, 3843, 3851, 3861, 3873; 1982 Census of Manufacturers, Industry Series MC82-1-38B; Bureau of the Census, Washington, DC 20233.

Selected Electronic and Associated Products, Including Telephone and Telegraph Apparatus, Current Industrial Reports 1983, MA-36N(83)-1; Bureau of the Census; Washington, DC 20233.

Electronic Market Data Book 1985, Electronic Industries Association, Washington, DC 20006.

Health—United States 1984, National Center for Health Statistics, Public Health Service, DHHS Pub. No. 85-1232, Hyattsville, MD 20782.

Medical Device & Diagnostic Industry, Canon Communications, Inc., Santa Monica, CA 90403.

Health Industry Today, Cassak Publications, Inc., Springfield, NJ 07081.

Modern Healthcare, Crain Communications Inc., Chicago, IL 60611.

CASE 9

Toys 'R' Us

CARON ST. JOHN
Georgia State University

In 1948, Charles Lazarus began selling baby furniture in the back of his father's Washington, D.C., bicycle repair shop, located below the apartment where Lazarus's family lived. Within a few months, and in response to customer requests, he added a few toys to his line of baby furniture. Before long he realized parents who bought toys returned for more toys—but parents who bought furniture rarely came back. "When I realized that toys broke," he said, "I knew it was a good business."[1] Soon his entire business was focused on toys.

His first store was successful, and he opened his second store in Washington as a self-serve, cash-and-carry business. In 1958, he opened his third store—a 25,000-square-foot "baby supermarket" with discount prices and a large selection of products. Within a few years, a fourth supermarket-style store was introduced. By 1966, the four stores in the Washington, D.C., area were achieving $12 million in annual sales.

In order to have the capital necessary for continued growth, Lazarus sold his four stores in 1966 to Interstate Stores, a retail discount chain, for $7 million. Lazarus stayed on with Interstate and maintained operating control over the toy division. Between 1966 and 1974, the Toys 'R' Us division of Interstate Stores grew from 4 to 47 stores through internal growth and a merger with Children's Bargain Town.

In 1974, the parent company, Interstate Stores, filed for bankruptcy. When Interstate completed reorganization and emerged from bankruptcy in 1978, the new company name was Toys 'R' Us (TRU) and Charles Lazarus was chief executive officer. Since then, all but four of the Interstate Stores have been divested and all creditors have been paid.

Between January 1979 and January 1984, Toys 'R' Us grew from 63 stores with sales of just under $350 million to 169 stores with sales of over $1.3 billion, for a compound annual growth rate of 30%. During the same years, profits increased from $17 million to $92 million for a compound annual growth rate of 40%. TRU stock, which traded for $2 per share in 1978, split 3 for 2 for 4 years in a row and consistently trades above $40 per share. A $2 TRU stock investment made in 1978 was worth $200 in the spring of 1984.

Copyright © 1985. Reprinted by permission.
[1] Stratford P. Sherman, "Where the Dollars 'R'," *Fortune,* June 1, 1981 pp. 45–47.

STRATEGY FORMULATION

Toys 'R' Us is currently the largest toy retailer in the world, with an estimated 12.5% share of the U.S. market.[2] With 169 retail toy supermarkets, Toys 'R' Us is now represented in all but six of the top-20 retail toy areas in the United States.

Charles Lazarus has consistently been the motivating force behind the growth of Toys 'R' Us. Lazarus, a man without a college education, is now worth over $75 million. His vision is for Toys 'R' Us to become the McDonald's of toy retailing: "We don't have golden arches, but we're getting there."[3] He credits his success in toy retailing to his love of the business. "What we do is the essence of America—making a business grow," he says. "If you're going to be a success in life you have to want it. I wanted it. I was poor. I wanted to be rich. . . . My ego now is in the growth of this company."[4]

TOY INDUSTRY

Retail toy sales in the United States were $10.5 billion in 1983. Primarily because of the national interest in electronic games, sales growth in the previous years had exceeded 18% per year. Excluding the electronic games category, industry sales growth has averaged 11% since 1980. Exhibit 1 shows the percent of total dollar sales by product category for 1980 through 1982.

In 1980, electronic games accounted for 18.4% of total U.S. toy market sales. By 1982, electronic games represented 30.9%, or almost one-third, of total toy sales. Industry analysts estimate that sales of traditional toys, such as Slinky, Silly Putty, and Etch-A-Sketch, account for 50% of nonelectronic

[2] TRU annual report and 10-K report for fiscal year ended January 1984.
[3] Dan Fesperman, "Toys 'R' Us is a Giant in Kids' Business," *The Miami Herald*, Nov. 22, 1982.
[4] Subrata N. Chakravarty, "Toys 'R' Fun," *Forbes*, Mar. 28, 1983 pp. 58–60.

EXHIBIT 1 Percentage of U.S. Retail Toy Dollar Sales by Product

PRODUCT	1980	1981	1982
Preschool	11.2	9.6	8.8
Arts/crafts/models/kits	6.6	7.1	5.1
Activity	10.9	10.8	8.5
Dolls	11.3	11.4	10.4
Games/puzzles	12.2	12.3	9.5
Infant toys	2.3	1.7	1.9
Non-riding toys	12.5	14.6	12.0
Riding trans.	7.1	6.5	7.0
Electronic games	18.4	18.5	30.9
All other	7.4	7.4	5.9

Source: "National Toy Chains Increase Market Share; Discounters Decline," *Playthings*, October 1983.

EXHIBIT 2 Percentage of U.S. Retail Toy Dollar Sales by State

STATE	1982*
California	11.72
Texas	7.75
New York	6.66
Illinois	5.01
Florida	4.99
Ohio	4.86
Pennsylvania	4.66
Michigan	4.19
Remaining 42 states	50.16

* Column will not sum to 100%, due to rounding.

Source: "U.S. Retail Toy Sales Up Slightly," *Playthings*, December 1983.

games sales each year.[5] Highly publicized toys, like Cabbage Patch dolls and ET products, account for the remaining 50% of sales.

Toy retailing is a very seasonal business. Well over 50% of toy sales are reported in the fourth quarter—with much of those sales generated in the 6 weeks before Christmas. To balance the unevenness of toy sales, most toy stores sell other seasonal items like swimming pool supplies and lawn furniture.

Retail toy sales are tied to population. In 1982, the state with the largest share of retail sales was California (see Exhibit 2). The states with the smallest shares of retail sales were Vermont (.18% of sales), Wyoming (.21%), and Alaska (.23%). The metropolitan areas with the largest retail toy sales were New York, Los Angeles, Chicago, Detroit, and Houston.

Discount stores are the primary outlet for toy sales in the United States (see Exhibit 3). Although all categories of retailers compete with each other, they use different approaches to appeal to customers. The larger department stores compete on the basis of convenience—the customer can purchase toys while shopping for other items. The national toy chains offer a much larger selection of products at lower prices with a minimal level of in-store service. The discount stores frequently offer similar low prices and minimal service, but their selection is not as extensive as that of the toy chains. The small, independent toy stores provide personalized service and specialty items but ask higher prices.

With 169 stores, Toys 'R' Us is the largest national toy chain. Child World, a division of Cole National, follows TRU with 89 stores. Lionel Corporation, a company reorganizing under Chapter 11 in 1984, operates 59 stores.

---

[5] Paul B. Brown, "Staying Power," *Forbes*, Mar. 26, 1984 pp. 186–188.

STRATEGY FORMULATION

EXHIBIT 3 Percentage Distribution of Unit Sales by Type of Outlet

TYPE OF OUTLET	1980[1]	1981[1]	1982[1]
Discount	37	36	35
Sears-Penneys-Wards	5	5	6
Other department stores	6	6	6
Variety	11	10	9
National toy chains	10	11	12
All other toy stores	4	3	3
Catalog showrooms	3	3	3
Other	25	25	26

[1] Columns will not sum to 100% due to rounding.
Source: "National Toy Chains Increase Market Share; Discounters Decline," *Playthings*, October 1983.

Industry Trends

Some demographic and industry trends that are expected to continue to influence in a positive way the demand for toys in the next several years are:

1. *Increased numbers of children.* Since the late seventies, members of the baby boom generation, who delayed having children while in their twenties, have started having babies. Consequently, the 2 to 5 age group has been growing steadily for several years.
2. *More money to spend on toys.* These older parents are having children after their households are formed and careers are established, so family incomes are higher. In many families, both parents are employed full-time. The higher family incomes mean there is more money for discretionary items like toys.
3. *Broader market appeal of toy stores.* As noted earlier, the toy market has joined with the video games and home electronics markets to form a broader category of "toys." The objective is to appeal to the teen and young adult market segment and draw this new group of buyers into the toy stores.
4. *Increased visibility of toys because of licensing.* Licensing, or basing a product on a motion picture, television program, or comic strip character, has accelerated in importance in the eighties and is expected to continue. Toys based on popular characters appeal to an already established market.

TOYS 'R' US

The aim of Toys 'R' Us is to be the customer's only place of purchase for toys and related products.[6] Management is proud that TRU attracts the least-

---

[6] Chakravarty, "Toys 'R' Fun."

affluent purchasers because of the everyday discount prices and also attracts the most-affluent purchasers because of the extensive product selection. In order to provide total service to all customer segments, the company maintains tight operating procedures and a strong customer orientation.

Retailing Operations

According to Charles Lazarus, "Nothing is done in the stores."[7] What he means is that all buying and pricing decisions are made at corporate headquarters in Rochelle Park, New Jersey. The corporate buying and pricing decisions are made using an elaborate computerized inventory control system where sales by item and sales by store are monitored daily. Those actual sales numbers are compared to forecasts, and when substantial differences exist, the slow items are marked down to get them out of the stores and the fast-selling items are reordered in larger quantities.

By closely following the buying habits of the consumer, TRU is able to pick up on trends before the crucial Christmas buying season and to maintain more flexibility than competitors. In 1980, when sales of hand-held video games fell off sharply before Christmas, Toys 'R' Us had been forewarned by its extensive monitoring system and had moved much of its stock of video games, at reduced prices, before the Christmas season. TRU was fully stocked with the big Christmas items that year—the Rubik's Cube and Strawberry Shortcake—unlike virtually all its competitors.

The TRU stores are regionally clustered with a regional warehouse within 1 day's driving distance of every store (see Exhibit 4). The company also owns a fleet of trucks to support its warehousing operations. The 15 regional warehouses allow TRU to keep the stores well stocked and make it possible for TRU to order large quantities of merchandise early in the year, when manufacturers are eager to ship. Since most manufacturers will defer payments for 12 months on shipments made in the months immediately following Christmas, TRU is able to defer payment on about two-thirds of its inventory each year. TRU's competitors typically buy closer to Christmas, when buying terms are tighter.

All 169 TRU stores have the same layout with the same items arranged on exactly the same shelves—all according to blueprints sent from the corporate office. A TRU store is typically 43,000 square feet and is characterized by wide aisles and warehouse-style shelving stocked to the ceiling with over 18,000 different items. A substantial percent of the floor space is devoted to computers and computer-related products and to nontoy items like diapers, furniture, and clothing. However, toys, games, books, puzzles, and sports equipment are the major focus of the stores.

Each store is jointly managed by a merchandise manager and an operations manager. The merchandise manager has full responsibility for the merchandising effort in the store: content, stock level, and display. The operations manager is responsible for the building, personnel, cash control, customer

---

[7] Sherman, "Where the Dollars 'R'."

EXHIBIT 4 Existing and Proposed 1984 Locations

Map labels:
- Seattle warehouse
- Cincinnati warehouse
- Chicago warehouse
- Detroit warehouse
- Toronto warehouse
- Boston warehouse
- Rochelle Park, N.J. National office
- Secaucus warehouse
- Philadelphia warehouse
- San Francisco warehouse
- Los Angeles warehouse
- Washington, D.C. warehouse
- Dallas warehouse
- Atlanta warehouse
- Miami warehouse
- Houston warehouse

Rochelle Park, N.J.

WASH. D.C. WHSE
- Marlo Hts., MD
- Rockville, MD
- Baileys Crossroads, VA
- Adelphi, MD
- Fairfax, VA
- Lanham, MD
- Catonsville, MD
- Towson, MD
- Richmond (South), VA
- Glen Burnie, MD
- Tyson's Corner, VA
- Hampton, VA
- Norfolk, VA
- Richmond (North), VA
- Golden Ring, MD
- Salisbury, MD

L.A. WH3E
- Van Nuys, CA
- Torrance, CA
- Covina, CA
- Anaheim, CA
- Ontario, CA
- La Mesa, CA
- Rosemead, CA
- San Diego, CA
- Woodland Hills, CA
- Cerritos, CA
- San Bernardino, CA
- Culver City, CA
- Burbank, CA
- Oceanside, CA
- Bakersfield, CA
- Santa Ana, CA
- Chula Vista, CA
- La Mirada, CA
- Las Vegas, NV

S.F. WHSE
- Sunnydale, CA
- Pleasant Hill, CA
- Colma, CA
- Hayward, CA
- San Jose, CA
- Arden Way, CA
- Citrus Heights, CA
- Redwood City, CA
- Newark, CA
- Fresno, CA
- Sacramento, CA
- E. San Jose, CA
- Santa Rosa, CA

CHICAGO WHSE
- Burbank, IL
- Melrose, IL
- Niles, IL
- Calumet City, IL
- Highland Park, IL
- Schaumburg, IL
- Downers Grove, IL
- Chicago (Southeast), IL
- Milwaukee (South), WI
- Milwaukee (North), WI
- Moline, IL
- Merrillville, IN
- N. Riverside, IL
- Aurora, IL
- Joliet, IL
- Riverview, IL
- Bloomingdale, IL
- Matteson, IL
- W. Dundee, IL
- Orland Park, IL
- Rockford, IL

N.Y/N.J. WHSE
- Levittown, NY
- Commack, NY
- Totowa, NJ
- E. Brunswick, NJ
- Paramus, NJ
- Watchung, NJ
- Brooklyn, NY
- Massapequa, NY
- Valley Stream, NY
- Carle Place, NY
- Staten Island, NY
- Eatontown, NY
- Colonie, NY
- Jersey City, NJ
- Huntington Station, NY
- Lake Grove, NY
- Woodbridge, NJ
- Livingston, NJ
- Yonkers, NY
- Toms River, NJ
- Douglaston, NY
- Bay Parkway, NY
- Bayshore, NY
- Nanuet, NY
- Milford, CT

HOUSTON WHSE
- Houston (Gulf), TX
- Houston (North), TX
- Houston (Katy), TX
- San Antonio (NW), TX
- Beaumont, TX
- San Antonio (NE), TX
- Houston (SW), TX
- Willowbrook, TX
- Austin, TX

DETROIT WHSE
- Southgate, MI
- Madison Heights, MI
- Southfield, MI
- Livonia, MI
- Roseville, MI
- Flint, MI
- Saginaw, MI
- Grand Rapids, MI
- Lansing MI
- Toledo, OH
- Dearborn, MI
- Sterling Heights, MI

BOSTON WHSE
- Warwick, RI
- Peabody, MA
- Auburn, MA
- Framingham, MA
- Woburn, MA
- Dedham, MA
- Springfield, MA
- Waterbury, CT
- Corbins Corner, CT
- Manchester, NH
- Swansea, MA
- Newington, NH
- Portland, ME

DALLAS WHSE
- Fort Worth, TX
- Dallas, TX
- Oklahoma City, OK
- Mesquite, TX
- Arlington, TX
- Tulsa, OK
- Red Bird, TX
- Hurst, TX
- Shreveport, LA

SEATTLE WHSE
- Clackamas, OR
- Jantzen Beach, OR
- Seattle, WA
- Tukwila, WA
- Tigard, OR
- Spokane, WA
- Tacoma, WA

PHILA. WHSE
- Montgomeryville, PA
- King of Prussia, PA
- Lawrence Township, NJ
- Port Richmond, PA
- Deptford, NJ
- Cherry Hill, NJ
- Phila. (NF), PA
- Phila. (So.), PA
- Granite Run, PA
- Oxford Valley, PA
- York, PA

MIAMI WHSE
- Palm Beach, FL
- Altamonte Springs, FL
- Hollywood, FL
- Hialeah, FL
- Plantation, FL
- Tampa, FL
- Cutler Ridge, FL
- Miami, FL

ATLANTA WHSE
- Nashville, TN
- Montgomery, AL
- Birmingham, AL
- Cumberland, GA
- Northlake, GA
- Southlake, GA

KUWAIT CITY, KUWAIT

CINCINNATI WHSE*

TORONTO, CANADA whse*

*Opening in 1984

Source: "Welcome to Toys 'R' Us," booklet prepared by Toys 'R' Us for new employees.

service, and everything else that is not directly related to merchandise. Area supervisors oversee the total operations of three or four stores in a given area, and area general managers are responsible for the performance and profitability of all the TRU stores in a given market.

Marketing

As indicated earlier, each Toys 'R' Us store carries over 18,000 items. Although toys represent, by far, the majority of the items stocked, other products include baby furniture, diapers, and children's clothing. The feeling at TRU is that the parent will go to the store to buy a necessity or nonseasonal item and will leave with at least one toy purchase. The average TRU customer spends $40 per visit.[8]

In recent years, TRU expanded its product line to include home computers and software in addition to the traditional toys. The move has served to broaden the company's customer base to include teenagers and adults, and to create add-on business at each retail unit. According to company statistics, products for these "older children" accounted for 18% of sales in 1983 compared with 11% in 1982.[9] TRU strongly feels this is not a change in its basic business—computers and software are toys for adults.

This strategy of carrying a wide selection of merchandise has benefited TRU in another way. The company has been successful in encouraging year-round buying at its stores (see Exhibit 5). In 1980, 7.5% of profits were made in the 9 months of January through September compared with 20% in 1982 (see Exhibit 6).[10]

TRU has a strong policy of year-round discount prices. Because TRU buys most of its merchandise during the off-season, when manufacturers are offering discounts, the company is able to pass the discounts on to the customer. TRU has a policy of not having store sales. Individual items will be marked down if they are not selling, but TRU does not have sales that are categorywide or storewide.

Virtually all the Toys 'R' Us stores are located on an important traffic artery leading to a major shopping mall. A location of this type serves two purposes: it allows TRU to attract mall patrons without paying high mall rents, and it gives TRU the space to do business the way it wants to—as a large "supermarket" for toys, complete with grocery-type shopping carts.

Other customer conveniences include the stock availability and return policy. Product availability is virtually guaranteed. Because of extensive inventory monitoring and attention to consumer buying habits, TRU rarely has a "stock out." Also, TRU boasts of a liberal return policy. The company claims it will accept all returns with no questions asked—even if a toy with no defect is broken by a child after several months of play.

Since TRU is not represented in all regions of the United States (see Exhibit 4), it does no national advertising. Before opening stores in a new region, TRU

---

[8] Ibid.
[9] TRU annual report for fiscal year ended January 1983.
[10] Chakravarty, "Toys 'R' Fun."

STRATEGY FORMULATION

EXHIBIT 5 Net Sales by Quarter

(in thousands of dollars)

END OF FISCAL YEAR	FIRST QUARTER	SECOND QUARTER	THIRD QUARTER	FOURTH QUARTER	TOTAL
1/29/84	$181,717	$213,945	$220,689	$703,291	$1,319,642
1/30/83	138,523	167,781	189,930	545,501	1,041,735
1/31/82	97,349	123,730	132,938	429,268	783,285
2/1/81	70,247	92,660	101,922	332,503	597,332
2/3/80	56,515	75,768	78,304	269,730	480,317
1/28/79	38,000	53,583	57,478	200,038	349,099

Source: Annual Reports and 10-K reports for fiscal years 1979 through 1984.

EXHIBIT 6 Net Earnings (or Loss) by Quarter

(in thousands of dollars)

END OF FISCAL YEAR	FIRST QUARTER	SECOND QUARTER	THIRD QUARTER	FOURTH QUARTER	TOTAL
1/29/84	$5,357	$7,113	$6,061	$73,786	$92,317
1/30/83	2,516	4,431	4,734	52,481	64,162
1/31/82	618	3,221	3,182	41,899	48,920
2/1/81	(193)	298	44	28,744	28,893
2/3/80	(180)	1,552	725	24,800	26,897
1/28/79	(1,556)	183	564	18,017	17,208

Source: Annual reports and 10-K reports for fiscal years 1979 through 1984.

does concentrated television and newspaper advertising. Once the stores are open, TRU may continue very limited television and newspaper advertising.

Domestic and Foreign Expansion

Toys 'R' Us pursues a corporate objective of 18% expansion of retail space per year. In order to meet this objective, it has opened 24 or 25 new stores each year for the last few years.

All of the expansions are made as a total entry into a new region. First, TRU builds a warehouse, then it clusters several stores within 1 day's driving distance of the warehouse so that prompt merchandise delivery is ensured. Typically, the warehouse and all the stores are up and running within the same fiscal year and in time for the Christmas season. Once TRU enters a local market with more than one store, it immediately becomes the low-price leader in the area—forcing competitors to bring down their prices.

Charles Lazarus keeps a file of 300 locations that have already been selected as potential sites for future U.S. stores.[11] The regions are selected on the basis

[11] Ibid.

EXHIBIT 7 Company Rankings by Capital Expenditures, 1983

(in thousands of dollars)

1.	Safeway	$500,000	11.	Lucky	140,000
2.	Dayton Hudson	475,000	12.	Carter Hawley Hale	138,000
3.	Kroger	410,000	13.	Stop & Shop	125,000
4.	Sears, Roebuck	400,000	14.	Supermarkets General	110,000
5.	J.C. Penney	395,000	15.	Allied Stores	100,000
6.	Federated	325,000	16.	Albertsons	95,000
7.	K Mart	320,000	17.	Toys 'R' Us	90,000
8.	Winn-Dixie	176,600	18.	Wal-Mart	90,000
9.	Jewel Cos.	166,000	19.	Melville	85,000
10.	May	140,000	20.	Associated Dry Goods	85,000

Source: Prepared by casewriter.

of demographic patterns and toy buying statistics. The individual store locations are decided after an analysis is completed of the area shopping malls, traffic patterns, and local retail toy competition. The fiscal 1984 and 1985 plans call for regional expansion into the midwest, upstate New York, and Pennsylvania.

In addition to domestic expansion, TRU is embarking on a plan of growth into the large non-U.S. toy market. The first Canadian and European stores are scheduled to open in late 1984. Arrangements are under way for a store in Singapore, and plans have been made with Alghanim Industries, a major Kuwait-based corporation, to provide technical and buying assistance for a series of toy stores that Alghanim has planned for the Middle East.

TRU is ranked as one of the top-20 U.S. retailers in annual capital expenditures (see Exhibit 7). It finances expansions exclusively with internally generated funds. It is able to build the capital necessary for expansion by not paying dividends (see Exhibits 8 and 9).

KIDS 'R' US, TOO

TRU's only venture outside of toy retailing has been into children's clothing—a $6 billion industry in the United States alone. According to a TRU press release, the corporate objective in creating Kids 'R' Us was to "provide one stop shopping with an overwhelming selection of first quality, designer and brand name children's clothing in the seasons' latest styles at everyday prices. . . . We have taken the knowledge and systems we have refined for our toy stores over the past 30 years and applied some of these principles to our Kids 'R' Us stores."[12]

In 1983, TRU opened two Kids 'R' Us stores in the New York area. Corporate plans call for a total of eight to ten Kids 'R' Us stores by the end of 1984. Each

---

[12] "Kids 'R' Us—The Children's Clothing Store Both Parents and Kids Will Choose," press release from Toys 'R' Us, July 1983.

EXHIBIT 8 Statements of Consolidated Earnings (in thousands of dollars)

	END OF FISCAL YEAR					
	Jan. 29, 1984	Jan. 30, 1983	Jan. 31, 1982	Feb. 1, 1981	Feb. 3, 1980	Jan. 28, 1979
Net sales	$1,319,642	$1,041,735	$783,285	$597,332	$480,317	$348,099
Costs and expenses:						
Costs of sales	881,258	705,260	522,808	409,886	319,964	234,389
Selling, advertising, general and administrative	254,448	206,378	166,930	131,430	101,548	71,867
Depreciation and amortization	13,428	11,060	8,900	7,124	5,457	4,658
Interest expense	2,404	4,285	4,086	2,933	4,502	6,398
Interest income	(10,138)	(9,570)	(11,649)	(4,997)	(4,065)	(3,413)
Gain on sale of property			(1,910)	(1,507)	(355)	(202)
	1,141,400	917,413	689,165	544,869	427,051	313,687
Earnings before tax	178,242	124,322	94,120	52,463	53,266	35,402
Taxes on income	85,925	60,160	45,200	23,570	26,490	18,255
Net earnings	$ 92,317	$ 64,162	$ 48,920	$ 28,893	$ 26,776	$177,147

Source: Annual reports and 10-K reports for fiscal years 1979 through 1984.

store offers a full assortment of first-quality, discount-priced clothing and accessories for children up to age 12. The surroundings are spacious and well decorated with neon signs, color-coded departments, fitting rooms with platforms for small children, changing areas for infants, play areas for children, and color-coded store maps.

Some observers feel TRU will meet more resilient competition in children's clothing than it did in toys. Department and discount stores make more money on children's clothing than they do on toys and are not willing to give up that market easily. "Department stores fight when it comes to soft goods. That's their bread and butter, it's the guts of their business."[13] Some department store managers feel the purchase of children's clothing sets a family's buying patterns for years—so the implication of losing the children's departments as a way to draw in families goes beyond the immediate loss of profits in that area.[14]

COMPETITOR REACTION

TRU has an excellent reputation with consumers—a reputation that precedes the company into new market areas. Toys 'R' Us also has a reputation—one

[13] Claudia Ricci, "Children's Wear Retailers Brace for Competition from Toys 'R' Us," *The Wall Street Journal*, Aug. 25, 1983.
[14] Peter Kerr, "The New Game at Toys 'R' Us," *The New York Times*, July 4, 1983.

EXHIBIT 9 Consolidated Balance Sheets

(in thousands of dollars)

	END OF FISCAL YEAR		
	Jan. 29, 1984	Jan. 30, 1983	Jan. 31, 1982
ASSETS			
Current Assets:			
Cash and short-term investments	$235,838	$134,516	$123,383
Accounts and other receivables	17,909	17,508	14,524
Merchandise inventories	264,192	191,950	140,657
Prepaid expense and other	1,537	705	4,010
Total current assets	519,476	344,679	282,574
Property and Equipment less dep.			
Real estate	184,500	120,836	78,625
Other	85,264	65,882	53,892
Leased property under capital leases net dep.	15,998	17,138	18,685
Other assets	14,990	10,473	8,721
	$820,228	$559,008	$442,497

	END OF FISCAL YEAR		
	Jan. 29, 1984	Jan. 30, 1983	Jan. 31, 1982
LIABILITIES AND STOCKHOLDERS' EQUITY			
Current Liabilities:			
Accounts payable	$184,504	$ 82,278	$ 65,740
Accrued expenses, taxes	79,281	66,011	47,051
Federal tax payable	33,167	36,948	30,853
Current portion:			
Long-term debt	1,260	1,281	788
Oblig. under capital leases	822	756	962
Total current liabilities	299,034	187,274	145,394
Deferred income tax payable	8,708	8,540	5,414
Long-term debt	30,913	17,047	62,177
Obligations under leases	21,850	22,671	23,663
Stockholders' Equity	5,405	3,600	2,115
Additional paid-in capital	191,732	147,745	90,902
Retained earnings	274,205	183,750	120,674
Less: Treasury shares at cost	(4,352)	(4,352)	(4,352)
Receivables from exercise of stock options	(7,267)	(7,267)	(3,490)
	459,723	323,476	205,849
	$820,228	$559,008	$442,497

Source: Annual reports and 10-K reports for 1982 through 1984.

that is feared and respected—with its competitors. Examples of comments from competitors include:

Toy store owner:

"We were going, 'oh, nooo,' because they were coming in right across the street from us."

(*The Miami Herald*, Nov. 22, 1982)

President of a buying guild about a children's store owner:

"All I can tell you is his face turned white. You come up against a giant like this, with every major line discounted, and where do you go? If you're the average kiddy shop next door, do you take gas or cut your throat?"

(*The Wall Street Journal*, Aug. 25, 1983)

Manufacturer about a buyer:

"One department store buyer, arriving at the [TRU] store, said it caused her instant depression."

(*The Wall Street Journal*, Aug. 25, 1983)

Atlanta toy retailers about TRU's entry into the Atlanta market:

"I admire Toys 'R' Us. They will own the town."

"I hope they take the business from Zayre, Richway, Lionel and not us. We may have to start looking outside Atlanta for locations."

"The new Toys 'R' Us will saturate the market."

(*Toys, Hobbies & Crafts*, May 1983)

Michael Vastola, chairman of the board of Lionel Corporation:

"They have paid a lot of attention to real estate and location, and it has paid off. You have got to say that they have a very disciplined, well-managed operation."

(*The New York Times*, Sept. 4, 1983)

INDUSTRIAL HIGHLIGHT

Dolls, Toys, Games, and Children's Vehicles Industries

Below is a capsule summary of environmental factors that could affect the strategic management of Toys 'R' Us during the approximate period of time covered in the case. Information used in this highlight was compiled by the U.S. Department of Commerce. Keep in mind that this industrial highlight is not intended as a complete synopsis of key environmental trends but as a profile of certain issues that can be relevant to the case situation.

CURRENT SITUATION

The rapid and widespread rise in real personal incomes in 1984 led to a 12.5 percent growth in personal consumption expenditures for dolls, toys, and other such items. While much of the new demand was met through increased imports, shipments of U.S. doll and toy producers increased an estimated 4.6 percent to $4.4 billion in 1984, or 6.0 percent growth after adjustment for inflation. Producer prices for dolls, toys, games, and children's vehicles generally were either unchanged or down slightly. Industry employment rose by 7 percent to an estimated 53,700 thousand.

    The continuing poor performance of the video games sector reduced the overall growth of toy and game shipments to 3.0 percent in current dollars. The meteoric rise in consumer demand for home video games in the 1979 to 1982 period occurred largely at the expense of demand for traditional toys and games. While U.S. video game shipments rose from less than $100 million in 1979 to $1.3 billion in 1982, shipments of traditional toys and games fell from $3.0 billion to $2.6 billion in the same period. Traditional toys have gained in popularity since 1982. Estimated U.S. shipments rose 5.8 percent in 1983 and 15.0 percent in 1984. Conversely, estimated U.S. home video game shipments fell 35 percent annually in 1983 and 1984.

    Doll shipments continued their upward trend begun in 1980. The U.S. doll market has been strongly influenced by faddish trends: in the early 1980's,

Source: U.S. Industrial Outlook, Department of Commerce, 1985, pp. 49-1–49-3.

plush or stuffed dolls were popular; more recently, cloth-covered stuffed dolls and traditional plastic dolls. Shipments of U.S.-made dolls and stuffed animals rose an estimated 15.6 percent in 1984 to $670 million. In constant dollars, this was a 16.7 percent increase.

Despite some slight producer price increases for dolls and toys in 1983 and 1984, the general index measuring price changes for each industry actually fell through the first six months of 1984. The producer price index for stuffed toys increased 2.0 percent annually through the first six months of 1984 while the index for children's vehicles (excluding bicycles) rose 3.3 percent annually in the same period. Strong import competition helped keep price increases down.

The U.S. doll and toy market is very dependent on foreign suppliers. Foreign trade data, therefore, provide the most useful and timely information reflecting industry trends.

The strong U.S. dollar and changing consumer preferences led to a 30 percent annual increase in U.S. imports of dolls, toys, games, and children's vehicles during the January-July 1984 period and a 33 percent annual decline in U.S. exports of those products during the same period. Imports of these items totaled an estimated $2.1 billion while exports declined to an estimated $260 million in 1984.

The surge in imports was led by doll and stuffed toy imports, which more than doubled in the first seven months of 1984 compared to the same period of 1983 and totaled an estimated $810 million in 1984. Hong Kong, Taiwan, and South Korea have historically dominated U.S. trade in dolls and stuffed toys, accounting for 80 percent of U.S. imports since 1979. The People's Republic of China (PRC) became a major supplier in the last six months of 1983 and had 7 percent of U.S. doll imports in 1984. Most of the larger U.S.-based producers either own factories in these countries or have locally owned manufacturers produce to U.S. specifications for the U.S. market. Almost all of the PRC trade apparently is between one U.S. manufacturer and the Chinese producers.

The import data reflect the rapid decline in video games' popularity. Imports of video games, including coin- or token-operated games, rose from $15.6 million in 1979 to $610.0 million in 1982, the zenith for domestic video game production. Imports then fell 42 percent in 1983 and another 39 percent in 1984 to an estimated $215 million, a decline which parallels the decline in U.S. production.

Imports of traditional toys rose an estimated 28 percent in 1984 to a total of $1.12 billion, reversing a 1983 decline of 14 percent. As with dolls, the major foreign suppliers are Far East producers who enjoy a substantial wage advantage over U.S.-based producers. Hong Kong and Taiwan together accounted for 53 percent of U.S. traditional toy imports in 1983 and 48 percent in 1984.

Dolls, toys, games, and children's vehicle exports from the United States in 1984 were severely hurt by both the warning of the video game craze and the strong U.S. dollar. The major markets for U.S.-made dolls and toys are Western Europe and Canada, countries which have tastes and income levels similar to the United States. Doll and toy exports to those countries declined

38 percent in 1984 as the dollar generally appreciated against foreign currencies. The largest declines were in video games, which fell 74 percent to an estimated $48.5 million worldwide.

OUTLOOK FOR 1985

The 1985 U.S. market for dolls, toys, games, and children's vehicles should grow 8 percent after inflation. This forecast is based on U.S. economic conditions combined with historical relationships between changes in real incomes, the child population, and real apparent consumption of dolls and toys. Long-term industry trends also indicate that imports will supply more of the U.S. market growth than U.S. production. Shipments of U.S.-made dolls are expected to increase 5.5 percent after adjustment for inflation while the value of domestically produced toys, games, and children's vehicles may increase 6.8 percent after inflation despite a continuing decline in video game shipments.

These growth rates are predicated on real personal incomes growing 4.0 percent and the general unemployment rate falling from 7.5 percent to 6.9 percent in 1985. Also, foreign markets for U.S.-produced dolls and toys are expected to grow more rapidly in 1985, stimulating demand for those items.

LONG-TERM PROSPECTS

Consumer purchases of dolls and toys, including games and children's vehicles, are largely discretionary and faddish, fluctuating greatly from year to year. The variations in doll and toy purchases largely occur within the doll and toy products areas rather than between doll and toy purchases and other expenditures. In constant dollars, annual U.S. apparent consumption of dolls and toys fell only four times from 1965 to 1984. Consumer expenditures on toys and other like items increased almost continually as a share of total constant dollar personal consumption expenditures in the same period.

Many factors help explain this strength in apparent consumption, including strong long-term growth in personal incomes and, more recently, the resurging numbers of children. The expected changes in these variables over the next five years indicate that real apparent consumption of dolls and toys may accelerate its long-term growth pattern, increasing an estimated 6.5 percent annually by 1989. Real personal income, minus transfer payments, is expected to grow 2.6 percent annually from 1984 to 1989 while the population of primary doll and toy users, i.e., children under 10 years of age, is expected to increase 1.0 percent annually in the same period.

Domestic production may not keep pace with the expected market growth, instead continuing to lose market share to foreign manufacturers. Most major U.S. doll and toy producers are multinational entities which shift production to least cost sites; those sites are increasingly in the Far East and Mexico where wages are often less than 20 percent of the U.S. level. Shipments of U.S.-made dolls are expected to increase 3.5 percent annually after inflation while U.S.-produced toys may increase 4.3 percent annually from 1984 to 1989.

CASE 10

Turner Broadcasting Systems, Inc.

WILLIAM H. DAVIDSON
University of
Southern California

G. ROBERT JOSEPH
University of
Virginia

In October 1983, Ted Turner, Bill Bevans (Vice-President of Finance), Steven Korn (Deputy Counsel), and Tench Coxe (Senior Partner, Troutman and Sanders), were discussing Turner Broadcasting's plans to acquire the Satellite News Channel (SNC) from the American Broadcasting Company and Westinghouse Electric Corporation. The purchase could boost Turner Broadcasting System's (TBS) revenues by adding up to seven million SNC subscribers to 23 million who already received Cable News Network (CNN) or CNN Headline News in their homes. Not only would TBS collect more in subscriber fees, but advertisers would pay higher sums to buy airtime on the 24-hour-a-day all-news stations. And if Turner acquired SNC, it would put an end to the ruinous price war that had eroded TBS revenues over the past 18 months.

But TBS had finished 1982 with its third consecutive net loss, and the company's balance sheet showed liabilities totaling $153 million on assets of only $135 million (financial data is presented in Exhibits 1 and 2). Turner wondered whether adding more debt to buy SNC was realistic, and, if so, what price he should pay.

TURNER BROADCASTING

Robert Edward "Ted" Turner III first came to national attention in the summer of 1977 when he skippered the 12-meter yacht "Courageous" to win the America's Cup off Newport, Rhode Island. An outsider to the Northeastern yachting elite, the sports media portrayed him as a newcomer who beat the established champions at their own game, providing Turner with an underdog image that suited him well for his later battles with the television networks:

> Do you know why we're going to be such a big success and why I'm going to make a billion dollars? It's because people know that things are screwed up, and they're looking for a change. It's not that I'm a genius, it's that television is lousy, and the three networks have it all to themselves and they want to keep it lousy. The networks are like the Mafia. The networks are the Mafia. Do you know they spent a quarter of a million dollars in Washington trying to stop my SuperStation from showing movies and sports in people's houses? Well, their day is finished now. It's over. They've made unbelievable profits, and what have they brought us? Mr.

This case was written by G. Robert Joseph, The Darden School, University of Virginia, under the supervision of Associate Professor William H. Davidson, School of Business, University of Southern California, Los Angeles. Copyright © 1984 by The Darden Graduate Business School Sponsors, Charlottesville, Virginia.

TURNER BROADCASTING SYSTEMS, INC.   175

Whipple squeezing the toilet paper. "The $1.98 Cheap Show." "The Newlywed Game." "Love Boat." The networks are run by a greedy bunch of jerks that have hoodwinked the American public, and now I'm riding in on a white horse. (C. Williams, *Lead, Follow or Get out of the Way: The Story of Ted Turner*, New York: Times Books, 1981.)

Although the America's Cup spectators hadn't seen anyone like Turner before, around Atlanta Turner had been considered a local hero for some time. The stories about Turner made him seem larger than life: his maneuvering to rescue his father's billboard business from a consortium of Northern busi-

EXHIBIT 1   TBS Consolidated Income Statement (figures in thousands, except per share data)

	1983	1982	1981	1980
Revenues				
Broadcasting	$136,217	$ 96,647	$ 55,329	$ 35,495
Cable productions	65,169	49,708	27,738	7,201
Professional sports	21,401	16,263	8,840	9,211
Management fees from affiliated company	1,462	2,717	2,835	2,473
Other	283	306	305	230
	$224,532	$165,641	$ 95,047	$ 54,610
Cost and expenses				
Cost of operations	$105,685	$ 81,187	$ 49,036	$ 33,391
Selling, general, and administrative	80,722	60,343	37,067	26,951
Amortization of player, film, and other contract rights	8,674	7,497	4,010	4,013
Depreciation	4,706	4,182	3,469	2,172
Interest expense and amortization of debt discount, restructuring fees, and imputed interest	14,383	13,084	9,673	4,437
	$214,170	$166,293	$103,255	$ 70,964
Operating income (loss)	10,362	(652)	(8,208)	(16,354)
Equity in losses of limited partnerships	(3,350)	(2,698)	(8,208)	(2,905)
Income (loss) before gains on dispositions of properties	7,012	(3,350)	(13,423)	(19,259)
Gains on dispositions of properties	—	—	—	15,684
Income (loss) before provision for income taxes	7,012	(3,350)	(13,423)	(19,259)
Provision for income tax	—	—	—	200
Net income (loss)	$ 7,012	$ (3,340)	$ (13,423)	$ (3,775)
Net income (loss) per common share	0.34	(0.16)	(0.66)	(0.19)
Common shares outstanding	20,393	20,402	20,358	20,062

STRATEGY FORMULATION

EXHIBIT 2 TBS Consolidated Balance Sheet (in thousands, except per share data)

	1983	1982	1981	1980
Assets				
Cash	$ 594	$ 538	$ 504	$ 489
Accounts receivable	31,768	23,731	17,701	9,869
Current portion of film contract rights	12,613	4,516	3,495	2,521
Prepaid expenses	2,177	3,868	1,086	552
Other current assets	4,965	2,585	1,433	1,591
Total current assets	$ 51,667	$ 35,238	$ 24,222	$ 15,022
Property, plant and equipment	71,505	33,555	28,698	26,647
Intangible assets	25,567	34,000	—	—
Film contract rights, less current portion	26,057	15,633	9,464	5,660
Player and other contract rights, less amortization	1,246	1,583	2,084	2,784
Investment in limited partnerships	1,633	1,900	900	2,027
Deferred charges	13,926	6,585	9,623	—
Deferred program production costs	11,432	4,460	—	—
Other assets	2,805	2,232	1,970	1,878
Total assets	$205,838	$135,186	$ 76,961	$ 54,018
Liabilities and Stockholders' Deficit				
Current liabilities				
Short-term borrowings	$ —	$ 49,924	$ 42,783	$ 17,907
Accounts payable	6,954	7,548	3,926	2,079
Accrued expenses	22,551	16,750	11,152	7,196
Deferred income	7,083	7,220	2,226	700
Current portion of long-term debt	14,473	4,266	3,005	8,430
Current portion of obligations for film contract rights	11,317	5,613	3,465	2,456
Current portion of debt-restructuring fees	3,650	3,000	2,253	—
Total current liabilities	$ 66,028	$ 94,321	$ 68,810	$ 38,931
Long-term debt, less current portion	122,404	42,802	7,165	9,825
Obligations for film contract rights, less current portion	13,959	7,379	3,943	2,662
Obligations under employment contracts, net of imputed interest	5,201	3,442	2,560	2,221
Deferred income	562	646	1,313	—
Debt restructuring fees	650	3,000	4,207	—
Other liabilities	7,507	1,097	3,117	1,201
Total liabilities	$216,311	$152,687	$ 91,115	$ 54,840

(Continued)

EXHIBIT 2 (Continued)

	1983	1982	1981	1980
Stockholders' deficit				
Common stock	2,663	2,663	2,663	2,663
Capital in excess of par value	1,508	1,508	1,508	602
Accumulated deficit	(12,734)	(19,746)	(16,396)	(2,973)
Less 906,000 shares of common stock in treasury	(754)	(474)	(474)	(605)
Notes receivable from sales of common stock in treasury	(1,156)	(1,452)	(1,455)	(509)
Total treasury stock	(1,910)	(1,926)	(1,929)	(1,114)
Total stockholders' deficit[1]	$ (10,473)	$ (17,501)	$ (14,154)	$ (822)
Total liabilities and stockholders' deficit	$205,838	$135,186	$ 76,961	$ 54,018

[1] Approximately 87 percent of TBS stock was owned by Ted Turner.

nessmen, rambunctious telethons to gain viewers for his Atlanta television station, and his purchase of the Atlanta Braves to keep them from moving to Toronto. When Turner announced in 1979 that he planned to build an international, 24-hour-a-day news network for cable television there were skeptics—but few of them lived in Atlanta.

In 1963, when Turner was 24, his father took his own life. Turner's father had left his son the family billboard business, Turner Outdoor Advertising, which operated in Atlanta, Macon, and Columbus, Georgia; and Norfolk, Richmond, and Roanoke, Virginia. But Ed Turner also had sold the company to a trio of businessmen from Minneapolis. Ted Turner asked the buyers to nullify the purchase agreement for the business, but the buyers insisted the deal was final. Before the property was transferred, however, Turner fired all the employees of his father's company, rehired them to work for a subsidiary over which he had control, and transferred the billboard-location leases to the subsidiary. The consortium agreed to accept $200,000 worth of stock in Ted Turner's billboard company and returned control of the company to him.

Turner's billboard company soon became a cash generator, and with the proceeds Turner bought a radio station in Chattanooga. Soon after, he acquired four more radio stations, and by 1969 he also owned a sailboat manufacturer, a direct-marketing enterprise, and a silkscreening company. In 1970 he sold most of these companies to buy Channel 17, an unprofitable UHF television station in Atlanta.

It took one year before the television station too became profitable. Turner's strategy was to "counterprogram" the network affiliates in Atlanta, starting all shows five minutes past the hour or half hour to attract viewers as they flipped their channel selectors during the first network commercial break. Turner ran "Star Trek" when the networks were running the national news, showed old movies and Atlanta Braves baseball games, and the station soon had a substantial local audience.

Turner bought the Atlanta Braves in January 1976 and the Atlanta Hawks basketball team in December 1976 to insure that sports programming would continue to be available on Channel 17. Although the baseball team had consistently finished near last place in its division for years, he attracted new players by offering large contracts. A team owner with a high profile, Turner was known for leaping onto the playing field when one of the Braves hit a home run so that he could shake the player's hand as he crossed home plate.

In December 1976, Turner Broadcasting beamed the Channel 17 signal onto RCA's communications satellite. The signal was made available free of charge to cable TV operators, making SuperStation WTBS, as Turner renamed it, the first advertiser-supported cable television network. A year earlier, Home Box Office, the first programming service to offer uninterrupted current movies to cable subscribers, had begun satellite broadcast, so cable systems were already installing satellite receiver dishes when the SuperStation went "on the bird." The installation of satellite antennas accelerated rapidly after the SuperStation became available.

CABLE NEWS NETWORK

In 1979, Turner announced he would broadcast a second satellite-distributed cable programming service, Cable News Network. On June 1, 1980, CNN originated its first day of programming. Broadcasting from a converted private clubhouse on Atlanta's near north side, CNN relied on satellite technology both to distribute its programming to cable subscribers around the nation and also to receive reports from news bureaus in major American and European cities.

The main studio of CNN, located on the first level of the Atlanta headquarters, resembled a cross between a newspaper newsroom and a commodity trading floor. Islands of desks arranged together by functions—reporting, editing, reviewing incoming videotape and satellite transmissions, and reading the news to a camera and national audience—filled an area the size of two basketball courts with computer monitors, television cameras, lighting equipment, typewriters, control panels, and telephones. By combining the studio and work areas, CNN achieved a look on camera that seemed improvised but in fact was meant to enhance its atmosphere of up-to-the-minute timeliness: in the foreground, the anchors read the latest news while viewers could see reporters, editors, and graphics technicians scurrying about behind the main CNN logo.

Because CNN broadcast around the clock, the editorial team had continuous deadlines to meet. Most videotape footage, text, and telephone "voicers" arrived through the assignment desk, an elevated platform where three to five coordinators selected stories for broadcast, told reporters in bureaus around the world when their deadlines were, and routed the flow of news within the CNN studio. From the assignment desk, a story went to videotape and copy editors, who polished and timed each piece and then submitted it to the producer. The producer set the order in which stories would appear on the air, made sure the scripts appeared in front of the anchor men and women at the right time, and supervised the technicians. In the background, graphic artists created the letters and backgrounds that accompanied stories, and special staffs prepared the daily business, sports, and interview shows. The Atlanta headquarters employed about 600 people. Across the hall, another 100 technicians, anchors, editors, and producers summarized CNN's broadcasts into a half-hour short form for CNN Headline News.

Subscriber Revenue

WTBS was offered "free" to cable systems—the cable operators paid no fee to TBS for carrying the service, although they had to pay 10 cents per subscribing household per month to the company that beamed WTBS to the satellite, as required by FCC regulations.

Because of its low cost, WTBS was carried as part of the "basic" channel line-up on cable systems. Cable operators offered their subscribers both basic and several optional tiers of television channels. The basic channels included all television stations operating within thirty-five miles of the subscriber's community, as well as selected national cable networks such as ESPN, USA, and The Weather Channel. This basic service was available for the minimum monthly fee, generally $10 to $20 per month. Tier service cost an additional $5 to $10 per month and included a line-up of premium channels such as HBO, Showtime, or the Disney Channel. CNN was offered on either basic or tier service, depending on the cable system.

For CNN however, Turner charged 20 cents per subscriber household per month from cable operators. This subscriber revenue augmented the advertising fees that CNN collected. That gave Turner Broadcasting two major sources of revenue—advertising sales for airtime on the two channels, and subscriber fees. Because the SuperStation cost relatively little to operate, the cash flow it generated helped to cover the considerable expense of running CNN (see Exhibit 3).

Turner had been the first entrepreneur to put together a national cable network that cable systems could carry on their basic channels. TBS, therefore, provided a valuable marketing tool for the cable operators because they did not have to charge their customers extra for a service that was available only on cable. This innovation, combined with Turner's swashbuckling image, contributed to his favorable relations with cable operators. As a result, the two Turner services were the most widely carried cable services in the U.S. except for ESPN, the sports network. Turner was consistently one of the most requested speakers at cable conventions.

THE CABLE TELEVISION INDUSTRY

The first cable TV system began operations in 1948 in rural Pennsylvania, where hills blocked out TV signals. To sell more television sets, a local storeowner erected an antenna on top of a hill and connected it to the

EXHIBIT 3 Turner Broadcasting System, Inc., Statement of Operations, Itemized by Business Unit (unaudited, figures in thousands)

	1983	1982
Revenue, net of commissions		
Management services	$ 1,473	$ 2,727
WTBS	100,797	78,323
Direct Response revenues	9,000	
TB Sales	7,884	6,393
TPS (program syndication)	11,486	6,393
CNN	51,073	41,787
CNN Headline News	5,526	1,677
Braves	22,456	17,386
Total net revenues	$209,695	$155,609
Expenses		
Management	$ 3,373	$ 3,139
WTBS	60,416	43,308
TB Sales	10,066	7,297
TPS	13,265	9,487
TBS Productions	1,549	—
Turner Educational Services	111	—
CNN	54,085	47,035
CNN Headline News	14,331	10,775
Braves	22,193	17,049
Total expenses	$179,389	$138,090
Operating income	30,306	17,519
Interest	14,383	13,084
Income before noncash charges and equity in limited partnerships	15,923	4,435
Depreciation and amortization	5,763	5,869
Equity in limited partnerships	(3,313)	(2,698)
Net income (loss)	$ 6,847	$ (3,350)

Source: TBS controller

neighborhood's television sets with copper wire. Jack Benny's monologues and Milton Berle's slapstick came in more clearly in those Pennsylvania homes than on the flickering TV sets sold to the rest of the nation, and cable systems began to spring up around the country. Thereafter, hundreds of entrepreneurs built Community Antenna Television (CATV) systems in areas that had poor over-the-air television reception, and the cable industry grew rapidly.

Cable television systems generally operated under a franchise license from the local community, which regulated their fees. As the number of subscribers climbed, the Federal Communications Commission became increasingly involved as it became apparent that CATV systems were competing with broadcast stations under the FCC's authority. The regulatory environment was influenced partly by lobbying from the major networks and their broadcast affiliates. At first NBC, ABC, and CBS welcomed the growth of cable systems because more viewers could see their programming. But they objected when cable systems because more viewers could see their programming. But they objected when cable systems began carrying independent broadcast stations that took viewers away from the networks.

By 1983, cable systems could carry independent broadcast signals provided they paid a fee to the common carrier (the telephone line, microwave, or satellite system that delivered the signal). Independent stations could beam their signals to cable systems around the country, but they were required to pay a royalty for the shows they broadcast to the Copyright Tribunal, a government agency set up to distribute these royalties to the syndicators that owned the TV shows.

The cable industry was highly fragmented; for the most part local entrepreneurs built the systems. Almost 6,000 cable systems operated in the United States in 1983. Increasingly, small systems were being purchased and operated by conglomerates, called Multi-System Operators (MSOs). The largest MSO, Telecommunications Inc., owned 270 cable systems and served 2.5 million subscribers, or 8.6 percent of all the cable households in the nation. The trend toward consolidation of cable systems was accelerating. In 1983, the top 73 MSOs accounted for 20 percent of the cable subscribers in the country (see Exhibit 4).

The chief advantage that an MSO held over the small cable system operator was marketing expertise. The corporate headquarters commonly sent marketing managers to visit the smaller systems and inform them of techniques for boosting the number of subscribers and viewership of their systems. On a street that already was served by the cable company, the cost of adding an additional household was low. By increasing "penetration" (the ratio of cable households to total households available), the cable operator could increase revenues and profitability.

EXHIBIT 4 Turner Broadcasting System, Inc., Systems and Subscribers Analyzed by Number of Subscribers

Number of Suscribers	Systems	Percent of all Systems	Basic Subscribers	Percent of all Subscribers
0–1,000	2,518	43.29	1,126,153	3.88
1,001–5,000	1,916	32.94	4,622,469	15.91
5,001–10,000	551	9.47	3,980,607	13.70
10,001–20,000	384	6.60	5,373,067	18.49
20,001–50,000	249	4.28	7,639,286	26.29
50,000+	73	1.26	5,591,355	19.58
Not available	125	2.15	627,819	2.16
Total	5,816		29,060,756	

Source: ICR, Titsch Communications, September 1983.

The Role of Advertising

Another source of revenue for cable operators was available from sales of advertising on their systems. Most advertiser-supported national services, including CNN, ESPN, USA, CBN, and Lifetime, made a certain number of time slots each hour available for local advertising. For example, at 23 minutes past the hour, CNN ran a public service announcement on its national feed, and cable operators had permission to preempt the spot with a 30-second commercial from the local community. The cable operator would put on a videotape cassette with the commercial recorded on it into a playback machine that would automatically start when it heard the computerized "cue tone" come over the national network. By setting the machine on automatic, the cable operator could collect advertising fees with little incremental labor cost.

The advertising rates charged at the local level followed the same principle that had governed television since the beginning of the networks. Advertisers paid rates that were based on the number of households that were tuned into a certain channel at a given time. Television audience sizes were measured by the A. C. Nielsen Co. and Arbitron, among others. In sample households, a meter connected to the television sent information about the time and channel that the set was tuned to through telephone lines to a central computer. Other households reported their viewing with diaries that contained time schedules for family members to record the shows they watched and the time they spent viewing. Meter data were considered to be more accurate, but diary data provided demographic information about the audiences for various shows. Viewership data were used to determine fees for advertising slots. Broadcasters, ad agencies, and advertisers used Nielsen and Arbitron ratings to calculate the size of the viewing audience for any ad slot. The expected audience size was multiplied by a revenue rate, expressed as a cost per thousand households, to determine fees. For example, if the rating services estimated that NBC delivered 6.7 million households for an episode of "Cheers," and the cost per thousand was $2.50, then a 30-second national commercial would cost $16,750.

Audience size was critical in determining broadcasting revenues, but the revenue rate also varied sharply. The major networks, which established prevailing price levels, set very different rates for different times of day and individual programs. A typical rate for daytime programming would be in the two-dollar range. Rates during prime time averaged about five dollars per thousand households. Advertisers would pay a premium for a show with a 30 rating (30 percent of all viewing households) to ensure a broader audience for their commercial. The purchase of three slots with 10 ratings would not reach as many unique households because of overlap among the viewer populations. Shows with high ratings had the highest cost per thousand households.

CNN used revenue rates that were slightly lower than the major networks. Don Lachowski, Director of Advertising Sales for TBS, explained:

> It's more expensive to buy cable ad slots. The ad agency doesn't get higher fees for working with cable broadcasters, but their costs go up because they have to deal with more runs, duplications, and more work. It used to be simple for them.

They would just talk to the three networks. Life has gotten complicated for the ad people. We have to give them an incentive to use cable. We started out 30% below the networks in terms of cost; now we're about 10% below the third network.

Although ad fees on WTBS or CNN were negotiable, Turner Broadcasting had a policy of enforcing integrity in pricing for ad slots. The advertising sales department frequently had to reject business because of pricing considerations.

Cable networks were in competition with the national networks and independent broadcasters for ad revenues. Before the boom of cable service, the networks had enjoyed a 95 percent share of household viewership. But by 1977, the networks' share had declined to 86 percent, and by 1983 it was estimated that only 77 percent of the viewing audience was tuned to the networks during primetime. The networks were losing viewers to the national cable networks, to local independent stations, and to the Public Broadcasting System. However, the major networks' share of advertising revenues remained at over 90 percent of total spending on television media.

NEW TECHNOLOGIES

Both the networks and the cable services were threatened by the advent of new television technologies. Although still experimental in 1984, direct broadcast satellite television (DBS) opened the possibility that homeowners could buy their own three-foot-diameter satellite dish antennas to receive the same programming that the cable services provided—but without the monthly subscription charge. A second technology, low-powered television, was being encouraged by the FCC. Local stations broadcasting at low wattage would be able to program their signals without the usual requirements that the FCC required of larger stations: public service programming, news programming, and local access that added to the overhead expense of regular television stations. An additional development, satellite master antenna television (SMATV), allowed owners of hotels and apartment complexes to buy their own seven-meter-diameter satellite dish antennas and receive cable programming, which they could provide to living units through a small-scale cable system. Already widespread in 1984, SMATV systems provided the same service as the local cable franchise but without the monthly charge. They had resulted in substantial erosion of cable-system revenues.

Cable itself promised to change rapidly during the next few decades. Since 1974, most new cable laid was designed for two-way communication under the expectation that consumers could shop, bank, and even subscribe to magazines and databases at home. Some industry analysts foresaw an age of electronic mail, where paper documents would be replaced by communication over television. And while the divestment of AT and T's operating subsidiaries had injected ambiguity into the role that the telephone company would play in the future, there was speculation that by the end of the century telephone and television service would have merged.

OUTLOOK

Despite these competing technologies, the number of households wired for cable television was forecast to increase through the end of the decade. Industry forecasts projected that the number of cable households would reach 58.9 million in 1990, an annual growth rate of 9.8 percent. That would represent 62 percent of all U.S. television households (see Exhibit 5).

The increasing popularity of cable meant that advertisers could no longer reach their intended audiences merely by buying time on the three networks, as they had done for decades. In 1982, the advertising industry spent $12.7 billion for national and local spot television advertising. Cable programmers received $200 million of that total. By 1990, according to projections by RCA Corporation, advertising expenditures would reach $32.3 billion, of which the cable industry would receive $3.5 billion. The network and network-affiliated stations would receive a total of $24.6 billion in 1990, up from $11.1 billion in 1982, according to RCA. The projections assumed that the advertising industry would shift substantial portions of their budgets to cable.

To advertisers, cable presented the advantage of reaching an audience with more buying power per person than the American public as a whole. Surveys showed that cable households tended to be younger, more affluent, and more disposed toward owning household appliances, sports equipment, and other consumer durables.

Cable programmers like Turner Broadcasting used these superior demographics to sell advertising. For example, they argued that companies that made sports equipment, nutritional supplements, and other health-oriented products would reach the right consumers by advertising on Cable Health Network. ESPN, a national network that broadcast sports events, pitched its airtime as appealing to males aged 25–54 and attracted advertising from automobile, beer, and tool companies. MTV, a station that presented rock and roll videos, attracted a teen-aged audience. The Financial News Network, on the other hand, broadcast only during business hours and advertised subscriptions to business publications like the Wall Street Journal.

In addition to SuperStation WTBS, two other "superstations" were reaching subscribers outside their broadcast areas. WOR in New York City and WGN in Chicago both transmitted a satellite signal that could be carried by cable system. But they were "passive" superstations. Station management placed almost no emphasis on attracting a national audience. The impetus for national distribution came instead from the common carrier that collected a subscriber fee for providing the satellite link. Thus viewers in places like Portland, Oregon, found they were frequently urged to bring their car-repair needs to West Diversey Street in Chicago, or to buy tickets to the latest Broadway hits.

Although most national cable networks hoped to attract specific audiences, Turner Broadcasting had aimed its programming at the general public. SuperStation WTBS showed old movies and television series that had previously succeeded on network television, including "Hogan's Heroes," "The Andy Griffith Show," "The Munsters," and "Rat Patrol." Together with its sports events (Atlanta Braves baseball, Atlanta Hawks basketball, and Big Time

EXHIBIT 5   Penetration of TBS Services

	December 1982	December 1983 (estimated)
Superstation WTBS		
Homes (thousands)	24,990	28,492
Percent of U.S.	0.30	0.34
Number of systems	4,885	5,803
Cable News Network		
Homes (thousands)	17,493	25,140
Percent of U.S.	0.21	0.30
Number of systems	3,240	4,278
CNN Headline News		
Homes (thousands)	2,393	9,860
Percent of U.S.	0.03	0.12
Number of systems	340	983

Subscriber Forecasts through 1990

	Estimated households	U.S. TV households (%)
Cable penetration		
1985	40,619	84,800 (48)
1986	44,359	85,800 (52)
1987	48,348	86,800 (56)
1988	52,241	87,800 (60)
1989	55,944	88,800 (63)
1990	59,537	89,800 (66)
SuperStation WTBS		
1985	33,750	84,800 (40)
1986	36,894	85,800 (43)
1987	40,796	86,800 (47)
1988	44,778	87,800 (51)
1989	48,840	88,800 (55)
1990	52,084	89,800 (58)
Cable News Network		
1985	32,817	84,800 (39)
1986	38,009	85,800 (44)
1987	42,359	86,800 (49)
1988	46,358	87,800 (53)
1989	50,438	88,800 (57)
1990	53,700	89,800 (60)

Source: TBS Research.

wrestling), WTBS positioned itself as classic family entertainment. CNN, on the other hand, broadcast news and features that viewers could tune in for up-to-the-minute reports of major happenings. Nielsen research showed that CNN viewership increased dramatically whenever an unpredicted, major news event took place, such as the assassination attempt on President Reagan. Although the channel showed news all day and night, however, its programming was not confined to breaking news. The schedule included a daily talk and news show at noon, and evening business report at 7 P.M. Eastern Time, and an interview show at 10 P.M.

Because viewership ratings determined the advertising sales revenue that Turner services would receive, the company was concerned with two components of viewership. First was the number of households that could receive WTBS and CNN, that is, the number of cable systems that allocated a channel to each service. Because WTBS had been available to cable systems for a longer time than CNN, it was available in more households: 28.5 million in October 1983 on 5,803 cable systems, representing 74 percent of all cable homes and 34 percent of all television homes. CNN was available in 25.1 million cable homes via 4,278 cable systems.

The second component of viewership was the number of households that were actually tuned into one of the two services during a given hour. Exhibit 6 shows an itemization of ratings by time of day, revealing that WTBS reached its highest viewership levels during weekend afternoons, when it ran old movies.

EXHIBIT 6 WTBS Ratings by Daypart

Daypart		Rating	Households Delivered (thousands)	Programming
M–Su	8–11 P.M.	4.0	1,173	Prime movies
M–F	7 A.M.–9 P.M.	2.8	821	Kids sitcoms
M–F	9 A.M.–3 P.M.	2.2	645	Movies/soaps
M–F	3 A.M.–6 P.M.	3.1	909	Kids programs
M–F	6 P.M.–8 P.M.	3.8	1,115	Sitcoms
M–F	11 P.M.–1 A.M.	1.3	381	Callins/late show
Sat	8 A.M.–1 P.M.	3.4	997	Morning movies
Sat	1 P.M.–6 P.M.	5.4	1,584	Afternoon movies
Sun	8 A.M.–1 P.M.	5.3	1,554	Sitcoms/Academy Award Theater
Sun	1 P.M.–6 P.M.	6.2	1,818	Afternoon movies
Sa–Su	6 P.M.–8 P.M.	4.7	1,379	Wrestling

Cable News Network Ratings by Daypay/Program

Time		Program	Rating	Households (thousands)
M–F	6 A.M.–9 A.M.	Daybreak	0.3	75
M–F	9 A.M.–12 N	Daywatch	0.7	176
M–F	12 N–2 P.M.	Take Two	0.7	176
M–F	2 P.M.–5 P.M.	Afternoon News	0.5	126
M–F	5 P.M.–7 P.M.	Newswatch	0.8	201
M–F	7–7:30 P.M.	Moneyline	1.0	251
M–F	7:30 P.M.–8 P.M.	Crossfire	1.3	327
M–F	8 P.M.–10 P.M.	Prime News	0.7	176
M–F	10 P.M.–11 P.M.	Freeman Reports	0.6	151
Sa–Su	6 A.M.–12 N	Weekend News	0.9	226
Sa–Su	12 N–6 P.M.	Weekend News	1.1	277

These viewership ratings were dwarfed by the networks, however. On a typical evening, more than half of all the televisions in the United States were tuned to the networks. In cable homes, however, the number of households watching network programming was estimated to be 13 percent lower than in noncable homes.

Cable News Network attracted considerably fewer viewers. With the average cost per thousand for a 30-second national commercial at $2.00 on CNN, the company was very concerned about ratings. They calculated that a gain of one-tenth of a rating point would result in $10 million in additional advertising revenue over the course of a year.

Turner Broadcasting advertised its services through two main channels. National advertising appeared in general circulation magazines like *Time, Esquire,* and *TV Guide*. These ads were administered by the advertising and promotion department. Also, each Turner network ran commercials for the other networks during regular programming. For example, CNN devoted two minutes an hour to promotions for WTBS, featuring upcoming movies and sports events.

The second mechanism for advertising WTBS and CNN was carried out by Turner Cable Sales, the division charged with signing up cable systems to carry the services. As a sales incentive, Turner Cable Sales provided funds to each cable system, based on the number of subscribers it had, for spending on local advertising. Turner Cable Sales also provided free "marketing materials" to cable systems, including radio scripts, newspaper advertising layouts, T-shirts, baseball caps, direct mail inserts to be included with monthly cable system bills, coffee mugs, and even copies of a biography of Ted Turner. The two advertising and promotion departments were budgeted to spend $11.8 million in 1984.

SATELLITE NEWS CHANNEL

Despite the above efforts, Turner Broadcasting had been unprofitable since the startup of CNN in 1980. CNN had lost $2 million per month in 1983. One factor that contributed to CNN's continuing losses was the advent of a competitor, Satellite News Channel. A joint venture of the American Broadcasting Company and Group W Communications (the media subsidiary of Westinghouse Electric Corporation), Satellite News Channel began broadcasting on June 1, 1982. The channel provided 24-hour-a-day news reports in 18-minute segments.

ABC and Group W had announced in late 1981 that they would form Satellite News Channel. One month later, Ted Turner announced his company would begin a new programming service, CNN Headline News, which would broadcast half-hour summaries of the latest news in a format similar to SNC's. Turner's news service began broadcasting on December 31, 1981. When SNC came on line six months later, the two companies found themselves competing head-to-head for limited channel capacity on the nation's cable systems.

The Turner Cable Sales organization, faced for the first time with competition from another all-news channel, stepped up the pace of signing on new cable systems to carry the Turner services. Whereas Turner Broadcasting had charged cable systems 20 cents per subscriber per month for CNN, it offered to provide CNN Headline News for free. The rate for CNN was 15 cents for cable systems that also carried SuperStation WTBS on its basic selection channels, providing an incentive for the operator to carry both services at once. SNC, however, offered to pay each cable system that carried it as much as 25 cents per subscriber. SNC also offered large sign-up bonuses to new cable customers. The consequence was an erosion in the price that cable systems were willing to pay for CNN. Where Turner Broadcasting had intended to collect an average of between 16 and 18 cents per subscriber, the average monthly rate per subscriber stood at only 7 cents by September 1983. These price cuts usually took the form of fixed fee contracts where large MSOs were guaranteed a maximum total charge for CNN regardless of the number of households served. Where CNN had been budgeted to bring $300 million in subscriber fees in 1983, the actual number was estimated to be $21 million.

At the same time, it was difficult to trim CNN's costs because of the high broadcast standards that the station strove to uphold. Said TBS controller Paul Beckham:

> News is a bottomless pit. There's always something happening somewhere that someone would like to cover. Anyway, about 90 percent of the cost of running CNN is fixed, so that when we saw that revenues were coming in under budget there wasn't a lot of play in the system for us to work with.

CNN's budget for 1983 had been $59.1 million. The CNN budget for 1984 was $70.9 million.

The SNC Acquisition

In March 1983, Turner launched a legal salvo against SNC and its corporate parents. It sued Group W for allegedly preventing Turner access to cable systems owned by Group W Cable, an MSO owned by Westinghouse. These systems totaled about two million subscribers in 1983 and included several key markets, such as most of Manhattan. Turner Broadcasting charged Group W with restraint of trade, and charged that it was forcing cable systems it owned to carry SNC rather than the Turner news services.

Lawyers for both sides spent the spring of 1983 in the discovery phase, photocopying internal documents and analyzing details of each other's businesses. At the same, Turner filed a second suit against Group W, charging them with failure to pay overdue fees and cancellation payments owed to Turner Broadcasting from cable systems acquired by Group W. This suit had become the focal point of the confrontation between SNC and Turner by June 1983. In July, Griffin Bell (former Attorney General under President Carter), as the chief lawyer for SNC, suggested that the two parties search for a "larger settlement." In September, Dan Ritchie, chairman of Group W, suggested that Mr. William Daniels mediate the negotiations between Turner and SNC. Mr. Daniels, Chairman of Daniels and Associates, was an exmarine who was considered the founding father of the cable TV industry. Daniels conducted "shuttle diplomacy" between New York and Atlanta to communicate offers and counteroffers as they developed.

On September 16, the *Wall Street Journal* reported that Turner Broadcasting was negotiating the acquisition of SNC. The TBS stock price rose 5¾ points to 31 in the first three hours before trading was halted by the Securities and Exchange Commission. Turner's lawyers met with the SEC to establish that no leak or insider trading had occurred. They also met with officials of the Regulated Industries Section of the Anti-Trust Division to review plans for the acquisition.

By early October, a preliminary agreement had been worked out in the on-going sessions between SNC and Turner lawyers and management. All major obstacles had been cleared except the issue of acquisition price. It was difficult to establish a value for the company as it was unclear when the service would become profitable. SNC had lost an estimated $80–90 million since its founding. SNC had generated less than $3 million in ad revenue during that period. In addition, field salesmen from Turner Cable Sales Division were reporting that cable system operators had begun to inquire about switching from SNC to CNN. With these issues in mind, the Turner team began their strategy session to prepare for the final round of negotiations with the SNC representatives in Atlanta. Exhibits 7, 8, and 9 provide additional information about the industry.

EXHIBIT 7 Pro Forma Income Statement of a Typical Cable System
(figures in thousands)[1]

Pay-TV	Price to Subscriber	Cost to Cable Operator	Pay-TV Penetration
HBO	$7.00	4.50	0.33
Showtime	$7.00	2.50	0.12
PRISM	$9.00	5.00	0.26
Cinemax	$4.00	1.50	0.08

Revenues	
Basic	$6,139.5
Installation fees	28.6
Pay-TV (net)	2,962.4
Total revenues	$9,130.5
Expenses	
Basic expense	$3,095.3
Franchise fee	456.5
Depreciation	1,658.4
Total	$5,210.2
Profit before tax	$3,920.3
Taxes	$2,254.2
Investment tax credit	$1,692.8

[1] Assumptions: miles of cable = 900; basic subscriber penetrations = 0.455; basic monthly fee = $7.00.

Source: G. Kent Webb (1983) *The Economics of Cable Television*. Lexington, MA: Lexington Books, pp. 134–135.

EXHIBIT 8 Twenty-five Largest Cable Satellite Services, 1983

Video Service	Programming	Subscribers (million)	Percent of U.S. homes
ESPN (Briston, CT)	Sports events	28.5	34.2
WTBS (Atlanta, GA)	Independent station	27.7	33.3
Cable News Network (Atlanta, GA)	News/special features	22.6	27.1
CBN Cable Network (Virginia Beach, VA)	Religion/family	22.2	26.7
USA Cable Network (Glen Rock, NJ)	Sports/entertainment	20.0	24.0
C-SPAN (Washington, D.C.)	House of Representatives and politics	15.7	18.8
MTV Music Television (New York, NY)	Video rock music	15.0	18.0
Cable Health Network (New York, NY)	Health	14.0	16.8
Financial News Network (Santa Monica, CA)	Finance	12.8	15.4
ARTS (New York, NY)	Culture	12.6	15.1
Home Box Office (New York, NY)	Movies/specials	12.5	15.0
WGN (Chicago, IL)	Independent station	10.9	13.1
The Nashville Network (Nashville, TN)	Country music	10.0	12.0
The Weather Channel (Atlanta, GA)	National/local weather	10.0	12.0
Daytime (New York, NY)	Women	9.5	11.4
Satellite Program Network (New York, NY)	Variety	8.8	10.6
MSN–The Information Channel (New York, NY)	Variety	8.7	10.4
PTL Satellite Network (Charlotte, NC)	Religion	8.5	10.2
CNN Headline News (Atlanta, GA)	News cycles	7.8	9.4
Black Entertainment Television (Washington, D.C.)	Black studies	5.1	6.1
Showtime (New York, NY)	Movies/specials	4.7	5.6
WOR (New York, NY)	Independent station	4.3	5.2
ACSN—The Learning Channel (Washington, D.C.)	Education/community	3.8	4.6
Trinity Broadcasting Network (Santa Ana, CA)	Religion	3.4	4.1

Source: NCTA Satellite Services Book, December 1983.

EXHIBIT 9 Estimated Cable TV Network Advertising Revenue
(figures in millions)

Network	1982 Gross Ad Revenue	1983 Gross Ad Revenue	1984 Projected Ad Revenue
ARTS	$ 2.1	$ 1.5	$ 1.3
BET	1.8	2.5	4.3
CBN	6.5	12.5	26.0
CHN	1.9	6.8	—
Country Music TV	—	—	0.8
CNN	24.0	31.5	45.0
CNN Headline	1.5	2.0	7.5
Daytime	1.5	2.2	—
ESPN	26.0	41.0	60.0
FNN	1.8	3.6	10.5
Lifetime	—	—	21.0
MSN	0.5	0.3	0.5
MTV	6.8	24.0	36.0
Nashville	—	5.9	17.5
SIN	1.5	1.8	2.2
SNC	1.5	1.9	—
SPN	0.7	0.9	1.8
USA	18.5	29.5	41.6
Weather Channel	0.9	2.5	4.1
WGN	8.0	10.0	12.0
WOR	5.0	5.0	5.0
WTBS	85.0	117.0	148.0
Totals	$195.2	$302.6	$448.7

Source: Paul Kagan Associates, Inc.

INDUSTRIAL HIGHLIGHT

Broadcasting Industry

Below is a capsule summary of the cable television segment of the broadcasting industry, of which Turner Broadcasting Systems, Inc. is a part. Information in this highlight was compiled by the U.S. Department of Commerce and focuses on this industry during the approximate period of time covered in the case. Keep in mind that industrial highlights contained in this text are not intended as a complete synopsis of an industry, but as a profile of certain issues that can be relevant to the case situation.

CURRENT SITUATION

The cable television industry continued to show strong growth in 1982. The number of subscribers to basic cable service increased an estimated 2.1 million, to 22.1 million. Basic revenues reached an estimated $2.4 billion, up nearly 17 percent from 1981. Of the basic cable subscribers, an estimated 15 million also paid an additional fee for one or more tiers of premium service. Revenues for this premium service—which primarily provides broadcasts of motion pictures and sports events—amounted to an estimated $1.4 billion. These revenues are shared by the cable systems, program suppliers, motion picture and program producers, and sports organizations.

Development of Cable TV

Cable TV service began as a means of bringing television to small communities lacking either a local station or adequate reception from distant television stations. Later, cable was introduced in suburban areas and in a few small cities, where it provided programs from one or two distant and local stations. But the higher cost of installing cable in larger cities, as well as the greater variety of TV programs already available, kept cable systems out of many urban markets.

Domestic communications satellites revolutionized the cable TV industry by providing a low cost method for distributing programming to individual cable systems. This was followed by the establishment of cable program

Source: U.S. Industrial Outlook, Department of Commerce, 1983, pp. 45-4 to 45-5.

services, such as Home Box Office, Showtime, the Movie Channel, Home Theater Network, and numerous others. These provide premium programs for delivery to cable subscribers willing to pay a premium fee. Approximately 50 firms were supplying video program service to cable systems by the latter part of 1982.

The additional revenues produced by premium program services are making it economically attractive for cable companies to wire the larger cities, and a number of major municipalities awarded cable franchises in 1982. The competitive award of cable franchises is now either underway or under study in most of the other unwired cities. The amount of time required between the initial study to the drafting of requirements for a franchise and the awarding of the franchise may be many months, particularly in larger communities. Consumer demand for a wider choice of programing than available from conventional TV broadcasting, and, especially, for the premium entertainment available through pay cable has now become the driving force for growth and profitability in the industry.

OUTLOOK FOR 1983

The cable TV industry will continue to expand in 1983. The number of basic subscribers is expected to increase 2.9 million, reaching a projected 25 million by the end of the year, while basic revenues are expected to rise 16 percent to approximately $2.8 billion, without adjustment for inflation. The number of premium pay cable subscribers is projected to reach 18.3 million, and premium pay cable revenues should reach about $1.8 billion, up 25 percent for the year.

New program suppliers will enter the market in 1983, and experiments with interactive cable technologies and with techniques for the cablecasting of news and information will continue during the year.

LONG-TERM PROSPECTS

Cable television will continue to increase its penetration of TV households during the 1980s. By the end of 1987, the number of basic cable subscribers is expected to reach 37 million, for a 42 percent share of total TV homes. These subscribers will provide about $5 billion in basic cable revenues annually. An expected 33 million of these basic subscribers will pay an additional fee for one or more tiers of premium program services, adding revenues of $3.3 billion. By the end of the decade, the number of basic cable subscribers may reach 49 million, providing $6.6 billion in revenues. Revenues from subscribers to premium service could amount to $5.9 billion, from 44 million subscribers, in 1990.

Cable systems are highly capital intensive. Many systems are highly leveraged financially. Despite high interest rates, capital has been available for the expansion of cable TV systems. During the 1970s, the sale price of an operating cable system ran about $300 per subscriber. By 1982, however, competition among investors had increased prices to the $600 to $1,000 per subscriber range. This increase reflected the prospects for increased revenues from premium services. The attractiveness of cable for investors lies in its predictability, its quasi-monopoly position as a municipally franchised operation, and its potential for future revenue growth from additional subscribers, new services, and rate increases.

The large number of channels available on newer cable systems and the growing number of cable program services are placing increasing demands on the suppliers of programs. Motion pictures, supplemented by sports, have been the mainstay of pay cable systems. Since the supply of revenue-producing motion pictures and sports events is not infinite, program suppliers are looking for new sources of entertainment programing and other video fare. Producers of motion pictures and other forms of entertainment will benefit from this rising demand and competition for their products. The already high production costs of feature programs made for TV—recovered at present through network, syndication, and overseas release—will become proportionately more costly if the programs are made primarily for cable. Cable program suppliers will also seek to increase the availability of special interest programing appealing to specific demographic or other groups.

The amount of advertising on cable remains small. An estimated $200 million was spent for advertising on cable TV channels during 1982. As the cable audience increases in size during the 1980s, and as more information on cable viewing becomes available, expenditures for advertising on cable will increase. Cable will share in the spending that heretofore had gone exclusively to broadcasters.

News and Information by Cable

The involvement of publishers in cable will expand during the 1980s. Cable systems, with their multiplicity of channels, are not subject to the pressures felt by the broadcast networks to offer programs attractive to mass audiences; they remain free, in other words, to devote some of their channels to the dissemination and retrieval of information. Newspaper and magazine publishers have already recognized this and have begun to enter the field, either by acquiring cable systems or by providing information services to cable systems.

The electronic delivery of news and information can take several forms. The simplest is the direct sequential transmission of textual material over one or more conventional cable channels to a conventional television receiver. A second technique, known as teletext, provides owners of decoder-equipped TV receivers with a choice of 60 to 100 periodically updated pages of information. Transmitted without interfering with conventional TV broadcasts, teletext information is invisible without a decoder. A third method involves two-way interaction between a special keyboard/keypad equipped TV receiver, which acts as a display device, and one or more computer data banks. The cable system can provide the two-way channel to the computer either directly or in conjunction with a telephone line. In addition to providing information, two-way systems can provide financial and shopping services.

The traditional television networks have also begun to enter the cable TV field, primarily as sources of programs. They expect to capitalize on their programing strength and to expand their participation in cable during the 1980s. Up until now, however, the FCC has not permitted TV networks to own cable systems. Any major relaxation of this policy would permit the networks to take equity positions in the cable industry.

Cable TV has been competing with the TV broadcasting industry for the viewing audience ever since it began to import "off the air" programs from distant TV stations. Cable will face further competition during the 1980s from stations in the multipoint distribution service (MDS), from satellite master antenna TV systems (SMATV) in apartment developments, from subscription television (STV) broadcasts from conventional TV stations, and from satellites that broadcast directly to homes.

MDS stations distribute premium programs by microwave to commercial and private subscribers. Satellite master antenna TV systems deliver premium programing from satellites by cable to paying subscribers within hotels, motels, and apartment complexes. Subscription TV (STV) services broadcast premium programs over conventional TV stations in scrambled form to descrambler-equipped receivers of paying subscribers. Direct broadcast satellite (DBS) service transmits premium programs directly to specially equipped receivers in the homes of paying subscribers.

The marketplace will determine the relative growth of these alternative means for the distribution of TV programing in the remainder of the 1980s. Nonetheless, cable TV, with its large number of channels, its capability for two-way interactive communication, and its ability to provide public service and public access channels, is expected to continue its strong growth.

ADDITIONAL REFERENCES

Broadcasting, Broadcasting Publications, Inc., 1735 DeSales Street, N.W. Washington, DC 20036.

Broadcasting Yearbook, Broadcasting Publications, Inc., 1735 DeSales Street, N.W. Washington, DC 20036.

Television Digest, published weekly by Television Digest, Inc., 1836 Jefferson Place, N.W. Washington, DC 20036.

Television Factbook, published annually by Television Digest, Inc., 1836 Jefferson Place, N.W. Washington, DC 20036.

Television/Radio Age, Television Editorial Corp., 1270 Avenue of the Americas, New York, NY 10020.

Video Age International, International TV Age Corp., 211 East 51st Street, New York, NY 10022.

C A S E   11

Pontiac Division of General Motors

PETER LANGENHORST
Pontiac Division
General Motors

WILLIAM E. FULMER
University of Virginia

"WE BUILD EXCITEMENT, PON-TI-AC!"

As he watched the sleek, sporty, black Firebird Trans Am and the fiery red Fiero in the new TV commercial, J. Michael Losh, the 40-year-old general manager of the Pontiac Division of General Motors, was convinced that Pontiac had returned to the tradition of a sporty image. According to Losh, "We're not going to be the low-priced division, we're not going to be selling luxury products, we're not going to have the broadest range of products. What we're going to sell are sporty and expressive cars." Although Pontiac's goals for 1987 were established—900,000 cars and 8.5 percent of the U.S. market—Losh needed to consider the direction Pontiac should take in the 1990s. Since GM's market share had dropped to 41 percent in 1986 and profits were expected to be under $3 billion, down more than $1 billion from 1985, new pressures were being felt at Losh's level. A significant pressure was Roger Smith's goal of reducing white-collar employment by 25 percent by 1990.

HISTORY OF PONTIAC IN GM[1]

The beginnings of Pontiac were credited to a successful young businessman named Edward M. Murphy, who in 1893 started the Pontiac Buggy Company in Pontiac, Michigan. In the next 10 years, Murphy became increasingly interested in the horseless carriages that began to appear around the streets of Pontiac. Sensing the automobile was here to stay and not just a rich man's novelty, he decided to enter the motor business by purchasing a two-cylinder engine from a well-known engineer in the field of engine design, A. P. Brush. Four years later, in 1907, Murphy equipped a section of his buggy-making facility for car production and founded the Oakland Motor Car Company. With an initial investment of $200,000, Murphy produced the two-cylinder Oakland, and in 1908 he introduced a four-cylinder Model K, a more powerful and competitively priced vehicle. Production of the Model K was 278 in 1908 and 1,035 in 1909.

This case was written by Peter Langenhorst, under the supervision of Professor William E. Fulmer, The Colgate Darden Graduate School of Business Administration, University of Virginia. Copyright © The Colgate Darden Graduate School Sponsors, 1987.

[1] Excerpts of the history of Pontiac were taken from *Automotive News*, GM 75th Anniversary Issue, September 16, 1983; *General Motors, The First 75 Years of Transportation Products*, from the editors of Automobile Quarterly; and *PMD Today*, an internal Pontiac newsletter.

Because of its initial success, the company attracted the attention of another automobile entrepreneur, William C. Durant. Durant had already started to buy automobile companies to form the nucleus of what would become the General Motors Corporation. In 1909 the GM board of directors approved the purchase of a half-interest in the Oakland Motor Car Company. Oakland joined the merging General Motors Company, which already included Buick and Oldsmobile car companies. (GM added Cadillac Motor Car Company in 1910 and Chevrolet Motor Car Company in 1918).

Murphy, considered by Durant to be a potential future leader in GM, died in 1909 at the age of 45. GM then took full control of the Oakland company, and a longtime friend and associate of Murphy's, L. L. Dunlap, succeeded him as manager. (A complete list of all Pontiac general managers is in Exhibit 1.)

In the following years, Oakland saw its production boom, even through tight financial times. It fast became a leader in ideas and products within the GM organization. The Model K grew to production of 4,639 vehicles in 1910. Following World War I, despite the warnings of skeptics, Oakland successfully put closed bodies on its light cars, and it pioneered a new, fast-drying Duco lacquer paint in 1923.

In 1926 Oakland introduced a new six-cylinder vehicle at the New York Auto Show. The Pontiac Six, or "Chief of the Sixes" as it was advertised, was named after Chief Pontiac of the Ottawas, who had ruled all Indian tribes bounded by the Great Lakes, the Alleghenies, and the Mississippi River. The new Pontiac, lighter than previous six-cylinder models, caught the public's favor, and 76,742 vehicles were sold in 1926.

EXHIBIT 1   Pontiac Division, General Managers

Oakland Motor Company	1907–08	Edward M. Murphy
	1909–10	Lee Dunlap
	1911–14	George P. Daniels
	1916–20	Fred W. Warner
	1921–23	George H. Hannum
	1924–30	Alfred R. Glancy
	1931	Irving J. Reuter
Pontiac Division	1932–33	William S. Knudsen/F. O. Tanner
	1933–51	Harry J. Klingler
	1951–52	Arnold Lenz
	1952–56	Robert M. Critchfield
	1956–61	Semon E. Knudsen
	1961–65	Elliott M. Estes
	1965–69	John Z. DeLorean
	1969–72	F. James McDonald
	1972–75	Martin J. Caserio
	1975–78	Alex C. Mair
	1978–80	Robert C. Stempel
	1980–84	William E. Hoglund
	1984–	J. Michael Losh

Source: *Automotive News*, GM 75 Years Anniversary Issue, 9/16/83.

Alfred P. Sloan, Jr., president of GM at the time, saw this entrant as another car to fill a slot in the wide range of automobile buyers' preferences. Backed by his famous statement, "A car for every purse and purpose," Sloan began to position the car divisions to meet that need, spanning the market with Chevrolet, Oldsmobile, Oakland, Buick Standard, Buick Master, and Cadillac. He had seen two gaps in the lineup, however, one between Chevrolet and Oldsmobile, and the other between Buick Master and Cadillac. The introduction of the new Pontiac Six filled the gap between Chevrolet and Oldsmobile, while the new LaSalle by Cadillac filled the other.

It was evident that production facilities were too small to accommodate both the new Pontiac and the existing Oakland car lines, so a new plant site was developed on 246 acres on the city's north side. Three assembly lines, an engine plant, a sheet metal plant, and a parts manufacturing plant were erected.

In the late 1920s, a shrinking automobile market and the onslaught of the Depression damaged the auto industry. While Pontiac's sales remained strong, Oakland's sales all but vanished, and with corporate cost cutting and consolidation, the Oakland Motor Car Company was terminated, as the Pontiac line became the new division, and was given a new name.

In 1933 Harry J. Klingler, then sales manager at Chevrolet, became general manager of Pontiac, the first to do so who was neither from engineering nor from manufacturing. GM felt Pontiac's engineering and manufacturing were satisfactory, so the concentration shifted to marketing. Klingler's first years were spent primarily on personnel changes, including bringing key marketing people from Chevrolet. The first two years of Klingler's management fell short of the long-range plan of 400,000 cars a year, but under Klingler, Pontiac made its greatest leap forward. In 1935 the first Pontiac engineered under his leadership was introduced. It had a distinctive silver streak on the radiator grille, which became the first identifying symbol of the Pontiac car. In 1935 sales hit 180,000 units, and production could not keep up with dealer orders. In 1941 Pontiac sold 330,061 units, becoming the largest producer in its price class ($3,000–$4,000) and the fifth largest in the nation.

Pontiac production ceased with the U.S. entrance into World War II, as auto facilities were converted to aid the war effort. Passenger-car manufacture resumed in 1945, at which time an expansion program was launched to increase production of Pontiacs by 50 percent.

In 1951 Klingler was moved to vice president of Vehicle Production at GM, and Arnold Lenz became general manager. Lenz's sudden death in 1952 led to R.M. Critchfield's taking over. Critchfield saw a need to expand and modernize the Pontiac operation. A new car-finish building and a newly modernized V-8 engine plant were completed in 1954. A sales record of 581,860 cars was set one year later.

Semon E. (Bunkie) Knudsen, the son of a former GM president, took over Pontiac in 1956. As the youngest GM general manager at the time (age 43), he proceeded to refocus Pontiac's image away from big, boxy cars. Knudsen put together a new engineering group headed by Chief Engineer Elliott (Pete) Estes from Oldsmobile and John Z. DeLorean from Packard. The team methodically went to work developing new models. An image of youthful cars emerged.

In three years the Knudsen/Estes/DeLorean team changed the product lineup. In the fall of 1960, following intensive R&D and testing, Pontiac introduced a completely new car line, the Tempest series. Fresh in styling, the Tempest became an immediate success and was recognized by the corporation and the media as the outstanding auto engineering achievement of the year.

When Knudsen became general manager of the Chevrolet Division in 1961, Estes was named the new general manager of Pontiac. He was credited with many engineering innovations in Pontiac cars. One of the most popular was the "wide track" principle, which supplied a car with a wider wheel base than before for better road handling. In addition to his engineering innovations, Estes was successful in raising Pontiac to a third-place position in U.S. sales, trailing only Chevrolet and Ford. Sales soared to nearly 700,000 units, and U.S. market share rose to nearly 9 percent.

In 1965 Fisher Body plants and most assembly plants were combined into the General Motors Assembly Division (GMAD) and a move was begun to standardize component parts among the five car lines. The same year, Estes followed Knudsen's footsteps to Chevrolet (and later became president of GM), and DeLorean, then chief engineer, was named the new general manager. DeLorean, a prolific inventor in his own right, claimed credit for over 200 patents and applications, and had participated in such Pontiac innovations as the wide track, the overhead cam engine, and the concealed windshield wipers. In early 1967 Pontiac introduced its first car targeted towards the youthful, sporty car market, the Firebird. In 1968 another sporty car was unveiled and became an instant hit, the legendary GTO. With its rubber-like bumper, the new GTO (the original version had been first introduced in 1964) attracted nationwide attention and was named *Motor Trend*'s "Car of the Year." Sales records were shattered as 866,826 Pontiac cars were sold, an all-time high, and Pontiac became a big name in auto racing. (See Exhibit 2 for Pontiac's historical model-year sales and Pontiac and GM domestic market shares.) For the first time, sales of specialty cars—Tempest, Grand Prix, and Firebird—exceeded those of the traditional Pontiac line.

As his two predecessors had done, DeLorean became general manager of Chevrolet (he later left the corporation to develop the DeLorean Motor Car Company in Europe), and F. James McDonald became Pontiac's new general manager in 1969. McDonald, a manufacturing expert, continued the division's momentum by steering Pontiac into the compact market segment with a low-priced vehicle, the Ventura II. Other new additions to the division were a new administration building on the original plant site and a new engineering test facility. By 1971 Pontiac was holding on to the third-spot ranking in the industry sales race for the 10th time in 11 years—following only Chevrolet and Ford.

In 1972 Martin J. Caserio became general manager of Pontiac, following McDonald's move to the general manager's position at Chevrolet (and later to the presidency of GM). Caserio, who had been general manager of the Truck and Coach division the previous six years, pushed Pontiac into the intermediate-car segment with a totally redesigned set of vehicles. These cars of the early 1970s were redesigned to be more luxurious.

STRATEGY FORMULATION

In late 1973 and early 1974, when the oil crisis left many carmakers scrambling to increase fuel economy and efficiency, Pontiac was harder hit than most. With its "gas guzzler," or "muscle car" image, Pontiac sales dropped to 557,726 vehicles in 1974 and then to 465,410 vehicles in 1975. As in the other GM divisions, Pontiac struggled to refocus its cars. The product line was changed to reflect more fuel-efficient vehicles, and scrambling for survival,

EXHIBIT 2 Pontiac Division: GM and Pontiac Unit Sales and Market Share, 1965–1985

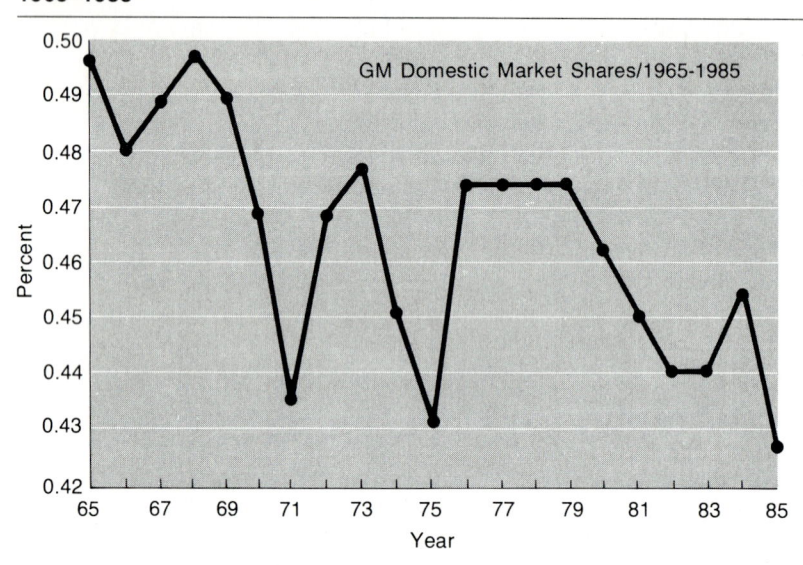

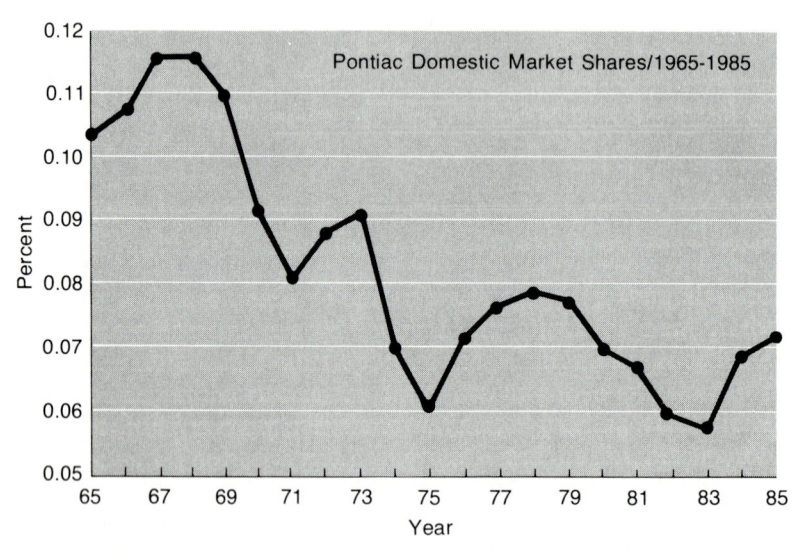

Source: Internal Pontiac Data Base

EXHIBIT 2 (Continued) Pontiac Division, GM and Pontiac Unit Sales and Market Share, 1965–1985

HISTORICAL MODEL YEAR (MY) SALES

	Unit Sales, $			Market Share, %	
Year	Pontiac	GM	U.S. Domestic	Pontiac	GM
1965	609,674	2,898,346	5,865,998	10.4	49.4
1966	831,684	3,764,493	7,849,318	10.6	48.0
1967	833,224	3,559,541	7,275,073	11.5	48.9
1968	866,826	3,739,136	7,521,926	11.5	49.7
1969	843,610	3,827,010	7,809,535	10.8	49.0
1970	664,879	3,357,229	7,190,992	9.2	46.7
1971	576,021	3,130,180	7,197,407	8.0	43.5
1972	741,691	3,988,972	8,523,645	8.7	46.8
1973	854,343	4,444,716	9,328,487	9.2	47.6
1974	557,276	3,591,776	7,957,617	7.0	45.1
1975	465,410	3,350,434	7,734,662	6.0	43.3
1976	700,931	4,607,895	9,731,181	7.2	47.4
1977	811,904	5,092,331	10,758,739	7.5	47.3
1978	871,391	5,245,719	11,065,501	7.9	47.4
1979	828,603	5,119,078	10,812,885	7.7	47.3
1980	638,656	4,228,231	9,137,507	7.0	46.3
1981	601,218	4,032,727	8,951,056	6.7	45.1
1982	461,845	3,387,607	7,683,154	6.0	44.1
1983	513,239	3,876,006	8,796,364	5.8	44.1
1984	707,033	4,659,818	10,256,021	6.9	45.4
1985	785,617	4,694,979	10,994,475	7.1	42.7

Source: Internal Pontiac Data Base.

Pontiac abandoned the sporty, "muscle car" image. The race was on to build the lowest priced car, with the plushest interior and the softest velour trim. According to a Pontiac spokesman,

> During the mid to late '70s, we tried hard to respond. We joined everyone else in trying to build smaller, lighter, more fuel-efficient products. We chased the Chevrolet price leaders, tried to out-plush Buick, and out-velour Oldsmobile.

In October 1975, Alex C. Mair was named the new general manager of Pontiac, as Caserio became group executive in charge of the Electrical Components Group. Pontiac's golden anniversary lineup in 1976 included a new sporty subcompact, the Sunbird, and a new platform for the Bonneville. These shorter and lighter weight vehicles were designed to meet the need for small and fuel-efficient automobiles, and helped increase sales in the short run.

When Mair was moved to the vice president's job of the Technical Staffs Group in 1978, Robert C. Stempel, then director of engineering at Chevrolet, became the new general manager of Pontiac. Considered one of the industry's leading engineering authorities, Stempel introduced a new lineup of vehicles that had major styling changes and engine updates to reflect even better fuel efficiency and handling than previously.

DEVELOPMENTS DURING THE 1980s

In August 1980, 45-year-old William E. Hoglund, formerly the corporate comptroller, became the new general manager of Pontiac. Hoglund was faced with a floundering division. Pontiac's market share and total sales were declining. As pressure rose from dealers and the corporation to reverse this trend, a group of concerned dealers met with GM's president, James McDonald, to discuss the future of Pontiac. Some dealers had sold or closed their Pontiac franchises, or added foreign car lines to help keep them afloat. The once successful image of sporty, youthful vehicles had been abandoned for a lineup that consisted of luxury vehicles—with wire wheels, whitewalls, and plenty of chrome—targeted for older car buyers. During the same time, other GM divisions had adopted strategies similar to Pontiac's; the result was a vehicle lineup that was almost parallel across all divisions. Except for some minor front and rear styling differences, the cars looked so similar that consumers had difficulty distinguishing among the divisions. By 1981 Pontiac had fallen to fifth position in U.S. industry sales, behind the third and fourth sister GM divisions, Buick and Oldsmobile, respectively.

New Mission and Direction

In early 1981 Hoglund formed an "image team" consisting of key people from every Pontiac staff area, the advertising agency, and the Pontiac design staff. The task force met off-site at what is now referred to as the first Pontiac Image Conference, with its goal to determine Pontiac's overall direction for the 1980s. One of the key tools used at the two-and-a-half day conference was the perceptual map. With the results of extensive research at hand, the team plotted Pontiac's position in relation to the perceived images of other car manufacturers (Exhibit 3). The results showed that Pontiac was perceived as relatively neutral, an ordinary American car division. People just did not get excited about Pontiac or its cars, and the sales figures showed it. A change in strategy was clearly needed.

As a result of the Image Conference, an agreement was made by top Pontiac managers to regain the sporty, youthful image that Pontiac had built in the 1960s—the strategy that had once made the division successful. Pontiac would now distinguish itself from its sister divisions by emphasizing performance and handling in the design and manufacture of its vehicles.

Armed with these new directives, the managers were ready to bring in the entire Pontiac organization. A mission statement was issued to all employees:

> This mission of Pontiac is to be a car company known for innovative styling and engineering that results in products with outstanding performance and roadability.

EXHIBIT 3   Pontiac Division: Perceptual Map, 1981

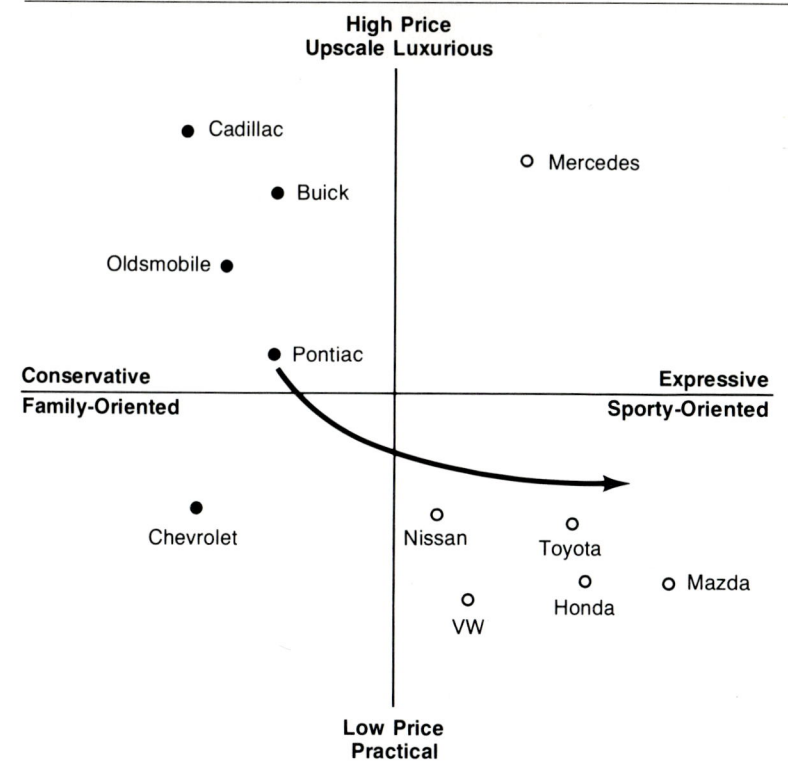

```
                        High Price
                        Upscale Luxurious
                              |
        ● Cadillac            |
                              |      ○ Mercedes
                ● Buick       |
                              |
  Oldsmobile ●                |
                              |
                  ● Pontiac   |
  Conservative                |                  Expressive
  Family-Oriented ─────────────────────────────── Sporty-Oriented
                              |╲
                              | ╲___
                              |     ╲___→
         ●                    |  ○        ○
       Chevrolet              | Nissan  Toyota
                              |                   ○ Mazda
                              |      ○       ○
                              |     VW     Honda
                              |
                        Low Price
                        Practical
```

Note: Arrow indicates direction of Pontiac after Image Conference.
Source: Automative News, *Sept. 15, 1986.*

A definition of the target market was formulated:

> Identified target market as a relatively young, better educated, higher income, 25- to 44-age group.

This group then represented 40 percent of the population but 55 percent of auto-buying power. By 1990 this group would compose 42 percent of the U.S. population and account for over one-half of all new car purchases. In 1981 the group's median household income was $32,000.

Results of focus-group discussions of the image were extremely positive. The results suggested that the upscale and/or luxury image fit more with Buick or Oldsmobile. Consumers remembered Pontiac as the excitement car of the 1960s and told management that's where they should be now.

Hoglund felt that consistent and continuous communication of Pontiac's new direction to all employees, the corporation, the dealer base, and the buying public was essential. He began working to instill a sense of teamwork in his staff. His personal dedication to change was viewed by many as the key to success. Meetings with corporate officials were frequent, because Pontiac wanted to identify the strategies it planned for the 1980s clearly, especially to gain top GM management support. These strategies had to fit into the overall corporate strategic direction of regaining lost market share and sales. The dealers were given an "image brochure" explaining the national marketing strategy so that they could begin implementing it on the local level.

Finally, and equally important, communication to the consumers through advertising played a key role. A clear and consistent advertising strategy was needed. As seen in Exhibit 4, this consistency began in 1982 with the slogan "Now the excitement begins." This base theme was the foundation for the 1983–1986 themes of "We build excitement." As the new vehicles began to be introduced throughout 1982–1985, consumers heard the same message relating Pontiac to excitement. To support the message, Pontiac started advertising on television and radio programs aimed at the young consumer.

Products Under the New Mission

The effort to reposition Pontiac to a more youthful market had to be accomplished first through the products. The redesigned sporty Firebird was

EXHIBIT 4 Pontiac Division, Advertising Campaign Themes, 1970–1986

Year	Theme
1986	We Build Excitement
1985	We Build Excitement
1984	We Build Excitement
1983	We Build Excitement
1982	Now The Excitement Really Begins
	Now The Excitement Begins
1981	More Pontiac Know-How For The Gallon
1980	More Pontiac Excitement To The Gallon
	More Pontiac Excitement For The Great Ones
	More Pontiac Know-How To The Gallon
1979	More Pontiac To The Gallon
	The 1979 Pontiacs—Our Best Get Better
1978	Pontiac's Best Year Yet!
1977	Mark of Great Cars
1976	Mark of Great Cars
1975	The Wide Track People Have a Way With Cars
	Pontiac Strikes Again
1974	The Wide Track People Have a Way With Cars
1973	The Wide Track People Have a Way With Cars
1972	That's What Keeps Pontiac a Cut Above
1971	Pontiac . . . A Cut Above
	Pure Pontiac
1970	Wide Track (Above All It's a Wide Track Pontiac)
	This Is the Way It's Going to Be
	(We Take the Fun of Driving Seriously)

Source: Internal Pontiac document.

introduced in 1982, but the first complete road car to be developed with the new mission and philosophy was the 1983 Pontiac 6000 STE. Although the mid-size 6000 STEs shared GM's "A" chassis with the Chevrolet Celebrity, the Olds Cutlass Ciera, and the Buick Century, its design was differentiated from its GM counterparts. From the interior to the exterior, the ride and handling, the 6000 STE was distinguished from its competitors with its European style, its wide body side molding, and its sporty flare. The 6000 STE won positive reviews by auto magazines such as *Car and Driver* and was listed as one of its top 10 cars for several years. Of the cars Pontiac advertised heavily, it attracted the highest age group on average. Exhibit 5 shows some 1984 demographics of Pontiac buyers.

The introduction of the 6000 STE, the "touring sedan of the '80s," was the first of many product changes for the division. Other cars that followed the new philosophy were the Fiero, the Sunbird, and the 1985 Grand Am (built on the same "N" chassis as the Olds Calais and the Buick Somerset). Exhibit 6 shows the 1987 Model Year lineup—a total of nine vehicle platforms.

The Fiero's introduction helped Pontiac's effort to regain the sporty image. The Fiero was innovative in using all-plastic body panels, which won acclaim from engineering and manufacturing experts, as well as from auto magazines, as the wave of the future. The plastic body panels were mounted over a 250-piece steel "birdcage" chassis. According to *Business Week*,

> GM first assembles the chassis, largely using robots and automatic welders. Then it shoves the completed chassis into a huge "mill-and-drill" machine that shaves down its body-panel "locator pads" to proper height. Next, workers install the drivetrain and other equipment. Once the chassis' running gear is installed and tested, the body panels are added. The result: chip-free fenders and doors that always line up perfectly.
>
> GM refuses to say whether this year-old, experimental method is as cost-effective as the traditional approach of building a car body first and then equipping it. But the system offers a fast and cheap way to restyle a car. To change its shape, GM can just bolt new body panels onto the same chassis. Restyling conventional cars usually means extensive reengineering.[2]

In addition, the Fiero created dealer traffic, which helped sell all Pontiac carlines. On average, Fiero had the youngest buyers in Pontiac's line.

The introduction of Fiero had not been without problems, however. *Fortune* magazine reported,

> GM's sporty little Fiero illustrates why Detroit can stumble even when it makes its best efforts to catch up. Conceived before the quality philosophy caught hold, the Fiero was originally designed as a cheap commuter car. The project was killed and revived twice before it came to life as a jazzy, midengine two-seater. Along the way it acquired the Chevette's leaden steering system, which had no power boost in the Fiero because of the great distance between the engine and the front wheels. The car's ridiculous 10.2-gallon gas tank, designed with frugal commuting in mind,

---

[2] "GM Moves Into a New Era," *Business Week*, July 16, 1984, p. 51.

EXHIBIT 5 Pontiac Division, Decision Makers for Passenger Cars Bought New, 1984

	Total U.S. '000	Decision Makers for Cars Bought New A '000	B % Down	C Across %	D Index	Pontiac A '000	B % Down	C Across %	D Index
Total adults	167,727	42,666	100.0	25.4	100	2,929	100.0	1.7	100
Males	79,263	23,340	54.7	29.4	116	1,379	47.1	1.7	100
Females	88,464	19,326	45.3	21.8	86	1,550	52.9	1.8	100
18–24	28,671	4,520	10.6	15.8	62	361	12.3	1.3	72
25–34	39,536	10,669	25.0	27.0	106	680	23.2	1.7	98
35–44	28,978	8,416	19.7	29.0	114	733	25.0	2.5	145
45–54	22,345	6,417	15.0	28.7	113	489	16.7	2.2	125
55–64	22,224	6,552	15.4	29.5	116	313	10.7	1.4	81
65 or older	25,973	6,093	14.3	23.5	92	352	12.0	1.4	78
18–34	68,207	15,189	35.6	22.3	88	1,042	35.6	1.5	87
18–49	108,058	26,742	62.7	24.7	97	2,038	69.6	1.9	108
25–54	90,859	25,502	59.8	28.1	110	1,902	64.9	2.1	120
35–49	39,851	11,553	27.1	29.0	114	997	34.0	2.5	143
50 or older	59,669	15,924	37.3	26.7	105	891	30.4	1.5	86
Graduated college	28,091	11,795	27.6	42.0	165	759	25.9	2.7	155
Attended college	28,938	8,414	19.7	29.1	114	671	22.9	2.3	133
Graduated high school	65,503	16,124	37.8	24.6	97	1,243	42.4	1.9	109
Did not graduate high school	45,195	6,334	14.8	14.0	55	257	8.8	0.6	33
Employed males	56,429	18,081	42.4	32.0	126	1,099	37.5	1.9	112
Employed females	43,971	11,895	27.9	27.1	106	959	32.7	2.2	125
Employed full-time	87,773	27,316	64.0	31.1	122	1,787	61.0	2.0	117
Employed part-time	12,627	2,660	6.2	21.1	83	270	9.2	2.1	122
Not employed	67,327	12,690	29.7	18.8	74	871	29.7	1.3	74
Professional manager	25,845	10,693	25.1	41.4	163	671	22.9	2.6	149
Tech/clerical/sales	30,895	9,388	22.0	30.4	119	653	22.3	2.1	121
Precision/craft	12,629	3,693	8.7	29.2	115	281	9.6	2.2	127
Other employed	31,031	6,203	14.5	20.0	79	454	15.5	1.5	84
Single	35,557	8,249	19.3	23.2	91	599	20.5	1.7	96
Married	103,585	27,748	65.0	26.8	105	1,913	65.3	1.8	106
Divorced/separated/widowed	28,585	6,669	15.6	23.3	92	417	14.2	1.5	84
Parents	59,295	14,255	33.4	24.0	95	1,217	41.6	2.1	118
White	146,081	38,647	90.6	26.5	104	2,681	91.5	1.8	105
Black	17,974	3,062	7.2	17.0	67	244	8.3	1.4	78
Other	3,672	957	2.2	26.1	102	4	0.1	0.1	6
Northeast-census	37,005	9,711	22.8	26.2	103	560	19.1	1.5	87
North central	42,642	11,104	26.0	26.0	102	1,078	36.8	2.5	145
South	56,777	13,466	31.6	23.7	93	979	33.4	1.7	99
West	31,303	8,385	19.7	26.8	105	313	10.7	1.0	57
Northeast-mktg	38,125	11,000	25.8	28.9	113	623	21.3	1.6	94
East central	24,794	6,209	14.6	25.0	98	587	20.0	2.4	136
West central	28,511	7,288	17.1	25.6	100	648	22.1	2.3	130
South	48,953	10,897	25.5	22.3	88	850	29.0	1.7	99
Pacific	27,344	7,272	17.0	26.6	105	221	7.5	0.8	46

(Continued)

EXHIBIT 5 (Continued)

	Decision Makers for Cars Bought New					Pontiac			
	Total U.S. '000	A '000	B % Down	C Across %	D Index	A '000	B % Down	C Across %	D Index
County size A	69,301	18,856	44.2	27.2	107	1,284	43.8	1.9	106
County size B	50,633	12,821	30.0	25.3	100	743	25.4	1.5	84
County size C	26,259	6,333	14.8	24.1	95	421	14.4	1.6	92
County size D	21,534	4,656	10.9	21.6	85	481	16.4	2.2	128
Metro central city	50,014	11,516	27.0	23.0	91	528	18.0	1.1	60
Metro suburban	76,832	21,783	51.1	28.4	111	1,638	55.9	2.1	122
Non Metro	40,881	9,367	22.0	22.9	90	763	26.0	1.9	107
Top 5 ADI'S	39,550	10,912	25.6	27.6	108	648	22.1	1.6	94
Top 10 ADI'S	54,877	15,118	35.4	27.5	108	960	32.8	1.7	100
Top 20 ADI'S	77,516	20,932	49.1	27.0	106	1,335	45.6	1.7	99
Hshld inc $50,000 or more	17,257	6,665	15.6	38.6	152	*359	12.3	2.1	119
$40,000 or more	33,235	12,188	28.6	36.7	144	837	28.6	2.5	144
$30,000 or more	59,693	20,989	49.2	35.2	138	1,456	49.7	2.4	140
$25,000 or more	76,275	26,029	61.0	34.1	134	1,806	61.7	2.4	136
$20,000–$24,999	18,607	4,666	10.9	25.1	99	*439	15.0	2.4	135
$15,000–$19,999	17,175	3,882	9.1	22.6	89	*242	8.3	1.4	81
$10,000–$14,999	24,569	4,429	10.4	18.0	71	*209	7.1	0.9	49
Under $10,000	31,101	3,660	8.6	11.8	46	*235	8.0	0.8	43
Household of 1 person	19,441	5,563	13.0	28.6	112	457	15.6	2.4	135
2 people	51,803	14,223	33.3	27.5	108	895	30.6	1.7	99
3 or 4 people	66,933	16,934	39.7	25.3	99	1,039	35.5	1.6	89
5 or more people	29,550	5,947	13.9	20.1	79	*538	18.4	1.8	104
No child in household	96,587	26,262	61.6	27.2	107	1,591	54.3	1.6	94
Child(ren) under 2 years	10,844	2,525	5.9	23.3	92	191	6.5	1.8	101
2–5 years	26,358	5,688	13.3	21.6	85	*419	14.3	1.6	91
6–11 years	30,453	6,517	15.3	21.4	84	*543	18.5	1.8	102
12–17 years	36,575	8,389	19.7	22.9	90	762	26.0	2.1	119
Residence owned	117,770	34,002	79.7	28.9	113	2,334	79.7	2.0	113
Value $50,000 or more	70,166	23,589	55.3	33.6	132	1,583	54.0	2.3	129
Value under $50,000	47,604	10,413	24.4	21.9	86	751	25.6	1.6	90

A is the projected number of people in thousands, in the cell defined by the heading and stub for the column and row concerned.

B is the result of percentaging this number "down" using the group defined by the heading as the base. For demographic stub items, this gives PROFILE.

C is the result of percentaging this number "across" using the group defined by the stub as the base. For demographic stub items, this gives PENETRATION.

D is an index of selectivity calculated by dividing C (Across %) by the across percent for the universe concerned (adults, males, females, etc.). Example: an index of 120 indicates that the group defined by the stub is 20% more likely to be in the group defined by the heading than is the total universe.

* Projection relatively unstable because of sample base—use with caution.
** Number of cases too small for reliability—shown for consistency only.

Source: *Simmonds Study of Media and Markets*, 1985. This report is the property of Simmons Market Research Bureau, Inc. and is distributed on loan to a limited group of clients pursuant to contract for their exclusive and confidential use. Any reproduction, publication, circulation, distribution or sale of this report or disclosure of the contents thereof in whole or in part is strictly forbidden and Simmons Market Research Bureau, Inc. will avail itself of every remedy in law and in equity respecting any unauthorized use. © 1984 by Simmons Market Research Bureau, Inc. All Rights Reserved.

208 STRATEGY FORMULATION

EXHIBIT 6 Pontiac Division: 1987 Product Lineup (Excluding Station Wagon)

Name: **Grand Am**
Base Price: $9,869
Platform: N

Name: **Grand Prix**
Base Price: $11,483
Platform: G-RWD

Name: **Firebird**
Base Price: $10,773
Platform: F

Name: **Sunbird**
Base Price: $8,369 (SE)
Platform: J

(Continued)

PONTIAC DIVISION OF GENERAL MOTORS 209

EXHIBIT 6 (Continued)

Name: **Fiero**
Base Price: $8,619
Platform: P

Name: **Pontiac 6000**
Base Price: $10,913
Platform: A

Name: **Bonneville**
Base Price: $13,874
Platform: H-FWD

Name: **Pontiac 1000**
Base Price: $6,389
Platform: T

was the smallest made in the U.S. When the four-cylinder engine proved too unexciting for a sports car, Pontiac added a six-cylinder engine, but the engine fits so tightly that it takes a skilled mechanic to change the spark plugs. Worst of all, in the early models coolant from the radiator up front got so chilled by the time it reached the hot engine farther back that cracks developed in the engine block. Pontiac tried to assuage its customers by replacing engines free long after warranties had expired. For the most part these design errors have been or are being corrected, so the Fiero is now, in Harbour's [James E. Harbour, auto industry consultant] view, "a class vehicle."

At the Pontiac, Michigan, plant where the car is assembled, managers, supervisors, and some line workers attend daily quality briefings that attest to Pontiac's desire to produce a fine car. A giant bulletin board on the plant floor keeps track of Fiero's quality. When it was first produced in 1984, Fiero scored 74 out of a possible 100, based on owner satisfaction surveys in GM's CAMIP (Continuous Automotive Marketing Information Process), conducted by Research Data Analysis. The bulletin board's most recent quarterly data show Fiero scoring 91, vs. 99 for Toyota's MR2, 97 for Mazda's RX7, and 89 for Nissan's Pulsar NX. Inside GM, Fiero looks good, since the company average CAMIP is 85.[3]

The shape and style of Fiero and the other new cars complemented the image the division was trying to regain. Pontiac's strategy of using image/specialty cars to sell other, lower-priced models was highly successful. While only accounting for a small portion of total sales, these image cars built a "halo" effect around the other Pontiac lines. For example, in 1986 the 6000 STE was the car most advertised, but the base 6000 was the most frequently purchased. As an image leader, the top-of-the-line STE was a performance-oriented vehicle with advanced technology in the powertrain, suspension, and steering. It also had an all-electronic dashboard and sporty trim packages. The base 6000 was more traditional, equipped with a standard engine and conventional dashboard, seats, and trim packages—a typical mid-size sedan. The base 6000 was $3,000–$4,000 less than the STE version.

Corporate Reorganization

The GM North American Car Group, of which Pontiac was a part in 1984 (see Exhibit 7), had in the past encouraged its car divisions to produce vehicles in certain ranges for specific consumer segments. For example, when a person first entered the car market, a Chevrolet was the most likely choice; this division provided a wide range of products at entry-level prices. As the consumer grew older and also increased household income, he or she was thought to trade up to different divisions (in this case, Pontiac). The consumer would eventually pass through the entire GM chain (Chevrolet, Pontiac, Oldsmobile, Buick, and Cadillac). In practice, however, consumers were forsaking this chain for competitor car manufacturers. The Japanese and European car manufacturers were now major players in the market, and GM was faced with fierce competition. In order to meet the challenges these competitors brought to the industry, a restructuring was announced in early 1984.

---

[3] Jeremy Main, "Detroit's Cars Really Are Getting Better," *Fortune*, February 2, 1987, p. 97.

EXHIBIT 7   Pontiac Division: Organization Charts

1986 Organization

- Chairman
- President
- Executive Vice-President
  - Buick, Oldsmobile, Cadillac Group B-O-C
    - Buick
    - Oldsmobile
    - Cadillac
    - Operations
    - Engineering
  - Chevrolet, Pontiac GM of Canada Group C-P-C
    - Chevrolet
    - Pontiac
    - GM of Canada
    - Saturn Corporation
    - Operations
    - Engineering

Note: This is a partial organization chart

Before 1984 Re-Organization

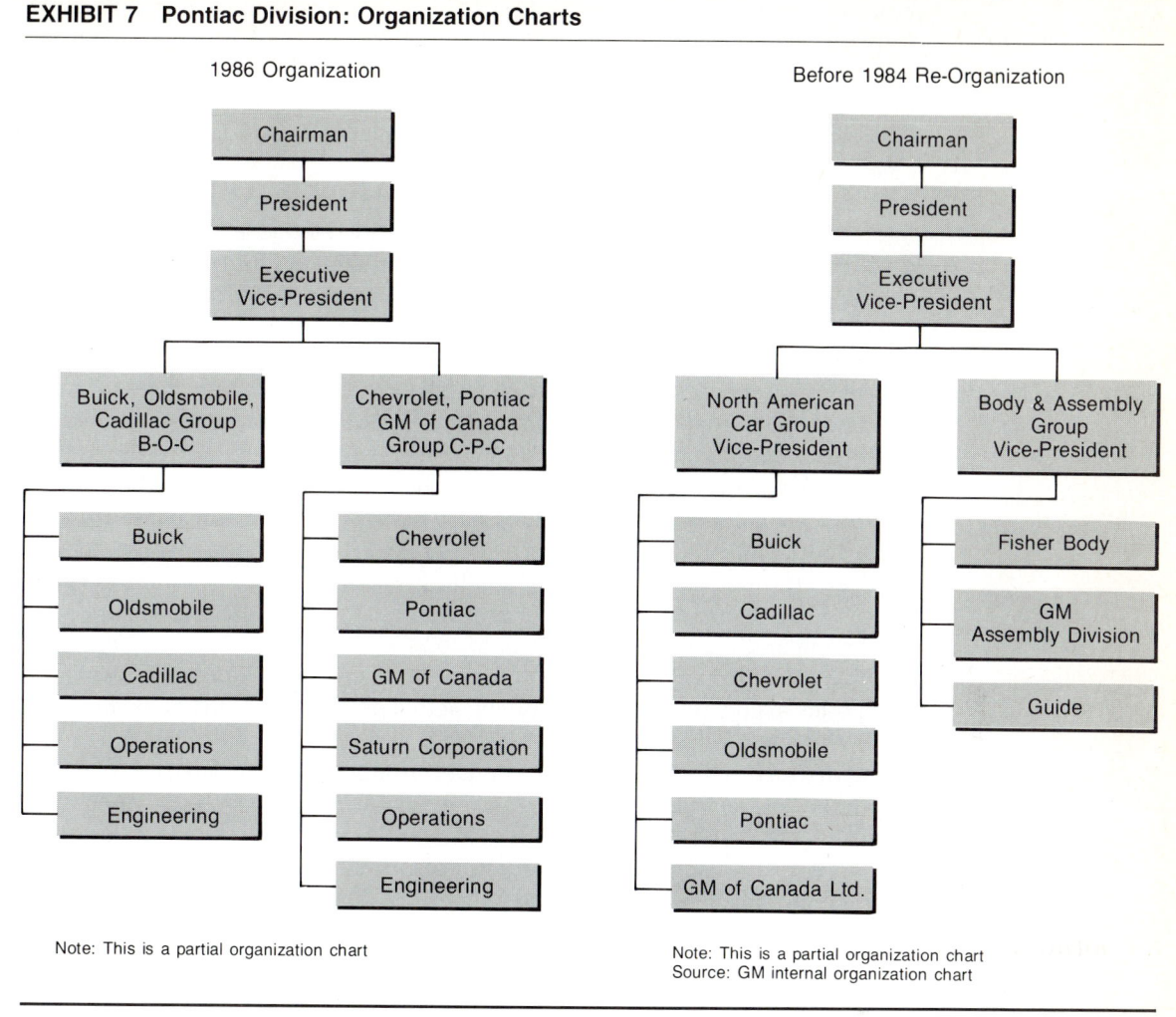

- Chairman
- President
- Executive Vice-President
  - North American Car Group Vice-President
    - Buick
    - Cadillac
    - Chevrolet
    - Oldsmobile
    - Pontiac
    - GM of Canada Ltd.
  - Body & Assembly Group Vice-President
    - Fisher Body
    - GM Assembly Division
    - Guide

Note: This is a partial organization chart
Source: GM internal organization chart

The restructuring of the North American automotive operations created two car groups or profit centers: the Chevrolet-Pontiac-Canada Group (CPC) and the Buick-Oldsmobile-Cadillac Group (BOC). This restructuring came after a two-year, internal comprehensive study of the company, assisted by McKinsey and Company, to shape GM for the future, and was expected by some GM officials to take three to five years to put into effect. The reasons for the reorganization were: (1) to compete for market share, (2) to compete with manufacturers throughout the world, and (3) to compete in world-class quality, value, and customer satisfaction.[4] The reorganization sought to focus the production of small-car platforms in CPC, and the larger-car platforms in BOC

---

[4] Material Management, BOC Group—an internal GM document, p. 2.

so that the company could make better use of its resources and make each group totally responsible for the value-added chain (from initial design to final delivery). The Fisher Body and GMAD plants were divided between the two groups, which had complete engineering and operational responsibilities. Most product platforms would still be shared by several car-marketing divisions.

Although originally rumored that Chevrolet and Pontiac would market small, inexpensive cars and Olds, Buick, and Cadillac would market larger cars with more dual dealerships (most frequently linking Chevrolet and Oldsmobile for buyers favoring more traditional styling and Pontiac and Buick for more distinctive styling), the announcement stressed that each group would build vehicles for its own car divisions as well as the other group's divisions. Thus, it would still be possible, if market conditions warranted, for Pontiac to sell a large car and Buick a small car. Exhibit 7 shows the GM organization before and after the reorganization.

The general managers of the nameplate divisions no longer had operational responsibilities for the plants at their respective locations. For example, the general manager of Pontiac no longer had responsibility for the Pontiac complex, which included a foundry, an engine plant, a parts plant, and the Fiero plant. CPC now controlled these activities. However, the general managers did have to meet CPC goals such as the five-year business plan and criteria such as cost-control programs. The divisions were to focus attention on marketing and planning activities, and to avoid confusing the consumer.

Pontiac went through a reorganization of its own. The orientation changed from sales to consumer marketing. The actual organization shrunk from nearly 10,000 people to approximately 1,500, but the responsibility of departments reporting to Hoglund—sales and service, product planning, market planning (including strategic and business planning), finance, and personnel—increased. (Product engineering was consolidated at the group level with an informal reporting relationship to Hoglund.) Engineers that remained at Pontiac were charged primarily with developing distinctions for their version of shared platforms and articulating those needs to CPC. Marketing and planning people were increased from less than 20 to approximately 50. A team approach to planning among market planning, product planning, and product engineering, was initiated.

J. Michael Losh

In mid-1984 Hoglund became group executive of the Operating Staff Group (he was later named president of the Saturn Corporation and at the time of the case was BOC Group executive), and Mike Losh, then managing director of GM de Mexico, became the 14th general manager of Pontiac. At the age of 38, he was GM's youngest VP and general manager. He arrived on July 1, just before the beginning of the 1985 model year in September.

Born in 1946 in Dayton, Ohio, Losh began his career with General Motors as a GMI (General Motors Institute) student sponsored by the Inland Division. He graduated with a BS in mechanical engineering and an MBA from the Harvard Business School in 1970. Upon graduation, Losh became a staff assistant, then a senior analyst for Inland. Two years later, he transferred to the GM central office in New York as a senior staff assistant in the treasurer's office. In 1974, he was promoted to director of Profit Analysis and Forecasts. In 1976, he moved to the Detroit central office as director of Product Programs for the financial staff. The following year, he became director of Finance at GM do Brasil in Sao Caetano do Sul. He joined GM de Mexico in early 1982 as deputy managing director and in December of that year was named president and managing director of GM de Mexico.

With the success of the Grand Am, Fiero, and 6000 STE, and the security of the stable Firebird and Sunbird, Losh seemed to have inherited a house in order. Sales were increasing, and Pontiac's market share for 1984 would be approximately 7 percent. With all its success, however, Pontiac faced many outside competitors who were making similar moves to target its specific market segment. The Europeans were already solid players, with their sporty vehicles. The Japanese were the most recent entrants with their technologically advanced cars—overhead cams, superior suspensions, and a tone of being generally sportier than U.S. cars. Losh believed the sporty; expressive market was going to become a battlefield for the world automakers. He predicted, "Sportiness and performance are emerging as major themes in a wide range of product segments for both import and domestic automakers."

In his first two years at the helm, Losh built on the changes initiated by Hoglund. In 1985, he initiated a series of annual marketing conferences, involving representatives from the total marketing process. A year later, three separate marketing conferences were held where, according to Losh,

> We established and developed the objectives and strategies for each 1987 carline taking into account the carline's specific image, the market segment in which it competes, and its competitive strengths and weaknesses. For example, we are placing our major marketing efforts behind key image cars within each class.
>
> The purpose of this "impact strategy" is not only to promote specific cars within each class but also to accentuate the Pontiac image as the excitement builder. For 1987 our featured carline leaders include the Grand Am SE, Bonneville SE, Fiero GT, 6000 STE, Sunbird GT, and the Trans Am GTA.
>
> In addition, we've devised a new multi-line strategy where we promote one image carline with another—in this case, Fiero, Firebird, and Sunbird. The result is a more efficient and cost-effective way to promote our cars and image philosophy.
>
> Another major benefit of our 1987 marketing conferences is that we established key divisional objectives and prioritized marketing and communications challenges. We integrated all areas into a single marketing plan. This way, Merchandising, Dealer Marketing Groups, Public Relations, and National Advertising all came away with a clear understanding of their roles. The end result is that marketing conferences now play a key part in our total planning process and an even more important role in keeping us ahead of our competition.

Pontiac also borrowed from the Japanese the concept of "option grouping"—special versions of cars that carried a particular group of options, with only limited variations allowed. By the fall of 1986, the concept had been extended to all Pontiac models.

By late 1986, Pontiac's aggressiveness and clear image had become known throughout GM, especially because Pontiac was GM's number one "import fighter." The Fiero, Grand Am, and 6000 STE ranked 1, 3, and 5 among all domestic makes in attracting import buyers.

In addition, Pontiac was getting good press for its new products. Publications like *Car and Driver* and *Road & Track* had written positively about Pontiac's improved performance. The newest product change, to be introduced at the beginning of the 1987 model year, was the redesigned Bonneville, built on the same chassis as the Olds Delta 88 and the Buick LeSabre. Although there were some internal concerns about whether the car really fit the image of sporty expressive vehicles (Exhibit 8 shows the placement of the Bonneville on the perceptual map for 1987 Pontiac vehicles and major competitors), an October 1986 preview by *Motor Trend* reported:

> The new Pontiac Bonneville . . . is destined to be the benchmark against which cars in this class are compared. An essentially full-sized car without giving up intangibles like fun and driving comfort. The '87 Bonneville is as first-cabin as any automobile in its class on the world scene today.

In addition to the new Bonneville, a replacement for the 1000, the LeMans, was scheduled for introduction in the 1988 model year. This front-wheel-drive subcompact would be designed by GM's Adam Opel division in West Germany and built in South Korea by the new GM-Daewoo Motor Company joint venture. The LeMans would be the second platform Pontiac would not have to share with other divisions. Approximately 80,000 to 100,000 would be imported the first year. Such a method of introducing a new vehicle was considerably cheaper than the substantial investment required to bring out a totally new vehicle, which would take three to five years' lead time.

Another positive development was the improvement in Pontiac quality. Whereas, in 1984, Pontiac's Customer Satisfaction Index ranked last among GM divisions, by 1986 it was about even with the other divisions. The lowest ratings were generally on the older design models, with the 1000 receiving the lowest and the STE the highest. The ratings were also low for Pontiac dealerships that also handled competing GM makes. For example, the rating on a Pontiac 6000 was usually lower than its sister cars—Buick Century and Olds Cutlass Ciera—if the Pontiac was sold from the same dealership.

Fully aware of the objective of the "sporty division" in GM, dealers still wondered if Pontiac's comeback was for real. In a recent study of dealer attitudes toward brand franchises, however, Pontiac ranks a strong fifth, up from its previous ninth-place position. In fact, the Pontiac franchise ranked first among all American-built brands.

Losh still felt he needed to build confidence and support in the dealer network. He was especially concerned that one-third of the approximately 3,000 dealerships accounted for 80 percent of sales. (Pontiac was the chief line for 800 dealerships.) Losh believed that Pontiac needed to strengthen its franchises. "In some cases that means different locations with the same guy; in some cases, that means better facilities where he is; and in some cases, it means we need a new operator."

He hoped to have all Pontiac dealers wired into GM's computerized marketing network by fall of 1987. Although the information would be

EXHIBIT 8 Pontiac Division: Bonneville Perceptual Map, 1987

The New Bonneville with the 1987 Pontiac Lineup

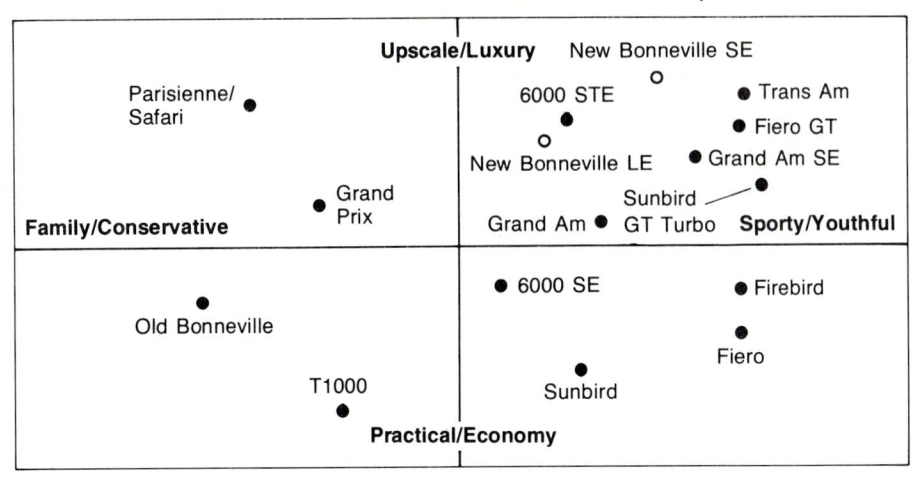

```
                    Upscale/Luxury    New Bonneville SE
                                           ○
      Parisienne/●            6000 STE          ● Trans Am
      Safari                     ●              ● Fiero GT
                                 ○        ● Grand Am SE
                          New Bonneville LE
                  ● Grand              Sunbird
  Family/Conservative  Prix       Grand Am ●  GT Turbo   Sporty/Youthful
                                           
                        ●              ● 6000 SE         ● Firebird
                  Old Bonneville                          ●
                                                         Fiero
                            ●
                          T1000           ●
                                       Sunbird
                              Practical/Economy
```

The Bonneville versus the Competition

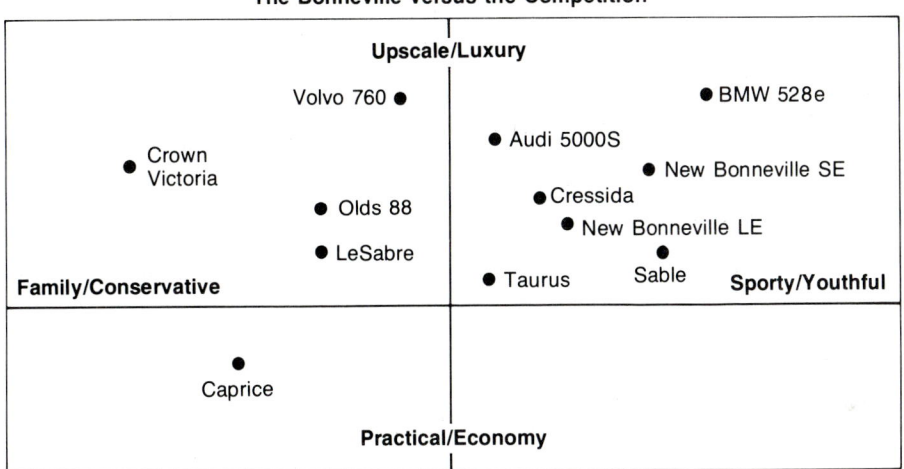

```
                        Upscale/Luxury
                  Volvo 760 ●                    ● BMW 528e
          ●                          ● Audi 5000S
       Crown                                     ● New Bonneville SE
      Victoria     ● Olds 88      ● Cressida
                                      ● New Bonneville LE
                   ● LeSabre                  ●
  Family/Conservative         ● Taurus      Sable   Sporty/Youthful

                        ●
                      Caprice
                        Practical/Economy
```

Who the New Bonneville is Designed to Attract

CAR NAME	MEDIAN AGE	MEDIAN HH INCOME	EDUCATION
Traditional Pontiac	57	$38,000	High Sch./Coll.
New Bonneville	48	$42,000	College
Pontiac 6000	43	$41,000	College

centralized, Pontiac had to decide whether to leave its local staffs in place or bring them into a single marketing center. Chevrolet was known to be favoring centralizing their "telemanagers."

Several other matters concerned Losh. To continue Pontiac's successful trend would require the division to become even more market-driven than it was. GM corporate parameters were starting to hamper that effort, however. As GM responded to its growing financial problems, capital reductions and program deletions were becoming a major concern for all GM managers. Not only was the widely reported all-plastic-body car project eliminated, which Pontiac had planned to use for some of its 1990 models, but CPC was applying strict cost controls in an effort to reduce spending. If new products or changes in current products were needed, Losh would have to convince CPC to implement them in light of these spending restrictions.

Losh thought another major challenge facing him was a corporate program that white-collar employment be reduced by 25 percent by 1990. Although some of his senior managers soon would be eligible for early retirement and a few employees could be transferred to other parts of GM, perhaps as many as 250 people might have to be released. When and how he should handle the situation was of increasing concern to Losh.

Losh also wondered what effort could best be taken to achieve GM Chairman Roger Smith's long-range corporate plan to optimize the corporation's efforts to regain lost market share and simultaneously increase corporate profitability. Smith, who had initiated the corporate reorganization in 1984, was concerned about the success of all the GM divisions. From 1982 to 1985, Pontiac was the only GM division to boost its share of the $130 billion U.S. car market. Pontiac's market share was up 1.1 percentage point, compared to a total GM drop of 1.4 percentage points. With the success of the sporty, expressive car niche clear and in light of the others' poor performance, would Smith encourage or restrict the other divisions' moves into the segment? In short, one of Losh's biggest concerns was how much distinctiveness Pontiac would be able to maintain.

Losh also had operations concerns. Pontiac had only recently been able to produce enough manual transmissions to satisfy demand, and it did not begin providing the Fiero with five-speed transmissions until the summer of 1986. In addition, by mid-1986, Pontiac's share of GM's "N"-body production had increased to 50 percent, so that Grand Am production now took up the entire output of the Lansing plant, and Buick Somerset Regal and Oldsmobile Calais were sharing another plant. (See Exhibit 9 for a list of GM plants and platforms by product.) With the Grand Am expected to be Pontiac's number-one selling model in 1987, Losh was not sure one dedicated plant was enough. For the time being, Losh thought the 1984 reorganization was working well.

> I don't know that we could have gotten the dedication and commitment out of the old organization that we've gotten today. And I don't know that we would have gotten the timely decisions on reallocating capacity under the old organization.
>
> Obviously, I'm influenced by the fact that things are going well for us in general, but the things that we need out of CPC are working. In many regards, perhaps it should be more difficult for us to deal with the reorganization than anybody else, because so many of our products are under the responsibility of BOC. [BOC's production accounted for more than half of Pontiac's sales.]

Expansion issues were also on Losh's mind. A recent Pontiac study indicated that by 1991, 144 nameplates would be on the marketplace, up from 111 in

EXHIBIT 9   Pontiac Division, GM Platforms and Plants

GENERAL MOTORS CORPORATION

	Chevrolet	Pontiac	Oldsmobile	Buick	Cadillac
A	Celebrity	**6000**	Cutlass Ciera	Century	—
B	Caprice, Caprice Classic	**Parisienne**	Custom Cruiser Wagon	Electra Wagon LeSabre Wagon	—
C	—	—	Ninety-Eight	Electra/ Park Avenue	De Ville, Fleetwood Limousine, Funeral Coach
D	—	—	—	—	Fleetwood Brougham
E	—	—	Toronado	Riviera	Eldorado
F	Camaro	**Firebird**	—	—	—
G	Monte Carlo	**Grand Prix**	Cutlass Supreme	Regal	—
H	—	**Bonneville**	Delta 88	LeSabre	—
J	Cavalier	**Sunbird**	Firenza	Skyhawk	Cimarron
K	—	—	—	—	Seville
L	Corsica, Beretta	—	—	—	—
M	Sprint	—	—	—	—
N	—	**Grand Am**	Calais	Somerset/ Skylark	—
P	—	**Fiero, Fiero GT**	—	—	—
R	Spectrum	—	—	—	—
S	Nova	—	—	—	—
T	Chevette	**1000**	—	—	—
V	—	—	—	—	Allante
Y	Corvette	—	—	—	—

GENERAL MOTORS

Arlington, Tex. . . . . Monte Carlo, Cutlass Supreme
Bowling Green, Ky. . . . . .Corvette
Detroit (Clark Ave.) . . . . Cadillac (rwd), Olds 88 (rwd), Caprice
Detroit-Hamtramck . . . . Toronado, Riviera, Eldorado, Seville
Doraville, Ga. . . . . Cutlass Ciera, Century
Fairfax, Kans . . . . .Chevrolet, Olds 88, LeSabre (rwd), Parisienne
Flint, Mich. . . . . LeSabre (fwd)
Flint (Buick City) . . . . . Estate Wagons, Caprice Classic, Cutlass Supreme, Regal
Framingham, Mass. . . . . .Celebrity, Cutlass Ciera
Janesville, Wis. . . . . Cavalier, Cimarron
Lake Orion, Mich. . . . . Cadillac/ DeVille (rwd), Olds 98, Electra
Lakewood, Ga. . . . . . . Chevette, 1000, Acadian
Lansing . . . . Calais, Grand Am, Somerset
Leeds, Mo. . . . . Cavalier, Firenza, Skyhawk
Linden, N.J. . . . . . GM-25 1987 models (fall 1986)
Lordstown, Ohio . . . . Cavalier, Sunbird
Norwood, Ohio . . . . . .Camaro, Firebird
Oklahoma City . . . . . Celebrity, Century
Pontiac . . . . Fiero
Pontiac (No. 8) . . . . . Cutlass Supreme, Regal
Tarrytown, N.Y. . . . . 6000, Century
Van Nuys, Calif. . . . . .Camaro, Firebird
Wentzville, Mo. . . . . . .Electra, Olds 98, Olds 88 (fwd)
Willow Run, Mich. . . . . . . Olds 88 (fwd)
Wilmington, Del. . . . . .Caprice, GM-25 1987 models (fall 1986)

Source: *Automotive News*, October 27, 1986, p. E40, and *Automotive News*, 1986 Market Data Book Issue, p. 14.

STRATEGY FORMULATION

1986. Although Pontiac's nine carlines were the most of any GM division, and there was growing corporate pressure to reduce the number of GM lines, Losh was considering introducing a minivan. There was a blurring of the market for vans and station wagons, and since 20 percent of such Pontiac lines as the 6000 and Parisienne were station wagons, Losh thought a minivan might soon be needed.

Losh was also concerned about the possibility of another energy crunch, and its effect on his sporty division and demographics. Also, how viable in the long term was this segment? The median age of a Pontiac buyer had dropped from 42 in 1981 to 37 in 1985, and the proportion of Pontiac buyers in the key 25- to 44-age group had increased from 43 to 51 percent. Sales among the age group had increased 65 percent, and their median household income in 1985 was nearly $40,000. An internal GM study indicated that, although the current ratio of people aged 55 and under to the over-55 age was 4 to 1, by the year 2010, it would fall to 3 to 1, and by 2050, 2 to 1.[5]

By late 1986, Losh's earlier projection of record-breaking sales of 900,000 Pontiacs was clearly not going to be achieved—in spite of GM's aggressively low interest rates for new purchases and Pontiac advertising expenditures of approximately $70 million. In fact, the number would be approximately 840,000 or 7.5 percent of the U.S. market and 17.8 percent of all GM sales. Losh and his team were convinced that they could have sold more if they could have produced more. In addition, the Fiero, facing similar cars from Toyota, Ford, and Honda, had experienced a drop in sales of 21 percent from 1985. (See Exhibit 10 for sales figures for Pontiac cars.)

As he prepared to enter 1987, Losh's staff was proposing a 40 percent reduction in the number of options on the 1987 cars, which would make it a leader among GM divisions in making option cuts. He wondered how the dealers would react to further reductions, especially in light of his team's 1987 sales goal of 900,000:

Sunbird	110,000
Grand Am	235,000
6000	170,000
Fiero	75,000
Firebird	90,000
Bonneville	140,000
1000	11,000
Grand Prix	24,000
LeMans	30,000
Safari Wagons	15,000
	900,000

[5] Taken from the article "EAS Studies Designs to Aid Aging Drivers" found in *GM Today*, a quarterly employee newsletter, October 23, 1986.

EXHIBIT 10 Pontiac Division, Annual Car Sales by Largest Selling Model and Major Categories, 1980–1986

	1980	1981	1982	1983	1984	1985	1986
TOTAL ECONOMY SEGMENT	1,416,758	1,821,461	1,550,609	1,610,411	1,596,685	1,724,210	2,063,990
Ford Escort	0	284,633	321,952	323,900	339,209	410,978	415,521
Nissan Sentra 210	188,695	161,573	176,678	212,438	192,186	212,071	221,012
Honda Civic	133,111	158,127	134,054	139,169	128,494	146,926	165,677
Plymouth Horizon Sedan	77,372	83,950	48,045	50,861	74,347	97,508	101,379
Chevrolet Spectrum	0	0	0	0	0	39,624	93,992
Volkswagen Domestic Golf/Rabbit	190,220	159,588	107,396	83,222	83,084	83,682	90,056
Dodge Omni Sedan	61,379	61,018	40,006	45,843	65,675	84,575	88,325
Mazda GLC	60,784	70,386	52,260	55,706	44,387	49,493	78,450
Chevrolet Chevette	375,396	376,758	233,858	183,970	180,341	135,261	75,761
Toyota Tercel	94,503	115,841	127,329	150,968	108,889	102,413	74,330
Pontiac 1000	0	43,097	52,558	38,286	28,900	24,180	20,066
TOTAL SUBCOMPACT SEGMENT	837,343	717,153	666,472	814,313	1,022,800	1,115,239	1,268,521
Chevrolet Cavalier	0	43,855	120,587	216,297	371,836	422,927	386,258
Chevrolet/Nummi Nova (fwd)	0	0	0	0	0	16,323	170,661
Subaru	81,094	104,274	99,856	109,622	99,706	153,350	159,888
Toyota Corolla	257,812	209,880	122,995	117,836	95,753	131,069	118,486
Pontiac 2000 Sunbird	0	34,424	59,018	79,509	123,937	120,207	109,807
Volkswagen Jetta	8,161	24,773	21,561	19,157	36,275	70,502	97,362
Buick Skyhawk (fwd)	0	0	32,952	69,946	116,276	90,700	77,966
Nissan Stanza	66,468	47,242	55,939	66,030	47,265	56,844	69,046
Oldsmobile Firenza	0	0	19,562	43,042	59,490	52,760	39,212
Mitsubishi Tredia	0	0	0	11,083	15,079	10,546	10,346
TOTAL COMPACT SEGMENT	1,627,388	1,730,358	1,249,854	1,158,459	1,292,511	1,665,911	1,967,387
Honda Accord	176,954	188,044	180,646	209,567	256,336	256,255	296,086
Ford Tempo	0	0	0	70,986	255,727	297,656	251,618
Pontiac Grand Am	0	0	0	0	26	98,567	190,994
Toyota Camry/Corona	37,352	25,549	6,656	35,054	85,477	117,539	144,405
Plymouth Reliant	0	180,103	151,279	161,757	141,377	137,074	131,372
Oldsmobile Calais	0	0	0	0	29	113,280	119,740
Buick Somerset Regal	0	0	0	0	66	88,103	113,862
Dodge Aries	0	137,066	112,761	124,650	110,939	117,742	104,572
Mazda 626	50,352	64,867	58,317	65,672	70,910	79,889	95,374
Chrysler LeBaron GTS	0	0	0	0	0	55,740	71,542
TOTAL MIDSIZE SEGMENT	1,994,295	1,885,261	1,566,210	2,091,446	2,512,523	2,500,540	2,472,094
Chevrolet Celebrity	0	0	67,475	155,953	307,777	360,167	395,860
Oldsmobile Ciera	0	0	78,542	169,939	252,669	315,569	330,572
Buick Century (fwd)	0	0	70,778	134,804	208,745	239,570	239,278
Oldsmobile Supreme	269,189	281,390	175,361	193,305	201,044	234,242	202,158
Pontiac 6000	0	0	36,564	84,816	124,407	156,994	196,209
Ford Thunderbird	164,795	80,942	47,903	99,176	156,583	169,770	144,577
Mercury Cougar Specialty	69,572	34,324	17,732	63,350	115,546	130,015	121,972
Chevrolet Monte Carlo	177,124	175,155	105,721	98,865	127,875	105,568	117,671
Buick Regal	192,507	223,992	148,893	155,906	134,282	127,386	82,904
Pontiac Grand Prix/Bonneville	208,258	215,863	162,876	169,034	152,470	117,719	82,478
Ford LTD	0	0	0	142,817	198,109	205,889	50,717

(Continued)

EXHIBIT 10 (Continued)

	1980	1981	1982	1983	1984	1985	1986
TOTAL REGULAR SEGMENT	964,235	763,567	677,403	855,614	1,086,663	1,057,901	948,473
Oldsmobile Delta 88	156,355	161,766	168,550	218,604	259,937	213,833	241,417
Chevrolet Caprice	307,395	216,630	205,861	226,750	264,625	251,693	228,706
Ford LTD Crown Victoria	161,537	120,410	118,527	124,154	157,068	173,509	128,280
Mercury Gran Marquis	58,007	52,552	69,784	97,341	131,515	145,242	112,225
Buick LeSabre	94,206	81,244	102,424	140,812	161,763	144,684	104,570
Pontiac Parisienne	119,880	98,955	12,257	14,459	55,736	73,109	72,909
Chrysler New Yorker (fwd)	0	0	0	33,494	56,019	55,831	59,455
TOTAL LUXURY SEGMENT	326,976	309,839	397,141	515,811	577,618	655,147	703,385
Cadillac DeVille (fwd)	0	0	0	0	46,356	139,718	164,979
Lincoln Town Car	35,845	31,038	34,620	59,335	77,475	116,015	119,180
Oldsmobile Regency 98	74,497	83,332	86,338	113,794	107,335	118,673	116,615
Buick Electra 225	68,890	59,722	57,704	75,691	88,397	90,922	111,245
Chrysler Fifth Avenue (rwd)	0	0	51,757	77,700	78,399	112,137	110,639
Cadillac DeVille/Fleetwood (rwd)	147,744	135,747	145,075	173,086	151,880	48,883	60,915
Lincoln Continental	0	0	21,647	16,205	27,776	28,799	19,812
TOTAL SPORTS SEGMENT	1,495,091	1,188,208	1,010,813	2,136,718	1,408,466	1,466,628	1,385,355
TOTAL HIGHSPORT	124,320	111,693	101,172	1,180,020	122,444	160,325	154,729
Nissan 300/280Z	71,594	64,487	59,853	68,575	71,617	67,826	57,187
Chevrolet Corvette	37,471	33,414	22,086	25,891	27,986	37,878	35,969
Porsche 944/924	0	0	2,567	12,142	12,716	14,725	19,871
Porsche 911	3,226	3,714	4,403	5,313	4,513	4,846	7,533
Alfa Romeo Spider/Spyder Veloce	2,749	1,329	1,486	1,981	2,461	4,485	5,103
Porsche 928	1,427	1,745	2,136	2,325	2,332	2,375	2,673
Ferrari Italian Total	570	912	757	541	585	606	656
TOTAL MIDSPORT	623,760	506,380	535,505	577,467	842,113	856,983	790,172
Chevrolet Camaro	131,066	109,707	148,649	175,004	207,285	206,082	173,674
Toyota Celica	145,485	103,505	113,599	119,140	90,784	72,265	108,725
Pontiac Firebird	95,449	61,460	83,810	93,378	105,628	101,797	96,208
Honda Prelude	47,041	49,025	37,137	35,538	65,694	72,011	75,409
Pontiac Fiero	0	0	0	2,015	99,705	90,691	71,283
Mazda RX7	46,021	44,053	46,422	53,402	53,178	54,656	53,511
Nissan 200SX	86,345	80,748	54,745	37,189	51,056	62,595	49,792
Dodge Daytona	0	0	0	802	42,596	51,299	40,504
Chrysler Laser	0	0	0	925	52,073	54,758	31,458
Toyota MR2	0	0	0	0	0	23,812	30,984
Isuzu Impulse	0	0	0	5,720	13,024	14,955	11,867
TOTAL LOWSPORT	747,011	570,135	374,136	379,231	443,909	449,320	440,454
Ford Mustang	246,008	173,329	116,804	116,120	131,762	159,741	175,598
Honda CRX	0	0	0	0	32,625	53,903	60,782
Dodge Charger (fwd)	49,329	50,129	41,534	45,238	51,799	49,501	51,695
Nissan Pulsar NX	0	0	0	43,841	42,319	45,423	49,458
Plymouth Turismo	57,434	52,959	38,776	37,079	47,226	45,385	47,053
Toyota Corolla	0	44,212	51,714	24,996	63,570	37,617	34,006
Mercury Capri	67,538	53,491	29,956	25,500	19,499	16,829	13,358
Mitsubishi Cordia	0	0	0	10,422	14,938	8,662	5,398
Renault Fuego	0	0	7,613	13,003	12,528	5,810	2,480
Ford EXP	0	41,601	43,049	26,471	24,040	26,450	626

This was at a time when there was growing concern that the domestic auto industry's low interest rates in late 1986 and the changing tax law would take business away from early 1987.

How he made his mark at Pontiac might well determine how far Losh would go at GM. Losh knew that many of the truly successful Pontiac general managers who had moved on to increasingly important positions at GM were those who, in some form or another, had implemented successful strategic moves in the divisions. Although Losh had been named "rookie of the year" in 1985 and "sales/marketing All-Star" in 1986 by *Automotive News,* he knew he couldn't let the division stand still. He had once commented to a group of GM managers, "I can tell you from firsthand experience, just when you think you're finished, you realize it's only the beginning." That seemed to be more true than ever in 1987.

INDUSTRIAL HIGHLIGHT

Motor Vehicles Industry

Below is a capsule summary of the passenger cars segment of the motor vehicle industry, of which General Motors is a part. Information in this highlight was compiled by the U.S. Department of Commerce and focuses on this industry during the approximate period of time covered in the case. Keep in mind that industrial highlights contained in this text are not intended as a complete synopsis of an industry but as a profile of certain issues that can be relevant to a case situation.

■ CURRENT SITUATION

Automobile Sales

U.S. retail sales of new passenger cars continued to grow steadily during 1984, building upon the strong sales recovery of 1983. Total car sales reached 10.4 million units, 13.2 percent above the 9.2 million units recorded in 1983.

Sales of domestic-make automobiles in 1984 totaled 8.0 million units, a 17.0 percent increase over 1983 sales, and 38.1 percent above the depressed 1982 level. Total import car sales, spurred by strong demand for European-built models, rose moderately to 2.4 million units. Sales of Japanese imports, including so-called "captive" imports of General Motors and Chrysler, declined slightly to 1.9 million units. This was due to Japanese restraint in exporting automobiles and continued strength in the U.S. demand for North American-built full-size, luxury, specialty, and performance automobiles.

As a result of these trends, imports' share of the U.S. car market fell by 2.5 percentage points in 1984, to 23.5 percent. The Japanese import share fell to an even greater degree, from 20.9 percent in 1983 to 18.3 percent in 1984. These were the lowest levels of Japanese and total import penetration since 1979.

Total U.S. sales of new automobiles were expected to be about 10.6 million units in 1985. Sales of domestic-make cars should be about 7.8 million units, while total import sales were expected to be about 2.8 million units. Japanese

Source: U.S. Industrial Outlook, Department of Commerce, 1986, pp. 36–1 to 36–3.

and total import penetration of the U.S. market were expected to increase to 20.8 and 26.4 percent, respectively, largely as a result of liberalization of Japanese exports in April 1985.

Labor Relations Trends

General Motors and Ford signed new 3-year contracts with the United Automobile Workers (UAW) in September and October 1984, respectively. Significant new job security provisions were included in those contracts. In addition, the new contracts provide workers with first-year wage increases of approximately 2.25 percent and lump sum payments equal to 2.25 percent of annual wages during the second and third years of the agreement. Pension benefits for both current and future retirees also will increase moderately under the new agreement; profit sharing and cost-of-living allowances will continue on the same basis as in previous agreements.

According to many industry officials, future changes in work rules are likely to have an important impact on the ability of U.S. producers to reduce labor costs and compete more effectively. While widespread implementation of major changes will require many years, it is likely that limited reforms will soon be introduced on a large scale. These reforms are likely to include reductions in the number of separate job classifications for both production and skilled trades workers, changes in worker "bumping" procedures to limit the frequency of costly job transfers within plants, the adoption of "pay for knowledge" systems, and increased use of semi-autonomous work teams.

Another development that could have a major impact on labor relations within the industry was the recent decision of the Canadian arm of the UAW to separate itself from the International UAW based in the United States. The implications of this split in the UAW for the manufacturers will not be clear until the UAW holds contract renewal discussions with Ford and General Motors in the fall of 1987.

Improving Productivity

Domestic automobile manufacturers continue to focus their attention on controlling fixed and variable costs. By containing variable cost increases as production expanded in 1984, the producers were able to hold constant the ratio of revenues to production costs. Gross profit per unit actually increased slightly between 1983 and 1984. However, 1984 was the first year since 1980 in which the ratio of revenues to costs of goods sold failed to increase from its year-earlier level (see Exhibit A). While this situation continued into the first half of 1985, the increasing ratio was expected to reappear in the second half.

Productivity gains will continue to play a key role in the industry's efforts to meet ambitious cost-control objectives. Industry output per worker increased 16 percent from 1983 to 1984, building upon the nearly 24 percent rise in productivity between 1982 and 1983 (see Exhibit B). Industry output per worker in the fall of 1985 stood at its highest level ever, and was expected to

EXHIBIT A Worldwide Costs and Revenues; GM, Ford, and Chrysler Combined

ITEM	1980	1981	1982	1983	1984
Revenue (billions)	$103.4	$110.9	$107.1	$132.3	$155.8
Costs[1] (billions)	$ 95.4	$ 98.7	$ 92.6	$108.9	$129.2
Revenue/Costs	1.08	1.12	1.16	1.21	1.21
Unit sales worldwide (millions)	12.65	12.36	11.69	14.20	15.96
Revenue/unit	$8,174	$8,972	$9,162	$9,317	$9,762
Cost/unit	$7,542	$7,985	$7,921	$7,669	$8,095
Gross margin/unit	$ 632	$ 987	$1,241	$1,648	$1,667

[1] "Costs" are costs of goods sold. Unit sales are worldwide factory sales of motor vehicles.

Source: Company annual and quarterly reports.

increase farther (though at a more moderate rate) during 1986. Industry investments in advanced manufacturing equipment (computer-controlled machine tools, robotics, etc.) and processes, as well as changes in the organization of work (greater use of modular assembly techniques, just-in-time material handling, and semi-autonomous work teams) will strengthen these favorable productivity trends.

OUTLOOK FOR 1986

New car sales are forecast to remain strong through 1986, reaching 10.7 million units, slightly above estimated 1985 sales. This forecast is based on continued strength in the overall economy and moderation in interest rates and fuel prices. Domestic car sales are projected to be about 7.5 million units, while imported car sales are forecast to reach about 3.2 million units. Import penetration is projected to rise from 26.4 percent in 1985 to 29.9 percent in 1986.

U.S. auto manufacturers are expected to enjoy another year of healthy profits in 1986. Given relatively favorable conditions, net earnings worldwide should reach $8.0 billion as nonrecurring startup costs incurred in 1985 taper off. These earnings will stengthen balance sheets by increasing liquidity and owners' equity, and provide funds for capital investment. The rate of increase in the value of the industry's product shipments is likely to be somewhat below

EXHIBIT B U.S. Vehicle Output Per Employee, 1979–84—GM, Ford, and Chrysler Combined (in thousands)

	1979	1980	1981	1982	1983	1984
Motor vehicle production	10,751	7,439	7,412	6,602	8,626	10,095
Employment	967	774	762	656	692	695
Vehicles/employees	11.1	9.6	9.7	10.1	12.5	14.5

Source: Company annual reports and Wards Automotive Reports.

the increase in general inflation, lending strength to the demand for its products.

LONG-TERM PROSPECTS

Domestic auto manufacturers now face the most challenging and competitive period in their history. Japanese manufacturers will soon begin to sell mid-size cars in the U.S. market, and new foreign manufacturers from such countries as Yugoslavia and South Korea are preparing to compete in the subcompact segment of the market. The U.S. companies are positioning themselves for increased competition by focusing on cost reductions, productivity increases, product quality improvement, and product line enhancement.

The Saturn, Alpha, and Liberty programs of General Motors, Ford, and Chrysler, respectively, embody the domestic manufacturers' hopes for the future viability of small car production in the United States, as well as increased productivity throughout the companies. But the Japanese manufacturers will not stand still. Continued gains in productivity and economies of scale by the Japanese will have to be matched by American producers if the domestic firms are to compete.

Capital Formation

The long-term success of U.S. carmakers will hinge on their ability to generate investment funds to fuel new programs. The ability of their suppliers to fund their own restructuring programs will also be crucial. U.S. auto manufacturers are planning to invest over $100 billion during the next 5 years in product development and plant improvements. In order to fund this level of investment, the companies will need to continue to reduce manufacturing costs while offering competitive products.

Demand Outlook

Growth in the overall automobile market will slow down over the longer term because of demographic trends and increases in ownership and operating costs. The driving-age population is projected to grow at an annual rate of 1 percent for the rest of the 1980s, compared to 2 percent during the 1970s. This trend will be partially offset by an increase in the percentage of the population between 25 and 44, the prime auto-buying years.

Another, and often overlooked, factor will be the average age of the domestic car population and vehicle scrappage rates. The average age of cars in use has reached its highest level since 1950. Meanwhile, scrappage rates in 1983–84 reached their lowest levels since the mid-1970s. Although the increased durability of automobiles has contributed to these trends, the high prices of new and used cars seem to have played a more important role. But given projections of continued growth of the U.S. economy, potential reductions in car and truck prices as a result of increased foreign competition, and the high average age of the cars presently on the road, car scrappage rates should rise over the next several years as replacement demand returns to a more normal level. Replacement demand should account for a signifcant portion of the moderate growth in U.S. car sales forecasted through the end of the decade.

Technological Developments

Technological developments in automotive electronics, plant communications systems, design and manufacturing control systems, materials engineering, and metalworking are being adopted by U.S. car manufacturers and their suppliers to improve their competitiveness. American producers are in the process of revolutionizing the assembly process and the manufacturing of components. Improvements under way include installation of computer-aided design and computer-aided manufacturing processes (CAD/CAM), computerized inventory controls, computer networking, and industrial robotics. Over the longer term, the U.S. auto industry's success in cutting costs will depend on its ability to develop and apply a wide range of new technologies to auto manufacturing, to incorporate product innovations, and to restructure organizational and managerial relations to help achieve these goals. These processes, which are already under way, will continue for the rest of the decade.

CASE 12

K mart Stores: Where America Shops and Saves

JOHN L. LITTLE
University of North Carolina at Greensboro

LARRY D. ALEXANDER
Virginia Polytechnic Institute and State University

The S. S. Kresge Company opened hundreds of K mart stores throughout the United States after its first store opened for business in the early 1960s. The company maintained a practice of keeping the stores uniform in layout and appearances throughout most of this period. Each store was a simple boxlike building, usually located free-standing and away from shopping malls. K mart stores sold low- to medium-quality merchandise priced lower than that of its competitors. This approach proved to be very successful, especially among price-conscious shoppers, who left full service department stores to shop at K mart and other discounters. The K mart logo itself became a symbol of low prices in the minds of many shoppers.

In the dynamic 1980s, important changes were taking place in the retail industry. Younger shoppers had become more discriminating than their parents. Many had a greater amount of disposable income to spend. These younger shoppers wanted higher quality merchandise and were willing to pay for it. While K mart stuck with its traditional approach, other retailers had moved in to satisfy this new consumer group. In the process, these competitors created a retail environment that had never been more competitive. Furthermore, the successful market penetration of warehouse clubs and specialty stores into the retailing industry meant even more intense competition for discount stores such as K mart.

How K mart should respond to these and other issues remained unclear. One thing did seem certain. Unless K mart made changes to remain aligned with a changing retail environment, its future financial performance would probably decline.

HISTORY

The S. S. Kresge Company was founded in 1899 with the opening of a single store in downtown Detroit, Michigan. Its founder, Sebastian Kresge, who

---

This case was written by John L. Little, Assistant Professor of Strategic Management at the University of North Carolina at Greensboro, and Larry D. Alexander, Associate Professor of Strategic Management at Virginia Polytechnic Institute and State University. Copyright © 1988 by John L. Little and Larry D. Alexander.

followed a slogan of "nothing over ten cents," rapidly opened more stores in new locations. He standardized the mix of merchandise, continued to emphasize low prices, and centralized the purchasing function. This latter move greatly increased the bargaining power that Kresge had over suppliers, while at the same time reducing administrative overhead. This reduction made the opening of new stores easier by spreading startup costs over a wider base. Kresge soon developed operating procedures that permitted centralized control over a growing number of uniform stores. The lower prices charged by Kresge caused individual store volume to increase and profits to rise, which provided the necessary funds to open still more stores. When the company was incorporated in 1912, Kresge's "five and ten" style stores numbered 85 and had a combined annual sales of more than $10 million.

Variety stores, which carried a variety of inexpensive kitchen, stationery, toy, soft goods, and hard goods items, grew in popularity throughout the 1920s and 1930s as a more convenient means of shopping than the earlier established speciality stores. A number of variety store chains had been established by 1940, with their limited selection of a wider array of product lines. The greater buying power available to these chain stores allowed them to underprice the specialty stores that concentrated in just one product line. The combination of lower prices and a wider selection of different product categories was a powerful attraction to customers. Furthermore, since more and more shoppers had their own cars, they were willing to travel further from home to save money.

During the 1950s, the introduction of shopping centers and supermarkets began to draw customers away from variety stores. To counter this, some variety retailers began looking for new ways to attract customers. In 1954, for example, Marty Chase converted an old mill in Cumberland, Rhode Island, into a discount store named Ann and Hope. The store sold ribbon, greeting cards, and women's clothing. As other discount stores opened throughout the 1950s, the then Kresge president, Harry Cunningham, began to consider a similar approach. Finally, in 1962, Kresge responded by opening its first K mart discount store in Garden City, Michigan.

K mart discount stores were nothing more than a large scale version of the earlier Kresge retail stores. They still emphasized low prices, a wide selection, and low overhead costs, which combined to create profits. The first K mart stores were stocked primarily with Kresge merchandise. A number of licensees, who operated departments within the store, added their merchandise to the selection. Later, licensee merchandise was replaced entirely with K mart's own merchandise. The initial stores were a great success, and by 1966, they numbered 162 with a combined sales of over $1 billion.

The K mart success formula remained relatively unchanged for many years. Many new stores were added each year, sometimes by the hundreds. Almost all of them were uniform, free-standing stores located away from large shopping centers. By erecting simple, free-standing buildings in suburban areas, K mart opened its stores more quickly than competitors, who had to wait for shopping centers to be completed. This also helped to keep overhead costs down since its free-standing stores were not located in expensive shopping malls, where rent was high. Over time, K mart stores became located in almost all major U.S. metropolitan areas. During the 1960s and 1970s, annual sales grew by an average of 20 percent per year, primarily due to the fact that consumers found K mart's blend of low price and wide selection very attractive. The company's smaller Kresge stores, unlike its K mart stores, were not as profitable and many were closed during this period.

By 1976, the Kresge Company had become the second largest general merchandise retailer in the United States, behind Sears. During the next year, the corporate name was changed from the Kresge Company to the K mart Corporation because K mart stores accounted for 94.5 percent of all corporate sales.

By the late seventies, several problems were impacting on K mart. Good locations for new K mart stores were becoming more difficult to find. Other discount chains were drawing some K mart shoppers away. Industry surveys indicated that the needs of the customers were changing. While other discounters started upgrading their stores and started emphasizing brand name merchandise, K mart continued to sell primarily low-priced K mart private label and generic goods in their same austere-looking stores. Furthermore, during these same years, K mart sales growth started to flatten.

In 1980, Bernard Fauber was named K mart's new chief executive officer. He replaced an unusual arrangement in which three men shared the office of the president. Fauber quickly moved to refurbish the dated K mart stores, and to upgrade the quality of goods which they carried. New display racks, better point of purchase displays, and improved traffic flow through the stores helped to make K mart stores more attractive to customers.

FUNCTIONAL AREA STRATEGIES WITHIN THE K MART STORES

Marketing

Early on, K mart stores emphasized low prices as an important marketing weapon. Its low prices often meant that the product being offered was of a lower quality. For hard goods such as kitchen appliances, this usually meant that just the basic product was carried, without the extra features that competing retailers' higher priced models offered.

K mart focused on satisfying the needs of low and middle income families with limited budgets. Customers in this market segment were unwilling to pay higher prices for similar products with extra features. Still, it was estimated in the 1980s that 80 percent of all Americans shopped at K mart at least once during a calendar year.

The sales promotion of K mart's products was accomplished in several ways. First, sales promotion was emphasized by more attractive in-store, point of purchase displays. Second, K mart's well known "blue light specials" were used to promote specific products for short periods of time during the day. Third, its products were promoted in numerous newspaper ads.

K mart relied heavily on newspaper advertising to promote its goods.

Newspaper inserts were designed at corporate headquarters and sent to newspapers throughout the country for publication. Advertising copy was sent to store managers in advance so they could prepare for the sales. The company placed approximately 120,000,000 inserts in 1,700 different newspapers each week throughout the U.S. by the mid-1980s. While the company continued to emphasize newspapers, increased attention was being given to television advertising. This advertising did not become relatively economical until K mart had opened thousands of stores across the nation.

With its high level of market penetration, K mart initiated a new effort to get customers to buy more goods per trip. Management felt this would be possible because the disposable family income of many K mart customers was rising. This rise in family income was partially the result of a significant increase in the number of two income families. K mart estimated that 19 percent of its customers were from households with annual incomes of at least $40,000; however, this customer group typically bought only low priced items such as tennis balls, batteries, and shampoo at K mart.

K mart added more national brand merchandise and higher quality private labels, and then displayed them in a more attractive manner. Brand name products such as Casio, Minolta, Nike, MacGregor, Wilson, and General Electric were increasingly found throughout the store. K mart hoped that this action would help attract higher income customers to other product areas and increase their per sale purchases. At the same time, the company hoped to retain its less affluent customers by continuing to offer an assortment of lower priced, lower quality merchandise.

K mart did extremely well in certain departments, but performed weakly in others. It was the leader in housewares and the second largest appliance retailer behind only Sears. Many customers were attracted to its brand name appliances and housewares by K mart's low prices. These same customers, however, were turned off by K mart's cheap clothing, which had a low image among many consumers. Its apparel departments, in fact, had been a major shortcoming for K mart throughout the years. K mart tried to address this problem by upgrading many lines of clothing. Furthermore, the responsibility for ordering apparel was taken away from store managers and given to professional staff buyers at corporate headquarters, who were more knowledgeable about fashion.

K mart had also moved into specialty discount stores through several acquisitions. The first Designer Depot, which was a discount price specialty apparel store, was started in Detroit during 1982. These stores sold quality brand name merchandise at discounts of 20 percent to 70 percent. Some stores also sold shoes, while others sold bedroom and bathroom soft goods.

The company also acquired several other impressive specialty chains. Walden Book Company, Inc., another K mart acquisition in 1985, operated 943 stores in all 50 states. Builders Square, Inc., a warehouse-type home improvement center chain, was acquired in 1984. By 1985, the company had 25 stores located in eight states. Fredrick Stevens, executive vice president of specialty retailing operations, argued that 400 locations across the country could support the volume requirements of these huge discount builders supply warehouses. Builders Square was hoping to capture a 25 percent share of that market.[1]

Pay Less Drug Stores Northwest, another K mart acquisition in 1985, was the tenth largest drug chain in the nation. Pay Less was a discount chain, supported by a very cost efficient operation, and strong management. With sales approaching $1 billion and 176 stores, the chain hoped to penetrate rapidly in its present markets in California, Oregon, Washington, Idaho, and Nevada.

Two final K mart acquisitions were in the restaurant industry. Furr's Cafeterias, acquired earlier in 1980, and Bishop Buffets, acquired in 1983, had a total of 162 units by 1985. Due to slow growth in the cafeteria industry, however, future growth for new cafeterias in this acquisition was expected to be limited to 10 percent per year.

K mart Corporation had limited involvement in overseas markets. It did have, however, a 20 percent interest in G. L. Coles and Coy Limited, a food and general merchandise retailer in Australia. It also had a 44 percent interest in Astra, S.A., which operated a food and general merchandise chain in Mexico.

Store Operations

During the 1980s, K mart was approaching market saturation, with its stores located almost everywhere throughout 48 states. Its 2,332 stores by the end of 1985 were located in 250 of the U.S. 255 Standard Metropolitan Statistical Areas (SMSA). From a record 271 new store openings in 1976, only 18 new K mart stores were opened in 1985.

Because of market saturation, K mart switched its emphasis from opening new stores to renovating existing ones. This effort, which started in the early 1980s, was intended to increase productivity as well as to upgrade the store image. Wider and taller display cases carried more merchandise and made better use of cubic space. This allowed for a wider assortment of merchandise to be displayed within the same square footage. It also reduced the need for additional backroom storage. A new store layout was developed around a wide center aisle that let consumers walk through every department without leaving the aisle. As one K mart store manager put it, "We want to encourage people to go into areas where they would not normally go . . . to pass by merchandise they were not planning to buy!"[2]

All K mart stores were designed around the same basic floor plan, shown in Exhibit 1. As shoppers entered the store, they were no longer confronted with the smell of popcorn and the sight of gumball machines. Instead, they might be greeted by the jewelry department with a wide selection of watches and jewelry of various price ranges. The main aisle down the center of the store separated soft goods from hard goods. Located on the soft goods side of the store were women's apparel, then men's apparel, with infants' wear and

---

[1] Anonymous, "K mart: A Look Inside the Nation's Largest Discounter," *Mass Market Retailers*, December 16, 1985, p. 42.
[2] *Ibid.*, p. 20.

EXHIBIT 1 Typical K mart Store Floor Layout

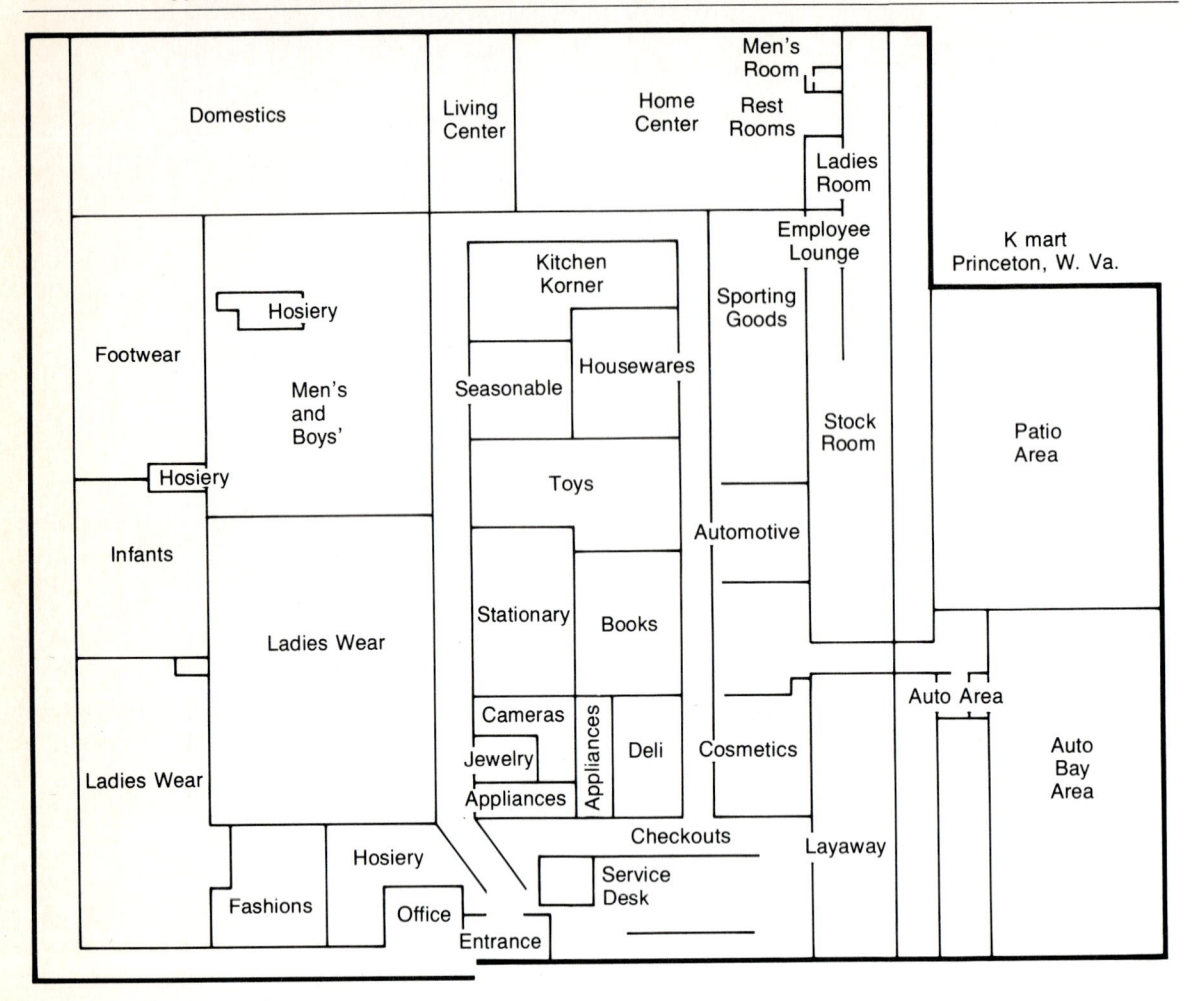

Source: K mart Pamphlet, 1985.

children's clothes nearby. Popular crafts and yarn were also located on this side, where homemakers were most likely to look for them. In the hard goods half of the store, housewares, sporting goods, automotive supplies, and hardware were located at the rear of the store, drawing men and women past the high impulse, high margin merchandise in the greeting cards, jewelry, and toy departments. The health and beauty items and the pharmacies, for the minority of stores that had them, were typically located in the right front section of the store.

Electronic communications systems connected all stores to 10 enormous regional distribution centers. These centers were located in California, Nevada,

Texas, Kansas, Minnesota, Michigan, Indiana, Ohio, Pennsylvania, and Georgia, as shown in Exhibit 2. These highly automated distribution centers contained a combined 15 million square feet of warehouse space. Together, they operated a fleet of 250 tractors and 1,000 trailers, which provided weekly delivery to every K mart store requesting it.

Approximately 25 percent of K mart's merchandise was handled by these distribution centers. In contrast, 75 percent of all store purchases were shipped directly from suppliers to the stores in order to minimize shipping cost. The delivery of products from suppliers was usually fast, in order to keep such a large account as K mart satisfied. This reduced inventory level requirements at stores to minimum levels. A significant reduction in reorder time had been achieved by installing optical scanners on cash registers at K mart stores. Scanning, coupled with a company wide computer network, permitted automated replenishment of merchandise and made it possible to differentiate the seasonal needs of each region.

As part of its efforts to upgrade its image, K mart was completing a major remodeling program of store interiors to present a more modern store appearance to shoppers. This new effort, called "The K mart of the '80s,"

EXHIBIT 2 Store Distribution Network

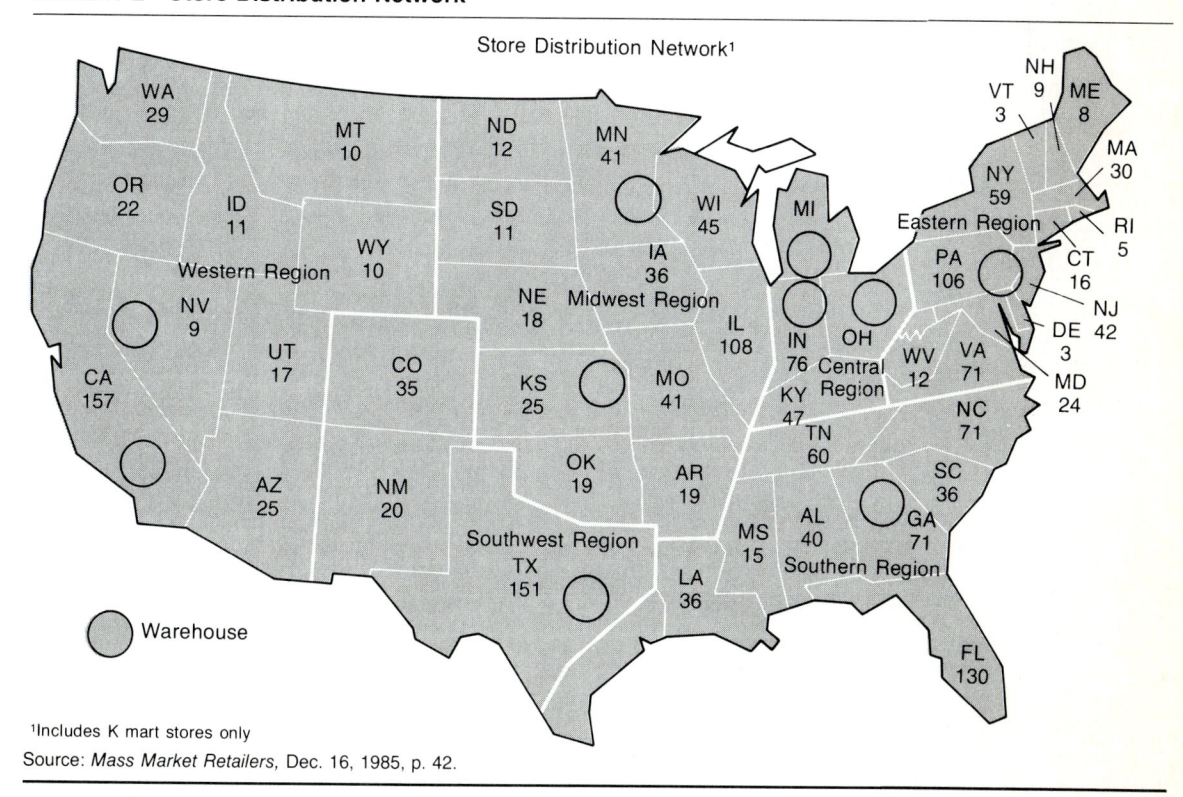

Store Distribution Network[1]

State	Stores
WA	29
MT	10
ND	12
MN	41
VT	3
NH	9
ME	8
OR	22
ID	11
WY	10
SD	11
WI	45
MI	—
NY	59
MA	30
RI	5
NV	9
UT	17
CO	35
NE	18
IA	36
IL	108
IN	76
OH	—
PA	106
WV	12
VA	71
CT	16
NJ	42
DE	3
MD	24
CA	157
AZ	25
NM	20
KS	25
MO	41
OK	19
AR	19
KY	47
TN	60
NC	71
SC	36
MS	15
AL	40
GA	71
TX	151
LA	36
FL	130

Regions: Western Region, Midwest Region, Southwest Region, Central Region, Southern Region, Eastern Region

○ Warehouse

[1]Includes K mart stores only

Source: *Mass Market Retailers*, Dec. 16, 1985, p. 42.

incorporated a new color scheme on interior walls and floors, broader aisles, and more attractive displays. Low volume lines were dropped or consolidated to achieve a store within a store format. The Kitchen Corner, Home Care Center, and Domestic Center were arranged along the back wall and emphasized fashion and style at discount prices. The early success of the plan was encouraging. Sales per square foot had risen from $139 in 1980 to $168 four years later. While this was superior to the $128 per square foot typical among discounter department stores, it was far behind such discounters as Target and Wal-mart.

Product categories no longer in demand were eliminated. For example, K mart's 360 automotive service departments in rural stores were closed in 1982. Unprofitable stores were closed altogether, freeing up more than $1 million each in capital for use elsewhere in the corporation.

The more than 2,000 K mart stores were organized into six regions, each of which had from 266 to 422 stores. Each region was comprised of about 20 districts, while each district had from 10 to 20 stores.

K mart stores came in five basic sizes. The smallest was the 40,000 square feet size store, which was placed in smaller markets. At the other end, the jumbo 120,000 square foot store was placed in large metropolitan markets. These free-standing stores were located in suburban areas with large parking lots, and were usually leased rather than owned. Buildings usually were erected by local contractors, but a K mart subsidiary built several stores each year to allow the company to remain knowledgeable about building costs and procedures.

K mart's decision to avoid shopping center locations was part of its low overhead philosophy. Leasing costs at shopping centers were very high compared to K mart locations. Shopping centers generally did not want discounters as tenants anyway, due to the negative image associated with them. Also, specialty stores did not want to locate next to a discount store because of the significant price difference between their products and a discounter's. Sometimes, K mart would buy existing buildings in shopping centers or develop properties in good locations and sublease retail space to specialty stores.

Finance

Total sales for the K mart Corporation, as shown in its consolidated statement of income in Exhibit 3, were $22.4 billion for fiscal year 1985, which ended on January 29, 1986. This represented a 6.3 percent increase over the sales for the previous year. Net income after taxes for that same year was $221.0 million. The consolidated balance sheet for fiscal 1985 and 1984 is shown in Exhibit 4. Finally, a comparison of sales and various financial data for K mart over a ten year period are presented in Exhibit 5.

Retail sales at K mart were extremely seasonal, with a high proportion of sales and profits coming during the Christmas shopping season. For example, some 33 percent of K mart's 1984 sales and 41 percent of its profits came during the fourth quarter alone.

EXHIBIT 3   K mart Corporation Consolidated Income Statements
(in millions, except per-share data)

	FISCAL YEAR ENDED		
	January 29, 1986	January 30, 1985	January 25, 1984
Sales	$22,420	$21,096	$18,598
Licensee fees and rental income	225	207	191
Equity in income of affiliated retail companies	76	65	57
Interest income	24	40	38
	22,745	21,408	18,884
Cost of merchandise sold (including buying and occupancy costs)	16,181	15,260	13,447
Selling, general and administrative expenses	4,845	4,428	3,880
Advertising	567	554	425
Interest expense:			
Debt	205	147	84
Capital lease obligations	191	193	189
	21,989	20,582	18,025
Income from continuing retail operations before income taxes	756	826	859
Income taxes	285	327	366
Income from continuing retail operations	471	499	493
Discontinued operations	(250)	0	(1)
Net income for the year	$ 221	$ 499	$ 492
Earnings per common and common equivalent share:			
Continuing retail operations	$3.63	$3.84	$3.81
Discontinued operations	(1.90)	—	(.01)
Net income	$1.73	$3.84	$3.80

Source: K mart Corporation, 1985 Annual Report, p. 30.

    K mart did not offer a charge card and did not encourage credit sales. By comparison, approximately 58 percent of arch-rival Sears' sales were on credit. MasterCard and VISA credit cards were accepted at K mart and limited in-house credit was provided on appliance sales. Many K mart stores required customers to follow a rigid two-step procedure for writing checks. The customer first had to get approval from the service desk, and then wait at a checkout line to pay for the purchased items.

    K mart's policy for granting exchanges or refunds, on merchandise which did not satisfy the customer, was quite liberal. Most items could be returned for cash by customers without a hassle. This policy was inherited from the old Kresge variety stores. Similarly, K mart customers could get a rain check on any advertised item not found in stock at the time of the sale.

STRATEGY FORMULATION

EXHIBIT 4   K mart Corporation Consolidated Balance Sheets
(in millions)

	January 29, 1986	January 30, 1985
ASSETS		
Current assets:		
Cash (includes temporary investments of $352 and $294, respectively)	$ 627	$ 492
Merchandise inventories	4,537	4,588
Accounts receivable and other current assets	363	231
Total current assets	5,527	5,311
Investments in affiliated retail companies	293	188
Property and equipment—net	3,644	3,339
Other assets and deferred charges	527	220
Investments in discontinued operations	0	204
	$9,991	$9,262
LIABILITIES AND SHAREHOLDERS' EQUITY		
Current liabilities:		
Long-term debt due within one year	$ 15	$ 2
Capital lease obligations due within one year	76	74
Notes payable	127	235
Accounts payable-trade	1,908	1,917
Accrued payrolls and other liabilities	548	362
Taxes other than income taxes	218	200
Income taxes	198	99
Total current liabilities	3,090	2,889
Capital lease obligations	1,713	1,780
Long-term debt	1,456	1,107
Other long-term liabilities	345	163
Deferred income taxes	114	89
Shareholders' equity	3,273	3,234
	$9,991	$9,262

Source: K mart Corporation, 1985 Annual Report, p. 31.

Innovation

The K mart approach to innovation was to adopt new ideas only after they had been developed and proven successful by someone else. This approach avoided risk and had served K mart well throughout the years. Once a good idea was identified, however, K mart showed its genius in applying and

EXHIBIT 5 K mart Corporation 10-Year Financial Summary

	1984	1983	1982	1981	1980	1979	1978	1977	1976	1975
SUMMARY OF OPERATIONS (millions)										
Sales	$21,096	$18,598	$16,772	$16,527	$14,204	$12,731	$11,696	$9,941	$8,382	$6,798
Cost of merchandise sold	15,260	13,447	12,299	12,360	10,417	9,283	8,566	7,299	6,147	4,991
Selling, general and administrative expenses	4,982	4,305	4,049	3,810	3,326	2,839	2,503	2,085	1,750	1,409
Interest expense—net	300	235	219	230	200	149	132	116	103	89
Income before income taxes	820	854	419	323	436	625	634	564	484	395
Net income	$ 499	$ 492	$ 262	$ 220	$ 261	$ 358	$ 344	$ 298	$ 262	$ 196
PER-SHARE DATA (dollars)										
Earnings per common and common equivalent share	$ 3.84	$ 3.80	$ 2.06	$ 1.75	$ 2.07	$ 2.84	$ 2.74	$ 2.39	$ 2.11	$ 1.61
Cash dividends declared	1.24	1.08	1.00	.96	.92	.84	.72	.56	.32	.24
Book value	$25.87	$23.35	$20.89	$19.81	$18.99	$17.79	$15.68	$13.56	$11.62	$ 9.69
FINANCIAL DATA (millions)										
Working capital	$ 2,422	$ 2,268	$ 1,827	$ 1,473	$ 1,552	$ 1,403	$ 1,308	$1,231	$1,074	$ 904
Total assets	9,262	8,183	7,344	6,657	6,089	5,635	4,836	4,489	3,983	3,336
Long-term obligations										
Debt	1,107	711	596	415	419	209	209	211	211	210
Capital leases	1,780	1,822	1,824	1,752	1,618	1,422	1,294	1,266	1,115	989
Shareholders' equity	3,234	2,940	2,601	2,456	2,343	2,185	1,916	1,649	1,409	1,169
Capital expenditures—owned property	622	368	306	361	302	292	217	162	123	112
Depreciation and amortization—owned property	$ 203	$ 168	$ 157	$ 141	$ 119	$ 93	$ 77	$ 65	$ 56	$ 52
Average shares outstanding	126	125	124	124	123	123	122	122	121	121

Source: K mart Corporation, 1984 Annual Report, pp. 16–17.

perfecting it. For example, when the discount store idea emerged, Kresge was the first to refine the concept with its K mart stores. K mart pursued rapid expansion while other retailers looked on with amazement. The idea of standardizing the store floor plan and layout was another example of how K mart borrowed a good idea from elsewhere and perfected it.

Human Resources/Personnel

K mart Corporation employed more than 290,000 people in 1985, but tried to encourage a small business feeling within its individual stores. Loyalty among store managers was unusually high; consequently, their turnover rate was low. Many K mart managers had never worked for any other employer, and 25-year service pins were common. Furthermore, promotion to managerial positions was almost entirely done from within. For those selected, management training consisted of a 16-week program on all phases of a K mart store's operation. After the program, the trainees became assistant managers with responsibility for several departments. Typically, trainees were rotated through various departments and stores for six to ten years before they were ready to manage their own stores.

The opportunity for promotion was strong in the 1970s when new stores were being opened at the rate of several per week. That changed in the 1980s when K mart greatly curtailed its new store openings. This threatened to increase employee turnover as assistant managers became impatient to move up. At the same time, K mart was reducing the number of assistant managers from three to two per store in order to cut administrative costs.

K mart relied heavily on part-time employees to operate its stores. The company goal was to have 60 percent part-time and 40 percent full-time employees with each store. This gave the store manager greater flexibility in matching the work force with the amount of traffic during different periods of the day. Also, the labor costs for part-time employees were considerably lower, because they started at minimum wage and were not paid benefits. The great majority of these employees were women who preferred to work part-time because of their family obligations. The company, however, did have an employee savings plan—even for part-timers—in which K mart contributed 50 cents in K mart stock for every one dollar that the employee contributed.

Management

Harry Cunningham developed the basic K mart strategy and led the company during its rapid growth from 1962 to 1972. When he stepped down in 1972, he appointed K mart's Robert Dewar, Ervin Wardlow, and Walter Tennga to collectively run the company. Dewar, with 32 years of legal and financial background but no store experience, was named chairman. Wardlow, with strong merchandising experience, was named president. Finally, Tennga, a real estate and financial executive, was named vice-chairman. These three executives ran the company for eight years. Although sales tripled during this period, the three could not agree on which direction K mart should take.

In 1980, Bernard Fauber was named the new chief executive officer at the suggestion of Dewar, who felt that K mart needed a store man at the top, rather than a staff man. Since then, K mart has made dramatic changes in its approach to business. As Fauber conceded:

> For 20 years we had been just about the most successful retailer in America, so it was not easy getting our people to admit that some changes were advisable and others were necessary.[3]

In explaining the reasons behind K mart's decision to diversify into other areas, Fauber added:

> We realized that we must do something else for growth since it was no longer possible to open 100 to 120 K mart stores each year.[4]

[3] Ibid., p. 54.
[4] Ibid.

Fauber, like all but one previous CEO, was not a college graduate. He first came to work for the company in 1941 as an 18-year-old stockroom boy in a Kresge store. Nine years later, he joined the management training program. Later he gained experience as a store manager and district manager, and in 1968 became vice president of the company's western region. Like nearly all K mart executives, Fauber had never worked for any other company.

K mart's philosophy was to train their store managers as generalists, then allow them wide discretion in running their stores. They had an incentive plan based on store profits to avoid the mistake Sears made in the 1970s when it tied its department managers' incentive plan to sales volume. The Sears incentive system, which has since been changed, caused its managers to focus on low margin merchandise which boosted sales and their bonuses, but which hurt profits.

Store managers at K mart were encouraged to involve themselves and the store in community activities, such as the United Way. One socially responsible effort K mart undertook was its "Lost Child Program" in 1985. The prime exposure available nationwide at its stores made K mart a good vehicle for the program and enhanced the corporate image.

THE RETAIL INDUSTRY

Market Segments

The retail industry was divided into several general segments which somewhat overlapped one another. There were full-line department stores, discount department stores, discount drug stores, specialty stores, supermarkets, and convenience shops. Exhibit 6 shows the top 15 general merchandise chains for 1985, which includes many of these store types. The trend towards one-stop shopping had blurred the distinctions among the various kinds of stores in recent years. For example, shoppers could find food items in drugstores and discount stores, and clothing and hardware in supermarkets. Within the discount department store category, the emerging warehouse stores were the fastest growing segment along with discount specialty stores.

External Threats

By the mid-1980s, the retail environment was extremely competitive. Retailers were also being squeezed by two powerful factors. One factor was slower growth in customer demand for general merchandise in recent years. Industry forecasts suggested a continuing trend in this direction, with a declining proportion of disposable income spent on general merchandise in coming years. The other factor was the excessive number of stores that existed in the industry. These two realities, along with several others, were making retail merchants somewhat worried about the future.

The decline in the teenage population had decreased per capita spending on apparel. Apparel chains, which had expanded so rapidly in the 1960s and 1970s to capitalize on the lucrative teenage market, were now facing an older

EXHIBIT 6 Top 15 General Merchandise Chains (sales and income in thousands)

Rank	Company	Net sales for 1985	Net income for 1985	Earnings per share for 1985	Location of Headquarters
1	Sears Roebuck	$40,715,300	$1,303,300	$3.53	Chicago
2	K mart	22,420,002	221,242	1.73	Troy, Mich.
3	J. C. Penney	13,747,000	397,000	5.31	New York
4	Federated Department Stores	9,978,027	286,626	5.88	Cincinnati
5	Dayton Hudson	8,793,372	283,620	2.92	Minneapolis
6	Wal-Mart Stores	8,580,910	327,473	1.16	Bentonville, Ark.
7	F. W. Woolworth	5,958,000	177,000	5.50	New York
8	BATUS	5,881,408	163,532	0	Louisville
9	Montgomery Ward	5,388,000	(298,000)	0	Chicago
10	May Department Stores	5,079,900	235,400	5.38	St. Louis
11	Melville	4,805,380	210,812	3.90	Harrison, N.Y.
12	Associated Dry Goods	4,385,019	119,696	3.00	New York
13	R. H. Macy	4,368,386	189,315	3.69	New York
14	Wiches Companies	4,362,454	76,130	0.47	Santa Monica, Cal.
15	Allied Stores	$ 4,135,027	$ 159,275	$3.70	New York

Source: "The 50 Largest Retailing Companies," *Fortune*, June 9, 1986, pp. 136–137.

customer base with less interest in fashion. As Americans grew older, their spending patterns were shifting toward health and leisure services and away from general merchandise.

Another source of trouble for retailers was the extremely high level of consumer credit in the mid-1980s. Some industry observers feared this would lead to a decline in consumer spending and to increased woes for retailers. Part of this fear was due to the catch-up spending that people did for consumer durables after the 1981–1983 recession.

Competition

A recent challenge within the retail industry was that of wholesale clubs and specialty stores. They were at opposite ends of the retailing spectrum. Still, both of these store types were very profitable and were making it harder for stores in the middle of the spectrum.

The wholesale club concept was first introduced in 1976 by Sal and Robert E. Price, with their first Price Club in San Diego. For a $25 membership fee, small businessmen could buy such diverse goods as food, office supplies, and appliances at wholesale prices. This membership approach meant that the Price Club got an interest-free loan in advance and locked in customers with switching costs if they decided to move to another such club. By stocking 4,000 high moving items, as compared to 60,000 items found in typical discount stores, Price Club stores turned over their inventory 15 times a year, compared to just five times for a full-line discount store. The Price Club had grown to 25 stores, and the concept was being copied by other retailers.

Specialty stores enjoyed strong growth in the early 1980s. A number of large retailers had established chains of small stores specializing in single product lines like shoes, women's apparel, and books. Woolworth had found success in stationery supplies with Herald Square, Lucky Stores with its Minnesota Fabrics, and Allied Stores with its Catherine's Stout Shoppes. The attraction of such stores was the greater depth of choice in a specific line for which many consumers were willing to pay extra.

Between the wholesale clubs and the specialty stores, were the full-line department stores. This was where the primary battle within the retailing industry was taking place. The saturation of the market with these one-stop shopping stores had caused many changes. For example, both Sears and J. C. Penney had curtailed most new store openings. Instead, they both were moving to upgrade their existing stores with higher quality, higher priced merchandise. Both sought to establish a fashion image to differentiate themselves from the discount chains.

Sears

K mart's greatest competition came from Sears, the world's largest retailer with its 435 full-line department stores, 397 medium sized department stores, and 1,971 catalog sales offices. Sears stores generated sales of $21.5 billion in 1985, which rose to a staggering $40.7 billion when all other Sears strategic business units were included. For its full line department stores, Sears' breadth in departments was unsurpassed by any competitor.

During the 1970s, Sears first moved to higher priced, more stylish merchandise. This confused many customers who preferred to go to discounters for lower prices and to specialty shops for greater product line depth. Under CEO Edward Telling, who took office in 1978, the company made drastic changes. Twenty percent of its work force was cut, 200 stores were closed, and the remaining stores renovated. Many Sears clothing labels were replaced by fashion labels associated with such names as Arnold Palmer, Joe Namath, and Cheryl Tiegs.

With its move into financial services, Sears envisioned the day when a customer could walk into a Sears store and buy a house through its Caldwell Banker realty division, insure it through its Allstate Insurance division, and furnish it before he or she left the store. Sears' charge card was already held by 58 percent of Americans. Visa cards, on the other hand, were held by only 53 percent of all households. The opportunity existed for Sears to convert its ordinary credit accounts into savings and checking accounts. Furthermore, the deregulated banking environment of the 1980s made it possible to offer multiple financial services in retail stores, an option Sears seemed to be pursuing.

J. C. Penney's

While Sears had its strength in hard goods, J. C. Penney's had a well established reputation for quality in soft goods. The company got its initials J. and C. from G. Johnson and T. Callahan, who founded the firm back in 1902. During the

1960s and 1970s, Penney's tried to move into hard goods to counter Sears' well established strength there. Penney's did this in several key instances by teaming up with well known suppliers. For example, it formed an alliance with General Electric to sell GE washers, dryers, refrigerators, stoves, etc., in Penney's retail stores.

During 1985, when Penney's had total sales of approximately $13.7 billion, it made a retrenchment of sorts. It discontinued its auto accessories department, eliminated children's toys, and even discontinued selling many hard goods such as GE appliances. Instead, it renewed its commitment to emphasize soft goods in its 574 metropolitan market stores, 133 metropolitan market soft line stores, and 696 geographic market stores in non-metropolitan markets. With this move, the firm refocused its efforts on selling quality clothing to men, women, boys, girls, and infants. In addition to clothing, Penney's continued to emphasize its underwear, towels, sheets, etc., for which it was noted.

Discount Chains

In 1985, there were more than 8,700 general merchandise discount stores in the U.S. Exhibit 7 gives a comparison of profitability and growth performance of the top discount, variety, and department store chains. The average discount store had 55,792 square feet of selling space, which had been rising in recent years. The average customer transaction was $12.35. The annual sales per square foot, as shown in Exhibit 8, varied from the $603 in the photography department to $132 in men's and boys' wear.

There were a number of regional chains within the discount segment of the retail industry. They included Mervyn's in the West, Target in the Midwest, Caldor in New England, and Richway in the Southeast. For the most part, they had done very well by differentiating themselves from K mart. Some firms had accomplished this by appealing to the high end of the discount market. Other discounters sold department store quality merchandise at discount prices in attractive stores. As a result, they succeeded in attracting many affluent shoppers who would not normally shop at K mart.

One of the most successful retailers in recent years was Wal-Mart, a discount chain headquartered in Bentonville, Arkansas. Much of its success was due to the location of its stores. Its 834 discount stores and 19 Sam's Warehouse Clubs were concentrated in small towns in the South and Midwest. By clustering up to 150 stores within several hours drive of a central warehouse and stocking only name brand merchandise, Wal-Mart consistently led the industry in return on investment.

SUPPLIERS

Retailers dealt with thousands of suppliers to stock the wide range of merchandise they carried. This was due in part to the fact that most retailers did not manufacture the merchandise they carried. The bargaining power of large retail chains in relation to their suppliers was great. Sears, J. C. Penney's, K mart, and others, were such large and welcome customers that suppliers often became overly dependent on them.

EXHIBIT 7 General Merchandise Retailers: 1985 Yardsticks of Management Performance

| | | PROFITABILITY ||||| GROWTH |||||
| | | Return on equity |||| Sales || Earnings per share ||
Company	% in segment sales/profits	rank	5-year average	latest 12 months	debt as % of equity	net profit margin	rank	5-year average	latest 12 months	rank	5-year average	latest 12 months
DEPARTMENT STORES
RH Macy	0/0	1	21.4%	16.3%	14.0%	4.3%	4	14.2%	7.5%	2	21.1%	−15.6%
Lucky Stores	25/13	2	19.2	17.5	61.3	1.1	12	9.5	6.5	12	−0.3	12.8
Dillard Dept Stores	0/0	3	18.6	19.8	70.4	3.9	1	25.2	49.3	1	40.5	32.0
Mercantile Stores	0/0	4	16.3	15.0	28.0	5.0	7	10.9	6.8	4	17.5	4.2
May Dept Stores	68/72	5	16.0	17.3	41.2	4.4	10	9.8	10.2	5	14.6	9.3
Federated Dept Stores	67/89	6	14.6	13.1	27.9	3.3	8	10.8	8.0	10	8.5	11.0
Allied Stores	0/0	7	12.8	15.3	70.9	3.9	5	13.8	5.7	9	9.9	25.5
JC Penney	79/na	8	12.7	10.1	54.7	2.9	13	3.0	2.3	8	13.3	−18.6
Strawbridge	0/0	9	12.5	16.0	125.8	3.7	6	11.5	12.5	3	20.1	16.6
Assoc Dry Goods	61/73	10	11.8	12.2	33.8	2.8	2	19.6	9.5	6	13.6	−0.7
Carson Pirie Scott	50/45	11	10.8	13.4	104.2	2.0	3	19.6	23.2	11	4.2	132.5
Sears, Roebuck	67/57	12	10.6	10.7	87.4	2.9	9	10.4	4.6	7	13.5	−19.9
Carter Hawley Hale	73/52	13	9.4	7.3	84.6	1.6	11	9.6	−2.0	13	−0.3	−50.0
Equitable of Iowa	41/2	14	7.0	4.3	9.2	2.6	14	2.7	4.9	14	−15.0	−10.2
Alexander's	0/0	15	1.4	7.4	87.0	1.0	15	1.9	0.5		NM	24.7
Medians			12.7	13.4	61.3	2.9		10.8	6.8		13.3	9.3
DISCOUNT AND VARIETY
Wal-Mart Stores	0/0	1	34.9%	30.7%	49.6%	3.9%	1	39.9%	32.2%	1	43.0%	24.1%
SCOA Industries	84/0	2	24.8	22.6	88.5	2.9	8	10.4	5.1	8	9.3	9.8
Ames Dept Stores	0/0	3	23.1	19.7	60.6	3.1	2	20.1	30.8	5	23.5	19.4
Stop & Shop Cos	48/73	4	19.2	12.8	52.8	1.3	7	11.2	12.8	2	33.6	−26.9
Dayton-Hudson	71/73	5	16.8	16.1	43.2	3.3	4	19.0	12.2	9	9.1	10.3
Zayre	70/65	6	15.7	19.0	46.5	2.6	5	16.0	19.9	3	28.7	22.1
Rose's Stores	0/0	7	15.6	14.2	16.6	2.1	6	14.0	9.2	4	28.1	−13.9
K mart	0/0	8	13.2	12.4	89.3	1.8	9	10.0	13.4	7	10.5	−23.2
Household Intl	26/8	9	12.0	13.6	236.0	2.6	10	9.1	5.3	10	4.7	−4.6
Assoc Dry Goods	38/26	10	11.8	12.2	33.8	2.8	3	19.6	9.5	6	13.6	−0.7
Heck's	86/DD	11	9.3	def	89.3	def	11	2.0	6.5		NM	P–D
FW Woolworth	68/39	12	3.5	14.5	35.4	2.6	13	−5.6	3.2		NM	20.6
Cook United	0/DD	13	def	def	NE	def	12	−2.8	−47.7		NM	D–D
Medians			15.6	14.2	49.6	2.6		11.2	9.5		10.5	−0.7

Source: "Industry Survey-Retailing," *Forbes*, January 13, 1986, p. 202.

Each year, many new products were introduced by the major chains, replacing old products which were discontinued. Each supplier knew that its products were expected to generate targeted levels of sales. Those that didn't achieve these goals were dropped with little regard for the supplier. On occasion, suppliers were encouraged to increase production capacity only to find their product dropped a short time later on. Often, orders were cancelled

EXHIBIT 8 Discount Store Sales by Category

Category	Volume (Bill $)	Sales per Store (in millions)	Annual Sales per sq. ft. (in dollars)	Annual turns	Initial Markup (%)	Gross Margin (%)
Women's apparel	$14.3	$1,763	$176	4.6	48.0	37.2
Men's & boys' wear	8.2	1,011	132	3.4	44.6	36.0
Housewares	6.3	777	135	3.2	41.1	30.2
Consumer electronics	5.9	728	316	3.2	31.4	19.4
Health & beauty aids	5.6	691	219	4.5	26.9	20.5
Automobile	5.2	641	279	2.8	34.9	28.7
Hardware	4.8	592	184	2.4	41.9	32.1
Toys	4.1	506	202	3.1	36.5	28.4
Sporting goods	3.8	469	187	2.0	36.9	26.9
Photo camera	3.3	407	603	3.2	24.5	16.6
Domestics	3.2	395	126	2.5	43.4	35.3
Personal care	2.9	358	421	3.3	30.4	20.0
Stationery	2.1	259	140	3.5	46.7	40.1
Paint	1.8	222	175	2.4	43.9	35.2
Electric housewares	1.7	210	238	3.4	33.2	21.4
Jewelry	1.4	166	290	1.8	49.9	37.7
Glassware	0.7	80	129	4.0	40.7	34.9

Source: *Standard and Poor's Industrial Survey*, July 4, 1985, p. 120.

at the last minute, leaving suppliers in a difficult position. At times, chain retailers would take merchandise on a consignment basis, paying for it only if sold, thus shifting the risk to the supplier. Payment to the suppliers was, at times, delayed by retailers in order to enhance cash flow and obtain free short-term financing.

Sears and K mart were good examples of firms making sizeable use of private label merchandise. Often their private label products were made by a brand name manufacturer to similar to, or the exact same specifications as, the brand label. The manufacture of private label products could then be contracted out to other manufacturers, giving a great deal of leverage to the retailer and reducing the bargaining power of suppliers.

In spite of such treatment by chain retailers, many suppliers were willing to take the risk and abuse. In return, they hoped to get the enormous volume and nationwide distribution that high volume retailers could provide. In response to this one-sided relationship, a number of general merchandise manufacturers had broadened their product lines. By producing a wide variety of items, a supplier could reduce dependence on a single product and increase its bargaining power with the retailer.

BUYERS: THE NEW CONSUMERS

Several important demographic shifts were affecting retailers during the mid 1980s. Population shifts from the cities to the suburbs were reducing the sales volume of urban stores while helping suburban stores. Population shifts from older industrialized areas of the northeast to the Sun Belt states had similar effects. The wave of baby-boom teenagers of the 1960s was approaching middle age. Better educated than their parents, their perception of value, their attitude towards quality merchandise, and their response to promotional techniques were changing the way retailers did business.

Price still remained a key consideration, but quality and brand image had increased in importance. Many consumers were willing to trade dollars for time, as was proven by the demand for fast-food, microwave ovens, and other time-saving products and services.

While the number of households was growing rapidly, the population growth was slowing. This caused changes in the type of merchandise demanded, the way to market it effectively, and the price/quality trade-off. Health-related products, prescriptions, and leisure products were in greater demand, reflecting the needs of older customers. At the same time, the market for baby food, toys, and children's clothing had declined.

Women were working in greater numbers than ever before. This contributed to the rise in discretionary income, and increased the demand for products needed by working women, such as clothes and cosmetics. A K mart survey showed that the percentage of K mart customers with household incomes from $25,000 to $40,000 had increased from 23.3 percent in 1980 to 28.1 percent in 1984.[5] Some 18.9 percent of K mart's customers in 1984 came from households with incomes greater than $40,000, as compared to 8.3 percent in 1980. A profile of K mart shoppers, broken down by income, occupation, education, sex, and age is shown in Exhibit 9.

With more women working, men were doing retail shopping more than ever before. Men tended to be less value conscious and more likely to trust the advertising of national brands. The trend was clearly towards a more mature, affluent customer with a preference for value, quality, and fashion in merchandise.

K MART AND THE FUTURE

Sales at the average K mart store were good, but there was tremendous room for improvement. Overall, K mart's per-store sales were about one-third that of Sears stores. K mart's appliances and housewares departments were strong areas; however, its clothing and other soft goods, which took up almost half of the typical K mart store, had low appeal to many customers. Clearly, K mart needed to address its clothing dilemma, perhaps by reducing store space allocated or by improving the clothing being offered. Overall, K mart needed to decide which product lines and departments should be emphasized. Exhibit 10 provides a breakdown of total retail trade by major product areas.

Since the appointment of Bernard M. Fauber as CEO in 1980, K mart had made a number of substantial changes. By the end of 1985, the store renovation

---

[5] K mart Corporation, *K mart Corporation Annual Report, 1984.*

EXHIBIT 9 Demographics of K mart Shoppers

	% of K mart shoppers
Occupation:	
Professional	12.5
Technical	5.5
Manager	13.4
Clerical	4.5
Salesworker	6.4
Craftsman	11.7
Operative/kindred worker	9.8
Service worker	4.7
Laborer	3.1
Retired	20.7
Income:	
Over $20,000	38.7
Under $20,000	60.6
Education:	
High school or less	52.2
Some college or more	46.5
Sex:	
Male	46.6
Female	53.4
Age:	
Under 25	12.8
25–34	24.1
35–44	19.6
45–54	12.7
55–64	14.5
65+	15.3

Source: *Chain Store Age*, December 1984, p. 54.

program had been going for some time, and the move toward higher quality national brand merchandise was well underway. Still, as 1986 began, there were a number of important issues still facing K mart. Would the repositioning program succeed in attracting more affluent customers to buy its higher priced name brand merchandise? What additional steps could be taken to upgrade K mart's stores? Would the new image result in a substantial loss of lower income customers which had historically been the backbone of its business? Might K mart customers be confused by the move, as happened to Sears in the 1970s? How could K mart improve the performance of its clothing and soft goods? If it did, could fashion seeking customers really be convinced that K mart was a trendy place to shop? These and other questions came to mind as CEO Fauber looked ahead to the remainder of the 1980s and into the 1990s.

EXHIBIT 10 Total Retail Trade (in millions of dollars)

	1984	% Chge. 1983–84	10-Year Growth Rate
Retail trade total	$1,297,015	+10.5	+9.0
Durable goods stores total	464,287	+17.1	+9.6
Nondurable goods stores total	832,728	+7.1	+8.8
General merchandise group	153,642	+10.2	+7.9
General merchandise stores	144,575	+10.6	+8.4
Department stores	129,284	+10.9	+8.6
Variety stores	9,067	+5.1	+1.8
Apparel group	66,891	+10.8	+8.8
Men's & boy's wear stores	8,432	+5.9	+3.1
Women's apparel accessary stores	27,899	+13.9	+9.3
Family & other apparel stores	17,567	+13.8	+11.1
Shoe stores	10,339	+5.6	+9.9
Furniture & appliance group	63,581	+16.3	+8.9
GAF total	325,938	+11.7	0
Automotive group	277,008	+19.0	+9.5
Gasoline service stations	100,997	+2.2	+10.2
Lumber, building material hardware	59,304	+15.2	+9.7
Eating and drinking places	124,109	+8.2	+10.8
Food group	269,959	+5.9	+8.3
Drug and proprietary stores	44,165	+10.3	+9.2
Liquor stores	19,494	+2.5	+6.3

Source: *Standard and Poor's Industrial Survey,* July 4, 1985, p. 111.

INDUSTRIAL HIGHLIGHT

Retail Trade Industry

Below is a capsule summary of the department store segment of the retail trade industry, of which K mart is a part. Information in this highlight was compiled by the U.S. Department of Commerce and focuses on this industry during the approximate period of time covered in the case. Keep in mind that industrial highlights contained in this text are not intended as a complete synopsis of an industry, but as a profile of certain issues that can be relevant to the case situation.

Department stores carry a general line of apparel, home furnishings, and housewares. Merchandise is physically arranged in separate departments, with accounting on a departmentalized basis. The stores usually provide their own charge accounts and deliver merchandise.

While the department store remains the mainstay of their business, some chains are diversifying into other types of merchandising. K mart, for example, made three major acquisitions in 1985—in the book, hardware, and drug store areas—designed to complement and expand its lines of merchandise.

In the fall of 1985, Sears, Roebuck and Co. introduced a new credit card on a regional basis. It is planned eventually to be nationwide. The card, named "Discover," is designed to compete with Visa, Mastercard, and other popular credit cards. Accepted in Sears stores and other service establishments across the nation, it is designed to provide entry to other financial services, including savings accounts, as well as access to automated teller machines. Sears is reputed to have about 28 million active credit cards and will draw upon the company's experience when it introduces the new card.

Dayton Hudson Corporation is initiating a specialty store operation with its R. G. Braden division, a home specialty chain, while aggressively expanding its Lechmere (appliance and hand goods) division. Federated Department Stores continues to place emphasis on its recently formed Main Street Group.

A number of department stores including Wal-Mart and Zayre Corp. are involved in developing deep-discount warehouse divisions. Both firms have found the concept profitable and capable of generating large sales volumes and profits. Sales for the Wal-Mart group are reported to be in excess of half

Source: *U.S. Industrial Outlook,* Department of Commerce, 1986, pp. 57-2 to 57-3.

EXHIBIT A Department Store Sales and Total Retail Sales

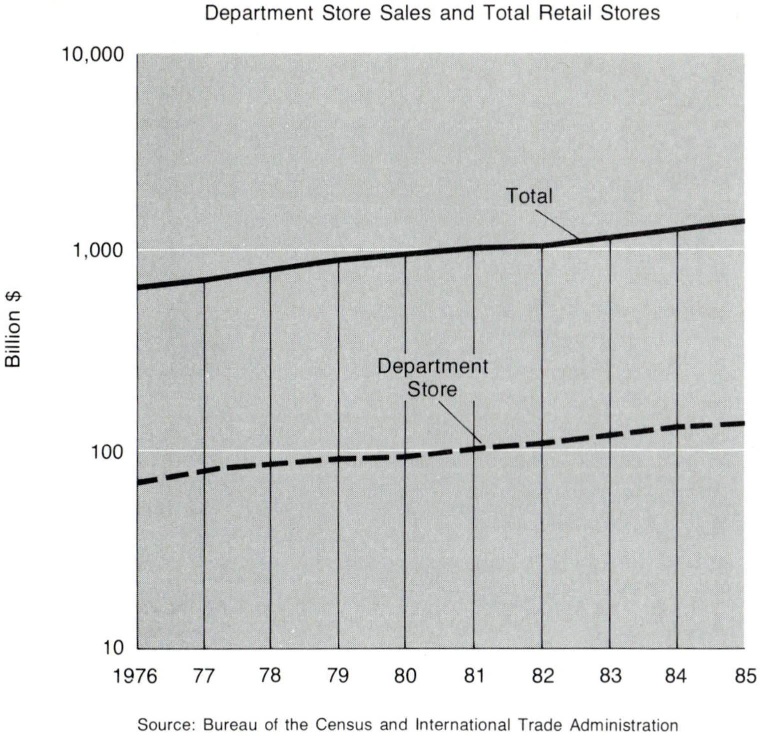
Department Store Sales and Total Retail Stores
10,000
1,000
100
10
Billion $
Total
Department Store
1976
77
78
79
80
81
82
83
84
85
Source: Bureau of the Census and International Trade Administration

a billion dollars and the company plans to increase the number of stores in the future. Deep discount warehouse stores sell at a smaller markup than traditional discounters, maintain a limited number of items in each category, and generally do not extend credit. The merchandising concept has found ready public acceptance and is currently a multibillion dollar business nationally with continued gains expected in future years.

Efforts by major retailers to sell commodities and services abroad has met resistance and competition. Depressed international commodity prices and the desire of each foreign nation to protect and insulate its own domestic sales structure have militated against major gains abroad by domestic marketers. In spite of recurring losses, one company plans to continue to expand its foreign sales and services.

LONG-TERM PROSPECTS

Trading up (an emphasis on better quality merchandise) should assume greater importance in the years ahead. Continued growth in disposable personal income should provide the finances required to pay for merchandise needed

STRATEGY FORMULATION

to complement existing or desired lifestyles. Consumer exposure to alternate modes of living has been stimulated in recent years by domestic and international travel and a proliferation of visual images created by television, video, and printed material.

The growth of specialty store retailers featuring specialized merchandise and service can be expected to grow in the future. Specialty stores have proliferated as consumer needs and wants have become more exacting. The department store as we know it today should continue in its present status for an indefinite period.

In the future, retailing will continue to expand and accommodate new types of stores and products. The proliferation of stores that sell or rent video cassettes and small computers and software are examples of new stores and products.

The remainder of the decade should witness the continued growth of retail stores that sell at less than full markup. These stores include discounters, off-price outlets, warehouse operations, and deep-discount stores. The retail market and the number and variety of customers are sufficiently broad to enable each retailing concept to be a success and to provide buying opportunities for a wide variety of customers.

CASE 13

Hershey Foods

RICHARD T. HISE
Texas A&M University

Milton S. Hershey, the founder of the giant chocolate manufacturing firm bearing his name, did not find the road to success an easy one. He tried a number of business ventures before eventually succeeding in the chocolate business. In his early teens, he found that he was not cut out to be an apprentice typesetter, but did enjoy his four-year stint as an apprentice candy maker for Joseph H. Royer, a Lancaster, Pennsylvania, confectioner.

At the age of 19, Hershey decided to go into the candy business for himself. His venture in Philadelphia failed, as did efforts with his father in Denver and Chicago. Another solo attempt in New York also failed.

Back in his native Lancaster, Hershey began to manufacture caramels, an operation with which he was experienced, and the caramel business expanded rapidly. In 1900, he sold his company for $1 million, an unheard of price in those days, and used the proceeds to begin construction of a chocolate processing plant in Derry Township, about 15 miles east of Harrisburg.

Within 10 years, the company prospered so much that Hershey and his wife were accumulating so much money they could not possibly spend it all. In 1909, Mrs. Hershey suggested they build a home for unfortunate boys. Hershey eagerly agreed, feeling that, although his own childhood had not been all he had wished it to be, he could try to provide security and love for others. Thus, 486 of the initial 1,000 acre construction tract were set aside for the Hershey Industrial School.

In subsequent years, other community projects were built by the Hershey Company. The Community Building, containing two theaters, a dining room and cafeteria, a gymnasium, swimming pool, bowling alley, fencing and boxing room, and photographic room was finished in 1933. The Hershey Hotel was also completed in 1933. The 7,200 seat Hershey Sports Arena was constructed in 1936, and the Hershey Stadium was finished in 1939. Later, Hershey's Chocolate World, which contains a free ride through a simulated chocolate manufacturing operation, Hershey Park, a theme park, the Hershey Museum of American Life, and the Hershey Gardens were constructed by Hershey.

In the 1920s, Milton Hershey decided to reorganize the company. The

---

This case was written by Richard T. Hise, Professor of Marketing, Texas A&M University, as a basis for class discussion rather than to illustrate either effective or ineffective marketing management. Reprinted with permission of the publisher from Richard T. Hise and Stephen W. McDaniel, *Cases in Marketing Strategy*, Columbus, Ohio: Charles E. Merrill Publishing Co., 1984.

Hershey Chocolate Company was dissolved, and three separate companies were organized. The Hershey Chocolate Corporation controlled all of the chocolate properties; the Hershey Corporation was responsible for the Cuban sugar interests; the Hershey Estates was established to conduct the various businesses and municipal services in the town of Hershey.

The Hershey Trust Company administers the funds of the Milton Hershey School. As trustee for this school, it owns or controls the other three companies because Milton Hershey provided the trust with a sizable block of shares of common stock. In 1981, the Hershey Trust Company owned about 51 percent of the company's common stock.

The Hershey Chocolate Corporation continued to prosper. During World War II, the army commissioned Hershey to develop a chocolate bar for troops in the field; the result was the "Field Ration D," and the company was soon producing 500,000 bars a day.

Milton S. Hershey died on October 13, 1945. For 15 years after his death, the Hershey Chocolate Corporation continued to emphasize its chocolate products. Since 1960, however, the company has pursued a strategy of becoming a multiproduct corporation. The name of the Hershey Chocolate Corporation was changed to the Hershey Foods Corporation, its current name. In 1961, the company's sales were $185 million, compared to over $1.4 billion in 1981.

MAJOR PRODUCT GROUPS

In 1982, Hershey had three major product groups. These included the chocolate and confectionery group, restaurant operations (Friendly Ice Cream Corporation), and the other food products and services group: San Giorgio-Skinner (pasta) and Cory Food Services, Inc. The chocolate and confectionery group has grown through both internal means and acquisitions, while the other two groups have grown primarily through acquisitions. Exhibits 1 and 2 show overall company performance between 1971 and 1981. Exhibit 3 shows performance figures for the various product groups between 1979 and 1981.

Chocolate and Confectionery Group

The company produces a broad line of chocolate and confectionery products. The major product lines in the chocolate and confectionery group are bar goods, bagged items, baking ingredients, chocolate drink mixes, and dessert toppings. Hershey uses a variety of packages, such as boxes, trays, and bags for bar products. Sizes include standard, large, and giant bars, and about 30 brand names are used. The most important of these are Hershey's Almond Bars, Hershey's Chips, Hershey's Cocoa, Hershey's Kisses, Hershey's Milk Chocolate Bar, Hershey's Miniatures, Hershey's Syrup, Kit Kat, Mr. Goodbar, Reese's Peanut Butter Cups, Reese's Pieces, Rolo, and Whatchamacallit.

While most of the company's chocolate and confectionery items have been developed internally, some were acquired or made available through licensing agreements. The Reese's products were added to Hershey's product lines

EXHIBIT 1 Five-Year Financial Summary, 1971–1975

(all figures in thousands—except market price and per share statistics)

	1975	1974	1973	1972	1971
Summary of earnings					
Continuing operations					
Net sales	$556,328	$491,995	$415,944	$392,004	$379,229
Cost of goods sold	368,992	357,830	294,174	255,162	247,784
Operating expenses	105,102	81,792	88,318	91,595	86,439
Interest expense (net)	1,259	2,190	4,848	3,246	2,610
Income taxes	41,682	25,812	13,929	20,679	21,947
Income from continuing operations	39,293	24,371	14,675	21,322	20,449
Losses from discontinued operations	(1,433)	(2,277)	(369)	(680)	44
Loss related to disposal of discontinued operations	(4,898)	—	—	—	—
Net income	32,962	22,094	14,306	20,642	20,493
Net income—per share of common stock					
Continuing operations	3.02	1.87	1.13	1.63	1.55
Discontinued operations					
Losses from operations	(.11)	(.17)	(.03)	(.05)	—
Loss related to disposal	(.38)	—	—	—	—
Net income	2.53	1.70	1.10	1.58	1.55
Dividends per—common share	.85	.80	1.10	1.10	1.10
Dividends per—preferred share	.60	.60	.60	.60	.60
Average number of common shares and equivalents outstanding during the year	13,024	13,024	13,024	13,064	13,212
Percent of net income to sales[1]	7.1%	5.0%	3.5%	5.4%	5.4%
Financial statistics					
Capital expenditures	$ 10,203	$ 10,887	$ 17,564	$ 25,137	$ 22,602
Depreciation[1]	7,541	7,912	7,010	5,622	5,597
Advertising[1]	9,325	1,744	9,565	13,954	10,506
Current assets	151,217	124,172	97,106	108,667	102,965
Current liabilities	52,494	57,579	23,456	29,789	44,486
Working capital	98,723	66,593	73,650	78,878	58,479
Current ratio	2.9:1	2.2:1	4.1:1	3.6:1	2.3:1
Long-term debt	$ 29,856	$ 31,730	$ 51,470	$ 51,364	$ 26,533
Debt-to-equity percent	15%	18%	32%	32%	17%
Stockholders' equity	$195,847	$173,173	$160,777	$159,714	$156,280
Stockholders' data					
Outstanding common shares at year-end	13,024	11,824	11,824	11,824	11,977
Market price of common stock—					
At year-end	$ 18⅝	$ 9¾	$ 12⅝	$ 23⅞	$ 28
Range during year	$10⅛–20⅞	$ 8½–15	$12½–24¾	$21⅛–28¾	$26–31⅜
Number of common stockholders	19,279	19,362	19,095	17,980	18,346
Employees' data					
Payrolls	$74,329	$72,936	$74,464	$67,700	$62,189
Number of employees—year-end	7,150	7,200	8,500	8,530	9,140

[1] Restated to reflect continuing operations only.

STRATEGY FORMULATION

EXHIBIT 2 Six-Year Financial Summary, 1976–1981
(all figures in thousands except market price and per share statistics)

	1981	1980	1979	1978	1977	1976
Summary of earnings						
Continuing operations						
Net sales	$1,451,151	$1,335,289	$1,161,295	$767,880	$671,227	$601,960
Cost of sales	1,015,767	971,714	855,252	560,137	489,802	417,673
Operating expenses	267,930	224,615	184,186	128,520	110,554	94,683
Interest expense	15,291	16,197	19,424	2,620	2,422	2,240
Interest (income)	(2,779)	(2,097)	(1,660)	(5,303)	(2,931)	(1,883)
Income taxes	74,580	62,805	50,589	40,450	35,349	45,562
Income from continuing operations	80,362	62,055	53,504	41,456	36,031	43,685
Income from discontinued operations	—	—	—	—	—	1,112
Gain related to disposal of discontinued operations	—	—	—	—	5,300	—
Net income	$ 80,362	$ 62,055	$ 53,504	$ 41,456	$ 41,331	$ 44,797
Income per common share						
Continuing operations	$ 5.61	4.38	3.78	3.02	2.62	3.18
Discontinued operations	—	—	—	—	—	.08
Gain related to disposal	—	—	—	—	.39	—
Net income	5.61	4.38	3.78	3.02	3.01	3.26
Cash dividends per common share	$ 1.75	$ 1.50	$ 1.35	$ 1.225	$ 1.14	$ 1.03
Average number of common shares and equivalents outstanding during the year	14,322	14,160	14,153	13,742	13,722	13,720
Percent of income from continuing operations to sales	5.5%	4.6%	4.6%	5.4%	5.4%	7.3%
Financial statistics						
Capital additions	$ 91,673	$ 59,029	$ 56,437	$ 37,425	$ 27,535	$ 20,722
Depreciation	27,565	24,896	20,515	8,850	7,995	7,539
Advertising	56,516	42,684	32,063	21,847	17,637	13,330
Current assets	287,030	221,367	170,250	216,659	221,202	169,872
Current liabilities	117,255	111,660	103,826	74,415	83,149	47,309
Working capital	169,775	109,707	66,424	142,244	138,053	122,563
Current ratio	2.4:1	2.0:1	1.6:1	2.9:1	2.7:1	3.6:1
Long-term debt and lease obligations	$ 158,182	$ 158,758	$ 143,700	$ 35,540	$ 29,440	$ 29,440
Debt-to-equity percent	34%	44%	45%	13%	11%	13%
Stockholders' equity	$ 469,664	$ 361,550	$ 320,730	$284,389	$259,668	$233,529
Total assets	$ 806,800	$ 684,472	$ 607,199	$422,004	$396,153	$331,870
Return on average stockholders' equity	19.3%	18.2%	17.7%	15.2%	16.8%	20.5%
Aftertax return on average invested capital	13.9%	12.8%	14.3%	13.0%	14.2%	17.1%
Stockholders' data						
Outstanding common shares at year-end	15,669	14,160	14,159	13,745	13,730	13,720
Market price of common stock						
At year-end	$ 36	$ 23½	$ 24⅝	$ 20⅝	$ 19⅞	$ 22⅜
Range during year	$ 41–23⅛	$ 26–20	$26½–17⅜	$23½–18½	$22⅜–16⅝	$27½–18½
Number of common stockholders at year-end	16,817	17,774	18,417	18,735	19,694	20,421
Employees' data						
Payrolls	$ 273,097	$ 253,297	$ 227,987	$112,135	$ 99,322	$ 88,848
Number of full-time employees at year-end	12,450	12,430	11,700	8,100	7,660	7,670

EXHIBIT 3 Product Group Information for the Years Ended December 31 (in thousands)

	1981	1980	1979
Net sales:			
Chocolate and confectionery	$1,015,106	$ 929,885	$ 822,813
Restaurant operations	302,908	274,297	224,072
Other food products and services	133,137	131,107	114,410
Total net sales	$1,451,151	$1,335,289	$1,161,295
Operating income:			
Chocolate and confectionery	$ 142,658	$ 118,435	$ 99,880
Restaurant operations	29,309	25,567	23,322
Other food products and services	7,250	5,148[1]	6,397
Total operating income	179,217	149,150	129,599
General corporate expenses	(11,763)	(10,190)	(7,742)
Interest expense (net)	(12,512)	(14,100)	(17,764)
Income before taxes	154,942	124,860	104,093
Less: income taxes	74,580	62,805	50,589
Net income	$ 80,362	$ 62,055	$ 53,504
Identifiable assets:			
Chocolate and confectionery	$ 445,815	$ 333,232	$ 297,296
Restaurant operations	223,265	219,196	207,125
Other food products and services	63,446	62,553	63,886
Corporate	74,274	69,491	38,892
Total identifiable assets	$ 806,800	$ 684,472	$ 607,199
Depreciation:			
Chocolate and confectionery	$ 9,554	$ 8,469	$ 7,389
Restaurant operations	14,379	13,015	10,283
Other food products and services	2,675	2,671	2,185
Corporate	957	741	658
Total depreciation	$ 27,565	$ 24,896	$ 20,515
Capital additions:			
Chocolate and confectionery	$ 57,504[2]	$ 27,061[2]	$ 29,472
Restaurant operations	22,098	24,468	20,965
Other food products and services	5,525	6,141	2,233
Corporate	6,546	1,359	3,767
Total capital additions	$ 91,673	$ 59,029	$ 56,437

[1] After a writeoff of deferred location costs of Cory Food Services in the amount of $1.4 million.
[2] Includes $37.8 million in 1981 and $6.5 million in 1980 for a new manufacturing facility currently being constructed.

through acquisition of the H. B. Reese Candy Company of Hershey, Pennsylvania, in 1963. H. B. Reese, a former Hershey employee, began operations in 1923. Since one of the major ingredients in the Reese's line is peanut butter, Hershey executives believe that these items reduce to some extent the firm's dependency on the cacao bean, the chief raw ingredient in chocolate. Y&S Candies, Inc. a licorice manufacturer with facilities in Lancaster, Pennsylvania; Moline, Illinois; Farmington, New Mexico; and Montreal, Canada, was acquired in 1977 to serve the same purpose.

STRATEGY FORMULATION

A licensing agreement with Rountree Mackintosh Limited of England gives Hershey the right to manufacture and market the Kit Kat and Rolo brands. The agreement with the English firm also allows Hershey to import, manufacture, and market After Eight, a thin dinner mint. This product was being test marketed in 1981.

Hershey has three other licensing arrangements. One is with AB Marabou of Sundbyberg, Sweden, the leading Scandinavian chocolate and confectionery company. Several AB Marabou products have been imported and marketed since 1978. Hershey owns 50 percent of Nacional de Dulces, S.A. de C.V., a manufacturer and marketer of chocolate and confectionery products in Mexico. The other licensing arrangement gives Hershey the right to import and sell various high quality licorice products of the Geo. Bassett & Co. of England. In 1981, Hershey executives did not consider any of these agreements to be large moneymarkets.

Exhibit 4 delineates the company's most important chocolate and confectionery products, and when they were developed. While Hershey has had a number of successful new products, there have also been several disappointments. Chocolate-covered raisins were introduced in 1975 and withdrawn the same year. The Rally Bar, a chocolate, caramel, and peanut candy bar, was removed from the market: one of its problems was that, in the initial formula, the peanuts became soggy on the retailers' shelves. The original formula was modified, but the product did not measure up to sales expectations. Exhibit 5

EXHIBIT 4   Development of Hershey Products

Year	Product
1894	The Hershey Bar and Almond Bar
	Hershey's Cocoa, Hershey's Baking Chocolate
1907	Hershey's Kisses
1923	Reese's Peanut Butter Cups
	Y&S Nibs
1925	Mr. Goodbar
1926	Hershey's Syrup
1928	Y&S Twizzlers
1938	Krackel
1939	Hershey's Miniatures
1940	Hershey's Hot Chocolate (now Hot Cocoa Mix)
1941	Dainties (now Semi-Sweet Chocolate Chips)
1952	Chocolate Fudge Topping
1956	Instant Cocoa Mix (Hershey's instant)
1970	Kit Kat
1971	Special Dark
1976	Reese's Crunchy
1977	Reese's Peanut Butter Flavored Chips
	Golden Almond
1978	Reese's Pieces, Giant Kiss
1979	Whatchamacallit

Source: Company document.

EXHIBIT 5   Sales of New and Present Chocolate and Confectionery Products, 1963–1977

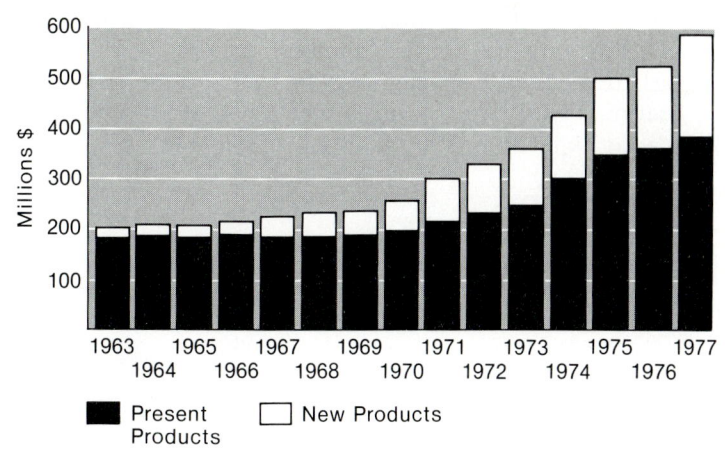

Source: *The Wall Street Transcript,* November 13, 1978, by permission.

shows the importance of new and current products for the Chocolate and Confectionery Division from 1963 to 1977.

Restaurant Operations

This division was acquired in January 1979. The Friendly Ice Cream Corporation consists of about 626 restaurants (1982) in 16 states, primarily in the Northeast and Midwest. Exhibit 6 shows the number of restaurants in each state. The division's headquarters and major plant are in Wilbraham, Massachusetts; another plant is in Troy, Ohio. Both plants manufacture the ice cream, syrups, and toppings used by the restaurants, and their capacities are considered sufficient for the current number of restaurants, as well as for some future expansion. The Wilbraham plant processes the meat required by the restaurants; it is shipped frozen to the individual restaurant units. Some items (milk, cream, baked goods, eggs, and produce) are purchased by the restaurants from local sources which are designated by Friendly's central purchasing department.

Friendly Restaurants serve high quality food at moderate prices, specializing in sandwiches, platters, and ice cream products. All units are owned outright by Friendly; there are no franchise agreements.

There are three major types of Friendly Restaurants. The *traditional* Friendly ice cream and sandwich shop offers a limited menu, featuring ice cream, hamburgers, breakfast items, platters, salad, french fries, beverages, and soup and sandwiches. Customers are served in booths or counters, or by take-out service. (The average seating capacity is 60.) There were 213 traditional operations in 1981. The 351 *modified* shop units offer most of the items available in the traditional shop, but serve a wider variety of full meals and

STRATEGY FORMULATION

platters. Unlike in the traditional shop, food is prepared out of the customer's sight. The modified units offer take-out service, but have a greater proportion of booth seats than the traditional restaurants. (Seating capacity averages 70 seats.) They also have more personalized service and a more pleasant dining atmosphere. The 50 *family* restaurants have the broadest menu, serving seafood, chicken, and other dinners, along with more varied breakfasts and platter meals. Desserts other than ice cream are available, and some units serve beer and wine. Seating is primarily booths and tables, and the floors are usually carpeted. (Seating capacity is from 90 to 120.)

EXHIBIT 6   Location of Friendly Restaurants

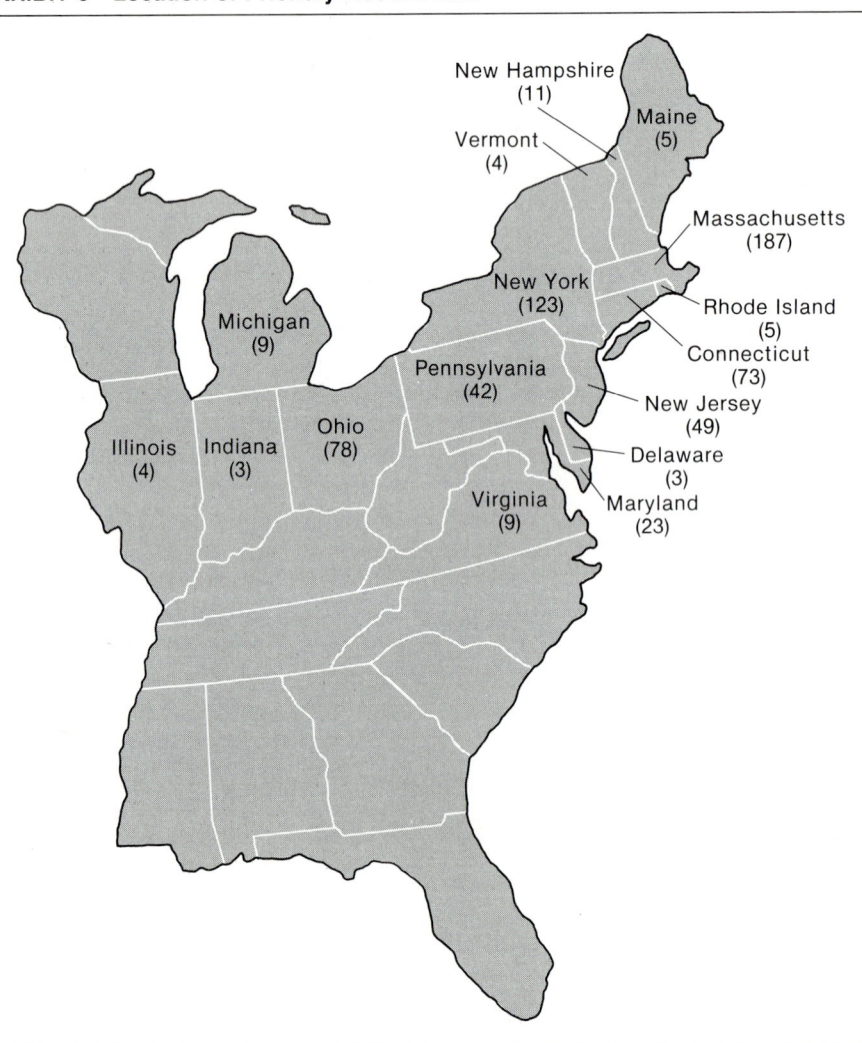

New Hampshire (11)
Vermont (4)
Maine (5)
Massachusetts (187)
New York (123)
Rhode Island (5)
Connecticut (73)
Michigan (9)
Pennsylvania (42)
New Jersey (49)
Ohio (78)
Delaware (3)
Illinois (4)
Indiana (3)
Virginia (9)
Maryland (23)

Menus and portions in each type of restaurant are standardized, but prices may vary, generally according to geographical location. Most of the units sell prepackaged ice cream for home consumption. Friendly restaurants feature a colonial decor, and free parking is available.

The Friendly Corporation has followed a policy of refurbishing its restaurants and opening newer ones. The remodeling policy involves converting traditional units into modified units; as of January 1, 1981, 351 units have been modified. Other units have been modernized. In 1980, 20 additional units, 14 of which are Family restaurants, were opened; 11 units were closed in 1980. All units use modern construction methods. Almost 400 Friendly units have opened since 1970.

As of January 1, 1981, 419 of the Friendly units were free-standing, while the rest were located in shopping centers. Seventy percent of the free-standing sites are owned by Friendly; the other 30 percent are leased, as are all the shopping center sites. Friendly's executives believe that the great majority of its customers are residents of the immediate area surrounding the restaurant. Virtually all units are in suburban areas.

Other Food Products and Services

Pasta

Four acquisitions comprise Hershey's pasta group. San Giorgio Macaroni, Inc. was acquired in 1966, with major markets in Philadelphia, Washington, D.C., Pittsburgh, and New York. Its primary plant is in Lebanon, Pennsylvania, about 20 miles from Hershey. San Giorgio produces 65 varieties of pasta and noodle products. Delmonico Foods, Inc. of Louisville, Kentucky was also acquired in 1966, and was merged with San Giorgio in 1975. Its manufacturing facility is in Louisville, and the company's products are distributed chiefly in Kentucky, Ohio, and parts of West Virginia. The Procino-Rossi Corporation was acquired in 1978. Its brands (P & R brands) are distributed chiefly in upstate New York. The largest pasta acquisition is the Skinner Macaroni Co. of Omaha, Nebraska. Purchased in 1979, it distributed its products to 20 states in the West, Southwest, and South. In 1980, Hershey merged all four pasta companies into one organization, called San Giorgio-Skinner Company.

San Giorgio–Skinner Company produces and sells a great variety of pasta items, including small shells, jumbo shells, large shells, manicotti, lasagna, rippled edge lasagna, macaroni, large elbow macaroni, shell macaroni, spaghetti, long spaghetti, thin spaghetti, curly spaghetti, mostaccioli, egg noodles, extra wide egg noodles, rigatoni, alphabets, linguine, perciatelli, fettucini, soupettes, cut ziti, and spaghetti sauce.

Cory Food Services

Cory Food Services, Inc., founded by Harvey Cory in 1933, was acquired in 1967. Cory developed a vacuum glass brewer with a glass filter that brewed a delicious coffee. In 1964, Cory introduced its coffee service to the business community in the United States and Canada. Cory's corporate headquarters is in Chicago, and the company has 51 branch offices in the United States. These branch offices are grouped into five regional offices: Arlington Heights, Illinois; Long Island, New York; Rockville, Maryland; Glendale, California; and Dallas, Texas. Six branch offices in Canada are serviced by the regional office in Toronto.

As a complement to its coffee business, Cory introduced leased water treatment units, compact refrigerator units, and microwave ovens suitable for offices. The latter two were expanded into more areas in 1981. Growth in these new ventures was good in 1981 and further expansion was anticipated in 1982.

STRATEGIC PLANNING

Hershey began to emphasize strategic planning in the late 1970s. William E. C. Dearden, Hershey's chief executive officer, stated that strategic planning was his number one priority. In 1978, Mr. Dearden established the position of vice president of corporate development, which reports directly to him.

Hershey's strategic plan for accomplishing its basic corporate objectives has centered on its efforts to diversify. In the company's 1980 annual report, Chairman of the Board Harold S. Mohler, Chief Executive Officer William E. C. Dearden, and the company's President and Chief Operating Officer, Richard A. Zimmerman, stated, "In keeping with our strategic plan, we shall continue our drive to become a major, diversified, international food and food-related company." This strategic plan is also reflected in the Statement of Corporate Philosophy developed by the same executives (see Exhibit 7). The statement also includes the company's basic objectives: "We are in business to make a reasonable profit, and to enhance the value of our shareholders' investment."

The company, however, faces strong competition. In the early 1970s, Hershey lost its lead in market share for candy bars to Mars, the privately owned, Hackettstown, New Jersey, company which markets such well known brands as Milky Way, Snickers, Three Musketeers, and m&m's. At one time, Mars had a 40 percent share of the candy bar market, compared to Hershey's 23 percent. By 1979, Mars had slipped to 36 percent of candy bar sales, while Hershey increased to 27 percent. Hershey executives maintained that in 1979 it was ahead of Mars in total candy sales.[1]

Another impediment is the slide in candy consumption. In 1978, Americans consumed an annual average of about 15 pounds of candy. A decade earlier, the figure was about 20 pounds. The highest per capita annual candy consumption was in the 1940s, and the 1978 figure was the lowest since 1935.[2] Competition is also stiff in the pasta division. In 1979, its San Giorgio, Delmonico, Procino-Rossi, and Skinner brands had a 10.2 percent market

---

[1] "Hershey Steps Out," *Forbes*, March 17, 1980, p. 64.
[2] "Indulge, Indulge! Enjoy, Enjoy!" *Forbes*, October 15, 1979, p. 45.

EXHIBIT 7 Hershey's Statement of Corporate Philosophy

Hershey Foods Corporation

STATEMENT OF CORPORATE PHILOSOPHY

As a major diversified company, we are in business to make a reasonable profit and adequate return on our investment and to enhance the value of our shareholders' investment.

We recognize that, to achieve this objective, we must use our resources efficiently, and we must provide for the proper balance among the fundamental obligations that we have to our shareholders, employees, customers, consumers, suppliers and within the society in which we operate.

In seeking to balance our desire for profitable growth with the obligations which we have to our other various constituencies, we shall:

I. **Protect and enhance the Corporation's high level of ethics and conduct.**
   - Honesty, integrity, fairness and respect must be key elements in all dealings with our employees, shareholders, customers, consumers, suppliers and society in general.
   - Our operations will be conducted within regulatory guidelines and in a manner that does not adversely affect our environment.
   - We continually strive to be good neighbors and to support community projects.
   - Employees are encouraged to take an active part in improving the quality of community life.

II. **Maintain a strong "people" orientation and demonstrate care for every employee.**
   - Employees will be treated with respect, dignity and fairness.
   - Employees will be given the opportunity to participate in and contribute to the Corporation's success.
   - We strive to provide attractive, competitive wages and benefits, good working conditions, and rewards for results.
   - We pursue our sincere commitment to our Affirmative Action Program in the letter and spirit of the law.
   - Promotion from within the Corporation is practiced to the fullest extent possible.
   - We constantly strive to improve two-way communication at every level and to work with each other in a spirit of constructive cooperation.

III. **Attract and hold customers and consumers with products and services of consistently superior quality and value.**
   - Our ongoing objective is to provide quality products and services of real value at competitive prices that will also insure an adequate return on investment.

IV. **Sustain a strong "results" orientation, coupled with a prudent approach to business.**
   - We strive to attain challenging objectives to insure a steady rate of real growth, while maintaining the financial strength of the Corporation.
   - We pursue profitable growth by maintaining excellence in our current businesses.
   - Growth opportunities are actively sought from within and outside the Corporation in areas which capitalize upon our strengths.
   - We constantly strive for positions of market leadership.

We shall continue to create a climate throughout the organization which causes this philosophy to become a way of life.

Adopted: July 26, 1976
Reaffirmed: April 22, 1986

Chairman of the Board and
Chief Executive Officer

President and
Chief Operating Officer

Source: Materials reprinted by permission of the copyright owner, Hershey Foods Corporation, Hershey, Pennsylvania, U.S.A.

share. This was well under the 18 percent shares of the industry leader, C. F. Mueller Co., a subsidiary of Foremost-McKesson, Inc.[3]

To implement its strategic plan, Hershey has developed the corporate organization presented in Exhibit 8. Gary W. McQuaid is the vice president of marketing for the chocolate and confectionery group, John D. Burke is Friendly's vice president of marketing, and Clifford K. Larsen serves in this capacity for San Giorgio–Skinner.[4]

[3] "Hershey Steps Out."
[4] *Advertising Age*, September 9, 1982. p. 106.

EXHIBIT 8 Hershey's Corporate Organization[1]

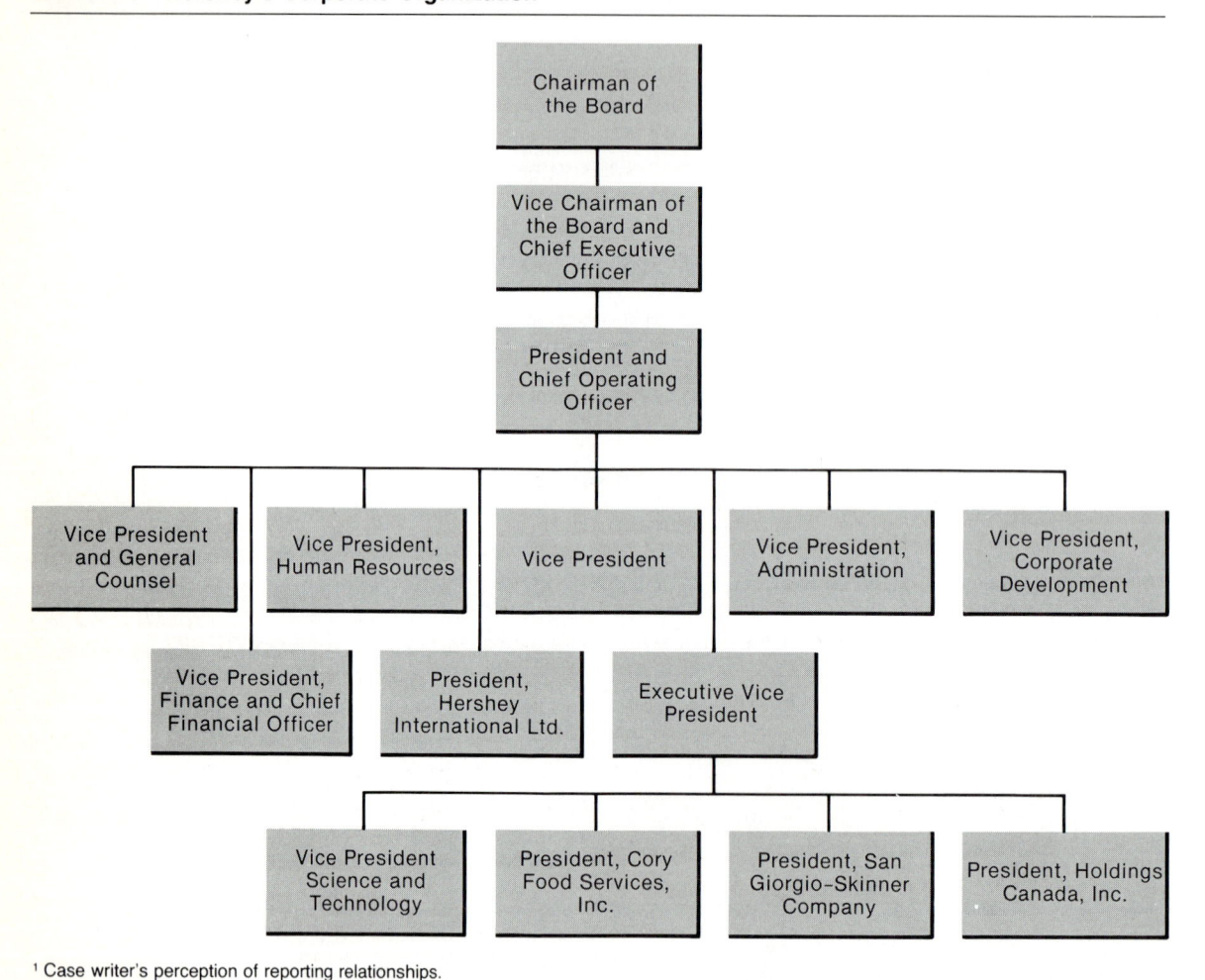

```
                    Chairman of the Board
                            |
              Vice Chairman of the Board and
                  Chief Executive Officer
                            |
              President and Chief Operating Officer
                            |
   ┌──────────┬─────────────┼─────────────┬──────────┐
 VP and    VP, Human    Vice President  VP,        VP,
 General   Resources                    Administration Corporate
 Counsel                                              Development
              |             |             |
         VP, Finance   President,    Executive Vice
         and Chief     Hershey       President
         Financial     International
         Officer       Ltd.
                            |
         ┌──────────┬──────────────┬──────────────┐
      VP Science  President,    President, San   President,
      and         Cory Food     Giorgio–Skinner  Holdings
      Technology  Services, Inc. Company         Canada, Inc.
```

[1] Case writer's perception of reporting relationships.

RESEARCH AND DEVELOPMENT

In 1979, Hershey's 114,000 square foot technical center was completed at a cost of $7.4 million. Management believes this facility and its staff will give it one of the best research and development capabilities in the industry. Included in the facility are offices, laboratories, a library, test kitchen, auditorium, animal testing facilities, and a pilot plant. A year before completion of the technical center, a major reorganization of the company's R&D effort was announced, and a new vice president of science and technology was named. This office, consisting of four groups, is responsible for heading up the company's entire R&D effort.

The *research group's* efforts have focused on three areas: vegetable fat chemistry, chocolate flavor research, and raw materials, such as peanuts and almonds. There are three subgroups in the research group. The analytical research group emphasizes chocolate analysis, and has received international acclaim for its efforts; it has compiled one of the world's largest data banks on the nutritional content of chocolate and cocoa. Microbiological research focuses on cocoa bean microbiology. This group's importance has increased as the company has purchased more chocolate liquor and less raw cocoa. The nutrition group engages in basic nutrition research projects, on subjects like tooth decay, acne, chocolate allergies, and nutrition, and it works closely with the technical committee of the Chocolate Manufacturers Association.

The *product and process development group* continually monitors consumer trends and behavioral patterns to define product opportunities. San Giorgio's Light 'n Fluffy Noodles and the Whatchamacallit candy bar were developed in response to consumers' demand for "lightness."

The *engineering group* is mainly responsible for assisting capital programs, and it also provides some engineering skills for moving new products into production.

The *equipment design and development group* provides support for producing new products and improving existing manufacturing systems. This group designs special equipment not generally available and integrates purchased equipment into the production line. In addition, it is responsible for designing special methods and devices unique to Hershey's products and conditions.

One of the major reasons for Hershey's purchase of Marabou in Sweden was to exchange technological information, with special emphasis on new confectionery products. An interest in Chadler Industrial de Bahia of Brazil was purchased for the same reason. Hershey was interested in Chadler's conversion processes which make chocolate liquor, cocoa butter, and cocoa powder from cacao beans. Hershey has also acquired interests in several cocoa growing ventures in Costa Rica, the Dominican Republic, and Belize, to try to increase yields from cacao bean production. Hershey is committed to continued support of the American Cocoa Research Institute, which works to improve the volume and quality of cacao bean production in the western hemisphere.

The company's R&D efforts have paid important dividends. Whatchamacallit and Reese's Pieces are two successful products which were developed by the company, and their success has encouraged further research. A significant technological breakthrough was the development of a peanut butter-flavored ingredient which reduces dependence on high-priced cacao beans.

Future corporate research and development is expected to continue to work toward creating new ingredients that are readily available domestically and will reduce the dependency on imported commodities. Two major emphases have been testing alternate fat products for cocoa butter and experimenting with new high-fructose corn syrup, which could be used as a sucrose alternate in certain kinds of products.

INTERNATIONAL OPERATIONS

In recent years, Hershey has increased its overseas marketing efforts. As of 1981, the company believes that "overall sales and earnings from international operations remain modest in comparison with the corporation's total performance." However, the company is pleased with its expansion in international sales.

Hershey's major foreign market is Canada. Although some sales growth occurred in Canada in 1980, the company executives considered these results well below expectations. As in the United States, higher operating costs forced the company to raise prices to 35 cents for the standard size candy bar.

During 1979 and 1980, several new products were successfully introduced in Canada. Brown Cow proved to be an immediate success, and became one of the company's leading brands in Canada. Brown Cow is a chocolate syrup milk modifier in a plastic dispenser bottle. Top Scotch, a butterscotch sundae topping, was introduced in 1979. Three other products entered the Canadian market in 1970: Special Crisp, the Canadian version of Whatchamacallit; Reese's Crunchy Peanut Butter Cups; and a boxed version of Y&S All Sorts (licorice). 1980 saw the introduction of Reese's Pieces and two clear plastic bag packages of Y&S All Sorts.

Hershey has a number of supply points for cacao beans. The major ones are La Guaria, Venezuela; Guayaquil, Ecuador; Ilheus, Brazil; Abidjan, Ivory Coast; Accra, Ghana; Lagos, Nigeria; and Douala, Cameroon.

Hershey has a policy of joint ventures in entering foreign markets. This strategy allows the company to work with well-established partners with considerable knowledge of local market conditions. Hershey entered a joint venture in 1979 with the Fujiya Confectioning Company, Ltd. of Tokyo. This Japanese firm has been in existence since 1910, and is a leader in chocolate and confectionery products, snack foods, beverages, ice cream, and bakery products in that country; it also has important restaurant operations. The joint venture agreement enables Hershey's products to be imported, manufactured, and sold in Japan, and company executives believe that this arrangement has already resulted in increased Japanese sales. Another joint venture arrangement in Mexico with Nacional de Dulces, S.A. has resulted in increased sales and earnings in that country. The company expects demand for its products to increase, and a new Mexican manufacturing facility is under construction. Two joint ventures exist in Brazil: one with Chadler Industrial de Bahia S.A. involves sales of chocolate and confectionery products. A new joint venture with S.A. Industrias Reunidas F. Matarazzo is concerned with pasta sales. Early indications were that the pasta joint venture was successful. However, the continued devaluation of the cruzeiro has adversely affected the firm's Brazilian operations.

In Sweden, AB Marabou acquired Göteborgs Kex, that country's leading cookie and cracker manufacturer. These additional sales contributed to Hershey's revenues; Hershey has a 20 percent interest in AB Marabou. In the Philippines, Hershey began in 1980 to furnish technical manufacturing assistance and cocoa growing advice to the Philippine Cocoa Corporation.

In 1981, Hershey formed a new subsidiary company, Hershey International Ltd. This company is responsible for Hershey's international operations outside Canada, especially those in Mexico, Brazil, the Philippines, Sweden, and Japan. Company executives believed this "consolidation will further strengthen the overall monitoring, control, and reporting of international operations." Richard M. Marcks, vice president, international, was named president of the new subsidiary company and his old position was abolished.

DISTRIBUTION

The company believes that its distribution system is critical in maintaining sales growth and providing service to its distributors. Hershey attempts to anticipate distributors' optimum stock levels and provide them with reasonable delivery times. To achieve these objectives, Hershey uses 35 field warehouses throughout the United States, Puerto Rico, and Canada. Hershey uses public carriers, contract carriers, and some private trucks to move its products from manufacturing plants to field warehouses, and then to customers. For example, a fleet of company-owned refrigerated trucks transports food and supplies from the two Friendly production sites to the individual restaurants. Some shipments go directly from manufacturing plants to customers. Hershey's executives believe that the distribution system has been very helpful in successfully introducing new products nationally.

Hershey has five major manufacturing plants in the United States and Canada for chocolate and confectionery products, with an additional manufacturing site under construction. Four of the present plants (two in Hershey, one in Oakdale, California, and one in Smith Falls, Ontario) produce primarily chocolate products. The Lancaster, Pennsylvania, plant produces licorice products. A future manufacturing plant in Stuart's Draft, Virginia, will produce chocolate items.

Hershey's chocolate and confectionery products are sold mainly to wholesale, chain, and independent grocers, candy and tobacco stores, syndicated and department stores, vending and concessions, drug stores, and convenience stores. Exhibit 9 shows the percentage of sales of each of these distribution

EXHIBIT 9 Percentage of Chocolate and Confectionery Sales by Type of Distribution Outlet

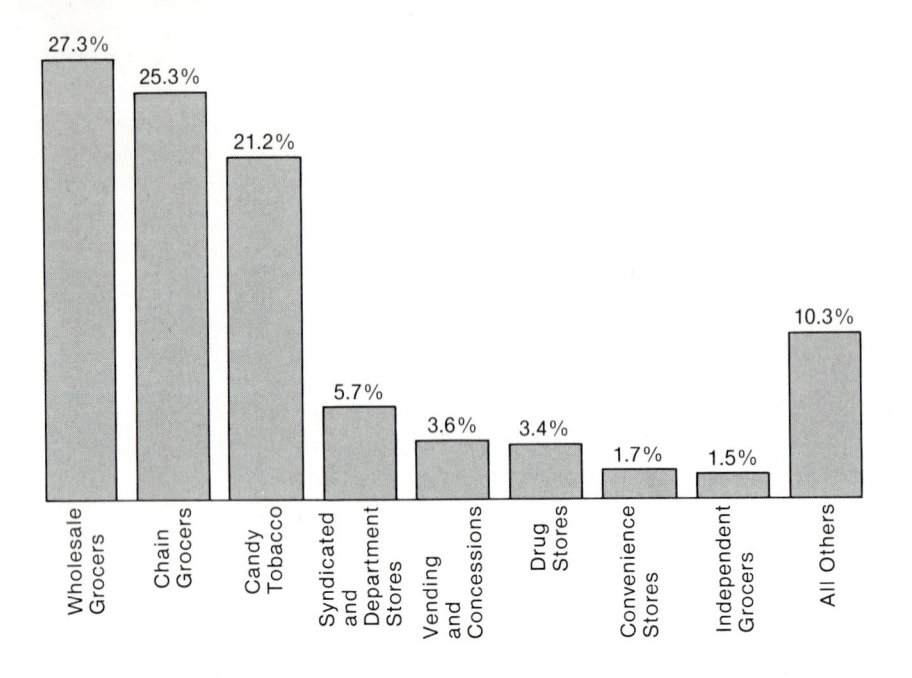

- Wholesale Grocers: 27.3%
- Chain Grocers: 25.3%
- Candy Tobacco: 21.2%
- Syndicated and Department Stores: 5.7%
- Vending and Concessions: 3.6%
- Drug Stores: 3.4%
- Convenience Stores: 1.7%
- Independent Grocers: 1.5%
- All Others: 10.3%

Source: *The Wall Street Transcript*, November 13, 1978, by permission.

outlets. Exhibit 10 shows the geographical sales pattern for chocolate and confectionery products. Over 375 sales representatives throughout the United States and Canada service over 20,000 direct sales customers. Company executives estimate that over 1 million retail outlets are served in 20,000 cities and towns, and that no single customer accounts for more than 4 percent of the total sales of chocolate and confectionery items. The company's sales representatives are specialized according to the product sold. One type is responsible for candy bars, packaged items, and grocery products. The other handles specialty products, food service, and industrial products. Hershey's pasta products are sold to supermarket chains, cooperatives, independent wholesalers, and wholesaler-sponsored volunteers. Four brand names are marketed (San Giorgio, Skinner, Delmonico, and P&R), but some private label merchandise is also marketed.

ADVERTISING

For its first 66 years, Hershey did not advertise. The company relied on the quality of its products and its extensive channels of distribution system to gain

EXHIBIT 10   Geographical Sales

REGION	PERCENTAGE OF SALES	PERCENTAGE OF U.S. POPULATION
North	31.9%	27.6%
South	24.2%	27.4%
Midwest	25.9%	27.9%
West	18.0%	17.1%
Total U.S.	100.0%	100.0%

Source: *The Wall Street Transcript*, November 13, 1978, by permission.

acceptance in the marketplace. Milton Hershey said, "Give them quality. That's the best kind of advertising in the world." However, Hershey did use various forms of sales promotion, such as the plant tour, to promote sales. The plant tour, seen by almost 10 million people, was replaced by Hershey's Chocolate World in 1973.

In 1968, over 20 years after the death of its founder, Hershey announced plans to initiate a consumer advertising program for its confectionery and grocery products. On July 19, 1970, the program was launched with a full page ad for Hershey's Syrup, which appeared in 114 newspaper supplements. National radio and television advertising appeared in September.

Hershey decided to advertise for several reasons. There was increased competition in the confectionery industry—increased competition which often involved heavy advertising. There was the need to better acquaint people under 25 with Hershey products. In 1970, these people accounted for half of the U.S. population. As Hershey developed new products, executives believed that advertising would promote mass distribution, which would, in turn, spur mass production.

Exhibit 11 shows advertising expenditures from 1971 through 1981. Hershey's $43 million of advertising in 1980 moved it into the top 100 of U.S. advertisers, and its 1981 expenditures ranked it 86th. Mars, Inc. spent $78.4 million on advertising in 1981, good for the 69th spot. Exhibit 12 shows 1981 advertising expenditures for Hershey's major brands. Sales promotion efforts are directed to consumers by such point-of-purchase materials as shelf-takers and case cards, and by coupon and premium offers.

The company has had to defend its advertising from attacks on two fronts: some of the advertising is directed toward children, and some of its products may promote tooth decay. Hershey estimates that about 30 percent of its advertising is directed to children. The Federal Trade Commission on May 28, 1980 began considering a trade regulation which would adversely affect the advertising of many of the company's products. At that time, however, Congress narrowed the FTC's authority to adopt such a trade rule. As of January 1, 1981, company executives were not sure whether the FTC would continue its efforts to regulate advertising to children. In most cases, it would take several

STRATEGY FORMULATION

EXHIBIT 11 Annual Advertising

YEAR	AMOUNT
1971	$10,506,000
1972	13,954,000
1973	9,565,000
1974	1,744,000
1975	9,499,000
1976	13,330,000
1977	17,637,000
1978	21,847,000
1979	32,063,000
1980	42,684,000
1981	56,516,000

Source: Company Annual Reports.

years to adopt such a trade rule. Hershey executives announced they were opposed to "any attempt to limit its rights to advertise truthfully its products to any audience." Hershey has developed material about the controversy surrounding tooth decay and nutrition. An example of these materials is presented in Exhibit 13.

PRICING

Pricing is a particularly important element of the marketing mix for Hershey, and it is difficult for a number of reasons. Hershey's chocolate and confectionery products depend on raw materials. The suppliers of these raw materials are usually in foreign countries and their supplies are frequently curtailed because of bad weather or other factors.

EXHIBIT 12 Most Heavily Advertised Products in 1981

PRODUCT	ADVERTISING EXPENDITURE
Hershey's Candy Bars	$7.0 million
Reese's Candies	4.6 million
Hershey's Chocolate Kisses	3.7 million
Whatchamacallit	3.7 million
Hershey's Chocolate Syrup	3.1 million
Reese's Pieces	2.9 million
Chocolate Chips	2.3 million
Rolo Candy	1.6 million
Hershey's Candies	1.4 million

Source: Reprinted with permission from the September 9, 1982 issue of *Advertising Age*. Copyright 1982 by Crain Communications, Inc. All rights reserved.

Cacao beans are the major raw materials for the Chocolate and Confectionery Division: two thirds of the world's supply is grown in West Africa, chiefly in Ghana. Prices fluctuated widely in the 1970s because of weather conditions, consuming countries' demands, sales policies of the producing countries, speculative influences, worldwide inflation, and currency movements. Hershey attempts to minimize the effects of bean price fluctuations through

EXHIBIT 13 Example of a Hershey's Advertisement

Good Nutrition Makes Good Sense

Everyone agrees that good nutrition makes good sense. But what is good nutrition? Nowadays many people are readily willing to answer this question, but many of their answers are contradictory.

While we do not advertise our chocolate products as especially nutritious foods, they do have nutritional value and do contribute to the overall diet since they are composed of such food ingredients as milk, various nuts, chocolate and sugar.

Nearly all Hershey's Chocolate and Confectionery Division products have nutrition information printed on their labels. This practice was begun voluntarily in 1973, and to date we are the only manufacturer in the chocolate and confectionery industry to provide this consumer service. Our effort to convey this information is one clear indication of Hershey's concern for good nutrition and our respect for the consumer's right to know.

Good nutrition comes from a balanced diet; one that provides the right amounts and the right kinds of proteins, vitamins, minerals, fats and carbohydrates. The chart following [Exhibit 14, p. 271] provides an interesting basis of comparison between Hershey Foods' products and other snack items commonly cited as "more nutritious."

Chocolate and confectionery products and other sugar containing snacks have been coming under attack recently. They are accused of being "empty calorie" or so-called "junk" foods.

We all have substantial caloric needs. At Hershey Foods we believe obtaining the right amount of calories is especially important for active, growing children. Calories come from nutrients; namely carbohydrates, fats and proteins. Our products supply these nutrients and do contribute to good nutrition.

Throughout the world, carbohydrates are the largest single component of the diet. In the United States, about half of all calories (i.e., energy) are provided by carbohydrates commonly referred to as sugars and starches. As far as the body is concerned, all carbohydrates must be reduced to simple sugars before they can be used. Once sugars and starches reach the stomach, their dietary origin is lost. It makes no difference whether they come from fruits, vegetables, milk, honey, or Hershey Bars—before entering the blood stream, they are all alike.

Sugar is currently bearing the brunt of the attack from a variety of sources. Since sugar is a significant component of many Hershey Foods' chocolate and confectionery products, we are naturally concerned about these attacks and the types of evidence used to support them.

At present sugar is not linked in substantive research to the variety of health problems usually mentioned in this context. As for dental caries, a complex issue, there is evidence that sugar, both naturally occurring and added, plays a role. On the other hand, a number of studies in dental literature show that chocolate, especially milk chocolate, does not cause an increase in dental caries.

Researchers report that milk chocolate has a high content of protein, calcium, phosphate and other minerals, all of which have exhibited positive effects on tooth enamel. In addition due to its natural fat (cocoa butter) content, milk chocolate clears the mouth quickly in

EXHIBIT 13 (Continued)

comparison to some other foods. These factors are thought to be responsible for making milk chocolate less likely to cause dental caries than certain other foods.

The American public is being inundated with numerous attacks on sugar and the role it plays in the diet. Many assertions are made on a partial understanding of the facts or without substantiating research.

Unfortunately the crusade against sugar containing products is well underway despite a lack of adequate, factual support. Federal, state, and local governmental bodies have entered the fray, and considerable media interest has been generated. We fear that great misunderstanding will be created before the issue is resolved, although as a company and an industry, we are trying to raise the information level on all fronts.

One aspect of this very complex situation is the role the Federal Trade Commission has been asked to play regarding the advertisement of products containing sugar. At the present time, the FTC is considering various means of limiting our industry's ability to advertise its products.

Hershey Foods has and will continue to oppose any attempt to limit its right to advertise. We believe we have the right to advertise to all of our audiences and we do not think our advertising has been out of balance. In 1978, less than one third of all our advertising impressions will be received by children.

Hershey Foods has always been concerned about the content of its advertising as well as the type of programs it supports. We have helped in the development of voluntary codes through the Children's Review Unit of the National Advertising Board, and our ads are constantly reviewed by child psychologists and public affairs specialists to make sure they are not misleading and cannot be misunderstood.

Our standard bar line, which accounts for the majority of advertising expenditures, represents an inexpensive group of products. We feel that children can be appropriately informed about them, especially in light of their nutritional value and the parental approval they have received for generations in the United States. We believe we have the right to remind consumers of our products and to inform new consumers about products their parents have used, enjoyed, and approved.

Perhaps the most paradoxical aspect of this issue is the fact that chocolate and confectionery consumption in the United States is not excessive, representing only about one percent of total food intake. What's more, consumption of these foods has not increased in the last 40 years. Since mass media advertising did not really come into being until the 1950s, it is evident that television advertising has not contributed to increased consumption of chocolate and confectionery products. As far as our industry is concerned, however, advertising has simply fostered competition.

The so-called "junk" food issue in all its complexity will continue to be an important challenge to Hershey Foods Corporation. We shall stand firmly in our position that Hershey's products are mixtures of ingredients which inherently have nutritional value. Hershey has manufactured chocolate and confectionery products of the highest quality for over 80 years. We are very proud of these products and the role they play in the lives of people throughout the world.

---

forward purchasing of large quantities of cacao beans, cocoa butter, and chocolate liquor. Cocoa future contracts are purchased and sold, and the company holds memberships in the London Cocoa Terminal Market Association and the Coffee, Sugar, and Cocoa Exchange, Inc. in New York. Crop forecasts, chiefly in West Africa and Brazil, are also made.

Despite these efforts, the prices of cacao beans skyrocketed in the 1970s.

EXHIBIT 14 Nutritional Value per Serving of Various Foods[1]

	A	B	C	D	E	F	G	H	I
	MILK CHOCOLATE	MR. GOODBAR	REESE CUP	ICE CREAM	SALTINE CRACKERS	GRAHAM CRACKERS	CHEESE/ PEANUT BUTTER CRACKERS	APPLE	DRIED DATES
Serving size	1.05 oz	1.3 oz	1.2 oz	8 fl oz (1 cup)	1 oz	1 oz	1.5 oz	3¾ in. diam.	1.4 oz
Calories	160	210	190	260	120	110	210	120	120
Protein (grams)	2	5	4	6	2	2	6	0	1
Carbohydrate (grams)	17	18	18	28	20	20	24	30	29
Fat (grams)	10	13	11	14	3	2	10	1	0
Vitamin A[2]	2	2	2	2	2	2	2	2	2
Vitamin C[3]	2	2	2	2	2	2	2	10	2
Thiamine[3]	2	2	2	2	2	2	2	2	2
Riboflavin[3]	4	4	2	15	2	4	2	2	2
Niacin[3]	2	8	8	2	2	2	8	2	4
Calcium[3]	6	4	2	20	2	2	2	2	2
Iron[3]	2	2	2	2	2	2	2	2	6

[1] Information for foods other than Hershey products derived from U.S.D.A. Handbook No. 456 *Nutritive Value of American Foods*. Items A, B, & C, according to at least one state's legislators' list, would be included in a "low-nutritious" category. Items D through I are identified on that list as nutritious food.
[2] Contained less than 2 percent of the U.S. RDA of these nutrients.
[3] Vitamin and mineral levels are expressed as a percentage of the U.S. RDA.
Source: Company Document

The following is the average price of cacao beans for October 1 through September 30, the normal crop year:

YEAR	CENTS PER POUND
1969–70	32.5
1970–71	26.3
1971–72	26.3
1972–73	44.5
1973–74	62.7
1974–75	57.3
1975–76	72.1
1976–77	150.1
1977–78	141.1
1978–79	156.4
1979–80	138.8

Source: Company document.

The other major ingredient is sugar. Like cacao beans, many factors affect the price of sugar, including quantities available, demand by consumers, speculation, currency movements, and the International Sugar Agreement. Another price determinant is the price support provided domestic sugar by the Agriculture Adjustment Act of 1978. The average price per pound of refined sugar, as reported by the U.S. Department of Agriculture, FOB Northeast, has been steadily increasing:

1977	17.3 cents
1978	20.8 cents
1979	23.2 cents
1980	41.0 cents
1981	36.1 cents

Three other raw materials are important. The company is the largest domestic user of almonds, using only almonds grown in California. The price of almonds doubled in 1979 due to a poor California crop in 1978, and has remained high despite a good 1979 California crop. Marginal crops in the rest of the world kept prices high. In 1980, the peanut crop in the United States was poor, causing significant price increases. The supply of peanuts is expected to be low in 1981, but Hershey did not expect any problem obtaining enough for production. The price of milk has also increased greatly in recent years; both milk and peanut prices are affected by various Federal Marketing Orders and by U.S. Department of Agriculture subsidy programs.

More expensive cacao beans, sugar, almonds, peanuts, and milk have forced Hershey to raise prices. The sizes of various products have also been modified. Below are the price/size adjustments for Hershey's Standard Milk Chocolate Bar since 1949:

Common Retail Price: 5 Cents

1949	1 oz.
March 1954	7/8 oz.
June 1955	1 oz.
January 1958	7/8 oz.
August 1960	1 oz.
September 1963	7/8 oz.
September 1965	1 oz.
September 1966	7/8 oz.
May 1968	1/4 oz.
Discontinued	11-24-69

Common Retail Price: 10 Cents

November 1969	1½ ozs.
November 1970	1 3/8 ozs.
January 1973	1.26 ozs.
Discontinued	1-1-74

Common Retail Price: 15 Cents

January 1974	1.4 ozs.
May 1974	1.2 ozs.
September 1974	1.05 ozs.
January 1976	1.2 ozs.
Discontinued	12-31-76

Common Retail Price: 20 Cents

December 1976	1.35 ozs.
April 1977	1.2 ozs.
July 1977	1.05 ozs.
Discontinued	12-1-78

Common Retail Price: 25 Cents

December 1978	1.2 ozs.
March 1980	1.05 ozs.

Source: Company Documents.

Friendly Restaurants use many raw materials. Rising prices of items such as beef, cream, condensed milk, whole milk, and sugar and corn syrup in the late 70s forced Friendly to raise menu prices. Pasta is made from durum wheat flour grown almost exclusively in North Dakota. Poor weather conditions in 1980 sharply reduced the quality of the durum wheat crop, resulting in a 60 percent increase in price. Hershey was forced to raise prices twice in 1980. Coffee prices declined in 1980 from 1979 levels, down from historic highs earlier in the decade, and the Cory Division was able to reduce its prices during 1980.

Hershey uses price concessions to induce its distributors to carry its products. The company hopes that the distributor will feature the item because the price reductions provide them with a higher-than-normal profit.

TOWARD THE FUTURE

As Hershey Foods Corporation moved into 1982, company executives decided to thoroughly review past performance and strategy, and use these assessments to chart the future direction of the firm. Several aspects of the company's operations were chosen for appraisal:

1. Have the company's diversification efforts been effective in accomplishing its objectives? What should Hershey's future diversification strategy be?
2. How effective has Hershey's advertising been? How much emphasis should the company place on advertising in the future?
3. How effective has the company's distribution strategy been? What changes would be appropriate in the future?
4. Has Hershey been able to reduce the risks which appear to be inherent in the kinds of products it sells? What can be done to reduce these risks?
5. How viable is the company's corporate organization? What are its strengths and weaknesses? What modifications are needed?

INDUSTRIAL HIGHLIGHT

Confectionery Products Industry

Below is a capsule summary of the confectionery products industry, of which Hershey Foods is a part. Information in this highlight was compiled by the U.S. Department of Commerce and focuses on this industry during the approximate period of time covered in the case. Keep in mind that industrial highlights contained in this text are not intended as a complete synopsis of an industry but as a profile of certain issues that can be relevant to a case situation.

CURRENT SITUATION

Shipments of confectionery products (SIC 2065) were expected to total about $6.4 billion in 1982, an increase of 6.5 percent over the 1981 level. Adjusted for inflation, confectionery shipments (chocolate and nonchocolate candy, some kinds of cough drops, packaged nuts, and candied fruits) reached an estimated $3.3 billion for the year, an increase of about 5 percent over the 1981 level.

Chocolate and nonchocolate candies continued to dominate the industry, accounting for over 85 percent of confectionery product sales in 1982. The estimated value of shipments in this category totaled $5.6 billion, about 8 percent over the 1981 level. Per capita consumption of chocolate and nonchocolate candies was expected to reach 16.2 pounds in 1982. Concerns about children's safety appeared to reduce candy consumption during Halloween, but it was hard to predict whether this concern would have any lasting effect on the industry.

Consumer prices for confectionery products rose about 3 percent during the year, largely because of stable sugar prices and declines in cocoa and peanut prices. In contrast, retail prices rose 11 and 12 percent respectively in 1980 and 1981, reflecting volatile sugar, peanut, and cocoa markets.

Source: U.S. Industrial Outlook, Department of Commerce, 1981, p. 371; 1982, p. 289; 1983, pp. 37-19–37-20; 1984, pp. 38-23–38-25.

Candy Bars Are Larger

Because the weight of candy bars increased in 1982, the average retail price per ounce declined for the first time since 1977. Following the lead of one large firm, virtually all producers increased candy bar weights more than candy bar prices. As a result, the price paid by consumers per ounce in 1982 was about the same as in 1979. Between 1977 and 1981 the average price per ounce of a candy bar rose about 10 percent.

Advertising expenditures rose an estimated 15 percent in 1982, to about $200 million. Confectionery producers spent heavily to introduce new items and to promote sales of larger candy bars.

Ingredient Supplies Ample

Sugar, cocoa, and peanuts account for about 60 percent of the raw material costs of confectionery manufacturers. In 1982 the price of sugar remained essentially unchanged from 1981, but peanut prices declined about 9 percent. The price of cocoa continued to decline, and by mid-1982 cocoa bean prices were at a 2-year low.

Industry Structure

Confectionery product manufacturers tend to be either small, closely held firms, or subsidiaries of large diversified food companies. Of the 10 firms that dominate the industry, eight are divisions of large diversified companies.

Employment in the industry was estimated at 58,000 in 1982, up almost 4 percent from the previous year. Production workers account for about four-fifths of the industry workforce.

Average hourly earnings of confectionery production workers reached $7.10 in 1982, about 7 percent higher than a year earlier. Output per hour dropped slightly in 1982, after having grown during the preceding 10 years.

Foreign Trade

The quantity and value of confectionery product exports, including nutmeats, declined in 1982, reflecting the continued strength of the U.S. dollar and a slowdown in economic activity in Canada and Mexico, our major North American trading partners. The ratio of exports to total product shipments declined for the third consecutive year. In 1982, imports of confectionery products in terms of quantity and value rose 7 percent and 4 percent, respectively. An increasing share of imports consists of candies produced abroad by subsidiaries of U.S. confectionery manufacturers.

Because of the strong dollar, the average value per pound of chocolate candy exports increased to $1.60 in 1982, while the average dollar value per pound of imported candies declined about 3 percent, to $1.16.

EXHIBIT A Chocolate and Nonchocolate Confection Shipments

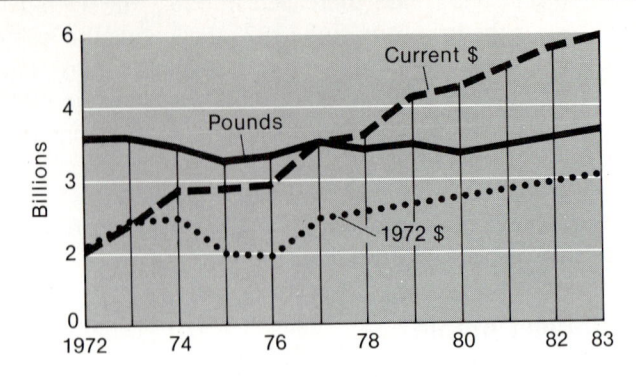

Source: Bureau of the Census, Bureau of Industrial Economics.

LONG-TERM PROSPECTS

Consumer spending on confectionery products is expected to continue upward in the next several years, reflecting a rising demand for a greater variety of products and higher quality candies. Young people between the ages of 8 and 17, traditionally the largest purchasers of candy bars, are expected to provide expanding markets for confectionery products as their numbers increase.

Price changes for confectionery products are expected to be moderate in the years ahead unless ingredient costs are affected by sharp changes in sugar and cocoa supplies. From 1982 to 1987, shipments of confectionery products are expected to increase at a 3.4 percent compound annual rate.

CASE 14

Anheuser-Busch Companies, Inc.*

DOUGLAS J. WORKMAN   JOHN CARY   NEIL H. SNYDER
SCOTT McMASTERS   RICH BONAVENTURA   KAREN COOK
all of the University of Virginia

BACKGROUND OF THE FIRM

In 1852, George Schneider opened the Bavarian Brewery on the south side of St. Louis, Missouri. Five years later, the brewery faced insolvency. In 1857, it was sold to competitors who renamed it Hammer and Urban. The new owners launched an expansion program with the help of a loan from Eberhard Anheuser, a successful soap manufacturer at the time. By 1860, the brewery had faltered once again, and Anheuser assumed control. Four years later, his son-in-law, Adolphus Busch, joined the brewery as a salesman. Later Adolphus became a partner and finally president of the company. Busch was the driving force behind the company's success, and in 1879, the company name was changed to Anheuser-Busch Brewing Association.

An important reason for the brewery's success was Adolphus Busch's innovative attempt to establish and maintain a national beer market. In 1877, he launched the industry's first fleet of refrigerated freight cars. He also pioneered the application of a new pasteurization process. Busch's talents were not limited to technology alone; he concurrently developed merchandising techniques to complement his technological innovations. By 1901, annual sales had surpassed the million-barrel mark for the first time.

August A. Busch succeeded his father as president of Anheuser-Busch in 1913. With the advent of Prohibition, he was forced to harness the company's expertise and energies into new directions (corn products, bakers' yeast, ice cream, commercial refrigeration units, truck bodies, and nonalcoholic beverages). These efforts kept the company from collapsing during the dry era. With the passage of the 21st Amendment, Anheuser-Busch was back in the beer business. To celebrate, a team of Clydesdale horses was acquired in 1933—the Budweiser Clydesdales.

In 1946, August A. Busch, Jr., became president and chief executive officer. During his tenure, the company's beer operation flourished. Eight breweries were constructed, and annual sales increased from 3 million barrels in 1946 to more than 34 million in 1974. The corporation also diversified extensively, adding family entertainment centers, real estate, can manufacturing, transportation, and a major league baseball franchise.

---

* This is a classic case in the strategic management literature.

This case was prepared by Douglas J. Workman, Neil H. Snyder, Rich Bonaventura, John Cary, Scott McMasters, and Karen Cook of the McIntire School of Commerce of the University of Virginia.

August A. Busch III was elected president in 1974 and chief executive officer the following year, making him the fifth Busch to serve in that capacity. Thus far under his direction, Anheuser-Busch has accomplished the following: opened its 10th brewery; introduced Michelob Light, Anheuser-Busch Natural Light, and Würzburger Hofbräu; opened a new Busch Gardens theme park; launched the largest brewery expansion projects in the company's history; vertically integrated into new can manufacturing and malt production facilities; and diversified into container recovery, soft drinks, and snack foods.

THE INDUSTRY AND COMPETITION

Ninety percent of Anheuser-Busch's sales come from their beer products. (Generically, the term *beer* refers to any beverage brewed from a farinaceous grain.) The type of beer consumed in America today originated in the 1840s with the introduction of lager beer. Lager beer is bottom fermented (meaning yeast settles to the bottom during fermentation). The beer is then aged (or lagered) to mellow, resulting in a lighter, more-effervescent potation. Prior to 1840, Americans' tastes closely resembled British tastes (that is, heavily oriented toward ale, porter, and stout). The influx of German immigrants in the 1840s initially increased the importance of lager beer because of the influence of German tastes and brewing skills.

By 1850, there were 430 brewers in the United States producing a total of 750,000 barrels per year, and by the end of the decade, there were 1,269 brewers producing over 1 million barrels per year. At that time, brewers served relatively small local areas. In the latter half of the 19th century, several significant technological advances were adapted to the beer industry, including artificial refrigeration, mechanized bottling equipment, and pasteurization. The latter innovation enabled brewers to ship warm beer and store it for a longer period of time without refermentation. With developments in transportation technology, the 20th century saw the rise of the national brewer. The combined impact of these technological advances resulted in greater emphasis on marketing as the primary instrument of competition.

The modern era of the brewing industry begins with the end of World War II. Prior to that time, only a few brewers sold beer nationally, and they primarily operated out of a single plant. To offset additional transportation costs not incurred by local or even regional brewers, the national firms advertised their beers as being of premium quality and charged a premium price. This structural change in the industry (from predominantly local or regional to national producers) in the post-World War II time period has resulted in a steady decline in the number of brewers and plants and an increase in the market concentration of the large national brewers. Exhibit 1 shows the number of breweries and brewery firms for 1946–1976. Exhibit 2 shows concentration ratios for 1935–1977.

In the period following World War II, annual beer sales hit a record high in 1947 and then declined and stagnated until 1959. Exhibit 3 shows per-capita demand trends in total beer, packaged beer, and draft beer for this time period.

ANHEUSER-BUSCH COMPANIES, INC.

EXHIBIT 1 Number of Breweries and Brewery Firms, 1946–1976

YEAR	PLANTS	FIRMS
1946	471	
1947	465	404
1948	466	
1949	440	
1950	407	
1951	386	
1952	357	
1953	329	
1954	310	263
1955	292	
1956	281	
1957	264	
1958	252	211
1959	244	
1960	229	
1961	229	
1962	220	
1963	211	171
1964	190	
1965	179	
1966	170	
1967	154	125
1968	149	
1969	146	
1970	137	
1971	134	
1972	131	108
1973	114	
1974 (June)	108	
1976	94	49

Source: For the years 1946–74: *Brewing Industry Survey* (New York: Research Company of America, 1973, 1974); 1947–72 (for number of firms): U.S. Bureau of the Census, *Census of Manufactures;* and 1976: *Brewers Digest Brewery Directory, 1977.*

EXHIBIT 2 National Beer Sales Concentration Ratios, 1935–1977 (percent)

YEAR	FOUR FIRM	EIGHT FIRM
1935	11	17
1947	21	30
1954	27	41
1958	28	44
1963	34	52
1966	39	56
1967	40	59
1970	46	64
1972	52	70
1973	54	70
1974	58	74
1975	59	78
1976	59	80
1977	63	83

Source: For the years 1935–72: U.S. Bureau of the Census, *Census of Manufactures* (based on value of shipments, establishment basis); 1973: based on share of total sales of U.S. brewers in *Brewing Industry Survey* (New York: Research Company of America, 1974); 1974–75: based on sales data in *Advertising Age,* November 3, 1975, and December 27, 1976; and 1976–77: based on sales data in *Modern Brewery Age,* February 14, 1977, and February 13, 1978, by permission.

Many analysts blamed the lack of growth in demand upon demographic factors. According to *Brewers Almanac 1976* (p. 82), past industry surveys have shown that persons in the 21–44 age group account for about 69 percent of beer consumption. Since this age group exhibited little growth during 1948–1959, population demographics offer a good explanation for stagnated demand during this period. However, other factors must be introduced to account for post-59 growth, because beer sales grew more than twice as fast as the number of people in this age group.

Economies of Scale

A major reason for the growth of national firms is the economies of scale obtained in their plant operations. Economies of scale in plant size enable

EXHIBIT 3 Analysis of Per Capita Beer Demand in the United States, 1935–1963

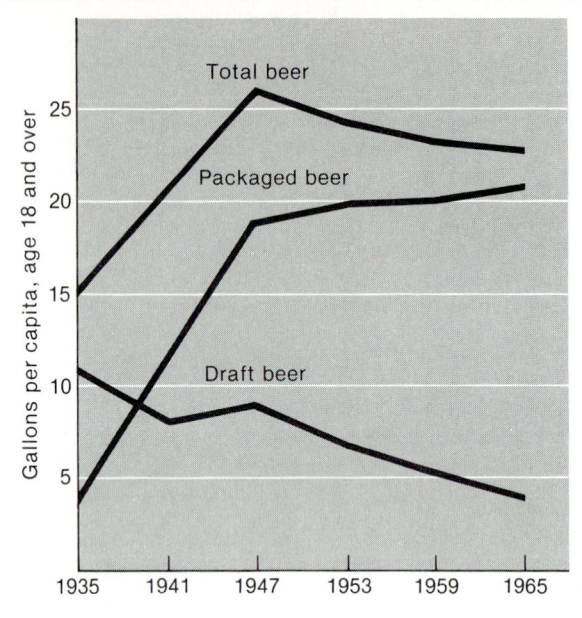

Source: John G. Keane (Ph.D. diss., University of Pittsburgh).

brewers to obtain the lowest possible unit cost. According to Dr. Kenneth G. Elzinga of the University of Virginia (an authority on the brewing industry), the minimum efficient size (MES) plant capacity for the brewing industry is 1.25 million barrels per year. Cost savings accrue from water-processing equipment, sewage facilities, refrigeration equipment, management, laboratories, and custodial cost reductions. Scale economies from most of these sources continue to plant capacities of 10 million barrels per year, but beyond the size of 4.5 million barrels, cost savings are negligible. Exhibit 4 shows one method used to estimate the extent of economies of scale: the survivor test.

Economies of scale played a central role in the restructuring of the brewing industry which led to the demise of hundreds of breweries between 1945 and 1970. Moreover, according to Charles F. Keithahn of the Bureau of Economics of the Federal Trade Commission, an analysis based solely on economies of scale would indicate a decline in firm concentration over the 1970s (in a world in which all plants are of minimum efficient size but no larger). Exhibit 5 shows the minimum market share a firm with a MES plant would need for survival.

The Effects of Mergers on Industry Concentration

Leonard Weiss of the University of Wisconsin at Madison developed a means of delineating the impact of mergers on an industry's structure. Using his

EXHIBIT 4 Surviving Breweries by Capacity, 1959–1973

LISTED CAPACITY (THOUSANDS OF BARRELS)	1959	1961	1963	1965	1967	1969	1971	1973
0–25	11	9	8	7	3	3	2	2
26–100	57	51	46	44	33	23	19	11
101–250	51	44	39	30	26	23	19	11
251–500	40	37	33	24	18	14	14	10
501–750	14	15	13	12	13	15	12	5
751–1,000	16	19	20	20	22	20	20	15
1,001–1,500	14	14	12	13	15	13	13	13
1,501–2,000	4	5	5	3	3	8	8	7
2,001–3,000	5	6	6	7	5	6	9	9
3,001–4,000	3	3	4	5	5	3	3	3
4,001+	2	2	3	3	4	7	7	11

Source: Compiled from plant capacity figures listed in the *Modern Brewery Age Book* (Stamford, Conn.: Modern Brewery Age Publishing Co., various years), and from industry trade sources. These figures do not include plants listed only on a company-consolidated basis (in the case of multiplant firms) or single-plant firms not reporting capacity in the *Blue Book*. Most plants list their capacity.

methodology, Dr. Elzinga found that mergers accounted for a negligible amount of the concentration occurring in the brewing industry. In fact, concentration trends in the brewing industry are rather unique in that most of the increased concentration was brought about by internal expansion rather than by merger or acquisition. Strict enforcement of the antitrust laws by the Justice Department (DOJ) is the reason mergers have accounted for such a small share of the increase in concentration. But the DOJ, through its rigid enforcement of the antitrust laws, may have promoted the end result it was seeking to prevent—increased national concentration. With the elimination of the merger route, the national brewers were forced to expand internally. They built large new breweries, which were more efficient than the older, smaller ones. If mergers had been permitted, the national firms might have acquired old, small breweries and might have grown more slowly than they actually did.

EXHIBIT 5 Economies of Plant Scale Expressed as a Percentage of Total Industry Production for 1970, 1975, 1980

	PRODUCTION (MILLIONS OF BARRELS)	MES PLANT AS A PERCENT OF PRODUCTION
1970	134.7	.9
1975	150.3	.8
1980 (estimated)	176.8	.7

Source: Dr. Willard Mueller, from testimony before the Subcommittee on Antitrust and Monopoly of the Committee of the Judiciary, United States Senate, 95th Congress, 2d sess. (1978).

The Effect of Advertising

Forced to expand internally in a capital-intensive industry (it costs between $25 and $45 for each additional barrel of capacity), the national firms sought to ensure a steady demand for their products. The need for larger markets resulting from increased capacity coincided with the development of television which led to an increase in the firm's desired level of product identification. Advertising, particularly television spots, became the key to product differentiation in an industry where studies have shown that under test conditions, beer drinkers cannot distinguish between brands. Exhibit 6 shows comparative advertising expenditures for 10 brewers. Exhibit 7 shows relative advertising effectiveness.

In the last decade, a new rivalry has developed among major national brewers (this time at the instigation of Miller Brewing Company). In 1970, Philip Morris completed an acquisition of Miller, and according to Dr. Willard

EXHIBIT 6 Barrelage Sold, Measured Media Advertising Expenditures, and Advertising Expenditures Per Barrel, 10 Leading Brewers, 1972–1977

PHILIP MORRIS–MILLER

Year	Barrels (000)	Advertising[1] ($000)	A/B[2]
1977	24,410	$42,473	$1.74
1976	18,232	29,117	1.60
1975	12,862	20,894	1.62
1974	9,066	12,140	1.34
1973	6,919	10,002	1.45
1972	5,353	8,400	1.57

ANHEUSER-BUSH

Year	Barrels (000)	Advertising[1] ($000)	A/B[2]
1977	36,640	$44,984	$1.23
1976	29,051	25,772	.89
1975	35,200	19,237	.55
1974	34,100	12,359	.36
1973	29,887	12,936	.43
1972	26,522	14,808	.56

SCHLITZ

Year	Barrels (000)	Advertising[1] ($000)	A/B[2]
1977	22,130	$40,830	$1.85
1976	24,162	33,756	1.40
1975	23,279	23,173	1.00
1974	22,661	17,977	.79
1973	21,343	16,615	.78
1972	18,906	17,782	.94

PABST

Year	Barrels (000)	Advertising[1] ($000)	A/B[2]
1977	16,300	$10,843	$ .67
1976	17,037	9,112	.53
1975	15,700	9,007	.57
1974	14,297	7,711	.54
1973	13,128	6,422	.49
1972	12,600	6,142	.49

COORS

Year	Barrels (000)	Advertising[1] ($000)	A/B[2]
1977	12,824	$ 3,966	$ .25
1976	13,665	1,626	.12
1975	11,950	1,093	.09
1974	12,400	801	.06
1973	10,950	699	.06
1972	9,785	1,332	.14

OLYMPIA (HAMM 1975)

Year	Barrels (000)	Advertising[1] ($000)	A/B[2]
1977	6,831	$ 8,470	$1.24
1976	6,370	5,430	.85
1975	5,770	5,555	.96
1974	4,300	2,764	.64
1973	3,636	2,323	.64
1972	3,330	2,491	.75

EXHIBIT 6 (Continued)

	HEILEMAN (GRAIN BELT 1975)			STROH		
Year	Barrels (000)	Advertising[1] ($000)	A/B[2]	Barrels (000)	Advertising[1] ($000)	A/B[2]
1977	6,245	$ 4,636	$ .74	6,114	$ 7,212	$1.18
1976	5,210	3,616	.69	5,765	5,017	.87
1975	4,535	2,864	.63	5,133	3,950	.77
1974	4,300	2,329	.54	4,364	3,477	.80
1973	4,420	2,243	.51	4,645	3,145	.68
1972	3,675	2,260	.61	4,231	3,567	.84

	SCHAEFER			C. SCHMIDT		
Year	Barrels (000)	Advertising[1] ($000)	A/B[2]	Barrels (000)	Advertising[1] ($000)	A/B[2]
1977	4,700	$ 4,219	$ .90	3,571	$ 3,912	$1.10
1976	5,300	2,516	.47	3,450	2,703	.78
1975	5,881	2,637	.45	3,330	2,269	.68
1974	5,712	2,308	.40	3,490	3,035	.87
1973	5,500	2,438	.44	3,520	2,916	.83
1972	5,530	2,994	.54	3,194	2,104	.66

[1] Advertising expenditures in six measured media as reported in *Leading National Advertisers,* various issues.
[2] Advertising per barrel.
Source: Company sales for 1970–77 from *Advertising Age,* various issues.

EXHIBIT 7 Relative Media Advertising Effectiveness by Beer Brand, 1975–1978

	MEDIA ADVERTISING EXPENSE ($ MILLION)	TOTAL BARRELS (MILLIONS)	ADVERTISING EXPENSE PER BARREL	BARREL CHANGE 1978 VERSUS 1974	ADVERTISING EXPENSE PER INCREMENTAL MILLION BARRELS
Premium category					
Budweiser	$71.5	100.2	$ .71	1.1	$65.00
Miller High Life	60.5	61.3	.99	13.5	4.48
Schlitz	70.4	59.3	1.18	(5.2)	n.a.[1]
Light category					
Lite	63.8	22.9	2.79	8.4	7.60
Anheuser-Busch Natural Light	24.0	3.8	6.32	2.3	10.43
Michelob Light	6.5	0.9	7.22	0.9	7.22
Schlitz Light	30.3	3.6	8.42	0.7	43.29
Super premium category					
Michelob	35.9	23.0	1.56	4.3	8.35
Lowenbrau	29.4	1.7	17.29	1.2	24.50

[1] n.a. = Not available.
Source: C. James Walker III, *Competition in the U.S. Brewing Industry: A Basic Analysis* (New York: Shearson Hayden Stone, September 26, 1979).

F. Mueller of the University of Wisconsin, Philip Morris's multiproduct and multinational operations in highly concentrated industries enabled it to engage in cross-subsidization of its brewing subsidiary. This capacity, coupled with the relatedness of the marketing function between Philip Morris and Miller, provided a powerful vehicle for industry restructuring. Miller adopted aggressive market segmentation and expansion strategies, thus increasing their capacity fivefold between 1970 and 1977. According to Dr. Mueller, a doubling of 1977 capacity was planned by 1981. Exhibit 8 shows comparative financial data on Philip Morris and the rest of the leading brewers.

In 1975, Miller found a successful method for promoting a low-calorie beer, Lite, which they had purchased from Meister Brau, Inc., of Chicago in 1972. They spent heavily, around $6.00 per barrel, to introduce it nationwide. However, Lite's success was not wholly attributable to heavy advertising. Low-calorie beers were promoted in the past with a notable lack of success. Through marketing research, Miller discovered that a significant portion of the beer market is comprised of young and middle-aged men who are sports fans with dreams of athletic prowess. In advertising Lite, Miller relied predominantly on retired athletes renowed for their speed and agility. The message was that one could drink a lot of Lite and still be fast, not that one should drink Lite to keep from getting fat.

By 1975, Schlitz and, to some extent, Anheuser-Busch began to increase their own advertising expenditures and made plans to enter the low-calorie beer market. This was done not only as a response to Miller's aggressiveness but also because of a general lack of growth in demand in the face of increasing industry capacity. By 1978, 9 of the 10 largest brewers had light brands on the market. Exhibits 9 through 11 show brand shipment breakdowns for the three major brewers.

EXHIBIT 8 Assets, Sales, Net Profit, Net Income on Stockholders' Investment, and Total Advertising Expenditures, 1977 ($ millions)

COMPANY	ASSETS	SALES	NET PROFIT	TOTAL PROFIT ON EQUITY	TOTAL ADVERTISING
Philip Morris (Miller)	$4,048	$3,849[1]	$335	19.8%	$277
Anheuser-Busch	1,404	1,838	92	13.5	79
Joseph Schlitz	727	937	20	5.5	55
Pabst Brewing	396	583	22	8.1	27
Adolph Coors	692	593	68	12.2	12[3]
Total 2d to 5th	3,219	3,951	202	9.8[2]	176
Philip Morris as a percent of 2d to 5th	126%	97%	166%	202%	157%

[1] Excludes U.S. and foreign excise taxes.
[2] Unweighted average.
[3] Estimate.

Source: "500 Largest Industrials," *Fortune*, May 1977; advertising data reported in individual company Securities and Exchange Commission's Form 10-K reports for 1977.

EXHIBIT 9 Estimated Anheuser-Busch Brand Breakdown: 1974–1978 (shipments in barrels—millions)

	1978	1977	1976	1975	1974
Budweiser	27.5	25.4	21.1	26.2	26.4
Michelob	7.4	6.4	5.0	4.2	3.1
Michelob Light	0.9	—	—	—	—
Busch	3.5	3.3	3.0	4.8	4.6
Natural	2.3	1.5	—	—	—
Total	41.6	36.6	29.1	35.2	34.1

Source: C. James Walker III. *Competition in the U.S. Brewing Industry: A Basic Analysis* (New York: Shearson Hayden Stone, September 26, 1979).

EXHIBIT 10 Estimated Miller Brewing Brand Breakdown: 1974–1978 (shipments in barrels—millions)

	1978	1977	1976	1975	1974
High Life	21.3	17.3	13.5	9.2	7.8
Lite	8.8	6.4	4.6	3.1	0.4
Lowenbrau	1.2	0.5	0.1	0.0	—
Other	0.0	0.0	0.2	0.5	0.9
Total	31.3	24.2	18.4	12.8	9.1

Source: C. James Walker III. *Competition in the U.S. Brewing Industry: A Basic Analysis* (New York: Shearson Hayden Stone, September 26, 1979).

EXHIBIT 11 Estimated Schlitz Brewing Brand Breakdown: 1974–1978 (shipments in barrels—millions)

	1978	1977	1976	1975	1974
Schlitz	12.7	14.3	15.9	16.8	17.9
Old Milwaukee	4.3	4.9	5.5	5.2	3.9
Schlitz Light	0.7	1.3	1.4	0.2	—
Malt Liquor	1.7	1.4	1.3	1.0	0.8
Primo	0.2	0.2	0.1	0.1	0.1
Total	19.6	22.1	24.2	23.3	22.7

Source: C. James Walker III. *Competition in the U.S. Brewing Industry: A Basic Analysis* (New York: Shearson Hayden Stone, September 26, 1979).

Currently, the only company with the financial resources to battle Miller and its multinational conglomerate backer is Anheuser-Busch, the industry leader, and Anheuser-Busch responded aggressively to Miller's program. In 1977, Anheuser-Busch surpassed Miller and Schlitz in advertising expenditures by spending over $44 million.

Exhibit 12 shows market share performance for the top five brewers and all others in the 1974–1978 period.

Clearly, Anheuser-Busch's and Miller's growth have been at the expense of the regional brewers and the faltering national brewers (Schlitz and Pabst). C. James Walker III, an industry analyst for Shearson Hayden Stone, Inc., estimates only 2.7 percent per year industry growth for the early 1980s. The capital-intensive nature of the industry, coupled with huge advertising outlays, make it very unlikely that any firm will be able to challenge the two leaders. To quote August Busch III, "This business is now a two-horse race."

ORGANIZATION OF ANHEUSER-BUSCH

Effective October 1, 1979, Anheuser-Busch, Inc., became a wholly owned subsidiary of a new holding company, Anheuser-Busch Companies, Inc., and the outstanding shares of Anheuser-Busch, Inc., were exchanged for an equal number of shares of the holding company. Concerning this change, August A. Busch III said:

> The holding company's name and structure will more clearly communicate the increasingly diversified nature of our business, thereby reflecting not only our position of leadership in the brewing industry but also our substantial activities in yeast and specialty corn products, family entertainment, transportation, can manufacturing, real estate, and other businesses. The new structure will also provide management with increased organizational and operational flexibility.
>
> Each of our businesses can eventually be operated as a separate company under Anheuser-Busch Companies, Inc., with responsibilities divided among management personnel.
>
> This reorganization will help facilitate our long-range plan to not only continue to grow in production and sales of beer but also to continue to expand and diversify into other areas which offer significant opportunities for growth.

Additionally, Busch announced that Fred L. Kuhlmann, executive vice president, had been elected vice chairman of the board of Anheuser-Busch Companies, Inc., and that Dennis P. Long had been elected president and chief operating officer of Anheuser-Busch, Inc., a subsidiary of the holding company. Long has overall responsibility for the conduct of the company's beer business, and he reports to Busch. (Busch is chairman and chief executive officer of Anheuser-Busch, Inc.)

Also, Long was elected a member of the corporate office of Anheuser-Busch Companies, Inc. Three individuals comprise the corporate office. They are Busch, Kuhlmann, and Long. Kuhlmann and Long consult with Busch on major corporate matters and assist him in implementing corporate policy.

Busch announced that the operating executives of two other divisions and subsidiaries have been named presidents of their respective operating units. W. Robert Harrington was named president of Industrial Products, and W. Randolph Baker was named president of Busch Gardens.

ANHEUSER-BUSCH COMPANIES, INC.

EXHIBIT 12   Market Share Performance

	1978				1977			
	Barrel Shipments (millions)	Market Share	Barrel Increment (millions)	Percent Increase (decrease)	Barrel Shipments (millions)	Market Share	Barrel Increment (millions)	Percent Increase (decrease)
Anheuser	41.6	25.1%	5.0	13.7%	36.6	22.9%	7.5	25.8%
Miller	31.3	18.9	7.1	29.3	24.2	15.2	5.8	31.5
Schlitz	19.6	11.8	(2.5)	(11.3)	22.1	13.9	(2.1)	(8.7)
Pabst	15.4	9.3	(0.6)	(3.8)	16.0	10.0	(1.0)	(5.9)
Coors	12.6	7.6	(0.2)	(1.6)	12.8	8.0	(0.7)	(5.2)
Top 5	120.5	72.7	8.8	7.9	111.7	70.0	9.5	9.3
All others	41.7	25.2	(3.5)	(7.7)	45.2	28.3	(3.0)	(6.2)
U.S. industry	162.2	97.9	5.3	3.4	156.9	98.4	6.5	4.4
Imports	3.45	2.1	0.8	30.8	2.6	1.6	0.2	8.3
All beer	165.6	100.0	6.1	3.8	159.5	100.0	6.7	4.5

	1976				1975			
	Barrel Shipments (millions)	Market Share	Barrel Increment (millions)	Percent Increase (decrease)	Barrel Shipments (millions)	Market Share	Barrel Increment (millions)	Percent Increase (decrease)
Anheuser	29.1	19.0%	(6.1)	17.3%	35.2	23.4%	1.1	3.2%
Miller	18.4	12.0	5.6	43.8	12.8	8.5	3.7	40.7
Schlitz	24.2	15.8	0.9	3.9	23.3	15.5	0.6	2.6
Pabst	17.0	11.1	1.3	8.3	15.7	10.4	1.4	9.8
Coors	13.5	8.8	1.6	13.4	11.9	7.9	(0.4)	(3.3)
Top 5	102.2	66.9	3.3	3.3	98.9	65.8	6.4	6.9
All others	48.2	31.5	(1.5)	(3.0)	49.7	33.1	(3.3)	(6.2)
U.S. industry	150.4	98.4	1.8	1.2	148.6	98.9	3.1	2.1
Imports	2.4	1.6	0.7	41.2	1.7	1.1	0.3	21.4
All beer	152.8	100.0	2.5	1.7	150.3	100.0	3.4	2.3

	1974		1974–1978		
	Barrel Shipments (millions)	Market Share	Increased barrel shipments (millions)	Market Share Point Change	Compounded Annual Shipment Growth
Anheuser	34.1	23.2%	7.5	+ 1.9	5.1%
Miller	9.1	6.2	22.2	+12.7	36.2
Schlitz	22.7	15.4	(3.1)	− 3.6	(3.3)
Pabst	14.3	9.7	1.1	− 0.4	1.9
Coors	12.3	8.4	0.3	− 0.8	0.4
Top 5	92.5	63.0	28.0	+ 9.7	6.8
All others	53.0	36.0	11.3	−10.8	(4.9)
U.S. industry	145.5	99.0	16.7	− 1.1	2.7
Imports	1.4	1.0	2.0	+ 1.1	24.9
All beer	146.9	100.0	18.7	0.0	3.1

Source: C. James Walker III. *Competition in the U.S. Brewing Industry: A Basic Analysis* (New York: Shearson Hayden Stone, September 26, 1979).

Key Executives[1]

August A. Busch III was born June 16, 1937, and attended public and private schools in St. Louis, the University of Arizona, and the Siebel Institute of Technology, a school for brewers in Chicago. Chairman of the board and president of Anheuser-Busch Companies, Inc., he began his career with the company in 1957 in the St. Louis Malt House. Since that time, he has worked in practically every department of both the brewing and operations divisions. In 1962, he moved into marketing, working in the field with wholesalers as well as in company-owned branches in all areas of the country. Returning to St. Louis, he was promoted to assistant sales manager—regional brands and later was named sales manager for regional brands where he was responsible for the marketing of Busch throughout the product's marketing area.

Busch was named a member of the company's board of directors and appointed vice president—marketing operations in 1963. He became general manager in July 1965, executive vice president and general manager in April 1971, president in February 1974, chief executive officer in May 1975, and chairman of the board in April 1977.

Fred L. Kuhlmann, a native of St. Louis, is vice chairman of the board of directors and executive vice president of Anheuser-Busch Companies, Inc. He joined Anheuser-Busch, Inc., in August 1967 as general counsel and was elected a vice president in January 1971, senior vice president—administration and services and member of the board of directors in February 1974, and executive vice president—administration in June 1977. He was elected to his present position in October 1979.

Kuhlmann received his A.B. degree from Washington University in St. Louis and his LL.B. from that institution's school of law. He also has an LL.M. degree from Columbia University School of Law in New York. He has been active in a number of business and civic groups and serves as a director of the St. Louis National Baseball Club, Inc., and Manufacturers Railway Company. He is also a director of Boatmen's National Bank of St. Louis, Civic Center Redevelopment Corporation, and St. Louis Regional Commerce and Growth Association.

Dennis P. Long, 44, president of Anheuser-Busch, Inc., attended Washington University in St. Louis, Missouri. He has extensive experience spanning more than 25 years at Anheuser-Busch in both brewing and nonbrewing areas. After serving as national price administrator in beer marketing from 1960 to 1964, he was promoted to assistant to the vice president of beer marketing operations and worked in the field with the nationwide beer wholesaler network as well as with the company-owned branch distribution centers. He was promoted to assistant to the vice president and general manager in 1965.

In 1972, Long was elected group vice president responsible for the Busch Gardens and industrial products division and Busch Properties, Inc. Under his leadership, the industrial products division became the nation's leading producer of bakers' yeast; the division's sales of both yeast and corn products

---

[1] The information presented in this section was obtained from the corporate headquarters of Anheuser-Busch Companies, Inc.

and profitability increased to record proportions. He also headed the transition of Busch Gardens from beer promotional facilities to a separate profit center. Since then, a new Busch Gardens has been opened in Williamsburg, Virginia, and that division also operates profitably. Since he took charge of Busch Properties, Inc., the real estate subsidiary has embarked further into residential and resort development in addition to the commercial-industrial field, and the performance of Busch Properties has improved markedly.

In June 1977, Long became vice president and general manager of the beer division and since that time, has embarked upon a strong effort to increase beer sales volume and profitability. His efforts include new and expanded marketing efforts, increased productivity in brewing and packaging, and a strong cost control and cost reduction effort.

PRODUCTS OFFERED BY ANHEUSER-BUSCH

Over the past five years, Anheuser-Busch's beer division has accounted for approximately 90 percent of consolidated net sales. It produces Budweiser, Michelob, Busch, Michelob Light, Classic Dark, and Anheuser-Busch Natural Light. The remaining 10 percent of the consolidated net sales come from family entertainment (Busch Gardens Division), can manufacturing, container recycling, transportation services (St. Louis Refrigerator Car Company and Manufacturers Railway Company), major league baseball (St. Louis Cardinals), real estate development (Busch Properties, Inc.), and the manufacture and sale of corn products, brewer's yeast, and bakers' yeast (industrial products division). Anheuser-Busch is the nation's leading producer of bakers' yeast with a market share of well over 40 percent. Exhibit 13 presents data by product line.

During 1978, Anheuser-Busch made significant progress in redefining its diversification objectives as a means of building for the future. A corporate policy was established to concentrate initially on developing new food and beverage products which are compatible with the existing capabilities and, where possible, on distributing these products through the company's existing wholesaler network. The company is presently working on developing a line of snack foods, reportedly called Eagle Snacks, which would also be compatible with existing production and distribution facilities.

The company began test marketing Würzburger Hofbräu beer in the United States early in 1979. This full-bodied, premium, German beer will be brewed in Wurzburg, West Germany, and shipped in large insulated barrels to the United States where it will be bottled by Anheuser-Busch and distributed through the company's wholesaler network.

Anheuser-Busch has a new installation in St. Louis, Missouri, which annually produces 1.8 million pounds of autolyzed yeast extract, a flavoring agent for processed foods. As the only producer of the extract in the United States with its own captive supply of brewer's yeast, Anheuser-Busch entered this new venture with a decided competitive advantage.

EXHIBIT 13 Revenue Generated by Product Class (in thousands of dollars)

	1978	1977	1976	1975	1974
Consolidated sales	$2,701,611	$2,231,230	$1,752,998	$2,036,687	$1,791,863
Federal and state beer taxes	441,978	393,182	311,852	391,708	378,772
Consolidated net sales	$2,259,633	$1,838,048	$1,441,146	$1,644,979	$1,413,091
Beer division	2,056,754	1,691,004	1,282,620	1,480,481	1,271,782
Percent of consolidated net sales	91%	92%	89%	90%	90%
Other divisions*	$ 202,879	$ 147,044	$ 158,526	$ 164,498	$ 141,309
Percent of consolidated net sales	9%	8%	11%	10%	10%

*All other divisions include: industrial products division, Busch Gardens division, Busch Properties, Inc., transportation, and the St. Louis Cardinals.

Source: Anheuser-Busch Company, Inc., annual reports, 1974–1978.

Anheuser-Busch's well-known family of quality beers includes products in every market segment. Budweiser has been brewed and sold for more than 100 years. Premium Bud, available in bottles, cans, and on draught nationwide, is the company's principal product and the largest selling beer in the world. Michelob was developed in 1896 as a "draught beer for connoisseurs." Superpremium Michelob is sold nationally in bottles, cans, and on draught.

With a greater percentage of the population entering the weight-conscious 25–39-year-old range, Anheuser-Busch has introduced Michelob Light. It has 20 percent fewer calories than regular Michelob, and when introduced in 1978, it was the first superpremium light beer. In order to capitalize on this by transferring the consumer appeal for Michelob to Michelob Light, Anheuser-Busch communicates "the heritage of Michelob and the taste of Michelob Light" in its advertising. Michelob Light is available nationwide in cans, bottles, and on draught. Anheuser-Busch also offers Natural Light for weight-conscious beer drinkers.

Busch Bavarian beer was introduced in 1955 as a low-priced beer in direct competition with subpremium regional beers. In April 1978, a smoother, sweeter, and lighter Busch beer was successfully test marketed in New England as a premium-priced brand to capitalize on anticipated growth of the premium segment of the market in future years. In 1979, with new package graphics and advertising, premium Busch was introduced in areas where the company previously marketed Busch Bavarian.

Anheuser-Busch's expanding corporate programs of vertical integration into can manufacturing and barley malting play an important role in overall beer division activities and profitability. The company's various vertically integrated enterprises provide an added advantage in controlling the cost and supply of containers and ingredients. Vertical integration helps to reduce cost pressures in brewing operations and to ensure continuity and quality of supply.

Metal Container Corporation, a wholly owned subsidiary of Anheuser-

Busch Companies, produces two-piece aluminum beer cans at facilities in Florida, Ohio, and Missouri. Container Recovery Corporation, another wholly owned subsidiary of Anheuser-Busch Companies, operates container recovery facilities in Ohio and New Hampshire which are actively involved in collecting and recycling aluminum cans.

The company's materials acquisition division is responsible for purchasing all agricultural commodities, packaging materials, supplies, and fuel. Its objective is to increase stability and flexibility in the procurement of commodities and materials. This division investigates alternative methods of supply, analyzes vertical integration opportunities available, and monitors the supply and cost of all commodities purchased by the company.

Anheuser-Busch processes barley into brewer's malt at plants in Manitowoc, Wisconsin (total capacity of 8.5 million bushels annually), and Moorhead, Minnesota (annual capacity of 6.4 million bushels). These two malt production facilities provide the company with the capability to self-manufacture approximately one third of its malt requirements.

The industrial products division produces corn syrup and starch for numerous food applications, including the processing of canned frozen foods and the manufacture of ice cream and candy. Additionally, the division markets starch and resin products used in the manufacture of paper, corrugated containers, and textiles. The company's corn processing plant in Lafayette, Indiana, currently has a grind capacity of 11 billion bushels of corn yearly.

The company's brewer's yeast food plant in Jacksonville, Florida, has a yearly capacity of 3 million pounds. The debitterized brewer's food yeast is sold to health food manufacturers for use in a variety of nutritional supplements. Busch Entertainment Corporation, the company's family entertainment subsidiary, operates theme parks in Florida and Virginia. Unique blends of natural beauty and family entertainment activities and attractions are featured in both locations. Busch Properties, Inc., is the company's real estate development subsidiary. It is currently involved in the development of both residential and commercial properties at sites in Virginia and Ohio. St. Louis Refrigerator Car Company, Manufacturers Railway Company, and five other companies compose Anheuser-Busch's transportation subsidiaries. They provide commercial repair, rebuilding, maintenance, and inspection of railroad cars, terminal railroad switching services, and truck cartage and warehousing services.

MARKETING

Anheuser-Busch has a coast-to-coast network of 11 breweries which are selectively situated in major population and beer-consumption regions. Once the beers leave the breweries, distribution to the consumer becomes the responsibility of 959 wholesale distribution operations and 11 company-owned beer branches which provide the company with its own profit centers within the distribution system. The beer branches perform sales, merchandising, and delivery services in their respective areas of primary responsibility. The company's beer branches are located in Sylmar and Riverside, California; Denver, Colorado; Chicago, Illinois; Louisville, Kentucky; New Orleans, Louisiana; Cambridge, Massachusetts; Kansas City, Missouri; Newark, New Jersey; Tulsa, Oklahoma; and Washington, D.C.

The beer industry has always been a highly competitive industry. Success depends on volume, and sales by the nation's top five brewers account for an estimated 70 percent of the total market. There is intense competition between the industry leaders. According to *Value Line,* it was expected that by 1980, the top five brewers would account for approximately 80 percent of the market.

Competitive pressures have led Anheuser-Busch to take an aggressive stance in its marketing strategy. It is the country's largest brewer in terms of barrel sales per year and the 34th largest national advertiser. The 1978 annual report of Anheuser-Busch said their marketing efforts were "the most extensive and aggressive in company history," stressing product and packaging innovations, brand identity, and off-premise merchandising. The company entered the 1980s with new packaging innovations and new marketing programs. The aggressive packaging is aimed at further market segmentation and penetration. Presently, the company sells more than 80 basic packages.

Anheuser-Busch's advertisements have traditionally been aimed at communicating the quality of the company's beer products which appeal to virtually every taste and price range. Television advertisements and sports sponsorships continue to be the major focal point for marketing the company's beer brands. Television advertisements focus on prime-time programming and sports. To increase its presence on college campuses, Anheuser-Busch utilizes a unique marketing team of 400 student representatives at major colleges and universities across the country.

Anheuser-Busch has enlarged its marketing staff in the beer division. A field sales task force has been established to provide immediate and concentrated assistance in markets needing a sales boost. The national accounts sales department was created to provide better marketing coordination and communication between the company's sales staff and large national chain accounts such as grocery stores, convenience stores, fast-food outlets, hotels, motels, liquor chains, and athletic stadiums. The marketing services department coordinates and expands activities in the areas of sales promotion, merchandising, special markets, point-of-sale, and incentive programs.

PRODUCTION FACILITIES

Reviewing the production facilities utilized by Anheuser-Busch provides insight into the growth pattern of the organization. Devotion to investment in plant capacity has been extensive in the past decade, and the future capital expenditure program allows for future expansion and modernization of facilities (annual report, 1978).

The largest subsidiary of Anheuser-Busch Companies is the beer production sector. Exhibit 14 is a listing of the geographically dispersed breweries with

EXHIBIT 14 Production Facility Locations and Capacities

	MILLIONS OF BARRELS	BEGINNING OF SHIPMENT
St. Louis, Missouri	11.6	1880
Los Angeles, California	10.0	1954
Newark, New Jersey	4.7	1951
Tampa, Florida	2.2	1959
Houston, Texas	2.6	1966
Columbus, Ohio	6.2	1968
Jacksonville, Florida	6.5	1969
Merrimack, New Hampshire	2.8	1970
Williamsburg, Virginia	7.5	1972
Fairfield, California	3.5	1976
Baldwinsville, New York	6.0	1982

Source: Aneuser-Busch annual reports.

their corresponding annual capacity in millions of barrels and dates of first shipments.

As can be seen from this exhibit, many of the beer production facilities are quite new. Plants in St. Louis and Newark have undergone extensive modernization programs to upgrade older plants and equipment and ensure consistent quality regardless of brewery location. In 1980, Anheuser-Busch purchased a brewery formerly owned and operated by Schlitz. The seller was forced to close the plant because of declining sales due to competitive pressures.

Commitments to plant expansion have been extensive in the past few years. For example, capital expenditures will approach $2 billion for the five years ending 1983, with 93 percent for beer-related activities, according to industry analyst Robert S. Weinberg. Expansion is currently being undertaken at several of the 11 breweries. At the Los Angeles plant, the largest expansion project, capacity is being increased by more than 6 million barrels. Capacity in Williamsburg, Virginia, is being increased threefold.

Plant expansion in the areas of can manufacturing and industrial products manufacturing is being conducted at rapid rates. Vertical integration into can manufacturing and malt production is requiring substantial increases in plant investment. Can-production facilities were completed in Jacksonville, Florida, in 1974, Columbus, Ohio, in 1977, and Arnold, Missouri, in 1980. Nearly 40 percent of cans used were provided internally by 1980. In addition, two can recycling facilities are currently in operation.

RESEARCH AND DEVELOPMENT

According to the 1978 Securities and Exchange Commission's Form 10-K report, Anheuser-Busch

> does not consider to be material the dollar amounts expended by it during the last two fiscal years on research activities relating to the development of new products

or services or the improvement of existing products or services. In addition, the company does not consider the number of employees engaged full time in such research activities to be material.

The company is, however, extensively involved in research and development. R&D funds are currently being used to develop new food and beverage products which are consistent with the company's production and distribution capabilities. The organization has a corn products research group which recently developed a number of new and very profitable modified food starches. In addition to these, Anheuser-Busch's research on possible new beer products helped to place Michelob Light and Anheuser-Busch Natural Light beers on the market.

Along with research on new and profitable products, the company is striving to cut packaging costs by doing research in the production of aluminum. Anheuser-Busch paid $6 million in 1978 to a major international aluminum company, Swiss Aluminum, Ltd., for access and participation rights in this company's ongoing research in the development of certain new technologies in aluminum casting. This area should greatly reduce costs in the future.

Besides product and container research, Anheuser-Busch's R&D departments are studying matters of social concern. The reasons for this type of research are so the company can remain active in its social responsibility as a public corporation and also to strengthen its influence in reducing government regulations and thus avoid possible costly restrictions to its operations. Research to determine the causes of alcoholism and develop effective treatment and prevention programs, in cooperation with the United States Brewers Association, is one example of the company's effort here. Other examples relate to environmental matters. In an independent effort toward developing and utilizing alternative energy systems, other than scarce natural gas and oil, Anheuser-Busch is researching solar energy. In 1978, the company installed a new pilot project at its Jacksonville, Florida, brewery. At this plant, solar energy is being tested in pasteurizing bottled beers. In addition, the company is developing new land application programs aimed at soil enrichment and energy conservation. Under these programs, rich soil nutrients are taken from the breweries' liquid wastes and used to grow various crops, primarily sod, grass, and grains.

MONEY MATTERS AT ANHEUSER-BUSH

Exhibits 15, 16, 17, and 18 contain relevant financial data on Anheuser-Busch.

FUTURE

In his letter to the stockholders in the 1978 annual report, August A. Busch III discussed Anheuser-Busch's expansion and diversification plans. He wrote:

> We continue to commit substantial resources to provide the capacity necessary to support our planned sales growth and to maintain our industry leadership. Future

growth and profitability also depend, however, on our willingness to commit funds and energies to the development of new products and new areas of business activity.

For a number of years, we have been investing considerable sums of money and a great deal of effort in the area of vertical integration of our beer business ... new can and malt plants and, more recently, in exploring the possibility of producing our own aluminum sheet used in the manufacture of cans. These activities have proved to be successful in controlling costs, and we will continue to pay close attention to vertical integration.

We are also exploring opportunities to diversify into other business ventures which are not beer related. We can do this either through acquisitions or through

EXHIBIT 15 Per Share Data ($)[1]

YEAR-END DECEMBER 31

	1978	1977	1976	1975	1974	1973	1972	1971	1970	1969
Book value	16.71	15.07	13.72	13.17	11.93	11.11	10.25	9.20	8.02	7.03
Earnings[2]	2.46	2.04	1.23	1.88	1.42	1.46	1.70	1.60	1.40	1.01
Dividends	0.82	0.71	0.68	0.64	0.06	0.60	0.58	0.53	0.42½	0.40
Payout ratio	33%	35%	55%	34%	42%	41%	34%	33%	30%	39%
Prices—High	27¾	25¼	38⅝	39⅝	38	55	69	57½	39⅝	36⅞
Low	17½	18¾	20¾	24½	21	28⅝	51	37	27⅛	28½
Price-earnings ratio	11–7	12–9	31–17	21–13	27–15	38–20	41–30	36–23	28–19	36–28

[1] Data as orginally reported. Adjusted for stock dividends of 100 percent April 1971.
[2] Before results of discontinued operations of —0.09 in 1972.

Source: *Standard OTC Stock Reports* 46, no. 125, sec. 5 (October 31, 1979). Copyright © 1979 Standard & Poor's Corporation. All rights reserved.

EXHIBIT 16 Income Data ($ millions)

YEAR ENDED DECEMBER 31	REVENUES	OPERATING INCOME	PERCENT OPERATING INCOME OF REVENUES	CAPITAL EXPEND-ITURES	DEPRECI-ATION	INTEREST EXPENSE	NET BEFORE TAXES	EFFECTIVE TAX RATE	NET INCOME	PERCENT NET INCOME OF REVENUES
1978	2,260	288	12.8%	229	66.0	28.9	206	46.0%	111	4.9%
1977	1,838	246	13.4	157	61.2	26.7	170	45.9	92	5.0
1976	1,441	181	12.6	199	53.1	26.9	103	46.4	55	3.8
1975	1,645	226	13.8	155	51.1	22.6	165	48.7	85	5.2
1974	1,413	164	11.6	126	45.0	11.9	122	47.3	64	4.5
1973	1,110	162	14.6	92	41.1	5.3	126	48.1	66	5.9
1972[1]	978	184	18.8	84	39.0	6.0	147	48.0	76	7.8
1971	902	170	18.9	73	35.0	6.6	136	47.3	72	7.9
1970	793	155	19.5	65	33.8	7.1	121	48.2	63	7.9
1969	667	122	18.2	71	30.1	7.4	93	51.2	45	6.8

[1] Before results of discontinued operations of—0.09 in 1972.

Source: *Standard OTC Stock Reports* 46, no. 125, sec. 5 (October 31, 1979). Copyright © 1979 Standard & Poor's Corporation. All rights reserved.

EXHIBIT 17 Ten-year Financial Summary (thousands of dollars, except per share and statistical data)

CONSOLIDATED SUMMARY OF OPERATIONS:	1978	1979	1976
Barrels sold	41,610	36,640	29,051
Sales	$2,701,611	$2,231,230	$1,752,998
Less federal and state beer taxes	441,978	393,182	311,852
Net sales	2,259,633	1,838,048	1,441,146
Cost of products sold	1,762,410	1,462,801	1,175,055
Gross profits	497,223	375,247	266,091
Less marketing, administrative, and research expenses	274,961	190,470	137,797
Operating income	222,262	184,777	128,294
Interest income	11,693	7,724	10,304
Interest expense	(28,894)	(26,708)	(26,941)
Other income net	751	4,193	1,748
Loss on partial closing of Los Angeles Busch Gardens[1]			10,020
Income before income taxes	205,812	169,986	103,385
Income taxes	94,772	78,041	47,952
Income before extraordinary item	111,040	91,945	55,433
Extraordinary item[2]			
Net income	$ 111,040	$ 91,945	$ 55,433
Per share[3] income before extraordinary item	2.46	2.04	1.23
Net income	2.46	2.04	1.23
Cash dividends paid	37,013	32,036	30,646
Per share[3]	.82	.71	.68
Dividend payout ratio	33.3%	34.8%	55.3%
Average number of shares outstanding[3]	45,138	45,115	45,068
Book value per share	16.71	15.07	13.72
Balance sheet information:			
Working capital	236,396	188,069	194,814
Current ratio	1.9	1.9	2.2
Plant and equipment, net	1,109,243	951,965	857,073
Long-term debt	427,250	337,492	340,737
Debt to debt plus total equity	34.5%	31.7%	34.0%
Deferred income taxes	153,080	125,221	99,119
Deferred investment tax credit	58,053	48,371	43,174
Shareholders' equity	754,423	680,396	618,429
Return on shareholders' equity	15.1%	14.2%	9.2%

[1] Notes to 10-year financial summary:
In December 1976, the company decided to close a portion of the Los Angeles Busch Gardens and convert the remainder to a sales promotion facility. Closing a portion of the Gardens resulted in a nonoperating charge of $10,020,000 (before reduction for income tax benefits of approximately $5 million). This nonoperating charge, which reduced earnings per share by 11 cents, has been reported in accordance with *Accounting Principles Board Opinion No. 39* which was effective September 30, 1973.

[2] In December 1972, the company decided to close a portion of the Houston Busch Gardens and convert the remainder to a sales promotion facility. Closing a portion of the Gardens resulted in an extraordinary aftertax charge against 1972 earnings of $4,093,000, or 9 cents per share, net of applicable income tax benefits of $4,006,000.

[3] Per share statistics have been adjusted to give effect to the two-for-one stock split in 1971.

EXHIBIT 17 (Continued)

Other information:
Capital expenditures	228,727	156,745	198,735
Depreciation	66,032	61,163	53,105
Total payroll cost	421,806	338,933	271,403
Effective tax rate	46.0%	45.9%	46.4%

1975	1974	1973	1972	1971	1970	1969
35,196	34,097	29,887	26,522	24,309	22,202	18,712
$2,036,687	$1,791,863	$1,442,720	$1,273,093	$1,173,476	$1,036,272	$871,904
391,708	378,772	333,013	295,593	271,023	243,495	205,295
1,644,979	1,413,091	1,109,707	977,500	902,453	792,777	666,609
1,343,784	1,187,816	875,361	724,718	658,886	579,372	490,932
301,195	225,275	234,346	252,782	243,567	213,405	175,677
126,053	106,653	112,928	108,008	108,087	92,660	84,113
175,142	118,622	121,418	144,774	135,480	120,745	91,564
10,944	9,925	4,818	3,299	3,102	3,715	3,604
(22,602)	(11,851)	(5,288)	(6,041)	(6,597)	(7,104)	(7,401)
1,816	4,840	5,287	4,855	4,065	3,420	5,171
165,300	121,536	126,235	146,887	136,050	120,776	92,938
80,577	57,517	60,658	70,487	64,412	58,227	47,627
84,723	64,019	65,557	76,400	71,638	62,549	45,311
			4,093			
$ 84,723	$ 64,019	$ 65,557	$ 72,307	$ 71,638	$ 62,549	$ 45,311
1.88	1.42	1.46	1.70	1.60	1.40	1.02
1.88	1.42	1.46	1.61	1.60	1.40	1.02
28,843	27,041	27,037	26,109	23,784	18,991	17,843
.64	.60	.60	.58	.53	.425	.40
34.0%	42.3%	41.1%	36.0%	33.1%	30.4%	39.2%
45,068	45,068	45,063	45,020	44,887	44,686	44,616
13.17	11.93	11.11	10.25	9.20	8.02	7.03
268,099	145,107	82,352	88,711	92,447	85,102	80,963
2.7	2.3	1.8	2.1	2.2	2.1	2.3
724,914	622,876	541,236	491,671	453,647	416,660	387,422
342,167	193,240	93,414	99,107	116,571	128,080	134,925
35.6%	25.7%	15.3%	17.2%	21.4%	25.6%	29.2%
80,748	66,264	54,281	41,456	34,103	27,274	23,212
24,293	21,157	17,225	14,370	14,276	13,563	12,577
593,642	537,762	500,784	461,980	413,974	358,476	314,121
15.0%	12.3%	13.6%	16.5%	18.6%	18.6%	15.1%
155,436	126,463	91,801	84,217	73,214	65,069	66,396
51,089	45,042	41,059	38,970	34,948	33,795	30,063
268,306	244,437	221,049	190,517	176,196	156,576	133,872
48.7%	47.3%	48.1%	48.0%	47.3%	48.2%	51.2%

Source: Anheuser-Busch Companies annual reports, 1969–1978.

EXHIBIT 18 Balance Sheet Data ($ million)

DECEMBER 31	Cash	CURRENT Assets	CURRENT Liabilities	Ratio	TOTAL ASSETS	RETURN ON ASSETS	LONG-TERM DEBT	COMMON EQUITY	TOTAL CAPITAL	PERCENT LONG-TERM DEBT OF CAPITAL	RETURN ON EQUITY
1978	196	492	255	1.9	1,648	7.3%	427	754	1,393	30.7%	15.5%
1977	154	400	212	1.9	1,404	6.9	337	680	1,191	28.3	14.0
1976	135	347	167	2.1	1,268	4.5	341	618	1,101	30.9	9.1
1975	224	420	161	2.6	1,202	7.9	342	594	1,041	32.9	15.0
1974	89	252	113	2.2	931	7.5	193	538	818	23.6	12.3
1973	60	176	100	1.8	765	9.0	93	501	666	14.0	13.6
1972[1]	69	166	81	2.0	698	11.3	99	462	617	16.1	17.4
1971	69	163	75	2.2	654	11.3	117	414	579	20.1	18.5
1970	61	158	78	2.0	605	10.8	128	358	527	24.3	18.6
1969	45	142	65	2.2	550	8.4	135	314	485	27.8	15.1

[1] Before results of discontinued operations of—0.09 in 1972.

Source: *Standard OTC Stock Reports* 46, no. 125, sec. 5 (October 31, 1979). Copyright © 1979 Standard & Poor's Corporation. All rights reserved.

internal development of new products. At the present time, we are emphasizing a program aimed at maximizing use of existing capabilities. We are in the process of developing internally a line of soft drinks and other consumer products which can be distributed through our wholesale network. We recognize from the outset that we may not achieve success in every one of these new ventures. However, the financial risks are relatively small, and the potential rewards are considerable.

C. James Walker III, an industry analyst, predicted a 1981 shipment level of 55 million barrels indicating a 9.2 million barrel growth in the 1979–1981 period. This is comparable to that achieved in 1977–1979. However, without the presence of a visible new major category similar to "Light" in size, Walker doubts that growth in the 1980s can match the expansion of the late 1970s. According to Walker, new brands such as Würzburger and Busch Premium seem unlikely to garner the growth that Natural Light and Michelob Light may attain. Exhibit 19 shows Walker's estimate for 1981, which would make Anheuser-Busch fall 6 percent shy of its goal of 98 percent capacity utilization.

Busch, on the other hand, was more optimistic. He wrote:

> In anticipation of what we can expect to encounter in the marketplace, we have developed strong and aggressive marketing and promotion programs to enhance our position as industry leader. We will be introducing more new products and new packages to keep Anheuser-Busch in the forefront of market segmentation. And we will be intensifying our emphasis on the quality of our products.
>
> Competitive pressures will demand the most dedicated and creative efforts that we can muster, but we are confident that with our strong sales momentum, our quality products, our great wholesaler family, and the team effort of our employees, we will have another successful year and will continue to build a solid corporate foundation for future growth and profits.

EXHIBIT 19 Estimated Volume by Brewer, 1978 and 1981

	1978		1981[1]		1978–1981	
	Barrel Shipments (millions)	Market Share	Barrel Shipments (millions)	Market Share	Barrel Increment (millions)	Compounded Annual Rate of Growth
Anheuser-Busch	41.6	25.1%	51.5	28.7%	+ 9.9	7.4%
Miller	31.3	18.9	44.9	25.0	+13.6	12.6
Schlitz	19.6	11.8	17.2	9.6	− 2.4	(3.8)
Pabst	15.4	9.3	14.7	8.2	− 0.7	(1.2)
Coors[2]	12.6	7.6	17.2	9.6	+ 4.6	11.1
Top 5	120.5	72.8	145.5	81.1	+25.0	6.6
All others[3]	41.7	25.2	28.4	15.8	−13.3	(9.7)
U.S. industry	162.2	97.9	173.9	97.0	+11.7	2.3%
Imports	3.4	2.1	5.4	3.0	+ 2.0	16.5
All beer	165.6	100.0%	179.3	100.0%	+13.7	2.7%

[1] Estimated.
[2] Coors was in a 16-state market in 1978 and an estimated 19-state market in 1981 (additions: Arkansas, Louisiana, and Minnesota).
[3] In 1981, the operations of Blitz-Weinhard are included with Pabst; in 1978, about 600,000 barrels of Blitz are in the all-other group.

Source: C. James Walker III, *Competition in the U.S. Brewing Industry: A Basic Analysis* (New York: Shearson Hayden Stone, September 26, 1979).

INDUSTRIAL HIGHLIGHT

Alcoholic Beverages Industry

Below is a capsule summary of the alcoholic beverages industry, of which Anheuser-Busch Companies, Inc., is a part. Information in this highlight was compiled by the U.S. Department of Commerce and focuses on this industry during the approximate period of time covered in the case. Keep in mind that industrial highlights contained in this text are not intended as a complete synopsis of an industry but as a profile of certain issues that can be relevant to a case situation. A list of additional references at the end of this highlight can be used for further industry analysis.

■ CURRENT SITUATION

The alcoholic beverage industry consists of three major groups: malt beverages (SIC 2082), wines and brandy (SIC 2084), and distilled spirits (SIC 2085). Shipments of alcoholic beverages are expected to reach $12.4 billion in 1979, an increase of 10 percent over estimated 1978 shipments of $11 billion. Real growth for the year, based on increased consumer expenditures on heavily advertised new products and modest price rises, should be 3 percent.

Malt Beverage Production Up Slightly

Shipments of malt beverages, which include ale, porter, stout, and beer, should reach an estimated $7.9 billion in 1979, a 9 percent increase over 1978 shipments. After gaining only 0.4 percent in the first six months of 1978, beer production for the year should exceed the 1977 record of 157 million barrels by 2 percent.

Decline in Number of Companies Continues

The number of brewing companies continued to decline in 1978, down to 44 from 81 in 1970. Small, regional companies have been unable to compete with the aggressive advertising and marketing campaigns of the national breweries. This trend toward concentration will continue as smaller companies either fail

Source: U.S. Industrial Outlook, Department of Commerce, 1979, pp. 346–351.

or are acquired by larger breweries; larger breweries will continue to grow through mergers and acquisitions.

Total employment in the malt beverage industry continued to rise in 1978 to an estimated 46,600 persons. The number of production workers decreased slightly to 32,200 in 1978 from 32,400 in 1977. Production worker earnings averaged an estimated $9.31 an hour in June 1978, 37 percent higher than the average for all beverage industry workers.

Increased Competition Among Breweries

Intense competition among the brewing companies has resulted in fewer companies vying for larger shares of the market. The top 10 companies held 66 percent of the market in 1970; by 1977, their share had grown to 87 percent. The search for new markets has resulted in several new products such as the "light" beers and domestically brewed foreign brands that have been introduced and marketed with extensive advertising campaigns. Sales of these products, as well as other higher-priced imported and super-premium brands, will continue to rise as status-conscious consumers show a willingness to pay higher prices for quality beer.

Industry estimates show per capita consumption of beer reached 22.4 gallons in 1977, 20 percent higher than in 1970. Adult consumption (18 years and older) increased to 32.1 gallons.

Container Legislation

Container legislation is still an important issue in the malt beverage industry; estimates show that 88 percent of all packaged beer sold in 1977 was in nonreturnable cans and glass containers. Sixteen states and seven local jurisdictions have enacted legislation concerning beverage containers and packaging. Of these, six states and some local jurisdictions have enacted bottle bills requiring mandatory deposits on beer and soft drink beverage containers. Other states have bans on pulltabs and nonbiodegradable plastic connecting devices. Many other states are now considering such bills as well as alternative responses to increased consumer and industry concern.

The malt beverage industry has supported positive litter reduction programs in local communities as an alternative to mandatory deposits and taxes on beverage containers. They are expected to continue these efforts in the foreseeable future.

Exports Increase

Estimated malt beverage exports for 1978, valued at $23 million, show an increasing trend as markets in the Near East and Asia continue to grow. Iran and Hong Kong were the principal export markets in 1978. Exports to Nigeria, the principal market in 1977, dropped off considerably in 1978 as a result of that country's ban on certain luxury imports.

Imports rose 40 percent in 1978 to reach an estimated $221 million, reflecting the growing demand for higher-priced imported beers. Major suppliers are the Netherlands, Canada, Federal Republic of Germany, and Mexico.

Shipments of Wine and Brandy Continue to Grow

Shipments of wine and brandy should reach $1.7 billion in 1979, an increase of 12 percent over estimated 1978 shipments of $1.5 billion. Industry figures show the quantity of domestic wine shipped to U.S. markets in the first half of 1978 increased 2.5 percent over the comparable 1977 period.

Marketings of Wine Double

Total sales of wine in the United States have nearly doubled in the past decade, reaching 400 million gallons in 1977. California wines continued to dominate sales with 286 million gallons or 71 percent of 1977 marketings. California's share of the wine market dropped slightly from 1976 in spite of a 6 percent increase in gallonage, while sales of imported wines rose to 69 million gallons to capture 17 percent of the market. Sales of wines produced in other States dropped from 48 million to 46 million gallons.

There are now 676 bonded wineries and cellars in the United States. More than half, 377, are in California. New York has the second largest number with 45, followed by Ohio with 38, Oregon with 26 and Pennsylvania with 23.

Wine Consumption Increases

Latest industry figures show that per capita consumption of wine has increased 41 percent since 1970 to reach 1.85 gallons in 1977. Consumer preference for table wines continues to grow. Table wines now account for more than half of all wine sales, while dessert wines have dropped to only 14 percent. Sparkling wine sales remain strong while sales of flavored wines, after jumping to an all-time high in 1972, are dropping off slightly.

New BATF Regulations

In August 1978, the Bureau of Alcohol, Tobacco, and Firearms (BATF) announced new wine-labeling regulations designed to provide more information for the consumer on the origin and grape type of wines. The regulations will go into effect January 1, 1983. The major provisions state that if a label indicates the wine comes from a specific county, State, or country, at least 75 percent of the wine must come from that place. The percentage increases as the area of origin labeled gets more specific. Varietal wines must contain at least 75 percent of the labeled grape-type wine instead of the present 51 percent, with the exception of the stronger, Labrusca type wines. If two or more grape types are listed, their percentages must be shown and must total 100. Many of the provisions were recommended by the industry and should not dramatically alter current wine production methods.

EXHIBIT A U.S. Wine Market Nearly Doubles in Decade

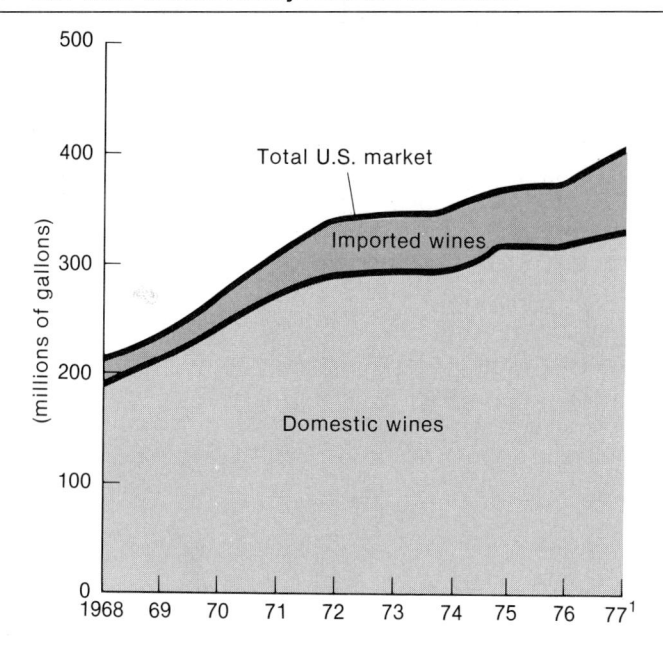

[Area chart showing U.S. wine market in millions of gallons from 1968 to 1977, with Domestic wines rising from about 190 to about 330 million gallons, and Imported wines added on top bringing Total U.S. market to about 400 million gallons by 1977.]

[1] Estimated.
Source: The Wine Institute and Industry and Trade Administration (BDBD).

Foreign Trade Grows

Wine and brandy imports continued to climb in 1978 to an estimated $560 million. This represents an increase of 33 percent over 1977 imports valued at $420 million. Major suppliers are Italy, France, Federal Republic of Germany, Spain, and Portugal. Exports of domestic wines have tripled since 1973, with estimated shipments of $9 million in 1978. The major markets are Canada, the Bahamas, and the Netherlands Antilles.

Distilled Spirits Advance Moderately

Shipments of distilled spirits increased 9 percent in 1978 to a value of $2.5 billion. With increased prices and slightly higher production, the value of shipments should increase by 10 percent in 1979 to reach $2.8 billion.

The trend toward white spirits—vodka, gin, and rum—continues. According to a major national magazine's survey, of the top 10 brands in 1977, six were the traditional whisky types. Increased advertising for the established brands and new, flavorful products such as coconut-flavored rum will help bolster sales in 1979. Industry estimates show total U.S. consumption of 433 million gallons of distilled spirits in 1977.

Exports of distilled spirits rose to an estimated $42 million in 1978, an 8 percent increase over 1977. Major markets included the Federal Republic of Germany, Australia, Canada, and the United Kingdom.

Imports increased to an estimated $680 million in 1978. During the first six months of 1978, distilled spirits imports showed an increase in volume of 17 percent over the comparable 1977 period, while the value increased 25 percent. The volume of imported white spirits increased 20 percent and imports of whisky grew 15 percent. Major supplying countries are the United Kingdom, Canada, Mexico, Italy, and France.

LONG-TERM PROSPECTS

The alcoholic beverage industry should continue to grow at a compound annual real rate of 3.5 percent through 1983. Growth in the wine industry will remain strong as per capita consumption continues to rise. Increased advertising and the introduction of new products will allow for steady growth in the malt beverage and distilled spirits industries.

ADDITIONAL REFERENCES

U.S. Department of Commerce, Washington, D.C. 20230. Bureau of the Census, 1976 *Annual Survey of Manufacturers.*

Wines and Vines, published by Hiaring Company, San Francisco, California 94103.

Beverage World, published by Keller Publishing Company, E. Stroudsburg, Pennsylvania 18301.

Modern Brewery Age, published by Business Journals, Inc., Norwalk, Connecticut 06856.

1977 National Association of Alcoholic Beverage Importers Annual Statistical Report, prepared by the National Association of Alcoholic Beverage Importers.

1977 Distilled Spirits Industry Annual Statistical Review, prepared by the Distilled Spirits Council of the United States.

SECTION FOUR

Strategy Implementation and Control

CASE 15

Lema Supply Company

MARY COULTER   CHARLES BOYD
both of Southwest Missouri State University

866-NUTS and 866-BOLT. These two unique telephone numbers describe the basic products that Lema Supply Company currently handles. Located in Springfield, Missouri, Lema is a small wholesale and retail distributor of bolts, nuts, screws, washers and other types of threaded fasteners. However, Lema has not always specialized solely in the fastener business.

BACKGROUND

The name Lema was derived from the first two letters of the first and last names of the company's president, Les Mace. He and his father started the company in 1954 as an army surplus business. Excess tools, machinery, and equipment were purchased from governmental sources and resold to wholesalers, retailers, and other businesses using these goods. For example, when the Paducah, Kentucky, Atomic Power Plant was completed, Lema purchased for resale the machinery and tools used in the plant's construction. In the process of purchasing excess materials from the military and other plant liquidations, Lema found itself handling fasteners as well.

Due to an expressway expansion in 1957, the company had to move from its initial place of operation on the west side of the city into its current more central location north of the downtown area. During this time, they also began to purchase for resale surplus aircraft hydraulics (hoses, cylinders, fittings, etc.) and other aircraft parts.

The company carried such a variety of products that their regular customers began to call them by the nickname "nuts and bolts." Since the correct spelling of "nuts and bolts" is a generic name that cannot be trademarked, Les Mace devised the unique spelling Nutz-n-Boltz and trademarked this name in 1975. This is the name of the centrally located store.

Les Mace indicated that, in the mid- to late-1970's, the company gradually found it necessary to shift its focus from surplus equipment, machinery, and hydraulics because it could not afford to compete with other distributors who specialized in these goods. By 1980, the company began to concentrate its operations solely on fasteners. A wide variety of stock ranging from small

Distributed by North American Case Research Association. All rights reserved to the authors and the North American Case Research Association. Reprinted by permission of the authors and the North American Case Research Association.

household screws to large industrial bolts is carried by Lema and sold at both the wholesale and retail levels. Selling in both wholesale and retail markets is common practice for most distributors in the industry.

THE FASTENER INDUSTRY

The fastener industry has an industry association, Fastener Industry Management, that conducts semi-yearly business surveys. The results of these surveys are transmitted to the industry members via a publication called *Fastener Industry News*. Information from the Survey of Business Conditions for the first half of 1984 was given by 52 companies that manufacture fasteners and 112 companies that distribute fasteners. Those manufacturers and distributors providing figures had total annual sales of $963 million, employed 10,486 people, and operated 246 plants and/or warehouses. Only the distributors' responses are included in the following industry information.

Sales during the first half of 1984 were considerably higher than either the first or second half of 1983. Profits in the first half of 1984 were also higher than either half of 1983. Sales and profits for the second half of 1984 were forecasted by one-third of the respondents to be higher than for the first half of 1984. The remainder believed that sales and profits would either be lower or the same in the second half of 1984 as compared to the first half. Taken together 91.5 percent of the respondents believed that sales for all of 1984 would be greater than sales in 1983 and 79.6 percent believed that profits for all of 1984 would be higher than profits in 1983. When asked what markets or products suffer the most during periods of declining sales, distributors replied (parentheses enclose the number of firms responding; asterisk indicates that Lema carries these items):

Most	*Least*
Automotive (8)	*Screws (all kinds) (6)
All Products (8)	Capital Equipment (5)
Construction (7)	Petrochemical (4)
*OEM (Fasteners for Original Equipment Manufacturers) (6)	Farm Equipment (3)
	*Standard Items (3)
*Nuts & Bolts (6)	Construction (2)
*Stainless Steel Products (5)	*Maintenance (2)
Industrial Transportation (4)	*MRO (Maintenance, Repair, and Operating Supplies) (2)
Specials (4)	Electronics
*Socket Screws (4)	*Imports
Electronics (3)	*Tools
Small Machine Shops (3)	Saw Manufacturers
Farm Equipment (2)	*Proprietary Fasteners
*Cap Screws (2)	Aerospace
Common Fasteners	

Most

Consumer Items
Spiral Pins
Metric Fasteners

Least

*Furniture
*Allen-type Screw & Spring Pins
*Metrics

High interest rates affected the fastener industry as they did other industries. This was especially evident in the collection of accounts receivable. Distributors reported the following speed of payments on their accounts receivable:

Collected within 30 days:

27 said 70–99 percent of accounts were collected.

36 said 40–69 percent of accounts were collected.

25 said 0–39 percent of accounts were collected.

45-day payments:

3 said 70–79 percent of accounts were collected.

19 said 40–69 percent of accounts were collected.

66 said 0–39 percent of accounts were collected.

60-day payments:

2 said 70–99 percent of accounts were collected.

5 said 40–69 percent of accounts were collected.

81 said 0–39 percent of accounts were collected.

Longer payments (61 or over):

1 said 50–59 percent of accounts were collected.

5 said 20–49 percent of accounts were collected.

82 said 0–19 percent of accounts were collected.

For Lema, 75 percent of accounts are collected within 30 days, 15 percent within 45 days, 5 percent within 60 days, and 5 take longer than 60 days. Lema also offers a 1 percent discount if payment is made within 10 days. An additional ½ percent discount is given if cash is paid on delivery.

Foreign competition in the fastener industry has been increasing during recent years. In the survey, distributors identified a wide variety of specific types of screws, nuts, bolts, and washers for which foreign competitors had gained U.S. market shares ranging from 60 percent to 100 percent. Mr. Mace estimated that for each of these items the percentage of imports was as follows:

nuts	100 percent
bolts	85–90 percent
washers	60–70 percent
screws	85–90 percent

In addition, the distributors were asked to identify their company's biggest problems in order of importance for the first half of 1984 (parentheses enclose the number responding; asterisk indicates Lema's responses):

*Product availability (32)	*Cost of freight (6)
Price competition (27)	Cost increases (6)
Vendor deliveries (27)	Sales levels (6)
Collections (accounts receivable) (20)	Small orders (5)
Cash flow (17)	*Import price changes (5)
Personnel (13)	Interest rates (4)
Product quality (10)	Credit terms (4)
Inventory control (10)	Too many competitors (4)
Qualified sales people (10)	Employee training (4)
Importers selling direct (9)	Strong yen (2)
Profit margins (8)	Packaging (2)
Back orders (8)	Inflation (2)
Lead times (7)	Canadian competition (2)
Import delays (7)	New buyers (2)
Stainless product shortages (6)	

Here are representative open-ended comments from the survey that indicate some of the concerns and frustrations the distributors were experiencing in mid-1984:

- Imports are beginning to take over.
- When the industry left list and discount methods of price for a cost plus method it was the beginning of the end for a good profitable industry.
- Very competitive with manufacturers who sell in dual market, serving warehouse distributors and retailers. Basically the market is good but real competitive among warehouse distributors. (Note: this comment was made by Les Mace.)
- The distributor as always needs more support from our domestic manufacturers.
- Where have all the domestic fastener manufacturers gone? Will they ever return?
- It is an in and out mess. No leaders in the industry (manufacturers) and too many inexperienced people selling too cheaply.
- U.S. manufacturers do not have stock. Don't care if you buy or not. Complain about imports. Want large production runs. Most are difficult to deal with.
- Manufacturers should strive for cost reduction programs. I don't believe in protectionist policies; however, some arrangement should be made to restrict imports. If we don't take action now we will become a service-oriented country as opposed to a leader in the manufacture of goods. We are heading towards more closures of manufacturing plants.

- Price firming. Danger of distributor over-inventory. Lack of enthusiasm by manufacturers for expansion, either in modern equipment or personnel.
- Importers should be more selective to whom they sell or at least use different price levels for the small or wagon jobber. Large U.S. firms favor certain distributors and in the long run hurt themselves. Young and new distributors are outperforming many old line distributors.

The business recovery of the past few years has not favored fastener distributors. During the good business climate, customers bypass the distributor and go straight to the source (i.e. manufacturer) for fasteners. However, during poor economic times, the distributor is needed and depended upon more because of his knowledge of sources of supply.

In addition to economic factors, external environmental events also impact upon the fastener industry. A recent (1981) disaster, the Kansas City Hyatt Regency hotel skywalk collapse, has had more impact on the fastener industry than anything in the last 50–70 years. What resulted from this was that only U.S.A.-manufactured fasteners can be used in bridges and public buildings that are constructed with government funding. This forces the distributor to provide documentation on traceability of fasteners to domestic manufacturers.

CURRENT OPERATIONS AT LEMA

As described earlier, Lema's basic product line includes bolts, nuts, screws, washers, and other types of fasteners. Eighty percent of Lema's fastener purchases are imported and Mr. Mace believes that this figure will increase 10–15 percent during 1985. The fastener business was conducted prior to this year out of the Nutz-n-Boltz location. This location includes a small store area and a large warehouse. Only a small fraction of sales out of this location are over-the-counter retail; the majority of sales are wholesale.

Wholesale

Lema Supply Company wholesales fasteners primarily in four states: Missouri, Arkansas, Kansas, and Oklahoma. Percentage sales distribution for each of these areas is as follows:

Missouri	80 percent
Arkansas	15 percent
Kansas and Oklahoma	5 percent

Sales of fasteners are made to manufacturers, retailers, and other wholesalers in the four-state and other geographic areas. Two customers constituted 55 percent of Lema's wholesale sales in 1984. One of these was a retailer constituting 17 percent of total sales, and the other was an original equipment manufacturer (OEM) constituting 38 percent of total sales. Mr. Mace indicated that the OEM customer had switched to a competitor; however, he was not overly concerned about the loss of this customer. It appears that this particular customer was very slow in paying or would delay shipments, forcing Lema to hold the inventory and incur carrying costs. Therefore, the $50,000 in lost sales cost him approximately $60,000.

Prices on the wholesale level range from $.70 to $.90 per pound. "We initiated the price/lb. concept 30 years ago when we didn't know how to sell our stock. We couldn't keep up with price lists, so we started selling at 15¢/lb., then went to 20¢/lb.," stated Mace. Prices have risen accordingly over the years.

Competition in the fastener industry occurs mostly on the wholesale level, according to Mr. Mace. In Springfield alone there are five wholesalers who compete directly with Lema Supply. These include: Shamrock Screw and Bolt, Trico, Rost Distribution, Sligo, and BTM Fasteners. The stock carried by each of the distributors varies. Shamrock concentrates on stainless machine screws (less than ¼") and automotive fasteners. Trico carries packaged machine screws, wood screws and sheet metal screws. Rost specializes in automotive, domestic and metric fasteners. BTM concentrates on structural and construction fasteners as does Sligo. However, Sligo also carries maintenance fasteners. Lema sells all of the above types of fasteners. Tulsa, Little Rock, and Kansas City also furnish many competitors. Because of the intense competition in the large cities in Lema's geographical area, the majority of Lema's wholesale customers are in towns with 3,000–8,000 population.

Mr. Mace and other wholesale distributors share a concern about buying practices which tend to squeeze them out of the channel of distribution. Specifically, some of their manufacturing customers have begun to buy directly from fastener manufacturers rather than from distributors like Mr. Mace. In one particular example, a manufacturing customer asked Mr. Mace to find him the cheapest source of supply, with the clear implication that Lema would then continue to serve as the wholesale intermediary. However, when Mr. Mace found and identified the lowest-price source, his customer began to buy directly from this source, eliminating Lema from the channel of distribution. Questionable practices such as this are causing concern among distributors.

Retail

In January, 1985, Lema expanded its business to include a retail fastener outlet, The Bolt House. Mr. Mace considered this expansion for three weeks prior to making this strategic move. The Bolt House is located close to the original location of the company. When asked about the decision to move into retail, Mr. Mace stated that he personally was more at ease with face-to-face negotiation with the customer rather than dealing over the phone with purchasing managers and other people. But even more important was the fact that during the last two or three years, competition in the wholesale fastener business had become much keener, necessitating another source of cash flow. Mr. Mace also felt that the retail outlet would open a new niche in the market.

The retail operation will be characterized by being cash 'n' carry, self-service, and no frills (gunny sacks will be used for bags). Mace stated, "This will be kind of a supermarket-type of place: self-service, offering assorted nuts, bolts, screws, and other metal fasteners at $1 a pound." Prices will be the competitive edge. The owner believes that the price will be approximately 30¢/lb. cheaper than other retailers. Potential customers include both individuals (home handymen and do-it-yourselfers) and businesses (contractors and small independent businessmen doing their own building and repair work). Mace indicated that the do-it-yourselfer will make up only 5 to 10 percent of his retail market. His main push will be towards the self-employed individual or small businesses who do small contracts.

A wide variety of items is kept in stock at the store. Markup varies depending on the item. Normally, it is about 200 percent, but some items carry a 300 percent markup. Most of the merchandise carried will be from liquidation sales (i.e., merchants who have gone out of business and sold their stocks at bargain prices). Mace states, "I feel that this will be just another part of the market that will be available to any and everybody at a warehouse-type price."

Advertising for The Bolt House is carried by a local radio station 50 times/month. Publicity in the local newspaper about the opening of the retail operation created some confusion. The headline of the article, "Nuts, bolts supermarket planned in city," led some people to believe that the business was not open yet.

Mr. Mace stated that he felt he would not be competing much with Meeks, Payless Cashways, and Lowes (large, retail lumberyards and home building supply stores located in Springfield). The stock carried at The Bolt House won't be plated and pretty like that carried by the other retailers, but it will be functional. Some businessmen in Springfield have been skeptical of the possibility of such a retail supermarket succeeding. To this criticism Mr. Mace replies, "Now I can fortify myself to find ways to put their fears to rest."

Organizational Structure

Les Mace is the President of the Company and his wife is the Vice President and Treasurer. Together they own all the stock of Lema Supply Company. Wally Springer, Jr. (the company's attorney) acts as Secretary. Mr. Frank Kunnanz is the Wholesale Operations Manager and Mr. Rick Norton is in charge of Inside Sales and Inventory Control.

Financial Information

Exhibit 1 presents income statements and Exhibit 2 presents balance sheets for Lema Supply Company for the years 1980 to 1984 (first nine months of 1984). Inventory is reported at the lower of cost or market. Cost is determined by the average cost method. Depreciation of property and equipment is computed using the straight-line method with the assumption of the following useful lives:

Machinery and Equipment	7–10 years
Fixtures and Office Equipment	5–10 years
Autos and Trucks	3–10 years
Warehouse Equipment	7–10 years
Leasehold Improvements	5–10 years

FUTURE PLANS

Mr. Mace believes that employee additions will be necessary in the future. These would include a retail manager and an inventory and stock control manager at The Bolt House.

Also, future plans involve ways of dealing with foreign competition. When the governor of Missouri traveled to the Far East in the summer of 1984 promoting Missouri products and Missouri as a good economic trading partner, Mr. Mace was in close communication with the organizers of the trip. One thing that resulted was the possibility of Lema Supply becoming an importer of fasteners. However, Mr. Mace has indicated that his current responsibility is to make the retail operation a success and to continue to be able to compete at the wholesale level.

EXHIBIT 1   Lema Supply Company, Inc. Statement of Operations (Unaudited)

	1984	1983	1982	1981	1980
Sales	$171,493	$151,154	$119,735	$122,920	$118,394
Cost of sales:					
Beginning Inventory	107,140	54,300	49,800	45,507	38,147
Purchases	103,945	81,147	31,811	24,053	20,174
Freight	6,237	1,248	1,227	959	414
	217,322	136,695	82,838	70,519	58,735
Ending Inventory	140,140	108,000	54,300	49,800	45,507
Cost of Sales	77,322	28,695	28,538	20,719	13,228
Gross Margin on Sales	94,171	122,459	91,197	102,201	105,166
Operating Expenses	97,761	109,432	104,074	103,086	102,629
Income (Loss) from Operations	(3,590)	13,027	(12,877)	(885)	2,537
Other Income (Expense):					
Other Income	—	—	101	93	36
Commissions	—	—	5,000	—	—
Loss on Disposal of Assets	—	(526)	—	—	—
Interest Income	—	—	—	100	60
Interest Expense	(3,131)	(2,693)	(1,697)	(1,432)	(2,253)
Net Income (Loss)	$ (6,721)	$9,808	$ (9,473)	$ (2,124)	$ 380[1]
Retained Earnings, Beginning of Year	$ 23,592	13,784	23,257		
Retained Earnings, End of Year		$ 23,592	$ 13,784		

[1] After-tax income for 1980 was $333.

EXHIBIT 2 Lema Supply Company, Inc. Balance Sheet (Unaudited)

	1984	1983	1982	1981	1980
ASSETS					
Current Assets					
Cash	$ 599	$ 443	$ 4,635	$ 496	$ 833
Accounts Receivable	13,974	10,160	2,460	6,424	1,635
Notes Receivable	600	—	—	—	4,513
Inventory	140,140	108,000	54,300	49,800	45,507
Total Current Assets	155,313	118,603	61,395	56,720	52,488
Property and Equipment, at Cost					
Machinery and Equipment	4,291	4,291	4,291	4,291	4,291
Fixtures and Office Equipment	3,479	3,287	3,287	2,653	2,653
Autos and Trucks	12,843	12,843	12,843	12,843	19,422
Warehouse Equipment	10,400	10,047	10,047	10,047	10,047
Leasehold Improvements	3,635	3,635	4,655	4,655	4,241
	34,648	34,103	35,123	34,489	40,654
Less accumulated depreciation	30,290	29,096	27,802	25,537	26,402
Total Property and Equipment	4,358	5,007	7,321	8,952	14,252
Other Assets					
Utility Deposits	—	50	50	50	50
Note Receivable	2,254	3,203	3,603	4,513	—
	2,254	3,253	3,653	4,563	50
Total Assets	$161,925	$126,863	$ 72,369	$ 70,235	$ 66,790
LIABILITIES AND STOCKHOLDERS' EQUITY					
Current Liabilities					
Accounts Payable	$ 32,543	$ 24,720	$ —	$ —	$ —
Current Portion of Long-Term Debt	24,973	9,800	12,286	5,184	5,077
Accrued Expenses	1,958	2,318	2,001	1,967	2,637
Income Taxes Payable	—	—	—	—	47
Due to Stockholders[1]	30,450	11,400	4,167	11,595	4,600
Total Current Liabilities	89,924	48,238	18,454	18,746	12,361
Long-Term Debt	45,130	45,033	30,131	18,232	19,048
Total Debt	135,054	93,271	48,585	36,978	31,409
Stockholders' Equity:					
Common stock, $100 Par Value Authorized—300 Shares Issued and Outstanding	10,000	10,000	10,000	10,000	10,000
Retained Earnings	16,871	23,592	13,784	23,257	25,381
Total Stockholders' Equity	26,871	33,592	23,784	33,257	35,381
Total Liabilities and Stockholders' Equity	$161,925	$126,863	$ 72,369	$ 70,235	$ 66,790

[1] Money loaned to the company by Mr. Mace.

INDUSTRIAL HIGHLIGHT

General Components Industry

Below is a capsule summary of the industrial fasteners segment of the general components industry, of which Lema Supply Company is a part. Information in this highlight was compiled by the U.S. Department of Commerce and focuses on this industry during the approximate period of time covered in the case. Keep in mind that industrial highlights contained in this text are not intended as a complete synopsis of an industry but as a profile of certain issues that can be relevant to the case situation. A list of additional references at the end of this highlight can be used for further industrial analysis.

CURRENT SITUATION

In 1984, rapidly increasing imports continued to hold down gains in U.S. manufacturers' shipments of industrial fasteners in spite of substantial expansion in the automotive, capital equipment, and appliance markets. Only the very strong rise in shipments to the automotive market enabled the industry to record a growth in shipments of about 4 percent in 1984. Total employment increased about 5 percent in 1984 to 50,400 after successive significant declines each year from a 70,000 record rate in 1979. Production worker employment grew at the same rate to 35,600. The average annual earnings of production workers increased 4.5 percent in 1984 to $10.32. The industry price deflator increased 3 percent.

U.S. exports increased 20 percent in 1984 to $225 million, accounting for about 5.9 percent of total U.S. manufacturers' shipments. Exports to Canada, the largest single export market for automotive and specialty fasteners jumped over 30 percent in 1984 to over $105 million. Exports to Mexico and to the United Kingdom each increased to about $14 million.

In 1984, imports of industrial fasteners rose sharply by 45 percent to $805 millions, representing over 17 percent of total new supply. Imports from Canada, a large supplier, increased over 40 percent to roughly $150 million. Imports from Japan, the major supplier, increased almost 50 percent to over $360 million and those from the third major supplier, Taiwan, by more than 100 percent to about $130 million.

Source: U.S. Industrial Outlook, Department of Commerce, 1985, pp. 24-1–24-6.

The projected expansion in most industrial equipment markets combined with some further growth in the automotive market will increase fastener industry shipments by about 3 percent.

Continuing growth in imports will limit any further gains in 1985. Imports are expected to expand 20 percent in 1985 to over $965 million, representing close to 19 percent of the total new supply in domestic markets. Imports will continue to dominate the "standards" (multipurpose products) segment of the U.S. market. Most of the growth in U.S. shipments will occur in "specials" or products designed to fit a particular customer's needs.

A petition to the International Trade Commission in 1981 (under Section 203 of the Trade Act of 1974) alleged economic injury due to imports. Another to the Department of Commerce in 1982 from the Department of Defense under section 232 of the U.S. Trade Expansion Act of 1962) expressed concern about erosion of the U.S. industry's capability to meet national defense needs. Neither produced relief for the domestic industry from imports of nuts, bolts, and large screws. Measured in tonnage, imports have grown from 20 percent of apparent U.S. consumption for bolts and large screws in 1972 to about 50 percent in 1983. The comparable market share for nuts expanded from 40 percent in 1972 to about 70 percent in 1983. These ratios of imports to apparent consumption are expected to continue to rise in 1985.

LONG-TERM PROSPECTS

Continuing but slower expansion is expected for the fastener industry through 1989. The 3 percent real annual growth rate expected in 1985 could continue during the rest of the 1980's provided the automotive industry expands at a moderate rate and the aircraft and capital goods markets show substantial growth. The 3 percent average annual rate of growth falls below the projected 4.8 percent average annual rate for all fabricated metal products during the 1984–89 period and the forecasted 5.2 percent rate for GNP. U.S. firms are concentrating in short run, higher unit priced "special" fastener products. Loss of markets to imports in the high volume, more profitable, "standard" product areas is expected to continue through the 1980's.

ADDITIONAL REFERENCES

1982 Census of Manufacturers, MC 82-I-34F-2(P), Bureau of Census, U.S. Department of Commerce, Washington, DC 20233.

Hydraulics and Pneumatics, Penton/IPC, 614 Superior Avenue, West Cleveland, OH 44113.

CASE 16

Nike, Inc.

ROBERT G. WIRTHLIN   ANTHONY P. SCHLICHTE
both of Butler University

In June 1984, the senior management met to review the events of the past fiscal year that ended May 31. Although the company reported a net income of $40.6 million, this represented a 29 percent decrease from the previous year despite a 6 percent increase in revenues. All were aware of the problems facing the company. The athletic-footwear industry had become keenly competitive, forcing price reductions. In addition, the domestic market for athletic shoes was decreasing. Consumers were changing their preference from the athletic look to a more fashionable and traditional style. Furthermore, the demand for running shoes, the company's leading revenue producer, was declining very rapidly. This was partly due to demographics. The industry's primary market was the baby boomers born between 1946 and 1964. With that market saturated and its leading-edge age approaching 40, the industry was hard pressed to maintain the substantial early growth it enjoyed.

At the beginning of fiscal 1984, Nike was caught in this changing market with an all-time-high inventory of 22 million pairs of shoes. Although by year end the inventory level had been reduced to 17 million pairs, this buildup was costly. The effects of price cutting, slow-moving merchandise, and inventory write-downs to market value decreased the gross margin by 3.5 percent. This translated into $32 million of additional costs.

No one was happy. Fiscal 1984 was the first year since the company was founded that had failed to produce an increase in net income.

COMPANY HISTORY

In 1958, Phil Knight was an aspiring miler at the University of Oregon. His coach, Bill Bowerman, was considered by many to be the premier track coach in the United States. In 1960, Knight went on to Stanford's Graduate School of Business. While fellow students were doing their market research papers on computers and electronics, Knight was only interested in running. His research paper asserted that there was an enormous potential in the United States for athletic shoes. Furthermore, he concluded the Japanese could become a dominent market force in athletic shoes. Following his graduation in 1962, Knight celebrated with a trip around the world. He stopped in Japan and placed his first shoe order with Onitsuka, which manufactured Tiger running shoes. When his shipment of 300 pairs of shoes finally arrived in December 1963, nearly 14 months after the order, Knight took the shoes to his former coach for his opinion. Bowerman was enthusiastic and joined Knight in a partnership called Blue Ribbon Shoes (BRS). They each put up $500 to order more shoes. In the first year, BRS sold 1300 pairs of shoes for a total revenue of $8000. Within two years, BRS had opened its first office and warehouse in Tigard, a Portland suburb. Then in 1969, Knight resigned his accounting position with Coopers and Lybrand to devote his full time to the company. Now employing 20, and having three retail outlets, BRS attained $100,000 in revenues.

In 1972, a dispute over their distribution agreement led to litigation between BRS and Onitsuka. BRS launched a new shoe line under its own label. The name Nike, after the Greek goddess of victory, was chosen. Bowerman was selected as head track and field coach for the U.S. Olympic team. Several members of his team wore Nike shoes in competition. Sales for the first year were $1.90 million.

In 1973, John Anderson won the Boston Marathon wearing Nike shoes. Ilie Nastase, playing in Nike, was ranked number 1 tennis player in the world. One year later, the company opened its first manufacturing facility in Exeter, New Hampshire. Nike also expanded its sales overseas to Australia. Worldwide revenues reached $4.8 million.

In 1975, taking a clue from his traditional Sunday breakfast, Bill Bowerman created the first "waffle" sole using raw rubber and a kitchen waffle iron. The resulting studded design revolutionized running by providing a high-traction, lightweight, durable outsole. This invention was patented and the design was quickly grasped by the emerging jogging boom. Sales for the year shot to $8.3 million.

In 1977, Nike made a commitment to amateur sports by organizing Athletics West (AW). This club was the first track and field training club for Olympic contenders. AW members included Mary Decker, Alberto Salazar, Willie Banks, and Carl Davis. In the same year, Nike established factory sources in Taiwan and Korea. Nike shoes were sold for the first time in Asia. Sales more than doubled over 1976 to $28.7 million.

By 1979, Nike had signed agreements with distributors in all European countries. In that same year, Nike shoes became the most popular athletic shoes in the United States and Canada. In 1980, the Company went public and offered 2 million shares of common stock. In 1980, the company also signed new manufacturing contracts in Thailand, Malaysia, and the Philippines.

In October 1981, the company formed a 51 percent owned subsidiary in Japan with Nissho Iwai Corporation to market Nike products in Japan. The company continued its explosive growth in sales, and by May 1984, revenues had grown to $919 million. In just 12 years, the company's revenues went from $1.96 million to $919 million and the company was in a strong financial position to continue this growth. (See financial statements, Exhibits 1–3.)

PRODUCTS

The company produces a broad line of athletic shoes for men, women, and children for competitive and recreational wear. The majority of the footwear products are designed for a specific athletic use. However, more and more shoes are being purchased and worn for casual or leisure purposes.

The company also manufactures a line of active-sports apparel including running shoes and shirts, tennis clothing, warmup suits, socks, jackets, athletic bags, and accessories. Apparel and accessories are designed to complement the company's footwear products featuring the "swoosh" design and the Nike trademark.

Shown in Exhibit 4 is a breakdown of revenues in the United States by product category, and revenues from foreign markets.

The company's products are designed for the high-quality market. At the end of 1984, the company's product line included 235 basic footwear models. Running, basketball, racquet, and children's shoes were expected to continue to account for the majority of the company's shoe sales in the near future. However, the company planned to continue to place significant emphasis on the development and production of a broader line of leisure shoes.

EXHIBIT 1   Nike, Inc. Consolidated Statement of Income (in thousands except per share data)

	1983	1982	1981
	YEAR ENDED MAY 31		
Revenues	$867,212	$693,582	$457,742
Costs and expenses			
Cost of sales	589,986	473,885	328,133
Selling and administrative	132,400	94,919	60,953
Interest	25,646	24,538	17,859
Other expenses	1,057	435	92
	749,089	593,777	407,037
Income before provision for income taxes and minority interest	118,123	99,805	50,705
Provision for income taxes	60,922	50,589	24,750
Income before minority interest	57,201	49,216	25,955
Minority interest	197	180	—
Net income	$ 57,004	$ 49,036	$ 25,955
Net income per common share	$ 1.53	$ 1.37	$ .76
Average number of common and common equivalent shares	37,158	35,708	34,031

EXHIBIT 2 Nike, Inc. Consolidated Balance Sheet (in thousands)

	MAY 31 1983	MAY 31 1982
ASSETS		
Current assets		
Cash	$ 13,038	$ 4,913
Accounts receivable, less allowance for doubtful accounts of $3,751 and $3,877, respectively	151,581	130,438
Inventories	283,788	202,817
Deferred income taxes and purchased tax benefits	10,503	2,145
Prepaid expenses	6,625	5,198
Total current assets	465,535	345,511
Property, plant, and equipment	61,359	41,407
Less accumulated depreciation	21,628	12,485
	39,731	28,922
Other assets	2,762	1,040
	$508,028	$375,473
LIABILITIES AND SHAREHOLDERS' EQUITY		
Current liabilities		
Current portion of long-term debt	$ 2,347	$ 3,936
Notes payable to banks	132,092	112,673
Accounts payable	91,102	74,064
Accrued liabilities	19,021	22,894
Income taxes payable	11,102	19,774
Total current liabilities	255,664	233,341
Long-term debt	10,503	9,086
Commitments and contingencies	—	—
Minority interest in consolidated subsidiary	948	−86
Redeemable preferred stock	300	300
Shareholders' equity		
Common stock at stated value Class A convertible—18,837 and 11,976 shares outstanding	225	166
Class B—18,434 and 5,555 outstanding	2,646	1,414
Capital in excess of stated value	77,457	27,020
Unrealized translation gain (loss)	70	(67)
Retained earnings	160,215	103,427
	240,613	131,960
	$508,028	$375,473

DOMESTIC SALES AND MARKETING

Nearly 83 percent of the company's sales in fiscal 1984 were made in the United States to approximately 12,000 retail accounts consisting of department stores, shoe stores, sporting good stores, specialty stores, tennis shops, and other retail outlets. During fiscal 1984, no single customer accounted for more

EXHIBIT 3 Nike, Inc. Consolidated Statement of Changes in Financial Position (in thousands)

	YEAR ENDED MAY 31		
	1983	1982	1981
Financial resources were provided by			
Net income	$ 57,004	$ 49,036	$25,955
Income charges (credits) not affecting working capital			
Depreciation	9,421	5,135	3,774
Minority interest	197	180	—
Other	(188)	194	131
Working capital provided by operations	66,434	54,545	29,860
Net proceeds from sale of class B common stock in October 1982 and December 1980	51,442	—	27,890
Purchased tax benefits becoming current	14,270	—	—
Additions to long-term debt	4,135	4,477	4,392
Disposal of property, plant, and equipment	584	343	134
Proceeds from exercise of stock options	100	—	450
Minority shareholder contribution	—	648	—
	136,965	60,013	62,726
Financial resources were used for			
Additions to property, plant, and equipment	21,031	18,228	9,914
Purchase of tax benefits	15,277	—	—
Long-term debt becoming current	2,368	4,002	7,049
Additions to other assets	527	161	670
Unrealized loss from translation of statements of foreign operations, including minority interest	31	109	—
Dividends on redeemable preferred stock	30	30	30
	39,264	22,530	17,663
Increase in working capital	$ 97,701	$ 37,483	$45,063
ANALYSIS OF CHANGES IN WORKING CAPITAL			
Increase (decrease) in current assets			
Cash	$ 8,125	$ 3,121	$ (35)
Accounts receivable	21,143	43,202	23,375
Inventories	80,971	82,588	64,288
Deferred income taxes and purchased tax benefits	8,358	845	1,165
Prepaid expenses	1,427	2,711	336
	120,024	132,467	89,129
Increase (decrease) in current liabilities			
Current portion of long-term debt	(1,589)	(2,684)	2,753
Notes payable to banks	19,419	51,483	24,690
Accounts payable	17,038	31,572	5,560
Accrued liabilities	(3,873)	7,493	5,102
Income taxes payable	(8,672)	7,120	5,961
	22,323	94,984	44,066
Increase in working capital	$ 97,701	$ 37,483	$45,063

than 9.0 percent of the company's sales, and the three largest customers accounted for only 17 percent of sales.

Sales are solicited in the United States by 24 independent regional sales representative firms which are compensated on a commission basis. These firms do not take title to the inventory. Additionally, the company supports its reps with in-house sales personnel. Company sales and credit personnel review all orders and new accounts and are responsible for collecting receivables. Bad-debt losses have been minimal.

The company operates seven Nike retail stores which carry a full line of products. One store carries primarily close-out merchandise. The company feels these stores are valuable for promotional purposes as well as a training ground for employees.

During 1984, nearly 60 percent of the company shipments were made under the "futures" program. This program, started in 1982, allows dealers to order six months in advance of delivery and be guaranteed that 90 percent of their order will be shipped within 15 days of the requested delivery date at a specified price. Retailers benefit from this program because prices are fixed, promotional activities are planned in advance, and sufficient inventories are assured to meet seasonal peak demands. These orders can be cancelled with penalties.

The company distributes its footwear products in the United States through three large warehouse facilities. The western United States is served from Portland; the East is served from Greenland, New Hampshire; and, the Midwest

EXHIBIT 4 Breakdown of Nike's Revenues in the United States and Abroad

	YEAR ENDED MAY 31[1]							
	1981		1982		1983		1984	
U.S. Revenues								
Footwear								
Running	$149,300	33%	$236,300	34%	$267,600	31%	$240,200	26%
Court								
Basketball	104,500	23	144,400	21	122,400	14	125,100	14
Racquet	60,700	13	58,600	9	62,100	7	81,400	9
Field sports	8,700	2	13,600	2	41,300	5	42,200	5
Other								
Children's	64,300	14	106,100	15	120,800	14	97,100	10
Leisure/other	11,400	2	21,300	3	52,300	6	53,600	6
	398,900	87	580,300	84	666,500	77	639,600	70
Apparel	33,100	7	70,300	10	107,400	12	121,800	13
Total United States	432,000	94	650,600	94	773,900	89	761,400	83
Foreign revenues	25,700	6	43,000	6	93,300	11	158,400	17
Total revenues	$457,700	100%	$693,600	100%	$867,200	100%	$919,800	100%

[1] Dollars in thousands.

and South by Memphis, Tennessee. Apparel products are distributed from Beaverton, Oregon, and Memphis, Tennessee.

FOREIGN SALES

Nike products are sold in 50 countries in addition to the United States. In most countries, Nike is represented by independent distributors, several of whom are licensed to manufacture and sell Nike brand products. Licensing arrangements provide for the company's approval of product lines and on-site quality control inspection.

In larger foreign markets, Nike has become directly responsible for the marketing of its products by opening its own branches and acquiring subsidiaries (Nissho Iwai Corporation to market Nike products in Japan and the acquisition of the Canadian distributorship).

PROMOTION AND ADVERTISING

Since 1972, the company has spent the majority of its annual promotion and advertising budget on having athletes wear and endorse Nike products. Shoes and equipment are provided to outstanding athletes and teams, athletes are hired as consultants, and product endorsements are obtained from leading professional athletes. The company uses this form of promotion to establish product credibility with customers.

The company founded Athletics West in 1972 to provide coaching, training, and financial support for postgraduate athletes. Presently there are 80 athletes in this club. During 1984, the company sponsored or assisted nearly 1000 road races, marathons, and other sporting events across the United States.

Although the company spends the majority of its advertising budget on promotional activities, it does limited advertising on television and in athletic and trade magazines, and it assists retailers with local advertising. The company supplies dealers with brochures, posters, and other point-of-purchase promotional material.

MANUFACTURING

Nearly 95 percent of the footwear produced for the company is manufactured by 35 foreign suppliers, primarily in South Korea and Taiwan. The remaining portion is manufactured by three contract suppliers in the United States and its own plants in Massachusetts, Ireland, and England. The U.S. facilities produce approximately 100,000 pairs of shoes per month, or roughly 2 percent of the current requirements. U.S. production is concentrated on the most expensive models. In fiscal 1984, South Korea and Taiwanese suppliers accounted for 63 percent and 15 percent respectively of total footwear production for the company. The company also obtains production from contract suppliers in the People's Republic of China, Spain, Yugoslavia, Malaysia, the Philippines, Brazil, and Italy. No single supplier accounted for more than 12 percent of that 1984 production.

All foreign and domestic contract manufacturing is performed to detailed specifications furnished by the company. The company closely monitors such production to ensure compliance with such specifications. Foreign operations are subject to the usual risks such as revaluation of currency, export duties, quotas, restrictions on the transfer of funds, and political instability. To date, Nike has not been materially affected by any such risk. However, the company has developed alternative sources of supply for such products.

Since 1972, Nissho Iwai American Corporation (NIAC), a subsidiary of Nissho Iwai Corporation, a large Japanese trading company, has performed significant financing and export-import services for the company. The company purchases through NIAC substantially all of the athletic shoes and apparel it acquires from overseas suppliers for sale in the United States. The company's agreements with NIAC expired on September 30, 1985.

COMPETITION

There are approximately 50 companies worldwide that produce athletic footwear and apparel. The industry has experienced substantial growth the past ten years and is becoming increasingly competitive. Adidas is the leader in worldwide sales. Nike is the largest producer in the United States and second largest in the world and estimates it has 30 percent of the worldwide market. Although there is no comprehensive independent trade statistics, Nike believes its running, basketball, and tennis shoes have the highest sales volume in the United States. (See Exhibit 5.)

RESEARCH AND DEVELOPMENT

Nike has always relied heavily on its technical competence and innovation and feels its success will depend on continued emphasis on research and development for the elimination of injury and performance maximization of its products. Many of the 150 people employed in R&D hold degrees in biochemics, exercise physiology, engineering, industrial design, and chemistry. The company also utilizes advisory boards, which include coaches, athletes, trainers, equipment managers, podiatrists, and orthopedists to review designs and concepts aimed at improving shoes.

TRADEMARKS AND PATENTS

The Nike trademark and "swoosh" design are two of the company's most valuable assets. Both are registered in over 70 countries.

The company has an exclusive worldwide license to manufacture and sell

EXHIBIT 5 Income Statements for Two of Nike's Competitors

Converse Inc.

	YEAR ENDED DECEMBER 31		TEN-MONTH PERIOD ENDED DECEMBER 31,
	1984	1983	1982
Net revenues	$265,598,000	$209,470,000	$150,844,000
Cost of sales	179,730,000	137,580,000	97,824,000
Gross profit on sales	85,868,000	71,890,000	53,020,000
Other expenses			
Marketing, general and administrative	52,910,000	44,043,000	27,548,000
Research and development	2,107,000	1,588,000	1,031,000
Income from operations	30,851,000	26,259,000	24,441,000
Other income, net	842,000	236,000	141,000
Interest expense	(7,581,000)	(7,601,000)	(10,207,000)
Income before income taxes	24,112,000	18,894,000	14,375,000
Income taxes	9,645,000	7,784,000	6,564,000
Net income	14,467,000	11,110,000	7,811,000
Less cumulative preferred dividends and amortization	—	(309,000)	(707,000)
Net income available to common stockholders	$ 14,467,000	$ 10,801,000	$ 7,104,000
Net income per common share	$ 2.54	$ 2.07	$ 1.63

Hyde Athletic Industries

	1984	1983	1982
Net sales	$ 47,313,237	$ 44,556,716	$ 36,877,503
Costs and expenses			
Cost of sales	28,176,286	27,381,355	23,663,233
Depreciation and amortization	487,516	316,948	279,813
Selling and administrative expenses	13,160,584	10,557,907	6,939,945
Total costs and expenses	41,824,386	38,256,210	30,882,991
Operating income	5,488,851	6,300,506	5,994,512
Interest expense	890,104	492,656	1,065,482
Income before income taxes	4,598,747	5,807,850	4,929,030
Income taxes	1,917,721	2,944,111	2,440,000
Net income	$ 2,681,026	$ 2,863,739	$ 2,489,030
Net income per share of common stock based on the average number of shares outstanding	$ .92	$ 1.06	$ 1.01

footwear using the patented Nike-Air midsole unit. This unit utilizes pressurized gas encapsulated in a polyurethane midsole. The company also has a number of patents covering component features used in various athletic shoes.

MANAGEMENT AND EMPLOYEES

Nike management in 1984 is shown in Exhibit 6.

Nike employs 4100 people. Approximately 1300 are engaged in footwear production, 600 in apparel operations, 375 in sales and marketing, 100 in retail stores, 500 in footwear warehousing, 150 in product research and development, 600 in foreign operations, and 475 in general management and administration. Except for 120 employees in Ireland, none of the company's employees are represented by a union.

EXHIBIT 6

NAME	AGE	TITLE	YEARS WITH NIKE	BACKGROUND
Philip Knight	46	Chairman and president	14	Accountant
William J. Bowerman	73	Vice-chairman and vice-president	14	Track coach
Robert L. Woodell	40	Executive vice-president	14	Salesman
Delbert J. Hayes	49	Executive vice-president	9	Accountant
Henry C. Carsh	45	Vice-president and manager—international operations	7	Accountant
David P. C. Chang	54	Vice-president—foreign production	3	Architect
Neil Goldschmidt	43	Vice-president—international marketing	3	Former secretary of treasury under President Carter and Portland mayor
John E. Jaqua	63	Secretary	14	Attorney
Gary D. Kurtz	38	Treasurer	3	Banker
James L. Manns	46	Vice-president—finance	5	Accountant
Ronald E. Nelson	41	Vice-president—apparel division	8	Accountant
George E. Porter	53	Vice-president—footwear division	2	Accountant
Robert J. Strasser	36	Vice-president—marketing and planning	8	Attorney
Richard H. Werschkul	38	Vice-president and counsel	1	Attorney

INDUSTRIAL HIGHLIGHT

Sporting and Athletic Goods Industry

Below is a capsule summary of the sporting and athletic goods industry, of which Nike, Inc., is a part. Information in this highlight was compiled by the U.S. Department of Commerce and focuses on this industry during the approximate period of time covered in the case. Keep in mind that industrial highlights contained in this text are not intended as a complete synopsis of an industry but as a profile of certain issues that can be relevant to the case situation. A list of additional references at the end of this highlight can be used for further industrial analysis.

CURRENT SITUATION

Domestic product shipments of sporting and athletic goods are estimated to have been at an all-time high of $3.7 billion, in current dollars, in 1984. Constant-dollar shipments rose an estimated 7 percent, mirroring the continued strength in the overall economy, particularly in the durable goods sector. Real disposable income grew an estimated 7 percent in 1984, while unemployment dropped to approximately 7.5 percent. Personal consumption expenditures on durables rose an estimated 11 percent in 1972 dollars.

The sporting goods industry is composed of more than 1,400 firms of various sizes that produce a wide range of products for use in athletic competition, exercise, and recreation. The major categories of sports equipment they produce are golf, gymnasium and exercise, fishing, tennis, bowling, and team sports. Total retail sales of sporting goods, including clothing, footwear, camping gear, and hunting equipment, were predicted to total $14.8 billion in 1984 by the National Sporting Goods Association.

The 1982 *Census of Manufactures* preliminary report on sporting goods revealed 1,428 firms (1,514 establishments) in this industry (SIC 3949 only). This number was down from 1,878 establishments of 1,757 companies in 1977. Although several of the leading producers are divisions of large diversified multinationals, 1,063 plants had fewer than 20 employees in 1982. The smaller establishments are sometimes one- or two-person operations that emphasize craftsmanship and that easily enter and exit the industry.

Source: U.S. Industrial Outlook, Department of Commerce, 1985, pp. 50-7–50-11.

The large multinationals generally produce goods that require substantial capital investment and technological sophistication. These firms benefit from brand-name recognition and economies of scale in marketing, research, and development. The major manufacturers often engage in importing, exporting, overseas production, contract work, and licensing the use of their trade names. Some of the major companies are Wilson Sporting Goods, a division of Pepsico, Inc.; AMF, Inc., which has several sporting goods divisions; Brunswick Corporation, which is known for its billiard tables and which competes with AMF in the bowling products market; and Questor Corporation, parent of Spalding Sports. Other large companies that have interests in the sporting goods industry include Alleghany International, American Brands, Anthony Industries, Campbell Soup, Cheseborough-Pond's, Coleman, Dart & Kraft, Kidde, Figgie International, Fuqua Industries, and MacGregor Sporting Goods.

During the industry's difficult period between 1978 and 1982, when product shipments declined at an annual rate of 0.3 percent, several firms stopped producing sporting goods. Others, in response to high interest rates of the late 1970's and the 1980–82 recession, shut down unprofitable factories and consolidated manufacturing facilities, reducing production costs and trimming corporate staffs.

The results of this cost cutting were felt in 1983. According to the *Value Line Investment Survey*, the recreation industry had an earnings gain of 19 percent in 1983 on increased sales of only 1 percent. Value line expected that sales increases in 1984 would improve profitability, as plants utilized more capacity. Several public companies reported record quarterly sales in the first half of 1984.

A Sporting Goods Manufacturers Association study of the financial performance of 74 sporting goods companies, including manufacturers of footwear and apparel, showed that profitability for these firms in 1983 rose to the highest level in a decade. The median value of the sales increases in 1983 for all firms was 9.7 percent. The median sales increases for hard goods companies only was 8.9 percent. The median value for return on sales before taxes was 5.7 percent for hard goods companies, up from 4.4 percent in 1982. Median return on investment was 16.3 percent for these firms. Companies with sales exceeding $50 million, including soft goods producers, outperformed the smaller sized firms.

Employment in the sporting goods industry declined irregularly from its peak of 61,900 workers in 1974 to an 11-year low of 47,500 workers in 1982. This represented a compound annual rate of decline of 3.3 percent. During the same period, the constant-dollar value of industry shipments grew at a compound annual rate of 1.1 percent. Value-added per production worker hour has risen from $9.84 in 1972 to $10.78 in 1977 and $12.32 in 1981, measured in 1972 dollars. These measures of productivity reflect the increased capital intensity and higher concentration in the industry.

The United States has traditionally had a trade deficit in sporting goods. In 1983, it totaled $462 million and, in 1984, it reached an all-time high estimated at $795 million as imports broke the $1 billion mark for the first time and exports declined slightly. Estimated imports as a percentage of apparent consumption also reached a record high in 1984 of 25 percent. This deterioration in trade performance can be partially attributed to the high value of the dollar, which appreciated 21 percent against a trade-weighted index of 67 countries' currencies in 1983 and set new highs against many of the major foreign currencies in 1984.

The majority of sporting goods imports originate in three East Asian countries: Taiwan, Korea, and Japan. Together these three countries supplied 62 percent of all U.S. sporting goods imports in 1983. Taiwan and South Korea tend to specialize in low-end, labor-intensive products geared toward the mass market. These countries have well-developed sporting goods industries that benefit from high tariffs at home, generally low tariffs in foreign markets due to preferential treatment, and cheap labor.

OUTLOOK FOR 1985

Following 2 years of strong growth in 1983 and 1984, constant-dollar product shipments of sporting goods are expected to slow somewhat to a 4-percent growth rate in 1985 as the expansion matures. Real disposable income growth is expected to slow from a 7 percent rate in 1984 to 2.5 percent in 1985. Unemployment is expected to continue its decline from its average of 7.5 percent in 1984 to below 7 percent in 1985. Personal consumption expenditures on durable goods are also expected to grow more slowly in 1985.

The trade deficit in sporting goods will set an annual high for the third consecutive year. U.S. exports are expected to decline again in 1985, although more slowly as foreign economies recover. U.S. imports will grow more slowly as the value of the dollar begins to return to more normal levels.

LONG-TERM PROSPECTS

According to a 1984 survey published by the *Sporting Goods Dealer,* 38 percent of the U.S. population engaged in some kind of exercise. The exercise participation rate among women is much higher than for men—43 percent to 32 percent. Women account for 54 percent of the population aged 35 and over, ages at which the exercise participation rate among women is high. As women continue to enter the workforce, they are expected to become an important component of the demand for sporting goods.

Another important observation of the survey is the high correlation between income and sports participation. Households with annual income exceeding $35,000 have the highest incidence of participation in aerobic dance, bicycling, bowling, golf, ice skating, jogging, skiing, swimming, and tennis. Between 1985 and 1990, the percentage of households with constant-dollar incomes exceeding $35,000 is projected to increase from 10.4 to 13.8, an annual compound growth rate of 7.7 percent.

Buoyed by these positive demographics, an apparently permanent shift toward greater participation in sports and exercise, and the migration of the population to the Sunbelt states, where weather and space permit more leisure activities, shipments of sporting goods are expected to continue growing. Import competition will dampen the growth in domestic shipments somewhat. Real domestic shipments of sporting goods will grow at an estimated rate of 2.5 percent annually during the next 5 years.

ADDITIONAL REFERENCES

1982 Census of Manufacturers Preliminary Report, Sporting and Athletic Goods, SIC industry 3949, Series MC82-I-39B-4(P). Bureau of the Census, U.S. Department of Commerce, Washington, DC 20233.

The Sporting Goods Dealer, The Sporting News Publishing Company, 1212 N. Lindbergh Boulevard, St. Louis, MO 63132.

The Sporting Goods Market in 1984, National Sporting Goods Association, 1699 Wall Street, Mount Prospect, IL 60056.

Sporting Goods Industry Financial Performance, Sporting Goods Manufacturers Association, 200 Castlewood Drive, N. Palm Beach, FL 33408.

"Fitness Marketing Special Report," *Advertising Age,* May 24, 1984.

CASE 17

The Lincoln Electric Company, 1989

ARTHUR SHARPLIN
McNeese State University

People are our most valuable asset. They must feel secure, important, challenged, in control of their destiny, confident in their leadership, be responsive to common goals, believe they are being treated fairly, have easy access to authority and open lines of communication in all possible directions. Perhaps the most important task Lincoln employees face today is that of establishing an example for others in the Lincoln organization in other parts of the world. We need to maximize the benefits of cooperation and teamwork, fusing high technology with human talent, so that we here in the USA and all of our subsidiary and joint venture operations will be in a position to realize our full potential. (*George Willis, CEO, The Lincoln Electric Company*)

The Lincoln Electric Company is the world's largest manufacturer of arc-welding products and a leading producer of industrial electric motors. The firm employs 2,400 workers in two U.S. factories near Cleveland and an equal number in eleven factories located in other countries. This does not include the field sales force of more than 200. The company's U.S. market share (for arc-welding products) is estimated at more than 40 percent.

The Lincoln incentive management plan has been well known for many years. Many college management texts make reference to the Lincoln plan as a model for achieving higher worker productivity. Certainly, the firm has been successful according to the usual measures.

James F. Lincoln died in 1965 and there was some concern, even among employees, that the management system would fall into disarray, that profits would decline, and that year-end bonuses might be discontinued. Quite the contrary—twenty-four years after Lincoln's death, the company appears as strong as ever. Each year, except the recession years 1982 and 1983, has seen high profits and bonuses. Employee morale and productivity remain very good. Employee turnover is almost nonexistent except for retirements. Lincoln's market share is stable. The historically high stock dividends continue.

A HISTORICAL SKETCH

In 1895, after being "frozen out" of the depression-ravaged Elliott-Lincoln Company, a maker of Lincoln-designed electric motors, John C. Lincoln took out his second patent and began to manufacture his improved motor. He

Copyright © 1989 by Arthur Sharplin, McNeese State University, Lake Charles, LA 70601.

opened his new business, unincorporated, with $200 he had earned redesigning a motor for young Herbert Henry Dow, who later founded the Dow Chemical Company.

Started during an economic depression and cursed by a major fire after only one year in business, the company grew, but hardly prospered, through its first quarter century. In 1906, John C. Lincoln incorporated the business and moved from his one-room, fourth-floor factory to a new three-story building he erected in east Cleveland. He expanded his work force to thirty and sales grew to over $50,000 a year. John preferred being an engineer and inventor rather than a manager, though, and it was to be left to another Lincoln to manage the company through its years of success.

In 1907, after a bout with typhoid fever forced him from Ohio State University in his senior year, James F. Lincoln, John's younger brother, joined the fledgling company. In 1914, he became active head of the firm, with the titles of general manager and vice president. John remained president of the company for some years but became more involved in other business ventures and in his work as an inventor.

One of James Lincoln's early actions was to ask the employees to elect representatives to a committee which would advise him on company opeations. This advisory board has met with the chief executive officer every two weeks since that time. This was only the first of a series of innovative personnel policies which have, over the years, distinguished Lincoln Electric from its contemporaries.

The first year the Advisory Board was in existence, working hours were reduced from 55 per week, then standard, to 50 hours a week. In 1915, the company gave each employee a paid-up life insurance policy. A welding school, which continues today, was begun in 1917. In 1918, an employee bonus plan was attempted. It was not continued, but the idea was to resurface later.

The Lincoln Electric employees' association was formed in 1919 to provide health benefits and social activities. This organization continues today and has assumed several additional functions over the years. In 1923, a piecework pay system was in effect, employees got two-week paid vacations each year, and wages were adjusted for changes in the Consumer Price Index. Approximately 30 percent of the common stock was set aside for key employees in 1914. A stock purchase plan for all employees was begun in 1925.

The board of directors voted to start a suggestion system in 1929. The program is still in effect, but cash awards, a part of the early program, were discontinued several years ago. Now, suggestions are rewarded by additional "points," which affect year-end bonuses.

The legendary Lincoln bonus plan was proposed by the advisory board and accepted on a trial basis in 1934. The first annual bonus amounted to about 25 percent of wages. There has been a bonus every year since then. The bonus plan has been a cornerstone of the Lincoln management system and recent bonuses have approximated annual wages.

By 1944, Lincoln employees enjoyed a pension plan, a policy of promotion from within, and continuous employment. Base pay rates were determined by formal job evaluation and a merit rating system was in effect.

In the prologue of James F. Lincoln's last book, Charles G. Herbruck writes regarding the foregoing personnel innovations:

> They were not to buy good behavior. They were not efforts to increase profits. They were not antidotes to labor difficulties. They did not constitute a "do-gooder" program. They were expressions of mutual respect for each person's importance to the job to be done. All of them reflect the leadership of James Lincoln, under whom they were nurtured and propagated.

During World War II, Lincoln prospered as never before. By the start of the war, the company was the world's largest manufacturer of arc-welding products. Sales of about $4 million in 1934 grew to $24 million by 1941. Productivity per employee more than doubled during the same period. The Navy's Price Review Board challenged the high profits. And the Internal Revenue Service questioned the tax deductibility of employee bonuses, arguing they were not "ordinary and necessary" costs of doing business. But the forceful and articulate James Lincoln was able to overcome the objections.

Certainly since 1935, and probably for several years before that, Lincoln productivity has been well above the average for similar companies. The company claims levels of productivity more than twice those for other manufacturers from 1945 onward. Information available from outside sources tends to support these claims.

COMPANY PHILOSOPHY

James F. Lincoln was the son of a Congregational minister, and Christian principles were at the center of his business philosophy. The confidence that he had in the efficacy of Christ's teachings is illustrated by the following remark taken from one of his books:

> The Christian ethic should control our acts. If it did control our acts, the savings in cost of distribution would be tremendous. Advertising would be a contact of the expert consultant with the customer, in order to give the customer the best product available when all of the customer's needs are considered. Competition then would be in improving the quality of products and increasing efficiency in producing and distributing them; not in deception, as is now too customary. Pricing would reflect efficiency of production; it would not be a selling dodge that the customer may well be sorry he accepted. It would be proper for all concerned and rewarding for the ability used in producing the product.

There is no indication that Lincoln attempted to evangelize his employees or customers—or the general public for that matter. Neither the chairman of the board and chief executive, George Willis, nor the president, Donald F. Hastings, mention the Christian gospel in their recent speeches and interviews. The company motto, "The actual is limited, the possible is immense," is prominently displayed, but there is no display of religious slogans, and there is no company chapel.

Attitude toward the Customer

James Lincoln saw the customer's needs as the *raison d'etre* for every company. "When any company has achieved success so that it is attractive as an investment," he wrote, "all money usually needed for expansion is supplied by the customer in retained earnings. It is obvious that the customer's interests, not the stockholder's, should come first." In 1947 he said, "Care should be taken ... not to rivet attention on profit. Between 'How much do I get?' and 'How do I make this better, cheaper, more useful?' the difference is fundamental and decisive." Willis, too, ranks the customer as management's most important constituency. This is reflected in Lincoln's policy to "at all times price on the basis of cost and at all times keep pressure on our cost ..." Lincoln's goal, often stated, is "to build a better and better product at a lower and lower price." "It is obvious," James Lincoln said, "that the customer's interests should be the first goal of industry."

Attitude toward Stockholders

Stockholders are given last priority at Lincoln. This is a continuation of James Lincoln's philosophy: "The last group to be considered is the stockholders who own stock because they think it will be more profitable than investing money in any other way." Concerning division of the largess produced by incentive management, he wrote, "The absentee stockholder also will get his share, even if undeserved, out of the greatly increased profit that the efficiency produces."

Attitude toward Unionism

There has never been a serious effort to organize Lincoln empoyees. While James Lincoln criticized the labor movement for "selfishly attempting to better its position at the expense of the people it must serve," he still had kind words for union members. He excused abuses of union power as "the natural reactions of human beings to the abuses to which management has subjected them." Lincoln's idea of the correct relationship between workers and managers is shown by this comment: "Labor and management are properly not warring camps; they are parts of one organization in which they must and should cooperate fully and happily."

Beliefs and Assumptions about Employees

If fulfilling customer needs is the desired goal of business, then employee performance and productivity are the means by which this goal can best be achieved. It is the Lincoln attitude toward employees, reflected in the following comments by James Lincoln, which is credited by many with creating the success the company has experienced:

> The greatest fear of the worker, which is the same as the greatest fear of the industrialist in operating a company, is the lack of income. ... The industrial manager is very conscious of his company's need of uninterrupted income. He is completely oblivious, evidently, of the fact that the worker has the same need.

> He is just as eager as any manager is to be part of a team that is properly organized and working for the advancement of our economy. ... He has no desire to make

profits for those who do not hold up their end in production, as is true of absentee stockholders and inactive people in the company.

If money is to be used as an incentive, the program must provide that what is paid to the worker is what he has earned. The earnings of each must be in accordance with accomplishment.

Status is of great importance in all human relationships. The greatest incentive that money has, usually, is that it is a symbol of success. . . . The resulting status is the real incentive. . . . Money alone can be an incentive to the miser only.

There must be complete honesty and understanding between the hourly worker and management if high efficiency is to be obtained.

LINCOLN'S BUSINESS

Arc-welding has been the standard joining method in shipbuilding for decades. It is the predominant way of connecting steel in the construction industry. Most industrial plants have their own welding shops for maintenance and construction. Manufacturers of tractors and all kinds of heavy equipment use arc-welding extensively in the manufacturing process. Many hobbyists have their own welding machines and use them for making metal items such as patio furniture and barbecue pits. The popularity of welded sculpture as an art form is growing.

While advances in welding technology have been frequent, arc-welding products, in the main, have hardly changed. Lincoln's Innershield process is a notable exception. This process, described later, lowers welding cost and improves quality and speed in many applications. The most widely-used Lincoln electrode, the Fleetweld 5P, has been virtually the same since the 1930s. The most popular engine-driven welder in the world, the Lincoln SA-200, has been a gray-colored assembly including a four-cylinder continental "Red Seal" engine and a 200 ampere direct-current generator with two current-control knobs for at least four decades. A 1989 model SA-200 even weighs almost the same as the 1950 model, and it certainly is little changed in appearance.

The company's share of the U.S. arc-welding products market appears to have been about 40 percent for many years. The welding products market has grown somewhat faster than the level of industry in general. The market is highly price-competitive, with variations in prices of standard items normally amounting to only a percent or two. Lincoln's products are sold directly by its engineering-oriented sales force and indirectly though its distributor organization. Advertising expenditures amount to less than three-fourths of a percent of sales. Research and development expenditures typically range from $10 million to $12 million, considerably more than competitors.

The other major welding process, flame-welding, has not been competitive with arc-welding since the 1930s. However, plasma-arc-welding, a relatively new process which uses a conducting stream of super heated gas (plasma) to confine the welding current to a small area, has made some inroads, especially in metal tubing manufacturing, in recent years. Major advances in technology which will produce an alternative superior to arc-welding with the next decade or so appear unlikely. Also, it seems likely that changes in the machines and techniques used in arc-welding will be evolutionary rather than revolutionary.

Products

The company is primarily engaged in the manufacture and sale of arc-welding products—electric welding machines and metal electrodes. Lincoln also produces electric motors ranging from one-half horsepower to 200 horsepower. Motors constitute about eight to ten percent of total sales. Several million dollars has recently been invested in automated equipment that will double Lincoln's manufacturing capacity for ½ to 20 horsepower electric motors.

The electric welding machines, some consisting of a transformer or motor and generator arrangement powered by commercial electricity and others consisting of an internal combustion engine and generator, are designed to produce 30 to 1,500 amperes of electrical power. This electrical current is used to melt a consumable metal electrode with the molten metal being transferred in super hot spray to the metal joint being welded. Very high temperatures and hot sparks are produced, and operators usually must wear special eye and face protection and leather gloves, often along with leather aprons and sleeves.

Lincoln and its competitors now market a wide range of general purpose and specialty electrodes for welding mild steel, aluminum, cast iron, and stainless and special steels. Most of these electrodes are designed to meet the standards of the American Welding Society, a trade association. They are thus essentially the same as to size and composition from one manufacturer to another. Every electrode manufacturer has a limited number of unique products, but these typically constitute only a small percentage of total sales.

Welding electrodes are of two basic types: (1) Coated "stick" electrodes, usually 14 inches long and smaller than a pencil in diameter, which are held in a special insulated holder by the operator, who must manipulate the electrode in order to maintain a proper arc-width and pattern of deposition of the metal being transferred. Stick electrodes are packaged in 6- to 50-pound boxes. (2) Coiled wired, ranging in diameter from 0.035 to 0.219 inches, which is designed to be fed continuously to the welding arc through a "gun" held by the operator or positioned by automatic positioning equipment. The wire is packaged in coils, reels, and drums weighing from 14 to 1,000 pounds and may be solid or flux-cored.

Manufacturing Processes

The main plant is in Euclid, Ohio, a suburb on Cleveland's east side. The layout of this plant is shown in Exhibit 1. There are no warehouses. Materials flow from the half-mile long dock on the north side of the plant through the production lines to a very limited storage and loading area on the south side. Materials used on each work station are stored as close as possible to the work station. The administrative offices, near the center of the factory, are entirely functional. A corridor below the main level provides access to the factory floor from the main entrance near the center of the plan. *Fortune* magazine recently

EXHIBIT 1 Main Factory Layout

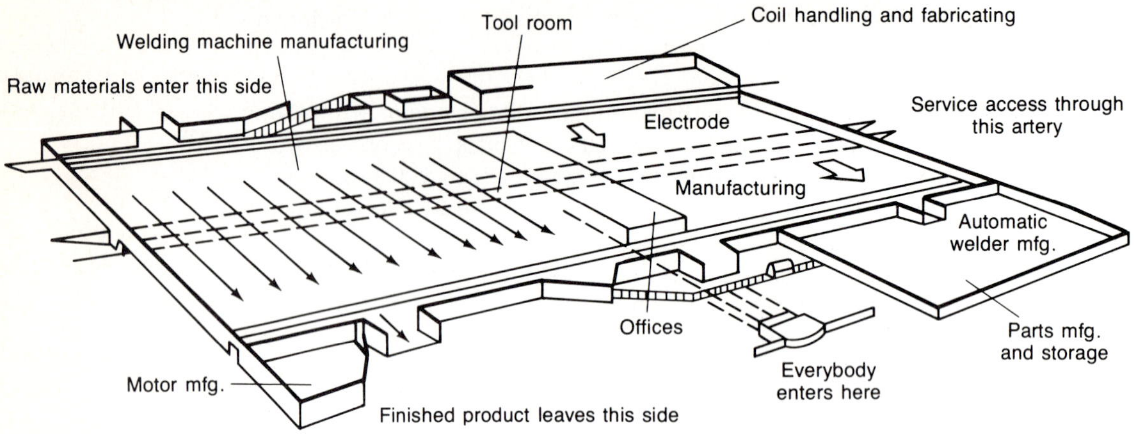
Tool room
Coil handling and fabricating
Welding machine manufacturing
Raw materials enter this side
Service access through this artery
Electrode
Manufacturing
Automatic welder mfg.
Offices
Parts mfg. and storage
Everybody enters here
Motor mfg.
Finished product leaves this side

declared the Euclid facility one of America's ten best-managed factories, and compared it with a General Electric plant also on the list:

> Stepping into GE's spanking new dishwasher plant, an awed supplier said, is like stepping "into the Hyatt Regency." By comparison, stepping into Lincoln Electric's 33-year-old, cavernous, dimly lit factory is like stumbling into a dingy big-city YMCA. It's only when one starts looking at how these factories do things that similarities become apparent. They have found ways to merge design with manufacturing, build in quality, make wise choices about automation, get close to customers, and handle their work forces.

A new Lincoln plant, in Mentor, Ohio, houses some of the electrode production operations, which were moved from the main plant.

Electrode manufacturing is highly capital intensive. Metal rods purchased from steel producers are drawn down to smaller diameters, cut to length and coated with pressed-powder "flux" for stick electrodes or plated with copper (for conductivity) and put into coils or spools for wire. Lincoln's Innershield wire is hollow and filled with a material similar to that used to coat stick electrodes. As mentioned earlier, this represented a major innovation in welding technology when it was introduced. The company is highly secretive about its electrode production processes, and outsiders are not given access to the details of those processes.

Lincoln welding machines and electric motors are made on a series of assembly lines. Gasoline and diesel engines are purchased partially assembled, but practically all other components are made from basic industrial products, e.g., steel bars and sheets and bar copper conductor wire.

Individual components, such as gasoline thanks for engine-driven welders and steel shafts for motors and generators, are made by numerous small

THE LINCOLN ELECTRIC COMPANY, 1989

"factories within a factory." The shaft for a certain generator, for example, is made from a raw steel bar by one operator who uses five large machines, all running continuously. A saw cuts the bar to length, a digital lathe machines different sections to varying diameters, a special milling machine cuts a slot for the keyway, and so forth, until a finished shaft is produced. The operator moves the shafts from machine to machine and makes necessary adjustments.

Another operator punches, shapes, and paints sheetmetal cowling parts. One assembles steel laminations onto a rotor shaft, then winds, insulates, and tests the rotors. Finished components are moved by crane operators to the nearby assembly lines.

Worker Performance and Attitudes

Exceptional worker performance at Lincoln is a matter of record. The typical Lincoln employee earns about twice as much as other factory workers in the Cleveland area. Yet the company's labor cost per sales dollar in 1989, 26 cents, is well below industry averages. Worker turnover is practically nonexistent except for retirements and departures by new employees.

Sales per Lincoln factory employee currently exceed $150,000. An observer at the factory quickly sees why this figure is so high. Each worker is proceeding busily and thoughtfully about the task at hand. There is no idle chatter. Most workers take no coffee breaks. Many operate several machines and make a substantial component unaided. The supervisors are busy with planning and record keeping duties and hardly glance at the people they "supervise." The manufacturing procedures appear efficient—no unnecessary steps, no wasted motions, no wasted materials.

The Appendix includes summaries of interviews with employees.

ORGANIZATION STRUCTURE

Lincoln has never allowed development of a formal organization chart. The objective of this policy is to insure maximum flexibility. An open-door policy is practiced throughout the company, and personnel are encouraged to take problems to the persons most capable of resolving them. Once, Harvard Business School researchers prepared an organization chart reflecting the implied relationships at Lincoln. The chart became available within the company, and present management feels that had a disruptive effect. Therefore, no organizational chart appears in this report.

Perhaps because of the quality and enthusiasm of the Lincoln work force, routine supervision is almost nonexistent. A typical production foreman, for example, supervises as many as 100 workers, a span of control which does not allow more than infrequent worker-supervisor interaction.

Position titles and traditional flows of authority do imply something of an organizational structure, however. For example, the vice-president of sales and the vice-president of the electrode division report to the president, as do various staff assistants such as the personnel director and the director of purchasing. Using such implied relationships, it has been determined that production workers have two or, at most, three levels of supervision between themselves and the president.

PERSONNEL POLICIES

As mentioned earlier, it is Lincoln's remarkable personnel pratices which are credited by many with the company's success.

Recruitment and Selection

Every job opening is advertised internally on company bulletin boards and any employee can apply for any job so advertised. External hiring is permitted only for entry level positions. Selection for these jobs is done on the basis of personal interviews—there is no aptitude or psychological testing. Not even a high school diploma is required—except for engineering and sales positions, which are filled by graduate engineers. A committee consisting of vice presidents and supervisors interviews candidates initially cleared by the personnel department. Final selection is made by the supervisor who has a job opening. Out of over 3,500 applicants interviewed by the personnel department during a recent period, fewer than 300 were hired.

Job Security

In 1958 Lincoln formalized its guaranteed continuous employment policy, which had already been in effect for many years. There have been no layoffs since World War II. Since 1958, every worker with over two year's longevity has been guaranteed at least 30 hours per week, 49 weeks per year.

The policy has never been so severely tested as during the 1981–83 recession. As a manufacturer of capital goods, Lincoln's business is highly cyclical. In previous recessions the company was able to avoid major sales declines. However, sales plummeted 32 percent in 1982 and another 16 percent the next year. Few companies could withstand such a revenue collapse and remain profitable. Yet, Lincoln not only earned profits, but no employee was laid off and year-end incentive bonuses continued. To weather the storm, management cut most of the nonsalaried workers back to 30 hours a week for varying periods of time. Many employees were reassigned and the total workforce was slightly reduced through normal attrition and restricted hiring. Many employees grumbled at their unexpected misfortune, probably to the surprise and dismay of some Lincoln managers. However, sales and profits—and employee bonuses—soon rebounded and all was well again.

Performance Evaluations

Each supervisor formally evaluates subordinates twice a year using the cards shown in Exhibit 2. The employee performance criteria, "quality," "dependability," "ideas and cooperation," and "output," are considered to be independent of each other. Marks on the cards are converted to numerical scores which are forced to average 100 for each evaluating supervisor. Individual merit rating scores normally range from 80 to 110. Any score over 110 requires

EXHIBIT 2   Merit Rating Cards

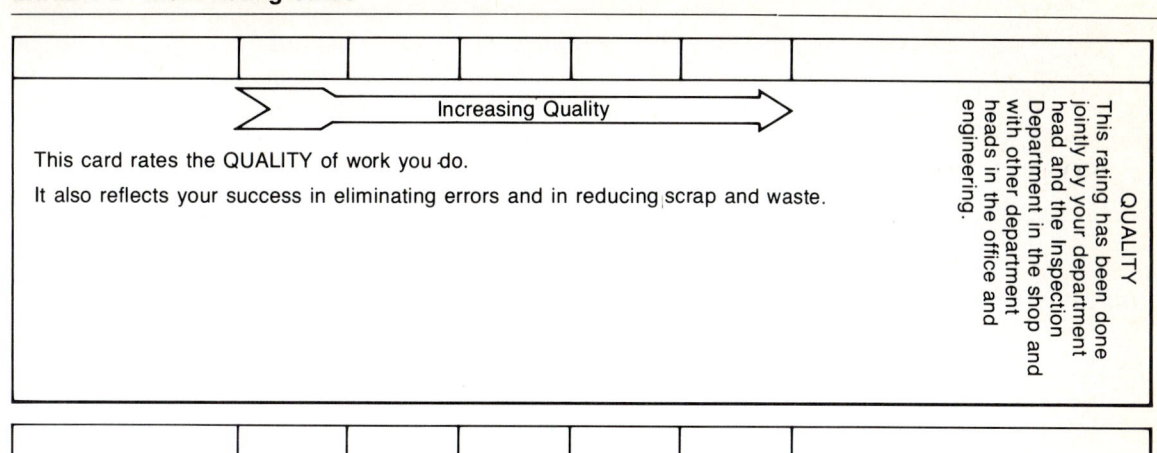

⟶ Increasing Quality ⟶

This card rates the QUALITY of work you do.

It also reflects your success in eliminating errors and in reducing scrap and waste.

QUALITY — This rating has been done jointly by your department head and the Inspection Department in the shop and with other department heads in the office and engineering.

⟶ Increasing Dependability ⟶

This card rates how well your supervisors have been able to depend upon you to do those things that have been expected of you without supervision.

It also rates your ability to supervise yourself, including your work safety performance, your orderliness, care of equipment, and the effective use you make of your skills.

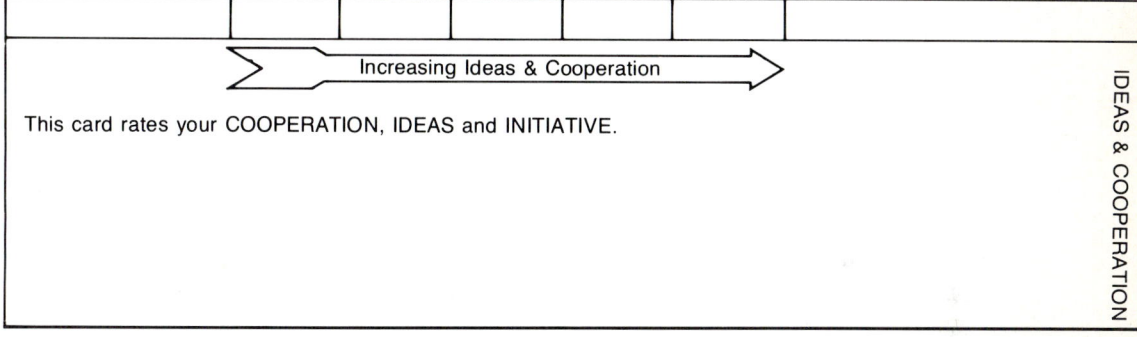

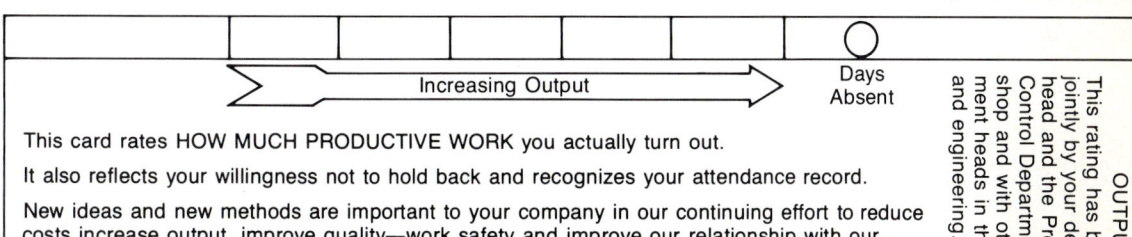

DEPENDABILITY — This rating has been done by your department head.

⟶ Increasing Ideas & Cooperation ⟶

This card rates your COOPERATION, IDEAS and INITIATIVE.

IDEAS & COOPERATION

⟶ Increasing Output ⟶   ○ Days Absent

This card rates HOW MUCH PRODUCTIVE WORK you actually turn out.

It also reflects your willingness not to hold back and recognizes your attendance record.

New ideas and new methods are important to your company in our continuing effort to reduce costs increase output, improve quality—work safety and improve our relationship with our customers. This card credits you for your ideas and initiative used to help in this direction.

It also rates your cooperation—how to work with others as a team. Such factors as your attitude towards supervision, co-workers, and the company; your efforts to share your expert knowledge with others, and your cooperation in installing new methods smoothly are considered here.

OUTPUT — This rating has been done jointly by your department head and the Production Control Department in the shop and with other department heads in the office and engineering.

a special letter to top management. These scores (over 110) are not considered in computing the required 100 point average for each evaluating supervisor. Suggestions for improvements often result in recommendations for exceptionally high performance scores. Supervisors discuss individual performance marks with the employees concerned. Each warranty claim is traced to the individual employee whose work caused the defect. The employee's performance score may be reduced, or the worker may be required to repay the cost of servicing the warranty claim by working without pay.

Compensation

Basic wage levels for jobs at Lincoln are determined by a wage survey of similar jobs in the Cleveland area. These rates are adjusted quarterly in accordance with changes in the Cleveland area wage index. Insofar as possible, base wage rates are translated into piece rates. Practically all production workers and many others—for example, some forklift operators—are paid by piece rate. Once established, piece rates are never changed unless a substantive change in the way a job is done results from a source other than the worker doing the job.

In December of each year, a portion of annual profits is distributed to employees as bonuses. Incentive bonuses since 1934 have averaged about ninety percent of annual wages and somewhat more than after-tax profits. The average bonus for 1988 was $21,258. Even for the recession years 1982 and 1983, bonuses had averaged $13,998 and $8,557, respectively. Individual bonuses are proportional to merit-rating scores. For example, assume the amount set aside for bonuses in 80 percent of total wages paid to eligible employees. A person whose performance score is 95 will receive a bonus of 76 percent (0.80 × 0.95) of annual wages.

Vacations

The company is shut down for two weeks in August and two weeks during the Christmas season. Vacations are taken during these periods. For employees with over 25 years of service, a fifth week of vacation may be taken at a time acceptable to superiors.

Work Assignment

Management has authority to transfer workers and to switch between overtime and short time as required. Supervisors have undisputed authority to assign specific parts to individual workmen, who may have their own preferences due to variations in piece rates. During the 1982–1983 recession, fifty factory workers volunteered to join sales teams and fanned out across the country to sell a new welder designed for automobile body shops and small machine shops. The result–$10 million in sales and a hot new product.

Employee Participation in Decision Making

Thinking of participative management usually evokes a vision of a relaxed, nonauthoritarian atmosphere. This is not the case at Lincoln. Formal authority is quite strong. "We're very authoritarian around here," says Willis. James F.

Lincoln placed a good deal of stress on protecting management's authority. "Management in all successful departments of industry must have complete power," he said, "Management is the coach who must be obeyed. The men, however, are the players who alone can win the game." Despite this attitude, there are several ways in which employees participate in management at Lincoln.

Richard Sabo, assistant to the chief executive officer, relates job enlargement/enrichment to participation. He said, "The most important participative technique that we use is giving more responsibility to employees. We give a high school graduate more responsibility than other companies give their foremen." Management puts limits on the degree of participation which is allowed, however. In Sabo's words:

> When you use "participation," put quotes around it. Because we believe that each person should participate only in those decisions he is most knowledgeable about. I don't think production employees should control the decisions of the chairman. They don't know as much as he does about the decisions he is involved in.

The advisory board, elected by the workers, meets with the chairman and the president every two weeks to discuss ways of improving operations. As noted earlier, this board has been in existence since 1914 and has contributed to many innovations. The incentive bonuses, for example, were first recommended by this committee. Every employee has access to advisory board members, and answers to all Advisory Board suggestions are promised by the following meeting. Both Willis and Hastings are quick to point out, though, that the Advisory Board only recommends actions. "They do not have direct authority," Willis says, "and when they bring up something that management thinks is not to the benefit of the company, it will be rejected."

Under the early suggestion program, employees were awarded one-half of the first year's savings attributable to their suggestions. Now, however, the value of suggestions is reflected in performance evaluation scores, which determine individual incentive bonus amounts.

Training and Education

Production workers are given a short period of on-the-job training and then placed on a piecework pay system. Lincoln does not pay for off-site education, unless very specific company needs are identified. The idea behind this latter policy, according to Sabo, is that everyone cannot take advantage of such a program, and it is unfair to expend company funds for an advantage to which there is unequal access. Recruits for sales jobs, already college graduates, are given on-the-job training in the plant followed by a period of work and training at one of the regional sales offices.

Fringe Benefits and Executive Perquisites

A medical plan and a company-paid retirement program have been in effect for many years. A plant cafeteria, operated on a breakeven basis, serves meals at about 60 percent of usual costs. The employee association, to which the company does not contribute, provides disability insurance and social and athletic activities. The employee stock ownership program has resulted in employee ownership of about fifty percent of the common stock. Under this program, each employee with more than two years of service may purchase stock in the corporation. The price of these shares is established at book value. Stock purchased through this plan may be held by employees only. Dividends and voting rights are the same as for stock which is owned outside the plan. Approximately 75 percent of the employees own Lincoln stock.

As to executive perquisites, there are none—crowded, austere offices, no executive washrooms or lunchrooms, and no reserved parking spaces. Even the top executives pay for their own meals and eat in the employee cafeteria. On one recent day, Willis arrived at work late, due to a breakfast speaking engagement, and had to park far away from the factory entrance.

FINANCIAL POLICIES

James F. Lincoln felt strongly that financing for company growth should come from within the company—through initial cash investment by the founders, through retention of earnings, and through stock purchases by those who work in the business. He saw the following advantages of this approach:

1. Ownership of stock by employees strengthens team spirit. "If they are mutually anxious to make it succeed, the future of the company is bright."
2. Ownership of stock provides individual incentive because employees feel that they will benefit from company profitability.
3. "Ownership is educational." Owners-employees "will know how profits are made and lost; how success is won and lost. . . . There are few socialists in the list of stockholders of the nation's industries."
4. "Capital available from within controls expansion." Unwarranted expansion would not occur, Lincoln believed, under his financing plan.
5. "The greatest advantage would be the development of the individual worker. Under the incentive of ownership, he would become a greater man."
6. "Stock ownership is one of the steps that can be taken that will make the worker feel that there is less of a gulf between him and the boss. . . . Stock ownership will help the worker to recognize his responsibility in the game and the importance of victory."

Until 1980, Lincoln Electric borrowed no money. Even now, the company's liabilities consist mainly of accounts payable and short-term accruals.

The unusual pricing policy at Lincoln is succinctly stated by Willis: "At all times price on the basis of cost and at all times keep pressure on our cost." This policy resulted in the price for the most popular welding electrode then in use going from 16 cents a pound in 1929 to 4.7 cents in 1938. More recently, the SA-200 Welder, Lincoln's largest selling portable machine, decreased in price from 1958 through 1965. According to Dr. C. Jackson Grayson of the American Productivity Center in Houston, Texas, Lincoln's prices increased only one-fifth as fast as the Consumer Price Index from 1934 to about 1970. This resulted in a welding products market in which Lincoln became the undisputed price leader for the products it manufactures. Not even the major Japanese manufacturers, such as Nippon Steel for welding electrodes and Osaka Transformer for welding machines, were able to penetrate this market.

Substantial cash balances are accumulated each year preparatory to paying the year-end bonuses. The bonuses totaled $54 million for 1988. The money is invested in short-term U.S. government securities and certificates of deposit until needed. Financial statements are shown in Exhibit 3. Exhibit 4 shows how company revenue was distributed in the late 1980s.

HOW WELL DOES LINCOLN SERVE ITS STAKEHOLDERS?

Lincoln Electric differs from most other companies in the importance it assigns to each of the groups it serves. Willis identifies these groups, in the order of priority ascribed to them, as (1) customers, (2) employees, and (3) stockholders.

Certainly the firm's customers have fared well over the years. Lincoln prices for welding machines and welding electrodes are acknowledged to be the lowest in the marketplace. Quality has consistently been high. The cost of field failures for Lincoln products was recently determined to be a remarkable 0.04 percent of revenues. The "Fleetweld" electrodes and SA-200 welders have been the standard in the pipeline and refinery construction industry, where price is hardly a criterion, for decades. A Lincoln distributor in Monroe, Louisiana, says that he has sold several hundred of the popular AC-225 welders, which are warranted for one year, but has never handled a warranty claim.

Perhaps best-served of all management constituencies have been the employees. Not the least of their benefits, of course, are the year-end bonuses, which effectively double an already average compensation level. The foregoing description of the personnel program and the comments in the Appendix A further illustrate the desirability of a Lincoln job.

While stockholders were relegated to an inferior status by James F. Lincoln, they have done very well indeed. Recent dividends have exceeded $11 a share and earnings per share have approached $30. In January 1980, the price of restricted stock, committed to employees, was $117 a share. By 1989, the stated value, at which the company will repurchase the stock if tendered, was $201. A check with the New York office of Merrill Lynch, Pierce, Fenner, and Smith at that time revealed an estimated price on Lincoln stock of $270 a share, with none being offered for sale. Technically, this price applies only to the unrestricted stock owned by the Lincoln family, a few other major holders, and employees who have purchased it on the open market. Risk associated with Lincoln stock, a major determinant of stock value, is minimal because of the small amount of debt in the capital structure, because of an extremely stable earnings record, and because of Lincoln's practice of purchasing the restricted stock whenever employees offer it for sale.

EXHIBIT 3 Condensed Comparative Financial Statements ($000,000)[1]

BALANCE SHEETS

	1979	1980	1981	1982	1983	1984	1985	1986	1987
Assets									
Cash	$ 2	$ 1	$ 4	$ 1	$ 2	$ 4	$ 2	$ 1	$ 7
Bonds & CDs	38	47	63	72	78	57	55	45	41
N/R & A/R	42	42	42	26	31	34	38	36	43
Inventories	38	36	46	38	31	37	34	26	40
Prepayments	1	3	4	5	5	5	7	8	7
Total CA	121	129	157	143	146	138	135	116	137
Other assets[2]	24	24	26	30	30	29	29	33	40
Land	1	1	1	1	1	1	1	1	1
Net buildings	22	23	25	23	22	21	20	18	17
Net M&E	21	25	27	27	27	28	27	29	33
Total FA	44	49	53	51	50	50	48	48	50
Total assets	$189	$202	$236	224	$227	$217	$213	$197	$227
Claims									
A/P	$ 17	$ 16	$ 15	$ 12	$ 16	$ 15	$ 13	$ 11	$ 20
Accrued wages	1	2	5	4	3	4	5	5	4
Accrued taxes	10	6	15	5	7	4	6	5	9
Accrued div.	6	6	7	7	7	6	7	6	7
Total CL	33	29	42	28	33	30	31	27	40
LT debt		4	5	6	8	10	11	8	8
Total debt	33	33	47	34	41	40	42	35	48
Common stock[1]	4	3	1	2	0	0	0	0	2
Ret. earnings	152	167	189	188	186	176	171	161	177
Total SH equity	156	170	190	190	186	176	171	161	179
Total claims	$189	$202	$236	$224	$227	$217	$213	$197	$227

INCOME STATEMENTS

	1979	1980	1981	1982	1983	1984	1985	1986	1987
Income	$385	$401	$469	$329	$277	$334	$344	$326	$377
CGS	244	261	293	213	180	223	221	216	239
Selling, G&A[3]	41	46	51	45	45	47	48	49	51
Incentive bonus	44	43	56	37	22	33	38	33	39
Income before taxes	56	51	69	35	30	31	36	27	48
Income taxes	26	23	31	16	13	14	16	12	21
Net income	$ 30	$ 28	$ 37	$ 19	$ 17	$ 17	$ 20	$ 15	$ 27

[1] Columns totals may not check and amounts less than $500,000 (0.5) are shown as zero, due to rounding.
[2] Includes investment in foreign subsidiaries, $29 million in 1987.
[3] Includes pension expense and payroll taxes on incentive bonus.

EXHIBIT 4 Revenue Distribution

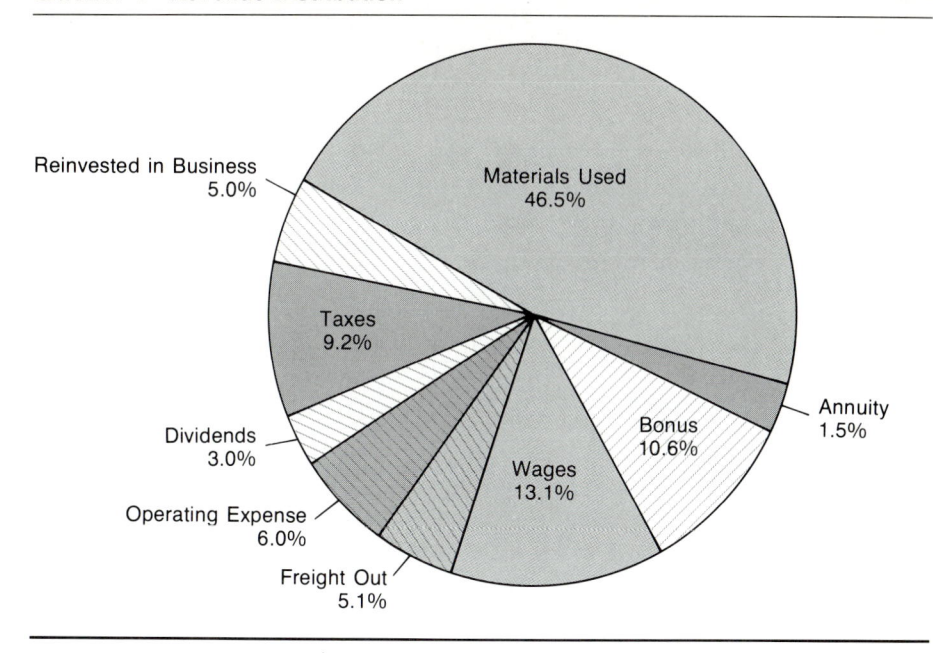

- Reinvested in Business 5.0%
- Materials Used 46.5%
- Taxes 9.2%
- Dividends 3.0%
- Operating Expense 6.0%
- Freight Out 5.1%
- Wages 13.1%
- Bonus 10.6%
- Annuity 1.5%

A CONCLUDING COMMENT

It is easy to believe that the reason for Lincoln's success is the excellent attitude of the employees and their willingness to work harder, faster, and more intelligently than other industrial workers. However, Sabo suggests that appropriate credit be given to Lincoln executives, whom he credits with carrying out the following policies:

1. Management has limited research, development, and manufacturing to a standard product line designed to meet the major needs of the welding industry.
2. New products must be reviewed by manufacturing and all producing costs verified before being approved by management.
3. Purchasing is challenged not only to procure materials at the lowest cost, but also to work closely with engineering and manufacturing to assure that the latest innovations are implemented.
4. Manufacturing supervision and all personnel are held accountable for reduction of scrap, energy conservation, and maintenance of product quality.
5. Production control, material handling, and methods engineering are closely supervised by top management.

6. Management has made cost reduction a way of life at Lincoln, and definite programs are established in many areas, including traffic and shipping, where tremendous savings can result.
7. Management has established a sales department that is technically trained to reduce customer welding costs. This sales approach and other real customer services have eliminated nonessential frills and resulted in long-term benefits to all concerned.
8. Management has encouraged education, technical publishing, and long range programs that have resulted in industry growth, thereby assuring market potential for the Lincoln Electric Company.

Sabo writes, "It is in a very real sense a personal and group experience in faith—a belief that together we can achieve results which alone would not be possible. It is not a perfect system and it is not easy. It requires tremendous dedication and hard work. However, it does work and the results are worth the effort."

APPENDIX

Employee Interviews

Typical questions and answers from employee interviews are presented below. In order to maintain each employee's personal privacy, fictitious names are given to the interviewees.

Interview 1

Betty Stewart, a 52-year-old high school graduate who had been with Lincoln thirteen years and who was working as a cost accounting clerk at the time of the interview.

Q. What jobs have you held here besides the one you have now?
A. I worked in payroll for a while, and then this job came open and I took it.
Q. How much money did you make last year, including your bonus?
A. I would say roughly around $25,000, but I was off for back surgery for a while.
Q. You weren't paid while you were off for back surgery?
A. No.
Q. Did the employees association help out?
A. Yes. The company doesn't furnish that, though. We pay $8 a month into the employee association. I think my check from them was $130.00 a week.
Q. How was your performance rating last year?
A. It was around 100 points, but I lost some points for attendance for my back problem.

Q. How did you get your job at Lincoln?
A. I was bored silly where I was working, and I had heard that Lincoln kept their people busy. So I applied and got the job the next day.
Q. Do you think you make more money than similar workers in Cleveland?
A. I know I do.
Q. What have you done with your money?
A. We have purchased a better home. Also, my son is going to the University of Chicago, which costs $13,000 a year. I buy the Lincoln stock which is offered each year, and I have a little bit of gold.
Q. Have you ever visited with any of the senior executives, like Mr. Willis or Mr. Hastings?
A. I have known Mr. Willis for a long time.
Q. Does he call you by name?
A. Yes. In fact, he was very instrumental in my going to the doctor that I am going to with my back. He knows the director of the clinic.
Q. Do you know Mr. Hastings?
A. I know him to speak to him, and he always speaks, always. But I have known Mr. Willis for a good many years. When I did Plant Two accounting I did not understand how the plant operated. Of course, you are not allowed in Plant Two, because that's the electrode division. I told my boss about the problem one day, and the next thing I knew Mr. Willis came by and said, "Come on, Betty, we're going to Plant Two." He spent an hour and a half showing me the plant.
Q. Do you think Lincoln employees produce more than those in other companies?
A. I think with the incentive program the way that it is, if you want to work and achieve, then you will do it. If you don't want to work and achieve, you will not do it no matter where you are. Just because you are merit rated and have a bonus, if you really don't want to work hard, then you're not going to. You will accept your ninety points or ninety-two or eighty-five because, even with that you make more money than people on the outside.
Q. Do you think Lincoln employees will ever join a union?
A. I don't know why they would.
Q. So you say that money is a very major advantage?
A. Money is a major advantage, but it's not just the money. It's the fact that having the incentive, you do wish to work a little harder. I'm sure that there are a lot of men here who, if they worked some other place, would not work as hard as they do here. Not that they are overworked—I don't mean that—but I'm sure they wouldn't push.
Q. Is there anything that you would like to add?
A. I do like working here. I am better off being pushed mentally. In another company if you pushed too hard you would feel a little bit of pressure, and someone might say, "Hey, slow down; don't try so hard." But here you are encouraged, not discouraged.

Interview 2

Ed Sanderson, a 23-year-old high school graduate who had been with Lincoln four years and who was a machine operator in the electrode division at the time of the interview.

Q. How did you happen to get this job?
A. My wife was pregnant, and I was making three bucks an hour and one day I came here and applied. That was it. I kept calling to let them know I was still interested.
Q. Roughly what were your earnings last year including your bonus?
A. $45,000.00.
Q. What have you done with your money since you have been here?
A. Well, we've lived pretty well and we bought a condominium.
Q. Have you paid for the condominium?
A. No, but I could.
Q. Have you bought your Lincoln stock this year?
A. No, I haven't bought any Lincoln stock yet.
Q. Do you get the feeling that the executives here are pretty well thought of?
A. I think they are. To get where they are today, they had to really work.
Q. Wouldn't that be true anywhere?
A. I think more so here because seniority really doesn't mean anything. If you work with a guy who has twenty years here, and you have two months and you're doing a better job, you will get advanced before he will.
Q. Are you paid on a piece rate basis?
A. My gang does. There are nine of us who make the bare electrode, and the whole group gets paid based on how much electrode we make.
Q. Do you think you work harder than workers in other factories in the Cleveland area?
A. Yes, I would say I probably work harder.
Q. Do you think it hurts anybody?
A. No, a little hard work never hurts anybody.
Q. If you could choose, do you think you would be as happy earning a little less money and being able to slow down a little?
A. No, it doesn't bother me. If it it bothered me, I wouldn't do it.
Q. Why do you think Lincoln employees produce more than workers in other plants?
A. That's the way the company is set up. The more you put out, the more you're going to make.
Q. Do you think it's the piece rate and bonus together?
A. I don't think people would work here if they didn't know that they would be rewarded at the end of the year.
Q. Do you think Lincoln employees will ever join a union?
A. No.
Q. What are the major advantages of working for Lincoln?
A. Money.

Q. Are there any other advantages?
A. Yes, we don't have a union shop. I don't think I could work in a union shop.
Q. Do you think you are a career man with Lincoln at this time?
A. Yes.

Interview 3

Roger Lewis, a 23-year-old Purdue graduate in mechanical engineering who had been in the Lincoln sales program for fifteen months and who was working in the Cleveland sales office at the time of the interview.

Q. How did you get your job at Lincoln?
A. I saw that Lincoln was interviewing on campus at Purdue, and I went by. I later came to Cleveland for a plant tour and was offered a job.
Q. Do you know any of the senior executives? Would they know you by name?
A. Yes, I know all of them—Mr. Hastings, Mr. Willis, Mr. Sabo.
Q. Do you think Lincoln salesmen work harder than those in other companies?
A. Yes. I don't think there are many salesmen for other companies who are putting in fifty to sixty-hour weeks. Everybody here works harder. You can go out in the plant, or you can go upstairs, and there's nobody sitting around.
Q. Do you see any real disadvantage of working at Lincoln?
A. I don't know if it's a disadvantage but Lincoln is a spartan company, a very thrifty company. I like that. The sales offices are functional, not fancy.
Q. Why do you think Lincoln employees have such high productivity?
A. Piecework has a lot to do with it. Lincoln is smaller than many plants, too; you can stand in one place and see the materials come in one side and the product go out the other. You feel a part of the company. The chance to get ahead is important, too. They have a strict policy of promoting from within, so you know you have a chance. I think in a lot of other places you may not get as fair a shake as you do here. The sales offices are on a smaller scale, too. I like that. I tell someone that we have two people in the Baltimore office, and they say "You've got to be kidding." It's smaller and more personal. Pay is the most important thing. I have heard that this is the highest paying factory in the world.

Interview 4

Jimmy Roberts, a 47-year-old high school graduate, who had been with Lincoln 17 years and who was working as a multiple-drill press operator at the time of the interview.

Q. What jobs have you had at Lincoln?
A. I started out cleaning the men's locker room in 1967. After about a year I got a job in the flux department, where we make the coating for

welding rods. I worked there for seven or eight years and then got my present job.
Q. Do you make one particular part?
A. No, there are a variety of parts I make—at least twenty-five.
Q. Each one has a different piece rate attached to it?
A. Yes.
Q. Are some piece rates better than others?
A. Yes.
Q. How do you determine which ones you are going to do?
A. You don't. Your supervisor assigns them.
Q. How much money did you make last year?
A. $53,000.
Q. Have you ever received any kind of award or citation?
A. No.
Q. Was your rating ever over 110?
A. Yes. For the past five years, probably, I made over 110 points.
Q. Is there any attempt to let the others know?
A. The kind of points I get? No.
Q. Do you know what they are making?
A. No. There are some who might not be too happy with their points and they might make it known. The majority, though, do not make it a point of telling other employees.
Q. Would you be just as happy earning a little less money and working a little slower?
A. I don't think I would—not at this point. I have done piecework all these years, and the fast pace doesn't really bother me.
Q. Why do you think Lincoln productivity is so high?
A. The incentive thing—the bonus distribution. I think that would be the main reason. The pay check you get every two weeks is important too.
Q. Do you think Lincoln employees would ever join a union?
A. I don't think so. I have never heard anyone mention it.
Q. What is the most important advantage of working here?
A. Amount of money you make. I don't think I could make this type of money anywhere else, especially with only a high school education.
Q. As a black person, do you feel that Lincoln discriminates in any way against blacks?
A. No. I don't think any more so than any other job. Naturally, there is a certain amount of discrimination, regardless of where you are.

Interview 5

Joe Trahan, 58-year-old high school graduate who had been with Lincoln 39 years and who was employed as a working supervisor in the tool room at the time of the interview.

Q. Roughly what was your pay last year?
A. Over $56,000; salary, bonus, stock dividends.

Q. How much was your bonus?
A. About $26,000.
Q. Have you ever gotten a special award of any kind?
A. Not really.
Q. What have you done with your money?
A. My house is paid for—and my two cars. I also have some bonds and the Lincoln stock.
Q. What do you think of the executives at Lincoln?
A. They're really top notch.
Q. What is the major disadvantage of working at Lincoln Electric?
A. I don't know of any disadvantage at all.
Q. Do you think you produce more than most people in similar jobs with other companies?
A. I do believe that.
Q. Why is that? Why do you believe that?
A. We are on the incentive system. Everything we do, we try to improve to make a better product with a minimum of outlay. We try to improve the bonus.
Q. Would you be just as happy making a little less money and not working quite so hard?
A. I don't think so.
Q. Do you think Lincoln employees would ever join a union?
A. I don't think they would ever consider it.
Q. What is the most important advantage of working at Lincoln?
A. Compensation.
Q. Tell me something about Mr. James Lincoln, who died in 1965.
A. You are talking about Jimmy, Sr. He always strolled through the shop in his shirt sleeves. Big fellow. Always looked distinguished. Gray hair. Friendly sort of guy. I was a member of the advisory board, one year. He was there each time.
Q. Did he strike you as really caring?
A. I think he always cared for people.
Q. Did you get any sensation of a religious nature from him?
A. No, not really.
Q. And religion is not part of the program now?
A. No.
Q. Do you think Mr. Lincoln was a very intelligent man, or was he just a nice guy?
A. I would say he was pretty well educated. A great talker—always right off the top of his head. He knew what he was talking about all the time.
Q. When were bonuses for beneficial suggestions done away with?
A. About eighteen years ago.
Q. Did that hurt very much?
A. I don't think so, because suggestions are still rewarded through the merit rating system.

Q. Is there anything you would like to add?
A. It's a good place to work. The union kind of ties other places down. At other places, electricians only do electrical work, carpenters only do carpenter work. At Lincoln Electric, we all pitch in and do whatever needs to be done.
Q. So a major advantage is not having a union?
A. That's right.

INDUSTRIAL HIGHLIGHT

Metalworking Equipment Industry

Below is a capsule summary of the welding apparatus segment of the metalworking equipment industry, of which The Lincoln Electric Company is a part. Information in this highlight was compiled by the U.S. Department of Commerce and focuses on this industry during the approximate period of time covered in the case. Keep in mind that industrial highlights contained in this text are not intended as a complete synopsis of an industry, but as a profile of certain issues that can be relevant to a case situation.

CURRENT SITUATION

Technological innovation in the welding industry and overall economic growth in the United States helped spur 1988 production of welding equipment and consumables to a record high. Shipments in 1988 amounted to $2,322 million and exceeded those for 1987 by 15 percent. This large gain came on the heels of a record-breaking year in 1987 which saw production of welding products rise about 11 percent, reaching $2,019 million.

Exports of welding machinery rose 15 percent between 1986 and 1987 and another 25 percent in 1988, reaching $276 million. The lower valued U.S. dollar combined with the aggressive foreign marketing strategies adopted by many welding equipment manufacturers account for these substantial increases. U.S. producers have expanded their market shares in foreign countries with particular success achieved in Canada, the United Kingdom and Mexico.

Imports of welding equipment rose from $185 million in 1986 to $203 million in 1987, a 10 percent increase. Imports of these products soared 58 percent to about $320 million in 1988. Most of this increase occurred in electric, non-arc welding equipment such as resistance welders. Imports of electric, non-arc equipment from Japan increased from $54.4 million in 1987 to approximately $150 million for 1988. U.S. imports of this equipment from West Germany roughly doubled from 1987.

About 40 percent of U.S. welding imports came from Japan. Canada contributed about 15 percent and Switzerland and West Germany slightly over 10 percent each to the U.S. welding import market.

Source: U.S. Industrial Outlook, Department of Commerce, 1989, p. 20-8.

Outlook for 1989

Domestic production of welding equipment and consumables will rise substantially in 1989, possibly increasing 10 percent. Much of this expansion results from aggressive export marketing by companies, which are seizing foreign market shares while the dollar remains relatively weak, and from continued innovation.

Throughout 1988, several advances in welding technology centered around plasma arc cutting and welding and the use of lasers in welding applications. These developments will accelerate in 1989 as companies move away from gas welding and towards electric processes.

Even at the current, relatively low value of the dollar vis-a-vis major European currencies and the Japanese yen, the welding industry will record its second consecutive trade deficit in 1989 as imports rise roughly 30 percent, reaching $415 million. Exports will post a more modest 20 percent increase, amounting to $330 million.

Long-Term Prospects

Over the next 5 years, the industry will grow at a rate of about 7 percent in constant dollars. The introduction of several new products will mark the period as will marketing to countries which are undergoing rapid economic development, particularly in the construction, automotive, shipbuilding and maintenance industries.

The long-term outlook for the industry appears good. As the industry continues to develop new applications for welding technology, and barring a substantial recession in user industries, sales will continue to increase.

CASE 18

Polaroid Corporation/Inner City, Inc.

JOHN A. SEEGER
Bentley College

Bill Skelley, manager of Polaroid Corporation's Inner City subsidiary, gazed intently across his circular conference table, emphasizing his concerns with the company's future:

> We are a 40-million dollar company, just as responsible for its operations as any other profit-center firm. We assemble parts for Polaroid's cameras . . . we package film . . . we do silk screen printing. At the same time, we help people who have never before succeeded at work to develop the skills they need, to hold a job anywhere. When we finish training somebody to be productive, we place them in a mainstream job with some other employer, to make room for a new trainee here.
>
> We're held responsible for the bottom line. Since 1978, we've returned more than our budgeted contribution to Polaroid headquarters. (Exhibit 1 shows Inner City's financial statements for 1985 and 1986.)
>
> Now, though, the whole economy is changing, with serious implications for us. Our history and skills lie in the manufacturing area, but all the economic growth is in the service sector: that's where the entry-level jobs are. To give our graduates a chance, we have to change the work we train them to do. We have to decide what work Inner City should take on—what new business we should go into.
>
> And the low unemployment rate here in Massachusetts makes it hard to attract new trainees. Our waiting list for employment used to have a thousand to fifteen hundred names; now there is virtually no waiting list at all. A skeptic might say our whole reason for existing is obsolete.

POLAROID CORPORATION

Polaroid Corporation was founded in 1937 by Edwin H. Land, who continued to lead the firm until his retirement in 1980. Through those years the company was based entirely on the products of Dr. Land's inventive genius—polarized filters and instant photography. Polaroid experienced rapid growth in sales, employment, and profitability, through 1978, when sales grew 30 percent over the previous year, reaching $1.4 billion with a return on equity of 13.8 percent. In 1979, however, several factors—including Kodak's penetration of the instant

---

This case was prepared by John A. Seeger, Associate Professor of Management at Bentley College, and Marie Rock, Senior Policy Analyst at Data General Corp. All rights reserved to the authors and to the North American Case Research Association. Permission to re-publish should be obtained from NACRA and from the authors. Copyright © 1987 by John A. Seeger.

EXHIBIT 1 Inner City Financial Statements (in thousands)

INNER CITY, INC. STATEMENT OF OPERATIONS
FOR THE YEAR ENDING DECEMBER 31ST

	1985 Budget	1985 Actual	1986 Budget	1986 Actual
Sales	$44,576	$38,457	$30,407	$35,401
Cost of sales				
Direct material	42,078	35,857	27,666	32,595
Direct labor	490	610	536	621
Total	42,568	36,467	28,202	33,216
Other direct costs	0	0	113	154
Gross margin	2,008	1,990	2,092	2,031
Other income	0	16	0	2
Subtotal	2,008	2,006	2,092	2,033
Operating costs				
Indirect labor (I.C. staff)	646	655	860	693
Staff labor (Polaroid staff)	798	793	840	746
Overhead	564	499	392	496
Total	$2,008	$1,947	$2,092	$1,935
Surplus (deficit) from operations	0	59	0	98[1]

INNER CITY, INC. STATEMENT OF FINANCIAL CONDITION
AS OF DECEMBER 31ST

Assets	1985	1986	Liabilities and Owner's Equity	1985	1986
Cash	$ 6	$ 44	Accounts payable	$ 7	$ 30
			Accrued expenses	16	42
Accounts receivable:			Total current liabilities	23	72
Polaroid	558	480			
Trade-Net	64	36	Advance from parent		
Other	3	5	corporation	2,778	3,019
Inventories	544	904			
Prepaid expenses	4	1	Total liabilities	2,801	3,091
Total current assets	1,179	1,470	Capital stock	1	1
			Paid in surplus	24	24
Plant and equipment—Net	99	98	Retained earnings (deficit)	(1,548)	(1,548)
Total assets	$1,278	$1,568	Total liabilities & owners' equity	$1,278	$1,568

[1] Redistributed to parent corporation

photography market, the failure of Polaroid's instant motion picture system, and an oil-starved economic recession—put an end to the growth. (Exhibit 2 shows ten years' operating results for Polaroid.)

From its inception, Polaroid Corporation reflected the values of its founder. The company was an innovator in participative management systems and responsiveness to community needs. In the late 1960s, autonomous worker teams were introduced in Polaroid's film manufacturing plant. When public criticism in 1970 focussed on the use of instant photography in South Africa's "Apartheid" identification pass program, Polaroid sent an employee team to investigate; supporting that group's analysis, the company refused to supply film to the government there. In 1978, Polaroid discontinued *all* sales in South Africa.

Richard Lawson, Director of Corporate Materials Management and Services for Polaroid and President of Inner City, Inc., commented:

> Dr. Land believed in helping people to grow and attain their limits. He created the Polaroid philosophy, recognizing that it takes people to produce a quality product and that everyone, even the sweeper, had good ideas. Here, the sweeper has a chance to become a lab technician.
>
> Our first goal is to build a company that makes a quality product we can all feel proud of. Hand in hand with this is a belief that we have to be good community members.

INNER CITY, INC.

Inner City, Inc. was a subcontract manufacturing firm, processing materials or assembling parts for Polaroid or other companies. Bill Skelley described his operation, as it might appear to a potential customer:

> We tell prospective customers, "We'd like to work for you. Send us your raw materials inventory. We'll process it and send it back to you. We're located on Columbus Avenue in Roxbury, and our work force is 95 percent minority." To tell the whole story, we might add, "Most of our people are unskilled. They've been with us, on average, only a couple of months. Most have no previous work history, or they've had problems at earlier jobs. Some have served time.
>
> We hire from the bottom of the labor force; our incoming trainees don't attach any importance to timeclocks or absenteeism or discipline or dress. Most just don't know what real work is, or how an employer expects them to behave."
>
> When you ask prospective customers to send their work into that environment, all sorts of perceptions start running through their minds. But when they come to visit, they find our trainees obviously working hard, and they're surprised. They say, "Wow, you guys have a very efficient, neat, well-organized, and clean operation! How do you do it?" We say, "That's what we expect. You can't run a place like this unless that's the order of business."

The Environment

Inner City occupied the top four floors of a freshly-painted, six-story brick and concrete building in Roxbury, a poor, predominantly black neighborhood of

EXHIBIT 2 Polaroid Corporation and Subsidiary Companies—Ten-Year Financial Summary
(Un-audited. Years ended December 31. Dollars in millions, except per-share data)

Consolidated Statement of Earnings	1986	1985	1984	1983	1982	1981	1980	1979	1978	1977
Net sales										
United States	$ 964.3	$ 779.3	$ 743.5	$ 730.1	$ 752.5	$ 817.8	$ 791.8	$ 757.2	$ 817.4	$ 645.8
International	664.9	515.9	528.0	524.4	541.4	601.8	659.0	604.3	559.2	416.1
Total net sales	1,629.2	1,295.2	1,271.5	1,254.5	1,293.9	1,419.6	1,450.8	1,361.5	1,376.6	1,061.9
Cost of goods sold	921.7	756.0	735.2	698.3	769.6	855.4	831.1	876.8	778.3	575.7
Marketing, research, engineering and administrative expense	571.8	505.6	492.6	462.1	472.6	520.8	483.9	449.4	418.2	337.3
Total costs	1,493.5	1,261.6	1,227.8	1,160.4	1,242.2	1,376.2	1,315.0	1,326.2	1,196.5	913.0
Profit from operations	135.7	33.6	43.7	94.1	51.7	43.4	135.8	35.3	180.1	148.9
Other income	18.1	28.9	39.5	32.5	45.5	49.2	25.4	13.3	20.3	19.0
Interest expense	18.6	22.3	20.9	26.5	35.5	29.9	17.0	12.8	5.9	6.4
Earnings before income taxes	135.2	40.2	62.3	100.1	61.7	62.7	144.2	35.8	194.5	161.5
Federal, state, foreign income taxes	31.7	3.3	36.6	50.4	38.2	31.6	58.8	(3)	76.1	69.2
Net earnings	$ 103.5	$ 36.9	$ 25.7	$ 49.7	$ 23.5	$ 31.1	$ 85.4	$ 36.1	$ 118.4	$ 92.3
Earnings per share	$ 3.34	$ 1.19	$ .83	$ 1.61	$ .73	$ .95	$ 2.60	$ 1.10	$ 3.60	$ 2.81
Cash dividends per share	$ 1.00	$ 1.00	$ 1.00	$ 1.00	$ 1.00	$ 1.00	$ 1.00	$ 1.00	$ .90	$ .65
Selected balance sheet information										
Working capital	$ 637.0	$ 697.8	$ 734.2	$ 769.0	$ 745.4	$ 749.5	$ 721.9	$ 525.9	$ 609.5	$ 589.6
Net property, plant, equipment	357.7	349.0	306.6	277.0	281.8	332.9	362.2	371.6	294.8	225.9
Total assets	1,479.2	1,384.7	1,346.0	1,319.1	1,323.6	1,434.7	1,404.0	1,253.7	1,276.0	1,076.7
Long-term debt	0	124.6	124.5	124.4	124.3	124.2	124.1	0	0	0
Stockholders' equity	994.7	992.2	916.3	921.6	902.9	958.2	960.0	907.5	904.3	815.5
Other statistical data										
Additions to property, plant, equip.	$ 82.9	$ 104.5	$ 82.7	$ 51.8	$ 31.5	$ 42.5	$ 68.1	$ 134.6	$ 115.0	$ 68.7
Number of employees	14,765	12,932	13,402	13,871	14,540	16,784	17,454	18,416	20,884	16,394
Return on stockholders' equity	10.8%	4.0%	2.0%	5.4%	2.5%	3.2%	9.1%	4.0%	13.8%	11.8%

Boston. The building was flanked on two sides by vacant lots awaiting urban redevelopment; behind it were 19th Century brick row houses, deteriorated by time and characteristic of much of historical Boston. Many houses were boarded up and abandoned, symbolizing the area's chronic unemployment—three times higher than that of surrounding neighborhoods. Across the street, bustling, dusty construction work continued on a new rapid transit line, spearhead of a major redevelopment program. According to plans for urban development, the area surrounding Inner City would eventually boast of cobblestone streets, brick walkways and new housing.

When Inner City was incorporated in 1968 as a subsidiary of Polaroid Corporation, the city of Boston, along with the rest of the nation, was experiencing great social unrest. Only four years earlier, the first federal civil rights laws had been enacted. Equal employment opportunity had not yet been legislated; discrimination was commonplace in employment, housing, voting, education, transportation, and in the daily lives of many Americans. Organizations which had represented the black community since 1910 were joined by college students to protest social injustices. Often, demonstrations intended to be non-violent broke into rioting and destruction—sometimes initiated by law enforcement personnel, sometimes by extremists among the protesters. Press and television coverage brought the violent encounters into public consciousness.

Reacting to spreading social unrest and violence, President Johnson launched a number of projects, including the War on Poverty in 1964, designed to derail the accelerating problems of the nation's youth and unemployed. Antipoverty programs, including training programs conducted by public agencies and private corporations, sprang up around the country. Still, social upheaval continued. In the mid- to late 1960s, several civil rights leaders and activists were assassinated, sparking even more social dissension across the country. Protesters against racism, against the Vietnam war, and against "the Establishment" marched through city streets and across college campuses, including those in Boston.

Riots erupted in major U.S. cities. Large areas of Rochester burned, as did Washington's black neighborhood. In Los Angeles, the vast area called Watts burned for days as snipers prevented fire fighters from entering and looters vandalized those stores still standing; 35 died in the riot, as 833 others were injured and 3600 more were arrested. In May of 1970, National Guard troops opened fire on students at Kent State University, killing 4 and wounding 10. Across the country, colleges closed until the following September, in sympathy with the slain students and to prevent further violence on their own campuses. Nervous civic leaders in Boston eyed the Roxbury ghetto, anticipating the worst.

The Founding of Inner City, Inc.

Governments, businesses, and civic minded groups of minorities and whites attempted to cope at the local level with the nation-wide illnesses of racism and unemployment. At Polaroid Corporation, black employees and the management executive committee focused on the issues. Richard Lawson, a member of the original planning team, recalled its formation:

> We had formed a "volunteer committee," where we shared ideas related to company business. At first, we met on our own time. Then Polaroid let us meet on company time, and allowed us to do more and more. As the volunteer committee grew in size, its running became a fulltime job held by elected officials who represented to management Polaroid's black employee viewpoint.
>
> At this same time, a movement was taking place in Washington which called for private enterprise to respond to the problem of hard-core unemployment in the nation's inner cities. We came up with the idea of establishing a small manufacturing plant in Boston's inner city, that would be a stepping stone for people coming to work at Polaroid or elsewhere.
>
> I worked at Inner City during its first year, and then went back to Polaroid. From there, I went to the Harvard Business School. About a year after I returned to Polaroid, Inner City was in financial turmoil. Community leaders felt the troubles resulted from mismanagement, and because I was a recent Harvard graduate, I was made manager of Inner City in 1973. Nowadays, assignments to Inner City are voluntary. Mine, in 1973, was not.
>
> Inner City was losing $700,000 to $800,000 a year, with no apparent end in sight, and turning out only about 50 graduates a year. It was costing us $9,000 to train a single graduate, far more than it would cost to send them to college. Inner City's operating systems duplicated all the overhead of the parent corporation; by simplifying things, I got the average cost down to $3,000 per graduate.
>
> For the life of me, I couldn't run a business to see it lose money. And I didn't think it was right for a successful business to carry a losing business. Now we run Inner City like any business in the United States. It makes money. If it doesn't, it had better answer why. Inner City now has to answer questions like, "What did you do?," and "What do you plan to do?" (Exhibit 3 summarizes operating results for ten years, ending in 1986.)

EXHIBIT 3   Surplus (Deficit) from Operations

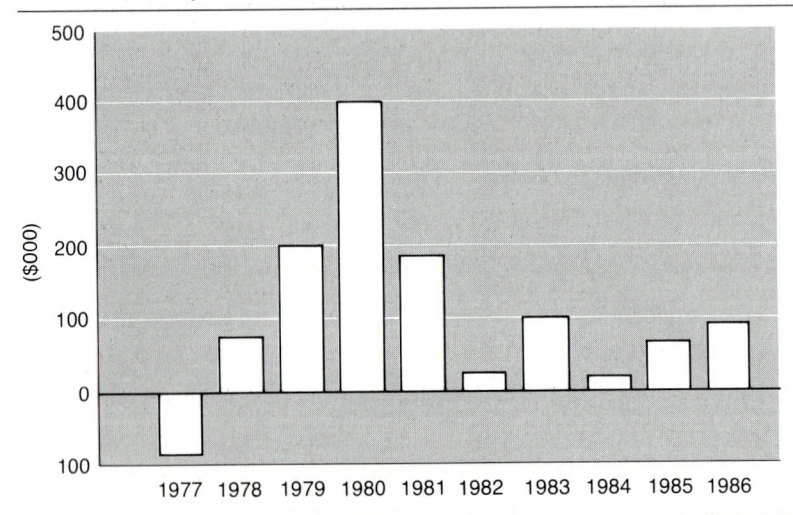

Organization

In 1987, Richard Lawson served as president and chairman of the board of directors of Inner City, Inc. Twelve other Polaroid executives, four of them members of the firm's executive committee, served as members of the Inner City board.

Inner City's own staff numbered about 30, of whom 17 were Polaroid employees on loan to the subsidiary. Bill Skelley noted that many of the needed skills in counseling, training, and placement areas were more available to Inner City in the open employment market than in the Polaroid staff. Some staff members were graduate students or interns from local universities.

Although small, the organization provided room for advancement for its people. One production supervisor had recently become a company planner, and several positions were held by former trainees. (Exhibit 4 shows the 1987 organization chart.)

EXHIBIT 4   The Inner City Organization: Polaroid Staff Members

```
                              President
                              R. Lawson
                                  |
                        Manager          Admin. Secretary
                        W. Skelley ——    L. Epps
                            |
   ┌────────────────┬───────┴────────┬────────────────┐
Sr. Personnel    General         Sr. Planner/        Sr. Financial
Administrator   Supervisor       Operations          Analyst
J. Wells        J. Hayes         G. Reid/R. Brennan  D. Farrell
   |                |                 |                  |
Education       Orientation     ┌─────┴──────┐      Financial Reporting
Training        Facilities      Production   Material Management  Forecasting
Placement       Safety          Training     Production Planning  Accounting
Counseling      Security        Performance  Quality Control      Product Pricing
Personnel       Admin.          Eval.        Purchasing           Receivables
Services        Management      Equipment    Product Training     Inventions
Trainee         Trainee         Maint.       Trainee Development  Trainee Development
Development     Development     Trainee
Community/                      Development
Public
Relations
```

Personnel Admin.
L. Mello

Prod. Supervisor
L. Joseph
|
Prod Supervisor
R. McCain
|
Prod. Supervisor
V. Valentine
|
Prod. Supervisor
R. Ashley
|
Camera Assy. Team
Coordinator
D. Gordon

Planner
M. Muther
|
Eval. Tech IV
B. Newell
|
Eval. Tech III
J. Huff
|
Mech. Specialist
W. Callahan

Fin. Analyst
A. Cohen

Salaried	12
Hourly	5
Total	17

Manufacturing Operations

Inner City's various material products included film and camera products, silk screen and offset printing products and special products. Typically, Inner City purchased raw materials from its customer, processed them, and then sold the finished product back to the customer. According to Bill Skelley,

> Polaroid was reluctant at first to give us some of their work, as you can imagine, but we proved that we could package film worth many millions of dollars. Some of the products we manufacture are essential to Polaroid. If we couldn't make the production and delivery schedule, whole divisions could be shut down or wouldn't be able to build their final products. Camera drive trains are an example.

Inner City's manufacturing operations occupied the top four floors of the Roxbury building, receiving raw materials by truck from Polaroid locations in Needham, Norwood, and Waltham. The work day began at 7 AM and continued until 3:30 PM, with trainees allowed one-half hour for lunch. Primary demand for Polaroid's products determined the number of trainees, which varied between 70 and 130 people. Bill Skelley had attemped to develop work from sources other than the parent company, but the jobs had not provided the kind of challenging work he felt was appropriate for the trainees.

Film packing operations were located on the sixth floor and occupied some 25 to 50 workers (of a total work force numbering 100 people.) Packs of film for the "Sun 600" camera and the "Spectra" line arrived by pallet loads, totaling 30,000 to 80,000 packs per day, depending on the schedule. Inner City's people packaged this film into groups of two, three, four, and five packs. The work involved little skill and could be expanded quickly as demand changed.

On the fifth floor, another 10 to 15 trainees worked at assembling a portion of the "hard body" for the "Sun" camera, applying the lens panel, trim button and retainer, and decorative stripe. Approximately 7,000 to 10,000 bodies per day were shipped to the Norwood plant. Photocopying and silk screening operations—the only department to serve a significant number of outside customers—employed eight trainees on the fourth floor.

The most complex jobs in Inner City involved the drive assembly for the "Sun" camera. Some 35 to 40 trainees on the third floor worked at the task, handling 26 intricate parts to build the drives. Five to six of these people, two of whom were Polaroid staff members, worked on quality control. Drive production remained relatively constant at 3,600 per day; the long learning times involved made it difficult to scale up operations quickly. Bill Skelley discussed quality control:

> We can't afford to have the slightest quality control problem. People will quickly take the work away from us. The standards that are applied to an operation like this versus the standards that are applied in the mainstream are really different. If you have a 2 percent rejection, somehow the 2 percent looks like 25 percent, because you are going to be held to a higher standard.

Competition

Competition for Inner City existed in both training and manufacturing. In training, government manpower development programs attempted to achieve similar goals. In manufacturing, the chief competition was with Polaroid's own internal production operations. Bill Skelley commented:

> I don't think there is anyone that quite does what we do, but we do have competitors. I have to convince managers within Polaroid to allow us to quote on increasing our subcontracting load. If we can't competitively quote and produce scheduled quality work, then we won't get that product. We have lost a number of lines because our quotes weren't competitive. However, in some cases we run a more efficient shop than Polaroid.
>
> There's also the offshore competition that the whole country is going through now. A lot of the type of work we do here, which is basic light hand-assembly, is what America is sending offshore.
>
> If you're looking from the training point of view, I guess our competition comes from those companies that offer entry level employment at low wages and with no future, like some segments of the fast-food industry. They take people off the street and employ them a while. It takes people some time to realize that they're not going anywhere.
>
> And there are competitors in the manufacturing arena, such as small subcontractors, that still tend to run on a sweatshop mentality, pay slightly above minimum wages with no benefits packages, offer people somewhat steady employment, yet no opportunity for career advancement.

At one time, Inner City competed with workshop-training programs contracted by various charities and state rehabilitation commissions. According to Bill Skelley, Inner City had moved away from that sort of work:

> Workshops are no longer competitors of ours and I think that's a significant transition. Years ago, we did the same kind of work—basic stuffing, putting components into a package. I think we've taken a significant step up: now we are focused on more intricate assembly, which is stepping into the high-tech arena, but requires much more in the way of quality control.

MANPOWER DEVELOPMENT OPERATIONS

In the 1960s, the federal government encouraged private industry to set up manpower training programs by paying companies to hire and train otherwise unqualified people. Jim Wells, Senior Personnel Administrator, commented:

> It was the thing to do, to take Federal money and set up a nice program. But we didn't want bureaucrats coming in saying, "Hey, Jim Wells, tomorrow we want you to do this." The next year they take half your budget and say, "Well, sorry, but we need to put the money somewhere else!"
>
> To our conscious knowledge, we did not borrow any program ideas from anyone. The program evolved. We didn't have a blueprint; we just built some things and they worked, so we expanded on them.
>
> There has always been a tremendous difference between how the people were treated here, versus how they were dealt with in the federally-funded city and state programs. I think it's the expectation levels we have here. Things are accepted in other programs that we just don't accept here.

Program Design

The program began with a four- to eight-hour orientation session where applicants heard in detail what would be expected of them. Those who decided to go ahead were hired into the first of the program's three phases, at the minimum wage of $3.55/hour.

During their first week of phase 1, trainees were introduced to the program, the staff, and all the products which were manufactured at Inner City. Trainees were moved through different tasks to find the area that best suited their skills. Here, they were told the quality and production standards that would be expected. Prominently displayed on the factory walls were easy-to-read charts, tracking each trainee's attendance record and hourly production (for individuals) or daily output (for groups).

After a month's demonstration of a cooperative attitude, good attendance, and work record, trainees were promoted to phase 2. Their pay was increased to $3.80 per hour. Trainees also attended required seminars on job performance, health and hygiene, and job-seeking skills. (Exhibit 5 shows the content of these seminars and lists the other seminars available.)

Each month, Inner City selected one of its trainees for the "employee of the month" award. Eligible people were at least six weeks into phase 2, had perfect attendance records, and had demonstrated an ability to get along with others. Supervisors recommended trainees to a rotating committee of staff members who picked the monthly winners. "Recruiters from other companies love to pick up our employees of the month," said Bill Skelley.

Production workers at Inner City were permitted to develop their own preferred methods of accomplishing the work. Millie Muther, production supervisor, commented:

> We'll show them how to run a machine, but if they have a better way of doing it, and if the quality is as good, then they can do it their own way. There's no set way that a trainee must work.
>
> I'm a firm believer: the person that's building the product, really knows how to do it better than anyone else. They'll try to get the most done. They're being paid for it.

Trainees

Although trainees joined the program in small groups, they completed it individually, depending on whether and when they were ready to work elsewhere. That decision was made by a group of Inner City staff, usually at the suggestion of the trainee's immediate supervisor. A trainee could be placed in an outside job in as little as four months or as long as nine months.

Other than a minimum age of 18, there were no eligibility requirements for Inner City trainees. Anyone could apply. Selection was on a first-come, first-served basis. Most trainees were in their early twenties. The oldest recruit was a man in his sixties; on occasion, the parent of a graduate became a trainee. Word-of-mouth communication was the program's only advertising up until 1985, when the thriving economy of Massachusetts had reduced the overall unemployment rate to just over three percent. At that time, Inner City began to use radio advertising to attract trainees.

EXHIBIT 5 Inner City Seminars

SEMINAR SUBJECTS

1. Health and hygiene
2. Job performance
3. Transition group
4. Financial literacy
5. Educational and vocational choices for adults
6. Planned parenthood
7. Nutrition and budgeting
8. Child development
9. The job entry phase
10. Emotions and behavior
11. Preparing your taxes
12. Understanding the judicial system
13. Jobs for the 1980s
14. The black contribution
15. Consumer education
16. Orientation to computers
17. Polaroid photography
18. Jobs in the service industry
19. Housing resources

MANDATORY SEMINAR: JOB PERFORMANCE
8 hours total (4 hours Inner City time)

Why people work
Components of good job performance
Importance of quality
Value of performance evaluations
Criteria for evaluating performance
Hierarchical structure of companies
Jobs for the 1980s

How to be successful on the job
Communicating effectively with supervisors
Understanding the supervisor's job
Job benefits
Job postings
Upward mobility
Resignations

MANDATORY SEMINAR: HEALTH AND HYGIENE
6 hours total (3 hours Inner City time)

Proper nutrition
Preventive medicine
Care of the body
Hair care
Skin care
Nail care
Dental care

Health clinics
Patients' rights
The physical exam
Birth control
Venereal disease
Sickle cell trait
Hypertension

MANDATORY SEMINAR: TRANSITION GROUP, JOB-SEEKING SKILLS
26 hours total (14 hours Inner City time)

Self-Assessment
Motivation
Getting what you want
Job applications
Resume preparation
Interviewing techniques

Role play interviews
In-House interviews
Off-Site interviews
Stress management
Fitting in
Adjustments to a new job

Bill Skelley summed up the plight of many trainees:

We have a lot of people in here who are really very bright, very sharp. Maybe because of social factors, maybe because of not knowing how to go about getting a job, or maybe because the places they apply to have certain criteria that exclude them because of color or some other factor. In any event, they have less than desirable work histories.

We take a couple of approaches to you as a trainee: we make you feel good about yourself initially; we tell you we expect an awful lot out of you; and we're not going to accept anything less. We say, "That's what you've got to do to be successful; now we'll help you with it. Are you willing to pay the price? That's the key question; if you are, you will be successful. If you're not, you'll probably wind up being terminated."

Trainee Gene Lang straddled a chair and chomped on a candy bar, hungry after working a full shift at Inner City, Inc.:

Before I came to Inner City, I only got jobs for one thing: quick cold cash, then I'd split. But this place really turned my head around. This is a place that wants you to work, to be on time, and to learn. They said to me, "You'll learn about holding on to a job by being here on time, by following the rules, and by taking pride in yourself and your work." Well, that sounded like so much crap to me. But you get here, man, and you see the other trainees. They been here a few weeks and so you see that they really work together. And that's the key, it's family. I mean, you might have some family scraps once in a while, but everyone starts to care about each other.

We all start to believe in each other, that we can make it through the program and graduate so that we can work in a permanent job someplace else. There *are* exceptions, the ones who don't want to be family; they usually goof off and get canned.

And it's tough here. They want you to know that you can make it through the program, but it's up to you to show your supervisor that you're serious about it, 'cause they sure as hell are.

Placement

Inner City placed approximately 100 trainees per year in a variety of manufacturing and service settings. Since 1968, over 1600 program graduates had been placed in 53 Boston-area companies, ranging from high technology to education to service. For the first ten years, the firm's trainees were placed with the parent company when their skills were sufficiently developed. In the business downturn of 1978, Polaroid's hiring policy changed; after that time, all graduates were placed with other Boston-area employers.

An important pre-placement activity was the "mock interview," with Inner City staff members playing the role of the potential employer. Millie Muther described the trainee's view of this experience:

One of my people had his first mock interview just today; that's his suit hanging there in the corner. He worked until 1:00, then changed into his suit and tie in the men's room. He says, "Are you sure I look all right?" Well, his collar was folded up, so he let me fix it. He says, "Can you see me shaking? Do you know how nervous I am? Is he going to say hello first or do I say it first to him?" He just got caught up, and so nervous. They're very proud to be all dressed up and going for their first interview. Even if it's only a mock interview, it's very important to them. He went downstairs and did a super job.

Brian Stebbins, a college senior in a management internship program, served as an assistant supervisor to Millie Muther and described the progress of a former trainee who had experienced a successful placement.

> You hear from former trainees every once in a while. I'm thinking of one who came back here to visit; he had had a really tough life before he came here and he had a tough beginning here, too. He was finally placed after a while. When he came back, he showed us his new bank book to show us his savings, and he wanted us to look out the window to see the car he just bought. But I remember that he had some very tough problems while he was here. We just kept telling him: "Willie, if you just keep working and do well here, you'll get a good job and you'll see a big turnaround." He came into our office one day and just broke down and started crying. He's over forty, but he broke down trying to tell us that he was a man and he wanted a job. That was heartbreaking. We kept encouraging him. We said there would be a change, but I don't think that he believed us completely until he went out and got the job.

Bill Skelley pointed out another placement potential for some trainees—promotion to Inner City staff positions:

> One trainee was just made a supervisor. We found after she came here, she had graduated from college in North Carolina; she's done very well. Another former trainee handles our whole payroll system; she's taking college courses at Northeastern now. Another former trainee is doing a fine job as a crew chief on the production floor. It really helps to see someone who works beside you go up the ladder. These people are excellent role models.

Retention

Typically, about one-quarter of the trainees entering Inner City's program graduated to "regular" full-time employment. Some thirty percent—referred to as "negative results" by the staff—were either fired or quit in the face of termination. Another large group left after a few months' training, to take other, higher-paying jobs. Nongraduates, Bill Skelley pointed out, benefitted from their training while employed in the program, even though they chose not to finish it. By year, the numbers of people hired and placed are shown in Exhibit 6.

Retention rates for Inner City graduates in their first jobs were tracked from 1982 to 1984 and indicated a substantial success during the graduates' first several months at work. Exhibit 7 shows that, of the total of 183 graduates covered by surveys, 158 or 85 percent stayed with their original employers for

EXHIBIT 6   Individuals Hired and Placed

	1982	1983	1984	1985	1986
Number hired	248	426	479	511	460
Number placed	62	94	130	106	102

EXHIBIT 7 Retention Rates: 1984 Study Group

Year Placed	Survey Total	Employees Still on the Job at			
		3 Months	6 Months	12 Months	18 Months
1982	57	50 (88%)	44 (77%)	42 (74%)	38 (67%)
1983	85	75 (90%)	68 (82%)	43 (52%)	17 (21%)
1984	41[1]	33 (80%)	28 (68%)		

[1] Small sample: first quarter placements only; this group not on job long enough to measure beyond six months

at least 90 days after placement. By the six-month point, retention had dropped only slightly to 140, or 77 percent. By year of placement, retention rates were measured as shown in Exhibit 7.

TRAINING POLICIES

Inner City emphasized its commitment to preparing people for long-term employment by implementing policies that might be considered stringent in many businesses.

Suspensions

Unruly and disruptive behavior or refusal to work was controlled through the use of suspensions. Millie Muther described handling a trainee's refusal to cooperate—a situation which might warrant a suspension:

> You say to yourself, "Why is that person doing that today? He is usually pretty good and has never refused to do a job." So you talk to that person and you get to the core of the problem and you solve it. It's usually a misunderstanding with someone else or a problem at home. But, if something like that continues, or is done more than once, we usually suspend them for three days because you can't refuse to do a job. You may not like to do it, but you can't refuse.
>
> An example might be a trainee—Eddie—who has just been placed. He started out really well—had no problems at all. Then all at once he changed. He came in one day with a certain attitude; it just wasn't him. He still came in on time, but he wouldn't communicate. You can't place people with an attitude like that. We talked about his behavior to get at the source of his problem.
>
> We had put up bars on all the sixth floor windows—kids were breaking in from the roof to steal film. The first day of the bars was when we saw the change in Eddie. It hadn't occurred to me that the bars would affect anyone. But Eddie had spent time in jail, and the bars had a special meaning for him. Knowing the problem helped me work with him. It made me feel pretty good when he finally did get a job—and it's a job he wants.
>
> There are different ways to deal with problems. I've had people refuse to do a job, and when I've talked to them, it's because they've had this back problem, or they've had this operation, and they can't help it. If they don't speak up or communicate in the correct manner, they could wind up getting terminated. So it's another lesson for them.

Terminations

Continued disruptive behavior is usually a way of testing the supervisor and can lead to termination early in the program. Millie Muther described some of the tactics used by trainees, and their results:

> They're brand new, so naturally they're going to put me through the test first. If there is a change in supervision, then they're going to put the new supervisor through the test to see if they can get away with more.
>
> They test you by coming back from lunch or breaks late. They're supposed to punch in for morning, at lunch, and when they leave for the day, but not for breaks. So if they are late from break, the first time I usually ignore it, but after that I'll talk to them. And I'll say, "I saw you the other day when you were late. I didn't say anything because I was hoping it was just a mistake on your part."
>
> I try to put the ownership back on them, and to make sure they realize that I'm not out to get them, that I want to help them. After that, they'll go on warning, and then they could be terminated if their behavior doesn't improve. You stress to them that no matter where they work, they have to come back on time, not one or two minutes late, or they're not going to keep their job. They learn eventually.
>
> We terminated a man on the spot, a couple of weeks ago. He put four packs of film underneath his hat. A lot of people saw that, so you can't let him get away with it. At first, we were going to wait—to catch him red-handed leaving the floor. But we've tried that before; you get interrupted for a few seconds, and the thief is gone. So we talked it over and said he's got it under his hat, and it shouldn't be there, so let's get rid of him now. A legal department in some big company would say the film doesn't cost you much; a lawsuit would cost a lot. But this is a training program. It's different. And even this guy has a right to appeal.
>
> Trainees know up front that I'm not here to fire them. I don't fire people; I never have. I've signed the termination papers, but they've done the firing to themselves. They'll say, "I don't know why you fired me, I don't know what I did." And so you show them the record, and point out that they didn't learn by going on warning or by being talked to. There are only so many breaks I can give them.

There was no specific rule at Inner City regarding the number of warnings prior to termination from the program. Rules were well defined, however, regarding processes for reinstatement of trainees.

Appeals Board

Not all terminations were permanent; Inner City gave its trainees a second chance. The terminated trainee received an appeals letter with his or her final check. The letter stated an appeal date, typically two weeks from the termination date, and a meeting time of 3:30 PM. According to Millie Muther, punctuality was considered to be an important indicator of a trainee's willingness to continue with the program.

> They have to be prompt and be here by 3:30. If they're a minute late, we don't see them because it proves that they really don't want their job. Ninety-nine percent of them are here before 3:30. Right now, I have 28 people on my floor; 6 of them have gone through the appeal process. When they come back, many of them seem to be okay for a while. Then all of a sudden some of them slip back again, and they end up being terminated. In the second termination, there is no appeal.

MEETING A CHANGING ENVIRONMENT

Long-term corporate commitment by Polaroid was essential to Inner City's ability to meet the challenges of an ever-changing environment.

Corporate Commitment

The commitment of Polaroid to Inner City's survival had been evident since its inception. Bill Skelley addressed this issue:

> When the parent company experiences difficult times—which we have gone through—it is forced to look at all facets of the company. Look at Inner City. Is it a cost or a drain on the company? If we lost a million dollars, there would be a lot of people sitting in Polaroid headquarters questioning the validity of this program. That could happen very quickly. Unemployment is 3.7 percent in this state; the lowest since sliced bread came on the board. Jobs are going begging; you have to bus people in from Timbuktu.
>
> It would be easy to ask, "Why do you need Inner City any more?" The people who make those decisions must have an in-depth understanding of what is happening in the real world. Polaroid went through a 30 percent reduction in personnel, beginning in 1978 or 1979. Today, the company is down to about 9,000 employees, domestically—some 14,000 world-wide. It really tested the corporate commitment to have products built by temporary people at Inner City, while full-time Polaroid employees were losing their jobs.
>
> Now the corporation is staying lean. Like most big companies, it hires *only* temporary people for entry-level manufacturing work. Last year they hired over 2,000 temps, and many of them came right out of Inner City's ranks. Say you were working here at $3.50 an hour, and you got a note saying, "Come to work at Polaroid and you can make $7 an hour." You'd say, "When do I report?" We told our people those were only temporary jobs; they'd be let go in three to six months, and they couldn't come back here if they left. Some held on there longer than we'd expected; others were back on the streets within three weeks. But such is life.

Current Problems and Alternatives

Bill Skelley summarized some of the current problems and alternatives for Inner City:

> For the first time in our history, the people we hire have options in their lives. Virtually *anyone* can get a job. Historically, our people had only us as a viable option.
>
> How do we motivate people to go through training when they can go out and get a job on their own, even though it's a dead-ended job? That's what we're struggling with—trying to convince younger people today to do some long-range planning. Long-range career planning for many of them is based on next Saturday night's party. Planning for six to nine months, never mind the next couple of years, is difficult.
>
> Do we have to pay them more? Then, how do we price our products competitively?

And if we pay more, we create another problem: people won't want to leave here. This is an environment geared to making them feel good about themselves, and we're also convenient to their homes. So, if we raise their pay by "x" cents per hour, whatever that may be, we reduce their incentive for leaving.

Also, for the first time in our history, the majority of our 1986 placements were in the service sector. Now "service sector" means a lot of things. For us, it *doesn't* mean flipping hamburgers—because we won't do that. But it *could* mean working in a bank as a teller. It could mean working in a hotel as a telephone operator or a receptionist or a bell captain or a housekeeper.

The skill levels needed for service sector jobs are higher than for entry-level manufacturing jobs. Which means that our people have to be better prepared. To go and sit on the production line at an electronics firm as an entry-level manufacturing person is pretty basic—it's just putting the piece parts together. To go and do a comparable job in a hotel requires a lot more from you. For instance, one of our women in a housekeeping function at a major hotel has to interface with a computer 5 to 6 times a day. She's got to go to the computer and punch numbers in to find out where her next assignment is, how many towels and bars of soap she needs. And this is in an entry-level job. We have to do a better job of preparing our people.

We're finding a population more in need at the same time that the jobs are more demanding. There's a widening gap. The schools are at an all-time low on preparing people for the world of work. There's a 47 percent noncompletion rate in the city's schools, and even those that *do* complete aren't prepared to get a job on their own.

We're trying now to tailor our training program to the service sector. I think 56 percent of our graduates last year went into service sector jobs; two years ago it was 14 percent. The advantage of service sector jobs is that they are mostly in Boston; we don't run into the transportation problem we normally have. See, our people don't drive; 99 percent of them don't own a car. And if you get jobs out on Route 128 or in some distant suburb, you are limited by a transportation problem.

We're trying to expand our silk-screening business with a new machine that more than quadruples our capacity. It teaches a specific skill. Hopefully, we can place somebody in that type of business.

We have to look at other service-related alternatives. For example, the fulfillment business is a multi-billion dollar industry. Let's say that you buy five six-packs of a soft drink and send the labels in and you get a free digital watch. Who sent you the watch? Companies don't do it themselves. We tried to do it once, but we got out of it because we weren't doing it right. Now we're looking at doing it again.

We're also looking at data entry. What if we set up a data entry business here? That sounds good but changes the way we approach things: it would require a higher skilled person. It means that we would have to keep people longer. Rather than turning people over in 6 months it means that they're going to be here for 2 or 3 years. And if that happens, then you've got to pay them a competitive market wage. You've got to add a benefits package and you can't serve as many people. Our costs skyrocket. How do you offset those costs?

Another idea is an "externship" kind of program, where we place our temporary employees in a Polaroid production operation and we supervise them there. Hopefully, it will be a good training tool for us. We're doing it now on a limited basis. We provide the supervisors, so we've got to make money at it.

We're still doing camera assembly, but some of it may be automated through robotics over the next few years, so I'm looking at products we can bring in for

1989. What happens if some of that gets automated? Then we switch to the service sector.

We've gone through our period of rapid growth. We're plateauing now, and looking at a redirection; new growth will come out of that. Redirection could mean that we'll be out of this building in a few years; I believe we'll have a new place to reside. There's going to be a *change* in direction. The world is changing around us. If we don't change with it, we limit what we can do.

INDUSTRIAL HIGHLIGHT

Photographic Equipment and Supplies Industry

Below is a capsule summary of the photographic equipment and supplies industry of which Polaroid Corporation/Inner City, Inc. is a part. Information in this highlight was compiled by the U.S. Department of Commerce and focuses on this industry during the approximate period of time covered in the case. Keep in mind that industrial highlights contained in this text are not intended as a complete synopsis of an industry, but as a profile of certain issues that can be relevant to the case situation. A list of additional references at the end of this highlight can be used for further industry analysis.

The photographic equipment industry covers a wide variety of products, including cameras, sensitized film and paper, and photocopier and micrographics equipment. Demand for traditional photographic products has continued soft in recent years due to domestic market saturation, competition from other leisure goods, and sluggish foreign markets. In addition, the challenge of electronic imaging systems has caused many producers to restructure their operations and adopt new manufacturing plans, which include diversified products and technologies that complement their silver-halide-based products.

CURRENT SITUATION

The photographic equipment and supplies industry had an average annual growth rate of 4.5 percent between 1972 and 1984, after adjusting for inflation. Increased purchases of consumer electronic products, manufacturer diversification into complementary products, and original equipment manufacturing agreements between U.S. and foreign firms all have depressed U.S. production. Shipments dropped 4 percent (in constant dollars) in 1985 and approximately 1 percent in 1986.

Containment of operating costs continues to be a major concern of photographic product manufacturers. Work force reductions have been an important contributor to lowering costs. During 1986, industry employment declined 2 percent, to 100,000 workers. The number of production workers,

Source: U.S. Industrial Outlook, Department of Commerce, 1987, pp. 35-1–35-4.

who accounted for about half of the total, dropped 4 percent, to 50,000. Employment has declined for 4 consecutive years at an average rate of 4 percent, to reach its lowest level since 1975.

Stable raw material prices also helped keep manufacturing costs down. The average producer price index for photographic equipment and supplies rose only 1 percent in 1986. The price index for equipment alone remained flat. Photographic supply prices increased only 1.5 percent, largely because the price index for silver, one of the more expensive inputs for sensitized photographic supplies, was 10 percent below the 1985 average.

Consumer Photography

The 10-year patent infringement case between Polaroid and Kodak, the two U.S. manufacturers of instant photographic products, came to an end in 1986. A Federal appeals court affirmed earlier judgments that Kodak had made unauthorized use of seven patents belonging to Polaroid. As a result, only Polaroid now produces, distributes, and markets instant photographic cameras and film. Photo dealers were able to return unsold products that had been discontinued, and Kodak offered camera owners several exchange options.

Demand for amateur instant photographic products has remained soft, and camera sales have declined each year since the peak year, 1978. In an effort to revive consumer interest, Polaroid introduced a new camera system, the first in 14 years. The system incorporates several electronic functions, including automatic focus, exposure, flash, picture ejection, and film advance. Technological advancements in instant color film chemistry were incorporated to improve the picture quality. In addition, the company offers a laser print service for computer-enhanced copies and enlargements. The success of this system may result in the first upturn in instant camera sales in 8 years. New medical, technical, and industrial applications of instant products continue to be developed, resulting in steady growth for these markets.

Disc camera sales were held down during 1986, primarily by the increased popularity of compact, automatic, non-SLR 35mm cameras. Improved film, telephoto models, and fashion colors failed to increase consumer interest in disc cameras. The dramatic drop of 40 percent in unit imports, to 600,000, was another indication of the weak demand for this camera format. Sales of the 110 cartridge camera, which was superceded by the disc camera in 1982, continued to decline: in 1986, sales were down 20 percent, to about 1.6 million units. Sales of 126 cartridge cameras were virtually nonexistent.

The introduction of autofocus SLR (single-lens reflex) 35mm cameras helped to renew consumer interest in this previously stagnant product group. SLR imports declined 12 percent in 1985, but rose 5 percent, to 3.5 million units, in 1986. Other automatic functions commonly incorporated on non-SLR 35mm cameras, such as automatic focusing, film loading, advancement and rewinding, exposure, and shutter speed setting, are available on some SLR models for both amateurs and professionals.

Sales of moderately priced non-SLR 35mm cameras continued to increase. Unit imports rose 30 percent, to 3.7 million units, during 1986. A major U.S.

manufacturer entered this segment of the U.S. market with imported cameras supplied through a marketing agreement. Very few 35mm cameras are actually produced in the United States. The import value of both SLR and non-SLR 35mm cameras exceeded $600 million in 1986.

Recent advancements in electronic imaging are based on a blend of technologies from the semiconductor, computer, and photographic industries. The formal introduction of an all electronic still camera/video system took place in 1986. Like the previous prototypes, this camera records images in electronic form for storage on a 2-inch magnetic video disk that can hold 50 pictures. The photographer can then view the images on a TV screen, reproduce them as a hard copy using a special printer, or transmit the image over telephone lines.

The system is presently targeted for the professional market and is priced near $40,000. Although several manufacturers are developing similar products, which include refinements in picture resolution, industry analysts do not expect the price of the electronic still camera to fall below $10,000 before the mid-1990s.

Photofinishing

Between 1981 and 1985, the retail market for amateur photofinishing grew at a compound annual rate of 11 percent. The continued quality and performance improvements and increased variety of photographic films are factors that contributed to the steady growth in recent years. In 1986, the market grew by 8 percent, to $3.8 billion. Meanwhile, the proliferation of onsite minilabs, which can process film within an hour, has increased the convenience of having film developed.

Film exposures by amateur photographers increased about 7 percent in 1986 to exceed 13 billion units. A breakdown of processing by film type showed 35mm film accounting for nearly 60 percent; disc film, 25 percent; cartridge film, 13 percent; and 2 percent for other roll films. Drug stores were the largest processing outlet, accounting for one-third of the total market by volume. Minilabs were second with about 25 percent.

Increased competition among operating minilab outlets has resulted in some photofinishing plant consolidations and closings. Some processors have begun to broaden services and increase advertising and promotional activities in an effort to attract more customers. Many of the best minilab locations are occupied. The largest and most sought after locations are in enclosed shopping malls. According to industry research, the mall location is the most prevalent site, accounting for nearly 40 percent, or 4,800, of the 12,000 minilab installations in the United States.

Photocopying

As a result of continual evolution in copier technology, features that were once only available on high-volume machines can now be found on low-end models that retail for less than $6,000. These standard features now include semiautomatic and automatic document feeders, sorters, and reduction capabilities. This standardization of low-end copiers increases the availability of identical models and results in aggressive pricing by the copier vendor. Price and reliable service have become the determining factors in purchase decisions. U.S. firms often rely on components sourced from foreign countries or market completely assembled copiers through original equipment manufacturing agreements as a way to participate in this competitive market segment. Personal copiers, typically priced at less than $1,000, incorporate a photosensitive drum, developing unit, and toner in a user-replaceable cartridge. An increased number of models, along with expanding distribution channels, including department and camera stores, have brought the U.S. installed base to an estimated 700,000 units in 1986.

Japanese suppliers furnish the majority of low-end machines to the U.S. market. Total U.S. photocopier imports from Japan in 1986 reached 1 million units, valued at $1.4 billion; this was 94 percent of all copier imports and 88 percent of total import value.

Advances in microprocessor technology have increased the sophistication and versatility of medium- and high-volume copiers. New capabilities that make possible the merging of two original images into a single document and the deletion of unwanted borders and margins are available on some models. In the more sophisticated laser copiers, the original image is converted into digital signals. Laser and electrostatic imaging allows the user to manipulate text and graphics electronically in a variety of ways, including selective copying and shifting text position prior to hard copy output. Microprocessors also simplify diagnostic displays, perform system checks, and make automatic returns to default settings.

Electronic copyboards are another new development in copiers. Sold under a number of different brand names, the copyboards are plastic panels on which information is written with water-based markers. Data can then be digitized by an image sensor. The electronic data can then be printed or copied onto paper. Industry analysts believe that ten companies, most of them foreign, were selling electronic copyboards by the end of 1986, with sales reaching about 40,000 units.

Foreign Trade

U.S. exports of photographic equipment and supplies in 1986 rose 5 percent, to $2.1 billion, after declining nearly 15 percent in 1985. The weakening of the U.S. dollar helped to boost sales in foreign markets. Photocopying and microfilming equipment was the only product grouping to decline in sales during the year. The 5 percent drop in exports of these products, to about $400 million, was partly due to an increase in U.S. overseas subsidiary production. Sensitized film, paper, and plates, the largest export category, rose 2 percent, to $1.2 billion. Both still and motion picture equipment exports rose about 15 percent, and photographic chemical exports were up 7 percent during the year.

In contrast to U.S. production and exports, imports of photographic products rose sharply in 1986, by 23 percent, reaching $4 billion. The increase exceeded the compound annual import growth rate of 11 percent for the 1981–85 period. Japan supplied about 70 percent of the import total. Although substantial increases in the yen's value occurred during 1986, photographic prices in the U.S. market have risen only slightly. Japanese manufacturers relied on other ways to offset the impact of the yen's strength in an effort to maintain market share and competitiveness, especially in sensitized products.

Photocopying and micrographics equipment imports rose 35 percent in 1986 and accounted for the largest share (40 percent) of the import total of $1.6 billion. Still picture equipment followed with one-third of the total, or $1.3 billion. About half the value of this category is attributed to 35mm cameras. Imports of sensitized film, paper, and plates rose about 15 percent and exceeded $1 billion for the first time.

Parallel imports, more commonly referred to as "gray market" goods, lessened during 1986 because of the decreased value of the U.S. dollar in relation to other world currencies. These exchange rate fluctuations resulted in higher prices for imported cameras and reduced the profit margins for gray marketeers. In addition, the campaign by various trade groups to educate consumers, along with state laws requiring retailers to inform consumers before they purchase gray market goods, helped to bring attention to the problem.

OUTLOOK FOR 1987

Some growth will likely occur among the wide range of products manufactured by the U.S. photographic industry. Any gains will be offset by declines in mature product markets, however. As a result, shipments are expected to remain at the 1986 level.

Many of the same competitive factors that have caused sluggish shipments in previous years will persist in 1987. Manufacturers will continue to restrain operating costs as they broaden product lines and test nontraditional products and markets.

Although U.S. imports will continue to outpace export growth, a continuation of favorable exchange rates and a healthy demand in foreign markets should help improve the U.S. export outlook.

LONG-TERM PROSPECTS

The photographic industry should experience periods of growth among its present diverse product offerings. Manufacturers will increase efforts to integrate traditional photographic technologies with emerging electronic technologies, which will result in broader product lines. Because of their initial high costs, many new electronic imaging products will be designed for the professional and industrial end-use markets.

The blurring of technologies in the office environment will lead to further refinements in digital copiers and the integration of previously separate functions such as copying, printing, and electronic mail. Further applications of imaging and printing will result in an increase of dual-purpose machines capable of desktop publishing.

The introduction of new products for the consumer market will be necessary to sustain interest in photographic equipment. Consumer electronic products, such as video cameras, video cassette recorders, and even home personal computers, will compete for consumers' disposable income.

Continued competition from foreign suppliers in both traditional and emerging products and further original equipment manufacturing agreements will cause U.S. producers to lose share in the U.S. market.

During the next 5 years, as the U.S. photographic industry moves into a period of transition from silver-halide products to electronic imaging, a period of very slow growth, with shipments not exceeding 2 percent compounded annually, is to be expected.

ADDITIONAL REFERENCES

Manufacturers' Shipments, Inventories and Orders, Current Industrial Reports, M3-1 (monthly) Bureau of the Census. U.S. Department of Commerce, Washington, DC 20233.

Wolfman Report on the Photographic Industry in the United States, 1985–86. ABC Leisure Magazines, Inc., 825 Seventh Avenue, New York, NY 10019.

Photographic Trade News. PTN Publishing Corporation, 210 Crossways Park Drive, Woodbury, NY 11797.

Photo Marketing. Photo Marketing Association International, 3000 Picture Place, Jackson, MI 49201.

"The Photofinishing Industry Report," *Photofinishing News,* 548 Goffle Road, Hawthorne, NJ 07506.

CASE 19

Mary Kay Cosmetics, Inc.

PHYLLIS G. HOLLAND
Valdosta State College

The story of the founding of Mary Kay Cosmetics, Inc., has been recounted in newspapers from Dallas to Wall Street. The version presented below is that of Mary Kay Ash herself in a speech which the company distributes.

I would like to take you back in time with me just how many years is none of your business—for as many of you know, I am a great-grandmother now, and I contend that a woman who would tell her age would tell anything. Nevertheless, let's go back to those early days, and I want you to picture in your mind a young wife and mother desperately in need of extra money for her family.

It was before the day of baby sitters and nurseries to keep your children, and so I had to depend upon kind neighbors and members of my family to help with my children if I were to work, so I decided upon the Stanley Home Products Company as a career, for it enabled me to be able to spend a few hours a day away from home and yet be able to be with my children some, too.

I had been with the Company just three weeks, and I was the worst recruit they ever had. After three weeks my Stanley Party average was, would you believe, $7.00—and when you consider that in those days we were giving away a $4.99 mop and duster when we walked across the Hostess's threshold, and then I sold only $7.00—I was in deep trouble.

Some of those Stanley dealers said they were selling $200 and $300 a week, but when you are selling $7.00, it is hard to believe.

However, they began to talk about a convention they were going to in the wicked city of Dallas. (I lived in Houston.) I was so well-traveled that I had never been to Dallas because it was 240 miles away. What they said about what they were going to learn at that convention intrigued me no end, and I decided that I just had to go.

There was a problem, however. It cost $12.00. That $12.00 paid for the chartered train fare, and it also paid for the hotel room—but nobody mentioned whether it included food for those three days, so I decided to take along a little sustenance.

I had no luggage, so I dumped out my Stanley suitcase, and that became my luggage. In my luggage I placed a box of crackers and a pound of cheese—and my other dress.

They talked about all the other clothes that they were going to wear and what not—but I really had none, so my luggage was packed in a hurry, and I went to that convention.

Reprinted by permission of the author.

On that train they did some very strange things. They sang some stupid songs like—

> "S-T-A-N-L-E-Y, Stanley all the time,
> That's the slogan you will hear
> Buzzing, buzzing in your ear."

I was so embarrassed that I pretended not to be part of those people.

We went to the hotel, and I had no money for a bellman. Can't you imagine what the bellman must have thought after he took up my luggage and my just saying "Thank you."

During those three days, when the others would go out to eat, I would say, "Oh, would you excuse me, please. There is something I need to do in my room," and I would go and eat my cheese and crackers.

However, something marvelous happened to me during that convention. I sat on the very back row because, believe me, that's where I belonged. At that convention they crowned a girl Queen. They placed a crown on her head and they gave her as a gift an alligator bag. Sitting on that back row, a burning, consuming desire swelled up within me, and I decided on the spot that next year I was going to be Queen.

I considered that there were thousands of people between me and that Queen, but none with the desire like mine. At that convention they said, "Get a railroad track to run on." In those days, the Stanley Home Products Company had no manual, no guide, nothing to go by. We learned everything orally, person to person—so I went up to the Queen and begged her to put on a Stanley Party during the time that we would be at the convention. She finally agreed. I guess I must have been like a little girl licking her shoes, and she put on a Party for me. I took 19 pages of notes, which became my railroad track to run on.

At the convention, they also stressed, "Tell somebody what you are going to do." I decided that there was no use to fool around with all those people in between, and I marched up to the President of that company. (Incidentally, I wore a hat they laughed about for ten years, and the worst of it is, I didn't know about it for nine.)

I declared to the President of that large company, "Next year I am going to be Queen." Had he known to whom he was talking, he might have laughed, but he looked me in the eye, took my hand in his, and he said, "Somehow I think you will." Those five words were the beginning of a career, an ambition that burned within me that ultimately took me to the top.

Do I need to tell you that next year I really was Queen? They forgot to give the alligator bag, but you see, that didn't matter because that really wasn't the important thing. It was the achievement that really mattered.

I stayed on with them for 15 years, and then I joined a gift company and began selling decorative accessories for the home. In that company I rose to National Training Director in a matter of a couple of years, and I learned the joy that goes with helping women to achieve their dreams, too.

In 1963 I retired, after approximately 25 years in the selling field—but I retired only for a month. I found out why they say in the obituary columns, "And he retired last year." I lived across the street from a mortuary, and I almost called them. I really felt that I had no reason to get up in the morning.

Thus I began to write down all of the good things that the companies I had been with had done, and then all of the problems that we encountered. All of this was in preparation for writing a book on sales for women which, incidentally, has never happened.

As I read over the notes that I had made over a period of a laborious month, I decided, "Wouldn't this make a magnificent company." My whole objective was to give women the chance that I felt I had always been denied. I wanted to provide a company and a climate for women to be able to do anything in the world that they were smart enough to do.

Along with a marketing plan designed especially for women, I decided to go into a field that was extremely feminine—cosmetics—even though I knew nothing about cosmetics, except the product that I had decided to use I had used for ten years. I felt that it was truly superior and that it had not succeeded simply because the woman who owned it had not had the proper marketing ability.

On Friday, September 13, 1963, we launched the company. We had a little Sears Roebuck $9.95 shelf, one tier filled with cosmetics the day we opened, and nine people who were just slightly interested in helping me get this Company off the ground.

My husband had died one month to the day before we were to start our Company, and he was to have been the administrator. I knew nothing of administration, so my twenty-year-old son joined with me to take his place. When God closes a door, He always opens a window—and Richard was the window. I must say that I didn't recognize it at the time. How would you like to turn your life's savings over to a 20-year-old son to administrate? I admit that it was traumatic, but God in all His wisdom knew that He had given Richard an "IBM Brain." Just five years later that young man was awarded the "Man of the Year" award in Texas, an award never given before to a man under 50.

Today, fifteen years later, those nine people have turned into approximately 46,000—and the retail sales this past year were $100 million. We are now listed on the New York Stock Exchange.

The success of our Company lies in all the lives that have been touched—the homes that have been built, the college educations that have been provided for children who otherwise would not have had them, the orthodonists' bills that have been paid—because the success of the multitude of women who have reached down inside themselves and found the seeds of greatness that God has planted there and who have brought these seeds into fruition.[1]

By December 31, 1978, the number of employees of Mary Kay Cosmetics, Inc., had grown to 530, while the independent sales force of beauty consultants numbered over 40,000. The company's assets were valued at slightly over $36 million. Net sales have grown steadily from $2.5 million in 1967 to $53.7 million in 1975. Earnings per share were $1.17 in 1978.

Mary Kay Ash is now chairman of the board. She is both spokesperson and symbol for the company which bears her name. Mrs. Ash's son, Richard R. Rogers, who took administrative and financial responsibility for the new enterprise at the age of 20, is now president. Exhibit 1 contains data on the top management team.

In addition to the vice presidents, two heads of subsidiaries report to the president. Exhibit 2 indicates supervisory responsibilities of the top executives.

---

[1] Adapted from a P.M.A. rally speech.

STRATEGY IMPLEMENTATION AND CONTROL

EXHIBIT 1   Top Management of Mary Kay Cosmetics, Inc.

NAME	OFFICE	BACKGROUND
Mary Kay Ash	Chairman of the board	Home sales (25 years); founded the company in 1963
Richard R. Rogers (35)[1]	President	Joined the company at age 20; president since 1964
Gerald M. Allen (37)	Vice president, administration	Joined the company in 1968; attended Arlington State University
Richard C. Bartlett (36)	Vice president, marketing	Marketing vice president—jewelry direct sales company; director of marketing services (MK)
Monty C. Barber (48)	Vice president and secretary	Joined the company in 1968; law degree, University of Texas
Phil J. Bostley, Jr.	Vice president, operations	Joined company in 1977; B.S., Penn State University
Phil Glasgow	Vice president, sales	Joined company in 1974; B.S., Oklahoma State University
J. Eugene Stubbs (39)	Vice president, finance; treasurer	Joined the company in 1971
John C. Beasley (37)	Vice president, manufacturing	Consultant—Arthur Young; director, operations (MK)
Judy Wheelock	Vice president, personnel	Joined company in 1979; B.B.A., Texas Tech. University

[1] Age in parentheses

EXHIBIT 2   Managers and Staff Reporting to Top Executives

TITLE	NUMBER OF MANAGERS REPORTING
Vice president, administration	4
Vice president, legal; secretary	2
Vice president, marketing	6
Vice president, finance; treasurer	10
Vice president, manufacturing	40
Vice president, operations	24
Vice president, personnel	4

PRODUCT LINES

Mary Kay Cosmetics stresses skin care in its product lines. The basic line consists of five preparations which should be used in conjunction: Cleansing Creme, Skin Freshener, Magic Masque, Night Cream (a skin conditioner), and Day Radiance (a foundation makeup). The total retail price of the basic line is $27.50. Although the rate of usage varies with the customer, this represents about a 6 month's supply of most of the products. There is a guaranteed refund to customers who are not completely satisfied.

Other products include makeup items, toiletry items for men and women, hair-care products, and skin-care items for men (these are identical to the women's line except for the packaging). Some accessory items are sold to beauty consultants to be used as hostess gifts, and some holiday gift sets are sold as limited editions. Mary Kay limits the lines so that consultants can be thoroughly familiar with each product and maintain complete inventories. The contribution of each product line to total sales is shown in Exhibit 3.

The company budgeted approximately $1 million for research and development in 1978, principally for the improvement of existing products. The director of research, who reports to the vice president of manufacturing, is Myra Barker. She holds a doctorate in biochemistry.

SALES

Mary Kay cosmetics are sold through independent sales representatives, who are called beauty consultants. Each consultant solicits customers through home beauty shows. Typically a consultant will ask a friend or customer to invite four or five friends to her home to participate in a demonstration of Mary Kay skin-care products and makeup (see the "Appendix" for a description of a beauty show). The hostess receives a gift for her help. The consultant uses demonstration products from her Mary Kay beauty kit, which she has purchased for $65 from the company. (This price represents the cost of the kit and is the only initial investment required of a consultant.) Each guest at the show actually uses the skin-care products and applies the makeup under the supervision of the consultant. State laws requiring the licensing of cosmetologists prevent the consultant from actually applying the makeup to the customers.

An advantage of the party system is that the consultant does not waste time knocking on doors where no one is home. She knows that the women

EXHIBIT 3   Contribution to Total Sales by Product Line

	YEAR ENDED DECEMBER 31,				
	1978	1977	1976	1975	1974
Skin-care products (women)	50%	48%	48%	52%	52%
Skin-care products (men)	1	2	2	1	1
Makeup items	21	18	18	21	21
Toiletry items (women)	12	14	14	11	10
Toiletry items (men)	3	2	2	3	4
Accessories	3	12	11	12	12
Hair-care products	10	4	5	0	0
Total	100%	100%	100%	100%	100%

attending the show will be fairly receptive to her message because they made the effort to come and that her time will be well used in making presentations to several women at once rather than to one at a time. Most shows are held at night, according to Richard C. Bartlett, vice president for marketing, so that the increasing number of women in the work force does not constitute a problem. Reorders are placed by phone, and the consultants are trained to ask customers the most convenient time to call and "not to bug them."

Mary Kay consultants are able to fill orders on the spot because the limited product lines allow them to stock most of the popular items. A typical consultant maintains an inventory worth about $400 wholesale (retail value—$800). Sales are also made on an individual basis to customers who were originally contacted through a home beauty show or who may contact the consultant. Mary Kay is presently experimenting with the use of Master Charge and Visa credit cards. Mrs. Ash says, "Women are impulse buyers. They buy more if they can have it right away."

Sales are made from the company to the consultant on a cash-in-advance basis, and only cashier's checks or money orders are accepted in payment. The company will buy back at 90 percent of cost any undamaged merchandise on which a consultant has made a refund to the customer. The company will buy back at 90 percent of cost any undamaged merchandise which a consultant has on hand at the termination of her association with Mary Kay Cosmetics, Inc.

The distribution system involves only one wholesale sale (from company to consultant) and one retail sale (from consultant to customer). There are no franchises or exclusive territorial rights, and a consultant is always able to obtain a product directly from the company. Marketing and promoting the lines is separate from actual distribution; this separation is the essence of what the company calls its "dual distribution system." The purpose of this dual system is to provide maximum support for the consultants without lengthening the distribution channel (see Exhibit 4).

MARKETING AND MOTIVATION

Before a consultant sells a product to a customer, the company must sell itself to the consultant. The Mary Kay recruiting literature assures the consultant that she will be in business "for yourself, but not by yourself." Motivation and support for the efforts of the sales force come from the sales directors—all former consultants who have sold and recruited their way up the ladder. As part of the qualifying procedure, potential sales directors must demonstrate performance in sales, recruitment, and leadership, as well as other skills, and they must participate in company-sponsored training sessions in Dallas.

While sales directors may continue to sell the products directly, much of their time is taken in recruiting new consultants for their units and motivating and training consultants. Five regional training and distribution centers (Dallas, Atlanta, Los Angeles, Piscataway, New Jersey, and Chicago) provide meeting

EXHIBIT 4 The Dual Distribution System

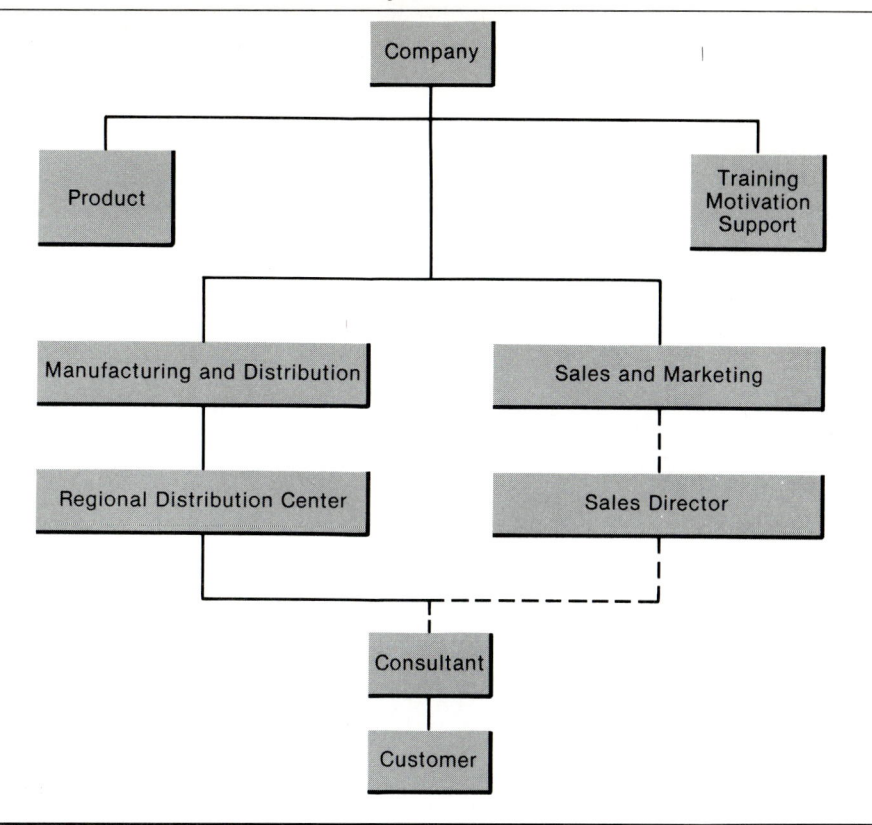

```
                          Company
              ┌──────────────┴──────────────┐
           Product                       Training
                                         Motivation
                                         Support

              ┌──────────────┬──────────────┐
    Manufacturing and Distribution   Sales and Marketing
              │                             │
    Regional Distribution Center       Sales Director
              │                             │
              └─────────────┬───── ─ ─ ─ ─ ─┘
                         Consultant
                            │
                         Customer
```

space for conference and workshops, although many local meetings are held in homes. The Mary Kay calendar is full of development opportunities:

July 1980	Jamboree and directors' meeting
September 1980	Leadership conference
January 1981	Seminar and directors' meeting

Each consultant also has the opportunity to attend weekly sales unit meetings, where problems are discussed and sales compaigns are introduced.

Personnel for the workshops include company executives, national sales directors, and sales directors. Much of the planning is done by the sales promotion department.

The seminar, to be held annually in January starting in 1980, is the high point of the sales year. Invitations must be earned by high performance, but as is the case for all conferences, participants must attend at their own expense. "Awards Night" at the 1978 jamboree was described in *The Wall Street Journal*:

The eyes of 7,500 Mary Kay beauty consultants are on the glittering black and silver stage set, dark except for a mountain of lighted stairs at stage center.

Then a sudden drum roll, and to the squeals, cheers and ecstatic applause of "her girls," Mary Kay Ash, company founder and chairwoman, rises slowly out of the top of the stairs on a hydraulic platform, like a golden figure emerging from a neon cake.

"Each of you can have all the applause," promises the round blond-wigged woman whose smooth face belies her 60-some years. "Each of you can have the spotlight." Dozens of the company's top saleswomen from the U.S., and Canada and Australia then proceed to claim just that onstage, along with expensive prizes—mink coats, gold and diamond jewelry, trips to Acapulco, and the use of new pale-pink Cadillacs and Buicks.

As she watches Mary Kay crown the 1978 Queen of Sales with a diamond tiara, a tearful consultant in the back row vows that she will be on stage next year. "I'm going to go home and sell Mary Kay to everything that moves," she says.[2]

RECRUITING AND COMPENSATION

No recruiting is done directly by the company, and no commissions are paid for recruiting, but the recruiter does receive a commission on the sales made by her recruit. Generous discounts and commissions are important recruiting tools. Consultants purchase cosmetics for resale at 50 percent of the suggested retail prices. They also may earn a commission on the sales of any recruits they have as long as both are active. For purposes of computing commissions, "active" is defined as maintaining $100 of wholesale sales per 3-month period. The commissions range from 4 percent to 8 percent, depending on the number of recruits the consultant has obtained.

Typical consultants' profits range from $600 to $800 a month for a 20-hour work week, according to company estimates. A typical consultant holds 1.5 parties a week. The 17 national sales directors earn an average of $56,000 annually, according to the company. The top-earning sales director in 1978 earned $118,000.

The company provides life insurance and disability insurance for sales directors and national sales directors.

Nonmonetary incentives are also provided to encourage the sales force. These incentives range from personal notes from Mrs. Ash to more substantial prizes, such as vacations, jewels, furs, and the use of a pink Buick Regal or a pink Cadillac for a year. (The Mary Kay account is much sought after by Texas car dealerships.)

Company survey data reveal the following facts about consultants:

1. The median age is 34.
2. Eighty percent are married.
3. Married consultants have 1.5 children at home.

---

[2] *The Wall Street Journal,* Sept. 28, 1978, p. 1.

4. The family income (including income from Mary Kay) is above average.
5. Consultants live in a suburb, small town, or rural area.

ADVERTISING

Most of Mary Kay's promotional spending is done to provide incentives for the sales force. Little money is spent on traditional advertising. Mrs. Ash says, "The company depends on word-of-mouth for publicity. It works. The three ways to get word out fast are telephone, telegraph, and tell a woman."

FINANCIAL DATA

Traditional financial data from annual reports are presented in Exhibits 5 and 6.

In 1976, the company began to buy its own stock, using both cash reserves and bank financing. Almost a million of the more than 5 million shares outstanding at the beginning of the program have been converted to treasury stock. Vice president of finance Eugene Stubbs commented, "Purchase of our own stock represents an attractive investment for us." The reduced number of shares outstanding resulted in an increase in earnings per share of 29 percent over 1976.

EXHIBIT 5   Consolidated Statement of Income
(in thousands)

	\multicolumn{4}{c}{YEAR ENDED DECEMBER 31}
	1978	1977	1976	1975
Net sales	$53,746	$47,856	$44,871	$34,947
Interest and other income, net	660	175	501	202
	$54,406	$48,031	$45,372	$35,149
Costs and expenses				
Cost of sales	$17,517	$14,562	$14,139	$10,509
Selling, general, and administrative expenses	27,402	21,394	19,192	15,050
Interest expense	504	212	43	60
	$45,423	$36,168	$33,374	$25,619
Income before income taxes	$ 8,983	$11,863	$11,998	$ 9,530
Provision for income taxes				
Current	$ 4,742	$ 5,590	$ 5,599	$ 4,365
Deferred	(632)	121	255	115
	$ 4,110	$ 5,711	$ 5,854	$ 4,480
Net income	$ 4,873	$ 6,152	$ 6,144	$ 5,050
Net income per common share	$ 1.17	$ 1.39	$ 1.26	$ 1.04
Cash dividends per share		$ 0.40	$ 0.36	$ 0.26

EXHIBIT 6 Consolidated Balance Sheet
(in thousands)

	YEAR ENDED DECEMBER 31			
	1978	1977	1976	1975
ASSETS				
Current assets				
Cash and cash equivalents	$ 4,048	$ 3,587	$ 6,734	$ 3,926
Accounts receivable	197	117	131	100
Inventories:				5,260
Raw materials	3,329	2,530	1,896	
Finished goods	3,189	4,551	3,992	
	6,518	7,081	5,888	
Prepaid taxes and expenses	1,031	280	313	303
Total current assets	$11,794	$11,065	$13,066	$ 9,589
Property, plant, and equipment, at cost	$27,848	$25,941	$21,810	$18,436
Less: Accumulated depreciation	4,931	3,752	2,962	2,047
	$22,917	$22,189	$18,848	$16,389
Other assets:				
Real estate not used in business, less accumulated depreciation	$ 1,066	$ 1,717	$ 1,295	$ 1,858
Cash surrender value of life insurance, net of policy loans	319	102	974	60
Other	209	71	148	100
	$ 1,594	$ 1,890	$ 2,417	$ 2,018
	$36,305	$35,144	$34,331	$27,996

	YEAR ENDED DECEMBER 31			
	1978	1977	1976	1975
LIABILITIES AND STOCKHOLDERS' EQUITY				
Current liabilities				
Accounts payable	$ 2,069	$ 2,533	$ 1,277	$ 1,105
Accrued liabilities	2,988	2,361	1,521	1,206
Income taxes	515	501	1,787	419
Dividends	498	417	486	388
Notes payable	—	—	16	22
Total current liabilities	$ 6,070	$ 5,812	$ 5,087	$ 3,140
Long-term debt	3,558	5,592	—	42
Deferred income taxes	730	756	637	412
Stockholders' equity	25,947	22,984	28,607	24,402
	$36,305	$35,144	$34,331	$27,996

On February 16, 1979, Mary Kay Cosmetics made an offer to purchase 700,000 shares of its common stock at $13 per share. (See Exhibit 7 for stock price data.) The company planned to finance the purchase with an unsecured long-term bank loan. Exhibit 8 depicts the *pro forma* effects of the offer,

EXHIBIT 7 Stock Prices

YEAR		HIGH	LOW
1977	First quarter	$20 3/8	$14 1/8
	Second quarter	15	13 1/4
	Third quarter	15 1/8	12 3/8
	Fourth quarter	14	10 3/4
1978	First quarter	12 7/8	10 7/8
	Second quarter	14	10 1/8
	Third quarter	12 5/8	10 1/8
	Fourth quarter	13 1/8	9
1979	First quarter		
	(through February 13)	11 1/2	9 1/4

EXHIBIT 8 Pro Forma Financial Statements

	DECEMBER 31, 1978	AS ADJUSTED FOR 350,000 SHARE TENDER (UNAUDITED)	AS ADJUSTED FOR 700,000 SHARE TENDER (UNAUDITED)
SELECTED BALANCE SHEET DATA AS OF DECEMBER 31, 1978			
Long-term indebtedness	$ 3,558,000	$ 8,397,000	$13,079,000
Stockholders' equity			
Preferred stock, $25 par value, 50,000 shares authorized, none issued	—	—	—
Common stock, $0.10 par value, 12,000,000 shares authorized, 4,906,676 issues	$ 491,000	$ 380,000	$ 345,000
Capital in excess of par value	7,642,000	4,338,000	3,365,000
Retained earnings	28,874,000	15,973,000	11,978,000
Less treasury shares, at cost	11,060,000	—	—
Total stockholders' equity	$25,947,000	$20,691,000	$15,688,000
Book value per share	$ 6.25	$ 5.44	$ 4.54
SELECTED INCOME STATEMENT DATA FOR THE YEAR ENDED DECEMBER 31, 1978			
Interest expense	$ 504,000	$ 1,307,000	$ 1,923,000
Net income	$ 4,873,000	$ 4,456,000	$ 4,135,000
Net income per common share outstanding	$ 1.17	$ 1.16	$ 1.19
Average common shares outstanding	4,176,000	3,826,000	3,476,000
Common shares outstanding at December 31, 1978	4,153,000	3,803,000	3,453,000

assuming tenders of 350,000 and 700,000 shares. The effects were explained further in the offer to purchase by the company:

> If a substantial amount is borrowed under the Loan Agreement, the Company will incur significant debt service requirements over the next several years. Application

or earnings to the payment of principal and interest will reduce funds that would otherwise be available for the payment of cash dividends, but the Company does not anticipate that the present level of dividends will need to be decreased in order to meet debt service requirements. The Loan Agreement imposes various restrictions, including restrictions on cash dividends, and requires the maintenance of operating ratios that could have the effect of restricting the payment of dividends. Under the most restrictive covenant in the Loan Agreement, the Company had $1,509,000 available for the payment of dividends at January 1, 1979.

The Company has under consideration the possibility of refinancing the loan at a more favorable fixed rate of interest. However, the Company has no commitment from any potential lender regarding refinancing of the loan, and there is no assurance that such refinancing could be arranged. In the absence of such refinancing, the Company expects to retire the indebtedness under the Loan Agreement from future earnings.

On February 13, 1979 (the last full day of trading on the New York Stock Exchange prior to the announcement by the company of its intention to make the offer), the closing price on the composite tape was $10⅛.

The company has made several purchases of common stock, as indicated in Exhibit 9. According to the company, such purchases are a "good investment," and the increased interest expense will be balanced by the decreased number of shares outstanding so that earnings per share will not be materially affected. Management denies any intention of "going private," avoiding SEC reporting requirements, or discontinuing its listing on the New York Stock Exchange.

As of January 31, 1979, directors and officers of the company and their spouses owned or voted an aggregate of 34.6 percent of the outstanding

EXHIBIT 9 Stock Purchases

PERIOD		NUMBER OF SHARES PURCHASED	RANGE OF PER-SHARE PURCHASE PRICES (EXCLUDING COMMISSION) Low	High	AVERAGE PER-SHARE PURCHASE PRICE (EXCLUDING COMMISSION)
1976	First quarter	0	—	—	—
	Second quarter	0	—	—	—
	Third quarter	0	—	—	—
	Fourth quarter	46,600	$17.75	$20.25	$18.50
1977	First quarter	293,400	15.125	15.50	15.20
	Second quarter	133,500	13.25	14.00	13.91
	Third quarter	265,771	13.375	13.75	13.74
	Fourth quarter	0	—	—	—
1978	First quarter	0	—	—	—
	Second quarter	0	—	—	—
	Third quarter	0	—	—	—
	Fourth quarter	14,000	10.125	10.125	10.125
1979	First quarter (through February 15, 1979)	0	—	—	—

common stock. Roughly half of this percentage was owned or controlled by Mrs. Ash and members of her family. None of these shares are expected to be tendered, so that the purchase will increase the voting power of directors and officers to 41.6 percent of the total shares entitled to be voted.

The financing arrangement has the following repayment schedule:

AMOUNT	DUE
$2,033,000	1979
2,033,000	1980
1,526,000	1981

The terms of the loan agreement limit the amount of additional debt which may be incurred and the amount of fixed assets which may be acquired, and future purchases of treasury stock and cash dividends may not exceed 75 percent of the consolidated net income of the preceding year.

Stock authorized and issued as of December 31, 1977, included:

Common stock ($0.10 par)	
Authorized	12,000,000 shares
Outstanding	4,906,676 shares
Treasury stock	739,271, shares
Preferred stock ($25 par)	
Authorized	50,000 shares
Issued	0 shares

There were stock splits in 1968, 1971, and 1973.

Mrs. Ash owned 15.7 percent of the outstanding shares at the end of 1977. Mr. Richard Rogers held 8.8 percent of the stock, and another son, Mr. Ben Rogers, held 5.7 percent. Approximately 8 percent of the outstanding stock is held in trusts for various family members. None of the other approximately 4000 stockholders held a significant percentage of the stock.

MANUFACTURING

Mary Kay's cosmetics (with the exception of eyebrow pencils) are formulated, processed, and packaged in its 240,000-square-foot Dallas manufacturing facility. Much of the equipment in the highly automated plant was designed and built by Mary Kay engineers. One feature of the design is the ease of converting from one product to another. This allows for flexibility in the production process, which, according to Mr. Bartlett, most other cosmetics manufacturers do not have.

Manufacturing costs have risen slowly, but the efficiency of the facility is credited by Mr. Bartlett as being the major reason why prices have not also risen steadily. Only three price increases have been recorded in 15 years, the latest in 1978. The company expected to be able to comply with federal price guidelines for 1979 without experiencing a profit squeeze.

All packaging materials are purchased, and much of the increase in manufacturing costs is attributed by company spokespeople to increased packaging costs. Many of the packages are made of either plastic, which is petroleum-based, or paper.

In addition to purchasing all packaging materials, the company purchases chemicals and essential oils for the manufacturing process. These are procured from a number of sources, and the company does not anticipate shortages. The company sells some of its products to other companies for marketing under their own brands, but these sales were less than 1 percent of total sales in 1977 and the 2 preceding years.

GROWTH

Mary Kay Cosmetics has grown through increases in the size and productivity of the sales force (see Exhibits 10 and 11). Growth has also come as a result of geographic expansion. The first distribution center was in Dallas; next, centers in Atlanta and Los Angeles were established. The center in New Jersey was added in 1975, and the newest center is in Chicago. The company has consultants in all 50 states, Puerto Rico, and Guam. Texas, Georgia, and California are leading states in the number of consultants, and Illinois is "coming on," according to Mr. Bartlett. There is a distribution center in each of these states. The Midwest, in Mr. Bartlett's words, has "a long way to go," and there is low penetration in the Northeast. In all regions, urban areas have a lower consultant-to-population ratio than suburbs, small towns, and rural areas.

Two subsidiaries market Mary Kay products internationally. The Canadian firm began operation in 1978, while the Australian subsidiary had 1610 consultants and 40 sales directors. The Australian operation accounted for 5 percent of consolidated net sales and 6 percent of consolidated net income in 1977. A symbol of the company's growth is the new international headquarters building in Dallas, located on the same property as the manufacturing plant. The headquarters facility cost $5.7 million, and its construction was internally financed. The company believes that the current facilities will support a sales level twice as large as that of 1977, or about $100 million in annual sales.

ORDER SYSTEM

The company leases a fleet of trucks to transport products from Dallas to the other regional centers. A common carrier is used to ship orders from regional

EXHIBIT 10   Growth of Beauty Consultants and Sales Directors
[Beauty consultants (dark) in thousands; sales directors (light) in hundreds.]

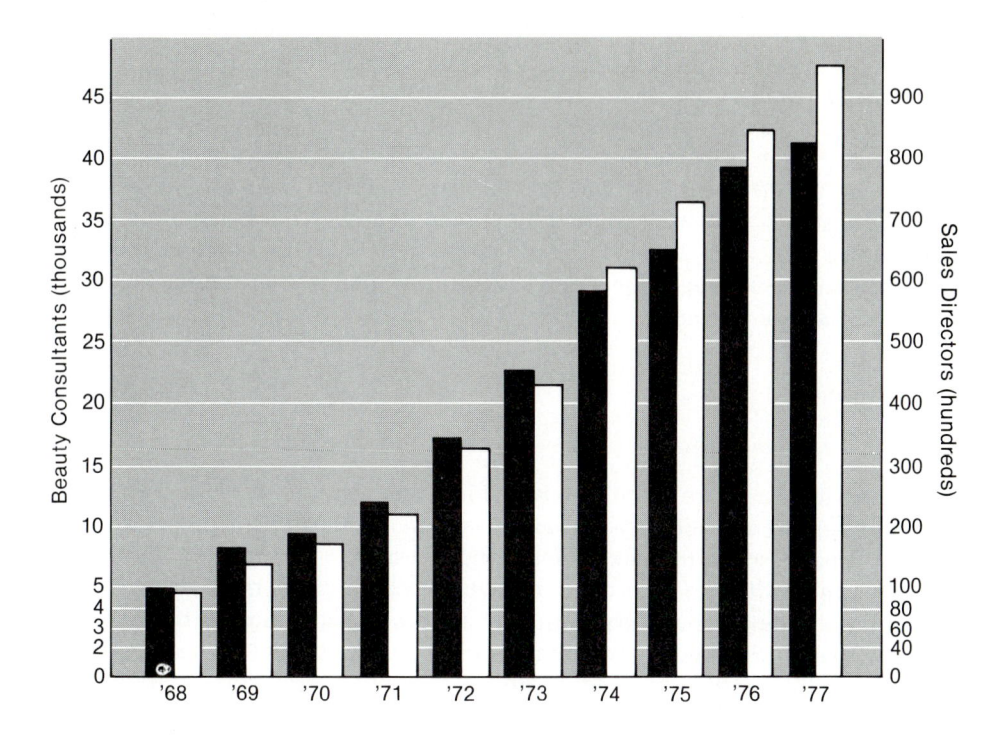

EXHIBIT 11   Productivity of Beauty Consultants and Sales Directors

	1977	1976	1975	1974	1973
Net sales (in thousands)	$47,856	$44,871	$34,947	$30,215	$22,199
Number of beauty consultants	38,630	35,199	32,401	27,662	20,458
Sales per consultant	$ 1,238	$ 1,274	$ 1,078	$ 1,092	$ 1,085
Number of sales directors	873	805	700	607	439
Sales per director	$54,817	$55,740	$49,924	$49,777	$50,567

centers to the consultants. The order system has been computerized so that orders are processed quickly and current information about sales by volume, product line, and sales unit is available to management. In 1977, the company achieved zero back orders.

PERSONNEL

Mary Kay employs approximately 530 people to manufacture, distribute, and promote its products. The majority are at company headquarters and the manufacturing facility in Dallas. None of the employees are represented by a union. Wages and benefits are described as comparable to those of similar firms in the Dallas area.

Although the company has women in some management positions (such as vice president of personnel, director of product marketing, and director of research and development) and Mrs. Ash is active in company affairs, one executive stated, "We wish we had more women in key roles—after all, this is a women's company." He also pointed out that the sales directors and national sales directors, though independent, are an essential part of the management team and are all female.

THE FUTURE

In discussing the future of the company, Mr. Bartlett emphasized the company's commitment to a quality product and to the methods which it presently uses. The company seeks to make its products "safer, easier to use, better for people" and to "make sure that we have solved all problems we can see for the future." The company is continually alert to the activities of the FDA, and when it learns of a new investigation, it immediately checks on its own use of the agent in question and looks for a substitute. Mr. Bartlett cited the investigation and subsequent banning of red dye number 2 as an example. Although the company used the dye not in lipstick but in skin freshener, where "the possibility of ingestion was as remote as my [Mr. Bartlett] going to Venus," it looked for alternatives when it heard of the investigation and was "not caught flat-footed" like others when the ban was announced.

Mr. Bartlett felt that the company was leading a cosmetics industry trend toward "more attention to the product itself. Cosmetics has put a lot of emphasis on fashion—'hope in a jar'—and not enough on what the product actually does for the customer. We have always been interested in providing products for good skin care and training the customer to use them properly."

The company has built its new facility to allow considerable growth, but it contemplates few basic changes. According to Mr. Bartlett:

> We are very conservative about line extensions, are cool to acquisitions and lukewarm to international expansion. Our Australian and Canadian subsidiaries are doing well but we aren't making an overt effort to expand into other international markets.
>
> We follow the simple country philosophy of Darrell Royal, a former football coach at the University of Texas, who said, "Dance with the one that brung you." Our methods have "brung" us a long way and we'll stay with them.

Future growth is expected to come from increased market penetration, both in urban areas and in all regions. "We will continue to do what we do best," said Mr. Bartlett. "Avon sales volume is not our goal. Sheer size is not a corporate objective. It is to have the finest skin care company in the world."

Appendix

A Mary Kay Beauty Show

In a living room in North Dallas, Zoe Hall, an 11-year veteran of Mary Kay home beauty shows, is telling three women how Mary Kay cosmetics evolved from the experiments of a tanner who used hide-tanning principles on his own skin and, at age 73, was said to have a remarkably youthful appearance.

Nicki, a perky Dallas woman, has come to the show at the urging of friends who were "overjoyed with the product," she says. Hazel and Dixie, two skeptical women from nearby Irving, Texas, were invited over their C.B. radio in a highway conversation with another Mary Kay consultant.

In front of each woman is a mirror and a square styrofoam palette with blobs of cream, different shades of foundation and rouge, and little heaps of colored powders. As Mrs. Hall gives instructions, each woman uses the cleansing cream, the oatmeal masque, and the skin toner and applies her own face and eye makeup.

Mrs. Hall has diagnosed Dixie's skin as especially oily and prescribes Mary Kay's special water-based products. "Oh, this is your lucky day," she exclaims, patting Dixie excitedly on the arm. Mrs. Hall has no doubt about the outcome of her sales talk. "You're going to be so pleased when you take this home," she tells Dixie.

Assuming a sale is part of the positive psychology the consultants are taught by their sales directors and their Mary Kay handbooks. "Nod your head yes when you're talking to your customers," Beverly Sutton, a senior sales director from Tulsa, told 300 consultants at a seminar class on selling techniques. "Look them in their right eye because the right eye controls—that's also a form of hypnosis. Phrase questions to get a yes answer. Touch the customer often to show you care. And when it comes time to sell, give them a full, complete set of all the products. If they hold it all, they'll want it all."

With Mrs. Hall's help, Nicki, Hazel, and Dixie have finished making up their faces, and with Mrs. Hall's help, they now are making up their minds about which Mary Kay products they can't live without. "You can really feel the difference in your skin, can't you?" Mrs. Hall asks, nodding.

Editor's note: This account is from a story by Beth Nissen, "Mary Kay Sales Agents Zero in on Prospects in Their Living Rooms" (*The Wall Street Journal*, Sept. 28, 1978, pp. 1, 24).

Hazel nods back. She buys $54 worth of Mary Kay products and wants to buy more, but can't afford to. Mrs. Hall tells her she can earn the money for more: Hazel can invite Mrs. Hall to come to her home in Irving to give a show to six of her friends. Hazel agrees. As the hostess, Hazel will get 10 percent of Mrs. Hall's sales in retail-value Mary Kay merchandise at that show—15 percent or 20 percent if she can get one or two of those friends to host shows, too. Mrs. Hall will get access to six new customers plus a chance to book more shows.

Nicki is so impressed that she is recruited to be a consultant herself. She buys $32 worth of Mary Kay and agrees to talk with Mrs. Hall later over coffee about the Mary Kay opportunity.

Dixie alone is unconverted. She says "no," she doesn't think she'll take anything today. But to Mary Kay consultants, "no" isn't a final answer. "Remember," reads the Mary Kay consultants' handbook, "when a woman says 'No' she means 'Maybe,' and when a woman says 'Maybe,' she means 'Yes.'" "O-Oh," Mrs. Hall says ruefully to Dixie, "and the special cream did such nice things for your problem skin. Isn't there some way you could take this home with you so you can get started on good skin care right away?" Alarmed by Mrs. Hall's tone of emergency, Dixie sneaks a worried look at herself in the mirror and says, "Well, maybe. . . ." She takes $37 worth of special skin products home to Irving with her.

At this afternoon's show, Mrs. Hall sells $123 worth of merchandise, retail. She will keep 50 percent of today's sales—$61.50 for 3 hours work.

INDUSTRIAL HIGHLIGHT

Cosmetics Industry

Below is a capsule summary of the cosmetics industry, of which Mary Kay Cosmetics, Inc., is a part. Information in this highlight was compiled by the U.S. Department of Commerce and focuses on this industry during the approximate period of time covered in the case. Keep in mind that industrial highlights contained in this text are not intended as a complete synopsis of an industry but as a profile of certain issues that can be relevant to a case situation.

CURRENT SITUATION

Cosmetics manufacturers are placing new emphasis on cost controls—streamlining operations with moderate capital expense; improving quality and productivity through advanced manufacturing practices under government guidelines; more effective materials management; and exercising better selectivity in choices of new product development projects to increase return on R&D investment.

Private label products will continue sales increases in 1978, but at a rate slower than established earlier in the seventies. Supermarket sales of cosmetics, toiletries and fragrances are becoming more pronounced as companies vie for increased mass market opportunities.

Manufacturers are adopting a more personalized approach to the sale of beauty products. There is an ongoing trend towards workable products that are within financial reach of the majority of cosmetics, toiletries and fragrance buyers.

The cosmetic industry's "free wheeling" entrepreneurial system is fast giving way to a more formalized, structured management which tends to dampen innovation. However, there is still a place for entrepreneurs. They have the flexibility to move quickly to take advantage of new product opportunities presented by changes in fashion, distribution or some other facet of the market.

Product liability claims are on the increase even though the industry has

Source: U.S. Industrial Outlook, Department of Commerce, 1978, pp. 133–136.

EXHIBIT A 1977 Profile[1]

COSMETICS
SIC Code: 2844

Value of industry shipments ($ million)	5,940
Number of establishments[2]	650
Total employment (thousands)	50
Exports as a percent of industry shipments	2.3
Imports as a percent of apparent consumption	0.8
Net profits as a percent of net worth	17.0
Compound annual rate of growth 1967–77 (percent):	
Value of industry shipments (current dollars)	9.0
Value of exports (current dollars)	18.0
Value of imports (current dollars)	13.7
Employment	1.8
Major Producing Areas—Northeast and North-Central Regions	

[1] Estimated by Bureau of Domestic Commerce.
[2] 1972 Census of Manufacturers.

a good record of safety. Liability insurance premiums are rising and there are some areas in which new product development has declined due to concern over potential liability claims.

Industry Perspective

There are about 1,000 cosmetic firms marketing 20,000 brands in the U.S. Ten firms account for about 55 percent of the business and 65 percent of the earnings.

From 1972–78, cosmetic product shipments are estimated to increase from $4.2 billion to $6.5 billion, an annual growth rate of 7.3 percent. Of this total, fragrances will have increased from $677 million to $1.1 billion for an annual growth rate of 8 percent. Hair preparations are estimated to rise from $1.1 billion in 1972 to $1.6 billion in 1978, at a 6.4 percent rate. Oral hygiene product shipments, valued at $485 million in 1972, are expected to move up to $638 million, for a modest increase of 4.5 percent per year.

A number of other products are expected to increase substantially in sales during 1978. Skin treatment products will have the greatest increase as the trend continues toward use of various moisturizers. Lipsticks and glosses, nail care products, male toiletries, makeup, and skin and sun-care products will also enjoy above average sales growth.

Cosmetic prices have increased only moderately since 1967 and are considerably below increases for many other commodities. The Wholesale Price Index at the end of 1977 is expected to have reached 144, as compared to the index for all commodities estimated at 195.

Marketing Perspectives

Consumers will use more care in selecting new products. They rely on known products, especially for skin care.

Smaller manufacturers may have more difficulty introducing new products because of increased brand name consciousness of the consumer.

In 1978, women will become more innovative in the use of cosmetics. Consequently, there will be more interest in fashion coordination, using cosmetics and fragrances.

Men and women are placing more emphasis on how to enjoy life rather than on how to make a living. Lifestyles vary and certain cosmetic products are associated with particular styles and fashion. These trends are certain to encourage more consumption of a variety of cosmetics, toiletries, and fragrances associated with a variety of daily routines.

Consumers are more knowledgeable in the purchase of cosmetic products. They are becoming more vocal concerning their likes and dislikes, expecting more from the industry and getting it.

Although a majority of consumers prefer major brands of cosmetics, there appears room for the private label companies, especially in mass merchandising arrangements such as supermarkets.

The market for cosmetic products is a big one. Almost half of all women work outside the home, most making frequent use of some forms of cosmetics and fragrances each day.

Fragrances

Fragrances are no longer seasonal. Various types of perfumes, colognes and toilet waters are purchased and used throughout the year to fit any number of different lifestyles.

The fragrance market is growing rapidly for a number of reasons: 1) considered part of good grooming, 2) more acceptance by men; 3) use of a variety of types; 4) use at younger ages; 5) more spending on luxuries; and 6) innovative marketing.

Most women in the U.S. use some form of fragrance product. An appreciation by women of a variety of fragrance strengths will create larger fragrance collections.

Fragrance sales will continue to outpace sales of cosmetics and toiletries but the competition in 1978 will be keener and the cost of new fragrance introductions higher.

Fragrance products are expected to move into such mass marketing areas as supermarkets. Distribution calls for good first impressions, samples and testers will increase and augment point of purchase and media promotion to assist consumers in choosing fragrances.

Fragrance sales represent about one fifth of the cosmetic, toiletry and fragrance product shipments. This share is increasing.

About 25 fragrances are capturing the majority of U.S. consumer sales. Over half of these are of U.S. manufacture. Reproductions of more expensive perfumes continue to make headway in the market.

Women will continue to buy fragrances for men, but this practice is changing due to promotional efforts aimed at men. There is also a consumer swing towards male use of colognes and skin moisturizers instead of after-shave lotions.

Ethnic Markets

Ethnic cosmetics, designed for particular shades and textures of skin, are developing into a fast selling line of products aimed primarily at the Black market, estimated at $500 million in sales potential per year.

The ethnic market demands a better understanding—more study—to evolve new products that will sustain the sales growth rate.

International Marketing

Exports of cosmetic, toiletries and fragrancies are estimated to reach $152 million in 1978, an increase of 10 percent over 1977. Between 1972–78 exports will have increased more than 3.5 times, while imports will have risen only about twice the 1972 level. In 1978, exports will exceed imports by $104 million, or three times more. In 1972, exports exceeded imports by only $20 million.

The trend towards a more favorable balance of trade will continue as exports continue to rise faster than imports. Disposable income abroad is increasing allowing more purchase of U.S. cosmetics, toiletries, and fragrances.

Although industry trade balance is good, exports could increase more substantially. U.S. firms do not dominate foreign markets. Foreign cosmetic manufacturers are big and getting bigger—and more are considering establishing U.S. operations.

The major foreign markets for cosmetics, toiletries, and fragrances are France, West Germany, Belgium, Italy, the United Kingdom, and the Netherlands. New markets are emerging in eastern Europe, the Middle East, and Africa.

Many U.S. firms, large and small, are looking to enter or expand their international markets. The task is difficult but it will result in greater corporate earnings and diversification.

Regulation

The cosmetic industry has embarked upon a self-regulatory program called the Cosmetic Ingredient Review (CIR), to determine which ingredients can be used safely and which should not. The CIR aims to simplify for cosmetic manufacturers the evaluation of product safety and reduce the burden of long-term testing.

EXHIBIT B Drug and Cosmetics Trade Surplus Increasing

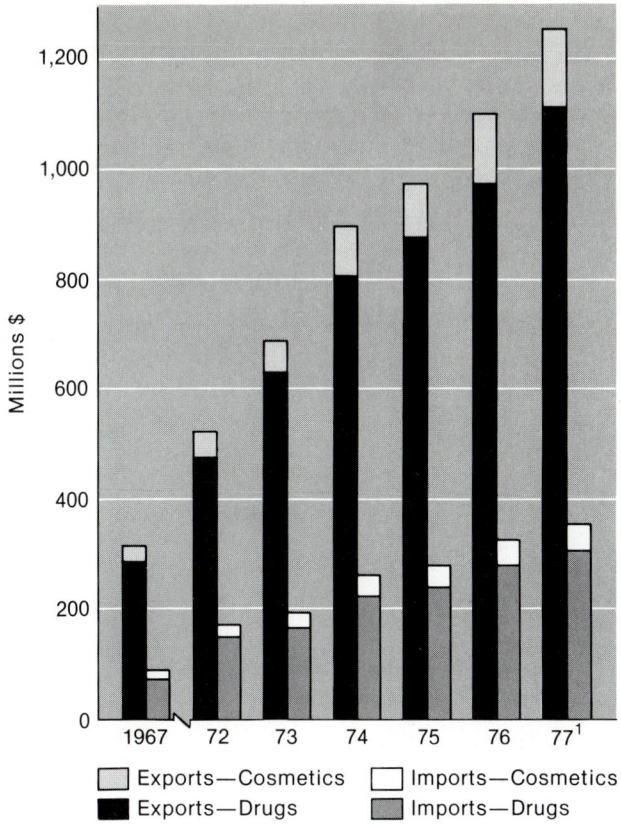

[Bar chart showing exports and imports of cosmetics and drugs in millions of dollars for years 1967, 72, 73, 74, 75, 76, 77¹. Legend: Exports—Cosmetics, Exports—Drugs, Imports—Cosmetics, Imports—Drugs.]

¹ Estimated.
Source: Bureau of the Census and BDC.

Consumer's safety is of prime importance and a direct challenge to the industry. There is growing emphasis by individual firms, large and small, on the evaluation of product safety. These quality assurance programs will involve more time, care, effort, and expense but are a necessary part of future cosmetic production.

More Federal government regulation of the cosmetic industry has been proposed but probably will not be forthcoming in 1978. However, additional regulation of the cosmetic industry appears inevitable.

LONG-TERM PROSPECTS

The outlook for continued annual growth in sales of cosmetics, toiletries and fragrances is excellent. By 1982 the value of product shipments in constant

1977 dollars should equal $7.4 billion, a real growth rate of 4.3 percent per year.

The consumer will be more knowledgeable in purchase of cosmetic products.

Future developments will be: 1) better skin moisturizers; 2) more effective anti-perspirants; 3) better hair coloring products; 4) more effective wrinkle masking and other geriatric treatment; 5) more involvement of the pharmaceutical industry in cosmetic products; and 6) more and better ethnic products.

CASE 20

Hines Industries, Inc.

ROBERT P. CROWNER
Eastern Michigan University

In June, 1984 Gordon Hines, the President of Hines Industries, Inc., reflected upon the first quarter of the 1985 fiscal year with mixed feelings. His marketing strategy of "niching" had been successful. He had started his second company in sixteen years when he began Hines Industries in 1979. The first three years were characterized by rapid growth in sales but the recession took its toll in 1983. Exhibits 1, 2, and 3 show the Balance Sheet, Income Statement, and Expense Statements for the fiscal years 1981 through 1984. The first quarter of 1985 looked like it would be near the entire sales of 1984 and a profit of 12% to 15% should be produced. Maybe this high growth rate would produce a new set of problems.

Gordon Hines is not new to the entrepreneur ranks. In February, 1968 he founded Balance Technology, Inc., in Ann Arbor, Michigan which manufactures and markets balancing equipment and vibration instruments. Bal Tec grew rapidly but Gordon lost absolute control of the company when he needed outside money, a mistake he is determined to not make again. Eventually he was squeezed out of the management and finally sold his stock at a considerable profit to an outsider who in turn squeezed out the management that followed Gordon.

Gordon Hines has an unusual background in relation to the businesses he founded. He has a degree in psychology and at one time was a social worker for the Chicago YMCA. Later, while selling insurance, he successfully sold policies to two partners in a balancing equipment company who really did not have the funds to buy insurance. They were so impressed by Gordon's sales ability that they made him an offer to enter their business. Gordon accepted and soon was successfully selling machines and became involved in redesigning and improving them as well.

Gordon, who is 54, has a natural aptitude for visualizing how things look and work and can quickly conceptualize his ideas. He is a problem solver. His

---

The research and written case information were presented at a Case Research Symposium and were evaluated by the Case Research Association's Editorial Board. This case was prepared by Robert P. Crowner, Associate Professor of Management of Eastern Michigan University, as a basis for class discussion.

Copyright © 1984 by Robert P. Crowner

Distributed by the Case Research Association. All rights reserved to the author and the Case Research Association. Permission to use this case should be obtained from the Case Research Association.

EXHIBIT 1 Hines Industries, Inc. Balance Sheet, Years Ending February 28

ASSETS	1981	1982	1983	1984
Current Assets				
Cash	$ 9,005	$ 5,027	$ 11,361	$ 26,707
Accounts Receivable	96,509	124,905	129,413	215,222
Inventories				
Materials	60,448	33,715	83,176	269,268
Work in Process	35,656	135,031	21,794	45,219
	$ 96,104	$168,746	$104,970	$314,487
Loan Receivable, officer				49,935
Total Current Assets	201,618	298,678	245,744	606,351
Property and Equipment				
Leasehold Improvements	7,386	7,386	7,386	7,386
Machinery and Equipment	21,894	38,871	52,358	96,188
Office Equipment	5,451	7,680	13,604	29,557
Transportation Equipment	0	19,933	30,247	58,768
Leasehold Interest in Communication Equipment	5,060	5,060	5,060	5,060
	$ 39,791	$ 78,930	$108,655	$196,959
Less Depreciation	6,485	20,747	42,084	82,258
	$ 33,306	$ 58,183	$ 66,571	$114,701
Intangible Assets	108	81	596	27
	$235,032	$356,942	$312,911	$721,079

LIABILITIES AND STOCKHOLDERS' EQUITY	1981	1982	1983	1984
Current Liabilities				
Notes Payable, Bank	$ 40,000	$ 0	$ 69,300	$170,000
Current Portion of Long-term Debt	6,632	2,626	12,100	27,353
Accounts Payable	77,273	88,765	72,432	181,684
Accrued Expenses	13,896	28,150	29,630	49,047
Accrued Taxes	5,930	8,579	6,748	20,288
Customer Deposits	30,074	117,513	10,000	218,091
Total Current Liabilities	$173,805	$245,633	$200,210	$666,463
Long-term Debt	6,051	67,131	25,178	24,641
Stockholders' Equity				
Common Stock, $1 par Value, 100,000 shares, 70,000 issued	70,000	70,000	70,000	70,000
Retained Earnings	(14,824)	(25,822)	17,523	(40,025)
	$ 55,176	$ 44,178	$ 87,523	$ 29,975
	$235,032	$356,942	$312,911	$721,079

father was an engineer and took Gordon into work on weekends with him so that Gordon learned early about machinery and the engineering behind machinery. He completed two years of engineering work at the University of Illinois before his intense interest in people drew him toward psychology.

EXHIBIT 2 Hines Industries, Inc. Income Statement, Years Ending February 28

	1981	1982	1983	1984
Net Sales	$394,498	$634,767	$1,114,201	$1,434,912
Cost of Sales				
Material	158,364	269,957	373,713	381,268
Direct Labor	36,345	107,362	174,321	209,747
Subcontract	63,842	27,514	8,288	7,063
Drafting	3,716	7,335	11,078	43,322
Installation	0	2,900	3,567	18,100
Manufacturing Overhead	27,605	80,317	207,173	281,656
	$289,872	$495,385	$ 778,140	$ 941,156
Gross Profit	104,626	139,382	336,061	493,756
Operating Expenses				
Research and Development	10,945	5,506	25,750	53,449
Selling Expenses	36,498	54,084	131,851	302,048
General and Administrative Expenses	68,204	79,000	128,123	173,892
	$115,647	$138,590	$ 285,724	$ 529,389
Operating Income	(11,021)	792	50,337	(35,633)
Nonoperating Income (Expense)				
Interest Income	0	0	0	790
Interest Expense	(4,473)	(11,790)	(6,992)	(22,705)
Miscellaneous	670	0	0	0
	$ (3,803)	$ (11,790)	$ (6,992)	$ (21,915)
Income Before Taxes	$ (14,824)	$ (10,998)	$ 43,345	$ (57,548)

It is certainly a fair statement to say that Gordon Hines is Hines Industries. His creativity is in evidence everywhere—marketing, design, manufacturing, and even finance.

PRODUCTS

Hines Industries presently has five basic product lines which are shown in Exhibit 4. These machines are known as hard bearing balancing machines. They come in a number of different models with different features as shown in the exhibit. All of the lines are available with microprocessor analyzers. The DL, Drive Line Balancing Machine, and the HC, Hard Crankshaft Balancing Machine, were the products which were first developed. The HC500A model has been sold to more than 120 customers in 33 states and 4 foreign countries. The HC Balancer is sold primarily to the automotive aftermarket for high performance and racing cars.

The DL line is used to balance the drive shaft for cars and trucks. Because of the heavy weights and usage given to trucks, their drive shafts, unlike cars,

EXHIBIT 3   Hines Industries, Inc. Years Ending February 28

	1981	1982	1983	1984
Manufacturing Overhead				
Supervisory Labor	$ 0	$ 0	$ 47,103	$ 67,654
Indirect Labor	2,638	2,829	8,635	12,640
Payroll Taxes	2,995	8,827	22,476	43,585
Insurance	2,662	6,469	26,642	37,200
Depreciation	3,469	10,874	15,019	22,710
Freight	4,799	14,118	13,657	30,099
Utilities	2,169	5,288	7,438	9,453
Maintenance	79	272	789	2,117
Tools	1,150	2,414	5,408	12,398
Rent	13,172	36,252	41,404	44,929
Supplies	4,618	4,442	7,885	10,584
Overhead Variance	(10,146)	(11,468)	10,717	(11,713)
Total	$27,605	$80,317	$207,173	$281,656
Selling Expense				
Advertising	$ 0	$ 0	$ 0	$ 8,175
Commissions	13,509	33,150	75,082	184,879
Payroll	0	0	20,990	35,747
Sales Promotion	11,616	11,158	18,018	49,460
Payroll Taxes	0	0	2,101	4,382
Travel and Entertainment	11,373	9,776	15,660	19,405
Total	$36,498	$54,084	$131,851	$302,048
General and Administrative Expenses				
Auto Operation	$ 8,171	$ 6,275	$ 6,473	$ 2,439
Airplane	510	3,408	3,688	1,876
Bad Debts	0	0	15,616	4,255
Contributions	0	270	394	3,741
Depreciation	1,332	3,388	8,586	17,464
Dues and Subscriptions	32	128	253	434
Equipment Rental	0	647	5,053	6,459
Insurance	1,785	724	8,641	13,956
Professional Fees	3,111	4,990	3,764	12,468
Maintenance and Repairs	0	382	0	1,048
Miscellaneous	942	1,761	2,175	2,511
Office Supplies	3,127	4,047	7,455	7,110
Clerical Payroll	24,781	35,046	39,083	65,275
Payroll Taxes	4,473	4,628	4,509	7,746
Sales Tax	406	273	715	667
Michigan Single Business Tax	219	960	3,900	4,100
Other Taxes	220	185	2,246	1,586
Telephone	8,515	11,888	15,572	20,757
Officer Salary	10,580	0	0	0
Total	$68,204	$79,000	$128,123	$173,892

EXHIBIT 4 Product Sheet

HINES

HARD BEARING BALANCING MACHINES

Standard features of Hines Balancers:

ELECTRONIC DIGITAL READOUT
PERMANENT CALIBRATION
DIRECT INDICATION OF ANGLE
AMOUNT IN OUNCES OR GRAMS
COMPLETE TOOLING PACKAGES

Hines Industries manufactures a variety of balancers for different applications, all of which are available with **Microprocessor Analyzers.**

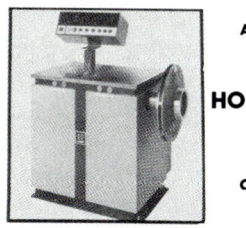

HO

ADDITIONAL STANDARD FEATURES:
- Single and two plane correction
- On machine correction capacity
- Automatic cycle
- Total enclosure of mechanicals
- Handles small and large unbalances
- Dynamic braking

OPTIONS AVAILABLE:
- Microprocessor analyzer
- Segmenting
- Tolerance function

APPLICATION:
Specifically designed for overhung part balancing like:
- Pump Impellers
- Blowers
- Fans
- and similar parts

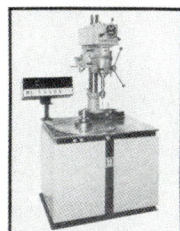

HVR

- Pure single plane balancing insensitive to couple unbalance
- On machine correction capacity
- Automatic cycle
- Low speed operation
- Dynamic braking

- Microprocessor analyzer
- Auto indexing
- Drill countdown
- Complete correction systems
- Tolerance function

Designed for single plane balancing of:
- Pulleys
- Clutches
- Impellers
- Flywheels
- and similar parts

HVS

- Microprocessor based electronics
- Automatic electronic centering
- Outstanding sensitivity

- Segmenting
- Tolerance function
- Part lift off device
- Display hold

This nonrotating static balancer is for fast part checking and balancing of:
- Grinding Wheels
- Fans
- Brake Drums
- Wheels
- and similar parts

HC

- Restraint/angle Indicator eliminates end stops
- On machine correction capacity
- Single and two plane balancing
- Simplified belt drive

- Microprocessor analyzer
- Segmenting
- Tolerance function
- Complete correction systems
- End drive

The HC Cradle Balancer will handle a variety of work pieces for job shop or production balancing, any part than can be run on 2 bearing surfaces or mounted on an arbor.
- Crankshafts
- Rolls
- Turbines
- Armatures

DL

The DL driveline balancer is available in several models from 3-3000 lb. capacities.
- Digital readout
- Direct angle indication
- Heavy motorized spindles

FOR MORE INFORMATION ON THESE AND OTHER BALANCERS AVAILABLE CALL OR WRITE.

HINES INDUSTRIES Inc.
661 AIRPORT BOULEVARD, SUITE 2, ANN ARBOR, MICHIGAN 48104
PHONE: (313) 769-2300

have to be replaced about every 50–75,000 miles and, of course, require balancing at that time. Dana Corporation is the exclusive sales agent for the Dana High Tech Driveline Package. In September, 1983, Dana placed a large order for ten units totaling $600,000. Shipments against this order began in February, 1984 and $321,000 remains in backlog as of April 30, 1984. A second order from Dana for $600,000 was received in June, 1984.

The other three product lines, which are sold in several sizes, are the HO or Horizontal Overhung Machine, the HVR or Hard Vertical Rotator Machine, and the HVS or Hard Vertical Static Machine. Balancing is important in parts which rotate in order to minimize or eliminate vibration. Parts which are not balanced create noise and excessive wear. These machines are sold to industrial customers to balance fans, pump impellers, pulleys, etc. These machines sell for about $22,000 each, but the HVR machine can reach $66,000.

Basically balancing can be done in one or two planes depending upon the size or shape of the part to be balanced. The balancing equipment finds the center of the mass and determines how much weight must be added to or removed from a determined point or points on the part to balance it. Elapsed time for balancing varies between 15 minutes to 1½ hours in the case of engine balancing plus time for loading and unloading the part. The heart of a balancing machine is the microprocessor, which quickly senses and performs the necessary calculations. Exhibit 5 shows a schematic diagram of a balancer.

ORGANIZATION

Hines Industries is organized along functional lines. Exhibit 6 depicts the organization as of June, 1984. Gordon Hines is the President and sole owner of the company. There are 46 employees, including 18 temporary or part-time employees. Temporary employees do not receive all of the fringe benefits and are subject to being laid off first should a cutback be necessary. Five of the key employees—Ron Anderson, Ken Cooper, Joann Huff, Mike Myers, and Len Salenbien—were with Gordon Hines at Balance Technology and came to Hines Industries at various times after Gordon organized his new venture.

MARKETING

Marketing is managed in an overall way by Gordon Hines through three employees. Joann Huff is responsible for the automotive aftermarket. She joined Hines in June, 1980, after being with Bal Tec in secretarial and sales positions for nine years. She supervises 20 manufacturer's representatives employing 45 salesmen, who sell the products to the ultimate customers. Mike Myers is responsible for the Drive Line machines, which are sold through several manufacturer's representatives. Industrial sales are handled by John Ramer through 3 manufacturer's representatives and some direct sales to customers. Bob Edwards was recently hired to cover the Ohio and West Virginia

EXHIBIT 5 How Imbalance Is Measured

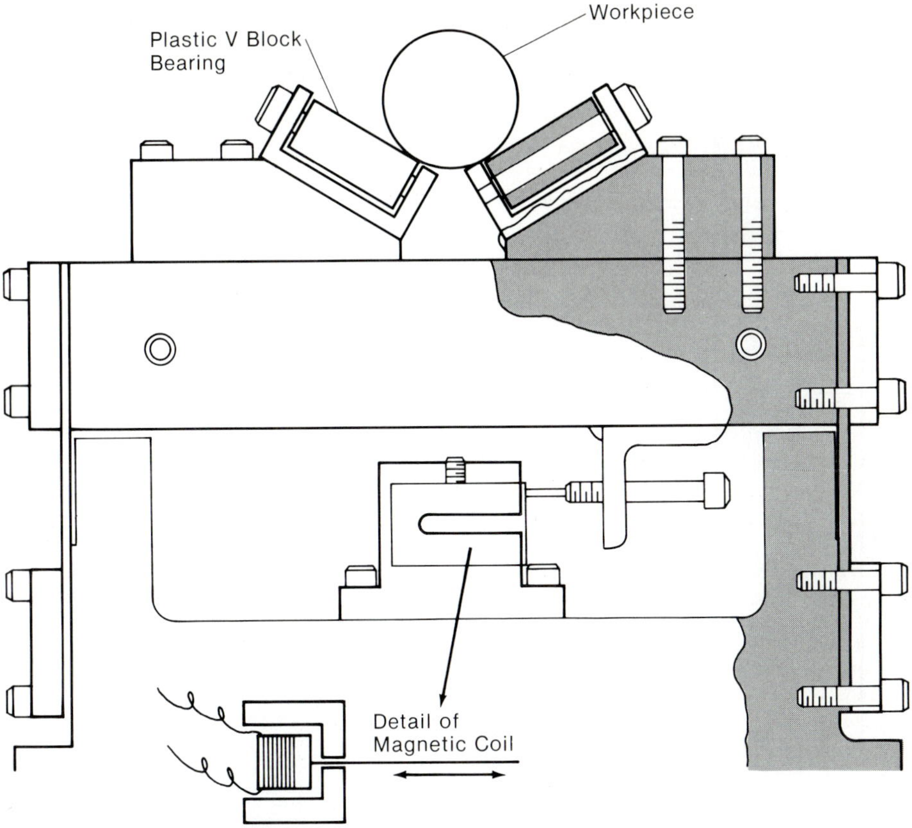
Workpiece
Plastic V Block Bearing
Detail of Magnetic Coil

territory directly for the company since it is difficult to get qualified general reps for this market.

Manufacturer's representatives are paid on a commission basis. A 15% commission is paid on the basic machine and 10% to 15% is paid on added components for the basic machine. Advertising support is provided in trade magazines to get inquiries. Exhibit 7 shows a typical advertisement which appeared in the June, 1984 issue of *Jobber Retailer*.

Products are built to order so no finished products are stocked. A substantial backlog of orders is considered desirable as an indicator of future sales and as an aid to scheduling production. Exhibit 8 is a sales analysis for the 12 months ending in April, 1984. It shows the monthly billings and bookings by product line and the backlog.

EXHIBIT 6 Organization Chart

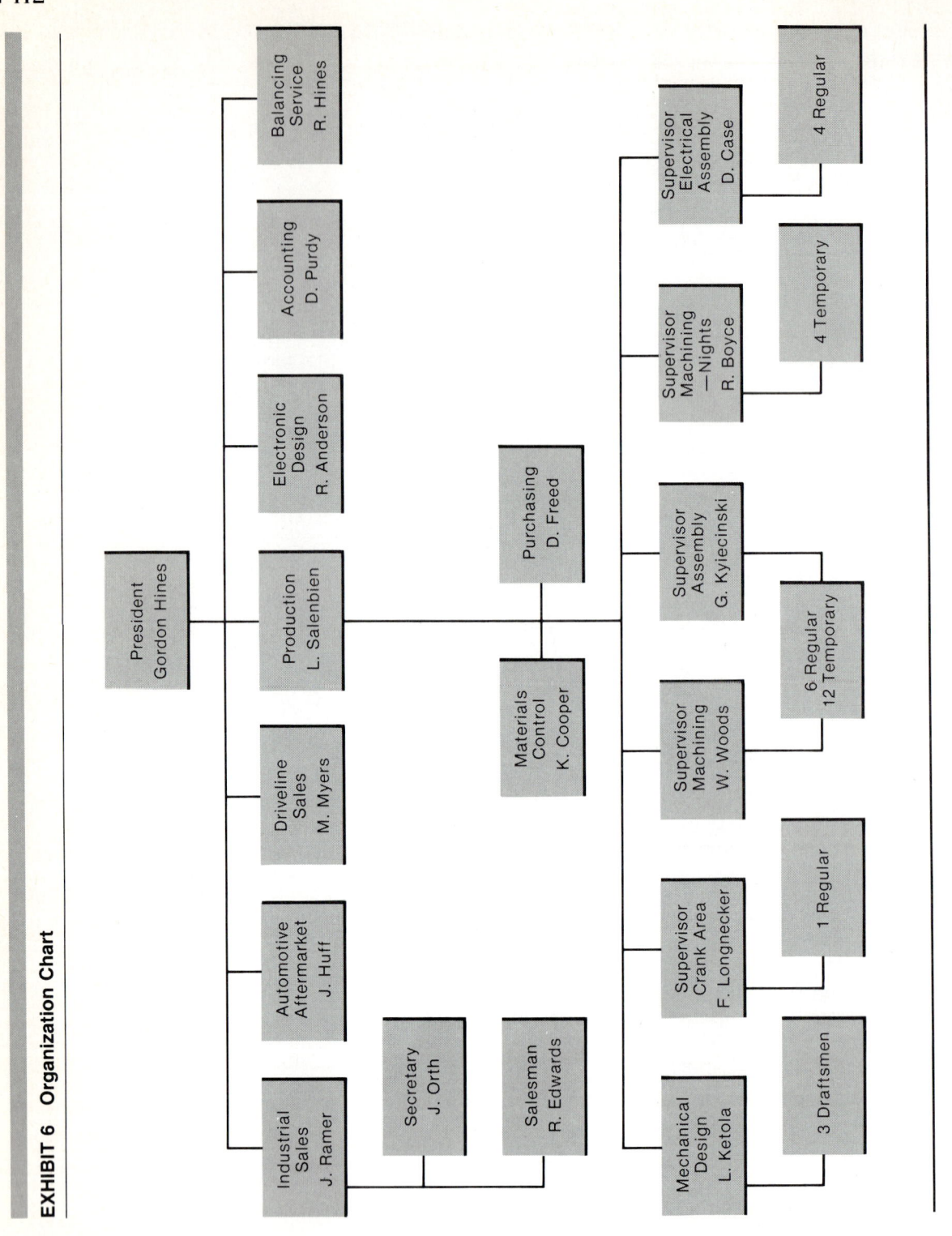

- President — Gordon Hines
  - Industrial Sales — J. Ramer
    - Secretary — J. Orth
    - Salesman — R. Edwards
  - Automotive Aftermarket — J. Huff
  - Driveline Sales — M. Myers
  - Production — L. Salenbien
    - Electronic Design — R. Anderson
    - Accounting — D. Purdy
    - Balancing Service — R. Hines
    - Purchasing — D. Freed
    - Materials Control — K. Cooper
    - Mechanical Design — L. Ketola
      - 3 Draftsmen
    - Supervisor Crank Area — F. Longnecker
      - 1 Regular
    - Supervisor Machining — W. Woods
      - 6 Regular, 12 Temporary
    - Supervisor Assembly — G. Kyiecinski
    - Supervisor Machining—Nights — R. Boyce
      - 4 Temporary
    - Supervisor Electrical Assembly — D. Case
      - 4 Regular

EXHIBIT 7 Sample Advertisement

Balancing is now...
SIMPLE!
VERSATILE!
PROFITABLE!
FAST!

with a
HINES
MICROCOMPUTER HARD BEARING BALANCER

MODEL HC500-2P for automotive and industrial parts. Options for larger components and drivelines available.

See us at AERA Booth 633

Circle 107 on Reader Service Card

WHAT USERS SAY:

SIMPLE!
"We have been using the machine for about 3 months. It couldn't be simpler. It's so easy a kid can run it. It tells you exactly how much to add and where to add it."
Greg James and Keven Lee,
Kleeco Motorsports, IL

VERSATILE!
"Although the purchase of our Hines balancer was for our high performance customers, we found the accuracy has been a tremendous asset in acquiring industrial accounts. We have balanced magnesium pulleys used in jet aircrafts, 8 oz., to steam turbines, 400 lbs."
Duane Saum,
Saum Engineering, KS

PROFITABLE!
"We have doubled our balance jobs in the last 9 months over what we did when we were sending them out... It also attracts other business. Once people find out you have a balancer, they call!"
Michael Heintz,
Heintz Bros., N.C.

FAST!
Using this machine is kind of like Fred Flintstone taking a ride on a jet plane. It is unbelieveable! I save so much time over what I had before."
Jim Totenbier, Jr.,
Superior Auto Machine, PA

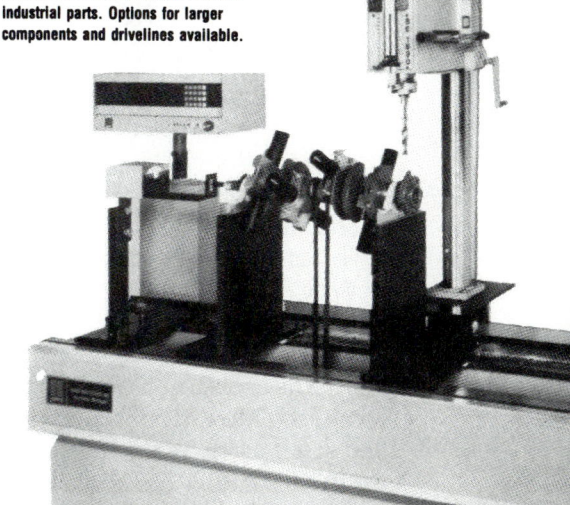

YES! I'm interested in balancing that's simple, versatile, profitable and fast.

Please send information to:

NAME_____
COMPANY_____
ADDRESS_____
CITY_____ STATE_____ ZIP_____
PHONE_____

Pat. No. 4,406,164

HINES INDUSTRIES

HINES

Ann Arbor, Michigan 48108 • 661 Airport Boulevard, Suite 2 • Phone: (313) 769-2300

EXHIBIT 8 Hines Industries, Inc. Sales Analysis

	MONTH ENDING						
	4/84	3/84	2/84	1/84	12/83	11/83	10/83
Billings							
Automotive	$ 74,510	$120,111	$ 191,071	$ 68,368	$ 128,572	$ 112,594	$ 42,305
Industrial	112,707	117,705		300	162,725	52,630	47,070
Driveline	125,610	124,770	55,555				
Parts and Service	2,373	1,159	2,372	1,281	1,201	1,269	2,231
Total	$315,200	$363,745	$ 248,998	$ 69,949	$ 292,498	$ 166,493	$ 91,606
Bookings							
Automotive	96,432	21,019	109,888	(22,942)	280,141	188,781	78,964
Industrial	31,808	29,652	132,100	83,470	85,190	114,739	129,615
Driveline		4,250	33,725	26,900			
Parts and Service	2,373	1,159	2,372	1,281	1,201	1,269	2,231
Total	$130,613	$ 56,080	$ 278,085	$ 88,709	$ 366,532	$ 304,789	$ 210,810
Backlog	$792,904	$977,491	$1,285,156	$1,256,069	$1,237,309	$1,163,275	$1,024,979

	MONTH ENDING						
	9/83	8/83	7/83	6/83	5/83	4/83	3/83
Billings							
Automotive	$ 59,193						
Industrial	105,510						
Driveline							
Parts and Service	1,268						
Total	$165,971	$111,202	$ 87,012	$ 94,507	$ 10,822	$ 41,224	$99,559
Bookings							
Automotive	87,560						
Industrial	54,310						
Driveline	600,000						
Parts and Service	1,268						
Total	$743,138	$165,471	$114,821	$142,277	$ 35,772	$182,654	$39,444
Backlog	$905,775	$328,608	$274,339	$246,530	$198,760	$173,810	$32,380

Automotive Aftermarket

The automotive aftermarket for balancing has been primarily for high performance cars. It is believed to include the potential for 100 to 150 balancers per year. Hines HC-500 balancer for this market sells for about $16,500. The market potential has improved since the EPA and OSHA have backed off interfering with racing.

The automotive aftermarket has two other competitors: Winona Van-Norman, which is now a foreign made copy of Hines equipment, and Stewart Warner, who is now engaging in "puffing" to overcome Hines advantage. To aid the marketing by manufacturer's reps, who also handle other machinery for rebuilding engines, Joann Huff advertises in five trade journals for the performance and rebuilding industry: *Automotive Rebuilder, Specialty and Custom Dealer, Jobber Retailer, National Dragster,* and *Circle Track.* Six half-page, two-color advertisements were placed in 1983 costing between $1,200 to $2,000, depending upon the publication. She has increased advertising in 1984 to one per month, including some full-page ads which are 1½ times the cost of the half-page ads. She would like to increase advertising to two per month in the latter part of 1984. She gets opinions from respected users as to which journals are most effective and tries to time Hines ads with articles about balancing, editorials about balancing, or issues preceding trade shows. Extra copies of the journals preceding trade shows are often distributed free at the shows. An example of an article about engine balancing is shown in Exhibit 9.

Special mailings, using articles such as Exhibit 9, and telephone campaigns are conducted to promote to the automotive aftermarket. Mailings typically range between 200 to 600 but have gone as high as 2,500. The membership lists of associations such as Automotive Engine Rebuilders Association, Automotive Service Industries Association, and Specialty Engine Machine Association are used for the mailings.

The company attends at least six trade shows per year. A balancing machine is displayed and Joann Huff as well as area manufacturer's reps are in attendance. Brochures describing the various machines made by Hines are available for use at trade shows as well as for use by manufacturer's reps and company sales personnel. Gordon Hines also attended the important Las Vegas AERA show in June, 1984. Seven orders totaling $175,000 were obtained as a result of the show. Other shows of the associations previously mentioned are held in March and October, respectively. The National Dragster show is held in September, the Oval Track show in February, and the Pacific Automotive Show in March. Other wholesaler shows in individual states are attended by manufacturer's reps and a balancer is sent.

Joann Huff sees her job as being an educational process—first manufacturer's reps and then customers. She said, "The market is there but needs to be made. About half of the rebuilders always balance and the other half never balance." An engine will last 50% longer if balanced, which is an important cost factor since the initial cost of engines is causing more and more to be rebuilt rather than replaced.

Diesel engine rebuilding is a new market which the company will be emphasizing. It is estimated by Gordon Hines that 5% of all truck engines are rebuilt each year and that 20 plus million trucks are on the road. Joann plans to use the trade journal *Renews* for advertising, which costs $2,600 for a full page. A heavy duty HC machine with extra bed length will be used for this market. Better drive line tooling has helped the servicing of this market.

Another market which has potential is rebuilding shops which also wish to do some industrial work such as repairing and rebuilding electric motor armatures, pump impellers, fans, and blowers. A microprocessor can be added to the balancers for shops doing this kind of work. The machines are designed and built in a modular form. Therefore, by simply adding or changing certain

EXHIBIT 9 Hines Industries, Inc. Engine Balancing Article

Engine Balancing

by Mike Mavrigian

It's high time that the bull stops concerning the area of engine balancing. When many machine shop owners/operators are asked to "balance" an engine, they automatically place the customer at hand into one category: racer/hot-rodder. For years, the only folks who offered balancing services out of their shop were regarded as "specialty speed shops," and out of the realm of the normal or "traditional" machine shop.

Wake up, folks. You cannot offer accurate and truly *complete* engine rebuilding services without including balancing as an integral part of your overall operation. It's called *doing the job right*.

That's right . . . we're suggesting that you go out and buy additional equipment if you don't already have it. That means increased operating bucks, right? Wrong. What it really means is additional profit opportunities.

An internal combustion engine features several moving parts, right? A crankshaft/damper-pulley/flywheel rotates within the engine block; and connecting rods/piston assemblies reciprocate up and down within their respective bores, while attached to the crankshaft. If there are unequal forces at work during engine operation, there is damaging stress being placed on engine bearings, and a loss of overall efficiency. Now, you know you can't dispute that fact, so why in the world are so many shops unwilling to look at balancing as the necessary service that it is?

Especially in these days of "downsized" powerplants that feature only six or four cylinders, balancing takes on a much more important role during engine rebuilding. Imbalance differences are proportionately more obvious and potentially damaging with the decrease in total number of cylinders. An imbalance condition in a V-8 engine that might go unnoticed has the potential to wreak havoc in a mill with only half the number of cylinders.

Let's take a look at a basic formula which illustrates how to determine the force that an unbalance condition produces. For a given unbalance condition, the force at the bearings is proportional to the speed of the engine *squared*. The relationship for force in pounds to do a given amount of unbalance in ounce-inches is as follows: Force = 1.7738 × unbalance × Engine RPM. For example, for one ounce-inch of unbalance at 1000 RPM, the force is 1.7738 pounds. For 2 ounce-inches at 2000 RPM, the force is 14.2 pounds (formula courtesy Hines Industries, Inc.).

That's 14.2 *pounds* of force applied to the crank bearings *constantly* at 2000 RPM. With OE factory tolerances being what they are (speaking in generalities), it's not at all uncommon to experience this level of uneven balance in a majority of engines that come into your machine shop. We just can't take balancing procedures for granted as so-called "luxuries" anymore. Our purpose within this industry is to give the end-user the *best* and most reliable rebuild that we can possibly achieve. Anything less should not be acceptable.

Let's take a look at the specific items that are included under the broad heading of balancing: the *rotating mass* includes the crankshaft, damper, flywheel and clutch pressure plate (if any). The *reciprocating mass* includes connecting rods, pistons, and pins.

Rotating Mass

Internally-balanced engines (where the flywheel and or damper has no counterweights) offer you a choice: you can either balance the pieces installed on the crankshaft as an assembly, or you can individually balance off the crank.

Externally-balanced engines (flywheel and or damper features counterweights) require these units to be installed on the crankshaft prior to crankshaft balancing.

In-line engines (four cylinder, straight sixes) allow their crankshaft assemblies to be balanced on the crank balancer machine without the use of bobweights, while V-type engines require bobweights to be installed on the crank prior to balancing (to simulate rod/piston thrusts during crank balancing).

EXHIBIT 9   (Continued)

Reciprocating Mass

Here we want to balance piston/pin assemblies and connecting rod assemblies. What we are essentially after here is to make all piston/pin assemblies weigh the same; and for all connecting rod large-ends to weigh the same; and for all connecting rod small-ends to weigh the same. To do this, we basically find the lightest unit and remove metal from other similar units so that they all come down to the weight of the lightest. For example, in balancing pistons, we weigh each piston (clean and dry, with pins), finding the one that weighs less than all the others. We record that lightest weight. All other pistons are then ground carefully in their pin boss areas until they each weigh the same as that lightest unit. Generally, your tolerance is thus: the piston/pin assemblies being lightened should weigh the same as the light assembly, within +.5 gram to .0 gram. Always constantly double-check your weights during and after all machining. Record the finished weight of each piston/pin assembly and mark each with cylinder number (if not already done).

The connecting rods are each weighed on a scale with the use of a special scale pan adapter. The rod ends (small and large) should be set up so that they are "square" with each other. Weigh each rod's large end and find your lightest end. Carefully grind material from all others to bring them down to this lightest rod-end's weight. The same procedure is followed for small ends. The tolerance to shoot for is +1 gram-.0 gram (for automotive engines). For heavy truck engines, the tolerance can be sometimes set at +2 grams to .0 gram. Most of the time, the very *end* surface of each rod end is the area from which material is ground. Be sure to record each rod's end weight as well as double-checking total rod weight. Identify them accordingly.

Record-keeping (on a bobweight card) is essential, not only for your immediate use, but for any future parts replacements that might be necessary. If you already know what weight a pison/pin assembly *must* be, you can choose an assembly for replacement that will maintain the balance job.

After rods and piston assemblies have been balanced, you can then set up the crank with the correct bobweights (if it's a V-block engine design).

Installation of bobweights, if needed, is critical from a centering standpoint. They must be accurately centered on the crank throws (spacing side-to-side across the bearing surface width). Orientation is not critical, so they do not need to be placed at right angles to each other. Bobweights, for those unfamiliar with this term, are the weights that are attached to the journals of the crankshaft of any V-type engine crank during balancing, on a dynamic crank balancer. They are adjustable, with flowable lead shot inside, and are there to cause the crank to respond to the balancer as if the rods and pistons were attached.

Determining Needed Bobweight

To determine bobweight needed, add up the figures on your bobweight card: add rod rotating weight (large rod end) plus rod bearing weight plus oil allowance (figure average 4 grams) plus piston/pin weight, plus locks (if any) plus piston rings plus the rod reciprocating weight. Add up all of these weight factors that a single rod throw of the crank has to handle, and you've got your total bobweight.

Again, keep in mind that straight-line engine crankshafts do not need the addition of bobweights in order to balance the crank.

Balancing, especially in today's marketplace, is a necessary service and not the grand luxury that some people deem it to be. Just imagine a clothes washer that has had an uneven load placed in it. The resulting vibration causes excessive wear in virtually every moving component in that machine, as well as eliminating the degree of efficiency that the machine is capable of. Translate that into engine operational terms. When a mechanical mass rotates, centrifugal force acts upon the entire mass. If the part is unbalanced, an *excess* of mass exists on one side. Everything is being pulled in the direction of the heavy side, or away from the mechanical axis of rotation. Definitely a no-win situation for main bearings, rod bearings, timing gear setup, transmission input shaft, etc.

(*Continued*)

EXHIBIT 9 (Continued)

Take Full Advantage of Balancing

If your shop is content with simple repair and replacement methods, you are not taking full advantage of the capabilities that balancing equipment offers in terms of *correcting* faulty OE traits, many of which can be traced directly back to unbalance conditions. If you want your customers to be supplied with rebuilt engine assemblies that will perform to the *design* level of efficiency and horsepower *and* offer reliable, extended life service, you must investigate the excellent balancing equipment that is currently available on the market.

Increasing horsepower is not the all-encompassing goal that the traditional machine shop strives towards; rather, it is the *beneficial* byproduct of simply *doing it right*. So please, don't just regard balancing as an act performed by the speed-freak seals of the racing world. It should be an integral part of the efficient, quality-conscious machine shop that is concerned with producing the best possible product with currently-available methods.

---

components, it is possible to "culture whole new products," which can be assembled to satisfy customer requirements. New market segments could be entered in this same way.

The company has a table top version of the HC500 called the HC10TC for turbo charger balancing. The machine sells for $10,000. The only competitor is a company which curiously is called Heins. One trade show, Automotive Diesel Specialists, can be used.

Another market is the 100 firms making up the Production Engine Rebuilders Association (PERA). A typical firm rebuilds as high as 70 engines per day using used parts obtained from tearing down used engines. Their business is increasing since the smaller engines used in production cars do not last as long because of higher speeds used in the engines.

Still another market is the clutch rebuilder. An HVR balancer without all of the "bells and whistles" is used for this job and costs about $11,000 versus the normal HVR price of $20,000. The size of this market is not known but is more like the PERA described previously. The trade group, Automotive Parts Rebuilder Association, puts on one show each year. Hines has three competitors in this business segment.

Driveline Market

The Drive Line Balancer is used primarily to balance the drive shaft for trucks which have to be replaced frequently because of the heavy weights involved and the many miles of use each year. The current DL balancer was redesigned from the original version to bring it into conformance with the other balancers Hines makes. It is similar to the crankshaft machine, HC series.

Gordon Hines, as he typically does, sold the original concept to Dana Corporation, which is now the exclusive sales agent for the Dana High Tech Drive Line Package. Gordon is intensively involved in the initial design and marketing of a new product for six months or so, often spending long hours at it, and, then, he "eases back so his whole body can come back up." Mike

Myers, who sells about one DL balancer to other customers a month, also tries to handle the big Dana account but really needs some help. Mike has a BA degree from the University of Michigan including 2½ years of engineering and worked at Bal Tec for 15 years in mechanical design, computer programming, and sales before joining Hines in December, 1983. Mike is Hines' internal computer expert and often provides help for those using Hines' three computers. He also is somewhat involved in mechanical design, although Gordon provides the major mechanical design concepts. Gordon Hines believes the Dana account has a potential for $2 million per year with another $500,000 of DL balancers sold to others.

In addition to the DL balancer, Hines makes two other products, which are related to the balancer and sold as part of the package Dana buys for $60–75,000. These are a push-up press and a specialty lathe. This group of machines allows Dana to do eight specific jobs essential to rebuilding shafts—weld cutoff, tube cut and chamfer, push up, pull out, straighten, weld, straighten, and balance. The package includes specialized tooling designed and built to Dana's specifications. Dana, in turn, sells the unit to the ultimate customer.

Industrial Market

The industrial market includes sales of the HO, HVR, and HVS products with several size models of each to industrial producers of original equipment (OEM) using impellers, fans, blowers, pulleys, etc. John Ramer heads this activity and he and Bob Edwards personally sell the products along with the three manufacturer's reps. John Ramer has a degree in business administration from the University of Michigan and is an artist. He joined Hines in 1982 as his first full-time job. It is believed that there is a great deal of business to be had within a 300 to 500 mile radius and, therefore, company sales personnel can be very effective.

Both John and Bob try to stay "off the road" and do most of their selling by telephone and sending out literature. They use lists of pump and blower manufacturers obtained from their trade association, as well as referrals, to make their calls. Thus they make only "hot calls." Gordon Hines believes the market is too narrow to advertise in publications like the *American Machinist* so he prefers the "rifle" approach instead of a "shotgun." He believes the HVR market is $4 million per year and, if the balancing could be done automatically, the market could be $20 million. HC balancers are also being sold for industrial use. Hines is being successful against established competitors.

Balancing Service

The company offers a balancing service for local customers who need relatively small quantities balanced. The idea behind this venture is to provide a service to smaller customers, gain experience with other items needing balancing, and, hopefully, sell balancers to the service customers when they grow large enough to warrant their own machine. For instance, Hines is now balancing 2,000 specialized parts per week for a Ford Motor supplier. This activity is managed by Robin Hines, Gordon's daughter. This activity will be housed in a third building, along with demo units, containing 3,200 square feet which will be available July 1. This move will free up some of the space in the main building.

MANUFACTURING

Leonard Salenbien, 40 years old, is the manager of production. Prior to joining Hines, he served in the same position at Balance Technology. He worked at Bal Tec for eleven years, starting as a check-out technician and progressing to head of the service department before he became production manager there.

Hines Industries rents two buildings located in the light industrial area north of the Ann Arbor Airport. The main facility consists of 9,600 square feet located on one floor plus 1,600 square feet located on the second floor. Exhibit 10 shows the floor plan of the main plant. The second building, which is located nearby, contains 3,200 square feet. It is used for painting machines, storage of large parts, lumber storage, fabrication of pallets for shipping machines, and storage of concrete bases for machines. Both buildings are quite crowded and thought has been given to the need for additional space. Unfortunately, the present buildings that are available or being built in the area are not big enough to house all of Hines' activities in one area.

The production area uses general-purpose machines for the fabrication work. Most of the machinery was purchased used at auctions at very favorable prices. Later these machines were reworked by Hines to bring them up to the standards required. Some have been converted to numerical control using the microprocessors which Hines produces. The production equipment includes four lathes, two horizontal milling machines, six vertical milling machines, one jig borer, one radial arm drilling machine, one cylindrical ID/OD grinder, one cylindrical ID grinder, one face grinder, a Burgemaster machining center which is being retrofit for numerical control (NC), and a lathe retrofit to CNC. Hines makes many of its own parts and does the mechanical and electrical assembly work. Electronics assembly, including the building of microprocessors, is done on the second floor of the main building, which also includes mechanical drafting.

One of the unique features of the machines produced by Hines is the use of a precision-formed concrete base to provide the mass needed to support and dampen the balancing machines. These concrete bases are purchased locally from a company that uses the forms which were designed and built by Hines. Delivery time on the bases is a week so that it is not necessary to have many of the bulky units in stock.

All machines are thoroughly tested at Hines using customer parts before they are shipped. Len Salenbien is often involved in the testing if trouble is encountered. An automotive aftermarket-type machine such as the HC takes about two days to assemble and test if all of the parts are available. Hines also trains the customer's maintenance men at the Hines plant so that little field repairs by Hines are required.

EXHIBIT 10 Hines Industries, Inc. Plant Layout

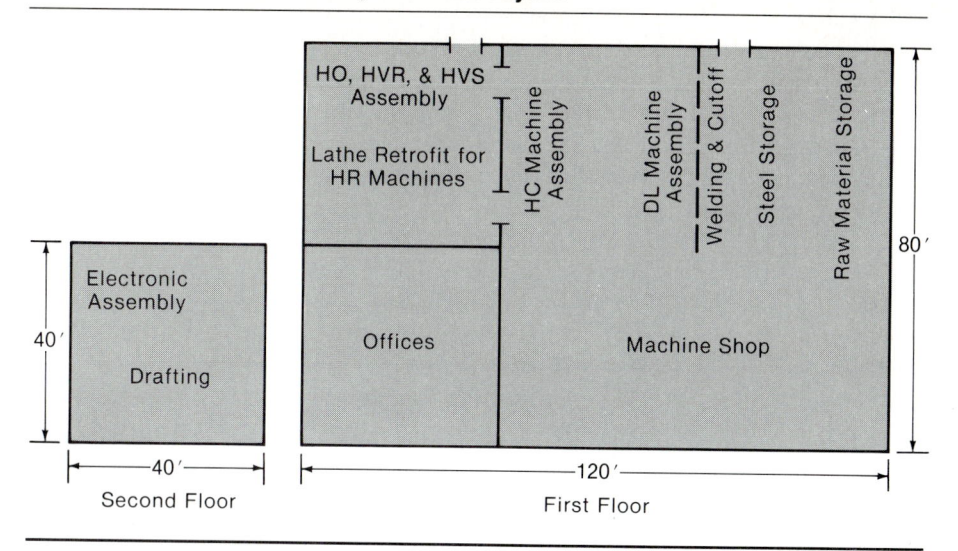

(Plant layout diagram: Second Floor (40' × 40') contains Electronic Assembly and Drafting. First Floor (120' × 80') contains Offices, Machine Shop, HO, HVR, & HVS Assembly, Lathe Retrofit for HR Machines, HC Machine Assembly, DL Machine Assembly, Welding & Cutoff, Steel Storage, and Raw Material Storage.)

Purchasing of standard parts from vendors is the responsibility of Dave Freed, who has been with Hines since August, 1983. He worked as a refrigeration contractor until three years ago, when he was injured while water skiing. He subsequently took training on computers at Washtenaw Community College before joining Hines.

Dave gets verbal or written lists of materials required from seven or eight people who keep track of their own stock and determine what they need. These people and their area of responsibility are as follows:

Fran Longnecker—crankshaft machines
Willie Woods—shop materials and supplies
Gary Kwiecinski—industrial machines, skidding and shipping
Dave Bloom (part time)—industrial machines
Keith Kwiecinski—painting
Larry Ketola—special tooling and special parts for each machine
Kay Lamay (Doug Case's employee)—electronics

Dave orders all of his parts by telephone. No purchase orders are sent to vendors. Dave maintains a list of purchase orders by number on the computer, including all of the pertinent data on each order. Orders are placed by description of the part. No part numbers have been assigned by Hines and vendor part numbers are not used. Although Engineering is beginning to assign part numbers to mechanical parts required for the company's products, it has not yet decided if company part numbers will be assigned to standard purchased parts. A Bill of Material is not generated for each machine although the company wants to do this. In fact, the company does not presently have a comprehensive part numbering system.

Dave does not know how many different parts are in the products but believes there are at least 1,000 purchased parts, not counting internally manufactured parts. Partial inventories may be taken every six months or so. Parts are not actually counted but the quantity is estimated. There is no definite stockroom used but rather a series of stock locations by product assembly area. Parts may be stocked in more than one area. Sometimes parts are ordered a second time if an item is on backorder. No production schedule is available.

Most of the parts Dave orders are available within a short time. Motors require a week and IC chips (integrated circuits) usually require a month. However, ICs could require 4 to 6 months if not in stock. Dave orders from vendors, with whom Hines is on good financial terms, based upon price, first, and delivery, second. Quality is important on some items.

Dave believes the company is "moving away from chaos" but not fast enough. He describes the big upswing in business in December, 1983: Dana was like a "cobra trying to swallow a pig." Although employees know basically how they fit in, what their job is, and how they do it, they are not enough aware of the company's goals and objectives, Dave believes. Items seem to be ordered on an emergency basis half of the time.

The big upswing in business created some cash flow problems, although Gordon Hines believes the worst is over. Since May, Dave has been required to check the price before ordering and he may be required to get approval for cash reasons. Sometimes he has ordered smaller quantities at a higher price in order to conserve cash. Sometimes he has delayed orders or challenged the size of orders. Sometimes, if a vendor required COD, Dave has had to find a new vendor, since Gordon has said no COD shipments will be accepted.

Gordon and Len sometimes disagree on product design and ordering. Dave feels caught in the middle. About half of the time Gordon discusses the issue directly with Dave, thus resolving it. Dave would like to see more formal planning. Purchase requisition forms are on order, which presumably will be used for preapproval before Dave sees them. The forms will be two-part—one for accounting and one for purchasing. If the originator wants a copy, a Xerox copy will be made.

Dave gets a copy of the Sales Order Information Form—Partial Release but is not sure why he gets it since he cannot order even long-delivery items based on this information. The form is used primarily by Ken Cooper to order outside mechanical items, he says.

Ken Cooper, whose responsibility is Materials Control, joined Hines in March, 1984. He worked at Bal Tec for 13 years and was Purchasing Manager when he left. Prior to Bal Tec, he worked in the machine shop at Bendix for 20 years. Ken orders some material directly and gets his purchase order numbers from Dave Freed. He subcontracts some of the mechanical parts work to outside firms on a time and material basis.

Ken schedules the shop and is supposed to schedule electronics but Doug

Case really does it. Ken keeps a cardex inventory system of common manufactured parts. Based upon this information, he initiates orders for parts through Machining or through outside suppliers. The lot size ordered is based on previous experience, with input from Willie Woods and Fran Longnecker. An inventory may be taken on individual items. Ken is trying to set up inventories by production area. He decides whether to make or buy an item.

Ken's goal is to get things running smoothly. He is getting shop costs by using the average actual hours, secured from job tickets, times $25 per hour, which includes burden. The actual cost of labor is about $7 per hour. If an item has not been made before, he estimates the cost based upon his previous experience.

Ken is concerned that production seems to always be behind and is "playing catch-up." He believes the men are learning but are operators and not machinists in that they cannot do setups well. Only Willie Woods and Bob Boyce can do setups. There is not a formal training program. The last thing that gets made is customer tooling, which is what often creates the delays. He also believes more space may be needed soon now that the second Dana order has been received. Under ideal conditions he estimates 2 to 3 Dana Machines, 3 IICs, and 3 HVRs or HOs could be assembled simultaneously if parts were available (maybe requiring multiple shifts) and if moves were carefully checked.

Ken describes the delivery commitment process in this way. Len Salenbien makes a tentative commitment to a sales person who has a potential order. If and when the order is actually received, it may be different than originally described. Also, other orders may have been received subsequent to the tentative commitment and be loaded into the shop. Thus the delivery commitment is frequently a problem. On the average, it takes two weeks from the beginning of assembly until the product is shipped, but shipment could be delayed 6 to 8 weeks because of production planning problems, inadequate pretesting of components, and delays in securing information and samples of customer parts for tooling fabrication.

ELECTRONIC DESIGN

The Electronic Design activity is conducted by Ron Anderson, who is 49 years old. Ron Anderson, who also worked for Gordon at Bal Tec, began working for Hines on a part-time basis but now is full-time. He has known Gordon personally for many years and began his work at Bal Tec as a consultant. He has a degree in electrical engineering and has specialized in electronic design. He had ten years previous experience at the University of Illinois as director of electronics for the Chemistry Department, which involved developing specialized instrumentation. Ron tries to use standard techniques and approaches in designing the electronics for the products so that common modules are used in the various models whenever possible. Ron is happiest when there is some new design to be developed and admits to being bored when things are too routine.

ACCOUNTING

Dean Purdy, who is 55 years old, was hired in late March, 1984 as Controller. Dean had previously worked for Fansteel for 17 years. His last position was Controller of their V. R. Wesson Division plant at Ferndale, Michigan, which made tungsten carbide cutting tools. The Ferndale plant had 125 employees and 50,000 square feet of floor area. He also had previous experience with Midwest Machine Company, which was an OEM for the auto industry. Thus Dean's background in the machining business fits well with Hines.

During his three months with Hines, Dean has learned the product line and internal workings of the company. He believes he has made progress in stabilizing the cash flow from receivables to payables. His personal priority is "to establish systems to do things in an orderly fashion," including inventory and production control and cost control.

The company presently uses two Altos computers, one with a 10 megabyte hard disk and one with 1 megabyte dual 8" floppy disks. The latter unit together with a small 64K dual 4½" floppy disk computer is used by Purchasing. Thought has been given to buying a Radio Shack 30 megabyte hard disk computer for additional applications, including accounting. Such a computer would cost about $15,000 including software.

Because the equipment for the industrial market and Dana typically have a longer delivery cycle than other products, Hines offers these customers, after receiving their order, a 2–5% discount if the customer will make an initial 30% downpayment and will pay the balance within ten days after delivery. Gordon Hines believes this policy gives the company a competitive advantage in addition to improving the cash flow.

MANAGEMENT

Gordon Hines began to draw a $40,000 per year salary in May, 1984. Prior to that he was living off his proceeds from selling his Bal Tec stock. When asked how he spends his time at the company, he estimated the following: sales—20%, design—20%, general business—20%, production—25%, and new business planning—15%. Gordon expects Dean Purdy will pick up a major share of his general business activities, which will free up some of Gordon's time to move into sales/design activities of other products or to develop new large accounts.

Gordon has also contemplated the need for a mechanical engineer who could handle design activities and manufacturing engineering activities. Such a person would be difficult to find and could be quite expensive in salary and relocation expenses. However, such a move would free Gordon from mechanical design activities which do require a substantial amount of his time.

Gordon also would like to see all of the company's activities in a common location. He would continue to rent since he does not want to put scarce cash into "bricks and mortar." The location would need to be near the present location for the convenience of employees. The airport location is also convenient, since Gordon shares an airplane with two other businessmen. Fortunately, the business which occupied the 3,200 square feet immediately adjoining Hines Industries is relocating to another part of the industrial park in July, and Hines will be able to rent this space and combine it with the main plant area.

Gordon sees a strong growth potential for the company over the next two years barring another prolonged recession. He thinks fiscal 1985 should see $4-plus million in sales, with the following year increasing another 50%. His overall management priorities are to manage cash first and profits second. In his view the October through December, 1984, period will set the stage for the following year.

INDUSTRIAL HIGHLIGHT

Pumps and Compressors Industry

Below is a capsule summary of the pumps and compressors industry. Information regarding this industry would probably be useful in managing Hines Industries, Inc. Information in this highlight was compiled by the U.S. Department of Commerce and focuses on this industry during the approximate period of time covered in the case. Keep in mind that industrial highlights contained in this text are not intended as a complete synopsis of an industry but as a profile of certain issues that can be relevant to a case situation. A list of additional references at the end of this highlight can be used for further industrial analysis.

CURRENT SITUATION

In 1984, shipments by the U.S. pump and compressor industries showed real growth of about 3 percent and 4 percent respectively, from 1983 levels. This rise in shipments represented a move toward recovery rather than an expansion. In constant dollars, the value of pump industry shipments in 1981 was $2.62 billion, compared with estimated shipments of $2.35 billion in 1984. Similarly, estimated shipments by the compressor industry were $1.47 billion in 1984, a 5-percent decline from the 1981 level.

Rising industrial production, particularly in the United States, was a major factor in improving the level of pump and compressor shipments. These products are major components in industrial process and assembly line operations.

Improved production levels at pulp and paper mills and food and beverage plants, in particular, aided recovery in the pump industry. Compressor sales were stimulated by increased production at automotive and other assembly plants using tools powered by compressed air.

Economic recovery lagged that of the general economy in both the pump and compressor industries because many manufacturers were exercising caution in making major expansions in plant production facilities using pumps and compressors. Production lead times of at least 6 months for large custom

Source: U.S. Industrial Outlook, Department of Commerce, 1985, pp. 22-3–22-5.

designed pump and compressor systems also created a lag in the recovery in shipments by these industries.

The low level of new orders and shipments of pumps and compressors for use in oil field drilling and production activities has hindered growth in this major market. The persistence of a worldwide surplus supply of petroleum has restricted the demand for large customized pumps and compressors for pipeline transmission.

The expansion in road and bridge repair, begun in 1983, continued to stimulate the demand for portable air compressors and pumps during 1984. Construction contractors often rent portable air compressors from private rental firms in lieu of purchasing, and rental firms have become a major market for compressor manufacturers.

The level of U.S. exports of pumps and compressors showed a small improvement in 1984. As in the United States, however, the recovery in demand for pumps and compressors lagged the general recovery in many foreign countries. In addition, the strength of the U.S. dollar made U.S. equipment less price competitive. The major export markets for U.S. pumps and compressors were Canada, Saudi Arabia, Mexico, the United Kingdom, and Japan.

U.S. imports of pumps and compressors rose sharply in 1984, by 11 percent and 33 percent, respectively. Imports as a percentage of U.S. apparent consumption were 7 percent for pumps and about 12 percent for compressors. The high value of the U.S. dollar made prices of foreign equipment very competitive. U.S. imports of pumps and compressors primarily originated from Canada, West Germany, Japan, and the United Kingdom.

U.S. pump and compressor industry shipments are expected to show growth of about 5 percent in 1985, in constant dollars. These increases will still not bring the industries to their 1981 level, however. This projection is based on the assumption that U.S. industrial production will continue to show strength and that foreign manufacturing levels will continue to improve. Industrial plant capacity utilization rates above 85 percent on a sustained basis will promote new plant and equipment investment. Interest rates low enough to encourage construction activity will also stimulate the markets for pumps and compressors.

The major markets for pumps and compressors in the petroleum industry should show some improvement if oil and natural gas supplies become more in balance with demand and prices remain relatively stable near current levels. Oil field pumps and gas compressors for pipeline production and transmission are high-value products that contribute importantly to the growth of the pump and compressor industries.

U.S. exports of pumps and compressors should show further improvement in 1985 as foreign industrial production expands and economic growth improves. International standards have been developed for many industrial pumps and compressors, so U.S. manufacturers must compete in many foreign markets on the basis of price, financing terms, and quality of service. U.S. imports of pumps and compressors are expected to show further growth, as foreign manufacturers continue to market aggressively in the United States.

STRATEGY IMPLEMENTATION AND CONTROL

LONG-TERM PROSPECTS

The long-range forecast for the U.S. pump industry is for a compound annual growth rate of 3.5 percent, in 1972 dollars, during the 1985–89 period. During the same time, the U.S. compressor industry is projected to have a compound annual growth rate of 3.4 percent.

Projected growth for these industries is based on the assumption that pumps and compressors will continue to be used in a wide range of industrial, commercial, and home uses. For example, automated machining centers in woodworking plants will continue to rely on compressors and vacuum pumps to move and then anchor work pieces in place. Power plants will use compressors to further improve combustion efficiency in fossil fuel plants, while specialty pumps will be used in nuclear power reactors for cooling operations. Municipal water and sewer systems are expected to continue to rely on large capacity pumps and compressors for transport and aeration operations. The arid countries of the world will depend on irrigation systems equipped with pumps to raise agricultural output. Many towns and households will need pumps for providing them with potable water.

In the future, pumps and compressors will often be designed into highly automated, high-capacity, and high-pressure manufacturing and process operations. Therefore, these products will be constructed of higher strength metals and lined with rubber or coated with plastics and other synthetic materials to reduce wear and maintenance requirements.

Computer-aided design (CAD) and manufacturing (CAM) systems will reduce pump and compressor design and production lead times for highly engineered projects. Computerized inventory control systems will aid manufacturers in carrying smaller and more efficient inventories for repair and replacement parts.

ADDITIONAL REFERENCES

1982 Census of Manufactures, "General Industrial Machinery and Equipment 356," Bureau of the Census, U.S. Department of Commerce, Washington, DC 20233.

Current Industry Reports, Pumps and Compressors 1983, MA 35P(83)-I, Bureau of the Census, U.S. Department of Commerce, Washington, DC 20233.

Compressed Air and Gas Handbook, fifth edition, Compressed Air and Gas Institute, 1230 Keith Building, Cleveland, OH 44115.

Pump Handbook, Igor Karassik, McGraw-Hill Book Company, 1221 Avenue of the Americas, New York, NY 10020.

CASE 21

Marion Laboratories, Inc.*

MARILYN L. TAYLOR   KENNETH BECK
both of the University of Kansas

Michael E. Herman, Senior Vice President of Finance for Marion Laboratories, had just received word that the Board of Directors was planning to meet in three days to review the company's portfolio of subsidiary investments. In particular, he and his senior financial analyst, Carl R. Mitchell, were to prepare an in-depth analysis of several of the subsidiaries so the board could be better positioned with respect to these subsidiaries' compatibility with Marion's overall strategic objectives. The analysis was part of a continuing process of self-assessment to assure future growth for the company. At the upcoming meeting the board was interested in a review of Kalo Laboratories, Inc.,* a subsidiary that manufactured specialty agricultural chemicals.

Kalo was profitable and in sound financial shape for the fiscal year just ended. (See Exhibit 1—Sales, Profits, and Assets of Major Industry Segments.) But Kalo, in the agricultural chemical industry, was unique for Marion and Mr. Herman knew that Kalo's long-term status as a Marion subsidiary would depend on more than just profitability.

Marion's future has been the subject of careful study following the first two years of earnings decline in the company's history. In fiscal 1975 net earnings for the company were 12 percent lower than in 1974. In fiscal 1976 Marion faced a more serious problem as earnings fell 30 percent below 1974 levels while sales decreased 4 percent and cost of goods sold rose by 12 percent above 1974 levels.

As a result of the interruption in the earnings growth pattern, Marion has sought to reexamine its corporate portfolio of investments. By fiscal year 1977 some results from the reappraisal were seen as earnings rose 28 percent from the previous year. Although sales continued to climb, earnings had not yet recovered to the 1974 level by the end of fiscal year 1978. Marion's long-range

---

* This is a classic case in the strategic management literature.

This case was prepared by Professor Marilyn L. Taylor and Kenneth E. Beck. M.S.—Finance, of the University of Kansas. The development of the case was supported in part by a grant from the University of Kansas Fund for Instructional Improvement. The research and written case information were presented at the 1980 Case Research Symposium and were evaluated by the Case Research Association's Editorial Board.
Copyright© 1981.

* Kalo Laboratories Inc. was utilized as the case subject due to the singular nature of the segment information available in Marion Laboratories Inc. SEC Submissions, and does not reflect Marion's intentions as to its investment in Kalo or any of its other subsidiary operations. Materials in this case were generally gathered from publicly available information.

EXHIBIT 1   Marion Laboratories Inc. Sales, Profits, and Identifiable Assets by Industry Segments
(thousands of dollars)

	YEAR ENDED JUNE 30				
	1978	1977	1976	1975	1974
Sales to unaffiliated customers					
Pharmaceutical and hospital products	$ 84,223	$ 72,299	$ 59,236	$ 64,613	$ 54,165
Specialty agricultural chemical products	9,302	5,227	2,880	4,522	4,044
Other health care segments	23,853	22,605	18,722	14,961	13,569
Consolidated net sales	$117,378	$100,131	$ 80,838	$ 84,096	$ 71,778
Operating profit					
Pharmaceutical and hospital products	$ 27,900	$ 23,439	$ 18,941	$ 28,951	$ 25,089
Specialty agricultural chemical products	905	382	(328)	881	620
Other health care segments	929	1,251	(593)	686	871
Operating profit	29,734	25,072	18,020	30,518	26,580
Interest expense	(1,546)	(1,542)	(898)	(97)	(83)
Corporate expenses	(5,670)	(4,474)	(3,106)	(2,795)	(2,475)
Earnings before income taxes	$ 22,518	$ 19,056	$ 14,016	$ 27,626	$ 24,022
Identifiable assets					
Pharmaceutical and hospital products	$ 75,209	$ 69,546	$ 60,376	$ 43,658	$ 35,103
Specialty agricultural chemical products	3,923	3,805	1,801	1,942	1,790
Other health care segments	14,635	14,875	13,902	14,229	12,217
Corporate	5,121	3,424	4,518	3,928	3,770
Discontinued operations	—	—	—	3,370	6,865
Consolidated assets	$ 98,888	$ 91,650	$ 80,597	$ 67,127	$ 59,745

Source: 1978 Annual Report.

planning was an attempt to define what the company was to become in the next ten-year period. Current analysis of subsidiaries and investments were analyzed within this ten-year framework. As part of this long-range planning, a statement of Marion's corporate mission was developed.

STATEMENT OF CORPORATE MISSION

1. Achieve a position of market leadership through marketing and distribution of consumable and personal products of a perceived differentiation to selected segments of the health care and related fields.
2. Achieve long-term profitable growth through the management of high risk relative to the external environment.
3. Achieve a professional, performance-oriented working environment that stimulates integrity, entrepreneurial spirit, productivity, and social responsibility.

In addition to these more general goals, Marion also set a specific sales goal of $250 million. No time frame was established to achieve this goal, as the major emphasis was to be placed on the stability and quality of sales.

Mr. Herman realized, however, that even though there was no written timetable for earnings growth it was well understood that to meet stockholder expectations, the company must grow fairly rapidly.

On June 8, 1978, in a presentation before the Health Industry's Analyst Group, Fred Lyons, Marion's president and chief operating officer, emphasized Marion's commitment to growth. In his remarks he stated:

> We expect to grow over the next ten years at a rate greater than the pharmaceutical industry average and at a rate greater than at least twice that of the real gross national product. Our target range is at least 10–15 percent compounded growth—shooting for the higher side of that, of course. Obviously we intend to have a great deal of new business and new products added to our current operations to reach and exceed the $250 million level. Our licensing activities and R&D expenditures will be intensified. ... At the same time we'll undertake some selective in-house research business into Marion through the acquistion route. It is our intention to keep our balance sheet strong and maintain an "A" or better credit rating, to achieve a return on investment in the 12–15 percent range, and to produce a net after tax compared to sales in the 8–12 percent range.

To finance this growth in sales Marion was faced with a constant need for funds. Most of these funds in the past had come from the company's operations. To finance a $25-million expansion in its pharmaceutical facilities, the company, in fiscal year 1976, found it necessary to borrow $15 million in the form of unsecured senior notes. The notes were to mature on October 1, 1980, 1981, and 1982 with $5 million due on each of those dates.

In regard to possible future financing, Mr. Herman made the following comments before the Health Industry's Analyst Group. "Most of you realize that industrial companies have a debt-equity ratio of 1:1 and, if we so desired to lever ourselves to that level, we could borrow $66 million. However, we would keep as a guideline the factor of always maintaining our "A" or better credit rating, so we would not leverage ourselves that far."

Although Marion was fairly light on debt, the potential for future borrowing was not unlimited. Besides maintaining an "A" credit rating, it was felt that a debt to equity ratio greater than 4:1 would be inconsistent with the pharmaceutical industry.

To analyze Kalo's future as well as the futures of the other nonpharmaceutical subsidiaries, Mr. Herman realized that he and his analysts would have to consider the impact of these financing constraints on Marion's future growth. With unlimited financing in the future he would have only had to make a "good" investment decision. However, to balance the goals of a strong balance sheet and a high growth rate, Mr. Herman was faced with making the optimal investment decision. It was with these constraints that Mr. Herman would eventually have to make his recommendation to the Board of Directors.

COMPANY HISTORY

In 1979, Marion Laboratories Inc. of Kansas City, Missouri, was a leading producer of ethical (prescription) pharmaceuticals for the treatment of cardiovascular and cerebral disorders. (See Exhibit 2—Marion's Major Ethical Products.) Marion also owned subsidiaries which manufactured hospital supplies, proprietary (non-prescription) drugs, eyeglasses, optical accessories, electrical home stairway elevators, and specialty agricultural chemicals.

Marion Laboratories was founded in 1950 by Ewing Marion Kauffman. Prior to establishing his own company, Mr. Kauffman held a job with a field sales force of a Kansas City pharmaceutical company. After four years on the job Kauffman's sales efforts were so successful that he was making more money in commissions than the company president's salary. When the company cut his commission and reduced his sales territory, Kauffman quit to establish his own firm.

In its initial year of operation the new company had sales of $36,000 and a net profit of $1,000. Its sole product was a tablet called OS-VIM, and was formulated to combat chronic fatigue. The company's three employees, counting Mr. Kauffman, worked from a 13′ × 15′ storeroom that served as manufacturing plant, sales office, warehouse, and headquarters.

From the company's inception, the major emphasis for Marion was on sales and marketing. Mr. Kauffman was successful in developing an aggressive, highly motivated sales force. During the mid-1960s the company's sales effort

EXHIBIT 2 Marion Laboratories Inc. Major Ethical Pharmaceutical Products

PRODUCT	PRODUCT APPLICATION	ESTIMATED MARKET SIZE (in thousands)	MARION'S PRODUCT	SHARE OF MARKET (percentage)
Cerebral and peripheral vasodilators	Vascular relaxant to relieve constriction of arteries	$90–$100	Pavabid™	22
Coronary vasodilators	Controlled-release nitroglycerin for treatment of angina pectoris	90–100	Nitro-Bid™	12
Ethical and OTC plain antacids	Tablets for relief of heartburn	37	GAVISCON™	26
Andogens–estrogens	Product for treatment of calcium deficiencies	12	OS-CAL™	46
Topical burn antimicrobials	Ointment for prevention of infection in third-degree burns	8	SILVADENE™	57
Urologic antispasmodics	Product for treatment of symptoms of neurogenic bladder	10	DITROPAN™	10

Source: Smith, Barney, Harris, Upham and Co. Research Report, January 19, 1978.

was concentrated on developing Pavabid, introduced in 1962, into the leading product in the cerebral and peripheral vasodilator market.

While other drug companies were spending large amounts on research and development, hoping to discover new drugs, Marion concentrated on the sales effort, spending very little on basic research. Nearly all of its research expenditures were directed at improving its current products or further developing products licensed from other drug companies. This particular approach to product development was still being followed in 1979.

Beginning in the late 1960s, Marion decided to reduce its dependence on Pavabid which acounted for more than half of Marion's sales. In the pharmaceutical area, the company continued to minimize basic research and worked to develop new drug sources. Marion also began diversifying into the hospital and health products sector primarily by acquiring existing firms in those areas. (See Exhibit 3 for a summary of Marion's acquisition and divestiture activities.) Taking advantage of the high market value of its common stock,[1] the company acquired several subsidiaries engaged in businesses other than pharmaceuticals.

[1] Price earnings ratios for Marion in 1968 and 1969 were 46 and 52, respectively.

EXHIBIT 3 Marion Laboratories Inc. Summary of Subsidiary Acquisitions and Divestitures

NAME OF SUBSIDIARY	TYPE OF PRODUCT(S)	DATE ACQUIRED	DATE DIVESTED
Marion Health & Safety	First-aid and hospital products	1968	—
American Stair-Glide	Manufacturer of home stairway lifts and products to aid the handicapped	1968	—
Kalo Laboratories	Manufacturer of specialty agricultural chemicals	1968	—
Rose Manufacturing	Industrial fall-protection devices	1969	Sold: 1978
Mi-Con Laboratories	Manufacturers of ophthalmic solutions	1969	Merged into MH&S: 1973
Pioneer Laboratories	Manufacturer of sterile dressings	50% in 1970	Sold out: 1971
Signet Laboratories	Vitamin and food supplements	1971	Discontinued operations, selling some assets: 1975
Optico Laboratories	Eyeglasses, hard contact lenses, and related products	1973	—
Certified Laboratories	Manufacturer IPC products	1969	Sold: 1978
IPC	Marketed IPC products	1969	Merged into Pharmaceutical Division: 1979
Marion International	Distributor of pharmaceutical products	Incorporated 1971	—
Inco	Industrial creams	1972	Merged into MH&S: 1974
Occusafe	Consulting services; re: OSHA regulation and compliance	Incorporated 1972	Discontinued operations: 1973
Nation Wide	Specialty AG-Chem products	1973	Merged into Kalo
Marion Scientific	Manufacturer and distributor of	Acquired by MH&S: 1973	—
Colloidal	Specialty agricultural products	1973	Merged into Kalo
WBC	Holding company for IPC	Incorporated 1976	Sold: 1978
SRC	Specialty AG-Chem products	1977	Merged into Kalo

ORGANIZATION

Marion's operations, in 1979, were divided into two separate groups, the Pharmaceutical Group and the Health Products Group. (See Exhibit 4—Marion Organization Chart.) The Pharmaceutical Group's operations were a continuation of the original ethical drug line of the company. The Health Products Group was composed of subsidiaries purchased by Marion in hospital and health-related fields.

Fred W. Lyons, 41, was president, chief executive officer, and member of the Board of Directors. As president, Lyons was responsible for the total operation and performance of the corporation. This responsibility included the company's pharmaceutical operating group as well as all subsidiary operations, corporate planning functions and corporate supportive activities.

Lyons joined Marion in 1970 as vice-president and general manager, and director. He came to Marion from a similar position with Corral Pharmaceuticals Inc., a subsidiary of Alcon Laboratories Inc. Lyons was a registered pharmacist and had received an MBA from Harvard University in 1959.

Also serving on the Board of Directors was Senior Vice President and Chief Financial Officer, Michael E. Herman, 37, who joined Marion from an investment banking firm of which he was a founding partner. Herman started with Marion as vice-president of finance in 1974 and in 1975 was named director of the company. His responsibilities were financial planning, financial control of operations, the management information systems, the treasury functions, product development, and strategic long-range planning. Mr. Herman was also chairman of the company's New Business Task Force Committee which was responsible for the financial review, planning, evaluation, and negotiation of acquisitions. Herman earned a bachelor's of science degree in metallurgical engineering from Rensselaer Polytechnic Institute and an MBA from the University of Chicago.

Gerald W. Holder, 48, was the senior vice-president in charge of administrative functions for Marion. Holder was responsible for all corporate administrative functions, including Marion's legal, personnel, facilities and engineering services, public relations and risk management staffs. He joined the company in 1973 rising to the senior vice-president level in March of 1978.

James E. McGraw, 46, was senior vice-president of Marion Laboratories Inc. and president of the company's Pharmaceutical Group. He was responsible for the manufacturing, marketing, quality control, and accounting functions within the two operating units of the Pharmaceutical Group: the Professional Products Division and the Consumer Products Division. McGraw joined Marion in 1974 from a position as president of the General Diagnostics Division of Warner-Lambert Company.

Tom W. Olofson, 36, was a senior vice-president and president of the Health Products Group. His responsibilities included financial and planning aspects for each of the subsidiaries in the Health Products Group.

Within the described organization, Marion made some of its operating decisions in small group or task force settings that brought together corporate

MARION LABORATORIES, INC. 435

EXHIBIT 4 Marion Laboratories Inc. Organization Chart

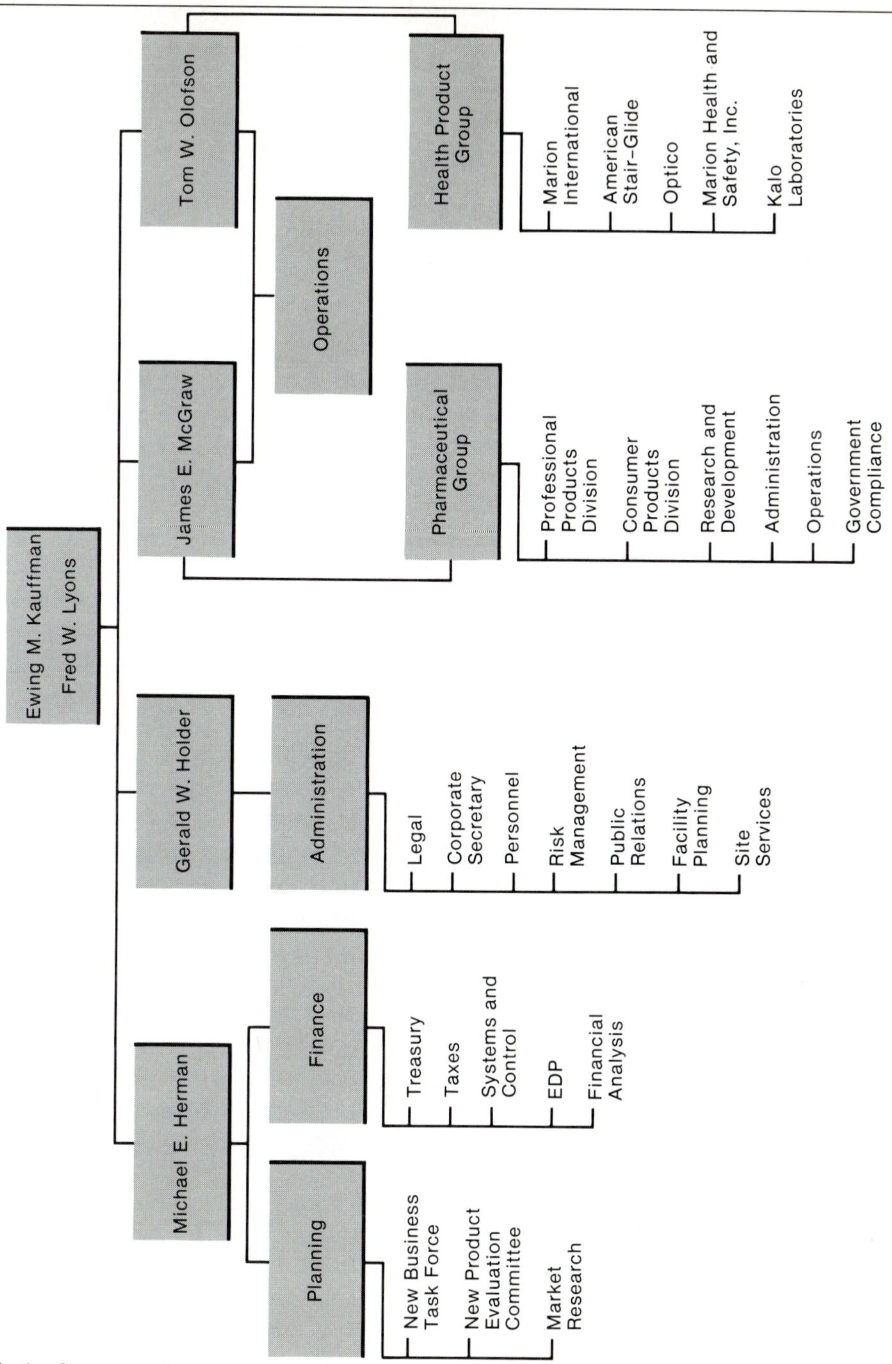

Ewing M. Kauffman / Fred W. Lyons

- Tom W. Olofson
  - Operations
- James E. McGraw
  - Health Product Group
    - Marion International
    - American Stair-Glide
    - Optico
    - Marion Health and Safety, Inc.
    - Kalo Laboratories
  - Pharmaceutical Group
    - Professional Products Division
    - Consumer Products Division
    - Research and Development
    - Administration
    - Operations
    - Government Compliance
- Gerald W. Holder
  - Administration
    - Legal
    - Corporate Secretary
    - Personnel
    - Risk Management
    - Public Relations
    - Facility Planning
    - Site Services
- Michael E. Herman
  - Finance
    - Treasury
    - Taxes
    - Systems and Control
    - EDP
    - Financial Analysis
  - Planning
    - New Business Task Force
    - New Product Evaluation Committee
    - Market Research

Organization Chart as rendered by authors.

personnel from several different disciplines. The process of approving certain capital expenditures was an example of the review and analysis process.

Marion had a formal capital expenditure review program for expenditures on depreciable assets in excess of $10,000. At the option of the group president, the review program could also be applied on expenditures of less than $10,000 with the modification that in these cases only the group president was involved in the review process.

A form that forced the requesting individual to discount the cash flows of the project was required to be completed and submitted, if the net present value of cash flows was positive, to a corporate planning group. This group consisted of corporate accounting and facilities planning personnel who, since the company was operating with limited funds, decided which projects, based on financial and strategic considerations, should be forwarded to Fred Lyons for final approval or rejection. This process occurred after the planning period and prior to the purchase of the asset. The capital expenditure review program was used for expenditures in both the Pharmaceutical Group and the Health Products Group.

PHARMACEUTICAL GROUP

Marion's ethical and over-the-counter drug operations were the major components of the Pharmaceutical Group. These operations were split into two divisions: the Professional Products Division and the Consumer Products Division. James E. McGraw headed the Pharmaceutical Group, which also was made up of the functions of research and development, administration, operations, and government compliance. Although Marion had been exclusively an ethical drugmaker prior to diversification efforts, the company had recently increased its operations in the proprietary drug area.

In 1978, Marion formed the Consumer Products Division from what had been International Pharmaceutical Corp. (IPC) to market its growing nonprescription product line. This market area, previously untapped for Marion, was expected to be a major ingredient for near-term growth. To aid in the marketing of its nonprescription line, Marion hired a full-scale consumer advertising agency for the first time in the company's history.

Sales for the Consumer Products Division were boosted when, in fiscal 1978, Marion purchased the product Throat-Discs from Warner-Lambert's Parke-Davis division. In addition, Marion also purchased two Parke-Davis ethical products, Ambenyl cough-cold products and a tablet for the treatment of thyroid disorders. Because of the timing of the acquisition, most of the sales and earnings were excluded from that year's earnings results. Sales for these three lines were expected to be nearly $8 million in 1979.

Marion's ethical pharmaceutical products were marketed by its Professional Products Division. The company sold its ethical product with a detail sales force of about 200 that called on physicians, pharmacists, and distributors within their assigned territories. The sales force was very productive by industry standards and was motivated by intensive training and supervision and an incentive compensation system. There was very little direct selling to doctors and pharmacists, the main purpose of the sales person visits being promotion of Marion's products. In addition, Marion had an institutional sales force that sold directly to hospitals, institutions, and other large users.

In fiscal 1978, 80 percent of Marion's pharmaceutical products were distributed through 463 drug wholesalers. All orders for ethical drug products were filled from the Kansas City, Missouri, manufacturing plant. Marion's pharmaceutical distribution system is diagrammed in Exhibit 5.

During 1978, the company decided to use its improved liquidity position to aid its wholesale drug distributors. Many wholesalers used outside financing to purchase their inventory and were unable to maintain profit margins when interest rates rose. By extending credit on key products, Marion helped its distributors maintain higher inventories and gave the company a selling edge over competitors.

One of Marion's major goals for each of its products was for the product to hold a market leadership position in the particular area in which it competed. This goal had been accomplished for most of the company's leading products. (See Exhibit 2.)

EXHIBIT 5 Pharmaceutical Distribution

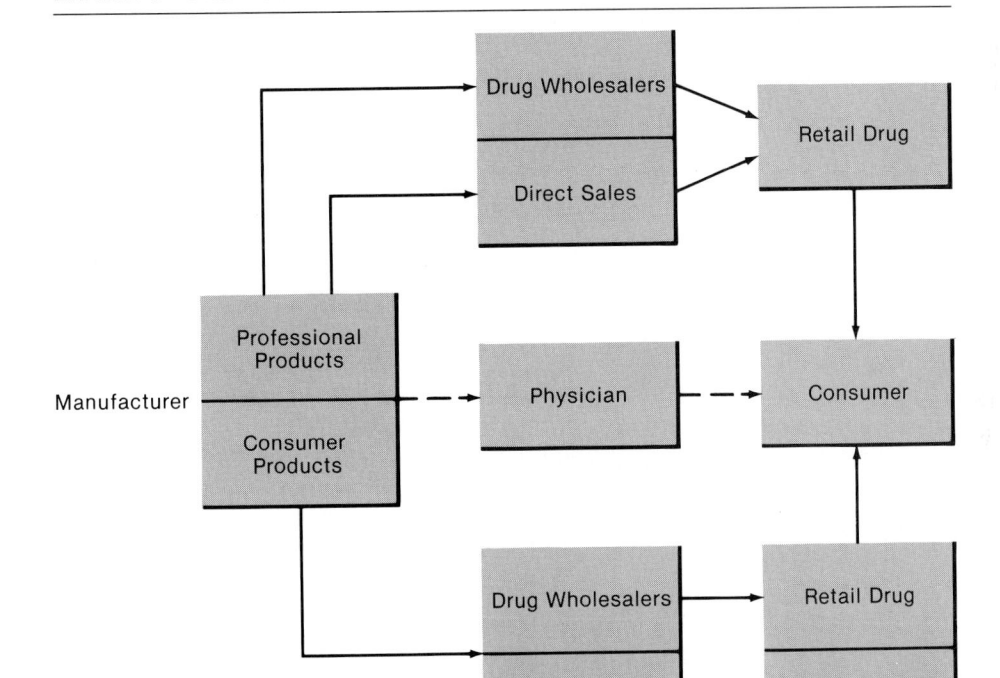

EXHIBIT 6 Marion Laboratories Inc. Changing Product Mix

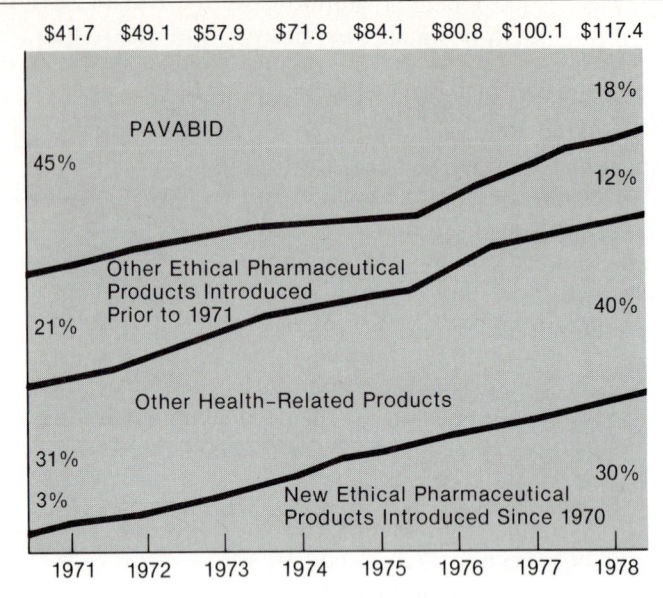

	1971	1972	1973	1974	1975	1976	1977	1978
Total ($)	$41.7	$49.1	$57.9	$71.8	$84.1	$80.8	$100.1	$117.4

- Pavabid: 45% (1971) → 18% (1978)
- Other Ethical Pharmaceutical Products Introduced Prior to 1971: 21% → 12%
- Other Health-Related Products: 31% → 40%
- New Ethical Pharmaceutical Products Introduced Since 1970: 3% → 30%

Source: 1978 Annual Report.

Capturing a large share of a market had worked particularly well for Marion's leading product, Pavabid, which in 1978 accounted for 18 percent of the entire company's sales. Marion was decreasing its reliance on Pavabid (see Exhibit 6) which, since its introduction in 1962, had been the company's most successful product. Through the 1960s Pavabid had been responsible for almost all of Marion's growth. In recent years, as the product's market matured, sales growth had slowed, forcing the company to become less dependent on Pavabid. The decrease in sales of 3.9 percent in fiscal year 1979 was due primarily to previous overstocking of Pavabid and the subsequent inventory adjustments at the distributor level.

In April of 1976 the Food and Drug Administration (FDA) had requested that makers of papaverine hydrochloride (sold by Marion as Pavabid) submit test data to support the safety and efficacy of the drug. Many small manufacturers were not able to submit the data and dropped out of the market. Marion complied with the request and had not yet been notified by the FDA of the outcome of the review by early 1979. A negative action by the FDA was not expected since it had taken so long for a decision and papaverine had been used safely for decades. However, if the FDA ruled that compounds such as Pavabid could not be marketed, either because they were not safe or were not effective, Marion would lose its leading product.

In August 1977, the FDA requested that manufacturers of coronary vasodilators, including nitroglycerin compounds like Marion's Nitro-Bid, submit test data to prove product safety and efficacy. This review was the same process that Pavabid was subject to and a negative ruling, although not expected, would adversely affect the company.

Proving its products to be safe and effective was only one area in which the company dealt with the FDA. Before any ethical drug product could be marketed in the United States, Marion had to have the approval of the FDA. Under the system effective at that time, the company was required to conduct extensive animal tests, file an Investigational New Drug Application, conduct three phases of clinical human tests, file a New Drug Application, and submit all its data to the FDA for final review. With the FDA's approval, the drug firm could begin marketing the drug.

The approval process from lab discovery and patent application to FDA approval took from 7 to 10 years. Often a company had only 7 to 8 years of patent protection left to market its discovery and recover the average $50 million it had taken to fully develop the drug from the initial discovery stages.

To avoid the R&D expenses necessary to fully develop a new drug entity into a marketable product, Marion's source for new products was a process the company called "search and development." Marion licensed the basic compound from other drug manufacturers large enough to afford the basic research needed to discover new drugs. Generally the licensers, most notably Servier of France and Chugai of Japan, were companies lacking the resources or expertise necessary to obtain FDA approval and marketing rights in the U.S. Marion's R&D effort then concentrated on developing a product with an already-identified pharmacological action into a drug marketable in the U.S. By developing existing drug entities, Marion was able to shorten the development time required to bring a new drug to market at a lower cost than discovering its own drugs. This enabled Marion to compete in an industry dominated by companies many times its own size. (See Exhibits 7 and 8 for drug industry information.)

EXHIBIT 7 Selected Ethical Drug Companies, 1977 (in thousands of dollars)

	NET SALES	COST OF GOODS SOLD	R & D EXPENSES	NET INCOME[1]
Pfizer Inc.	$2,031,900	$978,057	$ 98,282	$174,410
Merck & Co.	1,724,410	662,703	144,898	290,750
Eli Lilly & Co.	1,518,012	571,737	124,608	218,684
Upjohn Inc.	1,134,325	—	102,256	91,521
SmithKline Corp.	780,337	299,338	61,777	89,271
G. D. Searle & Co.	749,583	345,224	52,645	(28,390)
Syntex Corp.	313,604	132,710	27,648	37,643
A. H. Robbins Co.	306,713	122,374	16,107	26,801
Rorer Group Inc.	186,020	59,606	5,174	18,143
Marion Laboratories	100,131	37,300	5,907	10,652

[1] After tax

Source: "Drug and Cosmetic Industry," *Standard & Poor's Industry Survey*, June 1978.

EXHIBIT 8 Marion Laboratories, Inc. Ethical Drug Industry Composite Statistics

	1978	1977	1976	1975
Sales (millions $)	$12,450	$10,859	$10,033	$9,022
Operating margin (%)	22.5%	22.2%	21.9%	22.1%
Income tax rate (%)	36.5%	36.4%	36.2%	36.7%
Net profit margin (%)	11.8%	11.7%	11.7%	11.6%
Earned on net worth (%)	18.5%	17.9%	18.2%	18.4%

Source: Computed from company annual reports.

In addition to the FDA, the federal government was also affecting the drug industry with its activities that promoted generic substitution. In early 1979, 40 states had generic substitution that allowed nonbranded drugs to be substituted for branded, and often more expensive, drugs. The U.S. Department of Health, Education and Welfare and the Federal Trade Commission had also recently proposed a model state substitution law and a listing of medically equivalent drugs. Under other federal programs, the maximum allowable cost (MAC) guidelines, reimbursement for Medicaid and Medicare prescriptions was made at the lowest price at which a generic version was available.

Generics accounted for 12 percent of new prescriptions being written and were likely to increase in relative importance. To combat the decreasing profit margins that were expected, the industry was looking to its ability to develop new drugs to offset the shortfall that was expected in the 1980s caused by a loss of patent protection on many important drug compounds.

The effect that generic substitution laws would have on Marion was unclear. The company had always concentrated on products with a unique pharmacological action rather than those that were commodity in nature. Generic substitution required an "equivalent" drug be substituted for the brand-name drug and there were uncertainties about how equivalency would be defined.

Marion's pharmaceutical operations had not produced a major new product for several years. Products that were in various stages of development were diltiazen hydrochloride, an anti-anginal agent; sucralfate, a nonsystemic (does not enter the bloodstream) drug for the treatment of ulcers; and benflourex, a product that reduces cholesterol levels in the blood.

HEALTH PRODUCTS GROUP

Subsidiaries selling a wide range of products used in health care and related fields made up Marion's Health Products Group. The company had bought and sold several subsidiaries since beginning to diversify in 1968 (see Exhibit 3). By 1978 the group of subsidiaries was responsible for 39 percent of total company sales and 22 percent of earnings before taxes.

Several times after purchasing a company Marion had decided to sell or discontinue operations of a subsidiary. The divestment decision in the past had been based on considerations such as a weak market position, low-growth position, excessive product liability, or a poor "fit" with the rest of Marion.

In his presentation before the Health Industry's Analyst Group, Fred Lyons noted the importance of a subsidiary fitting in with the rest of Marion when explaining the company's decision to sell Rose Manufacturing. "You may have noticed that during this past year we determined through our strategic planning that Rose Manufacturing, in the fall-protection area of industrial safety, did not fit either our marketing base or our technology base. Therefore we made a decision to spin Rose off, and we successfully culminated its sale in November of 1977. Rose, like Signet Laboratories three years ago, just did not fit."

In adjusting its corporate profile Marion was always searching for companies that provided good investment potentials and were consistent with the company's goals. To provide a framework within which to evaluate potential acquisitions and to avoid some of the mistakes made in past purchases, Marion developed a set of acquisition criteria to be applied to possible subsidiary investments.

SEARCH CRITERIA FOR ACQUISITIONS

- Product Area: health care
- Market: $100 million potential with 8 percent minimum growth rate
- Net Sales: $3–30 million
- Tangible Net Worth: not less than $1 million
- Return on Investment: not less than 20 percent pretax
- Method of Payment: cash or stock

The Board of Directors made the ultimate decision on the acquisitions and divestment of Marion's subsidiaries. At the corporate level, Mr. Herman was responsible for evaluating changes in the corporate portfolio and, based on his analysis, making recommendations to the board. Since Mr. Herman was also on the Board of Directors his recommendations were heavily weighted in the board's final decision.

In early 1979 Marion had four subsidiaries in its Health Products Group: Marion Health and Safety Inc., Optico Industries; American Stair-Glide; and Kalo Laboratories. Following is a brief description of each:

MARION HEALTH AND SAFETY INC. sold a broad line of hospital and industrial safety products through its Marion Scientific Corp. and Health and Safety Products Division. Recently introduced, Marion Scientific products (a consumer-oriented insect bite treatment and a device for transporting anaerobic cultures) both showed good acceptance and growth in their respective markets. Distribution is generally through medical surgical wholesalers and distributors who in turn resell to hospitals, medical laboratories, reference laboratories, etc. Health and Safety Division manufactures and/or packages primarily safety-related products (hearing protection, eyewash, etc.) and first-aid kits and kit products, such as wraps, band-aids, and various OTC products. Sale of these products is made to safety-equipment wholesalers/distributors who resell to hospitals, industry, institutions, etc. Sales of Marion Health and Safety Inc. were estimated to have increased about 17 percent by outside analysts, to a level estimated at $19 million. Pretax margins were about 10 percent in this industry. Marion Health and Safety Inc. was headquartered in Rockford, Illinois.

OPTICO INDUSTRIES INC. participated in the wholesale and retail optical industry. Its main products were glass and plastic prescription eyeglass lenses and hard contact lenses. Outside analysts estimated this subsidiary recorded sales gains of about 26 percent for 1978 for sales estimated to be about $8 million. Optico had reduced profitability during 1978 due to expansion of its retail facilities. Pretax margins for 1978 were estimated at 6 percent, but this was expected to improve when the expansion program was completed. Optico's headquarters were located in Tempe, Arizona.

AMERICAN STAIR-GLIDE CORP. manufactured and marketed home stairway and porch lifts and other products to aid physically handicapped individuals. These products were principally sold to medical/surgical supply dealers for resale or rental to the consumer. In some instances distribution is through elevator companies. Sales were estimated at about $5 million annually by outside analysts. This subsidiary was expected to grow slowly and steadily and it had a very stable historical earnings pattern. The trend for greater access to buildings by the handicapped was expected to impact favorably on this Grandview, Missouri-based subsidiary.

KALO LABORATORIES INC.

Kalo Laboratories operated in the specialty agricultural chemical market and provided products to meet specialized user needs. In the past, Kalo had been successful in marketing its line of specialty products. (See Exhibit 9—Kalo's

EXHIBIT 9 Kalo Laboratories Sales, Investment, and Expense Information

	1978	1977	1976	1975	1974	1973
			(in millions of dollars)			
Sales	$9.0	$5.0	$2.0	$4.0	$3.0	$2.0
Total assets	5.0	4.0	2.0	2.0	2.0	1.0
Total investment[1]	3.0	3.0	1.0	1.0	1.0	0.5

	1978	1977	1976	1975	1974	1973
		EXPENSES AS PERCENT OF SALES				
COGS	43%	54%	61%	53%	55%	48%
R&D expense	8	7	7	5	5	3
Marketing, selling and general administrative expenses	37	31	42	23	24	27

[1] Includes Marion's equity in Kalo and funds lent on a long-term basis.
Authors' estimates.

Past Earnings Information.) In assessing Kalo's future there were many risks to consider. These risks included competition from large chemical companies, governmental regulatory actions, and uncertain future product potentials.

Competition and Industry

The United States and Canadian agricultural chemical market was estimated to be $3.2 billion in 1978 and growing at more than 15 percent a year.[2] The industry was dominated by large chemical manufacturers including Dow Chemical, DuPont, Stauffer Chemical, and Gulf Oil. The market was also shared by large ethical drug manufacturers including Eli Lilly, Pfizer, and Upjohn. (See Exhibit 10 for agriculture-related sales.) Economies of scale allowed the larger companies to produce large amounts of what might be perceived as a commodity product (herbicides, insecticides, and fungicides) at a much lower cost per unit than the smaller companies. Diversification of and within agricultural product lines assured the larger manufacturers even performance for their agricultural divisions as a whole.

Since smaller chemical companies like Kalo could not afford to produce large-enough amounts of their products to match the efficiency and prices of the large companies, these firms concentrated on specialty markets with unique product needs. By identifying specialty chemical needs in the agricultural segment, Kalo was able to produce its products and develop markets that were very profitable but weren't large enough to attract the bigger firms.

Products

Since the larger chemical companies dominated the large product segments, Kalo's products were designed to meet the specialized needs of its agricultural users. Kalo's product line was divided into four major classes: seed treatments, adjuvants, bactericides, and herbicides.

Seed treatments for soybeans accounted for the majority of Kalo's sales. One product in this area was Triple Noctin. Products in the seed treatment

[2] 1979 DuPont Annual Report and 1979 Upjohn Annual Report.

EXHIBIT 10   Marion Laboratories Inc. Total and Agriculture-Related Sales, Selected Companies, 1979

	TOTAL SALES (millions)	AGRICULTURE RELATED SALES (millions)	AGRICULTURE RELATED EARNINGS (before tax)
Eli Lilly	$2,520	$920[1]	28.6%
Pfizer	3,030	480[1]	9.8
Upjohn	1,755	280[1]	9.2
Marion (1978)	100	9	9.0

[1] Includes international sales.

Source: Company annual reports.

class were intended to act on soybean seeds to increase their viability once in the ground. Kalo manufactured seed treatments for soybeans only.

Adjuvants were chemicals that, when added to another agricultural product, increased the efficacy of the product or made it easier to use. For instance, Biofilmo prevented liquid fertilizer from foaming, which made it easier to apply, and Hydro-Wet enhanced the soil's receptiveness to certain chemicals, which reduced runoff into surrounding areas.

The newest product for Kalo was the adjuvant EXTEND, a chemical compound added to fertilizer that made it bind chemically with the soil or the plant. The binding process helped retain the fertilizer where it was applied, making each application longer-lasting and more effective. EXTEND was only recently introduced and its success was difficult to assess at such an early stage. Kalo's management was planning to build a family of products around EXTEND. Sales projections showed EXTEND contributing between 60–70 percent of Kalo's future growth through 1987.

Bactericides and herbicides were the final two product classes at Kalo. Bactericides were applied to the soil to either inhibit or encourage the growth of selected bacteria. One product, ISOBAC, was used to control boll rot in cotton. Herbicides, mainly for broadleaf plants, were used to control or kill unwanted weeds, leaving the desirable crop unharmed.

In the past, Kalo had acquired several of its products by acquiring the company that manufactured the product. When it purchased a going concern intact, Kalo was able to gain both manufacturing facilities and an existing distribution system. In the future Kalo expected to diversify its product line in a similar fashion. To enlarge its existing product lines Kalo was planning to use both internal and contract R&D. An example of enlarging the product family was the planned adaptation of its products to different numerous crop applications.

Because Kalo did not have a well diversified product line, its operations were more cyclical than the overall agricultural sector. Two major factors beyond Kalo's control made its annual performance extremely unpredictable, the weather and spot prices for commodities.

Kalo's operating results were seasonal as its products were primarily intended to be applied in the spring months. It was not unusual for the subsidiary to show a net loss from operations for the nine months from July until March and show a large profit in the three months April, May, and June, when the products were being purchased for immediate application. If the spring months were particularly rainy Kalo's profitability was adversely affected. Heavy farm equipment couldn't operate on wet fields without getting stuck and application was impossible until the fields dried out. Once the fields were dry, Kalo's agricultural users often did not have time to apply the herbicides or other products even though it would have been economically advantageous to do so.

The other factor that affected the demand for Kalo's products was the spot pricing of commodities. The price of commodities relative to each other had a large effect on the total amount of each type of crop planted. Because the producer was free to switch crops yearly based on the spot prices, Kalo's demand for the upcoming planting season was uncertain and variable. Kalo was particularly vulnerable to swings in demand caused by the substitutability of crops since many of their products were applicable only to soybeans.

Distribution and Marketing

The end user of Kalo's products was usually the individual farmer. Kalo and the rest of the agricultural chemical industry had a distribution system like the one shown below.

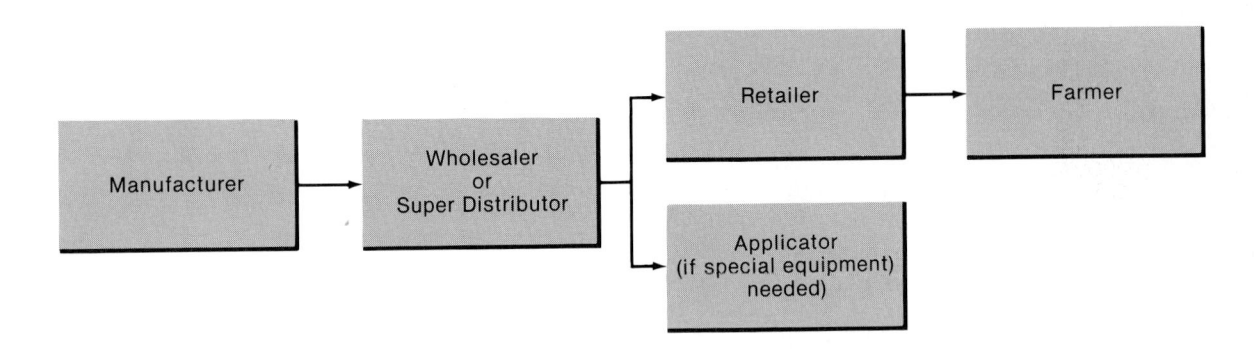

```
Manufacturer → Wholesaler or Super Distributor → Retailer → Farmer
                                               → Applicator (if special equipment) needed
```

Kalo promoted its products with a sales force of about 30 salesmen. The main task of these salesmen was to call on and educate wholesalers' distributors on the advantages, unique qualities, and methods of selling Kalo's products. In addition some end user information was distributed to farmers, using "pull" advertising to create demand. A limited amount of promotion was done at agricultural shows and state fairs but because of the expense involved, this type of promotion was not used often.

Kalo's Future

Sales forecasts prepared by the staff analysts for Mr. Herman looked very promising as they predicted sales gains of from $4 to 6 million in each of the next nine years. (See Exhibit 11.) There were, however, some important assumptions on which the forecasts were based.

As mentioned earlier, 60–70 percent of the forecasted growth was to come from a product family based on the new product EXTEND. A great deal of uncertainty surrounded the product, however. Since it was new, the current success of EXTEND was difficult to measure, particularly in determining how current sales translated into future performance. If the market evaluation for EXTEND and related products were correct, and if a family of products could be developed around EXTEND, then the sales potential for the proposed product family was very promising provided Kalo was able to exploit the available sales opportunities.

Additional growth projected in the sales forecasts was to come from existing products and undefined future products that were to be developed or acquired.

EXHIBIT 11 Kalo Laboratories Forecasted Sales and Asset Turnover

	1979	1980	1981	1982	1983	1984	1985	1986	1987
Net sales $MM (current dollars)	$12	$16	$20	$25	$30	$35	$40	$45	$50
Asset turnover	1.8x	1.8x	1.9x	1.9x	1.9x	1.9x	1.9x	1.9x	1.85x

Note: After-tax margin expected to increase to 7 percent by 1984.
Authors' estimates.

Approximately 20 percent of the growth was to come from the existing products in the next 4–5 years. Ten to 20 percent of the growth in the later years of the forecast was expected to come from currently unknown products.

For Kalo to realize the forecasted growth it was going to be necessary for Marion to provide financing. It was going to be impossible for Kalo to generate all the required funds internally. Kalo had been a net user of cash, provided by Marion, since 1976. (See Exhibit 9—Kalo's Sales and Earnings Information, Exhibit 12—Kalo's Balance Sheet at June 30, 1978, Exhibit 13—Balance Sheets, and Exhibit 14—Ten-Year-Financial Summary for information about Marion's investment in Kalo.) Marion's management did not consider the amount of cash provided through the first part of 1979 to be excessive so long as Kalo maintained adequate profitability and steady growth rates. In addition to the long-term funds provided by Marion, Kalo also required short-term financing of inventory during each year due to the seasonality of its sales.

Government Regulation

Another major uncertainty in Kalo's future was an unpredictable regulatory climate. Regulation of agricultural chemicals was under the jurisdiction of the Environmental Protection Agency (EPA). Compliance with the EPA was a similar process as with the FDA. The process of developing and introducing a new chemical product took from 8–10 years which included 2–5 years necessary to obtain EPA approval. The costs of developing and bringing a new product to market were generally from $5 to $10 million.

Once a product was on the market the EPA had powers of recall similar to the FDA and could require the company to do additional research after the product was introduced. The prospect of having a product removed from the

EXHIBIT 12 Kalo Laboratories Balance Sheet, June 30, 1978 (in millions)

Current assets	$2.5	Current liabilities	$1.4
PP&E (net)	1.9	Long-term debt	1.0
Other	.2	Capital	2.2
Total	$4.6	Total	$4.6

Authors' estimates.

market was an added element of risk for Kalo if any of its products were affected. No problems were expected for Kalo although several of the subsidiary's products (particularly its herbicides and bactericides) had a relatively high potential for environmental problems, if not applied correctly.

THE DECISION

Mr. Herman knew that in making his recommendation he would have to balance the immediate and long-term resource needs and the goals of Marion. Although Kalo looked promising from the forecasts, there were many uncertainties surrounding these subsidiaries' futures that had to be considered.

Since Marion had no new drug products ready to be introduced soon, the company would have to rely on other areas to reach its growth goals. Kalo was growing, but it was also requiring a constant input of funds from its parent.

EXHIBIT 13 Marion Laboratories, Inc. Consolidated Balance Sheet, 1977 and 1978

		JUNE 30 1978	JUNE 30 1977
ASSETS			
Current assets	Cash	$ 381,116	$ 961,588
	Short-term investments, at cost which approximates market	2,561,660	10,028,297
	Accounts and notes receivable, less allowances for returns and doubtful accounts of $1,845,466 and $2,305,793	28,196,199	20,576,412
	Inventories	19,640,945	15,568,170
	Prepaid expenses	2,305,403	1,461,367
	Deferred income tax benefits	757,585	895,110
	Total current assets	53,842,908	49,490,944
Property, plant, and equipment, at cost	Land and land improvements	2,832,588	2,935,671
	Buildings	24,456,746	25,224,652
	Machinery and equipment	19,671,607	18,110,907
	Aircraft and related equipment	1,670,904	1,670,904
	Construction in progress	365,311	357,338
		48,999,156	48,299,472
	Less accumulated depreciation	(10,725,533)	(8,585,190)
	Net property, plant, and equipment	38,273,623	39,714,282
Other assets	Intangible assets	4,774,055	2,042,762
	Notes receivable (noncurrent)	890,692	11,589
	Marketable equity securities, at market value	688,914	—
	Deferred income tax benefits (noncurrent)	318,434	249,647
	Miscellaneous	99,597	141,232
	Total other assets	6,771,692	2,445,230
Total assets		$98,888,223	$91,650,456

(Continues)

EXHIBIT 13 (Continued)

		JUNE 30	
LIABILITIES AND STOCKHOLDERS' EQUITY		**1978**	**1977**
Current liabilities	Current maturities of long-term debt	$ 82,102	$ 95,004
	Accounts payable, trade	3,979,341	4,224,105
	Accrued profit-sharing expense	1,752,515	243,096
	Other accrued expenses	3,864,168	3,008,238
	Dividends payable	1,260,612	1,198,938
	Income taxes payable	4,391,252	5,030,219
	Total current liabilities	15,329,990	13,799,600
Long-term debt, excluding current maturities		15,580,072	15,661,399
Deferred income taxes payable		1,107,000	733,000
Deferred compensation		177,975	172,889
Stockholders' equity	Preferred stock of $1 par value per share authorized 250,000 shares; none issued	—	—
	Common stock of $1 par value per share authorized 20,000,000 shares, issued 8,703,346 shares	8,703,346	8,703,346
	Paid-in capital	3,474,358	3,475,443
	Retained earnings	58,358,925	51,604,550
		70,536,629	63,783,339
	Less:		
	293,153 shares of common stock in treasury, at cost (189,500 shares in 1977)	3,819,243	2,499,771
	Net unrealized loss on noncurrent marketable equitable securities	24,200	—
	Total stockholders' equity	66,693,186	61,283,568
Commitments and contingent liabilities		—	—
Total liabilities and stockholders' equity		$98,888,223	$91,650,456

Source: 1978 Annual Report.

One possibility for growth was to purchase another drug manufacturer and add its products to Marion's, taking advantage of any distribution synergies that might exist. To make such a purchase, the company would need more resources. To sell a subsidiary could provide needed resources, but to do so quickly under less-than-optimum conditions would surely result in a significantly lower price than could be realized under normal conditions. The income and cash-flow impact of this approach would be undesirable.

With the board meeting so soon, Mr. Herman was faced with analyzing the complex situation quickly. In three days he would have to make his recommendation to the Board of Directors.

EXHIBIT 14 Marion Laboratories Inc. Ten-year Financial Summary
(dollar amounts in thousands except per share data)

		\multicolumn{10}{c}{YEAR ENDED JUNE 30}
		1978	1977	1976	1975	1974	1973	1972	1971	1970	1969
Sales:	Net sales	$117,378	$100,131	$80,838	$84,096	$71,778	$57,937	$49,066	$41,692	$35,322	$30,188
	Cost of sales	43,177	37,330	29,315	26,078	21,715	18,171	14,932	12,262	10,622	8,985
	Gross profit	74,201	62,801	51,523	58,018	50,063	39,766	34,134	29,430	24,700	21,203
	Operating expenses	51,718	43,397	37,292	31,699	26,991	21,155	19,164	17,181	13,828	12,453
	Operating income	22,483	19,404	14,231	26,319	23,072	18,611	14,970	12,249	10,872	8,750
	Other income	1,581	1,194	683	1,404	1,033	722	709	599	630	328
	Interest expense	1,546	1,542	898	97	83	109	116	88	198	260
Earnings:	Earnings from continuing operations before income taxes	22,518	19,056	14,016	27,626	24,022	19,224	15,563	12,760	11,304	8,818
	Income taxes	10,804	8,404	5,628	13,295	11,791	9,297	7,730	6,364	5,899	4,493
	Earnings from continuing operations	11,714	10,652	8,388	14,331	12,231	9,927	7,833	6,396	5,405	4,325
	Earnings (loss) from discontinued operations	—	—	—	(3,617)	(120)	76	488	—	—	—
	Net earnings	$ 11,714	$ 10,652	$ 8,388	$10,714	$12,111	$10,003	$ 8,321	$ 6,396[1]	$ 5,405	$ 4,325
Common share data:	Earnings (loss) per common and common-equivalent share:										
	Continuing operations	$ 1.38	$ 1.23	$ .96	$ 1.65	$ 1.40	$ 1.14	$ .90	$ .76	$ .65	$ .52
	Discontinued operations	—	—	—	(.42)	(.01)	.01	.06	—	—	—
	Net earnings	$ 1.38	$ 1.23	$ .96	$ 1.23	$ 1.39	$ 1.15	$ .96	$ .76[1]	$ .65	$ .52
	Cash dividends per common share	$ .59	$ .53	$ .52	$ .48	$ .28	$ .21	$ .20	$ .16	$ .12	$ .12
	Stockholders' equity per common and common-equivalent share	$ 7.87	$ 7.09	$ 6.63	$ 6.29	$ 5.52	$ 4.16	$ 3.16	$ 2.52	$ 2.01	$ 1.47
	Weighted average number of outstanding common and common share equivalents	8,475	8,640	8,707	8,708	8,689	8,715	8,651	8,396	8,377	8,354

[1] Before extraordinary charge of $916,000, equal to $.11 per common share resulting from the disposition of investment in affiliated companies.

Source: 1978 Annual Report.

INDUSTRIAL HIGHLIGHT

Drugs and Cosmetics Industry

Below is a capsule summary of the drugs segment of the drugs and cosmetics industry. Marion Laboratories, Inc., is a part of this industry segment. Information in this highlight was compiled by the U.S. Department of Commerce and focuses on this industry during the approximate period of time covered in the case. Keep in mind that industrial highlights contained in this text are not intended as a complete synopsis of an industry but as a profile of certain issues that can be relevant to the case situation.

DRUGS[1]

The current[2] value of drug product shipments in 1979 is expected to reach $15.7 billion, or 12 percent over an estimated $14 billion in 1978. Drug industry shipments will follow a similar pattern of growth, climbing to $17 billion in 1979, or 13 percent above the 1978 value of $15 billion.

Drug industry sales have grown at an annual rate of more than 10 percent since 1967. This trend should continue through 1983.

In 1977, the annual rate of profit for the industry was slightly over 18 percent measured against equity; and is estimated to have increased to 18½ percent in 1978. This favorable rate of return will continue for the near future. However, higher labor and material costs, coupled with more pronounced competition from generic drug sales, will have a tempering effect. A reduction in the number of new drugs being introduced during the next few years also is expected to adversely affect profits.

The drug industry has continued to resist inflationary price pressures. The Producers Price Index for drugs and pharmaceuticals will reach 150 in 1978 and 160 in 1979, or an annual rate of increase of 7.3 percent since 1973.

Source: U.S. Industrial Outlook, Department of Commerce, 1979, pp. 151–159.

[1] The term drug is defined in the Federal Food, Drug, and Cosmetic Act.
[2] All values are in current dollars unless otherwise stated.

Ethical Drugs Up 11 Percent

The value of ethical drug products shipped in 1979 will be $8.74 billion, an increase of 11 percent over 1978. Most ethical drugs are dispensed by prescription only.

Industry surveys show a slight decline in the number of prescriptions dispensed in 1977, for a total of approximately 1.4 billion. This could be due to the tendency of practitioners to prescribe higher initial dosages, thus reducing the number of refills.

According to the Consumer Price Index, prescriptions are estimated to have increased in price by 26 percent since 1967. However, during that time, the number of units in each prescription will have increased by one-third, thus reducing the average price increase to about 7 percent in 10 years.

Research and Development

The pharmaceutical industry is one of the most technologically oriented in the United States. Of 209,000 employees, more than 13,000 are college-trained scientists working in research and development.

About 150,000 chemical compounds will be screened in 1979 for possible medicinal use. Of these, approximately 15 will reach the market. However, some may be major medical breakthroughs like the pneumonia vaccine introduced in 1978.

According to a recent university research study it is estimated that the average cost of developing a new drug entity has risen to $55 million. The industry will be budgeting about $1.72 billion for research and development in 1979. The high cost of research is slowing innovation in the United States.

In 1977, the U.S. pharmaceutical industry spent 45 percent of the world total for research and development. However, of the 56 new drug entities introduced throughout the world that year, only nine were developed in the United States. This may be due to some extent to Federal regulations which cause more research funds to be channeled into safety and efficacy studies than are required abroad.

There is a trend toward shifting more U.S. research overseas. In 1977, more than $200 million of the $1.3 billion allocated for research by U.S. firms was spent on overseas projects. Partly as a result, six new U.S. drug entities were developed abroad that year.

International Activity

In 1979, the U.S. drug industry will contribute approximately $800 million to the balance of payments. Exports are expected to reach a level of $1.8 billion, an increase of 20 percent above estimated 1978 exports of $1.5 billion. Imports also will increase 20 percent, to $980 million.

Exports of medicinal chemicals and botanicals comprise about 66 percent of total U.S. exports of drugs. In 1979, medicinal exports will be valued at about 1.2 billion, an increase of 16 percent over 1978. Imports of medicinals and botanicals will be valued at $912 million in 1979, which is 20 percent above the value in 1978.

The value of biological exports in 1979 is expected to reach $225 million, about 20 percent above exports of $187 million in 1978. Imports will be minimal, not more than $10 million in 1979.

Benzenoid medicinal imports in 1977 were valued at $108.9 million, an increase of 28 percent over the value in 1976. There was a 2½ percent decrease in tonnage imported, however.

Half of the 14 leading drug manufacturers in the world are U.S. companies. Forty-five U.S. based firms have affiliates or subsidiaries abroad.

Major opportunities for greater sales exist in the international market primarily because of its faster rate of growth. In 1978, for example, only about 3 percent of the total value of U.S. pharmaceutical preparations shipments were exported. The potential for significantly increasing this segment of U.S. export trade, especially for small to medium-size generic firms, will be enhanced by the more favorable competitive situation that exists internationally as a result of the position of the U.S. dollar at this writing.

In 1979, about 65 percent of the Free World market for ethical drugs, estimated at $60 billion, will be concentrated in North America, Japan, and Western Europe. The United States, Japan, Germany, France, Italy, and Spain accounted for more than 50 percent of world consumption of ethical drug products. The U.S. is estimated to hold 15 percent of the market.

World health experts believe that only 200 essential drugs, equitably distributed throughout the world, could alleviate disease and suffering. However, along with this drug therapy and prophylaxis must come an awareness of hygiene and nutrition and an economical capability to maintain the basic essentials.

Generics Getting More Attention

More emphasis is being placed on the marketing of generic prescription drugs, multi-source products on which patents have expired. As late as 1977, only one-third of patients knew what a generic drug was, and only about 25 percent were concerned about prescription prices. This situation has changed considerably as more publicity is being given the price advantage of generic versus brand names drugs. The Food and Drug Administration's opinion that there was no essential difference between the products of large or small drug companies, or between generic or brand name products, also has boosted generic drug sales.

The rate of growth of generic drug shipments since 1970 has been three times that of branded prescriptions. More major pharmaceutical manufacturers are establishing generic drug lines to compete in this market. Approximately 600 drug entities are now being prescribed generically.

Generically prescribed products are expected to account for 14 percent of all new prescriptions dispensed in 1979. This trend will tend to slow the growth in value of industry shipments due to increased competition and price reductions.

The long-term potential for generic sales is excellent. By 1985, about 40 patents covering drugs having a current value of shipments of $800 million will expire.

Industry Outlook

In 1983, the value of drug and pharmaceutical shipments will reach $26.6 billion, an annual growth rate of 12 percent from 1978. A portion of this growth will result from the development of new drugs and increased export sales.

Within the next 10 years, U.S. research efforts should produce new antibiotics and antivirals, bacterial vaccines, a cure for schizophrenia, and deterrents to the aging process. Additional research funds will be budgeted to develop preventives for tuberculosis, the common cold, and dental caries.

Governmental restrictions probably will be tightened, resulting in higher production and research costs, and a greater concentration of sales among fewer companies.

SECTION FIVE

Special Issues in Strategic Management

CASE 22

Tylenol's Capsule Crisis: Part I

YAAKOV WEBER
Ben-Gurion University

On February 8, 1986, a 23-year-old woman in Yonkers, New York, died from a cyanide-contaminated Tylenol capsule. In 1982, when seven people in Chicago died after ingesting similarly tainted Tylenol capsules, the company Johnson & Johnson (J&J), recalled 31 million bottles and spent about $100 million on marketing and repackaging. The first move of the chairman, Jim Burke, was to stop the manufacture and sale of the over-the-counter (OTC) capsule, much as he did in 1982. The frustrating nightmare for Tylenol executives—seemingly random poisonous tampering with a few capsules of the company's best-known product—had returned. They faced a strategic crisis! How to respond? What to do with a $525 million-sales-per-year product? And when to do it?

BACKGROUND—JOHNSON & JOHNSON

J&J was incorporated in New Jersey in 1887 by Robert Wood Johnson and his two brothers with $100,000 of capital and 14 employees. During his tenure, he established the company as a leader in the health care industry by such moves as introducing revolutionary surgical dressings and establishing a bacteriological laboratory. Over the years, the company experienced a rapid growth through internal development by introducing new products, by acquiring established companies, and by international expansion. The company's 1985 earnings were $613.7 million on revenue of $6.42 billion.

J&J manufactures and sells a broad range of products in health care and other fields all over the world. The company's products are divided into four industry segments as follows:

Consumer. This segment consists of products that are marketed to the general public and distributed both through wholesalers and directly to independent and chain retail outlets. It includes toiletries and hygienic products, baby care items, first aid products, and nonprescription drugs.

Professional. This segment consists of ligatures and sutures, mechanical wound closure products, diagnostic products, dental products, medical equip-

---

This case was prepared as a basis for class discussion by Yaakov Weber, Ben-Gurion University. Department of Industrial Engineering and Management, Beer-Sheva 84105 Copyright © 1987 by Yaakov Weber.

ment and devices, surgical dressings, surgical instruments, and related items used principally by the professional fields, including hospitals, physicians, dentists, diagnostic laboratories, and clinics. These products are marketed principally through surgical supply and other dealers.

Pharmaceutical. This segment consists principally of prescription drugs, including contraceptives and therapeutics, and veterinary products. These products are distributed both directly and through wholesalers for use by health care professionals and the general public.

Industrial. These products are converted or consumed by industrial users and, in general, not available to or used by the general public. This segment consists of textile products, collagen sausage casings, and fine chemicals. Sales are directly to users and through a variety of industrial trade channels.

Sales and operating profit for the four industry segments are presented in Exhibit 1. Balance sheet and income statements appear in exhibits provided with Case 23. Exhibit 2 shows several financial ratios comparing J&J and its major competitors.

The international business began with the establishment of an affiliate in Canada in 1919 and one in Great Britain in 1924. Their international business is conducted by subsidiaries manufacturing many of J&J products in about 50 countries and selling in most countries of the world. The principal products marketed and the methods of distribution used by J&J's international subsidiaries vary across countries and cultures. About 40 percent of J&J's sales and more than half of its after-tax earnings came from overseas. Exhibit 3 shows the foreign sales of J&J and its major competitors.

J&J views research and development (R&D) as a key strength supporting its domestic and international business. Major research facilities are located not only in the United States but also in Belgium, Brazil, Canada, Switzerland, the United Kingdom, and West Germany. Exhibit 4 shows the costs of worldwide research activities relating to the development of new products, the improvement of existing products, the technical support of products, and compliance

EXHIBIT 1 Sales and Operating Profit by Business Segment
(in millions of dollars)

Segment	1981 Sales	1981 Operating Profit	1980 Sales	1980 Operating Profit
Consumer	$2,362.8	$338.4	$2,124.7	$263.7
Professional	1,734.4	177.9	1,540.5	191.5
Pharmaceutical	1,118.6	314.7	1,008.1	228.2
Industrial	243.7	32.9	303.4	29.5
Total	$5,399.0	$837.7	$4,837.4	$712.9

EXHIBIT 2 Financial Ratios of Major Drug Companies (corporatewide—includes All Products)

Company (OTC analgesic product)	1980 EPS[1]	1980 ROI[2]	1980 NI[3]	1980 D/C[4]	1981 EPS	1981 ROI	1981 NI	1981 D/C	1982 EPS	1982 ROI	1982 NI	1982 D/C	1983 EPS	1983 ROI	1983 NI	1983 D/C	1984 EPS	1984 ROI	1984 NI	1984 D/C
Johnson & Johnson (Tylenol)	2.17	12.9%	$400	3.0%	2.51	13.1%	$468	3.4%	2.79	13.0%	$523	4.8%	2.57	11.3%	$489	6.0%	2.75	11.4%	$515	6.8%
Bristol-Myers (Bufferin and Excedrin)	2.04	13.1	271	7.5	2.29	13.0	306	6.0	2.59	13.3	349	6.1	3.00	14.2	408	4.7	3.45	15.1	472	4.4
American Home Products (Anacin and Anacin 3)	2.84	20.0	446	0.2	3.18	20.1	497	0	3.59	20.7	560	0	4.00	21.2	627	1.9	4.26	21.4	656	1.9
Sterling Drug (Bayer Aspirin)	2.04	10.2	123	5.5	2.15	10.3	130	5.0	2.17	10.2	132	7.2	2.24	9.8	137	8.1	2.39	9.9	145	7.4

[1] EPS = Earnings per share.
[2] ROI = Return on investment (percent).
[3] NI = Net income (millions of dollars).
[4] D/C = Debt/capital ratio (percent).

EXHIBIT 3 Foreign Sales of Major Drug Companies

Company (OTC analgesic product)	1981 Foreign sales ($ millions)	1981 Percent of total sales	1982 Foreign sales ($ millions)	1982 Percent of total sales	1983 Foreign sales ($ millions)	1983 Percent of total sales	1984 Foreign sales ($ millions)	1984 Percent of total sales
Johnson & Johnson (Tylenol)	$2,373	44%	$2,457	43%	$2,389	40%	$2,389	39%
Bristol-Myers (Bufferin and Excedrin)	1,257	36	1,223	34	1,175	30	1,264	30
American Home Products (Anacin and Anacin 3)	1,387	34	1,412	31	1,360	28	1,050	23
Sterling Drug (Bayer Aspirin)	828	44	769	41	703	37	699	38

SPECIAL ISSUES IN STRATEGIC MANAGEMENT

EXHIBIT 4   Research Expenditure by Johnson & Johnson ($000)

Year	Expenses[1]
1984	$421,200
1983	405,100
1982	363,200
1981	282,900
1980	232,800
1979	192,688
1978	163,617

[1] These expenses are charged directly to income in the year in which they were incurred.

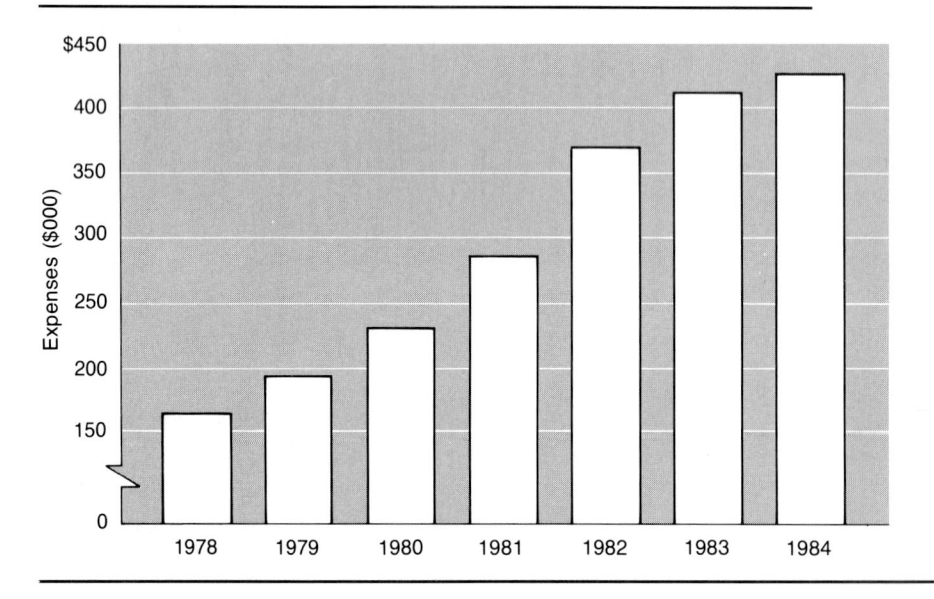

with governmental regulations for the protection of the consumer. These costs are charged directly against income in the year incurred. Exhibit 5 compares J&J's R&D expenditure with its major competitors'.

J&J was the last of the large, public companies to nominate outsiders for its board of directors, relenting in 1978 only under pressure from the New York Stock Exchange. The stock exchange required J&J to accept two outsiders, enough to dominate a three-member audit committee. But J&J has since brought 7 outsiders onto the board to join 10 insiders.

J&J articulates its business principles in a document called *Our Credo*—a code of corporate behavior that has a mystical but nonetheless palpable influence on the company. Chairman Jim Burke commented after the first Tylenol crisis: "All of us at McNeil Consumer Products and J&J truly believe that the guidance of the credo played the most important role in our decision making." The credo is a legacy of "the General," Robert Wood Johnson, the son of one of the founding Johnson brothers. He was the man who, during his long rule from 1938 to 1963, shaped the company's philosophy and culture.

EXHIBIT 5 Corporatewide R&D Expenditure of Major Drug Companies (in millions of dollars)

Company (Analgesic Product)	1981 Amount Spent	1981 Percent of Sales	1982 Amount Spent	1982 Percent of Sales	1983 Amount Spent	1983 Percent of Sales	1984 Amount Spent	1984 Percent of Sales
Johnson & Johnson (Tylenol)	$282	5%	$363	6%	$405	7%	$421	7%
Bristol-Myers (Bufferin and Excedrin)	144	4	161	4	185	5	212	5
American Home Products (Anacin and Anacin 3)	115	3	137	3	161	3	N.R.	N.R.
Sterling Drug (Bayer Aspirin)	67	4	70	4	81	4	88	5

First given to employees in 1947, the guiding principles of the credo have been renewed over the years, in part through credo challenge meetings. The beginning of a series of credo challenge meetings was in 1975, with an invitation for 24 officers from the United States and overseas to challenge the credo. They debated for hours before changing even a paragraph in the document. The final result, which was prominently displayed in every manager's office, is shown in Exhibit 6. It commands that the company serve customers first, employees second, the communities in which it operates third, and finally its stockholders. J&J has sometimes sacrificed earnings in what it perceived to be the best interests of the customers. For example, when sun worshipers discovered that Johnson's Baby Oil is an excellent tanning agent, J&J played along with an advertising campaign aimed at teenagers: "Turn on a tan, baby." As evidence began to accumulate that overexposure to the sun promotes skin cancer, J&J voluntarily killed the campaign in 1969, at an estimated cost of about 15 percent of baby oil sales.

J&J put a great emphasis on its decentralized organizational structure. The 1981 annual report revealed the main reasons for having decentralized units, which:

> share a commitment to meeting the special needs of a well-defined customer. In doing so, they create a wide variety of innovative ways to successfully run their businesses.
>
> We feel that the secret to liberating that productivity is decentralization—granting each company sufficient autonomy to conduct its business without unnecessary constraints. In short, we believe decentralization equals creativy equals productivity.

To accomplish this purpose, a new company was created whenever a new product or market handled by any unit was deemed important enough to warrant a separate dedicated effort. This was the case with McNeil Consumer Products Company, which was created in 1976 to focus exclusively on the consumer product opportunity for Tylenol products in the OTC analgesic business. McNeil Pharmaceutical, then, was able to concentrate on prescription products, including Tylenol with codeine.

EXHIBIT 6

Our Credo

We believe our first responsibility is to the doctors, nurses and patients
to mothers and all others who use our products and services
In meeting their needs everything we do must be of high quality
We must constantly strive to reduce our costs
in order to maintain reasonable prices
Customers' orders must be serviced promptly and accurately
Our suppliers and distributors must have an opportunity
to make a fair profit

We are responsible to our employees,
the men and women who work with us throughout the world
Everyone must be considered as an individual
We must respect their dignity and recognize their merit
They must have a sense of security in their jobs
Compensation must be fair and adequate
and working conditions clean, orderly and safe
Employees must feel free to make suggestions and complaints
There must be equal opportunity for employment development
and advancement for those qualified
We must provide competent management
and their actions must be just and ethical

We are responsible to the communities in which we live and work
and to the world community as well
We must be good citizens—support good works and charities
and bear our fair share of taxes
We must encourage civic improvements and better health and education
We must maintain in good order
the property we are privileged to use
protecting the environment and natural resources

Our final responsibility is to our stockholders
Business must make a sound profit
We must experiment with new ideas
Research must be carried on innovative programs developed
and mistakes paid for
New equipment must be purchased, new facilities provided
and new products launched
Reserves must be created to provide for adverse times
When we operate according to these principles
the stockholders should realize a big return

Johnson & Johnson

BACKGROUND—TYLENOL

Before the First Crisis in September 1982

On January 15, 1959, J&J acquired McNeil Laboratories, Inc., manufacturer of pharmaceutical products (including Tylenol), in exchange for 622,008 common shares ($32 million in 1959). Through the 1960s, McNeil carefully promoted Tylenol among doctors and pharmacists as an alternative pain reliever for people who suffer stomach upset and other side effects from aspirin. The drug—which is an acetaminophin-based, or nonaspirin, analgesic—found consumer favor because it is less irritating to the stomach than aspirin.

In 1974, J&J acquired StimTech, a fledgling health care company built around a new product. The product, an electronic pain-killing device, was intended as a substitute for analgesic drugs—including J&J's Tylenol. StimTech was founded in 1971 to market a transcutaneous electronic nerve stimulator (TENS). The unit, coinvented by Hagfors in the 1960s, blocks pain sensations electronically by stimulating nerve fibers in the patient's skin.

TENS is claimed effective against headaches, arthritis, and back pain, without any of the side effects of drugs used to treat the same infirmities. But while J&J's aggressive marketing made Tylenol the number one OTC drug in the United States, StimTech foundered. The three founders charged J&J with quashing StimTech as a potential competitor. A U.S. district judge in Minneapolis has upheld a jury's finding that J&J bought the company to suppress development of its product. Judge Miles W. Lord, who presided over the trial in summer 1981, said the evidence "fully justifies" a verdict of fraud, antitrust violations, and breach of contract. J&J had to pay $170 million to the three entrepreneurs who started StimTech. George S. Frazza, J&J's general counsel, noted that about 10 other companies now market TENS equipment, including Medtronic, Minnesota Mining, and Dow-Corning, and that the company will continue to invest in it and promote it. He was also confident that J&J will win its appeal.

In early 1975, Bristol-Myers decided to challenge Tylenol with a cut-rate imitation called Datril. At first, McNeil showed some hesitancy about all-out combat. But by late 1975 McNeil cut Tylenol's price by one third and began to advertise Tylenol heavily. Tylenol's spectacular rise is shown in Exhibit 7. After the battle was over, the 12 products in the Tylenol line had taken an overwhelming 37 percent share of the $1.3 billion analgesic market (over $400 million), more than Bayer, Bufferin, and Anacin combined—the three best-selling headache cures until Tylenol came along. Datril has been all but annihilated. For an illustration of the analgesic market share of the major competitors, see Exhibit 8.

While J&J was large and widely diversified, its Tylenol product line had a huge and direct impact on J&J. In late 1982, Tylenol contributed an estimated 7.4 percent of J&J's worldwide sales of $5.4 billion and 17 to 18 percent of its $476.6 million in net earnings in 1981. A rise of 25 percent in Tylenol-derived profits was estimated for 1982, compared to a corporatewide estimate of increased profits of around 16 percent. As the summer of 1982 drew to a close, McNeil executives were confident Tylenol would take over 50 percent of the market by 1986. J&J stock had risen in two years from a low of $20 to $46, reflecting in part the stock market's attraction to Tylenol's success. Within a few days, market share and stock prices would drop dramatically.

The First Crisis: 1982

On September 30, 1982, the Cook County (Chicago) Medical Examiner's Office reported that three people had been killed as the result of ingesting cyanide

EXHIBIT 7 Sales of 12 Products in Tylenol Line

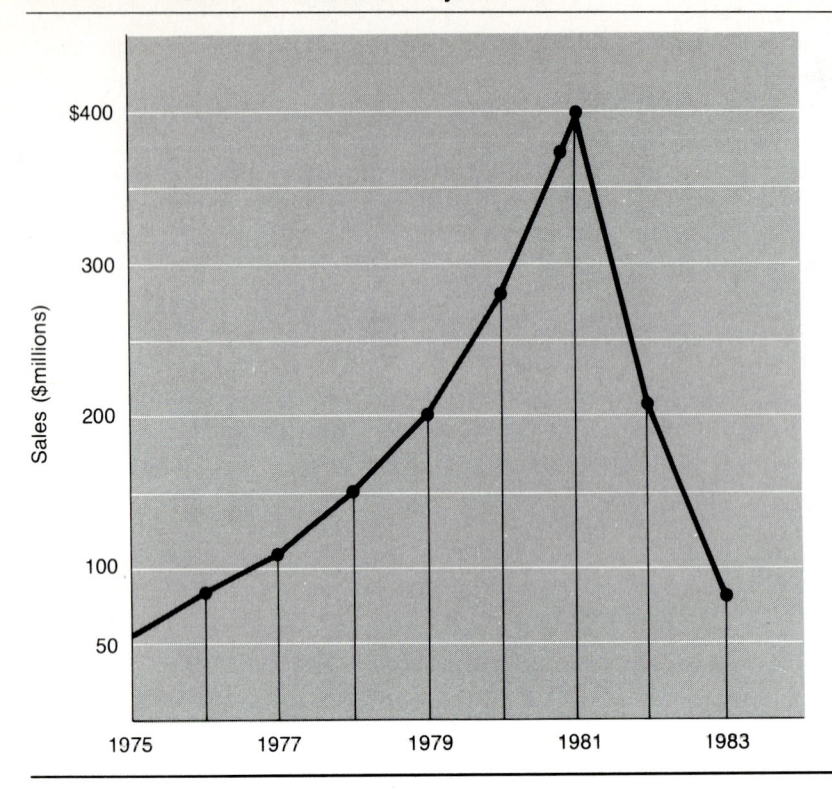

in Tylenol capsules. That morning, calls came from newspapers, TV, and radio stations as far away as Honolulu and Ireland. And, as the story started to break, even more calls began to pour in from pharmacies, doctors, hospitals, poison control centers, and hundreds of panicked consumers. Within a few days, Chicago's mayor, Jane Byrne, went on television urging her constituents to stop taking Tylenol.

Many retailers immediately removed the entire Tylenol line of tablets, capsules, and elixirs from their shelves. A senior vice president for marketing at Revco D.S., Inc., in Twinsburg, Ohio, said that buyers "are switching brands" and that the chain was getting "hundreds of phone calls" from people with Tylenol products not implicated in the scare. Tylenol's market share and J&J's stock price fell rapidly, as shown in Exhibit 9.

International sales were affected differently in each country. The governments of Guatemala and Puerto Rico banned sales of Tylenol, and the Venezuelan government ordered consumers to "break their bottles" of the painkiller. In the Philippines, where Tylenol capsules were introduced only three months earlier, yet where Tylenol tablets had been available for some time, the government's health minister banned the sale of the capsules and

EXHIBIT 8   The OTC Analgesic Market, 1982

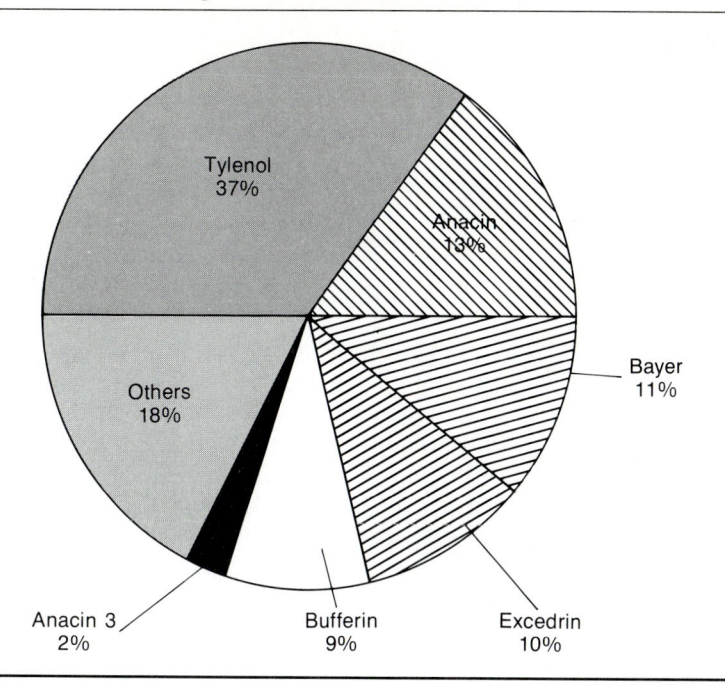

- Tylenol 37%
- Anacin 13%
- Bayer 11%
- Excedrin 10%
- Bufferin 9%
- Anacin 3 2%
- Others 18%

ordered a recall. All post offices and customs sections in ports of entry were ordered to seize capsules brought into the country. In Canada, sales were not banned, and Canada's Department of Health initiated industrywide discussions about ways to ensure that consumers could detect product tampering. In Europe, Tylenol was unaffected, primarily because it was not yet widely available.

First Reaction of J&J

Despite the commitment of J&J to decentralization, J&J Chairman James Burke elevated the management of the crisis to the corporate level. He personally took charge of the company's response and delegated responsibility for running the rest of the company to other members of J&J's executive committee. Burke's reason for doing this was "because the crisis was a major public health problem and a major threat to the company as a whole and to other products bearing the company's name." The crisis committee consisted of J&J Chairman James Burke, J&J President David Clare, Vice President of Public Relations Lawrence Foster, McNeil Consumer Products Chairman David Collins, General Counsel George Frazza, and executive committee member Arthur Quilty. This committee met twice daily.

Their first move was to immediately stop manufacturing and selling Tylenol capsules. Next they suspended all advertising for Tylenol and recalled 93,000

EXHIBIT 9   Changes in Sales, Stock Price, and Market Share

	Per Incident	Immediately Post-incident
Tylenol sales	$480 million (12 months preceding incident)	$90 million (12 months following incident)
Stock price (per share)	$46 (day before incident)	$38 (one week later)
OTC market share	37% (day before incident)	7% (three weeks later)

bottles scattered across Ohio. This was an expensive process—telegrams to doctors, hospitals, and distributors alone cost almost a half-million dollars. In a meeting with the FBI and the Food and Drug Administration (FDA), Burke advocated a recall of all Extra-Strength Tylenol capsules, but he was counseled against it. The FBI feared that this move would tell the murderer he could bring a major corporation to its knees, and the FDA feared it might cause more public anxiety. However, following the seventh victim and what appeared to be copycat strychnine poisoning with Tylenol capsules in California, the FDA agreed with Burke that he had to recall Tylenol capsules worldwide. This 31 million-bottle recall raised the expense of this incident to over $100 million.

While recognizing possible dangers in trying to manage the news media, J&J's crisis team decided to open its doors and to have a close relationship with the press. Burke and Foster felt the company could use the media to quickly get out maximum information to the public so as to both prevent a panic and gain credibility. For example, on the first day after the Chicago deaths, the crisis committee learned that cyanide was in fact used in the quality assurance facility next to the Tylenol manufacturing plant. The cyanide was used to test the purity of raw materials. Consistent with this "open" approach, the public relations department immediately released this information to the press. An obvious advantage from having close relationships with the media was that the company could get its most accurate and up-to-date information around the country (and the world) via reporters calling in for comments.

Making a Strategic Decision: 1982

Within weeks, consumer groups advocated immediate action and tamper-proof packaging for OTC drugs, but FDA Commissioner Arthur Hayes, Jr., argued that this was not possible. To quell consumer panic, the FDA and members of the OTC medicines industry formed a committee to develop standards for tamper-resistant packages. The FDA's recommendation for a tamper-resistant regulation was rumored to go along with industry suggestions allowing marketers to select from among many different types of tamper-resistant packagings. It also was expected to recommend that the special packaging would be required on all new products after 90 days and that all old packaging must be off the shelves after 15 months. The proposal put the cost of the regulation at

$20 million to $30 million annually, or about 1 cent per item. The FDA prepared a 30-second commercial that had Commissioner Arthur H. Hayes urging consumers to check medications carefully.

Most companies were awaiting word of the specifics of the FDA regulation before making public any marketing plans regarding permanent protective packaging or advertising. Several companies, including American Home Products and Norcliff-Thayer, were taking temporary steps to protect products, such as glued boxes and cellophane wrappings.

Despite the uncertainty surrounding final resolution of the packaging issue, Tylenol's competitors were not standing idly by. American Home Products had just introduced Anacin 3, a nonaspirin analgesic like Tylenol, and immediately benefited from the damage to Tylenol's reputation. AHP increased production at both of its Anacin 3 plants from two to three shifts on a round-the-clock basis. Bristol-Myers, producer of Excedrin, said that demand was up considerably. During the same time, Bristol-Myers reported that a poisoning incident occurred with Excedrin capsules in Colorado. This led Bristol-Myers to remove all Excedrin capsules from Colorado shelves, to urge consumers to switch to tablets, and to take out newspaper ads telling consumers how to exchange Excedrin capsules for tablets.

While the controversy over instituting tamper-proof containers swirled around it, J&J's crisis team sifted through its strategic options. Larry N. Feinberg, an analyst for Dean Witter Reynolds, Inc., said that it would take a great deal of time to reestablish the Tylenol brand and that "J&J may never be able to reestablish its credibility fully." Robert Benezra, an analyst for Alex, Brown & Sons, said that "destroying all Tylenol capsules wherever they can find them will be the only way they can effectively deal with the problem of consumer hesitancy." He contended that the company might eventually come up with a new brand name for the now-tainted capsules. Most analysts estimated that it would take J&J at least 18 months to repair the damage done to its product, based on the quick move of J&J to halt public distrust. Both analysts and retailers agreed that the company had earned its good reputation and deserved public support. Sumner H. Goldman, vice president of merchandising at Super Valu Stores, Inc., said that "They've done one of the best marketing jobs on Tylenol in the history of health and beauty aids marketing." But he too believed it would be a long road back for Tylenol.

David H. Talbot, a health care analyst with Drexel Burnham Lambert, estimated that Tylenol's initial recalls would cost $50 million after taxes—enough to hold its 1982 earnings rise to only 1 or 2 percent. Most of the recall costs were incurred in buying back Tylenol bottles from retailers and consumers and shipping them to disposal points. The cost of testing all the recalled capsules for the presence of poisons exceeded their value; therefore, all the withdrawn capsules were destroyed. The company estimated that costs would drop third-quarter earnings from 78 cents a share in 1981 to 51 cents in 1982. Security analysts projected a 70 percent drop in what normally would have been $100 million plus in sales for Tylenol's over-the-counter line of products in the fourth quarter. It was estimated that prescription sales of Tylenol with codeine, about $18 million a quarter, would not be affected. Some analysts said that the company would be lucky if Tylenol could make half of the sales that originally were expected for the next year (the precrisis estimate was half a billion dollars).

Joseph Chiesa, McNiel president, said that "There was a lot of noise out there, most of it associating Tylenol with death." One possible option was abandoning Tylenol and reintroducing the pain reliever under a new name. Another possibility was to switch to Tylenol tablets. There's a hidden danger, however, in the switch back to tablets: it may lead to a serious decline in the previously fast-growing revenues of the analgesics market as a whole. Michael LeConey, a health care analyst with Merrill Lynch, said that the more expensive extra-strength capsule format mass-marketed by Tylenol was a significant factor for the revenues per headache dosage: "The number of headaches certainly hasn't gone up by 15 to 20 percent a year, as the dollar growth in the market would indicate. A lot of this has been due simply to the upgraded capsule format." An extra-strength capsule in a jar of 100 cost about 5.5 cents, while an extra-strength tablet cost only 4.5 cents. Another alternative was simply to follow the FDA recommendation: keep Tylenol but use new packaging. The cost of the new packaging, which would give more protection than the minimum required by the FDA, would be about 2.4 cents per package.

James Burke called in Young & Rubicam, J&J's oldest advertising agency, to poll consumer attitudes about the Tylenol poisoning crisis. He said that one of the things which bothered him "was the extent to which J&J was becoming deeply involved in the affair. The public was learning that Tylenol was a J&J product, and the dilemma was how to protect the [J&J] name and not incite whoever did this to attack other J&J products." The results of the company surveys revealed that more than 47 percent of the American public were aware of the fact that J&J is the parent company behind Tylenol. Before the poisoning less than 1 percent of consumers knew this fact. Other results indicated that 94 percent of all Americans knew about the Tylenol tragedy; 90 percent knew that the problem involved only the capsule form; 93 percent thought that the problem could occur for any capsule, not just Tylenol; and 90 percent believed the maker was not to blame. According to a survey among Tylenol users, 87 percent said they realized the maker of Tylenol was not responsible for the deaths; 61 percent still were not likely to buy extra-strength capsules in the future; 50 percent felt that way about Tylenol tablets as well as capsules; and 35 percent of all Tylenol users threw away the product in their homes. A survey of individuals who were not regular Tylenol users showed that 80 percent had little interest in ever using the brand. Burke concluded that there was a strong residue of fear and anxiety. But crisis team member Joseph Chiesa said that "The problem with consumer research is that it reflects attitudes and not behavior. The best way to know what consumers are really going to do is put the product back on the shelves and let them vote with their hands."

The Decision

James Burke said that management looked at all options and was convinced, according to the surveys, that there was a core of loyal users who wanted the product in capsules as well as tablet form. The frequent Tylenol user was seen as much more inclined to go back to the product than the infrequent user. Thus, the company decided to concentrate on bringing back the loyal customers first. Burke argued that reintroducing the product under another name could very well be misleading, anyway. He noted that even if the brand lost half its business, which the company saw as the worst scenario, it would still be the leading analgesic in the marketplace. Therefore, J&J decided to rebuild the brand with a new Tylenol package in a triple-safety-sealed, tamper-resistant package. He declared that J&J had never been run for the short term and that he had no doubts about whether the brand would survive.

Still, the big question was how quickly—or whether—consumer confidence in Tylenol, and J&J, could be restored.

The Implementation

Timing was crucial. If J&J brought Tylenol back before the hysteria had subsided, the product might die on the shelves. If the company waited too long, the competition would gain an enormous lead.

To rebuild consumer confidence in Tylenol, J&J bought an estimated $1 million plus in TV time during a four-day period and ran a 60-second commercial at the same time on all three big networks. The commercials ran a total of 14 times from October 24 through October 27. In those spots, the medical director of McNeil Consumer Products Company, Dr. Thomas Gates, urged consumers "to continue to trust Tylenol." He reminded viewers of the 20 years of trust established by Tylenol and said that his company would do all it could to regain that trust. He noted that the company would be back on the market with capsules as soon as it developed tamper-resistant packaging and that, until then, viewers should take tablets. The commercials did not run in Chicago, where Tylenol products had not yet returned to the shelf; cut-ins were made locally, with spots for two other J&J products.

At the end of October, Burke mobilized 2,259 salespeople from all of J&J's domestic subsidiaries to persuade doctors and pharmacists to begin recommending Tylenol tablets to patients and customers. This was the same way Tylenol was marketed 22 years ago.

McNeil sued its insurers to recover at least $110 million in product recall and business interruption expenses incurred to remove its Extra-Strength Tylenol from the market (see Exhibit 10). The suit asked the court to decide whether there was coverage under the defendants' policies for costs associated with McNeil's production halt and nationwide recall of the capsules after some were laced with cyanide. McNeil's insurers were expected to vigorously oppose the suit.

J&J also took steps in the international market. Lawrence Freeman, president of J&J/Philippines, for example, appeared on prime-time TV to explain the difference between capsules, which are only 4 percent of all Tylenol sales, and tablets. Throughout Canada, J&J asked all pharmacists to place the product behind the dispensary counter to reassure the public that there was no possibility of tampering with the product. In Australia, the company continued with its original plans to go national by 1983, because Tylenol was

EXHIBIT 10 Insurers Sued by McNeil

Insurer	Coverage ($ millions)
North River	$19.9
Transit Casualty	0.5
Employers of Wausau	4.6
Aetna Casualty and Surety	12.5
American Centennial	5.0
Granite State	10.9
First State	5.0
Northbrook Excess and Surplus	9.0
Affiliated F. M.	50.0

sold in a locally made plastic blister pack, which J&J officials said was tamper proof.

In November 1982, in a closed-circuit press conference, carried live by satellite TV transmission to more than 1,000 media representatives in 30 cities, J&J introduced the new packaging for Tylenol and its future plans. The new capsules were being offered with triple safety protection even though any one of the three closures would comply with government regulations, which had been issued a few days before the conference. The protection included (1) glued flaps on the outer box, (2) a tight plastic neck seal, and (3) an inner foil seal over the mouth of the bottle. In addition, a bright yellow warning label read: "Do not use if safety seals are broken."

The plans included the following steps:

1. Newspaper ads running one full week in November and again in December, offering consumers a $2.50 coupon for any Tylenol product to replace any product they may have discarded. The coupon could be received by calling a toll-free number.
2. Implementation of a "Continue to Trust Tylenol" ad campaign similar to the earlier commercials.
3. Complete distribution of newly packaged capsules by 1982 year-end.
4. Resumption of product-oriented advertising early in 1983.
5. Attempting to persuade Chicago's Mayor Byrne to lift the total ban on the sale of Tylenol products in that city.
6. Repackaging of many J&J consumer products, including toiletries, in tamper-resistant containers.

After the Crisis

The results of the steps taken by J&J were impressive. AdWatch, a monthly survey of consumer awareness of advertising, conducted a telephone survey from November 1 through November 27, 1982, asking consumers to name the medicine and drug advertising that first came to mind. Tylenol was named by

EXHIBIT 11 Percent of Public Awareness of Advertising of Leading Brands in the Medicine and Drugs Industry

	Month (1982)					
Brand	June	July	August	September	October	November
Tylenol	18.7%	17.5%	16.6%	19.8%	16.6%	25.7%
Anacin	6.2	6.8	10.6	8.8	8.5	5.5
Anacin 3[1]	—	—	—	—	—	3.4
Bayer	4.6	2.8	4.6	6.8	7.0	3.3

[1] Not in top three until November.

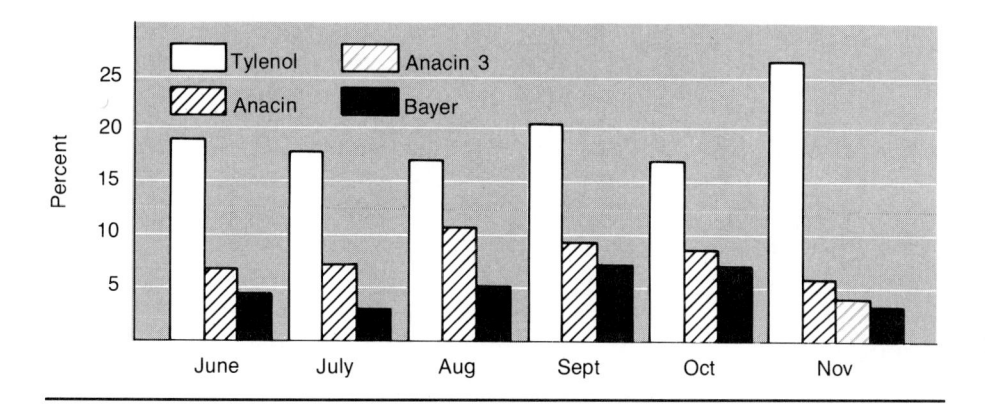

25.7 percent, up from 16.6 percent in October (see Exhibit 11)—an increase of 9.1 percent, which was the largest of any advertiser mentioned by consumers in this survey. These results were due to the "trust us" TV spots, which were cited by 80 percent of those mentioning Tylenol ads.

By the fifth week after the tragedy, 59 percent of regular Tylenol users said they would either definitely or very likely buy Tylenol in the future, up from 40 percent in the first week after the poisoning. That figure rose to 77 percent when the regular users were asked whether they would buy Tylenol in a tamper-resistant container, a result attributed by Jim Burke to the growing confidence due, in part, to the TV commercials of October 24–27.

Despite increasingly competitive advertising and promotion by rivals, research indicated a dramatic rise in Tylenol market share, as shown in Exhibit 12. The research measured sales of a variety of products via retail scanner data in grocery outlets in Massachusetts, Indiana, Wisconsin, and Texas. The sample base represented less than 1 percent of the population, but its primary value was in indicating trends and changes in market shares rather than absolute figures. Some 30 percent of purchases during week nine were with the $2.50 coupon McNeil ran in thousands of newspapers to help customers replace product they may have thrown away.

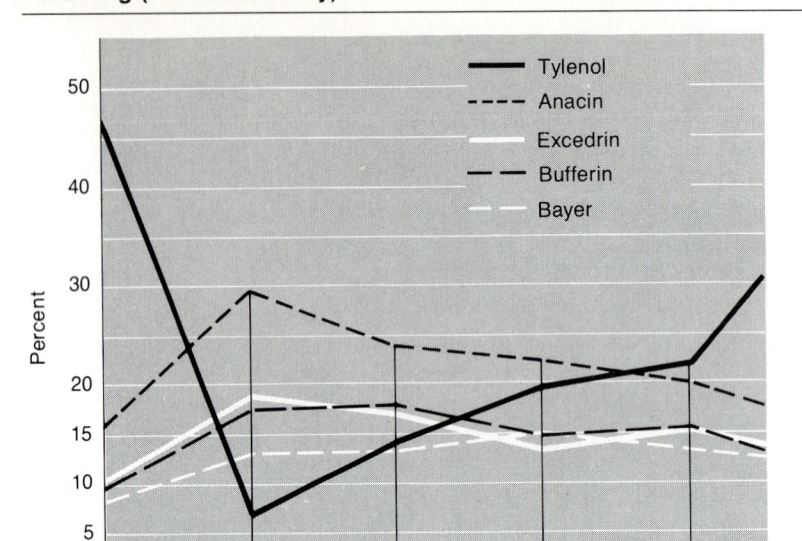

EXHIBIT 12 Analgesic Dollar Shares in Four U.S. Cities, before and after Poisoning (food stores only)

A year after the tragedy, Jim Burke referred to the fairness of the American public:

> A remarkable poll by the Roper organization taken three months after the tragedy showed 93 percent of the public felt J&J handled its responsibility either very well or fairly well. But the public also gave very high marks to the FDA, the law enforcement agencies, the drug industry in general, and the media! The public knew that all of these institutions were working—together—and in their interest! And what did our customers do? They gave us back our business. . . . Our latest Nielson, taken in July–August [1983], shows Tylenol has regained over 90 percent of the business we enjoyed prior to the tragedies.

In November 1983, Jim Burke received the Advertising Council's public service award. He spoke of the J&J credo and said that "If we do the other jobs properly, the stockholder will always be well served."

The drug industry, in general, recovered from the crisis. The total OTC drug volume amounted to about $6.5 billion in 1983, up 4.1 percent from 1982; the rise for 1984 was estimated at about 6 to 8 percent, and it was expected to expand by about 45 percent until the end of the decade. The modest growth in recent years reflected the growing number of elderly people in the population, the introduction of new proprietary drugs, the switching of prescription drugs

EXHIBIT 13 Estimated OTC Analgesic Markets, 1984 and 1985

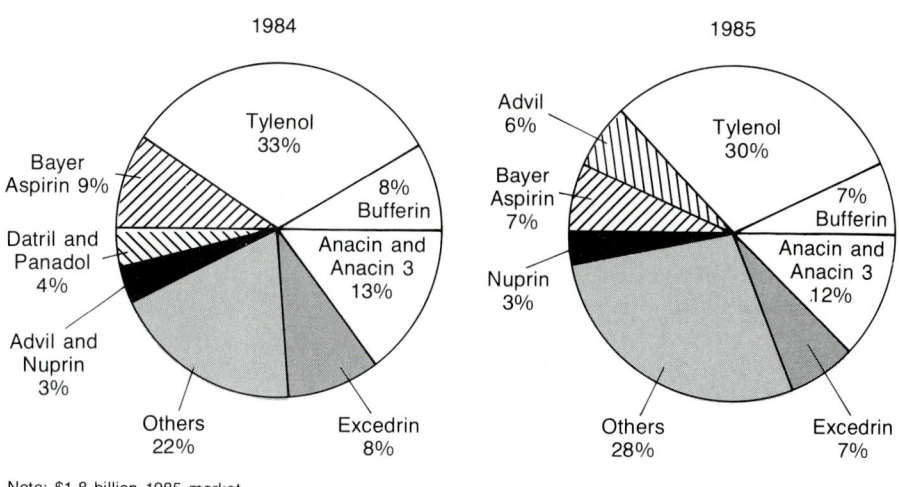

1984
- Tylenol 33%
- Bufferin 8%
- Anacin and Anacin 3 13%
- Excedrin 8%
- Others 22%
- Advil and Nuprin 3%
- Datril and Panadol 4%
- Bayer Aspirin 9%

1985
- Tylenol 30%
- Bufferin 7%
- Anacin and Anacin 3 12%
- Excedrin 7%
- Others 28%
- Nuprin 3%
- Bayer Aspirin 7%
- Advil 6%

Note: $1.8 billion 1985 market
Source: Standard & Poor's Corporation.

to OTC status, and increased self-treatment to avoid the high cost of medical care.

In the spring of 1984, the FDA approved two new Ibuprofen products for OTC sale, which caused important changes in the $1.5 billion analgesic market and were expected to affect negatively such drugs as Bayer's Aspirin, Bristol-Myers' Bufferin and Excedrin, and Tylenol (see Exhibit 13). The drug, which is the first new major nonprescription painkiller introduced in nearly 30 years, relieves pain as well as reduces inflammation and fever. It has been available for more than 10 years on a prescription basis under the Motrin name, which is manufactured and marketed by the Upjohn Company. Now the Ibuprofen products, Advil and Nuprin, are being produced (under license from Upjohn) by American Home Products and Bristol-Myers, respectively.

In August 1985, U.S. District Judge Fred Lacey ruled that McNeil could not recover lost profits under the business interruption clause of its property insurance policy. He found that J&J's loss of profits following the Tylenol recall didn't fit the definition of loss set forth in the business interruption clause. Yet even with this unfavorable ruling, the beginning of 1986 saw J&J's top management satisfied with Tylenol's performance, which generated about 18 percent of J&J's earnings. Tylenol capsules alone accounted for about 6 percent of the company's 1985 earnings of $613.7 million, or $3.36 a share, on revenues of $6.42 billion. The capsule business represented about one third of the $525 million in Tylenol sales in 1985.

INDUSTRIAL HIGHLIGHT

Drug Industry

Below is a capsule summary of the pharmaceutical preparations segment of the drug industry of which Johnson & Johnson, maker of Tylenol Capsules, is a part. Information in this highlight was compiled by the U.S. Department of Commerce and focuses on this industry during the approximate period of time covered in the case. Keep in mind that industrial highlights contained in this text are not intended as a complete synopsis of an industry, but as a profile of certain issues that can be relevant to the case situation. A list of additional references at the end of this highlight can be used for further industry analysis.

CURRENT SITUATION

The estimated value of pharmaceutical industry and product shipments in 1985 increased 4.1 percent. The International Trade Administration (ITA) has estimated the increase in the shipments price index for pharmaceutical preparations in 1985 as 6.8 percent. Other BLS price indexes covering the first 7 months of 1985, which use a different set of weights, imply that the price index increase might exceed 9 percent.

Employment in the industry declined slightly in 1983, increased about 4 percent in 1984, and leveled off in 1985. Wages have been rising about 5.5 percent a year since 1982. Productivity is estimated to have increased 3.9 percent in 1985, slightly more than the average of 3.6 percent a year since 1982.

The value of exports was estimated to have increased 12.9 percent, to $773 million, in 1985. Imports rose to $325 million, 31.5 percent above the 1984 level. Import gains have averaged 100 percent a year since 1982, while exports have risen only about 11 percent a year. In perspective, however, the positive net trade balance of the pharmaceutical preparation industry decreased only $74 million between 1982 and 1985, to $448 million.

According to a major industry survey, drugstores dispensed more than 1.5 billion prescriptions in 1984, 1 percent more than in 1983. This figure was estimated to have increased slightly in 1985. Mail order, health maintenance

Source: U.S. Industrial Outlook, Department of Commerce, 1986, pp. 17-3–17-4.

organizations, and hospital outpatient pharmacies probably account for another 300 million prescriptions. An estimated 150 million fewer prescriptions were dispensed in 1985 because some former prescription products were shifted to over-the-counter (OTC) status. The average annual number of prescription sales has been rising since 1980, but only by about 1 to 2 percent a year. The reasons for this slow growth are the public's wariness about taking drugs, the declining number of new products coming to market, and the shift of more prescription products to OTC status. About half of all prescriptions dispensed are wasted because patients do not adhere to the drug regimens prescribed for them and because about 20 percent of patients never fill their prescriptions.

People over the age of 65 make up 11 percent of the population but consume 25 percent of all prescription drugs in the United States. This is about three times the amount used by 25-to-44 year olds. Additional generic drugs will make prescriptions more affordable. In May 1985, five of the top seven leading prescription drugs became eligible for generic marketing in the United States. Sales of these five items exceeded $1.1 billion in 1984. By the end of 1985, 51 of the leading 200 prescription drugs will have achieved generic status.

More than 300 U.S. firms compete for nonprescription drug business, valued at more than $8 billion in 1985. Of these firms, 10 control 45 percent of the market. The OTC market is growing at the annual rate of 9 percent, after adjusting for price changes. The reason for this trend is the public's growing reliance on self-medication and an increasing variety of OTC products.

OUTLOOK FOR 1986

The value of pharmaceutical preparation industry and product shipments is forecast to increase 3.9 percent. The value of exports should increase to $875 million, or by 13.2 percent, while imports are expected to rise to $425 million, an increase of 30.7 percent.

Generic prescription products will be marketed in a more professional fashion in 1986. Techniques will include more aggressive promotion to physicians and pharmacists, more package information, and better package design. About 150 new generics will be approved in both 1986 and 1987. In addition, third-party payers, such as insurance companies, will apply more pressure to expand the use of generics because they cost less than brand-name products. More than 100 primary generic companies will market these new generic prescription products. The industry will show an increase in sales of generic products of more than $1 billion in 1986.

LONG-TERM PROSPECTS

The value of industry and product shipments in the pharmaceutical preparation industry will increase at an annual rate of about 3 to 4 percent through 1990. Prompting this continued growth will be an aging population that requires more prescription drugs. Tempering the increase in growth will be fewer introductions of new drugs. Prices will be lower, on the average, because of the heavy influx of generic drugs expected during the next 5 years. About 30 percent of all prescription drugs dispensed in 1990 will be generics. Smaller generic companies will merge with larger ones, some of which will be foreign, especially Japanese, that wish to enter the U.S. market. These mergers will allow some smaller generic companies to become innovators, expanding into new drug development.

By 1990, about 40 percent of all drugs sold will be OTC. Pharmacists will be prescribing as well as dispensing drugs in a number of states and will be a primary source of drug information.

The pharmaceutical market in Europe will decline 10 percent by 1990 because of a reduction in public health expenditures on drug products. Already, many U.S. companies with subsidiaries in Europe and Japan are feeling the pressure of price and promotion controls. German producers will continue to dominate the European market, followed by those in France, Italy, and Great Britain.

Research and development both in the United States and abroad, will continue to be maintained at the current high rate of expenditures. Applied research, which will produce short-term profits, will include development of new delivery systems, such as biocompatible polymeric substances, monoclonal antibody/chemotherapy, transdermals, and osmotic pump tablets. Longterm projects from basic research promise even greater rewards. Research on immunomodulators, such as interferon (for proper functioning of the immune system) and neurotropic hormones (to stimulate nerve cell growth and alleviate neurological disease), is especially promising.—*Leo McIntyre, Office of Chemicals and Allied Products, (202) 377-0128, September 1985.*

ADDITIONAL REFERENCES

Pharmaceutical, Preparations, Except Biologicals. Current Industrial Reports, MA28G(84)-1, Bureau of the Census, U.S. Department of Commerce, Washington, DC 20233.

Annual Survey of Manufactures. M83(AS)-Z, Bureau of the Census, U.S. Department of Commerce, Washington, DC 20230.

1982 Census of Manufactures, MC82-1-28c, Bureau of the Census, U.S. Department of Commerce, Washington, DC 20230.

CASE 23

Tylenol's Capsule Crisis: Part II

YAAKOV WEBER

Ben-Gurion University

On February 8, 1986, Diane Elsroth, a 23-year-old New Yorker, died after taking a tainted Extra-Strength Tylenol capsule. This sent an all-too-familiar shudder through J&J. At the end of the first week, J&J shares traded in the New York Stock Exchange had fallen to $47.25 from $52.50 before the death and were expected by some analysts to fall in the second week to about $40 to $42.

The immediate move of J&J was to stop the manufacture and sale of Tylenol. The company asked retailers to remove from their shelves only the remaining 200,000 bottles that were in the lot containing the suspect capsule. The recall and cost of rebuilding Tylenol's market share was expected, according to Jim Burke, to cost the company $100 million to $150 million after taxes for 1986.

INFORMATION FOR DECISION MAKING

There were several options available for J&J. The first was simply to abandon capsules for nonprescription drugs and to convince, if possible, capsule users to convert to the company's caplets (smooth-coated, capsule-shaped tablets developed in 1983). Since 1983, McNeil had aggressively promoted the caplets, which had grown to account for about 15 percent of Tylenol brand sales in 1985. Top company executives pulled out consumer surveys from three years ago that showed that 90 percent of capsule users would be willing to use caplets if given reason to try. But a telephone survey J&J conducted over the weekend of this second crisis found that only 59 percent of capsule users said they would be willing to use caplets or tablets if capsules weren't available. This alternative was expected to result in a $150 million pre-tax charge against first-quarter earnings. Analysts said the moves could expect to cost the company between 60 cents and 80 cents a share, reducing its previously anticipated per-share earnings for 1986 to about $3. See Exhibits 1–7 for sales and operating profit figures, balance sheets, and income statements. Frank Young, the FDA commissioner, said that the agency "did not suggest, direct, or pressure J&J" into such action and "This is a matter of J&J's own business judgment."

This case was prepared as a basis for class discussion by Yaakov Weber, Ben-Gurion University. Department of Industrial Engineering and Management, Beer-Sheva 84105. Copyright © 1987 by Yaakov Weber.

EXHIBIT 1 Sales and Operating Profit by Business Segment (in millions of dollars)

Segment	1985 Sales	1985 Operating profit	1984 Sales	1984 Operating profit	1983 Sales	1983 Operating profit	1982 Sales	1982 Operating profit	1981 Sales	1981 Operating profit	1980 Sales	1980 Operating profit
Consumer	$2,774.5	$ 408.7	$2,600.7	$305.0	$2,530.7	$412.9	$2,477.0	$362.4	$2,362.8	$338.4	$2,124.7	$263.7
Professional	2,207.0	149.2	2,004.2	111.6	2,043.1	121.5	1,931.5	152.6	1,734.4	177.9	1,540.5	191.5
Pharmaceutical	1,439.8	461.1	1,295.7	427.0	1,175.8	345.6	1,118.6	314.7	1,008.1	288.5	8,688.0	228.2
Industrial[1]	—	—	223.9	38.9	223.3	21.1	233.8	23.9	293.7	32.9	303.4	29.5
Total	$6,421.3	$1,019	$6,124.5	$882.5	$5,972.9	$901.1	$5,760.9	$853.6	$5,399.0	$837.7	$4,837.4	$712.9

[1] In 1985, sales and earnings of industrial products have been merged with the remaining three segments.

Industry officials argue that tablets often have to be larger than capsules to contain the same amount of active medicine, and this may make some tablets harder to swallow. Drug company executives say that consumers clearly prefer the capsules, which are easier to swallow and less foul tasting. Moreover, Burke said that "Some consumers have the impression that [the capsules] work better."

Most drug makers resisted the idea of abandoning the capsules, and Burke said that if "we get out of the capsule business, others will get into it" and also that pulling the capsules would be a "victory for terrorism." The spokesperson for the industry trade group said that "For the entire industry to walk away from capsules now would be like throwing out the baby with the bath water."

Some people called on the manufacturers to switch to new tamper-resistant gelatin capsules, which already are being manufactured by two companies. Eli Lilly's Qualicaps division was working on such capsules, which involved placing an easily visible band of gelatin around the capsule to seal the cap to the capsule body. The spokesperson of this company argued that it will enable drug makers to seal capsules at regular production line speeds. But drug industry officials said that they were reluctant to adopt this option because it was a costly step and the new capsules were too susceptible to breakage, both during the manufacturing process and after the capsules leave the plant.

Another alternative for tamper-resistant capsules had been available since 1983 from the Capsugel unit of Warner-Lambert Company. The top half of this capsule slips down entirely over the bottom half and snaps or locks into place. The spokesperson said that even if someone can open the capsule, it would be extremely hard to do so without damaging it.

Each alternative had been received coolly by the drug makers. The basic concern was the reliability of these methods and the feeling that until the capsule-tampering technology improved, there was little they could do. As a spokesperson of one drug maker said, "Nothing is 100 percent tamper proof."

It was with similar opinions that J&J executives sought to plan their long-range responses to this latest crisis. Chairman Burke quickly convened virtually the same crisis team. On their agenda was whether to respond much the same way they did in 1982, to take more drastic steps and either drop the Tylenol name or terminate the use of capsules[1] in OTC medicine, or some other response.

---

[1] J&J had over $500 million invested in capsule-making/filling facilities in the United States alone.

EXHIBIT 2 Summary of Operations and Statistical Data, 1975–1985
(dollars in millions except per share figures)

	1985	1984	1983
Earnings data			
Sales to customers			
Domestic	$3,989.9	3,735.9	3,610.5
International	2,431.4	2,388.6	2,362.4
Total sales	6,421.3	6,124.5	5,972.9
Interest income	107.3	84.5	82.9
Royalties and miscellaneous	48.1	38.0	49.4
Total revenues	6,576.7	6,247.0	6,105.2
Cost of products sold	2,594.2	2,469.4	2,471.8
Selling, distribution, and administrative expenses	2,516.0	2,488.4	2,352.9
Research expense	471.1	421.2	405.1
Interest expense	74.8	86.1	88.3
Interest expense capitalized	(28.9)	(35.0)	(36.9)
Other expenses including nonrecurring charges	50.3	61.8	99.9
Total costs and expenses	5,677.5	5,491.9	5,381.1
Earnings before provision for taxes on income	899.2	755.1	724.1
Provision for taxes on income	285.5	240.6	235.1
Earnings before extraordinary charge	613.7	514.5	489.0
Extraordinary charge (net of $50.0 taxes)	—	—	—
Net earnings	$ 613.7	514.5	489.0
Percent of sales to customers	9.6	8.4	8.2
Domestic net earnings	$ 376.6	305.6	281.8
International net earnings	$ 237.1	208.9	207.2
Per share of common stock	$ 3.36	2.75	2.57
Percent return on average stockholders' equity	19.5	17.3	16.8
Percent increase over previous year			
Sales to customers	4.8	2.5	3.7
Net earnings per share	22.2	7.0	2.0
Supplementary expense data[1]			
Cost of materials and services	$3,441.0	3,285.8	3,205.9
Total employment costs	1,941.1	1,935.8	1,920.8
Depreciation and amortization	250.5	226.3	209.8
Maintenance and repairs[2]	132.7	124.0	119.6
Total tax expense[3]	466.2	418.6	415.2
Total tax expense per share[3]	2.55	2.23	2.18
Supplementary balance sheet data:			
Property, plant and equipment—net investment	$1,839.9	1,720.6	1,668.2
Additions to property, plant and equipment	366.3	366.0	401.3
Total assets	5,095.1	4,541.4	4,461.5
Long-term debt	185.3	224.8	195.6
Common stock information:			
Dividends paid per share	$ 1.28	1.18	1.08
Stockholders' equity per share	$ 18.33	16.04	15.82
Average shares outstanding (millions)	182.9	187.4	190.5
Stockholders of record (thousands)	53.5	53.8	49.3
Employees (thousands)	74.9	74.2	77.4

[1] Excludes in 1982 an extraordinary charge of $100 million ($50 million after taxes or $.27 per share) associated with the withdrawal of Tylenol capsules.

1982	1981	1980	1979	1978	1977	1976	1975
3,304.0	3,025.9	2,633.6	2,372.1	1,991.3	1,713.6	1,493.2	1,268.0
2,456.9	2,373.1	2,203.8	1,839.5	1,506.0	1,200.5	1,029.3	956.7
5,760.9	5,399.0	4,837.4	4,211.6	3,497.3	2,914.1	2,522.5	2,224.7
88.9	78.8	50.0	43.3	28.7	18.9	19.3	11.8
49.3	28.6	26.4	23.1	17.2	16.8	16.7	15.6
5,899.1	5,506.4	4,913.8	4,278.0	3,543.2	2,949.8	2,558.5	2,252.1
2,450.9	2,368.4	2,194.3	1,950.2	1,580.3	1,368.0	1,222.9	1,071.7
2,248.8	2,030.6	1,794.2	1,505.3	1,258.9	1,002.3	847.9	746.6
363.2	282.9	232.8	192.7	163.6	131.8	112.5	97.8
74.4	60.7	37.0	21.9	13.5	8.5	6.3	8.8
(46.3)	(43.5)	(32.7)	—	—	—	—	—
20.9	23.4	12.9	16.2	12.7	7.0	7.4	8.4
5,111.9	4,722.5	4,238.5	3,686.3	3,029.0	2,517.6	2,197.0	1,933.3
787.2	783.9	675.3	591.7	514.2	432.2	361.5	318.8
263.8	316.3	274.6	239.6	215.1	184.9	156.1	135.0
523.4	476.6	400.7	352.1	299.1	247.3	205.4	183.8
(50.0)	—	—	—	—	—	—	—
473.4	476.6	400.7	352.1	299.1	247.3	205.4	183.8
8.2	8.7	8.3	8.4	8.6	8.5	8.1	8.3
235.8	262.2	184.6	172.4	144.4	129.3	107.5	90.5
237.6	205.4	216.1	179.7	154.7	118.0	97.9	93.3
2.52	2.51	2.17	1.92	1.67	1.41	1.18	1.06
17.8	19.5	18.8	19.1	18.8	17.8	16.7	17.1
6.7	11.6	14.9	20.4	20.0	15.5	13.4	14.8
.4	15.7	12.8	15.2	18.2	19.8	11.0	13.6
3,078.1	2,843.4	2,532.4	2,200.1	1,803.0	1,494.5	1,294.4	1,151.0
1,821.7	1,693.6	1,535.2	1,337.4	1,101.6	892.0	785.1	682.9
176.2	152.4	138.7	121.2	103.1	86.5	77.5	68.6
123.6	126.2	116.1	118.2	102.0	89.1	74.8	61.9
436.3	477.0	425.3	373.2	323.0	274.9	231.1	203.7
2.32	2.56	2.30	2.04	1.80	1.57	1.32	1.17
1,577.9	1,335.6	1,161.9	947.8	788.2	652.4	568.5	528.3
470.2	388.5	364.0	273.3	228.5	171.7	119.2	136.0
4,209.6	3,820.4	3,342.5	2,874.0	2,382.4	2,019.8	1,730.7	1,537.1
142.2	91.7	70.1	69.5	52.1	37.1	26.7	39.4
.97	.85	.74	.67	.57	.47	.35	.28
14.80	13.51	12.24	10.82	9.47	8.43	7.45	6.61
188.0	186.4	184.8	183.3	179.4	175.2	174.6	173.7
43.0	38.2	35.6	35.6	31.9	31.2	31.1	31.0
79.7	77.1	74.3	71.8	67.0	60.5	57.9	53.8

[2] Also included in cost of materials and services category.
[3] Includes taxes on income, payroll, property, and other business taxes.

EXHIBIT 3 Johnson & Johnson and Subsidiaries: Consolidated Balance Sheet
at December 29, 1985, and December 30, 1984 (dollars in millions)

	1985	1984
Assets		
Current assets		
Cash and cash items	$ 129.2	94.4
Marketable securities, at cost, which approximates market value	606.4	348.1
Accounts receivable, trade, less allowances $39.7 (1984, $32.0)	959.4	877.3
Inventories (Notes 1 and 3)	955.1	945.4
Prepaid expenses and other receivables	246.4	248.5
Total current assets	2,896.5	2,513.7
Marketable securities, non-current, at cost, which approximates market value	148.7	162.3
Property, plant and equipment, at cost (Note 1)		
Land and land improvements	170.6	157.1
Buildings and building equipment	1,210.6	1,103.9
Machinery and equipment	1,410.3	1,202.3
Construction in progress	151.6	156.0
	2,943.1	2,619.3
Less accumulated depreciation and amortization	1,102.3	898.7
	1,839.9	1,720.6
Other assets	210.0	144.8
Total assets	$5,095.1	4,541.4
Liabilities and Stockholders' Equity		
Current liabilities		
Loans and notes payable (Note 4)	$ 229.3	201.4
Accounts payable	401.4	301.6
Accrued liabilities	328.7	326.4
Taxes on income	65.3	87.1
Salaries, wages and commissions	95.1	80.2
Miscellaneous taxes	52.5	45.7
Total current liabilities	1,172.3	1,042.4
Long-term debt (Note 4)	185.3	224.8
Deferred taxes on income	121.3	91.7
Certificates of extra compensation (Note 10)	58.0	53.0
Deferred investment tax credits	40.2	42.2
Other liabilities	167.1	155.3
Stockholders' equity		
Preferred stock—without par value (authorized and unissued 2,000,000 shares)	—	—
Common stock—par value $1.00 per share (authorized 270,000,000 shares; issued 191,832,000 and 191,831,000 shares)	191.8	191.8
Additional capital	247.6	278.6
Cumulative currency translation adjustments (Note 6)	(291.9)	(366.4)
Retained earnings	3,499.6	3,119.1
	3,647.1	3,223.1
Less common stock held in treasury, at cost (8,980,000 and 8,986,000 shares)	296.2	291.1
Total stockholders' equity	3,350.9	2,932.0
Total liabilities and stockholders' equity	$5,095.1	4,541.4

See Notes to Consolidated Financial Statements

EXHIBIT 4   Johnson & Johnson and Subsidiaries: Consolidated Balance Sheet
at January 1, 1984 and January 2, 1983 (dollars in millions except per share figures)

	1983	1982[1]
Assets		
Current assets		
Cash and cash items	$ 122.6	140.4
Marketable securities, at cost, which approximates market value	303.9	225.1
Accounts receivable, trade, less allowances $28.1 (1982, $24.8)	836.4	758.1
Inventories (Notes 1 and 6)	992.2	957.5
Prepaid expenses and other receivables	202.0	172.0
Total current assets	2,457.1	2,253.1
Marketable securities, non-current, at cost, which approximates market value	181.5	222.1
Property, plant and equipment, at cost (Note 1)		
Land and land improvements	149.9	142.2
Buildings and building equipment	1,050.0	924.7
Machinery and equipment	1,106.2	1,005.9
Construction in progress	163.6	238.6
	2,469.7	2,311.4
Less accumulated depreciation and amortization	801.5	735.5
	1,668.2	1,577.9
Other assets	154.7	156.5
Total assets	$4,461.5	4,209.6
Liabilities and Stockholders' Equity		
Current liabilities		
Loans and notes payable (Note 7)	$ 214.4	213.9
Accounts payable	311.2	312.1
Taxes on income	13.6	1.3
Salaries, wages and commissions	78.1	75.0
Miscellaneous taxes	47.7	53.6
Miscellaneous accrued liabilities	258.8	244.3
Total current liabilities	923.8	900.2
Long-term debt (Note 7)	195.6	142.2
Certificates of extra compensation (Note 1)	46.6	42.9
Deferred investment tax credits	41.0	35.3
Other liabilities and deferrals	223.1	279.8
Minority interests in international subsidiaries	4.9	9.7
Stockholders' equity		
Preferred stock—without par value (authorized and unissued 2,000,000 shares)	—	—
Common stock—par value $1.00 per share (authorized 270,000,000 shares; issued 191,562,000 and 189,361,000 shares)	191.6	189.4
Additional capital	272.1	234.5
Cumulative currency translation adjustments (Note 4)	(260.7)	(163.5)
Retained earnings	2,824.5	2,540.1
	3,027.5	2,800.5
Less common stock held in treasury, at cost (234,000 shares)	1.0	1.0
Total stockholders' equity	3,026.5	2,799.5
Total liabilities and stockholders' equity	$4,461.5	4,209.6

[1] Reclassified to conform to 1983 presentation. See Notes to Consolidated Financial Statements.

EXHIBIT 5 Johnson & Johnson and Subsidiaries: Consolidated Balance Sheet at January 3, 1982 and December 28, 1980 (dollars in millions except per share figures)

	1981	1980
Assets		
Current assets		
Cash and cash items	$ 101.2	92.8
Marketable securities, at cost, which approximates market value	325.8	266.3
Accounts receivable, trade, less allowances $22.2	705.9	643.8
Inventories (Notes 1 and 5)	900.1	848.8
Prepaid expenses and other receivables	169.2	119.3
Total current assets	2,202.2	1,971.0
Marketable securities, non-current, at cost, which approximates market value	193.5	143.9
Property, plant, and equipment, at cost (Note 1)		
Land and land improvements	123.9	110.6
Buildings and building equipment	772.9	659.7
Machinery and equipment	899.1	810.2
Construction in progress	217.7	196.0
	2,013.6	1,776.5
Less accumulated depreciation and amortization	678.0	614.6
	1,335.6	1,161.9
Other assets	89.1	65.7
Total assets	$3,820.4	3,342.5
Liabilities and Stockholders' Equity		
Current liabilities		
Loans and notes payable (Note 7)	$ 195.4	167.0
Accounts payable, trade	247.0	232.3
Miscellaneous accounts payable	50.0	51.2
Taxes on income	90.8	72.2
Salaries, wages and commissions	70.9	67.1
Miscellaneous taxes	50.2	52.9
Miscellaneous accrued liabilities	176.9	130.8
Total current liabilities	881.2	773.5
Long-term debt (Note 7)	91.7	70.1
Certificates of extra compensation (Note 11)	38.3	32.8
Deferred investment tax credits	30.1	23.7
Other liabilities and deferrals	239.6	163.8
Minority interests in international subsidiaries	11.6	9.5
Stockholders' equity (Note 9)		
Preferred stock—without par value (authorized and unissued 2,000,000 shares)	—	—
Common stock—par value $1.00 per share (authorized 270,000,000 shares; issued 187,297,023 and 185,647,266 shares)	187.3	185.6
Additional capital	178.2	144.3
Cumulative currency translation adjustments (Note 3)	(85.7)	—
Retained earnings	2,249.1	1,940.1
	2,528.9	2,270.0
Less common stock held in treasury, at cost (235,299 and 234,399 shares)	1.0	.9
Total stockholders' equity	2,527.9	2,269.1
Total liabilities and stockholders' equity	$3,820.4	3,342.5

See Notes to Consolidated Financial Statements.

EXHIBIT 6 Johnson & Johnson and Subsidiaries: Consolidated Balance Sheet
at December 30, 1979 and December 31, 1978 (dollars in thousands except per share figures)

	1979	1978
Assets		
Current assets		
Cash and certificates of deposit	$ 127,340	147,475
Marketable securities, at cost, which approximates market value	184,025	253,740
Accounts receivable, trade, less allowances $19,763 (1978 $15,838)	596,421	468,997
Inventories (Notes 1 and 4)	745,434	601,322
Expenses applicable to future operations	64,950	29,945
Total current assets	1,718,170	1,501,479
Marketable securities, non-current, at cost, which approximates market value	144,694	45,494
Property, plant, and equipment, at cost, less accumulated depreciation and amortization $546,302 (1978 $479,929) (Notes 1 and 5)	947,783	788,240
Other assets	63,307	47,156
Total assets	$2,873,954	2,382,369
Liabilities and Stockholders' Equity		
Current liabilities		
Loans and notes payable (Note 7)	$ 96,382	58,058
Accounts payable	237,112	192,218
Taxes on income	84,577	59,808
Other accrued liabilities	210,816	158,636
Total current liabilities	628,887	468,720
Long-term debt (Note 7)	69,549	52,125
Certificates of extra compensation (Note 10)	30,104	28,341
Deferred investment tax credits	20,614	17,857
Other liabilities and deferrals	129,959	105,979
Minority interests in international subsidiaries	8,195	8,519
Stockholders' equity		
Preferred stock—without par value (authorized and unissued 2,000,000 shares)	—	—
Common stock—par value $2.50 per share (authorized 70,000,000 shares; issued 61,290,424 and 59,931,524 shares) (Notes 2 and 8)	153,226	149,829
Additional capital	158,069	105,506
Retained earnings	1,676,298	1,446,441
	1,987,593	1,701,776
Less common stock held in treasury, at cost (78,333 and 78,433 shares)	947	948
Total stockholders' equity	1,986,646	1,700,828
Total liabilities and stockholders' equity	$2,873,954	2,382,369

See Notes to Consolidated Financial Statements.

EXHIBIT 7 Johnson & Johnson and Subsidiaries: Consolidated Balance Sheet at January 2, 1977 and December 28, 1975 (dollars in thousands except per share figures)

	1976	1975[1]
Assets		
Current assets		
Cash and certificates of deposit	$ 47,509	38,300
Marketable securities, at cost, which approximates market value	230,591	199,921
Accounts receivable, less allowances $11,182 (1975 $11,320)	315,179	288,465
Inventories (Notes 1 and 3)	456,170	396,940
Expenses applicable to future operations	17,883	21,281
Total current assets	1,067,332	944,907
Marketable Securities, Non-Current, at cost (market value at year-end 1976—$58,092; 1975—$29,536)	59,612	34,147
Property, plant, and equipment, at cost, less accumulated depreciation and amortization (Notes 1 and 4)	568,456	528,252
Other assets	35,319	29,750
Total assets	$1,730,719	1,537,056
Liabilities and Stockholders' Equity		
Current liabilities		
Loans and notes payable (Note 6)	$ 26,290	27,575
Accounts payable	125,023	99,424
Taxes on income	56,304	29,927
Other accrued liabilities	94,223	109,698
Total current liabilities	301,840	266,624
Long-term debt (Note 6)	19,058	30,832
Capitalized long-term lease obligations	7,650	8,570
Certificates of extra compensation (Note 9)	29,001	28,579
Deferred investment tax credit	13,793	11,654
Other liabilities and deferrals (Note 12)	51,292	35,078
Minority interests in international subsidiaries	6,146	4,882
Stockholders' equity		
Preferred stock—without par value (authorized and unissued 2,000,000 shares)	—	—
Common stock—par value $2.50 per share (authorized 70,000,000 and 63,000,000 shares, issued 58,353,499 and 58,136,616 shares, 1976 and 1975, respectively) (Note 7)	145,884	145,342
Additional capital	74,738	68,545
Retained earnings	1,082,548	938,181
	1,303,170	1,152,068
Less common stock held in treasury, at cost (101,883 shares)	1,231	1,231
Total stockholders' equity	1,301,939	1,150,837
Total liabilities and stockholders' equity	$1,730,719	1,537,056

[1] Reclassified to conform to 1976 presentation. See Note 12.
See Notes to Consolidated Financial Statements.

INDUSTRIAL HIGHLIGHT

Drug Industry

Below is a capsule summary of the pharmaceutical preparations segment of the drug industry of which Johnson & Johnson, maker of Tylenol Capsules, is a part. Information in this highlight was compiled by the U.S. Department of Commerce and focuses on this industry during the approximate period of time covered in the case. Keep in mind that industrial highlights contained in this text are not intended as a complete synopsis of an industry, but as a profile of certain issues that can be relevant to the case situation.

CURRENT SITUATION

The value of shipments by the pharmaceutical preparations industry was $23.7 billion (current dollars) in 1984, equal to a growth rate of 3.1 percent after adjusting for price increases. The 1984 value of pharmaceutical preparation shipments was $20.9 billion, also equivalent to a price-adjusted increase of 3.1 percent.

Prescription drugs account for about 65 percent of the value of all pharmaceutical preparations used in the United States. Overall, prescription drug use is on the rise. One survey shows the number of prescriptions in 1983 to have reached 1.5 billion, 2.3 percent above the level of 1982. Although new prescriptions increased by only 0.5 percent, refills rose 7 percent, constituting 30 percent of the total number of prescriptions dispensed.

Average prices of prescriptions have been increasing considerably faster than prices for all nondurables. As a result, consumer interest in generics and direct sales is growing. Mail order catalog sales have been escalating, especially among the aged, with savings reported to exceed 50 percent on some generic prescription drugs to treat chronic geriatric conditions.

The generic drug industry is concerned that only 22 of a possible 125 generic drugs are certified under the Federal maximum allowable cost program. As a result, only those 22 can be substituted for higher cost prescription

Source: U.S. Industrial Outlook, Department of Commerce, 1985, pp. 17-4–17-6.

products, under Federally funded programs. The concern is that these Federal programs are not taking full advantage of the availability of lower cost generic substitutes.

About 35 percent of the value of shipments of all pharmaceutical preparations are sales of proprietary (nonprescription, over-the-counter) medications. Almost half the people in the United States treat health problems either with nonprescription medications or, to lesser degree, home remedies. More than one-third do not treat their ailments at all, which constitutes a large target market for self medication. Nonprescription drugs will continue to increase in sales volume because of the lower cost of self-treatment, the extensive promotion of over-the-counter products by producers, the trend towards reclassifying some prescription drugs to nonprescription status, and the increasing medical sophistication and education of the general population.

Americans suffer a minor ailment once every 3 days and self-treat nine out of ten of these ailments without the aid of a licensed medical practitioner. As the number and variety of nonprescription drugs increase, more self-treatment options will become available. Since 1956, more than 40 prescription ingredients and at least two combinations of ingredients have become available for use in nonprescription drug products.

New product development in pharmaceutical preparations is emphasizing geriatric, cardiovascular, anti-infective, and psychotherapeutic preparations. New product approvals by FDA decreased from 28 in 1982 to 14 in 1983. It is estimated that only 14 new products were approved in 1984 also.

LONG-TERM PROSPECTS

The value of shipments of pharmaceutical preparations, after adjusting for price increases, is projected to rise at an average annual rate of 3.0 percent through 1989. The value of exports is slowly diminishing, whereas imports are rapidly increasing because of the strong U.S. dollar. A negative trade balance may be expected by 1987.

Generic versions are planned for more than 100 prescription drugs with patents that have recently expired or that will expire during the next 3 years. Sales of these drugs currently exceed $2 billion a year. The small pharmaceutical companies will probably increase their generic sales of these drugs by 60 percent by 1989.

CASE 24

Coca-Cola Company

LINCOLN W. DEIHL
Kansas State University

THOMAS C. NEIL
Atlanta University

Before the United States put its first space vehicle into orbit, foreign cartoonists had assumed that American satellites would be built along the familiar lines of a Coca-Cola bottle. In their eyes, as in the eyes of many people abroad, Coca-Cola is a fluid that, like gasoline, is responsible for, and symbolic of, the American way of life. The two legends, indeed, are often thought of as compatible, even though gasoline is one of the few solutions around that has not yet been mixed with Coke. An English cartoon showed the space shuttle fueled in flight by a pair of aerial tankers, one furnishing gas to the engines, the other Coca-Cola to the crew.[1]

HISTORY

Coca-Cola entered the market originally as one of thousands of exotic medicinal products belonging to the nationwide patent medicine industry. Coca-Cola was created by founder Dr. John Styth Pemberton in May 1886. The extract of "Coca" was blended with the "Cola" extract to form a syrup base for a new and wondrous "Brain Tonic."

Dr. Pemberton sold 25 gallons of syrup the first year and spent $46, or about 90 percent of his receipts, for advertising. In 1886, Asa Candler purchased all the rights to the product. In 1892, the Coca-Cola Company was formed as a Georgia corporation with capital stock of $100,000. In 1893, the trademark Coca-Cola was registered in the U.S. Patent Office. In the same year, the company paid its first dividend. Candler, a firm believer in advertising, laid the foundation of promotion through coupons and souvenirs. The bottling of Coca-Cola started in 1894 in Vicksburg, Mississippi, and continued until 1899, when the company granted rights to bottle and sell Coca-Cola in practically the entire continental United States.

By 1904 the annual sales for Coca-Cola syrup reached one million gallons, and there were 123 plants authorized to bottle the finished drink. The Coca-

Reprinted by permission of Thomas C. Neil.
[1] E. J. Kahn, Jr., *The Big Drink, The Story of Coca-Cola* (New York: H. Wolff Manufacturing Co., 1960).

Cola Company was the first to introduce the glass containers in 1915 and the cans in 1954. The cans have been found well suited for the overseas shipment of the finished drinks.

In 1919, the company was sold to Ernest Woodruff, an Atlanta banker, and an investor group for $25 million. Robert W. Woodruff was elected president succeeding Howard Candler. Moving aggressively, the company established a foreign sales department. A concentrate for the syrup was developed which reduced transportation costs. At the present time, Coca-Cola is served in 155 countries.

Since 1960, the company has acquired more than 13 different kinds of businesses ranging from food, wine, and bottling to entertainment in the form of movies. In 1984, Coca-Cola decided to license its trademark to a complete line of leisure wear. The company has divested itself of selected businesses, the latest being its Wine Spectrum, Taylor California Cellars, in 1983.

GENERAL ORGANIZATION AND MANAGEMENT

Roberto C. Goizueta is the chairman of the board of directors and the chief executive officer of the Coca-Cola Company. His appointment as CEO was an important step forward, signaling an end to what many expected to be a messy fight to succeed J. Paul Austin (former CEO), orchestrated by the CEO himself. Austin, who was not known for his gentle methods ("He is the ice man," said a competing bottler), set up an intense competition for Coke's number two spot after he suddenly forced popular president Lucin Smith out of office in 1979. By creating an office of the chairman, made up of six vice-chairmen plus the chief financial officer, he forced the contenders to "tough it out" for the right to be president and, presumably, move on to the top spot.

Roberto C. Goizueta was born in Cuba and came to the United States when he was 18 to study chemical engineering at Yale University. A year later, Goizueta completed his prep-school studies at Cheshire Academy as class valedictorian. After Yale, Goizueta returned to Havana, joining Coke in 1954 as a quality control chemist at $500 a month.

Fidel Castro nationalized Coke's Cuban business in 1961. By then Roberto C. Goizueta had been transferred to Coke's Caribbean area headquarters in Nassau. His background was mainly technical, and many of Coke's 551 independent U.S. bottlers wish he had had direct experience with marketing soft drinks. Goizueta noted, "Mr. Austin was Coca-Cola's first lawyer and Mr. Woodruff didn't finish college." In any case, Goizueta preferred to describe his role as one of "an orchestra conductor," not "a first violinist."[2]

"Selecting Goizueta, a foreign born executive, is welcome recognition that Coke is truly an international company," said Kevin B. Skislock, investment officer of Brown Brothers Harriman, noting that almost all of Coca-Cola's earnings growth during 1970–1982 came from overseas. Timothy Griffith of

---

[2] "Coca-Cola Cuban Libre," *Fortune,* September 8, 1980, pp. 15–16.

Merrill Lynch pointed out that Goizueta's inexperience in soft drinks can work to his advantage. "He has a free hand in that he didn't come through any special branch of the company—he's not a soft drink man or a coffee man or whatever. Executives have a tendency to stay overly loyal to operations they once ran."[3]

Some observers thought that his appointment as chairman and CEO of the company was beneficial. Economic conditions in the United States were rough. They were very similar to conditions which many foreign countries had faced in the past: double-digit inflation, declining productivity, and escalating costs. Goizueta was one executive who had firsthand knowledge of dealing with these problems and managing successfully in spite of them. In addition, he brought a conciliatory brand of management philosophy to what was the world's largest beverage firm and to what, until his promotion, suffered from diffused executive management.

Discussing the operation of the company, for example, he stressed:

> ... and yet, our business is truly multilocal in nature, because our products are produced and sold for the most part by local independent entrepreneurs—our 1500 franchised bottlers of Coca-Cola. In the U.S. we are associated with over 500 of the best American Companies—our partners—our Coca-Cola bottlers. And that's where the real strength of our business system lies.[4]

Roberto C. Goizueta is a man of very definite opinions, "but only if they are right," and he takes the time to find out if they are right, commented a long-time supplier to the industry who knew the new chairman from his days in Latin America.[5]

In January 1980, Goizueta made what was at that time the most important decision in the 47-year history of the product: allowing its bottlers to substitute high-fructose corn-based syrup for sucrose. "Our bottlers are absolutely delighted," Goizueta said.[6] Fructose is roughly 40 percent cheaper than sugar, and Coke used 15 percent of the fructose consumed in the United States in 1982. He, naturally, wanted something in return. "It give the bottlers a nice edge, which I hope they will use to promote the product."

At a New York press conference on April 23, 1985, Coca-Cola said they had made the best better in a new formula. After a taste test of over 190,000 persons, with 55 to 45 percent preferring the new taste, Coke was changed. Eighty-eight days later, in response to a tidal wave of protest by devout Coke drinkers, the company brought back the old formula, renamed Coca-Cola Classic.

Roberto C. Goizueta has ruled out the possibility of acquiring fast-food businesses. "We will not compete with our customers, which include the fast

---

[3] Neal Gaff, "Coke Fights Back," *Financial World,* September 15, 1980, pp. 17–20.
[4] Paul E. Mullins, "Goizueta Clears Priorities at 'Multilocal' Coca-Cola," *Beverage Industry,* November 7, 1980.
[5] Ibid.
[6] Ibid.

food people and their fountain business," said Goizueta, aiming a swipe at rival PepsiCo and its ailing Pizza Hut restaurant chain.[7]

He was not altogether content with Coke's existing business either. Coffee, for instance, where Coke made Butter-Nut and Maryland Club, was not safe from his axe. Even though coffee was profitable, it had not been percolating. "It provides $400 million (sales) which helped with the overhead, but it was not growing," he observed.[8]

Donald R. Keogh was elected president, chief operating officer, and director of the Coca-Cola Company in March 1981. At age 56, he moved up from senior executive vice-president, with responsibility for all operating units and the corporate marketing division. He had also been president of the company's food division and Coca-Cola U.S.A.

Sam Ayoub, age 63, was senior executive vice-president and chief financial officer of the company. He was treasurer of the company from May 1976 to November 1977, and vice-president from November 1977 to March 1979. From March 1979 to May 1980, he served as senior vice-president of the company. On May 30, 1980, he was selected executive vice-president, general operations, of the company, and served in that capacity until August 1981, when he assumed his present position, senior executive vice-president and chief financial officer.

Employees

The company and its subsidiaries employed approximately 39,000 persons, of whom approximately 17,000 were located in the United States. Through its divisions and subsidiaries, the company had entered into numerous collective bargaining agreements and management had no reason to believe it would not be able to renegotiate any such agreements on satisfactory terms. Management of the company generally believed that its relations with its employees were satisfactory.

SOFT DRINK OPERATIONS

Coca-Cola began a dynamic new advertising campaign with the introduction of its caffeine-free versions of Coca-Cola, Tab, and Diet Coke brands. Coca-Cola was extremely successful with its ad themes. The important changes in attitudes and behavior occurring among the country's young people were carefully researched by the company, with expenditures totaling nearly $3.5 million.

Exhibit 1 illustrates the 1984 rankings by market share and sales of the top ten soft drinks in the industry. Coke was leading the market percentages with 24.8 percent of the total industry. The total volume of sales (millions of cases) had Coke heading the list with 1584 million cases.

Coca-Cola plunged into no-caffeine cola, introducing no-caffeine versions

[7] Ibid.
[8] Maurice Barnfather, "Coke's Cultural Revolution," *Forbes*, December 22, 1980, pp. 32–33.

EXHIBIT 1 Coca-Cola Company: The Top Ten Soft Drink Brands

BRAND	1984 MARKET PERCENT	1984 SALES (millions of cases)
Coke	24.8	1,584.6
Pepsi	18.1	1,155.6
Diet Coke	6.9	439.8
7UP	5.3	335.9
Dr. Pepper	4.7	298.0
Sprite	3.3	214.0
Diet Pepsi	3.1	198.5
Mountain Dew	2.8	176.6
RC	2.2	140.1
Tab	2.1	131.3
Top ten total	73.3	4,674.4
Other brands	26.7	1,720.3
Total industry	100.0	6,394.7

Source: *Beverage World*, March 1985.

of its Coke and Diet Coke brands, predicting that demand for decaffeinated colas would equal May 1983 levels of diet drink sales by 1985. Coke was capitalizing on its trademark name to catch up in the market. The company's strategy was to introduce the no-caffeine versions as line extensions in order to avoid the "cannibalization" of the company's main cola drinks.

A new marketing innovation gave the company a competitive edge, with the introduction of talking vending machines, each costing over $3000 and equipped with computerized voice synthesizers to converse with consumers. Other new designs included energy-efficient machines and vendors equipped with electronic games for play after purchase.

The number of soft drink vending machines in use throughout the United States ranged from 1.1 million to 1.8 million in late 1983. Of these, 600,000 to 800,000 were Coca-Cola's. PepsiCo was gaining a substantial footing in the race for the vending market share.

Diet Coke

The 1982 annual report highlighted Diet Coke as the "Company's most significant new product entry in 96 years," with greater than 60 percent of its volume coming from sales of competitive products or from new soft drink consumers. Extending its precious trademark to a new product in 1982, the company was committing itself to the rapid expansion of the new worldwide market for low-calorie beverages.

The commitment to Diet Coke returned tenfold with its movement into position number three in 1984. It appears, however, that this growth was supported in part by the decline by Tab from number five in 1982 to number ten in 1984.

Cherry Coke

With a bow to nostalgia, longtime soda fountain favorite Cherry Coke was introduced in April 1985 into four U.S. test markets. The product is an extension of the Coke line rather than a new product, and the company is anticipating a 2 percent market share. Cherry Coke is being positioned as an alternative cola taste with a target market of males and females aged 12 to 29.

Advertising

Since the slogan "Delicious and Refreshing" was first used in 1886, advertising for Coca-Cola has reflected the pleasant things in life. Advertising expenditures were over $11,000 by 1882, and by 1920 had reached $2 million. Radio has been used since 1927 and television since 1950. (See Exhibits 2 and 3.)

In 1929, the company's first universal slogan "The Pause That Refreshes" appeared and set a standard that was not matched until 1963. In 1963, "Things Go Better with Coke" emerged as a worthy successor to the pause. In the early

EXHIBIT 2 Coca-Cola Company: Estimated 1981 Total Media Spending

	TOTAL (millions)	PER GALLON
Coca-Cola	$72.0	$2.40
Dr. Pepper	14.2	2.58
PepsiCo	56.3	2.57
Royal Crown	10.2	2.67
7UP	36.9	6.80

Source: *Beverage World Periscope*, May 1983, p. 8.

EXHIBIT 3 Coca-Cola Company: Soft Drink Market, 1981–1982 Media Expenditures (in thousands of dollars)

	MEDIA DOLLARS	
	1981	1982
Magazines	$ 350,000	$ 276,000
Supplements	—	—
Newspapers	2,191,000	2,535,000
Network TV	15,203,000	17,197,000
Spot TV	20,446,000	26,878,000
Network radio	—	—
Spot radio	6,231,000	6,123,000
Outdoor	2,458,000	2,602,000
Total	$46,879,000	$55,611,000

Source: "Coca-Cola Soft Drink," brand report, *Marketing and Media Decisions*, July 1983, p. 90.

seventies, riding the tide of concern for world harmony, the jingle "I'd Like to Give the World . . ." sung by a multinational group of young people was presented.

The company's commitment to wholesome, high-quality advertisement has a history incorporating the works of Norman Rockwell and Hoddin Sundblom's "portraits" for holiday ads. Begun in the 1930s, Sundblom's pictures established the standard for the rosy-cheeked, red-suited Santa Claus. Famous names in Coke advertising included Jean Harlow, Johnny Weissmuller, Cary Grant, Clark Gable, and Bill Cosby. In an award-winning television commercial, "Mean" Joe Greene and a small admirer raised a lump in the throat and a tear in the eye.

Exhibit 4 shows the company's popular soft drink brands available in the United States.

Bottlers and Can Containers

Attempts to design a can for Coca-Cola originated in 1940, but it was only after the end of World War II, when steel became more plentiful, that the company made significant progress distributing the cans in the domestic markets. The sale of Coke in cans increased sharply between 1969 and 1976. After 1970, the dynamic contour design with the trademarks "Coca-Cola" and "Coke" was featured on all cans for Coca-Cola.

Distribution Channels

The company manufactures soft drink syrups and concentrates, which it sells to bottling and canning operations and to approved fountain wholesalers. Syrups are comprised of sweetener, water, and flavoring concentrate. The bottling and canning operations, whether independent or company-owned, combine the syrup with carbonated water and package the final product for sale to retailers. Packaged soft drinks are distributed to consumers in cans, returnable and nonreturnable glass bottles, and plastic packaging. Fountain wholesalers sell soft drink syrups to fountain retailers, who sell soft drinks to

EXHIBIT 4 Coca-Cola U.S.A.: Soft Drink Products of the Coca-Cola Company

New Coca-Cola	Fresca
Coca-Cola Classic	Mr. Pibb
Diet Coke	Sugar-free Mr. Pibb
Caffeine-free Diet Coke	Mello-Yello
Tab	Fanta
Caffeine-free Tab	Hi-C soft drinks
Sprite	Ramblin' Root Beer
Sugar-free Sprite	Sugar-free Ramblin' Root Beer

Source: Consumer Information Center, Coca-Cola U.S.A., a division of Coca-Cola Company, Atlanta, Ga.

consumers in cups and glasses. Some syrups and concentrates, however, are completely processed for sale to the ultimate consumer by the canning and bottling operations of the company's subsidiaries.

During 1984, the company sold about 70 percent of its soft drink syrup and concentrate gallonage in the United States to approximately 500 bottlers who prepared and sold the products for the food store and vending machine markets. The remaining 30 percent was sold to approximately 4000 authorized fountain retailers. The parent company provided promotional and marketing support to its bottlers and developed and introduced new products, packages, and equipment in order to assist its bottlers. Coca-Cola continued its bottler restructuring begun in 1981. In 1984, bottlers were acquired in Ohio, Michigan, Oregon, and California.

Coca-Cola is pushing ahead with technological changes. Bag-in-box nonreturnable fountain syrup packing systems, first tested on the West Coast, were made available nationally in 1984. The bag-in-box does away with the cumbersome metal cylinders, is cheaper to manufacture, and does away with pickup and recycling.

The third-generation vending machine with video display, voice simulation, and coupon dispensing is in the final testing phase. This machine will be unique in that it will offer a choice of products in several prices and sizes.

In the food sector, the company continues to push aseptic packaging. Aseptic packaging, especially for the fruit juices, is seen as opening previously untapped consumer consumption.

COMPETITION

Among Coca-Cola's leading competitors are PepsiCo, Seven-Up, Dr. Pepper, and Royal Crown.

PepsiCo

Pepsi-Cola U.S.A. had been playing the numbers game again, asserting that Pepsi-Free was the third-largest-selling cola in 1983. Pepsi-Free, it was claimed, held more than 50 percent of the caffeine-free segment and was the number-three cola in the United States (considering both sugar and sugar-free versions). This lead was lost to Diet Coke in 1984.) The Diet Pepsi commercials were found to be more traditional, warmer—targeting women, with increased focus on taste rather than low-calorie content.

The Pepsi-Free commercials focused on moods of celebration. The ads showed all sorts of people drinking Pepsi-Free, offering bottles and cans to TV viewers and singing, "We are Pepsi-Free."[9] The success of Pepsi-Free and Sugar-free Pepsi-Free, however, was due to fundamental shelf positioning. Sugar-free accounted for 40 percent to 50 percent of Pepsi-Free's total sales.

---

[9] Nancy Giges, "Colas Intensify Share Fight as Key Selling Season Heats," *The International Newspaper of Marketing,* August 8, 1983, Section I, pp. 1–2.

Health consciousness was the reason cited for its popularity. The lemon-flavored Pepsi Light was repositioned to appeal to men. Pepsi was making every effort to be the leader in the decaffeinated beverage market—the fastest-growing segment of the domestic soft drink industry.

PepsiCo netted sales of $7,499,000,000 for the year ending December 31, 1982. The projected sales for the calendar year 1984 was $8.3 billion. "The new advertising strategy calls for an approach based on segmentation," said the Pepsi vice-president of advertising. The company had slated an ad budget of $40 million for brand Pepsi.

Mountain Dew was sold mostly on a single-drink basis in cold boxes and vendors. The target market was the American teenager, particularly the male teenager.[10]

Seven-Up

Seven-Up Company, a division of Philip Morris, Inc., continued its assault on the soft drink industry with increased emphasis on the "no artificial flavoring or coloring" aspect, through commercials. Competitors did not feel good about Seven-Up.

In 1982, Seven-Up garnered 5 percent of the total market, superseding and pushing Dr. Pepper to the fourth position. Estimated sales for 1982 were $11,716,000,000, an increase from $10,886,000,000 over the previous year. A change in Seven-Up's advertising approach in 1983 resulted in increased market share and shipment gains, but with less than significant increases in earnings (as reflected in its remaining number four at 5.3 percent in 1984). Promotional outlays had been stepped up. Seven-Up used a new advertising approach—antiadditive for Like (caffeine-free) positioned against Coke and Pepsi, which had not been received well in the soft drink circles.

Dr. Pepper

The discounting effect by Coca-Cola and PepsiCo in many of Dr. Pepper's prime areas had an adverse effect on the company's unit volume. Dr. Pepper lost unit volume in 1982, and Sugar-free Dr. Pepper continued to lose market share. The company netted sales of $516.1 million in 1982, an increase from $364 million the previous year.

To compete with Coke and Pepsi, Dr. Pepper initiated a new marketing approach, seeking out "new markets" of opportunity. New markets of opportunity meant attempting to strengthen areas that were already strong, and not to do more than they were capable of doing. Dr. Pepper cut back on network television advertising for 1983, favoring regional spots funded jointly by the company and its bottlers. It introduced a caffeine-free product, Pepper-Free, during January 1983, with the idea of extending the life cycle of its products. It was acclaimed as a nationwide leader in the mixer category with Canada Dry, USA, which Dr. Pepper acquired in 1982, doing well in fiscal 1983.

---

[10] Larry Jabbonsky, "Segregating the Pepsi Generation," *Beverage World,* May 1983.

Canada Dry, the popular ginger ale, increased its unit volume a sound 15 percent in the first six months of 1982 and boasted a 37 percent share of the domestic ginger ale business in late 1983. The increase of 1982 sales by Dr. Pepper was primarily due to the Canada Dry acquisition.

Royal Crown

In 1983, Royal Crown was still a small factor in the highly competitive soft drink business, although it was the nation's fifth largest soft drink manufacturer in 1982. It introduced decaffeinated and sugarless RC 100 in the spring of 1980. The parent company recorded sales of $469.8 million in 1982, with sales of 18 million cases in 1981 and 35 million cases in 1982.

Royal Crown entered a new soft drink category with the distribution of Diet Rite Cola, which contained neither salt nor caffeine. Catering to the U.S. consumer's concern with health, RC's "no-salt" approach was geared to attack Seven-Up's marketing approach of combating others for containing artificial flavors or colors. In 1981, 33.1 million cases of Diet Rite were sold; in 1982, 32.1 million cases were sold.

FOODS BUSINESS SECTOR

The Foods Business Sector includes citrus products, Minute Maid and Hi-C, coffee, spring water, and household consumer goods. In 1984, the net operating revenues were $1.5 billion with operating income of $150 million.

Foods Division

The Coca-Cola Company Foods Division products mainly include Minute Maid fruit juices and ades; Hi-C fruit drinks and Five-Alive beverages; two regionally marketed coffees, Maryland Club and Butter-Nut brands; spring water; and nonedible products. In 1983, the operating income was $121 million in revenues of $1,285,000,000.

Citrus Products

Harvested at the peak of flavor, fresh fruit is quickly processed and the juice extracted and concentrated under strict quality controls at the division's processing plants. The concentrate is used to make Minute Maid juices and ades as well as Five-Alive fruit beverages, and as the basis for many Hi-C fruit drinks.

Keeping abreast of changing consumer needs is vital to the success of the Foods Division. Before a new product is introduced nationally, it has been tested extensively. This testing is a lengthy process—sometimes taking as long as seven or eight years.

The division faced difficulties when a freeze in January 1982 was followed by a devastating freeze on December 25, 1983. Approximately 40 percent of Florida's orange crop as well as its trees were destroyed. Also occurring in 1983 was the introduction of competitive brands backed by significant promotion. In response, Coca-Cola worked out an agreement with Brazilian fruit growers to supply concentrate and began an intense advertising campaign in 1984.

Minute Maid brand orange juice gained both record volume and record market in 1982. Overall unit sales for the division's frozen products increased 7 percent. Chilled products increased 3 percent. Despite the problems of 1983, Minute Maid remained the industry leader that year with 24 percent of the market.

Snow Crop Five-Alive, introduced in 1979, had become one of the division's strongest brands. This product ranked second in sales among all frozen products, surpassed only by Minute Maid brand orange juice.

The division extended the Minute Maid line with new products. Minute Maid frozen concentrated orange juice with more pulp was introduced successfully, and Minute Maid reduced-acid orange juice was tested in selected markets. It also introduced Hi-C in the Drink Box, teaming aseptic packaging with the nation's number one fruit drink, in January 1983. In 1984, aseptic packaging was used for Minute Maid orange juice and then for a fruit punch. The division was the first U.S. firm to market an aseptic-packaged fruit drink nationwide. The innovative package was sterilized to require no refrigeration or preservatives. From 1977 to 1982, the Foods Division introduced 35 new items or products in test markets, with 50 percent becoming successful. Continuing its aggressiveness learned from the cola fountain service, the division placed Minute Maid orange juice into Denny's, Days Inns, and Marriott.

Other Products

Coffee production is another facet of the division's operations. Unroasted coffee beans purchased from around the world are roasted to perfection, specially blended, and ground to the desired fineness at two Foods Division plants. Maryland Club is processed in Houston for distribution primarily in the Southwest, and Butter-Nut is processed in Omaha for Midwest distribution. The division maintained market share for its coffee products although both suffered from the U.S. decline in coffee consumption from 38 gallons per capita in 1966 to 27 gallons in 1982. In order to combat this downturn, decaffeinated was introduced under both brands while emphasis was given to the coffee food service business. In 1984, unit volume for coffee grew 2 percent. Exhibit 5 shows the division's market share of the regular coffee market.

EXHIBIT 5   Coffee Market Shares

	1982
General Foods	34.8
Procter & Gamble	23.0
Coca-Cola Maryland Club	1.0
Butter-Nut	2.4

Source: *Advertising Age*, May 9, 1983, p. 82.

Also in the Foods Division are pasta foods, spring water, and plastic wraps and films. In line with the strategy of developing or acquiring new product bases, the division acquired Ronco Foods Company, its first venture into the marketing of solid foods. Ronco manufactures high-quality pasta products, marketed primarily in the Southwest.

Belmont Spring Water Company, Inc., continued to grow in 1984 as a consumer demand for bottled water increased in the company's greater Boston market. Sales volume rose to 25 percent in 1984.

Presto Products, Inc., in Appleton, Wisconsin, is a leading private-label supplier of plastic wraps and films. In 1984, unit volume and revenue growth continued to be favorable, with revenues up 14 percent.

WINE SPECTRUM

The Coca-Cola Company announced on September 26, 1983, the sale of its Wine Spectrum, Taylor California Cellers, to the New York subsidiary of the world's largest distiller, the Montreal-based Seagram Company, for about $210 million. Coke sold out for only marginally more than it had invested—probably about $150 million in terms of their Wine Spectrum operations.

Operations

In 1975 and 1976, the Coca-Cola Company wanted to move into endeavors where there would be opportunity for growth. Since the fastest-growing beverage was wine, and Coke was a beverage company, a wine company seemed a natural choice. Coke took over the 97-year-old Taylor Wine Company in early 1977 and renamed it Taylor California Cellars in November 1977.

Wine Spectrum grew more quickly than any of its rivals during 1980–1982 (Exhibit 6), moving from 9.3 million 9-litre cases to 13.5 million. After Heublein Wines decided in 1983 to sell its lower-priced United Vintners brands back to its growers, Coke's unit rose to number two from number three in the industry. But growth and size alone were not enough for Coke.

EXHIBIT 6 Six Largest American Wineries—Total Wine Shipments
(millions of 9-liter cases)

1982 RANK	WINERY	1980	1981	1982
1	E & J Gallo	51.3	55.3	57.8
2	Heublein Wines	22.1	21.2	20.2
3	The Wine Spectrum	9.3	11.7	13.5
4	Almaden	13.5	12.8	12.1
5	The Wine Group	9.1	9.1	9.1
6	Paul Masson (Seagram)	7.4	7.8	8.1
	Total	112.7	117.9	120.8

Source: *Marketing & Media Decisions*, August 1983, p. 116.

According to Chairman Roberto C. Goizueta, Coke decided to "concentrate our resources in the areas of our business where the returns on assets are highest."[11] In 1982, the company had a net income of $512 million on $6.2 billion in revenues, but its wine business was estimated to have earned only $6 million on $220 million in sales.

A number of observers suggested that Coke's sale was at least prompted by pressure from Wall Street. Marvin Shanken, publisher of *Impact*, said "They were influenced by Wall Street's desire for immediate returns, and that made Coke unwilling to make the kind of long-term investment spending that was necessary to build the brands."[12] It expanded long-term contracts with growers and invested $34 million in its Gonzales Winery, the largest investments in a production facility Coke has made in its 97-year history. Part of the problem was that Coke banked on nonstop growth and "the market failed to keep up," says wine consultant Ed Everett.[13]

Market and Competition

California table wine shipments flattened at 273 million gallons in 1982 after a decade of 10 percent annual growth. Wine inventories soared 16 percent to 685 million gallons between 1981 and 1982.

But California's main problem mirrored that of Detroit and Pittsburgh. While domestic sales flattened, wine imports grew 6.5 percent, continuing their steady climb of the past decade. Their market share reached almost 24 percent compared with 13 percent in 1975. American producers reacted by offering the deepest discounts in memory. Prices of magnum-size jugs plunged by half after 1981.

If the future belongs to the low-cost producer, nobody was better positioned than E & J Gallo. Gallo enjoyed operating economies at every stage of making wine. Analysts admitted that their estimates of the dollar volume of its sales were $650 million to $700 million a year. One rival firm insisted, "Gallo has everything, just loves selling more wine, and earns a zero rate of return on sales." Few in the wine business took seriously the idea that the Gallo winery did not make money.[14]

Almaden's parent, National Distillers and Chemical Corp., reported that the winery's operating profits fell in 1981 and 1982 by 50 percent, to $10.5 million on revenues of $180.6 million in 1982. Its case sales dropped 5.3 percent in 1982.

In October 1982, R. J. Reynolds bought Heublein, which was facing a 6.6 percentage point drop in market share since 1975. Robert M. Furek, president of Heublein's wine division, said "Profits had become the biggest issue in the business."[15]

Lower prices seem destined to become permanent in the California wine business. The companies which survive are likely to be the efficient and

[11] Michael Emerson, "Why Coca-Cola and Wine Didn't Mix," *Business Week,* October 10, 1983.
[12] Ibid.
[13] Ibid.
[14] Gilbert T. Sewall, "Trouble for California Wine Makers," *Fortune,* April 18, 1983.
[15] Ibid.

aggressive wine makers who can keep costs down and spend heavily to build their brands.

COLUMBIA PICTURES INDUSTRIES, INC.

The Coca-Cola Company entered the dynamic and fast-growing entertainment industry on June 22, 1982, with the acquisition of Columbia Pictures Industries, Inc.

Columbia was a major producer and distributor of motion pictures and television programming. In addition, Columbia had become an important factor in the growing pay-television, videocassette, and videodisk markets. Throughout its 62 years of existence, it had built a vast library of more than 1800 film titles and thousands of hours of television programs.

Columbia's activities reflected its dedication to fulfill a well-defined strategy which called for an increase in annual volume of filmed entertainment, expansion of outside financing of film production costs, continued control of distribution of its products, maintenance of the properties in its library, establishment of profitable market share in the video game business, and formation of new lines of business. The record box-office receipts achieved by Columbia in 1982 clearly underscored the long-term growth potential of the newly formed entertainment business sector of the Coca-Cola Company.

The Motion Picture Industry

Most indications pointed to a continuing high in box-office receipts for the motion picture industry topping the 1982 record year.

Through the first half of 1983, receipts totaled $1.74 billion (based on data reported by *Industry Surveys*), 8.5 percent above year-earlier figures. Optimistic expectations for the year were based on the success of summer releases. Between Memorial Day and Labor Day, receipts rose about 8.1 percent to $1.50 billion. Although this approximately equaled the increase in ticket prices for 1983, the number of tickets sold remained at 1982 levels—when attendance set records by wide margins. In 1982, summer ticket sales totaled about 470 million, some 8 percent higher, year to year. Dollar volume exceeded the 1981 figure by 15 percent and the average for 1978–1980 by 40 percent.

The summer and Christmas seasons are critically important because they are periods of relative leisure for the principal movie audience—persons under 24 years of age. During 1978–1983, 37.5 percent of annual box office receipts were generated during the summer months.

Megahits Capture the Market

The heavy box office for the summer of 1983 followed a customary pattern: The bulk of consumer spending went to a few megahits, with relatively smaller amounts spread among all the rest. The big winners for the year shaped up as *Return of the Jedi, Tootsie, Trading Places, War Games,* and *Flashdance*. During 1984, the blockbuster was *Ghostbusters,* Columbia's all-time box-office attraction grossing over $88 million in just 19 weeks. Although not as dramatic in income, *Karate Kid,* grossing $25 million between September 1984 and April 1985, was acclaimed as a warm, sensitive picture.

The movie industry is characterized by inherent earnings volatility, reflecting changing public tastes, the individual nature of each film project, and the lack of continuity in the business. As a relatively inexpensive form of entertainment, motion pictures had historically exhibited little correlation to economic fluctuations. It had even been argued that box-office totals were helped by unfavorable economic conditions, since people tended to reduce outlays for other, more expensive diversions; films provided a convenient method of escaping unpleasant realities.

Production and Budgets Rise

In 1982, 184 films were produced by major studios and independents—compared with 205 in 1981, 209 in 1980, and 248 in 1979—largely due to rising production costs. During 1973–1983, however, rising costs caused a substantial drop in total production. In 1972, the average production cost $1.5 million to complete. By 1982, rising inflation, increasing studio overhead, rising interest rates, and large single-picture guarantees for stars pushed the average cost to $10 million.

However, in the first eight months of 1983, the number of films in production rose 31 percent to 145, from 111 in the comparable 1982 period. The record year had an impact and everyone wanted to be on the bandwagon.

Independent Production Continues to Grow

Rising costs had for some time prompted the major producer/distributors to spread their risk by increasingly distributing films made by outside production companies and by attracting capital from outside sources.

The major companies had various sources of cofinancing for in-house productions. Although tax shelter financing was largely eliminated by changes in U.S. tax laws in the mid-1970s, some were available in foreign countries. Other cofinancing arrangements included foreign sale and lease backs, joint ventures with nonentertainment companies, advances from pay-television exhibitors, and publicly sold limited partnerships.

Examples of the last were the Delphi I and Delphi II partnerships organized and marketed through syndicates of major underwriters. Each of these partnerships had raised $60 million through minimum subscriptions of $5000 for investment in Columbia Pictures productions.

Diversification Spreads Risk

Most film entertainment companies had diversified into other fields in recent years, either by making acquisitions or being acquired themselves. For example, MCA, Inc. (Universal Pictures) was active in the production of television programs and records, music publishing, retailing, mail order and book publishing, as well as its Universal Studio tour and other tours and services. Walt Disney Productions (Buena Vista) had a dominant position in the theme park area, while Warner Communications (Warner Bros.) had interests in recorded music, cable television, book publishing, traditional and electronic games, and direct-response marketing. Paramount Pictures was a part of Gulf + Western Industries, and Columbia Pictures was a 1982 purchase of the Coca-Cola Company.

Operations of Columbia

The 1978–1983 periods had been good ones for Columbia. It had seen its revenues advance at a compound growth rate of 17 percent to $780 million in the fiscal year which ended June 30, 1982. In 1984, the entertainment sector earned $121 million, an increase of 34 percent over 1983.

A vital element of Columbia's aggressive strategy was its library of some 1800 film titles and thousands of hours of television programming. The tremendous growth rate in the entertainment industry had enormous implications for Columbia because pay television had a virtually insatiable demand for programs, a demand which was being filled largely by showing movies produced by Columbia and other studios.

Its strategy was to increase the number of movies to catch up with its competitors (illustrated in Exhibit 7), improving its chances of producing more successful and profitable films. Toward that goal, Columbia planned to increase motion picture production levels to meet the full capacity of the excellent distribution system. It also continued its efforts to attract the best producers and creative talent to its studios to ensure further success.

In 1984, Columbia Pictures Television group, producer of prime-time and daytime series, miniseries, and made-for-television movies, was the largest contributor to the entertainment sector's earnings.

EXHIBIT 7 Coca-Cola Company: U.S. Film Distributors—Market Share Breakdown

	1980		1981		1982	
Company	Rank	Share %	Rank	Share %	Rank	Share %
Universal (MCA, Inc.)	1	20	3	14	1	30
Paramount (Gulf + Western Inc.)	2	16	2	15	2	14
20th Century-Fox	2	16	4	13	2	14
MGM/UA[1]	6	7	6	9	4	11
Warner Brothers	4	14	1	18	5	10
Columbia Pictures	4	14	4	13	5	10
Walt Disney Productions (Buena Vista)	7	4	8	4	7	4
Embassy	8	3	7	5	—	—

[1] MGM acquired UA from Transamerica Corp. in July 1981; prior to that, UA distributed MGM's films domestically.

Source: *Industry Surveys*, October 13, 1983.

INTERNATIONAL OPERATIONS

When Robert W. Woodruff was elected president of the Coca-Cola Company on April 28, 1923, the amount of Coca-Cola being sold outside the United States, Canada, and Cuba was infinitesimal. And that's why, as the 33-year-old Woodruff took office, he quickly became concerned as to the reason for such a poor showing. He was convinced that there was rewarding market potential the world over for a product of such demonstrated consumer appeal.

So it was logical that in 1926, President Woodruff launched the first organized effort to sell Coca-Cola overseas through establishment of a Foreign Department in New York City. At that time, there were fewer than a dozen plants bottling Coca-Cola offshore. By 1950, when the Foreign Department became the Coca-Cola Export Corporation, there were 65 bottlers of Coca-Cola in 30 offshore countries.

In 1983, seven of the world's ten largest bottling plants were offshore. The largest bottler of Coca-Cola and allied products in the world was in Buenos Aires, Argentina. The second largest bottler was in Mexico City. Exhibit 8 shows the total consumption and per capita consumption in selected countries.

In 1984, non-U.S. operating earnings increased 4 percent, with good performance in Europe, Africa, the Pacific, and Canada; earnings in Latin America declined primarily due to the economic environment. The modest increase was due to the strong dollar.

EXHIBIT 8 Coca-Cola Company: Soft Drinks Are International Favorites

COUNTRY	1981 TOTAL CONSUMPTION (million liters)	1981 PER CAPITA CONSUMPTION (liters)
United States	31,000	147
West Germany	4,310	70
Japan	2,680	54
United Kingdom	2,000	36
Canada	1,990	89
Spain	1,810	52
Benelux	1,750	63
Italy	1,350	24
Colombia	1,300	49
Venezuela	1,260	91
Australia	950	65
South Africa	800	27
Malaysia	260	19
Puerto Rico	230	69
Singapore	130	29

Source: *Beverage World Periscope*, December 4, 1982.

Coca-Cola was sold in over 155 countries through more than 900 local independent and company-owned bottlers in 1982. In 1982 also, markets outside the United States and Puerto Rico accounted for 64 percent of total unit sales of the soft drink operations.

In March 1982, a massive international rollout of the new Diet Coke was begun. By August 1982 Diet Coke was in 35 countries. By 1984, 41 markets had been penetrated with a unit volume increase of 105 percent. Diet Coke contributes an average of 8 percent of Coca-Cola sales on the international scene. In Japan, introduced as Coca-Cola Light, the beverage has garnered a 68 percent share of the low-calorie market.

The long-term strategic objective for Coca-Cola is to achieve growth in the international market by increasing per capita soft drink consumption. Outside the United States, soft drink consumption is only 15 percent of the U.S. total. Focusing on increasing frequency of use, emphasis is placed on product availability, product variety, and product positioning. Consumption increase is encouraged through occasion use, vending machine availability, and enlarging fountain outlet use. In 1985, Coca-Cola moved into the 275-million-person market of the Soviet Union. During the ten years ending in 1984, Coca-Cola experienced an average growth in unit volume of 6 percent.

Latin America

In Mexico, the company's second largest world market by sales volume, a 10 percent unit volume gain outperformed the industry in 1982. In 1984, the unit volume increase was a modest 3 percent in response to a slight easing of price controls. The company increased its share of the fountain segment, launched Tab in cans, and increased coverage of both Coke and Sprite. Economic pressures affected a unit sales decline of 7 percent in Brazil and more than 20 percent in Argentina. Rebounding in 1984, Coca-Cola experienced a 17 percent volume gain in Brazil, where the economy had improved. In Argentina, a 33 percent volume gain was due to the low prices of Coca-Cola products being held in place by price controls. In Ecuador, unit sales had doubled from 1977 to 1982. In 1982, Colombia became the seventh largest market for Coca-Cola worldwide.

In December 1982, a wave of poisonings in which caustic soda was put in bottles of Coca-Cola, and which involved threats of more poisons being added to other beverages—similar to the Tylenol poisonings in the United States—swept Brazil. Sales of Coke temporarily dropped an estimated 10 percent in the Rio area.

In the Diet Coke segment, the main barrier to Diet Coke's entry in Brazil was a tough government regulation that maximum recommended consumption of the diet beverage clearly be stated on the label. "You have to give maximum intake a day, not more than half a liter a day," said Coca-Cola Brazil's marketing director Jorge Giganti. "It's like a medicine. You can't launch it as a diet product."[16]

---

[16] Carolyn Hulse, "Diet Coke Faces Hurdles as It Spreads World Wide," *Advertising Age,* March 14, 1983, pp. 68–72.

In Argentina, three years after the introduction of Tab in 1980, category sales accounted for 55 percent of the overall soft drink market. Tab was soon followed by Coca-Cola's low-calorie Sprite in May 1981 and Seven-Up Company's Diet 7UP in September 1982.

But Seven-Up president Ruben Roys was not optimistic about the potential for growth in the segment in Argentina, since "market studies show that even the most emancipated diet drink consumer will seldom ask for such a drink at restaurants and pubs, and that diet drinks will continue to appeal mostly to women."[17]

Europe

The introduction of Diet Coke (called Coca-Cola Light in certain countries) in Germany, Great Britain, and other countries in 1983 spearheaded aggressive marketing that in 1982 earned an outstanding unit volume increase of approximately 10 percent for company products in Europe.

West Germany, the company's largest market in Europe, achieved 9 percent unit growth and an increase in corporate market share in 1982. Sluggish economic conditions in 1984 held volume gains to less than 3 percent. Germany had an underdeveloped diet-drink category that posed problems for Diet Coke. One reason was heavy mineral water consumption, and another was that laws permitted only limited use of sweeteners.

In Spain, the second largest European market, 1984 unit sales increased slightly. Aiding the sales effort were expanded availability of Sprite and growth in the fountain segment. In Italy, sales of Sprite continued strong following its 1981 introduction; overall unit volume gained 10 percent in 1982 but slipped to 5 percent in 1984 again due to slow economic growth.

Coca-Cola continued to lead the cola segment in Great Britain, where the company's unit sales rose 12 percent in 1982. Diet drinks accounted for 5 percent of Britain's total soft drink market, but as much as 45 percent of that was accounted for by Schweppes's slim line range and only 20 percent by colas. However, the diet cola segment grew by 30 percent in volume in 1982 with little promotional support, and many observers believed that it was ripe for expansion. Diet Pepsi held 55 percent of this business, with Tab trailing at 15 percent. The Diet Coke introduction could mean the end of Tab, or at least a dramatic cut in sales. In order to improve per capita consumption the southern United Kingdom bottler was purchased. New management was installed and directed to aggressively pursue increasing product availability and awareness.

In the Soviet Union, new bottling operations in the city of Tallin supported a good performance in 1982 by Fanta Orange. In 1985, the Moscow market became available. In France, there was no chance of introducing Diet Coke because of stiff rules preventing the use of all artificial sweeteners (including aspartame) except through pharmacies. The country's powerful sugar beet interests had been successful in their fight to prevent France from conforming with EEC standards, which permit the use of artificial sweeteners.

[17] Ibid.

In Norway, artificial sweeteners were forbidden except for use by diabetics, and the term diet or low calorie could not appear on labels; drinks like Tab were technically only for use by diabetics. Still, the irony was that 11 percent of soft drinks sold in Norway were diet; only the United States and Canada rank higher. In countries like Norway and Germany, where the word diet connotes illness, Diet Coke became Coke Light, but that may cause problems, too. Authorities warned that if there was a sharp increase in consumption of these drinks, they would ban the "Light" name and maybe diet drinks as well.

Africa

In Egypt, the company's business more than doubled during 1982 as new plants were brought into production. Unit volume was up 13 percent in South Africa, following the introduction of the 1.5-liter bottle, a new tangerine flavor for Fanta, and the launch of the 500-milliliter nonreturnable bottle. South Africa's continuing problems with apartheid influenced economic vitality and resulted in a volume growth of 3 percent. The company saw potential for growth and profits from Tab and the low-calorie segment in South Africa. Diet Coke was introduced in the market in June 1982. The diet segment held 4 percent of the soft drink market. Coke had to address image problems in South Africa, largely due to the race issue.

In this segmented market, where soft drinks were expected to grow 12 percent in 1983, blacks consumed 70 percent of the soft drinks. But only 4 percent of that was low-calorie. Among whites, however, 20 percent of the soft drinks consumed were in that category. In 1982, Tab held 80 percent of the diet segment, with Diet Pepsi (which was still not available nationwide) covering the rest.

In Nigeria, governmental import restrictions caused erratic shipment patterns and a 59 percent lower volume. The company hopes that new markets in the Sudan and Congo can lead to an overall upswing in volume in the African market.

Far East

For the Far East, excluding Japan, unit volume rose 8 percent. The standout performance came in the Philippines, where unit volume rose 16 percent. This market growth was fueled by introductions of the 12-ounce returnable bottle for Coke, the 1-liter resealable returnable bottle, and Mello Yello. In Korea, the company achieved a 3 percent gain in unit growth.

In Australia, where the diet segment was 12 percent of the total soft drink market in 1982, Tab had well over 50 percent of the cola category, with Diet Pepsi holding a smaller share. The company introduced Diet Coke in the Australian market in June 1982. A strengthening economy in 1984 led to a 7 percent volume gain.

The entire soft drink market had been undergoing a slow but steady decline in Australia, with diet drinks static over 1982, following the introduction and success of mineral waters (including new flavored varieties). Fortunately for the soft drink industry, this trend appears to be reversing.

EXHIBIT 9 Diet Drink Market as Percent of Total Soft Drink Market

COUNTRY	PERCENTAGE
United States	20.0
Canada	13.0
Australia	12.0
Norway	11.0
Argentina	5.5
Germany	5.3
England	5.0
South Africa	4.0
Japan	0.1

Source: *Advertising Age*, March 14, 1983.

Canada

Historically, the diet segment of the Canadian soft drink market ranged from around 8 percent to 10 percent of the total market until 1977, when saccharin was banned. By 1979, the diet share of the market had shrunk to 2 percent. In 1982, the first full year aspartame was available, the diet segment had not only regained historical levels, it had grown to 15 percent of the total market by year's end, while the total market itself had doubled.

Figures for April–May 1982 showed food store sales of diet soft drinks at a new high of 21.4 percent of the total and still growing. Roy Lockyer, president and CEO, Canada Dry Ltd., said, "It's 21% already and it could go to 30% by the end of 1983. It's heading that way."[18] Exhibit 9 shows the diet drink market as a percent of the total soft drink market. Coca-Cola Ltd. showed a 6 percent unit volume gain in 1984, double the Canadian industry growth rate of 3 percent. During the third quarter of 1984, Minute Maid orange was introduced in markets covering 40 percent of the Canadian population.

Coca-Cola Export Corporation

The Coca-Cola Export Corporation is a rare blend. On the one hand, it is thoroughly decentralized with as much decision making as possible pushed down through a hierarchy of zone, area, and regional offices to the person on the scene. On the other hand, its progress is increasingly the concern of Coke's people at the top.

Since most of the bottlers are local nationals, the company likes to think it is relatively immune to the dangers of expropriation. "It's a franchise business; if they nationalize the assets, they're nationalizing their own people," said J. Paul Austin, the former chairman of Coca-Cola Company.[19] Nevertheless,

---

[18] Special Report, "Canadian Bottlers See Diets at 30% of Market," *Beverage Industry*, September 1983, p. 1.
[19] "How Coke Runs a Foreign Empire," *Business Week*, August 25, 1973.

Coke was not entirely free of overseas hazards. Several Arab states shut them out some years ago because Coke refused to stop selling to Israel.

BUSINESS OBJECTIVES AND STRATEGY

Coca-Cola's core strategy is to increase shareholder value by achieving growth in earnings per share in excess of inflation and by increasing return on equity. The strategy will be achieved by focusing on the following:

1. *Increases in unit volume at rates in excess of industry rates for the soft drink and foods sectors:* Within the United States, the soft drink sector will accomplish this through marketing strength, positioning in the growing low-calorie segment, and the strengthening of the bottler system. The international focus will be on increasing per capita consumption through the mechanism of availability. The foods sector strategy will be one of product and package segmentation. Increases in unit volume will focus on layering new products into existing distribution systems.

The entertainment sector has as its key objective leveraging its distribution system through increased product flow without significantly increasing invested capital. Risk will be reduced through the use of equity and prelicensing agreements with such entities as Home Box Office and CBS, Inc.

2. *Profit margins:* Coca-Cola's objective is to improve real profits per unit. This can be accomplished through tight controls over pricing, operating expenses, and operating efficiencies. In 1984, 91 percent of the bottlers agreed to give Coca-Cola more pricing flexibility in return for additional marketing expenditures.

In 1984, high-fructose corn syrup was increased to the 100 percent level for Coca-Cola sold in bottles and cans. By January 1985, all diet drinks went to the use of 100 percent aspartame.

In 1984, the percentage of administrative and general expenses to gross profits was 16.8 percent compared to 17.7 percent in 1983. This reduction resulted in an operating income increase of over $30 million.

3. *Resource management:* Coca-Cola attempts to achieve its goals by concentrating its resources in consumer markets offering a strategic fit, attractive returns, and high growth potential. For investments with risk characteristics similar to the soft drink industry, cost of capital is estimated to be 14 percent after taxes.

In 1984, Coca-Cola reinvested $339 million excluding fixed assets of purchased companies. Reinvestment was allocated among the sectors as follows: soft drink, 72 percent; foods, 12 percent; entertainment, 9 percent; corporate,

7 percent. Additionally, Coke acquired over $100 million in soft drink bottling territories and product lines.

CAPITAL STRUCTURE

Coca-Cola attempts to maintain a strong financial position by using prudent amounts of long-term debt. During 1984, there were three $100 million long-term debt offerings with interest rates of 12.75, 11.75, and 11.375; at the close of 1984, long-term debt represented 17.9 percent of total capital. Future policy regarding the use of long-term debt will be on funding attractive investment opportunities. Exhibit 10 (pp. 997–998) details the financial review for 1974–1984. Exhibit 11 (p. 999) gives consolidated statements of income for 1982–1984.

FUTURE OUTLOOK

Top management at Coca-Cola will no longer hide under the blanket of brand popularity. Goizueta stated, "With the exception of putting out a fire here and there, I'm devoting 90% of my time to strategic planning." The clear implication is that Coke is looking hard for acquisitions. Will he buy big and will the spending be in the United States?

EXHIBIT 10 Selected Financial Data (dollars in millions except per share data)

YEAR ENDED DECEMBER 31,	1984	1983	1982[2]	1981	1980	1979	1978	1977	1976	1975	1974
Summary of operations[1]											
Net operating revenues	$7,364	$6,829	$6,021	$5,699	$5,475	$4,588	$4,013	$3,328	$2,928	$2,773	$2,425
Cost of goods and services	3,993	3,773	3,311	3,188	3,103	2,521	2,203	1,836	1,614	1,633	1,462
Gross profit	3,371	3,056	2,710	2,511	2,372	2,067	1,810	1,492	1,314	1,140	963
Selling, administrative, and general expenses	2,313	2,063	1,830	1,725	1,635	1,378	1,167	922	806	693	616
Operating income	1,058	993	880	786	737	689	643	570	508	447	347
Interest income	129	83	106	71	40	37	35	29	29	22	21
Interest expense	124	73	75	39	35	11	7	6	6	6	6
Other income (deductions)—net	5	(3)	7	(23)	(9)	(3)	(14)	(9)	(4)	(8)	5
Income from continuing operations before income taxes	1,068	1,000	918	795	733	712	657	584	527	455	367
Income taxes	439	442	415	355	329	318	300	268	245	218	170
Income from continuing operations	$ 529	$ 558	$ 503	$ 440	$ 404	$ 394	$ 357	$ 316	$ 282	$ 237	$ 197[5]
Net income	$ 529	$ 559	$ 512	$ 482	$ 422	$ 420	$ 375	$ 331	$ 294	$ 249	$ 204[5]
Per share data[3]											
Income from continuing operations	$ 4.76	$ 4.10	$ 3.88	$ 3.56	$ 3.27	$ 3.18	$ 2.89	$ 2.56	$ 2.29	$ 1.93	$ 1.60[5]
Net income	4.76	4.10	3.95	3.90	3.42	3.40	3.03	2.68	2.38	2.02	1.65[5]
Dividends	2.76	2.68	2.48	2.32	2.16	1.96	1.74	1.54	1.325	1.15	1.04
Year-end position											
Cash and marketable securities	$ 782	$ 611	$ 261	$ 340	$ 231	$ 149	$ 321	$ 350	$ 364	$ 389	$ 241
Property, plant, and equipment—net	1,623	1,561	1,539	1,409	1,341	1,284	1,065	887	738	647	601
Total assets	5,958	5,228	4,923	3,565	3,406	2,938	2,583	2,254	2,007	1,801	1,610
Long-term debt	740	513	462	137	133	31	15	15	11	16	12
Total debt	1,363	620	583	232	228	139	69	57	52	42	69
Shareholders' equity	2,778	2,921	2,779	2,271	2,075	1,919	1,740	1,578	1,434	1,302	1,190
Total capital[4]	4,141	3,541	3,362	2,503	2,303	2,058	1,809	1,635	1,486	1,344	1,259

COCA-COLA COMPANY

Financial ratios (percent)

Income from continuing operations to net operating revenues	8.5	8.2	8.4	7.7	7.4	8.6	8.9	9.5	9.6	8.5	8.1
Income from continuing operations to average shareholders' equity	22.1	19.6	19.9	20.2	20.2	21.5	21.6	21.0	20.6	19.0	17.1
Long-term debt to total capital	17.9	14.5	13.7	5.5	5.8	1.5	.8	.9	.7	1.2	1.0
Total debt to total capital	32.9	17.5	17.3	9.3	9.9	6.8	3.8	3.5	3.5	3.1	5.5
Dividend payout	58.0	65.3	62.8	59.5	63.2	57.6	57.4	57.5	55.7	56.9	63.0
Other data											
Average shares outstanding	132	136	130	124	124	124	124	123	123	123	123
Capital expenditures	$ 391	$ 384	$ 382	$ 330	$ 293	$ 381	$ 306	$ 264	$ 191	$ 145	$ 154
Depreciation	166	154	144	133	127	106	88	77	67	64	57

[1] In June 1982 the company acquired Columbia Pictures Industries, Inc., in a purchase transaction.
[2] In 1982 the company adopted Statement of Financial Accounting Standards No. 52, "Foreign Currency Translation."
[3] Adjusted for a two-for-one stock split in 1977.
[4] Includes shareholders' equity and total debt.
[5] In 1974 the company adopted the last-in, first-out (LIFO) accounting method for certain major categories of inventories. This accounting change caused a reduction in net income of $31.2 million (25 cents per share) in 1974.

New Operating Revenues ($ Billions) 1974–1984: 7.5, 6.0, 4.5, 3.0, 1.5

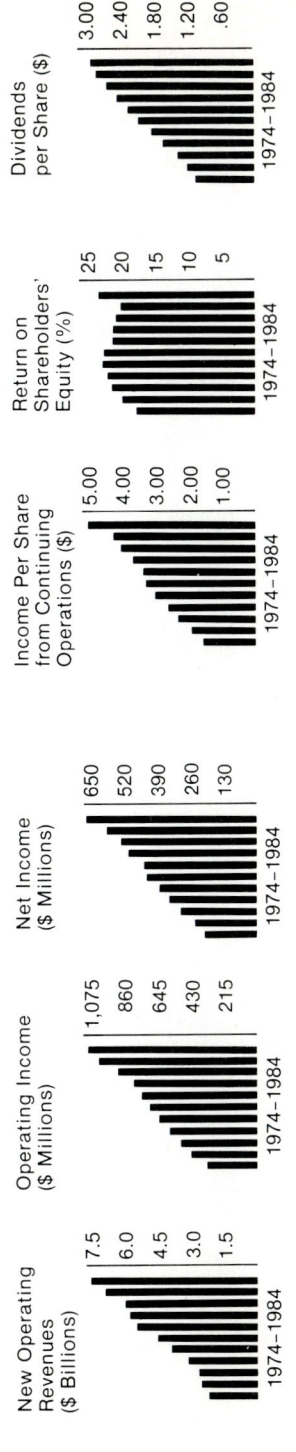

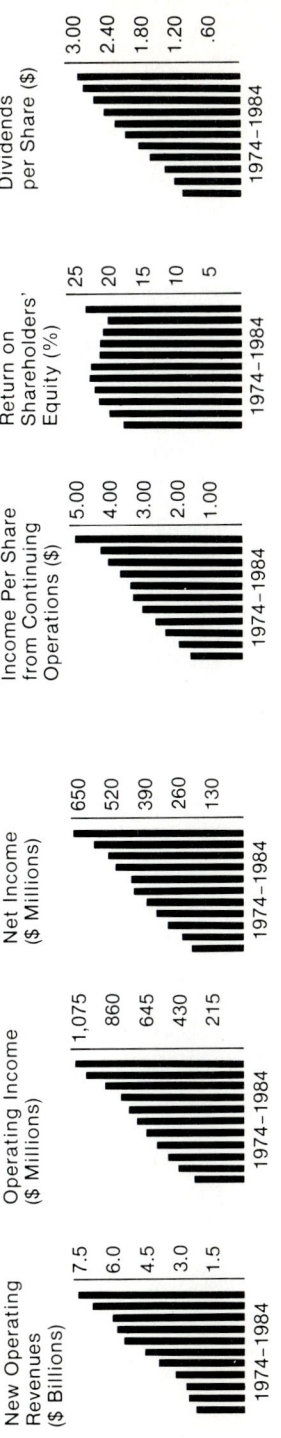

Operating Income ($ Millions) 1974–1984: 1,075, 860, 645, 430, 215

Net Income ($ Millions) 1974–1984: 650, 520, 390, 260, 130

Income Per Share from Continuing Operations ($) 1974–1984: 5.00, 4.00, 3.00, 2.00, 1.00

Return on Shareholders' Equity (%) 1974–1984: 25, 20, 15, 10, 5

Dividends per Share ($) 1974–1984: 3.00, 2.40, 1.80, 1.20, .60

EXHIBIT 11 Consolidated Statements of Income (in thousands except per share data)

YEAR ENDED DECEMBER 31,	1984	1983	1982
Net operating revenues	$7,363,993	$6,828,992	$6,021,135
Cost of goods and services	3,992,923	3,772,741	3,310,847
Gross profit	3,371,070	3,056,251	2,710,288
Selling, administrative, and general expenses	2,313,562	2,063,626	1,830,527
Operating income	1,057,508	992,625	879,761
Interest income	128,837	82,912	106,172
Interest expense	123,750	72,677	74,560
Other income (deductions)—net	5,438	(2,528)	6,679
Income from continuing operations before income taxes	1,068,033	1,000,332	918,052
Income taxes	439,215	442,072	415,076
Income from continuing operations	628,818	558,260	502,976
Income from discontinued operations (net of applicable income taxes of $414 in 1983 and $4,683 in 1982)	—	527	9,256
Net income	$ 628,818	$ 558,787	$ 512,232
Per share:			
Continuing operations	$ 4.76	$ 4.10	$ 3.88
Discontinued operations	—	—	.07
Net income	$ 4.76	$ 4.10	$ 3.95
Average shares outstanding	132,210	136,222	129,793

INDUSTRIAL HIGHLIGHT

Bottled and Canned Soft Drink Industry

Below is a capsule summary of the bottled and canned soft drink industry, of which the Coca-Cola Company is a part. Information in this highlight was compiled by the U.S. Department of Commerce and focuses on this industry during the approximate period of time covered in the case. Keep in mind that industrial highlights contained in this text are not intended as a complete synopsis of an industry but as a profile of certain issues that can be relevant to the case situation. A list of additional references at the end of this highlight can be used for further industrial analysis.

The bottled and canned soft drink industry includes establishments primarily engaged in manufacturing soft drinks (nonalcoholic beverages), carbonated water, and some non-carbonated drinks containing real juices. Pure fruit and vegetable juices, fruit syrups, cider, and bottled spring waters are excluded.

CURRENT SITUATION

Strong consumer demand for diet soft drinks and a strengthening in disposable income contributed to record soft drink consumption in 1984. For the year, the value of bottled and canned soft drink industry shipments reached an estimated $20 billion, up 8.4 percent compared to 1983. Adjusted for inflation, the value of soft drink industry shipments rose more than 5 percent in 1984; in comparison, inflation-adjusted industry shipments rose about 1.5 percent annually between 1980 and 1983. The quantity of soft drinks shipped during the year increased by an estimated 5 percent to 6 percent.

Demand Increases

Diet drink sales of the major franchise brands (Coca-Cola, Pepsi-Cola, Seven-Up) rose an estimated 18 to 28 percent in 1984. The recent introduction of aspartame-sweetened diet drinks, which reduce or eliminate the use of

Source: U.S. Industrial Outlook, Department of Commerce, 1985, pp. 42-6–42-9.

EXHIBIT A Per Capita Consumption Changes for Selected Beverages, 1979–1984

(annual percent change)

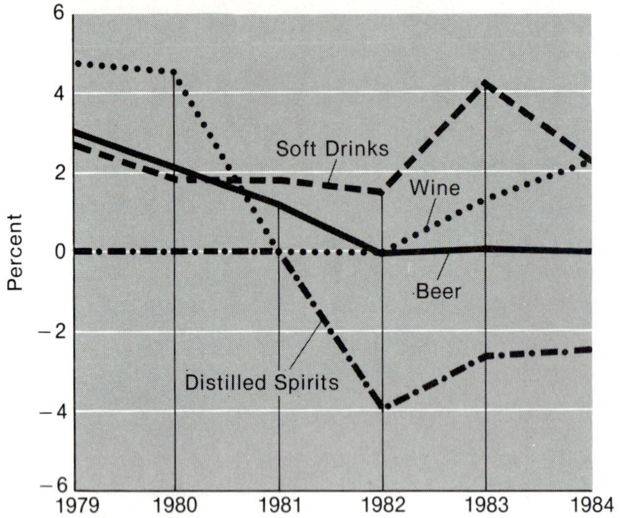
6
4
2
0
−2
−4
−6
Percent
Soft Drinks
Wine
Beer
Distilled Spirits
1979
1980
1981
1982
1983
1984

Source: International Trade Administration.

saccharin, provided a major boost for bottlers. Demand for soft drinks containing aspartame rose significantly in 1984, while consumption of saccharin drinks leveled off. In 1984, diet drinks represented about 21.5 percent of the market, up from a 20 percent share in 1982.

Initially, aspartame-sweetened soft drink formulas employed a blend of saccharin and the more costly aspartame. Attempting to accentuate product differentiation and capture a larger market share, some soft drink firms then introduced 100 percent aspartame-sweetened diet drinks. By mid-1984, diet drinks from Procter & Gamble, Shasta, Canfield, and the Squirt Company used only aspartame.

In November 1984 the Pepsi-Cola Company announced that all of its diet colas would use aspartame in the future rather than a saccharin blend. Currently, Pepsi-Cola is second in the diet cola market, but this move to all aspartame is expected to heighten competition with the leader, Coca-Cola. Industry observers believe that most diet soft drinks will ultimately use aspartame exclusively.

In spite of improving sales and rising volume, bottlers' profit margins did not keep pace, with bottlers of high-volume cola brands faring better than other bottlers. Competition for retail space and consumers' attention grew in 1984, and discounting was widespread as bottlers continued to provide price incentives to retailers and consumers. Thus, sharply increased volume was necessary to offset the negative effects of discounting, and some bottlers failed to make adequate volume gains. In addition, the use of aspartame also squeezed some bottlers' margins. Some analysts believe that continuing product segmentation, discounting, and competition for retail space will strain many less well-capitalized bottlers, prompting further industry realignment and mergers.

Other Soft Drink Trends

New products and packaging were introduced in 1984.

The Pepsi-Cola Co. introduced a citrus-based carbonated drink containing 10 percent real fruit juice. The product, in regular and an aspartame-blend diet version, is partially targeted to health-conscious consumers. The General Cinema Corporation, Pepsi-Cola's largest franchise, introduced a citrus-based caramel-colored carbonated drink. The product, which looks and tastes somewhat like a cola, is caffeine-free and contains vitamin C. The product contains no cola extract.

Many soft drink bottlers introduced aseptically packaged fruit drinks in 1984. These were an effort to diversify product lines and to bolster sagging profits. Industry analysts estimate the aseptic fruit beverage market, including pure juices and juice blends, at about $500 million. Soft drink bottlers' aseptic juice drink sales account for about 40 percent of this amount, about equally divided between bottler labels and national brands. Many bottlers believe that their access to smaller retailers and vending outlets gives them a competitive advantage in the aseptic market. Thus, it is likely that more bottlers will add aseptic juice products to their product lines.

Many soft drink bottlers, recognizing the increasing demand for larger containers, moved to add three-liter (101-ounce) plastic bottles to their product lines in 1984. The Coca-Cola Co. announced its intent to make eight of its brands available in this size, but grocery retailers expressed concern about the space demands of still another soft drink package variation. Since grocery shelf space is limited, it is likely that retailers will be more selective in allocating shelf space. Lower-volume brands may therefore be reduced or eliminated.

According to the Census Bureau, substantial changes occurred in the package mix between 1977 and 1982. Demand for carbonated drinks in single-service bottles and cans (16 ounces and less) declined as consumers sought greater value by purchasing larger bottle sizes.

Even more dramatic changes occurred in the bottled single-serving market. Between 1978 and 1982, demand for smaller bottles declined 78 percent for six to nine-ounce bottles and 42 percent for ten to twelve-ounce bottles. Shipments of 16-ounce bottles, on the other hand, rose 18 percent.

In November 1984, Pepsico, Inc. and the Coca-Cola Company announced that they would significantly increase their use of high-fructose corn sweeteners (HFCS-55) in their nondietetic cola drinks. Pepsico intends to use corn sweeteners exclusively for all regular cola drinks, while Coca-Cola will allow up to 100 percent corn sweetener use in bottled and canned drinks. Because HFCS-55 is less costly than traditional cane and beet sugar-based sweeteners, soft drink bottlers will benefit from reduced production costs. Investment analysts estimate that affected bottlers' profits will likely increase by 5 percent to 10 percent because of these decisions.

Industry observers estimate that domestic demand for high-fructose corn sweeteners will increase by the equivalent of about 44 million bushels of corn because of these moves. In contrast, hard-pressed sugar refiners confront the loss of up to 1.3 billion pounds of cane and beet sugar sweeteners entirely unless the domestic price of sugar becomes competitive with corn sweeteners.

Foreign Trade

U.S. trade in bottled and canned soft drinks is relatively small. Imports and exports of packaged drinks represent less than 1 percent of the value of soft drink product shipments. However, American soft drinks are very popular and are widely available worldwide. In order to avoid shipping costs, U.S. companies prefer to license overseas firms to produce the drinks locally. Thus, U.S. exports are limited to products not produced abroad. The value of U.S. exports of soft drinks in 1984 reached $28 million, down 23 percent from 1983. The quantity of soft drinks exported in 1984 declined an estimated 11 percent. The average price was $1.75 per gallon, down 8 percent from 1983.

The quantity and value of soft drink imports rose an estimated 5.3 percent and 18.9 percent, respectively, while the average price rose 5.3 percent, to $2.14 per gallon. France, Canada, Switzerland, Japan, and Mexico accounted for over 75 percent of the soft drink imports. Industry analysts noted a sharp increase in shipments from Japan, stimulated by the introduction of a new product which blends carbonated citrus juices with dry milk powder. The product is supposedly the third-largest-selling soft drink in Japan.

Observers also monitored the introduction of a new orange soda in Canada by Coca-Cola. The drink, which contains a small amount of orange juice, was introduced under the Minute Maid label.

OUTLOOK FOR 1985

The carbonated soft drink industry is expected to experience another good year in 1985; the value of industry shipments is forecast to increase about 5 percent over the 1984 level, after adjusting for inflation.

Price discounting is expected to continue as bottlers compete for market share and retail shelf space. Consequently, margins will continue to be thin and some bottlers dependent on slower-selling brands will be under pressure. Thus, bottlers are expected to place increased emphasis on aseptic juice drink production in 1985.

LONG-TERM PROSPECTS

Substantial structural changes are likely in the soft drink industry over the next five years. The major drink franchisers are expected to become more dominant and to further broaden their product lines; some smaller national and regional brands are expected to be acquired or to discontinue operation.

The number of bottling operations is also forecast to continue declining as multimarket bottlers consolidate manufacturing operations and increase distribution outlets. Some analysts believe manufacturing consolidation may help small brands remain competitive.

The industry is expected to come under increasing pressure as state and local governments seek new sources of revenue. As yet, soft drinks are not subject to state excise taxes. However, hard-pressed state and local governments confronting static or declining income from tobacco and alcoholic beverages excise taxes are expected to intensify efforts to tax soft drinks. Bottlers and drink companies are expected to react aggressively to efforts, but passage of such legislation in some areas is considered probable.

Adjusted for inflation, the value of soft drink industry shipments is forecast to increase 1.8 percent annually over the next five years. Demographic shifts and changing taste patterns will restrain demand growth.

ADDITIONAL REFERENCES

Bottled and Canned Soft Drinks, SIC 2081, *1982 Census of Manufacturers,* preliminary report industry series, Bureau of the Census, U.S. Department of Commerce, Washington, DC 20233.

National Soft Drink Association, 1101 16th Street, NW, Washington, DC 20036.

Beverage World, 150 Great Neck Road, Great Neck, NY 11021.

Beverage Industry, 1 East First Street, Duluth, MN 55802.

Advertising Age, 740 N. Rush Street, Chicago, IL 60611.

CASE 25

Ford of Europe

H. LANDIS GABEL   ANTHONY E. HALL
INSEAD (European Institute of Business Administration)

In mid-1983, the Management Committee of Ford of Europe (the company's senior decision-making committee) was once again examining the trends, opportunities, and threats offered by the European market (see Exhibits 1, 2, and 3). The principal threat perceived by management was the growing Japanese presence in Europe. Japanese manufacturers had increased their car sales in Western Europe from 750,000 units in 1979 to almost one million units in 1983 and they were beginning to establish a manufacturing foothold in Europe. Nissan, for example, was just beginning to produce automobiles in Italy, it would soon increase its production of vehicles for Europe from a Spanish plant, and, most worrisome, the company was expected to announce imminently a decision to proceed with a previously shelved plan to construct a new and very large assembly plant in the United Kingdom. Although Ford competed very successfully against the other European producers—and for the first time had captured the number one European market share position in the second quarter of 1983—Japanese producers' plants in Europe would constitute a new and severe challenge. What especially worried Ford was the possibility that Nissan's new U.K. plant would import major automobile components into Europe from Japan, assemble them into finished vehicles, and then claim that the vehicles were European in origin and thus not subject to any existing European–Japanese trade agreements or understandings.

This worry had led Ford executives back in 1981 to consider seriously local content regulations as a way of reducing this risk and helping to stem the growth of the Japanese producers' share of the European market. Local content regulations, most commonly employed by developing countries against multinational firms based in developed countries, defined the percentage of a product that must be produced in a specified geographical region as a precondition of sale in that region.

Although local content regulations had been discussed occasionally in the Management Committee for the past two years, no conclusions had been

---

This case study was developed after discussions with certain Ford personnel but it does not necessarily reflect the actual scope or manner of deliberations undertaken by Ford management or the conclusions of Ford management. This is a serial case; related cases will appear in subsequent issues of the journal.

Address reprint requests to H. Landis Gabel, Associate Professor of Industrial Economics, INSEAD (European Institute of Business Administration), Boulevard de Constance, 77305 Fontainebleau Cedex, France.

© H. Landis Gabel and Anthony E. Hall, 1985

EXHIBIT 1 Ford Motor Company and Consolidated Subsidiaries Consolidated Balance Sheet at December 31, 1982 ($ millions)

ASSETS	1982	1981
Current Assets		
Cash and cash items	$ 943.7	$ 1,176.5
Marketable securities (including $500 million of commercial paper of Ford Motor Credit Company in 1981), at cost and accrued interest (approximates market)	611.7	923.5
Receivables	2,376.5	2,595.8
Inventories	4,123.3	4,642.9
Other current assets	743.7	838.2
Total current assets	8,798.9	10,176.9
Equities in Net Assets of Unconsolidated Subsidiaries and Affiliates (Note 9)	2,413.4	2,348.2
Property		
Land, plant and equipment, at cost	17,014.9	16,395.7
Less accumulated depreciation	9,546.9	8,959.4
Net land, plant and equipment	7,468.0	7,436.3
Unamortized special tools	2,668.3	2,410.1
Net property	10,136.3	9,846.4
Other Assets	613.1	649.9
Total Assets	$21,961.7	$23,021.4

LIABILITIES AND STOCKHOLDERS' EQUITY	1982	1981
Current Liabilities		
Accounts payable		
Trade	$ 3,117.5	$ 2,800.2
Other	1,002.1	1,089.8
Total accounts payable	4,119.6	3,890.0
Income taxes	383.0	208.9
Short-term debt	1,949.1	2,049.0
Long-term debt payable within one year	315.9	128.7
Accrued liabilities	3,656.4	3,663.7
Total current liabilities	10,424.0	9,940.3
Long-Term Debt	2,353.3	2,709.7
Other Liabilities	1,922.7	1,856.2
Deferred Income Taxes	1,054.1	1,004.8
Minority Interests in Net Assets of Consolidated Subsidiaries	130.1	148.2
Guarantees and Commitments	—	—
Stockholders' Equity		
Capital Stock, par value $2.00 a share		
Common Stock, shares issued: 1982—108,870,062; 1981—107,859,065	217.8	215.7
Class B Stock, shares issued: 1982—11,717,738; 1981—12,717,003	23.4	25.5
Capital in excess of par value of stock	522.4	526.1
Foreign-currency translation adjustments	(623.2)	—
Earnings retained for use in the business	5,937.1	6,594.9
Total stockholders' equity	6,077.5	7,362.2
Total Liabilities and Stockholders' Equity	$21,961.7	$23,021.4

Source: Ford of Europe.

EXHIBIT 2 Ford Motor Company and Consolidated Subsidiaries Ten-Year

SUMMARY OF OPERATIONS	1982[1]	1981
Sales	$37,067.2	38,247.1
Total costs	37,550.8	39,502.9
Operating income (loss)	(483.6)	(1,255.8)
Interest income	562.7	624.6
Interest expense	745.5	674.7
Equity in net income of unconsolidated subsidiaries and affiliates	258.5	167.8
Income (loss) before income taxes	(407.9)	(1,138.1)
Provision (credit) for income taxes	256.6[3]	(68.3)[3]
Minority interests	(6.7)	(9.7)
Income (loss) before cumulative effect of an accounting change	(657.8)	(1,060.1)
Cumulative effect of an accounting change[4]	—	—
Net income (loss)	(657.8)	(1,060.1)
Cash dividends	—	144.4
Retained income (loss)	$ (657.8)	(1,204.5)
Income before minority interests as percentage of sales	*	*
Stockholders' equity at year-end	$ 6,077.5	7,362.2
Assets at year-end	$21,961.7	23,021.4
Long-term debt at year-end	$ 2,353.3	2,709.7
Average number of shares of capital stock outstanding (in millions)	120.4	120.3
A share (in dollars)		
Income (loss) before cumulative effect of an accounting change	$ (5.46)	(8.81)
Cumulative effect of an accounting change[4]	—	—
Net income (loss)[5]	$ (5.46)	(8.81)
Net income assuming full dilution		
Cash dividends	—	$ 1.20
Stockholders' equity at year-end	$ 50.40	61.06
Common Stock price range (NYSE)	$ 41½	26
	$ 16¾	15¾
▲ Pro forma amounts assuming the investment tax credits accrued after 1970 flowed through to		
Net income (in millions)	—	—
Net income a share	—	—
Assuming full dilution	—	—
Facility and Tooling Data		
Capital expenditures for expansion, modernization and replacement of facilities (excluding special tools)	$ 1,605.8	1,257.4
Depreciation	$ 1,200.8	1,168.7
Expenditures for special tools	$ 1,361.6	970.0
Amortization of special tools	$ 955.6	1,010.7
Employee Data—Worldwide		
Payroll	$ 8,863.0	9,380.1
Total labor costs	$11,756.7	12,238.3
Average number of employees	379,229	404,788
Employee Data—U.S. Operations		
Payroll	$ 5,352.7	5,507.5
Average hourly labor costs per hour worked[7] (in dollars)		
Earnings	$ 13.57	12.75
Benefits	9.80	8.93
Total	$ 23.37	21.68
Average number of employees	155,901	170,806

Share data have been adjusted to reflect the five-for-four stock split that became effective May 24, 1977.
* 1982, 1981 and 1980 results were a loss.
[1] See Note 1 of Notes to Financial Statements.
[2] Change to LIFO reduced net income by $81 million.
[3] See Note 5 of Notes to Financial Statements.

FORD OF EUROPE 523

Financial Summary (millions of dollars)

	1980	1979	1978	1977	1976[2]	1975	1974	1973
	37,085.5	43,513.7	42,784.1	37,841.5	28,839.6	24,009.1	23,620.6	23,015.1
	39,363.8	42,596.7	40,425.6	35,095.9	27,252.7	23,572.7	23,015.4	21,446.1
	(2,278.3)	917.0	2,358.5	2,745.6	1,586.9	436.4	605.2	1,569.0
	543.1	693.0	456.0	299.1	232.6	155.8	171.4	189.9
	432.5	246.8	194.8	192.7	216.6	301.0	281.5	174.7
	187.0	146.2	159.0	150.0	136.3	107.0	58.5	48.5
	(1,980.7)	1,509.4	2,778.7	3,002.0	1,739.2	398.2	553.6	1,632.7
	(435.4)[3]	330.1	1,175.0	1,325.6	730.6	151.9	201.5	702.1
	(2.0)	10.0	14.8	3.6	25.5	18.8	25.0	24.1
	(1,543.3)	1,169.3	1,588.9	1,672.8	983.1	227.5	327.1▲	906.5▲
	—	—	—	—	—	95.2	—	—
	(1,543.3)	1,169.3	1,588.9	1,672.8	983.1	322.7	327.1	906.5
	312.7	467.6	416.6	359.3	263.4	242.6	298.1	317.1
	(1,856.0)	701.7	1,172.3	1,313.5	719.7	80.1	29.0	589.4
	*	2.7%	3.7%	4.4%	3.5%	1.4%	1.5%	4.0%
	8,567.5	10,420.7	9,686.3	8,456.9	7,107.0	6,376.5	6,267.5	6,405.1
	24,347.6	23,524.6	22,101.4	19,241.3	15,768.1	14,020.2	14,173.6	12,954.0
	2,058.8	1,274.6	1,144.5	1,359.7	1,411.4	1,533.9	1,476.7	977.0
	120.3	119.9	119.0	118.1	117.6	116.6	116.8	124.1
	12.83)	9.75	13.35	14.16	8.36	1.95	2.80▲	7.31▲
	—	—	—	—	—	0.82	—	—
	(12.83)	9.75	13.35	14.16	8.36	2.77	2.80	7.31
	—	$9.15	12.42	13.08	7.74	2.65	2.69▲	6.86▲
	2.60	3.90	3.50	3.04	2.24	2.08	2.56	2.56
	71.05	86.46	80.77	71.15	60.14	54.09	53.58	51.66
	35¾	45⅜	51⅞	49¼	49½	36¼	43½	65⅞
	18⅛	29⅜	39	41⅜	34⅞	25⅞	23	30⅞

income in the year the assets were placed in service:

	—	—	—	—	—	—	$363.9	938.9
	—	—	—	—	—	—	$ 3.12	7.57
	—	—	—	—	—	—	$ 2.98	7.10
	1,583.8	2,152.3	1,571.5	1,089.6	551.0	614.2	832.5	891.7
	1,057.2	895.9	735.5	628.7	589.7	583.8	530.8	485.1
	1,184.7	1,288.0	970.2	672.7	503.7	342.2	618.7	594.3
	912.1	708.5	578.2	487.7	431.0	435.3	392.7	463.1
	9,519.0	10,169.1	9,774.9	8,338.3	6,639.2	5,629.2	5,892.6	5,769.2
	12,417.3	13,227.2	12,494.0	10,839.2	8,653.3	7,165.7	7,317.3	7,108.2
	426,735	494,579	506,531	479,292	443,917[6]	416,120	464,731	474,318
	5,248.5	6,262.6	6,581.2	5,653.4	4,380.4	3,560.5	3,981.9	4,027.0
	11.45	10.35	9.73	8.93	8.03	7.10	6.61	6.12
	8.54	5.59	4.36	3.91	3.98	3.86	2.88	2.31
	19.99	15.94	14.09	12.84	12.01	10.96	9.49	8.43
	179.917	239,475	256,614	239,303	219,698[6]	203,691	235,256	249,513

[4] Cumulative effect of change (as of January 1, 1975) to flow-through method of accounting for investment tax credit.
[5] See Note 7 of Notes to Financial Statements.
[6] Excludes effect of UAW strike.
[7] Excludes data for subsidiary companies.

Source: Ford of Europe.

EXHIBIT 3 Ford Motor Company and Consolidated Subsidiaries Ten-Year Summary of Vehicle Factory Sales

	1982	1981	1980	1979	1978	1977	1976	1975	1974	1973
U.S. and Canadian Cars and Trucks[1]										
Cars										
United States	1,270,519	1,385,174	1,397,431	2,044,461	2,632,190	2,625,485	2,197,039	1,867,713	2,336,415	2,685,423
Canada	118,721	148,515	162,576	236,437	248,285	247,427	210,049	225,293	258,980	231,598
Total cars	1,389,240	1,533,689	1,560,007	2,280,898	2,880,475	2,872,912	2,407,088	2,093,006	2,595,395	2,917,021
Trucks[2]										
United States	803,484	716,648	753,195	1,183,016	1,458,132	1,345,282	1,017,736	809,360	991,447	1,086,281
Canada	70,120	104,136	109,006	160,160	153,955	149,756	131,186	131,104	143,079	98,326
Total trucks	873,604	820,784	862,201	1,343,176	1,612,087	1,495,038	1,148,922	940,464	1,134,526	1,184,607
Total cars and trucks	2,262,844	2,354,473	2,422,208	3,624,074	4,492,562	4,367,950	3,556,010	3,033,470	3,729,921	4,101,628
Cars and Trucks Outside the United States and Canada[2]										
Germany	797,850	737,383	657,258	880,325	847,529	891,390	815,279	636,799	496,780	728,514
Britain	423,073	418,629	468,472	555,496	433,191	563,384	515,368	468,255	559,534	615,276
Spain	229,839	254,006	266,522	252,917	247,408	212,855	16,448	—	—	—
Brazil	145,110	125,346	165,703	169,631	158,935	129,466	169,707	172,235	177,698	144,739
Australia	141,990	127,181	93,490	115,148	107,389	112,376	108,549	124,600	131,393	130,881
Mexico	90,478	107,312	84,668	74,703	68,009	49,216	45,498	55,909	54,649	44,242
South Africa	59,171	66,962	52,671	40,447	46,201	34,156	33,638	36,878	40,155	35,473
Argentina	52,764	78,671	106,463	89,669	52,702	52,466	35,318	39,793	53,810	61,373
Other countries	51,790	43,225	10,995	7,894	8,139	9,042	8,629	9,833	14,993	8,902
Total outside United States and Canada	1,992,065	1,958,715	1,906,242	2,186,230	1,969,503	2,054,351	1,748,434	1,544,302	1,529,012	1,769,400
Total worldwide—cars and trucks	4,254,909	4,313,188	4,328,450	5,810,304	6,462,065	6,422,301	5,304,444	4,577,772	5,258,933	5,871,028
Tractors[2]										
United States	24,258	31,517	35,286	51,361	35,789	39,650	34,643	38,342	41,090	40,223
Overseas	48,905	57,757	62,415	82,267	59,448	90,880	83,177	73,981	68,202	61,624
Total worldwide—tractors	73,163	89,274	97,701	133,628	95,237	130,530	117,820	112,323	109,292	101,847
Total worldwide factory sales	4,328,072	4,402,462	4,426,151	5,943,952	6,557,302	6,552,831	5,422,264	4,690,095	5,368,225	5,972,875

[1] Factory sales are by source of manufacture, except that Canadian exports to the United States are included in U.S. vehicle sales and U.S. exports to Canada are included as Canadian vehicle sales. Prior year data have been restated for reclassification of Club Wagons from cars to trucks.
[2] Includes units manufactured by other companies and sold by Ford.

EXHIBIT 3 (Continued)

Ford Shares of Major Car and Truck Markets

	CARS				TRUCKS			
	1982		1981		1982		1981	
	Industry Unit Sales	Ford Market Share	Industry Unit Sales	Ford Market Share	Industry Unit Sales	Ford Market Share	Industry Unit Sales	Ford Market Share
United States	7,955,970	16.9%	8,514,956	16.6%	2,584,989	30.6%	2,281,879	31.4%
Canada	713,005	15.8	903,536	15.2	205,409	26.7	287,290	30.2
Germany	2,091,297	11.3	2,264,634	11.8	187,789	8.1	214,261	7.7
United Kingdom	1,552,926	30.5	1,484,250	30.9	229,346	36.6	213,832	30.5
Other European Markets[1]	6,171,231	8.2	5,913,692	7.8	874,626	6.1	842,626	7.0
Brazil	556,596	17.6	448,256	19.2	134,621	23.2	132,677	17.9
Mexico	288,253	12.9	342,724	15.9	181,948	27.7	230,939	25.6
Argentina	114,455	33.9	172,640	31.8	29,484	54.1	56,965	46.4
Other Latin American Markets[1]	288,423	15.9	439,635	11.1	171,138	17.5	249,266	13.8
Australia	454,250	26.0	453,806	23.0	162,104	13.0	152,476	13.1
South Africa	283,427	14.5	301,528	16.7	142,696	10.3	152,013	10.7
All Other Markets[1]	4,673,287	2.0	4,630,160	1.8	3,288,457	1.0	3,437,096	0.8
Worldwide Total[1]	25,143,120	12.5%	25,869,817	12.4%	8,192,607	14.6%	8,252,320	14.0%

[1] 1982 data estimated.

Source: Ford of Europe.

reached, and pressure was building to push the discussion through to a definitive policy stance. If the Committee were to decide to favor local content regulations, it would then have to decide on strategy and tactics. Regulations could take various forms, some of which might be more advantageous to Ford than others. And, of course, Ford would have to decide how to represent its position to the governmental bodies that would have to introduce, monitor, and enforce the regulations.

FORD OF EUROPE

Ford's European headquarters are based at Warley near Brentwood in southeast England. The sixth floor of its 2,500-person office building houses Ford of Europe's executive suites, where trade policy is a frequent—and often emotional—topic of conversation. The Ford Motor Company had a long tradition of favoring unrestricted international trade. Henry Ford declared in 1928, "I don't believe in anything else than free trade all 'round." Indeed, he exported the sixth car he made (to Canada). But the international trade environment of the 1920s was not that of the 1970s and 1980s, and although Henry Ford II was a strong free-trader like his grandfather, Ford U.S. had altered its official policy position in 1980 away from free trade toward fair trade with an element of protectionism. The management of Ford of Europe could follow this lead by lobbying for local content regulations, but they did not feel obliged to do so. They were sufficiently independent of their American parent that the decision was theirs to make.

Ford of Europe was a product of the Ford Motor Company's traditional internationalism. It was created in 1967 when the managing director of Ford of Germany, John Andrews, convinced Henry Ford II of the need to coordinate the design, development, production, and marketing operations of the Ford European national operating companies within the framework of the European Economic Community (EEC).

Ford now has 25 manufacturing sites in six European countries, and it is the most geographically integrated car producer in Europe. In the last five years the company spent more than $5 billion on automation and common design of its European cars, with the objective of making at least half the parts used in its European line interchangeable. Ford's European integration and focus and its image as a national producer in each national market gives it an important advantage in the growing trend of nationalistic car buying. The company proudly claims that 95 percent of the content of its European cars is European in origin.

Ford of Europe had sales of $9.9 billion in 1981 and would have ranked 34th on the FORTUNE 500 listing. From 1980 through 1982—one of the worst periods for the auto industry since the 1950s—Ford of Europe earned $1 billion in profit. (See Exhibits 4 and 5 for production information on world automobile manufacturers.)

EXHIBIT 4 Automobile Production by Producer, 1975, 1980, 1982
(thousands of units)

PRODUCER	1975	1980	1982
1. General Motors (United States)	4,649	4,753	4,069
2. Toyota (Japan)	2,336	3,293	3,144
3. Gr. Nissan (Nissan–Fuji)	2,280	3,117	2,958
4. Volkswagen–Audi	1,940	2,529	2,108
5. Renault-RVI (France)	1,427	2,132	1,965
6. Ford (United States)	2,500	1,888	1,817
7. Peugeot–Talbot–Citroën (France)	659	1,408	1,574
8. Ford (Europe)	1,099	1,395	1,450
9. Fiat–Autobianchi–Lancia–OM	1,231	1,554	1,170
10. Toyo–Kogyo (Mazda)	642	1,121	1,110
11. Honda	413	956	1,020
12. Mitsubishi	520	1,104	969
13. Chrysler Co. (United States–Canada)	1,508	882	967
14. Open (General Motors)	675	833	961
15. Lada (Fiat–U.S.S.R.)	690	825	800
16. Daimler-Benz	556	717	700
17. Suzuki	184	468	603
18. General Motors (Canada)	598	763	560
Talbot (France, United Kingdom, Europe)	719	642	—
19. British Leyland	738	525	494
20. Isuzu	244	472	404
21. BMW	221	341	378
22. Ford Canada	481	434	374
23. Volvo (Sweden–Netherlands)	331	285	335
24. Seat (Fiat)	332	297	246
25. Polski Fiat	135	330	240
26. Moskvitch	300	230	205
27. American Motors	463	252	194
28. Alfa Romeo	191	221	189
29. Vauxhall	190	151	164
30. Saporoskje (U.S.S.R.)	130	150	150

Source: *L'Argus de l'Automobile.*

THE GROWING JAPANESE PRESENCE IN EUROPE

Ford of Europe had identified Japanese automotive products as the principal threat in the 1980s. To respond to that threat, Ford's European companies launched a major education and development program in the late 1970s called "After Japan." The program had started with trips by management to Japan to tour Japanese automobile assembly plants. By 1983, "After Japan" was well established with emphasis on robotics, quality circles, "just in time" inventory controls, and other work practices imported from Japan. Already, over 700 robots were at work in Ford's European plants with 1,500 planned by 1986.

EXHIBIT 5 Automobile Industry in Leading Countries (data in thousands of units)

	1973	1980	1982[1]
Worldwide production	29,793	29,244	27,197
Federal Republic of Germany			
New car registrations	2,031	2,426	2,156
Imports	763	1,013	824
Exports	2,173	1,873	2,194
to Europe	1,150	1,381	1,785
to United States	786	335	257
Production	3,650	3,521	3,761
France			
New car registrations	1,746	1,873	2,056
Imports	461	675	972
Exports	1,446	1,530	1,464
to Europe	1,222	1,203	1,095
Production	2,867	2,939	2,777
United Kingdom			
New car registrations	1,664	1,516	1,557
Imports	505	863	934
Exports	599	359	313
to Europe	296	143	140
Production	1,747	959	888
Italy			
New car registrations	1,449	1,530	1,900
Imports	419	908	868
Exports	656	511	437
to Europe	505	385	383
Production	1,823	1,445	1,297
Spain			
Exports	158	492	495
Production	706	1,029	928
U.S.S.R.			
Production	917	1,327	1,307
Japan[2]			
New car registrations	2,919	2,854	3,038
Import	37	46	35
Exports	1,451	3,947	3,770
to Europe	357	1,003	896
to United States	601	1,887	1,741
Production	4,471	7,038	6,882
United States			
New car registrations	11,351	8,761	7,754
Imports	2,437	3,248	3,091
Exports[3]	579	560	353
to Europe	15	24	6
Production	9,667	6,376	5,073

[1] Figures are partly estimated.
[2] From 1978 on, actual figures are given, excluding major components.
[3] Including exports to Canada.
Source: Daimler-Benz.

Ford's top management believed, however, that it would still take at least five to ten years for their European plants to establish the cost and productivity levels necessary to match the landed price of Japanese imports. The Japanese cost advantage has been estimated to be about $1,500 ex-works per automobile.

A series of bilateral trade agreements between individual European countries and Japan currently capped Japanese automobile imports into Europe. A reciprocal trade treaty between Italy and Japan (ironically initiated by the Japanese in the 1950s) restricted exports to each other's market to 2,200 units annually. Japan's shares of the French and U.K. markets were informally limited to 3 percent and 11 percent, respectively. The French quota was imposed by President Valéry Giscard d'Estaing in 1976 after an abrupt increase in Japan's share of the French market. The U.K. quota was negotiated with the Japanese Ministry of International Trade and Industry (MITI) in 1978 after a previous, less formal agreement on export restraint failed. The Benelux countries and West Germany were technically open to the Japanese after the lapse of a 1981 informal one-year agreement in those countries establishing a maximum share of 10 percent of each market for the Japanese. Although there was no evidence that the Japanese were moving quickly to exploit this opening into Europe, Ford executives feared that the whole structure of trade understandings was very fragile.[1]

It was not only by exporting vehicles that the Japanese were making their presence felt in Europe, threatening European producers, and promoting European government concern. In 1981, British Leyland launched its Triumph "Acclaim." The Acclaim was a Honda "Ballade" assembled under license from Honda. Mechanical components were imported from Japan, and a royalty was paid to Honda on each car. The Acclaim was introduced to plug a gap in British Leyland's model range, and it precipitated a considerable outcry by some European governments. For example, although British Leyland argued that 70 percent of the car was British in origin, the Italian government refused to allow the first consignment of Acclaims to enter their country from Britain in 1982. The Italians classified the car as Japanese and thus subject to the strict quota agreement between Italy and Japan. British Leyland successfully mobilized support from the U.K. government and the EEC, and the Italians eventually backed down. Nonetheless, the nature of the future battle was becoming clear.

In August 1983, the French government announced that starting in 1984 the Acclaim would be subject to the French "voluntary" agreement with Japan; or rather 40 percent of it would be. That was the percentage that the French government deemed to be of Japanese origin. Again the threat to the Acclaim

---

[1] Ford also perceived an import threat from the emerging automobile industries of Eastern Europe. Many of the countries of Eastern Europe had established their industries with the help of Western European producers (e.g., Fiat in the Soviet Union and Poland, and Renault in Romania). The cars now produced in Eastern Europe were of outdated design, however, and with rapidly growing domestic demand, Eastern European countries were not expected to be a challenge in Western European markets on a scale close to that of the Japanese.

was withdrawn after a visit to Paris by U.K. Trade Minister, Cecil Parkinson, in August 1983.

The United Kingdom also experienced a similar situation on the import side. In 1983 a Mitsubishi automobile named the "Lonsdale" was imported for the first time into the United Kingdom from Australia, where it was assembled from Japanese components. Strong industry concern was again expressed about hidden loopholes in the network of orderly marketing agreements, but no action was taken.

Japanese components were also beginning to appear on the European market in the 1980s in what had been until then strictly European automobiles. In Milan, Innocenti replaced the old British Leyland miniengine in its small car with a Japanese Daihatsu engine. And in 1981 General Motors started to purchase gearboxes from Japan for its "Cavalier" (U.K.) and "Rekord" (Germany) models. General Motors was thought by many industry observers to be pursuing a policy of increasing the percentage of Japanese components in its European and U.S. models.

In addition to their direct export of vehicles, and their indirect exports through cooperative agreements with some European producers, the Japanese were beginning to explore direct foreign investment in Europe. Nissan (Datsun) had for some time been actively looking at sites for overseas automobile assembly plants. In 1981, Nissan commissioned the consulting firm of McKinsey and Co. to undertake a feasibility study for the location of an assembly plant in the United Kingdom. It was to produce up to 200,000 units annually by 1986, rising possibly to 500,000 by 1990. Employment on a greenfield site was to be 4,000–5,000, rising to perhaps 12,000 workers. The scheme would be eligible for government grants of £50–100 million.

Included in the negotiations between Nissan and the U.K. government was a discussion of the degree of voluntary local content. It was widely rumored at the time that Nissan was prepared to accept an EEC content level of 60 percent by value from the outset, rising to 80 percent later. The U.K. Department of Industry was rumored to want these percentages to apply to the ex-works price, after classifying Nissan's profit after tax on the operation as an import. British Leyland and Ford lobbied hard for an immediate 80 percent local content. Further uncertainty revolved around the impact of the new plant on the understanding between the U.K. Society of Motor Manufacturers and Traders and the Japanese Association of Motor Assemblers, which restrained the Japanese share of the U.K. market to 11 percent. The project had been temporarily shelved in 1982 because of uncertainty about future car sales, possible hostility from European governments (notably Italy and France), and fears of poor labor relations. It now threatened to come off the shelf.

Although the U.K. project was at least temporarily stalled, the first cars had just begun to roll off the line from a factory in southern Italy that Nissan built jointly with Alfa Romeo.[2] The production rate planned was 60,000 units

---

[2] This plant was a 50/50 joint venture in which Alfa Romeo mechanical components were installed in a Nissan "Cherry" body coming from Japan. Alfa Romeo ran the assembly operation. Half the finished vehicles went to Alfa Romeo and half to Nissan.

annually. The Italian government was said to be satisfied that no more than 20 percent of the value of the cars was being imported into Italy.

Finally, Nissan was sending four-wheel-drive vehicles into the EEC from a Spanish plant in which it held a two-thirds share. Next year, panel vans would follow.[3]

THE U.S. SITUATION

Much of what might be envisioned in Europe's future was already taking place in the United States. Japanese imports had been taking a progressively larger and larger share of the market until a voluntary limit of 1.68 million vehicles was negotiated between Washington and Tokyo in 1981. That agreement was due to expire in March 1984, and there was widespread speculation that the Japanese wanted at least a substantially higher ceiling in the future. In the meantime, Ford's share of the U.S. market had dropped alarmingly from 26 percent in 1976 to 16 percent in 1982. Analysts blamed much of this on a 1975 decision by Henry Ford II to postpone a major U.S.-based small car program. (A U.S.-based "Fiesta" had been planned.) Ford reengineered and restyled their existing "Pinto" line instead and relied on that for the small car market.

Regardless of the question of fault, Ford's deteriorating position in the late 1970s led the company in 1980 to reverse its historic free-trade policy, arguing for what was called "fair trade" instead. Fair trade was defined by its proponents as trade between countries with similar social and industrial infrastructures and similar national trade policies (for example, similar wage rates, indirect tax burdens, and export incentives).

In November 1980, Ford and the United Auto Workers Union lost a petition they had filed in June with the U.S. International Trade Commission[4] seeking protection from imports. A three-to-two majority of the commissioners ruled that imports were not the major cause of the industry's problems. The causes, according to the majority, were the recession and Detroit's own mistakes.

Ford had requested in its statement to the International Trade Commission that imports from Japan be limited to 1.7 million cars—the 1976 import level. Ford's setback by the Commission was short-lived, however. In April 1981, President Reagan announced the voluntary export restraint agreement with the Ministry of International Trade and Industry. Automobile imports would not exceed 1.68 million units for the next three years.

In spite of the voluntary export restraint, Ford continued lobbying for legislative relief from the pressure of Japanese imports. Ford favored a policy that combined a continuing cap on Japanese imports, a better yen/dollar

---

[3] In 1980 Nissan bought 36 percent of Motor Iberica and later increased that share to 66 percent.
[4] The International Trade Commission is an advisory commission that determines whether a given industry has been substantially injured by foreign imports, and if so, makes recommendations to the President. Traditionally, the Commission has been viewed as a valuable ally in the executive branch of the government of beleaguered U.S. industries. Thus its decision in this case was a surprise to everyone.

exchange rate, and tax incentives. The United Auto Workers Union, fearful of the threat to American jobs, was lobbying hard for domestic content legislation.

In February 1983, a bill was introduced in Congress entitled the "Fair Practices in Automotive Products Act" (see Exhibit 6). If passed, the bill would impose a graduated minimum domestic content percentage for automobile importers dependent on the total volume of the importer's sales. The percentages ranged from zero for foreign producers with U.S. sales of fewer than 100,000 units per year to an upper limit of 90 percent for those with annual sales of more than 500,000 units.

The conflicting positions on trade policy of General Motors (GM) on the one hand and Ford, Chrysler, and the American Motor Company on the other were brought into the open by the proposed bill. General Motors lobbied against the bill, arguing that any moves toward protectionism could cause a cascade of restrictive measures that would threaten global traders such as itself. Said Thomas R. Atkinson, GM's Director of International Economic Policy (*New York Herald Tribune,* June 29, 1983):

> Local content and other performance regulations decrease our flexibility as a corporation, and force us to do things we otherwise might not be doing. We wish these laws had never been invented, and would not like to see them increased or created in countries where they don't exist now.

General Motors' position was particularly suspect in the eyes of the other major U.S. manufacturers, given the 1982 announcement by GM and Toyota of a cooperative plan to produce 450,000 small cars annually by 1985 from a mothballed GM plant in Freemont, California. General Motors and Toyota would have equal shares in the venture, and half the output would be sold under the Toyota name, half under the GM name (to replace GM's "Chevette"). Ford and other U.S. manufacturers were strongly opposed to the deal, fearing that it was a precedent that could end up threatening the native U.S. industry. The implications of a joint venture by the world's first and third largest automobile manufacturers were obvious to all their competitors.

Of course, there were other risks involved in the proposed U.S. domestic content law that went beyond those cited by GM. The more restrictive the import regulations in the United States, for example, the greater the pressure on Europe from Japanese exports diverted from U.S. shores. And some analysts within Ford felt that the bill would stimulate Japanese direct investment in the United States, perhaps constituting a greater threat to the U.S. manufacturers than some limited degree of imports. On this point the interest of the U.S. labor unions and manufacturers could conflict. Finally, there was the general realization that the government could exact a "price" in return for protectionist favors granted the industry.

As of this writing, the bill was being debated in Congress where it was felt to have a reasonable chance of passage. Whether it would pass the Senate and survive a threatened presidential veto would likely depend on Japanese export pressure. A Data Resources International analyst argued that the passage of

EXHIBIT 6 Selected Testimony on "Fair Practices and Procedures in Automotive Products Act of 1983"

> Over one million jobs have been lost in the auto industry and its supplier industries since 1978. In many parts of our country, this has contributed to unemployment unheard of since the Great Depression.
>
> Quite simply, this bill requires that the more cars a company wants to sell in our country, the more they would be required to build here. If a company takes advantage of the biggest automobile market in the world, it ought to make some effort to put some of its manufacturing in that market—the economic times demand it, and so does the American worker.
>
> These are tough times—and much of the industrial base of our country has eroded. Without reviving this base, our national security is jeopardized and economic recovery will be stifled. We must act now, before our jobs and industrial base are permanently lost.
>
> *Congressman Richard Ottinger (D–N.Y.) (Sponsor of the Bill)*
>
> It is our belief that this legislation will (1) have a negative effect on U.S. employment, (2) impose substantial costs on consumers, (3) violate our international agreements, (4) invite retaliation by our trading partners against United States exports, (5) undermine the competitiveness of the domestic auto manufacturers, and (6) discourage foreign investment in the United States.
>
> When the Congressional Budget Office reviewed this legislation last September, it determined that, by 1990, this legislation would create 38,000 auto jobs but 104,000 jobs would be lost in the U.S. export sector. This would mean a net loss in American jobs of 66,000.
>
> The direct effect of H.R. 1234 would be to increase substantially the automobile prices paid by American consumers by reducing both the number of automobile imports and the competitive pressures that they exert on domestic manufacturers.
>
> A 1980 Commission staff analysis—commenting on a proposal to reduce foreign car imports from 2.4 million to 1.7 million units per year—estimated that prices of small cars would increase by between $527 and $838 per unit, and increase total consumer expenditures on the purchase of automobiles by $1.9 to $3.6 billion per year.
>
> *Statements by opposing Congressmen*
>
> (The Bill) would severely damage America's trading position, flout our international obligations under the General Agreement on Tariffs and Trade (GATT), subject us to challenge under bilateral Treaties of Friendship, Commerce and Navigation with many of our trading partners, and be of great cost to the American consumer and to the nation.
>
> *Secretary of State George Schultz*
>
> In addition to competitive pressures on price, foreign competition has also provided important incentives for U.S. manufacturers to engage in research efforts and to invest in new technologies. American car makers have been moving rapidly toward smaller "world cars" that are very similar to those produced abroad, and United States companies are already importing engines, transmissions, and other components. Confronted with the enormous cost of downsizing American cars and the lower production costs of many foreign companies, United States auto makers are reportedly planning even greater reliance on foreign sources for major components. The enactment of legislation requiring vehicles sold in the United States to be 90 percent "American-made" by 1987 would disrupt established supply lines and aggravate the demands upon scarce domestic capital resources now faced by the United States automobile industry and the economy as a whole. The resulting supply effects would increase car prices, leading to reduced sales and employment in the auto industry.
>
> *United States Federal Trade Commission*
>
> The difficulties of our industry ultimately will not be resolved in legislative halls, but rather in the marketplace where success is earned by offering superior products at competitive prices. Rather than seek shelter from competition—even temporarily—in laws and regulations, U.S. automakers must continue their efforts to meet and exceed foreign competition.
>
> *General Motors Corporation*

the bill would be a real possibility if the Japanese were to take much more than their current 20 percent of the U.S. market.

LOCAL CONTENT REGULATIONS

Local content regulations have long been a device used by developing countries to force multinational companies to increase the rate at which they transfer technology and employment to their local operations. With respect to automobiles, these regulations typically require that a certain percentage of a vehicle's content be produced in the country of sale. This percentage may be defined by value or by weight. Weight is generally thought to be a stricter criterion because it is not susceptible to manipulation by transfer pricing. Yet it can lead to only low-technology, high-weight items being produced locally (e.g., steel castings and chassis components).

Although simple in concept, local content regulations can often be quite complicated in practice. The treatment of overhead and profit is often a problem (see Exhibit 7). Some countries apply the regulations on the basis of fleet averaging, others to specific models. Mexico, where at least 50 percent of the value of all cars sold must be produced locally, strengthened its regulations by

EXHIBIT 7 Analysis of Automobile Construction Cost

		PERCENTAGE OF EX-WORKS PRICE
Freight		2
Administration, selling cost, warranty, and profit		7
Production and assembly overheads		22
Variable manufacturing costs:		69
Engine	10.4	
Gearbox	4.8	
Axles	6.9	
Other mechanical parts	8.3	
Body stamping	5.5	
Body assembly	6.9	
Accessories and seating	7.6	
Final assembly and painting	18.6	
	69.0	
Total		100%

Notes
1. The labor content of variable manufacturing costs accounts for 14 percent of the total ex-works price.
2. For a typical medium-sized salon at a production level of 200,000 annually.
3. Final retail price is usually 22 percent higher than the ex-works price.

Source: Yves Doz: "Internationalization of Manufacturing in the Automobile Industry," unpublished paper, and Ford of Europe estimates.

also requiring that the value of all component imports must be matched by component exports for each assembler. This led to a flurry of investments by Chrysler and Ford in engine facilities in Mexico.

Until recently, Spain had a 95 percent domestic content rule. All component imports were assessed a 30 percent customs duty, and 50 percent of all local manufacturing operations had to be Spanish owned. All this was changed in the 1975 negotiations between the Spanish government and Ford over Ford's "Bobcat" (or "Fiesta") project in Valencia. Contemplating the attractive prospect of a plant producing 225,000 cars annually, the Spanish government settled for 100 percent Ford ownership, 75 percent Spanish content, and 5 percent import duty on component parts. Concessions on import duty were also granted for machine tools and equipment unavailable in Spain. But two-thirds of automobile production had to be exported from Spain, and Ford's sales in Spain could not exceed 10 percent of the previous year's total Spanish market size. General Motors arranged a similar deal for a plant in Zaragoza, Spain, producing 280,000 small "S cars" ("Corsas") annually. Spanish accession to the EEC would phase out much of its protective legislation.

Local content regulations did not exist in any EEC or European Free Trade Association (EFTA) country except Portugal and Ireland. (The European Community's trade regime did have a scheme for defining local assembly with the EFTA countries for the purpose of trade classification—60 percent of value added had to be locally produced.) Nevertheless, there was a variety of statutory powers in the EEC and the General Agreement on Tariffs and Trade (GATT) that could protect specific industries. For example, Regulation No. 926 of the EEC allowed for the protection of specific industries and could be triggered by the Commission of the EEC after advice from the Council of Ministers.

At the GATT level, any member country could ask for temporary protection from imports from another member (under Articles 19–23) if those imports severely endangered national industry (see Exhibits 8 and 9). These "escape clause" articles were difficult for EEC countries to use, however, because each country delegated responsibility for all trade negotiations to the EEC Commission in Brussels. Thus the European automobile industry would have to coordinate campaigns in a number of EEC member countries before it could approach the EEC Commission. Even then, there was no guarantee that the Commission would agree to take a case to the GATT. Not surprisingly, existing import restrictions were essentially bilateral diplomatic agreements—varying widely from country to country—rather than statutory enactments.

FORD'S DELIBERATIONS

At least on the surface, informal local content regulations in Europe looked very attractive to Ford's executives. The Japanese threat was surely very real. Production levels in Europe in 1980 were about the same as they had been in 1970, and in the last decade, while European exports to non-European markets fell 42 percent, Japanese worldwide exports rose 426 percent (see Exhibits 10

EXHIBIT 8 EEC Market Share Analysis, 1973/1980/1982 (percent of total registrations)

	GERMANY	BELGIUM	DENMARK	FRANCE	UNITED KINGDOM	ITALY	HOLLAND	TOTAL[6]
Fiat[1]	7.2/3.6/4.3	9.1/5.4/5.7	7.1/8.7/4.9	4.8/3.7/4.9	3.0/3.3/3.0	64.6/49.4/51.7	8.8/4.1/5.5	16.9/12.2/14.9
Ford[2]	12.8/10.4/11.3	14.7/8.5/8.6	11.7/10.6/16.1	4.6/3.7/6.5	24.2/30.7/30.1	3.6/4.8/5.6	9.3/9.1/10.4	11.5/11.4/12.1
GM[3]	21.6/16.9/18.2	13.4/10.2/10.3	12.8/11.6/14.3	2.5/1.8/2.5	9.8/8.8/12.0	3.3/3.5/3.7	13.0/15.3/16.1	10.4/9.1/9.5
Renault	7.1/4.7/3.9	9.7/8.9/9.4	5.3/1.9/1.0	28.9/40.5/39.1	3.6/5.8/4.1	3.3/10.5/11.1	7.5/8.7/8.0	10.6/14.3/14.4
Peugeot[4]	6.7/4.7/4.0	24.3/15.2/13.8	11.6/8.6/7.4	51.8/36.4/30.2	12.4/5.1/4.4	10.2/11.0/8.5	27.8/12.9/11.8	20.6/14.1/12.2
VW[5]	24.9/21.7/23.5	10.3/8.9/10.4	19.1/5.1/5.3	2.4/4.0/4.9	4.1/3.4/4.5	3.8/4.4/5.3	8.4/7.5/8.2	9.9/9.6/10.0
Nissan	—/2.1/2.0	—/3.8/3.7	—/5.0/5.2	—/0.9/0.9	—/6.1/5.9	—/0.03/0.01	—/5.3/4.6	—/2.5/2.2
Honda	—/1.8/1.5	—/4.4/3.3	—/2.4/0.9	—/0.4/0.4	—/1.5/1.1	—/0.03/0.01	—/5.5/3.5	—/1.4/1.0
Mazda	—/1.9/1.9	—/3.2/3.6	—/8.9/9.4	—/0.7/0.7	—/1.0/1.0	—/0.02/0.01	—/3.9/3.7	—/1.4/1.3
Mitsubishi (Colt)	—/1.7/1.9	—/3.5/3.4	—/3.4/1.2	—/0.2/0.2	—/0.7/0.6	—/0.02/0.02	—/4.8/3.5	—/1.1/0.9
Toyota	—/2.4/1.9	—/9.1/6.1	—/8.2/7.1	—/0.7/0.7	—/2.3/1.8	—/0.02/0.03	—/6.0/4.4	—/2.1/1.5
For 1973 all Japanese vehicles	0.8	13.4	7.1	0.6	4.6	0.1	10.1	2.5

[1] Fiat includes Lancia and Autobianchi.
[2] Ford includes all sourced vehicles (e.g., Spain and Belgium).
[3] General Motors includes both Vauxhall and Opel.
[4] Peugeot includes 1973 Chrysler and Citroën, bought in 1979 and 1974, respectively.
[5] Volkswagen includes Audi.
[6] Ireland and Luxembourg figures (about 100,000 units) are not included.

Source: L'Argus de l'Automobile.

and 11). Ford's market analysts forecast slow growth for the European market in the future, indicating that higher Japanese sales in Europe would come directly from those of the established European producers. The existing structure of voluntary agreements to limit Japanese imports into individual European countries was fragile. Although "voluntary" was clearly a euphemism, any cracks in the agreements could quickly lead to more Japanese imports before new and possibly more lenient agreements were negotiated. West Germany and Belgium were thought to be the weak spots.

If a European local content rule were to be established on the basis of local sales (i.e., if a specified percentage of each manufacturer's European sales had to be produced in Europe), then the existing system of individual national voluntary trade agreements would become redundant. Alternatively, if a local content rule were to be applied to local production (i.e., if a specified percentage of the content of each manufacturer's cars assembled in Europe had to be sourced in Europe), then some controls on automobile imports would still be needed. A local content rule of this type would prevent the Japanese from circumventing the intent of import controls by importing the bulk of their components from Japan while establishing only token assembly operations in Europe.

Yet there were many potential negative consequences for European producers if local content regulations spread across Europe. It was not obvious that European producers should object to Japanese imports, even at a substantially higher level than at present, if the alternative was to be new

EXHIBIT 9　European Motor Industry, Net Profits
(in millions of British pounds, unless otherwise stated)

	1977	1978	1979	1980	1981	1982
Peugeot	226	526	1,800	−150	−184	−336
Renault	31[2]	19[2]	133[2]	140	−55	−112
Ford U.K.	116	144	347	204	165	192
Ford Werke	143	143	124	11	32	76
Ford Europe[1]	1,045	1,271	1,219	323	289	451
Vauxhall	−2	−2	−31	−183	−57	−29
Opel	84	128	65	−97	−130	22
General Motors Europe[1]	277	376	338	−359	−427	6
British Leyland	−52	−28	−145	−536	−497	−293
VAG	103	149	172	76	20	−11
Daimler Benz	145	154	164	261	181	217
BMW	31	39	45	28	32	47
MAN	—	17	18	13	12	7
Alfa-Romeo	−98	−77	−52	−28	−51	−29
Fiat	41	46	22	26	39	58
Seat	NA	NA	NA	−106.6	−104.7	−122.6
Motor Iberica	5.8	6.6	4.2	−2.3	−13.4	−17.2
Volvo	25	36	46	4	45	45
Saab	23	23	26	36	39	43

[1] Millions of U.S. dollars.
[2] Unconsolidated.
NA = Not available.
Source: Company accounts and University of East Anglia, finance and accountancy department; Krish Bhaskar.

EXHIBIT 10　Share of Japanese Exports in Registrations by Importing Country in Europe (percent)

COUNTRY	1966	1970	1975	1979	1981
Belgium	0.3	4.9	16.5	18.0	28
France	0	0.2	1.6	2.2	2
Germany	0	0.1	1.7	5.6	10
Italy	0	0	0.1	0.1	—
Netherlands	0.6	3.2	15.5	19.5	26
United Kingdom	0.1	0.4	9.0	10.8	10
Denmark	0.5	3.4	14.7	18.1	28
Ireland	0	0	8.9	25.2	30
Austria	0	0.9	5.4	12.4	23
Switzerland	0.1	5.6	8.4	16.0	26
Portugal	0	10.7	11.8	7.8	11
Finland	14.4	18.3	20.8	23.9	26
Norway	1.9	11.4	28.4	24.2	36
Sweden	0.2	0.7	6.5	10.0	14

Source: G. Sinclair, *The World Car*.

EXHIBIT 11 Restrictions on Japanese Car Sales in Developed Countries, 1981–1982

United Kingdom	10–11 percent market share ceiling, dating from 1975 package to nationalize British Leyland
Federal Republic of Germany	Growth limit of 10 percent per annum on 1980 sales (252,000 units)
Netherlands	No increase on 1980 level
Luxembourg	No increase on 1980 level
Italy	Quota of 2,200 units
France	3 percent market share ceiling
Belgium	Reduction of 7 percent on 1980 sales
EEC as a whole	Common external tariff is 10.9 percent
Canada	Shipments of "around 174,000" units as against 158,000 in 1980
Australia	All imports restricted to 20 percent of market; tariff of 57 percent; local content must be 85 percent to count as home-produced
United States	Shipments of 1.68 million for 1981 (Japanese fiscal year); subsequent shipment limits to be calculated taking account of U.S. market conditions; tariff is 2.9 percent
Denmark, Greece, Ireland	No restrictions
Japan	No quotas or tariffs on assembled cars, but internal taxes, depending on engine size; distribution and administrative checking systems alleged to operate as nontariff barriers

Note: The Benelux and Canadian restrictions are supposed to last only for 1981. The others appear to be more permanent.

Source: G. Sinclair, *The World Car.*

Japanese greenfield plants in Europe. Even if they complied scrupulously with local content rules, these new plants, employing the most advanced production technology and work methods, could be tough competitors, unshackled from any form of constraint. At the very least, they would add production capacity to a market already suffering from 20 percent excess capacity. A price war was certainly not impossible to imagine. And Ford, among others, was worried about the impact that these plants could have on fleet sales, particularly in the high-margin U.K. market, if nationalistic customers began to think of Nissan, for example, as a "national" producer.

Another problem was that local content rules could limit Ford's own manufacturing flexibility. The key new concept in the automobile industry in the 1970s was that of a "world car." A world car is assembled in local markets (tailored to local consumers' tastes) from a common set of components. Each component is produced in very high volume at one site, where it can be done least expensively, and then shipped around the world to the scattered assembly plants. Local content rules and world cars were seemingly incompatible.

Ford's "Erika" project (the 1981 "Escort") was the first of the world cars. In actual practice, the world car concept was of questionable success. The Escort that was marketed in the United States differed so much in style and design from its European sibling that there was little parts commonality, and transportation costs ate away at the efficiency gains from large-scale production of the common parts. The result was that although there was some international trade in components within Ford, most movement of parts was either within Europe or within the United States.

General Motors had similar problems with its "J car" (the Vauxhall "Cavalier" in the United Kingdom and Opel "Rekord" in West Germany) and "X car" (the Vauxhall "Royale" in the United Kingdom and Opel "Senator" in Germany). General Motors seemed to have been more successful than Ford, however, in standardizing components, and whereas Ford had primarily maintained an approach of European sourcing for European markets, GM had already moved to exploit its global reach.

To make matters even more complex, Ford had a 25 percent share in Toyo Kogyo (Mazda) and thus an option of working with Mazda to import inexpensive Japanese vehicles (see Exhibit 12). Indeed, a Mazda pickup truck was sold in the United States and Greece as a Ford truck, and the very successful Ford "Laser" in the Far East was a version of the Mazda 626 made in Japan. (In July 1983, Ford was threatening such a policy to counteract the proposed GM–Toyota production plant in California.)

TECHNICAL ASPECTS OF LOCAL CONTENT REGULATIONS

If the management of Ford of Europe were to support local content regulations, they felt they would have to answer four technical questions:

1. How should "local" be defined geographically?
2. How was local content to be measured?
3. To what should local content regulations be applied—individual cars, models, or a producer's entire fleet?
4. What should the minimum percentage of local content be?

The company had already done some thinking about each question.

Of all the producers, Ford was the most geographically integrated in Europe. It would therefore be important to encompass most or all of Europe in the term "local." A definition restricted to the EEC would exclude Ford's big Valencia plant in Spain and a 200,000-unit per year plant contemplated for Portugal. These plants represented critical low-cost sources for small cars for the other European markets. (Both Spain and Portugal had applied for admission to the EEC, however.) Ford regarded a nation-state definition as impractical and intolerable.

Defining local content was a very difficult task. One proposal was to define content by weight. This had the advantage of being difficult to manipulate by transfer pricing, but it might allow the importation of high-value, high-technology components that were light in weight.

The other common definition of local content was by value. Essentially the percentage of local content was established by subtracting the value of the

EXHIBIT 12 Foreign Sourcing—Recently Announced Commitments by U.S. Automobile Manufacturers to Purchase Foreign-made Components for Use in Domestic Vehicles Production

AUTOMOBILE MANUFACTURE	DESCRIPTION OF COMPONENT	INTENDED USE	MANUFACTURING SOURCE	APPROXIMATE NUMBER OF COMPONENTS	PERIOD
General Motors	2-8 lit V-6	Cars	GM Mexico	<400,000/year	1982–
	2-0 lit L-4 with transmission	Minitrucks	Isuzu (Japan)	100,000/year	1981–
	1-8 lit diesel L-4	Chevette	Isuzu (Japan)	Small numbers	1982–
	1-8 lit L-4	J-car	GM Brazil	250,000/year	1979–
	THM 180 automatic transmission	Chevette	GM Strasbourg (France)	~250,000/year	1979–
Ford	2-2 lit L-4	Cars	Ford Mexico	<400,000/year	1983–
	Diesel L-4	Cars	Toyo Kogyo	150,000/year	1983–
	2-0 lit L-4	Minitrucks	Toyo Kogyo	<100,000/year	1982–
	2-3 lit L-4	Cars	Ford Brazil	~50,000/year	1979–
	Diesel 6 cyl.	Cars	BMW/Steyr	100,000/year	1983–
	Turbo-diesel/4 cyl.	Cars	BMW/Steyr	—	1985–
	Manual transaxles	Front-disc cars	Toyo Kogyo	100,000/year	1980–
	Aluminum cylinder heads	1-6 lit L-4	Europe, Mexico	—	1980–
	Electronic engine control devices	Cars	Toshiba	100,000+/year	1978–
	Ball joints	Cars	Musashi Seimibu	1,000,000/year	1980–84
Chrysler	L-6 and V-8 engines	Cars	Chrysler Mexico	<100,000/year	Early 1970
	2-2 lit L-4	K-body	Chrysler Mexico	<270,000/year	1981
	2-6 lit L-4	K-body	Mitsubishi	1 million	1981–85
	1-7 lit L-4	L-body (Omni)	Volkswagen	1–2 million	1978–82
	1-6 lit L-4	L-body	Talbot (Peugeot)	400,000 total	1982–84
	2-0 lit Diesel V-6	K-body	Peugeot	100,000/year	1982–
	1-4 lit L-4	A-body (Omni replacement)	Mitsubishi	300,000/year	1984–
	Aluminum cylinder heads	2-2 lit L-4	Fiat		
AMC	Car components and power train	AMC-Renault	Renault in France and Mexico	300,000/year	1982–
VW of America	Radiators, stampings	Rabbit	VW Mexico	250,000/year	1979–
	L-4 diesel and gas	Cars	VW Mexico	300,000+/year	1982–

Source: Bulletin of the European Communities, *The European Automobile Industry: Commission Statement.*

imported components as declared on customs documentation from 1) the distributor's price, 2) the ex-works price, or 3) the ex-works price minus the labor and overhead content of the car. Then the local content residue was divided by the corresponding denominator.

Clearly the percentage of the imported components gets larger from 1) to 3) as the value of the domestic content gets smaller. Ford had not decided its position with regard to this issue, except that it did not want specific components identified for mandatory local production. It was also possible to devise other hybrid methods of valuing local content, but they were generally not under discussion.

Regarding the question of to what should the local content rules be applied, Ford favored applying them to the average of a producer's entire line of cars, rather than to each individual car or model. The former would jeopardize Ford's current importation from South Africa of small quantities of their P100 pickup truck (based on the "Cortina").

There was also a related question of whether automobile production or regional sales should form the basis of measurement. Ford preferred that a specified percentage of a producer's European sales be made in Europe, since such a rule was insurance against circumvention of the current import quotas. A production-based local content rule would only prevent circumvention of the intent of import quotas by token local final assembly.

Finally there was the question of what the appropriate percentage should be. Figures currently under discussion ranged from 60 to 80 percent, although the percentage clearly depended on the format of the specific proposals. Of particular significance in terms of these percentages was that a 60 percent rule might allow importation of engines and major parts of the drive train that would all be excluded by an 80 percent rule. Also, it might be very difficult for the Japanese to start up a new plant with an immediate 80 percent local content (even if that percentage were to be achieved with more time). Start-up at 60 percent would be substantially easier.

THE POLITICAL OPTIONS

Should Ford decide to support local content regulations and then find answers to the technical questions, it would still have to determine the best way to carry its case to the appropriate government body. And here again, the way was not clear.

Ford definitely did not want to act on its own. It would be much better to act in concert with the other European producers. (Despite the all-American image of the founder and his name, Ford of Europe unquestionably considered itself "European.") Not only was this desirable on general principles, but for one quite specific reason Ford preferred not to lobby the EEC directly. It had recently fought and was currently fighting other battles with the European

Commission. In 1982, the Commission had issued an interim order to Ford under Article 85 of the Treaty of Rome (an antitrust statute) requiring the company to offer right-hand-drive cars to the West German market. The background to this directive was that most European automobile producers charged significantly higher prices in the United Kingdom than on the Continent. To prevent consumers from ordering right-hand-drive cars in Germany and importing them to the United Kingdom, Ford had refused to make the models available on the Continent. This provoked a consumer response to which the EEC Commission reacted.

In June 1983 the Commission issued a draft regulation applicable to the distribution systems of all motor manufacturers operating in Europe. The regulation aimed at hamonizing vehicle availability and prices across Europe. Any model of vehicle sold in any EEC member state would have to be made available in all other member states. And if price differences exceeded 12 percent (net of taxes) between any EEC markets, new importers (not authorized by the manufacturer) could enter the market. Ford, along with all other European motor manufacturers, was opposing this proposal vigorously.

Although Ford preferred to have a common industry position to press on the governmental authorities, there was little likelihood of unanimity among the European producers even on the most basic question of whether local content rules were desirable. General Motors was an almost certain opponent to local content rules despite the fact that it too might welcome relief from Japanese competition. Fiat, Renault, and British Leyland, on the other hand, might be strong allies who could perhaps rally the support of their respective governments. They appeared to have much to gain from local content rules because they had most of their operations in Europe and they purchased most of their components locally.

There were a number of sourcing arrangements, however, which could undermine the support of some of these firms. Japanese cars assembled in Australia were entering the United Kingdom with a certificate of origin from Australia. British Leyland's Acclaim was of questionable origin. Fiat was bringing in "Pandas" from Brazil, and Volkswagen "Beetles" came into Europe from Mexico. Renault had extensive operations in the United States that could alter the company's outlook. And on July 27, 1983, the *Wall Street Journal* reported that Fiat was being indicted by the Italian authorities for selling cars made in Spain and Brazil under the guise of Italian manufacture. Fiat denied the charge.

Ford executives believed, nonetheless, that with the exception of GM, Ford was likely to find general support within the industry. In fact, in a 1981 draft paper, the CLCA[5] stated:

> The establishment of Japanese motor vehicle manufacturing plants should be subject to the following durable conditions:
>
> a. the CIF value of the components not originating from the EEC should not exceed 20 percent of the price ex-works of the vehicle.

---

[5] Comité de Liaison des Constructeurs Associations. The CLCA was basically a political liaison committee of the national automotive trade associations of France, the United Kingdom, Germany, Belgium, Holland, and Italy.

b. the manufacturing and assembly of mechanical components (engines, gearboxes and drivetrain) should be performed within the EEC.

THE EUROPEAN COMMISSION

Ford executives believed that the European Commission was prepared to take some action on the automobile imports issue. In January 1983 the Commission had held discussions with the Japanese in Tokyo and had obtained a nonbinding commitment to moderate vehicle exports to the EEC. The Commission was currently monitoring the agreement. Beyond this it was unclear what action the European Commission was considering. In principle, the EEC should be expected to favor relatively free trade between its member countries and the rest of the world. The history of international trade since World War II—a history in which the EEC featured prominently—was one of declining tariffs (from an average of 20 percent on manufactured goods in the 1950s to 8 percent in the mid-1970s), dramatically growing trade volumes, and greater interdependence of national economies. Two other principles dear to the EEC were that all member countries maintain a *common* trade policy vis-à-vis non-EEC countries, and that there be no barriers to trade between member countries. Clearly, the existing set of nonuniform bilateral trade agreements with the Japanese offended these principles.

Although the principles underlying the EEC were relatively unambiguous, the EEC often resorted to protective policies, and it was not immune to pressures to maintain jobs in the automotive sector. But granted this observation, it was still not evident just how job preservation might best be achieved. Formal local content rules would be inconsistent with EEC law and would violate the GATT. Thus any local content measures would have to be informal such as those that currently existed between the Japanese and the British. Would the EEC prefer to see a uniform (albeit informal) external quota and internal production-based local content rule? Or would it rather see a uniform internal sales-based content rule and no quota? Would its preference in either case be less restrictive than the status quo, shaky though it might be? And was it realistic to expect that an informal negotiating process could create a common position among the different EEC member states? A weak, contentious, and nonuniform set of local content rules established and enforced by each EEC member country could be the worst of all the imaginable alternatives.

The Japanese, of course, would have some influence on EEC thinking on this matter. Any EEC action would probably come in the context of trade negotiations—not simply unilaterally imposed trade sanctions. And what position might the Japanese take? It is conceivable that they might agree to some reasonable export restraints into the EEC in return for open markets within the EEC. That would give them access to the two big markets from which they were currently virtually excluded—France and Italy. But would those two countries agree? Each would face greater Japanese competition in its home market but less in its export markets in other EEC countries.

The executives on the Management Committee considered their alternatives. If they were to have any role in determining the public policies that would undoubtedly have a significant impact on their company, they would have to act quickly.

REFERENCE

New York Herald Tribune, June 27, 1983.

INDUSTRIAL HIGHLIGHT

Motor Vehicles Industry

Below is a capsule summary of the passenger car segment of the motor vehicles industry. The Ford Motor Company is a part of this industry segment. Information in this highlight was compiled by the U.S. Department of Commerce and focuses on this industry during the approximate period of time covered in the case. Keep in mind that industrial highlights contained in this text are not intended as a complete synopsis of an industry but as a profile of certain issues that can be relevant to a case situation.

CURRENT SITUATION

Following depressed years in 1980 and 1981, new car sales in 1982 were again disappointing, totaling only an estimated 7.9 million units, 7 percent below 1981. Domestic-make sales reached an estimated 5.7 million units, 8 percent below 1981's dismal performance. The weak market resulted from sluggish economic conditions, high car prices, and steep interest rates.

Unlike previous automotive recessions, the present slump is not entirely cyclical in nature. In addition to cyclical influences, the downturn in domestic-make car sales also reflects an apparent slowdown in the long-term growth rate of demand for automobiles together with the impact of sharply intensified international competition for the U.S. market.

Production of passenger cars in 1982 dropped 18 percent below 1981 to the lowest level since 1958. Operating at only half of capacity, the industry produced an estimated 5.1 million cars in 1982. As a result of sharply curtailed output, dealer inventories—which totaled an estimated 1.3 million new cars at the end of 1982—were at their lowest year-end level since 1970. Thus as the industry enters 1983, it finds itself well positioned to take advantage of a sales increase, and an upturn in the car market should trigger significant increases in production.

Source: U.S. Industrial Outlook, Department of Commerce, 1983, pp. 30-1–30-7.

EXHIBIT A New Car Retail Sales (thousands of vehicles)

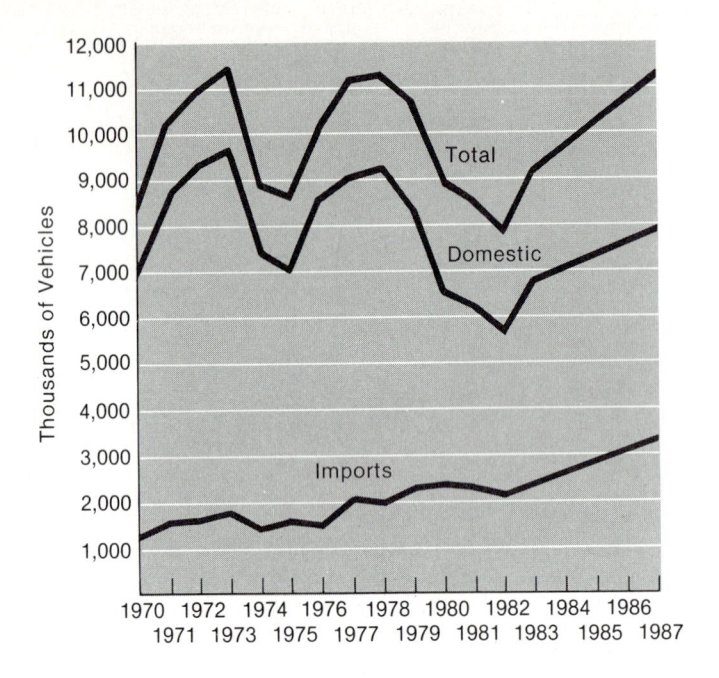

[1] Includes units built in the United States by foreign based manufacturers.
[2] Estimates by Bureau of Industrial Economics.
Source: Motor Vehicle Manufacturers' Association.

Small-Car Demand

One of the most noteworthy developments in recent years has been the dramatic shift of consumer demand toward smaller, more fuel-efficient cars in response to the rapid rise in petroleum prices in 1979 and 1980. Small cars (subcompacts and compacts, including imports) accounted for 47 percent of total new car sales in 1978; their market share increased to 55 percent in 1979, 62 percent in 1980, and 63 percent in 1981. With the peaking of gasoline prices in the spring of 1981, the smaller-car share appears to have reached a plateau. Providing the inflation-adjusted price of gasoline does not change significantly, the small-car share of the market is expected to remain stable at its present level for the next several years.

Japanese Competition

With the sudden shift in demand toward small cars beginning in 1979, import penetration of the U.S. car market increased sharply, rising from 17.7 percent in 1978 to 26.7 percent in 1980 and to 27.3 percent in 1981 and holding at about that level in 1982. Imported car shipments to the United States set a new record of 2.5 million units in 1980, dropping slightly to 2.4 million cars in both 1981 and 1982. The Japanese voluntary-restraint program caused the decline. The Japanese government established its export-limitation program in May 1981 and in early 1982 announced continuation of the program at the 1981 restraint level through March 1983. Japanese manufacturers have dominated the U.S. import market since the mid-1970's and now hold an 80-percent share.

Although motor vehicle imports from Japan have fallen below their 1980 peak in unit terms, the value of these shipments has increased because of higher vehicle prices and an upgraded product mix. As a result, the U.S. automotive products trade deficit with Japan continues to increase—from $11.2 billion in 1980 to an estimated $15 billion in 1982. The automotive trade deficit, which has sky-rocketed from $1.8 billion in 1973, accounts for the bulk of the total U.S. merchandise trade deficit with Japan. This large trade imbalance is straining U.S.–Japanese trade relations and is providing substantial stimulus for protectionist pressures in this country.

The Japanese manufacturers have been under pressure for several years to locate production facilities in the United States. Honda built a new car assembly plant in Ohio and launched production in late 1982. Nissan is constructing a new truck plant in Tennessee scheduled to start production in 1983. Toyota and General Motors are considering a joint venture to produce Toyota-designed cars in one or both of General Motors' idle assembly plants in California. These plants however, even at full production, will displace only a small portion of the motor vehicles Japan currently exports annually.

Exports of U.S. cars have been low for many years. Reflecting the declining value of the dollar in 1978 and 1979, car exports peaked in 1979 at 187,000 units. Because of intensified Japanese competition in European and other foreign markets and the strengthening of the dollar, U.S. exports dropped to 105,000 cars in 1980. Under the added pressure of a worldwide recession, car exports slipped further, to 76,000 cars in 1981, and then to an estimated 50,000 cars in 1982. The Near East, which for at least five years has accounted for almost 40 percent of U.S. car exports, is expected to continue as the leading export market for U.S. cars.

LONG-TERM PROSPECTS

The automobile industry is now moving through an extremely critical and challenging period. Its immediate challenge is recovery from the current recession. The outlook for this happening in 1983 is promising. Equally critical longer term challenges will remain, however, including acquiring the capital needed to rebuild the industry and meeting import competition. Meeting these challenges is becoming more difficult because of an apparent slowdown in the long-term growth rate of automotive demand.

Demand Outlook

The slower automotive demand growth rate results from demographic factors, the erosion of consumer purchasing power by inflation, and a sizable increase in the relative price of owning and operating a car.

- The driving-age population is projected to grow at an average annual rate of about 1 percent during the 1980's compared to roughly 2 percent in the 1970's; partially offsetting this negative factor, the portion of the population 25 to 44 years old—the primary new car buying ages—will increase.
- The rate of increase in consumers' real income has slowed markedly during the past five years. Moreover, because prices for food, energy, and shelter have increased at a more rapid pace than other items, the squeeze on discretionary real incomes has become even more pronounced.
- In recent years, the costs of financing, insuring, maintaining, and operating a car have increased at double the rate of increase in new car prices. Thus, though consumers spend a relatively constant share of their total expenditures on owning and operating automobiles, a smaller share of their transportation budgets is available for new car purchases. In addition, consumers have responded to higher operating costs by driving fewer miles per year. This reduced use of cars will lead ultimately to lower replacement demand.

Capital Shortages

The automobile industry will require an expenditure of $65 billion from 1978 through 1985 (about twice the real level of investment in the previous eight years) to redesign its products and retool; to modernize production facilities; and to convert production capacity to smaller, front-wheel drive, fuel-efficient cars.

Historically, the companies have met their capital requirements primarily through internal sources, i.e. retained earnings and depreciation and amortization allowances. However, inflation and depressed sales have resulted in massive losses. The companies have been able to finance their investment programs only through substantial increases in debt, sales of assets, and an erosion of working capital. This loss of liquidity has (1) diminished the companies' future borrowing ability, thus increasing each firm's vulnerability to future cyclical downturns, and (2) reduced each company's capability to sustain another major round of investment, should post-1985 world market conditions require it.

Although the current pressures on cash flow are expected to ease as the industry recovers from the recession, capital formation will continue to be a problem. The larger-size cars and the luxury models have historically returned higher profit margins, while small cars generally have had low and, in some instances, negative margins. This situation reflects the influence of import pricing which, to a considerable degree, controls domestic small-car pricing. Because profit margins tend to diminish as small cars increase their market share, domestic manufacturers will promote optional equipment and introduce small luxury and specialty models. During the 1980's, manufacturers will face a major challenge in developing and producing a fleet of cars with a product mix that can provide an adequate return on investment.

Increasing Competitiveness

In addition to capital formation and regaining a reasonable degree of profitability, import competition—primarily Japanese—presents another critical challenge for the industry in the 1980's.

Japanese manufacturers have been highly successful in producing high-quality cars at lower costs. Japanese manufacturing costs fall at least 20 percent below U.S. manufacturing costs for a comparable car because the Japanese have lower hourly labor costs and productivity advantages from more effective systems for controlling inventory, product quality, and workplace activity.

Obtaining reliable data on cost differentials between the U.S. and Japanese auto industries has proved difficult, but recent studies indicate that Japanese manufacturers can land cars in this country for roughly $1,500 per car less than U.S. producers can deliver comparable vehicles to the same locations. This cost advantage severely limits U.S. manufacturers in developing pricing strategies and, unless substantially reduced, threatens the long-term viability of the U.S. industry.

Lack of competitiveness in manufacturing costs constitutes the U.S. auto industry's most difficult challenge. A substantial portion of the industry's current investment program involves the modernization of manufacturing facilities to achieve the productivity improvements necessary for regaining competitiveness internationally. The eventual success of this program—scheduled for completion by the mid-1980's—evades prediction, particularly in view of the industry's current cash flow problems and their adverse effect on its investment programs. In addition, the Japanese industry will not stand still during this period; rather it will move to enhance its competitive position with further product and manufacturing advances.

Japanese manufacturers also have been successful in developing and maintaining product quality. Domestic-make cars have not been competitive in the visual areas of quality, such as paint and surface finishes, mating of sheet metal panels, and molding fits. The domestic industry must improve its products in these respects to gain consumer recognition of competitive quality.

Technological Advances

Changes that the U.S. industry has been and will continue to be making in its products will contribute importantly to its adjustment to international competition. Cars will be smaller and lighter to enhance fuel-efficiency. Front-wheel drive will be universal in small cars (compacts and subcompacts) and will also be incorporated in a majority of intermediate- and full-size cars because it allows more efficient use of space. By the mid-1980's, more than 95 percent of the cars produced will be front-wheel drive.

By 1985, 60 percent of the cars produced in this country will have four-cylinder engines, compared with only 6 percent in the 1977 model year. The standard engine for the full-size passenger car of the mid-1980's will be a V-6; by 1985, this engine will be installed in 20 to 25 percent of car production. Conventional V-8's will all but disappear by the mid-1980's. Assuming resolution of the diesel engine's environmental problems, diesels should capture 10-to-15 percent of the passenger car market within the next five years.

Major changes are also taking place in car components. For example, new devices for controlling air–fuel mixture, such as electronically controlled carburetors and variable venturi carburetors, are being introduced to improve fuel economy. Major advances in automotive transmissions, including lock-up torque converters and automatic transmission overdrives are also being adopted to save fuel. Continuously variable transmissions may be commercially available by the late 1980's.

A rapid increase in the use of electronic components is taking place because of the precise control they provide and their rapid feedback capability. Engine-control functions, such as air–fuel ratio, spark timing, and exhaust gas recirculation, are ideal applications. The new three-way catalytic converter requires very precise control of the air–fuel ratio and has led to the introduction of microprocessor-controlled systems for engine-control functions. Electronics also finds use in automatic speed control and driver-information systems (fuel consumption, average vehicle speed, and estimated arrival time). By the late 1980's, electronic control of automatic transmissions will be in widespread use.

The industry is also pursuing programs to improve today's conventional reciprocating engines and to develop alternative power plants. The reciprocating engine in its gasoline and diesel versions appears destined to remain the dominant automotive power plant until at least the end of this century inasmuch as all the alternatives require major technological breakthroughs to gain serious consideration for general automotive application.

Alternatives with long-term potential include the gas turbine, the Stirling-cycle engine, electric propulsion, and electric hybrids. The gas turbine and Stirling-cycle engine, totally different from current automotive power plants, require major technological breakthroughs for development of production designs. Then, complete rebuilding of production lines would have to follow. Under the most favorable circumstances, some gas turbines might be commercially available in limited volume by the mid-1990's; Stirling-cycle engines, a number of years later.

The electric propulsion automobile has attracted considerable interest. For practical, general automotive use, however, electric propulsion awaits a technological breakthrough in developing the needed high-energy-density battery.

Until then, the potential for electric propulsion extends only to short-range vehicles used primarily for stop-and-go driving, as in urban deliveries.

In summary, the automotive industry is undertaking new product and plant modernization programs of unprecedented scope to regain international competitiveness. These programs involve high risks, although the risks would be less severe if the industry were in a period of strong growth. The automotive market in the United States is now essentially mature. With the squeeze on discretionary real incomes, consumers can be expected to allocate less of their income to the purchase of automobiles. Taking these various factors into consideration, a real growth rate of only 1.0-to-1.5 percent annually for passenger car sales can be expected during the next decade.

CASE 26

Fourwinds Marina*

W. HARVEY HEGARTY
Indiana University

HARRY KELSEY, JR.
California State College

Jack Keltner had just completed his first day as general manager of the Fourwinds Marina. It was mid-August and though the Marina slip rentals ran until October 30, business took a dramatic downturn after Labor Day. It would be unwise to change any of the current operations in the next three weeks, but he would have to move swiftly to implement some of the changes he had been considering, and at the same time would have the better part of a year to develop and implement some short-range and long-range plans that were sorely needed if the Marina was to survive.

The day before, Jack had been called in by Sandy Taggart, president of the Taggart Corporation, owners of the Fourwinds Marina and the Inn of the Fourwinds. Leon McLaughlin had just submitted his resignation as general manager of the Marina. McLaughlin and Taggart had disagreed on some compensation McLaughlin felt was due him. Part of the disagreement concerned McLaughlin's wife who had been hired to work in the parts department, but had spent little time there due to an illness.

McLaughlin had been the fifth manager in as many years that the Marina had been in operation. He had had fifteen years of marine experience before being hired to manage the Marina. His experience, however, consisted of selling and servicing boats and motors in Evansville, Indiana, not in marina management. He took pride in running a "tight ship" and felt that the Marina had an excellent chance in turning around after some hard times. It was fairly easy to keep the marina staffed because the resort atmosphere was so attractive, and his goal was to have the majority of the staff on a full time basis year round. Even though the Marina is closed from November until April there is a considerable amount of repair work on boats needed during those months. McLaughlin was told when hired that he had a blank check to get the Marina shaped up. This open policy, however, was later rescinded. He and his wife have a mobile home near the Marina, but maintain a permanent residence in Evansville. For the most part he puts in six full days a week, but has an aversion to working on Sunday. McLaughlin was an effective organizer, but weak in the area of employee and customer relations.

* This is a classic case in the strategic management literature.
Copyright 1974 by W. Harvey Hegarty and Harry Kelsey, Jr. Reprinted with permission.

Keltner had no experience in marina management, but was considered a hard worker willing to take on tremendous challenges. He had joined the Taggart Corporation after four years as a CPA for Ernst and Ernst, an accounting firm. Functioning as controller of the corporation, he found that there was a tremendous volume of work demanded, necessitating late hours at the office and a briefcase full of work to take home with him most evenings. At this point, Keltner lived in a small community near the Marina, but still had to commute frequently to the home office of the Taggart Corporation in Indianapolis, an hour and a half drive from Lake Monroe. He had indicated that he hoped to move the offices to Lake Monroe, site of the Marina and Inn as soon as possible. Handling the accounting for the Marina, the Inn and other Taggart Corporation interests could be done effectively at the Marina. The Inn and the Marina comprise 90 percent of the corporation.

Much of the explanation for the heavy work load lay in the fact that there had been virtually no accounting system when he first joined Taggart. He had, however, set up six profit centers for the Marina and generated monthly accounting reports.

The other principal investors involved in the Taggart Corporation besides Sandy (A. L. Taggart III) were William Brennan, president of one of the state's largest commercial and industrial real estate firms, and Richard DeMars, president of Guepel-DeMars, Inc., the firm that designed both the Marina and the Inn.

Sandy Taggart is a well known Indianapolis businessman who is Chairman of the Board of Colonial Baking Company. This organization is one of the larger bakeries serving the Indianapolis metropolitan area and surrounding counties. He did his undergraduate work at Princeton and completed Harvard's A.M.P. program in 1967. He is an easygoing man and appears not to let problems upset him easily. He maintains his office at the Taggart Corporation in Indianapolis, but tries to get to the Marina at least once every week. He kept in daily contact with Leon McLaughlin, and continues to do the same with Keltner. He enjoys being a part of the daily decision-making and problem-solving that goes on at the Marina and feels that he needs to be aware of all decisions due to their weak financial position. Taggart feels current problems stem from a lack of knowledge of the marina business and lack of experienced general managers when they began operation some six years ago. He also admits that their lack of expertise in maintaining accurate cost data and controlling their costs hurt them, but feels Keltner has already gone a long way in correcting this problem.

Keltner has been intimately involved in the operation and feels that at a minimum the following changes should be made over the next 12 month period.

1. Add eighty slips on E, F, and G docks and put in underwater supports on these docks to deter breakage from storms. Cost $250–300,000. Annual profits if all slips are rented—$75,000+.
2. Add a second employee to assist the present secretary-receptionist-

bookkeeper. This will actually be a savings if the Indianapolis office is closed. Savings—$300+/month.
3. Reorganize the parts department and put in a new inventory system. Cost—$3,000. Savings—$2,500–3,000/year.
4. Keep the boat and motor inventory low. Boat inventory as of mid-August is approximately $125,000. It has been over $300,000.
5. Reduce the work force through attrition if a vacated job can be assumed by someone remaining on the staff.
6. Use E, F, and G for winter storage with the improved and more extensive bubbling system. Profits to be generated are difficult to estimate.
7. Light and heat the storage building so repair work can be done at night and in the winter. Cost—$12,000 which he estimates probably would be paid for from the profits in two winters.

Each of these changes would add to the effectiveness and profitability of the Marina operation and that was his prime concern. The operation of the Inn was under the control of another general manager and operated as a separate corporate entity. Keltner was only responsible for the accounting procedures of the Inn.

As he reviewed the structure, background, and development of the Inn and the Marina he realized the problems that faced him in his new role of general manager—and at the same time controller of Taggart Corporation. Managing the Marina was a full time 7-day-a-week job, particularly during the season. The questions uppermost in his mind were: 1) what would be the full plan he would present to Taggart for the effective, efficient and profitable operation of the Marina? and 2) how would it be funded? The financial statements presented a fairly glum picture, but he had the available back up data to analyze for income per square foot on most of the operations, payroll data, etc. as well as the knowledge he had gleaned working with the past general managers and observing the operation of the Marina. (See Exhibits 3, 4, and 5 at the end of the case for the organizational structure and financial statements of the Marina.)

BACKGROUND DATA ON FOURWINDS MARINA

The Setting

The Fourwinds Marina and the Inn of the Fourwinds are located on Lake Monroe, a manmade reservoir over ten thousand acres in size nestled in the hills of southern Indiana. Both facilities are owned and operated by the Taggart Corporation, but are operated as totally distinct and separate facilities. They cooperate in promoting business for each other.

The Inn occupies some 71,000 square feet on 30 acres of land. It is designed to blend into the beautifully wooded landscape and is constructed of rustic and natural building materials. It is designed to appeal to a broad segment of the population with rooms priced from $21–$33 for a double room. The Inn is comprised of 150 sleeping rooms, singles, doubles and suites, and has meeting rooms to appeal to the convention and sales meetings clientele. The largest meeting room will seat 300 for dining and 350 for conferences. Recreation facilities include an indoor-outdoor swimming pool, tennis courts, sauna, whirlpool bath, a recreation room with pool tables and other games. Added facilities include 2 dining rooms and a cocktail lounge. The Inn is open year round with heavy seasonal business in the summer months.

It is the first lodge of its nature built on state property by private funds. By virtue of the size of its food service facilities (in excess of $100,000 per annum) it qualifies under Indiana State Law for a license to serve alcoholic beverages on Sunday.

A brief description of the Pointe is also in order as its development promises a substantial boost to the Marina's business. The Pointe, located three miles from the Marina, consists of 384 acres on the lake. It is a luxury condominium development designed to meet the housing needs of primary and secondary home buyers. Currently 70 units are under construction. Twenty of these have been sold and the down-payment has been received on eighty more. These condominiums range from $25,000 to $90,000 with an average of $60,000. Approval has been secured for the construction of 1,900 living units over a seven year period. The development has a completed 18 hole golf course. Swimming pools and tennis courts are now under construction. The Pointe is a multi-million dollar development by Indun Realty, Inc., Lake Monroe Corporation, and Reywood, Inc. Indun Realty is a wholly owned subsidiary of Indiana National Corp., parent firm of Indiana National Bank, the state's largest fiduciary institution.

The Fourwinds Marina occupies four acres of land and is one of the most extensive and complete marinas of its type in the United States. It is comprised of the boat docks, a sales room for boats and marine equipment, an indoor boat storage facility and marine repair shop (see Exhibit 1).

There are seven docks projecting out from a main connecting dock that runs parallel to the shore line. The seven parallel docks extend out from 330 to 600 feet into the lake at a right angle to the connecting dock. The center dock houses a large building containing a grocery store, snack bar, and restrooms and a section of docks used as mooring for rental boats.

At the end of the dock is an office for boat rental, five gasoline pumps and pumping facilities for removing waste from the houseboats and larger cruisers.

The three docks to the right of the center dock (facing toward the lake) are docks A, B, and C and are designed for mooring smaller boats—runabouts, fishing boats, etc. A bait shop is on A dock. A, B, and C slips are not always fully rented. The three docks to the left are the prime slips (E, F, G) and are designed for berthing houseboats, large cruisers, etc.[1] There are a total of 460 rentable slips priced from $205–$775 for uncovered slips and $295–$1,125 for covered slips per season (April 1–October 30). Seventy-five percent of all the

---

[1] E, F, and G are the most profitable slips and are fully rented. There is a waiting list to get into these slips.

EXHIBIT 1 General Layout

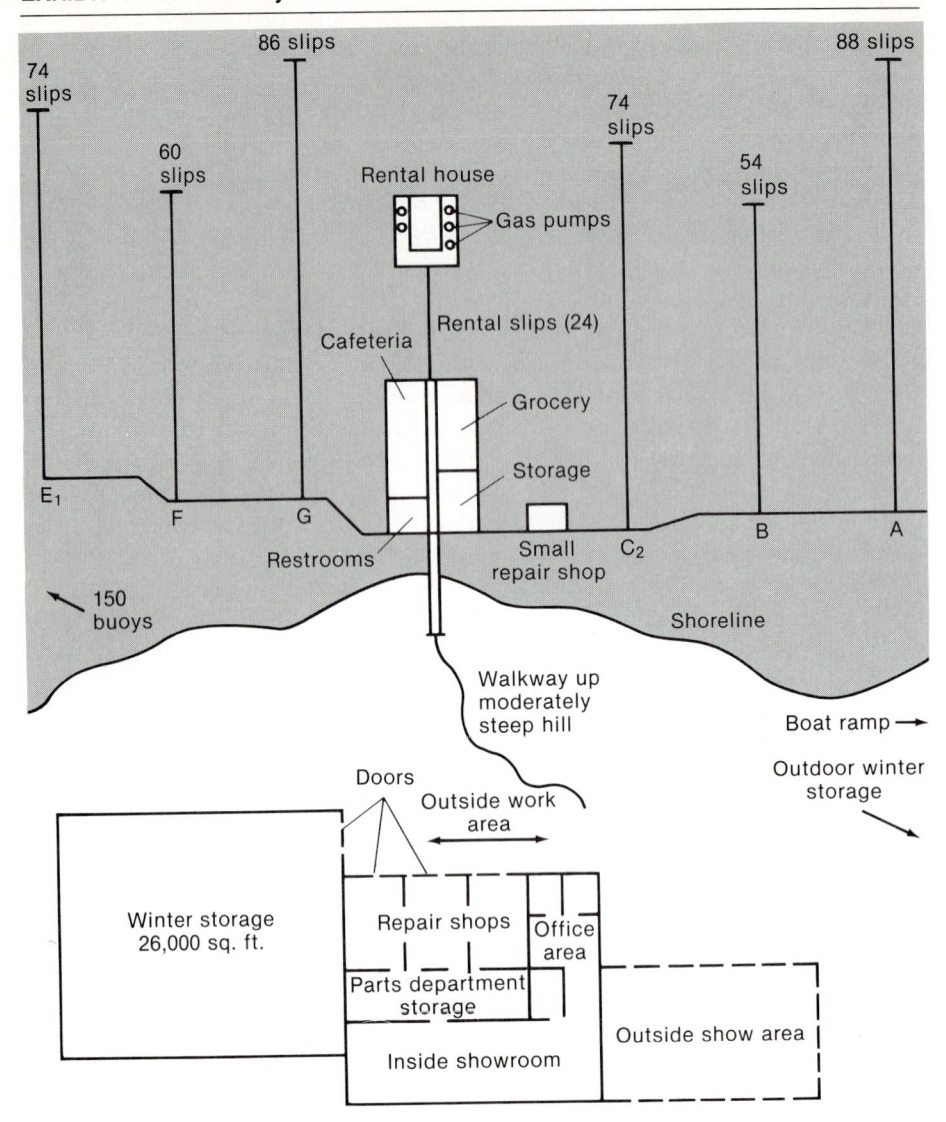

- 74 slips
- 86 slips
- 88 slips
- 60 slips
- 74 slips
- 54 slips
- Rental house
- Gas pumps
- Rental slips (24)
- Cafeteria
- Grocery
- Storage
- E₁
- F
- G
- Restrooms
- Small repair shop
- C₂
- B
- A
- 150 buoys
- Shoreline
- Walkway up moderately steep hill
- Boat ramp →
- Outdoor winter storage
- Doors
- Outside work area
- Winter storage 26,000 sq. ft.
- Repair shops
- Office area
- Parts department storage
- Inside showroom
- Outside show area

E, F, and G range from 15′ × 34′ to 18′ × 50′. About two-thirds of these slips are covered. A, B, and C slips range from 9′ × 18′ to 12′ × 32′. Over 80 percent of these slips are covered.

slips are under roof and are in the more desirable location, hence they are rented first. Electric service is provided to all slips, and the slips on E and F docks have water and trash removal provided at no extra cost. To the left of the prime slips are 162 buoys, renting for $150 per season. This rental includes shuttle boat service to and from the moored craft. Buoys are not considered to be a very profitable segment. The buoys shift and break loose occasionally requiring constant attention. Time is required to retrieve boats that break loose at night or during storms.

Lake Monroe, the largest lake in Indiana, is a 10,700 acre reservoir developed by the U.S. Army Corps of Engineers in conjunction with and under the jurisdiction of the Indiana Department of Natural Resources. With the surrounding public lands (accounting for some 80% of the 150 mile shoreline) the total acreage is 26,000. It is a multi-purpose project designed to provide flood control, recreation, water supply and flow augmentation benefits to the people of Indiana.

The Reservoir is located in the southwestern quadrant of the state, about 9 miles or a 15 minute drive southwest of Bloomington, Indiana, home of Indiana University, and a ninety-minute drive from Indianapolis. Indianapolis metropolitan area has a population of over one million with some $3.5 billion dollars to spend annually. It is considered a desirable site for future expansion by many of the nation's top industrial leaders, as reported in a recent FORTUNE magazine survey. The city is the crossroads of the national interstate highway system with more interstate highways converging here than in any other section of the United States. Its recently enlarged airport can accommodate any of the jet aircraft currently in operation, and is served by most of the major airlines. The per capita effective buying income is $4,264 as contrasted with $3,779 for the U.S. as a whole, with almost half of the households falling in the annual income bracket of $10,000 and above. While approximately seventy-five percent of the customers of the marina for boat dockage, etc., come from the Indianapolis area, it is estimated that there is a total potential audience of some 2.9 million inhabitants within a one hundred mile radius of Bloomington (see Exhibit 2).

The thirty-four acres of land on which the Fourwinds complex is located is leased to the corporation by the state of Indiana. In 1968 a prospectus was distributed by the Indiana Department of Natural Resources asking for bids on a motel and marina on the selected site. Only one other bidder qualified of the eight to ten bids submitted. The proposal submitted by the Taggart Corporation was accepted primarily based on the economic strength of the individuals who composed the group as well as the actual content of the bid.

The prospectus specified a minimum rental for the land of $10,000. Taggart Corporation offered in their bid a guarantee of $2,000 against the first $100,000 in marina sales and income and four percent of all income over that amount. For the Inn, they guaranteed $8,000 against the first $400,000 of income plus four percent of all room sales and two percent of all food and beverage sales over that amount.

An initial lease of thirty-seven years was granted to Taggart with two options of thirty years each. At the termination of the contract, all physical property reverts to the state of Indiana and personal property to Taggart. The entire dock structure is floating and is considered under the personal property category.

Prior to tendering a bid, the corporation visited similar facilities at Lake of the Ozarks, Lake Hamilton in Hot Springs and the Kentucky Lakes operations.

SPECIAL ISSUES IN STRATEGIC MANAGEMENT

EXHIBIT 2 Location of Fourwinds Marina in Relation to Urban Centers

Indiana

- Indianapolis — 1 hr
- Terre Haute — 1 hr 40 min
- Bloomington
- Cincinnati — 3 hr
- Louisville — 2 hr 15 min

They received a considerable amount of information from the Kentucky Lakes management.

Construction of the initial phase of the marina began in May 1969 and the first one hundred slips were opened in August under a speeded up construction schedule. The Inn had its formal opening in November of 1972.

Sources of Income

Note: The Indiana Department of Natural Resources exercises total control over the rates that can be charged on slip rental as well as room rates at the Inn.

Slip Rental

Reservations for slips must be made by November 15 of each year or the slip is subject to sale on a first come basis. Ordinarily all slips are rented for the year. Rental period runs from April 1–October 30. Rental varies from $205 to $1,125 depending on the size of slip and whether or not it is covered.

Buoy Rental

One hundred and sixty-two buoys are rented for the same April 1–October 30 season at a rate of $150. Shuttle boat service for transporting boat owners to and from their craft moored at the buoy area is operative twenty-four hours a day. It is not a scheduled service, but operates as the demand occurs. This requires the primary use of a runabout and driver. The charge for the service is included in the buoy rental fee for the season. As long as the buoy field is in existence the shuttle service must operate on a 24-hour basis in season.

Boat Storage—Winter

It is more expensive to remove a boat from the water than to allow it to remain moored at the dock all winter. The prime rate for storage is based on the charge for storage in the covered area of the main inside storage building. This area is not heated or lighted so repair work cannot be done in this building. An investment of about $12,000 would afford lighting and spot heating to overcome this drawback. When boats are stored, they are not queued according to those needing repair and those not needing service. As a result, time is lost in rearranging boats to get to those on which work must be performed. The storage facility is not utilized in the summer months. The addition of lights in the facility would allow display of used boats for sale which are currently stored out of doors. Rate for storage charges are:

- 100% base rate—inside storage
- 70% of base rate—bubbled area of docks covered
- 60% of base rate—bubbled area of docks open
- 50% of base rate—open storage areas out of water

Storage rate is computed by the size of the boat. A six-foot wide boat has a rate of $7. This is multiplied by the boat length to determine the total rate. So a twenty-foot long boat seven feet wide would cost $140. Last winter the storage facility was filled. One hundred boats were stored with the average size somewhat larger than the 7 × 20 example given above. This rate does not include charges for removing the boat (approximately $75) from the water and moving it to either inside or outside storage areas. There has been, in the past, vandalism on the boats stored in the more remote areas of the uncovered, out of water storage. The Marina claims no responsibility for loss, theft, or damage.

Boat and Motor Rental

Available equipment is up to date and well maintained and consists of:

- 15 houseboats—rental Monday to Friday $300; Friday to Monday $300
- 10 pontoon boats—hourly rental $20 for 3 hours; $35 for 6 hours
- 6 runabouts for skiing—$15–$20 per hour
- 12 fishing boats—$12 for 6 hours; $18 for 12 hours

Maximum hourly rental is 13 hours per day during the week and 15 hours per day on Saturday and Sunday (the rental rate does not include gasoline).

It is not uncommon to have all fifteen houseboats out all week long during the height of the season. (Season height is from Memorial Day weekend to Labor Day weekend.) Pontoons are about 50 percent rented during the week. Utilization of runabouts is 50 percent, while fishing boats is approximately 40 percent. The man who operates the boat and motor rental for the Marina has a one-third interest in all of the boat rental equipment. The Marina holds the balance. Funds for the purchase of the equipment were contributed on the same ⅓ to ⅔ ratio. Net profits after payment of expenses, maintenance, depreciation, etc. are split between the two owners according to the same ratio. The area utilized by the rental area could be converted to slips in the $500 range as a possible alternate use for the dock space. Rental income after expenses, but before interest and depreciation, was slightly less than $20,000 last season.

Small Boat Repair Shop

A small boat repair shop is located between C and D docks. It is well equipped with mechanical equipment and a small hoist for removing small boats from the water for repair at the docks. This facility is currently standing idle. One qualified mechanic could operate it.

Grocery Store

The grocery store is subleased and is effectively operated. Prices are those expected at a small grocery catering to a predominately tourist clientele. Income on the leased operation is approximately $500 month.

Snack Bar

The snack bar is operated by the Inn of the Fourwinds and returns a 5 percent commission to the Marina on food sales. Currently it is felt that the manager of the snack bar is not doing a reliable job in operating the unit. The snack bar is sometimes closed for no apparent reason. Food offered for sale includes hot sandwiches, pizza, snack food, soft drinks, milk and coffee. Prices are high and general quality is rated as good.

Gasoline Sales

Five pumps are located around the perimeter of the end of the center dock. They are manned thirteen hours per day, from seven a.m. to eight p.m., seven days a week. The pumps for the removal of waste from the houseboats and other large craft are located in this area. It takes an average of five minutes to pump out the waste and there is no charge. These gasoline pumps are the only ones available on the lake, permitting access from the water to the pump.

Boat and Boat Accessory Sales Room

A glass enclosed show room occupying approximately 1,500 square feet of floor space is located at the main entrance to the Marina property. Major boat lines Trojan Yacht, Kingscraft, Burnscraft, Harris Flote Bote, Signa, as well as Evinrude motors are offered for sale. In addition, quality lines of marine accessories are available. The sales room building also houses the executive offices of the Marina and the repair and maintenance shops. Attached to the building is the indoor storage area for winter housing a limited number of boats. Last year total boat sales were approximately $971,048. The boat inventory has been reduced from last year's $300,000, removing some lines while concentrating on others that offered higher profit on sales.

Fourwinds Marina is the only operation in the state that stocks the very large boats. They are also the only facility in Indiana with large slips to accommodate these boats. With E, F, and G filled and a waiting list to get in, selling the larger, more profitable boats has become nearly impossible.

MARINA DOCKING AREA FACTS

Dock Construction

The entire section is of modular floating construction. Built in smaller sections that can be bolted together, the construction is of steel frameworks with poured concrete surfaces for walking upon and styrofoam panels in the side for buoyancy. In the event of damage to a section, a side can be replaced easily, eliminating repair of the entire segment of dock. Electrical conduits and water pipes are inside the actual dock units. The major damage to the styrofoam dock segments comes from ducks chewing out pieces of the foam to make nests and from gasoline spillage that literally "eats" the styrofoam. An antigas coating is available. Damage from boats to the dock is minimal. The docks require constant attention. A maze of cables underneath the sections must be kept at the proper tension or the dock will buckle and break up. Three people are involved in dock maintenance. If properly maintained the docks will have 20–30 more years of use. Original cost of the entire dock and buoy system was $984,265.

Winter Storage

Winter storage can be a problem at a marina which is located in an area where a freeze-over of the water occurs. It is better for the boat if it can remain in the water. Water affords better and more even support to the hull. By leaving the craft in the water possible damage from hoists used to lift boats and move them to dry storage is avoided. These factors, however, are not common knowledge to the boat owner and require an educational program.

A rule of the marina prohibits any employee from driving any of the customers' boats. Maintaining a duplicate set of keys for each boat and the cost of the insurance to cover the employee are the prime reasons for this ruling. This means, however, that all boats must be towed, with possibility of damage to the boats during towing.

Bubbling Process

To protect boats left in the water during the winter season, Fourwinds Marina has installed a bubbling system. The system, simple in concept, consists of hoses that are weighted and dropped to the bottom of the lake around the individual docks and along a perimeter line surrounding the entire dock area.

SPECIAL ISSUES IN STRATEGIC MANAGEMENT

Fractional horsepower motors operate compressors that pump air into the submerged hose. The air escaping through tiny holes in the hose forces warmer water at the bottom of the lake up to the top, preventing freezing of the surface or melting ice that might have frozen before the compressors were started. The lines inside the dock areas protect the boats from being damaged by ice formations while the perimeter line prevents major damage to the entire dock area from a pressure ridge that might build up and be jammed against the dock and boats in high wind.

EXHIBIT 3 Organization Chart for Fourwinds Marina

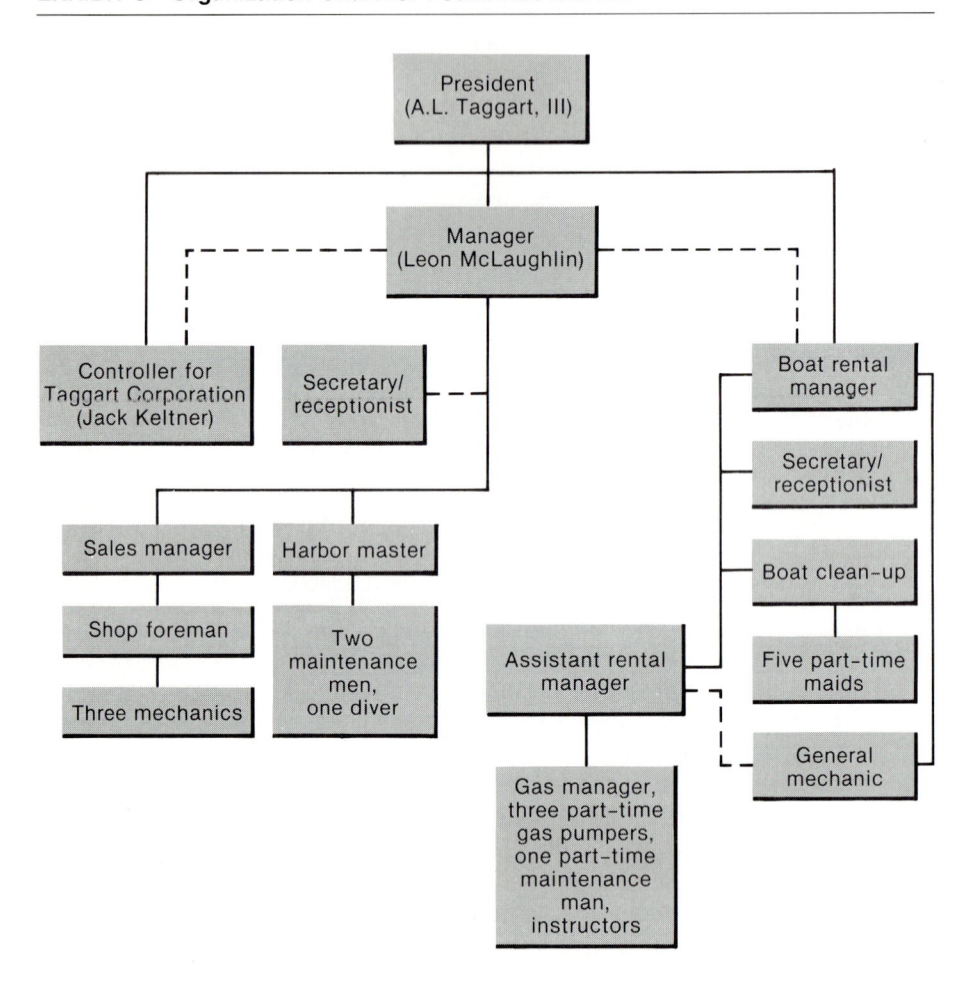

```
                        President
                     (A.L. Taggart, III)
                            |
                         Manager
                     (Leon McLaughlin)
                            |
    ┌───────────────────────┼───────────────────────┐
Controller for         Secretary/              Boat rental
Taggart Corporation    receptionist              manager
(Jack Keltner)                                      |
                                               Secretary/
                                               receptionist
                                                    |
                                               Boat clean-up
    ┌──────────┬──────────┐                         |
Sales      Harbor    Assistant rental          Five part-time
manager    master       manager                    maids
    |          |            |                       |
Shop       Two         Gas manager,            General
foreman   maintenance  three part-time         mechanic
    |      men,        gas pumpers,
Three      one diver   one part-time
mechanics              maintenance
                       man,
                       instructors
```

FOURWINDS MARINA

EXHIBIT 4 Profit Loss Statement (Fiscal year ending March 31, 1974)

REVENUE

Sale of new boats	$774,352	
Sale of used boats	179,645	
Sale of rental boats	17,051	
Total sales		$ 971,048
Other income:		
Service and repair	$128,687	
Gasoline and oil	81,329	
Ship store	91,214	
Slip rental	174,808	
Winter storage	32,177	
Boat rental	99,895	
Other income		608,110
Total income		$1,579,158

EXPENSES

Fixed costs:		
Cost of boats	$798,123	
Cost of repair equip.	56,698	
Ship store costs	64,405	
Cost of gasoline	51,882	
Boat rental costs	8,951	
Total fixed costs		$ 980,059
Operating expenses:		
Wages and salaries	$228,154	
Taxes	23,725	
Building rent	58,116	
Equipment rent	8,975	
Utilities	18,716	
Insurance	25,000	
Interest on loans	209,310	
Advertising	30,105	
Legal expense	19,450	
Bad debt expense	8,731	
Miscellaneous	39,994	
Total operating expenses		670,321
Total costs		$1,650,380
Operating loss		$ 71,222
Depreciation		122,340
Total loss[1]		$ 193,562

[1] This represents the total operating loss of the Fourwinds Marina in the fiscal year ending March 31, 1974. Fourwinds sold a subsidiary in 1973 (boat sales firm in Indianapolis) which they wrote off a loss on of $275,580.

EXHIBIT 5 Balance Sheet (March 31, 1974)

ASSETS				LIABILITIES	
Current assets:				Current liabilities:	
Cash		$ 31,858		Accounts payable	$ 89,433
Accounts receivable		70,632		Intercompany payables	467,091
New boats		199,029		Accrued salary expense	8,905
Used boats		60,747		Accrued interest expense	20,383
Parts		53,295		Accrued tax expense	43,719
Ship store		2,471		Accrued lease expense	36,190
Gas/oil		2,626		Prepaid dock rental	178,466
Total current assets		$420,928		Boat deposits	4,288
Fixed assets:		Less depr.		Current bank notes	177,600
Buoys and docks	$ 984,265	$315,450		Mortgage (current)	982,900
Permanent bldgs.	201,975	17,882		Note payable to floor plan	225,550
Office furniture	3,260	704		Note on rental houseboats	71,625
Houseboats	139,135	15,631		Notes to stockholders	515,150
Work boats	40,805	7,987		Dealer reserve liability	13,925
Equipment	72,420	38,742		Total current liabilities	$2,835,225
	$1,441,860	$396,396		Long term note on houseboats	117,675
Net fixed assets		$1,045,464		Common stock—1,000	
Other assets:				shares at par value $1/share	1,000
Prepaid expense		$ 2,940		Retained earnings deficit	(990,105)
Deferred interest exp.		25,321		Loss during year ending	
		$ 28,261		March 31, 1974[1]	(469,142)
Total assets		$1,494,653		Total liabilities	$1,494,653

[1] Loss during year ending March 31, 1974 is composed of an operating loss of $71,222 plus depreciation of $122,340, and a write-off loss of a sold subsidiary of $275,580.

INDUSTRIAL HIGHLIGHT

Hotels and Motels Industry

Below is a capsule summary of the hotels and motels industry, of which Fourwinds Marina is a part. Information in this highlight was compiled by the U.S. Department of Commerce and focuses on this industry during the approximate period of time covered in the case. Keep in mind that industrial highlights contained in this text are not intended as a complete synopsis of an industry but as a profile of certain issues that can be relevant to a case situation.

HOTELS AND MOTELS

Receipts of hotels and motels are expected to reach $10.3 billion in 1975, an increase of 10 percent over the estimated level of $9.4 billion for 1974. This continued growth will result from increased leisure time available to workers, sustained high levels of family income, and the steady uptrend in travel for business purposes. Recovery from the effects of the energy crisis should continue, but high gasoline prices will hamper recovery of motels along major highways and in some areas far from centers of population.

The energy crisis, particularly the problem of gasoline supplies during the early months of 1974, caused severe dislocations in the industry, but is not expected to halt its long-term growth. While the gasoline problem was at its height during the late fall and winter of 1973–74, some motels along interstate routes and in winter resort areas experienced serious occupancy rate declines, especially on weekends when gas stations were closed. On these weekends, occupancy rates at some motels fell to 20 percent.

Hotels in large cities, however, have experienced a slight increase of occupancy rates, contrary to the downward trend which had persisted for years. Year-round resort hotels also experienced a sizable increase in occupancy rates and revenues.

As drivers adjust to the gasoline supply situation, motels should regain much of the traffic lost during the period of severe shortage. Shorter station hours and higher gas prices will have a restraining effect on long automobile trips, however. Motels in out-of-the-way places, therefore, may not recoup the

Source: U.S. Industrial Outlook, Department of Commerce, 1975, pp. 416–417.

full decline in their occupancy rates. Hotels in downtown areas and those in resort areas within a 4- or 5-hour drive of large centers of population should continue to enjoy improved occupancy, especially in view of the greatly increased costs of foreign travel.

In some areas, overbuilding is a more severe industry problem than the gas supply. Where hotel and motel building booms have been based on overly optimistic estimates of a locality's potential, the establishments will experience low occupancy rates for several years, until traffic grows to a level closer to their capacity.

By 1980, receipts of hotels and motels should be approximately $16.5 billion. This represents a sustained annual growth rate of 10 percent.

EXHIBIT A   Hotels and Motels: Trends and Projections, 1967–1975

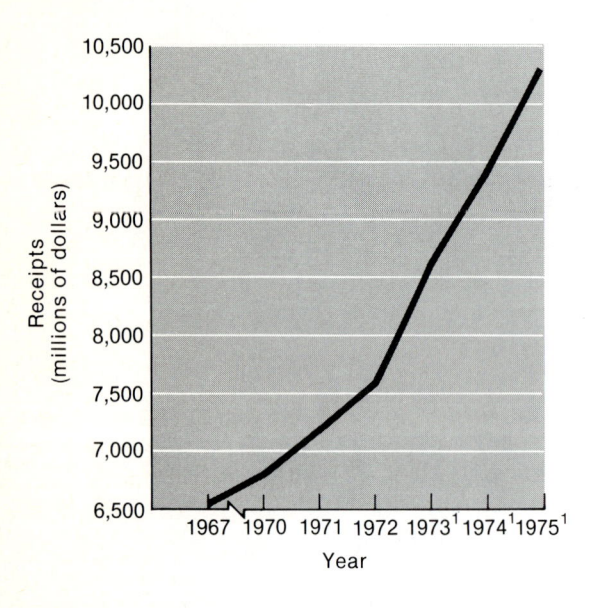

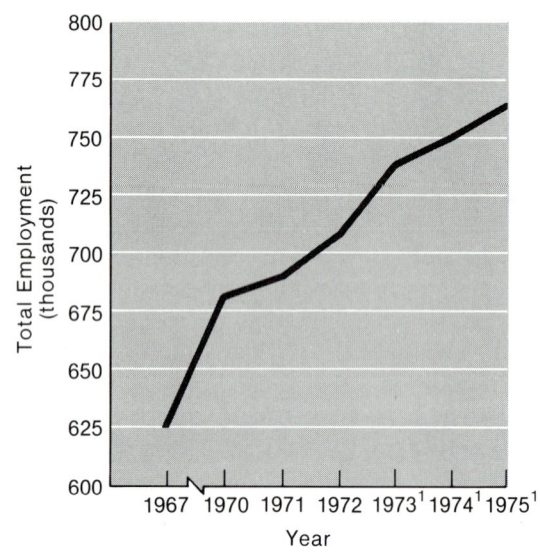

[1] Estimated by Bureau of Domestic Commerce (BDC).
Source: Bureau of the Census, Bureau of Labor Statistics, BDC.

SECTION SIX

A Comprehensive Approach to Analyzing Strategic Problems and Cases

A Comprehensive Approach to Analyzing Strategic Problems and Cases

Since its development at the Harvard Business School in the 1920s, case analysis has become a major tool of management education.[1] *Cases* are detailed descriptions or reports of strategic management problems. They are often written by trained observers who were actually involved with the organization and the problems or issues described in the case. Cases usually include both qualitative and quantitative data that students must analyze in order to determine appropriate alternatives and solutions.

Since there are many different types of strategic management problems, there are many different types of cases. Some cases involve large, diversified companies; others involve small, single-product companies. Some cases involve very successful companies seeking to maintain industry leadership; others focus on failing companies about to go bankrupt. Some cases involve a complicated mixture of strategic management problems; others focus on only a single issue.

A primary advantage of the case method is that it introduces a measure of realism into strategic management education. Rather than emphasizing the learning of concepts, the case method stresses

---

[1] This section is based on J. Paul Peter and James H. Donnelly, Jr., *A Preface to Marketing Management*, 4th ed. (Plano, Tex.: Business Publications, Inc., 1988), pp. 247–276.

the *application* of concepts and sound logic to real-world problems. In this way students learn to bridge the chasm between abstraction and application and to appreciate the value of both.

The purpose of this chapter is to outline a general approach to the analysis of strategic problems and cases. In addition, we suggest some common pitfalls to avoid in case analysis and some approaches to presenting cases. Remember, however, that although following the approach offered here is a logical and useful way to develop sound analyses, no single approach can be applied routinely or mechanically to all cases. Cases differ widely in scope, context, and amount of information available. Analysts must always be ready to "customize" this approach to the particular situation they face.

For example, in our approach, we offer a number of worksheets to assist analysts in various stages of case analysis. These worksheets are designed for broad, general cases and may have to be adapted to more specialized cases and problems. In short, there is no "magic formula" to guarantee an effective case analysis, and there is no substitute for logical, informed thinking on the part of the case analyst.

A major reason why instructors use the case method is that analyzing cases helps students develop and improve their skill at identifying problems and creating sound solutions to them. If this process required nothing more than routinely plugging information into a formula, there would be no need for strategic managers! Managers are paid to recognize problems and to formulate and implement sound solutions to them. Having a successful career in management depends on developing these skills. Highlight 1 lists some of the skills that case analysis helps student analysts develop.

A CASE ANALYSIS FRAMEWORK

The basic approach to case analysis that we propose is shown in Figure 1. This four-stage process suggests that analysts first clearly define the problem or issue to be resolved. Second, they should formulate reasonable alternatives that could potentially solve the problem. Third, analysts should evaluate each of the alternatives and compare them to find an effective solution. Finally, the alternative judged to be most effective and efficient should be selected and implemented to solve the problem.

When this process is carried out in a real situation, an additional step is included. Analysts would evaluate the effects of implementing the alternative to determine whether the problem had been solved. If so, they would continue to monitor the situation to ensure the sustained effectiveness of the alternative. If not, they would go "back to the drawing board" (to problem definition) and begin the whole process again in search of an effective solution.

This problem-solving approach to case analysis is the approach we advocate. However, for students who are not experienced in the analysis of strategic problems and cases, this basic framework may be inadequate and oversimplified because it does not explain how to approach each of these tasks.

A COMPREHENSIVE APPROACH TO ANALYZING STRATEGIC PROBLEMS AND CASES

HIGHLIGHT 1

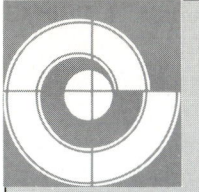

ILLUSTRATIVE EXAMPLE ■ A Case for Case Analysis

Cases assist in bridging the gap between classroom learning and the so-called real world of strategic management. They provide us with an opportunity to develop, sharpen, and test our analytical skills at:

- Assessing situations
- Sorting out and organizing key information
- Asking the right questions
- Defining opportunities and problems
- Identifying and evaluating alternative courses of action
- Interpreting data
- Evaluating the results of past strategies
- Developing and defending new strategies
- Interacting with other managers
- Making decisions under conditions of uncertainty
- Critically evaluating the work of others
- Responding to criticism

Source: Adapted from David W. Cravens and Charles W. Lamb, Jr., *Strategic Marketing: Cases and Applications,* 2nd ed. (Homewood, Ill.: Richard D. Irwin, 1986), p. 55. Reprinted by permission.

For example, consider the first stage, problem definition. What is desired here is a clear, unambiguous statement of the major problems or issues that the case hinges on. Yet just as in real situations that confront practicing managers, few cases offer a direct statement of what these pivotal problems are. In fact, after their initial reading of a case, students often conclude that the case is no more than a description of events in which there are no problems or important issues for analysis. Even in those cases that do include a direct statement about the problems or issues, there is almost always more of a problem than what first meets the eye, and much more analysis must be done.

For these reasons we have developed the more detailed framework for case analysis shown in Figure 2. This framework is designed to help students recognize case problems and issues and sequentially approach devising appropriate solutions to them.[2]

---

[2] For further discussion of the case method and approaches to analyzing cases, see Malcolm P. McNair, *The Case Method at the Harvard Business School* (New York: McGraw-Hill, 1954); Alfred G. Edge and Denis R. Coleman, *The Guide to Case Analysis and Reporting* (Honolulu: Systems Logistics, 1978); and Robert Ronstadt, *The Art of Case Analysis* (Dover, Mass.: Lord Publishing, 1978).

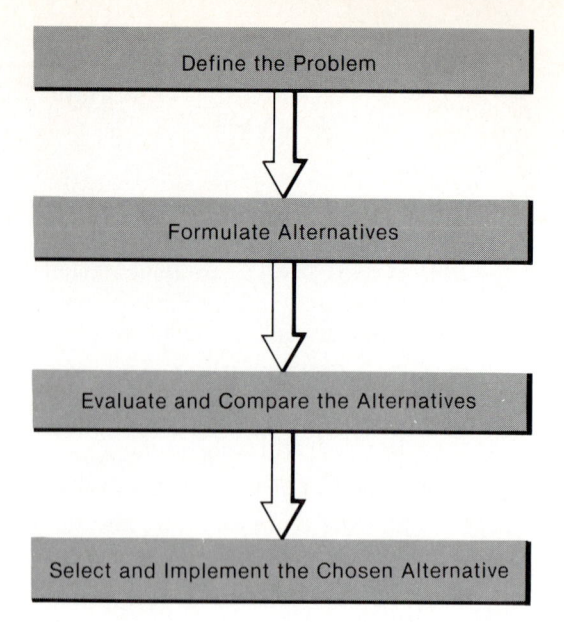

A COMPREHENSIVE APPROACH TO ANALYZING STRATEGIC PROBLEMS AND CASES

```
Define the Problem
        ↓
Formulate Alternatives
        ↓
Evaluate and Compare the Alternatives
        ↓
Select and Implement the Chosen Alternative
```

FIGURE 1 Stages in Case Analysis

```
Analyze and Record the Current Situation
        ↓
Analyze and Record Problems and Their Core Elements
        ↓
Formulate, Evaluate, and Record Alternative Courses of Action
        ↓
Select, Justify, and Record the Chosen Course of Action and Implementation
```

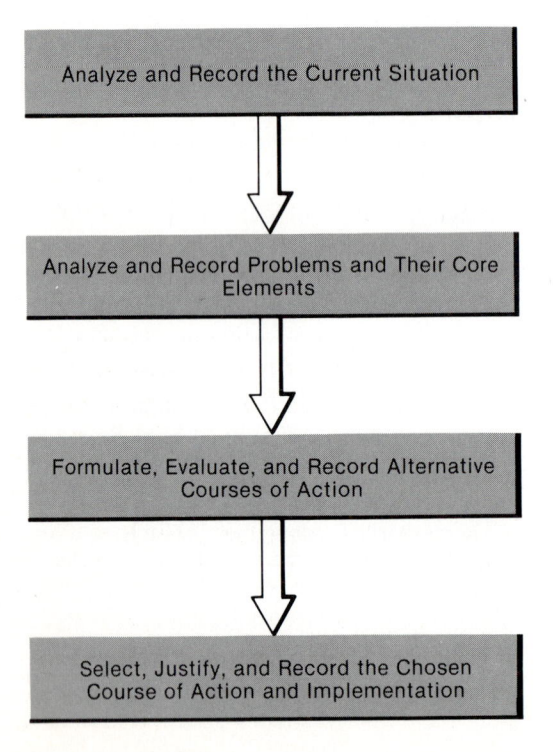

FIGURE 2 An Expanded Framework for Case Analysis

Analyze and Record the Current Situation

Whether the analysis of a strategic problem is conducted by a manager, a student, or an outside consultant, the first step is to analyze and record the current situation. This does not mean writing up a history of the organization or rewriting the case material. It involves the type of environmental analysis described below.

Analyzing and recording the current situation is critical for three reasons. First, until we have developed a clear understanding of the current situation, it is impossible to determine what courses of action are appropriate. In other words, we have no basis for deciding how to improve a situation until we know what that situation is.

Second, the major purpose of this stage of the analysis is to investigate the current and potential problems involved in the case. By sequentially analyzing all elements of the current situation, the analyst clarifies those problems and amasses evidence that they are the central issues.

Third, this stage is useful for delineating the level of analysis for a specific case. By "level of analysis" we mean the overall scope of the problem. For example, some cases emphasize issues arising at the industry level, whereas others focus on particular organizations, certain departments, individual executives, or particular strategic decisions. Clearly, determining the appropriate level of analysis is a very important aspect of case analysis.

In an effort to pinpoint case problems, it is useful to analyze sequentially each component or aspect of the general, operating, and internal environments. Table 1 provides a list of these elements and the types of questions that should be asked in the process of analyzing them.

In very few cases are all of these components or aspects crucial for the analysis. However, until each component or aspect is considered, there is no way to judge its relative importance. The analyst who considers each component and aspect in detail avoids missing critical issues. In other words, the key task at this stage of the analysis is to consider every possible environmental element in order to assess problems and opportunities in the case situation.

An analysis of any of the components or aspects of the environment may have important implications for defining case problems and for supporting appropriate solutions to the problems. Thus, keeping a detailed record of all of the relevant information uncovered in the environmental analysis is crucial. Table 2 presents a worksheet for recording this information and for further investigating its impact on the case.

In completing an environmental analysis, the analyst should keep six major points in mind:

1. Careful analysis is often required to separate relevant from superfluous information. Just like the situations facing a practicing manager, cases often include information that is irrelevant to the major issues. In order to get a clear understanding of the case problems, the analyst must decide what information is important and what should be ignored.
2. It is important to determine the difference between symptoms of

TABLE 1 Study Areas in Environmental Analysis

GENERAL ENVIRONMENT

1. *Economic component:* What is the state of such economic variables as inflation, unemployment, and interest rates? What are the trends in these variables, and how are they relevant to the case?
2. *Social component:* What is the state of such social variables as educational levels, customs, beliefs, and values? What are the trends in these variables, and how are they relevant to the case?
3. *Political component:* What is the state of such political variables as lobbying activities and government attitudes toward business? What are the trends in these variables and how are they relevant to the case?
4. *Legal component:* What is the level of such legal variables as federal, state, and local legislation? What are the trends in these variables and how are they relevant to the case?
5. *Technological component:* What is the level of technology in the industry? What technological trends are relevant to the case?

OPERATING ENVIRONMENT

1. *Customer component:* What are the target markets and customer profiles, and how are they relevant to the case?
2. *Competition component:* What are the major barriers to entry in this industry? What are the strengths, weaknesses, strategies, and market shares of major competitors, and how are they relevant to the case?
3. *Labor component:* What factors influence the supply of labor, and how are they relevant to the case?
4. *Supplier component:* What factors influence relationships between suppliers of resources and the firm, and how are they relevant to the case?
5. *International component:* What is the state of international factors? What international trends are relevant to the case?

INTERNAL ENVIRONMENT

1. *Organizational aspects:* What organizational or managerial issues, concepts, and analyses are relevant to the case?
2. *Marketing aspects:* What marketing issues, concepts, and analyses are relevant to the case?
3. *Financial aspects:* What financial issues, concepts, and analyses are relevant to the case?
4. *Personnel aspects:* What personnel issues, concepts, and analyses are relevant to the case?
5. *Production aspects:* What production issues, concepts, and analyses are relevant to the case?

problems and current and potential problems themselves. Symptoms of problems are indicators of a problem but are not problems per se. For example, a decline in sales in a particular sales territory is a symptom of a problem. The problem is the root cause of the decline in sales—

perhaps the field representative stopped making sales calls on minor accounts because she or he is dissatisfied with the firm's compensation plan.
3. In recording the current situation, the analyst must be mindful of the difference between facts and opinions. Facts are objective statements or accounts of information such as financial data reported in a balance sheet or income statement. Opinions are subjective interpretations of facts or situations. For example, when a particular executive says she believes sales will increase by 20 percent next year, she is expressing an opinion. The analyst must not place too much emphasis on unsupported opinions and must carefully consider any factors that may bias people's opinions.
4. It is often useful to collect additional information from outside the case when performing a situational analysis. The Appendix to this book offers a summary of sources of secondary data from which additional information can be obtained. This information can be very useful for putting the problem in context and for supporting an analysis. Remember, though, that the major problems are contained in the case, and the analyst should not need outside information to recognize them.
5. Regardless of how much information is contained in the case and how much additional information is collected, the analyst usually finds it

TABLE 2 General Worksheet for Analyzing the Current Situation

ENVIRONMENT	RELEVANT ISSUES (SPECIFIC TO CASE)	CASE IMPACT (FAVORABLE/ UNFAVORABLE)	CASE IMPORTANCE (IMPORTANT/ UNIMPORTANT)
General Environment			
Social			
Economic			
Political			
Legal			
Technological			
Operating Environment			
International			
Suppliers			
Competition			
Customers			
Labor			
Internal Environment			
Organizational aspects			
Marketing aspects			
Financial aspects			
Personnel aspects			
Production aspects			

impossible to characterize the current situation completely. At this point assumptions must be made. Clearly, because different analysts might make widely differing assumptions, assumptions must be stated explicitly. Doing so avoids confusion about how the analyst perceives the current situation and enables other analysts to evaluate the reasonableness and necessity of the assumptions.

6. When an analyst concludes that a certain aspect of an environmental analysis has no bearing on the case, he or she should say so explicitly. Moreover, analysts should avoid trying to force or stretch information to fit into each of the environmental components. Indeed some aspects are likely to be irrelevant to any specific case, although each must be evaluated to determine whether it is relevant.

Analyze and Record Problems and Their Core Elements

The environmental analysis just described is useful for developing a general understanding of the current situation. However, its primary purpose is to help the analyst recognize the major problems or issues. In other words, comparing the case situation with an optimal situation should highlight the inconsistencies between them. By an optimal situation we mean a situation in which activities are performed in a manner consistent with sound managerial principles and logic.

For example, suppose analysis of a particular case revealed that although an organization had done an excellent job of setting objectives, its current strategy was not designed appropriately for accomplishing these objectives. Because management principles strongly recommend that strategies flow from objectives, this inconsistency and the reasons for it should be carefully considered. The deviation in strategy is probably symptomatic of a deeper managerial problem.

Recognizing and recording problems and their core elements is crucial to a meaningful case analysis. Obviously, if the root problems are not determined and explicitly stated and understood, the remainder of the case analysis has little merit because it does not focus on the key issues.

Table 3 presents a worksheet to help analysts recognize and record problems. This table emphasizes the importance of providing evidence that a particular problem is a critical one. Simply stating that a particular issue is the major problem is not sufficient; analysts must also provide the reasoning by which they reached this conclusion.

Formulate, Evaluate, and Record Alternative Courses of Action

At this stage, the analyst addresses the question of what can be done to resolve the problems defined in the previous part of the analysis. Generally, several alternative courses of action that might help alleviate the problem are available. One approach to developing alternatives is to brainstorm as many as possible and then reduce the list to a workable number of the most feasible. Another approach is to screen each alternative as it is developed, saving for further evaluation and comparison only those that meet predetermined feasibility

A COMPREHENSIVE APPROACH TO ANALYZING STRATEGIC PROBLEMS AND CASES

TABLE 3 General Worksheet for Defining Problems and Their Core Elements

MAJOR PROBLEM OR ISSUE

Description of problem or issue:

Evidence that this is a major problem or issue:
1. Facts
2. Symptoms or other effects of the problem
3. Opinions
4. Assumptions

(Repeat as necessary for cases involving several problems or issues.)

---

criteria. Regardless of the method used to develop alternatives, the final list should usually include only three or four of the better solutions.

After listing a number of feasible alternatives, the analyst evaluates them in terms of their strengths and weaknesses. Strengths include anything favorable about the alternative (such as increased efficiency, increased productivity, cost savings, or increased sales and profits). Weaknesses include anything unfavorable about the alternative (such as its costs in time, money, and other resources or its relative ineffectiveness at solving the problem). Table 4 offers a worksheet for evaluating alternative courses of action.

Sound logic and the application of managerial principles are particularly important at this stage. It is essential to avoid alternatives that might alleviate the problem but could at the same time spawn a new, more serious problem or require a greater investment of resources than solving the problem warrants. Similarly, analysts must be as objective as possible in their evaluation of alternatives. For example, it is not uncommon for analysts to ignore important weaknesses of an alternative that they favor.

Select, Justify, and Record the Chosen Course of Action and Implementation

It is now time to select the alternative that best solves the problem, while creating a minimum of new problems. This alternative is selected via careful analysis of the strengths and weaknesses of each alternative scrutinized in the previous stage. Recording the logic and reasoning that precipitated the selection of a particular alternative is very important. Regardless of what alternative is selected, the analyst must justify the choice.

TABLE 4 General Worksheet for Evaluating Alternative Courses of Action

ALTERNATIVE 1

Description of alternative: _____

Strengths of alternative: _____

Weaknesses of alternative: _____

Overall evaluation of alternative: _____

ALTERNATIVE 2

Description of alternative: _____

Strengths of alternative: _____

Weaknesses of alternative: _____

Overall evaluation of alternative: _____

(Repeat as necessary for each feasible alternative.)

At this stage in the analysis, an alternative has been selected and the analyst has explained why she or he feels it is the appropriate course of action. The final phase in case analysis is the devising of an action-oriented implementation plan. Analysts should describe their proposed implementation plan in as much detail as possible.

Table 5 offers a worksheet to use in considering implementation issues. Although cases do not always contain enough information for the analyst to answer all of these questions in detail, reasonable recommendations for implementation should be formulated. In doing so, the analyst may have to make certain assumptions about commonly used and effective methods of implementing strategic alternatives.

TABLE 5 General Worksheet for Implementing the Chosen Alternative

1. What should be done to implement the chosen alternative effectively?
Specific recommendation: _____

Justification: _____

2. Who should be responsible for implementing the chosen alternative?
Specific recommendation: _____

Justification: _____

3. When and where should the chosen alternative be implemented?
Specific recommendation: _____

Justification: _____

4. How should the chosen alternative be evaluated for success or failure?
Specific recommendation: _____

Justification: _____

PITFALLS TO AVOID IN CASE ANALYSIS

Analysts commonly make a variety of errors in the process of case study. Below we discuss some of the mistakes analysts make most frequently. When evaluating your analyses or those of others, use this list as a guide to spotting potential shortcomings.[3]

Inadequately Defining the Problem

Analysts often recommend courses of action without adequately understanding or defining the problems that characterize the case. This sometimes occurs because analysts jump to premature conclusions upon first reading a case and then proceed to interpret everything in the case as justifying those conclusions—even factors that they should realize argue against them. Closely related is the error of analyzing symptoms without determining the root problems. Sound case analyses absolutely depend on a clear understanding of major case problems.

---

[3] Several of the items in this list are based on Ralph W. Reber and Gloria F. Terry, *Behavioral Insights for Supervision* (Englewood Cliffs, N.J.: Prentice-Hall, 1975), pp. 213–215.

Searching for "The Answer"

Analysts sometimes spend a great deal of time searching through secondary sources to find out what an organization actually did in a particular case and then present this alternative as though it were "the answer." However, this approach ignores the fact that the objective of undertaking a case study is to learn through exploration and discussion. There is no one "official" or "correct" answer to a case. Rather, many good analyses and solutions, as well as many poor ones, usually exist.

Assuming the Case Away

Analysts sometimes make such sweeping assumptions that the case problem is essentially assumed away. For example, suppose a case concerns a firm that has lost a major share of its market. Simply concluding that the firm will increase its market share by 10 percent per year for the next five years is an example of assuming the case away.

Not Having Enough Information

Analysts often complain that not enough information is given in the case for them to make a good decision. However, there is good reason for not presenting "all" of the information in a case. In real business situations, managers and consultants seldom have all the information they would need to make an optimal decision. Reasonable assumptions and predictions have to be made, and the challenge is to arrive at intelligent solutions in spite of uncertainty and limited information.

Relying on Generalizations

Analysts sometimes discuss case problems and recommendations at such a general level that their work has little value. Case analysis calls for specific problems and recommendations, not sweeping generalizations. For example, to recommend that the structure of the firm be changed is to generalize. However, to provide a detailed plan for changing the organizational structure, to explain just what the structure should be, and to give one's reasons for this solution is to make a specific recommendation.

Postulating a Different Situation

Analysts sometimes exert considerable time and effort contending that "if the situation were different, I'd know what course of action to take" or "if the manager hadn't already fouled things up so badly, the firm wouldn't have any problems." Such reasoning ignores the fact that the events in the case have already happened and cannot be changed. Even though analysis or criticism of past events may be necessary in diagnosing problems, the situation as it exists must be addressed in the end, and decisions must be based on it.

Focusing Too Narrowly

Too often, analysts ignore the effects that a change in one area has on the rest of the situation. Although cases are sometimes labeled as concerning specific types of issues, this does not mean that other variables can be ignored. For example, changing the price of a product may well influence the appropriate methods of promotion and distribution.

Abandoning Realism

In many cases, analysts get so obsessed with solving a particular problem that their solutions become totally unrealistic. For example, designing and recommending a sound $1 million advertising program for a firm with a capital structure of $50,000 is totally unrealistic, even though, if it were possible to implement, it might solve the given problem.

Setting Up "Straw Man" Alternatives

Analysts sometimes offer a single viable alternative and several others that are extremely weak and untenable. The evaluation and selection of an alternative then proceed (predictably enough) by discrediting the "straw man" alternatives and accepting the single viable solution. Such an approach to case analysis is inappropriate, because what is desired is a *set* of alternatives that it is worthwhile to evaluate. Case analysis can enhance the development of decision-making skills only when each alternative has some important strengths and analysts must make an informed choice.

Recommending Research or Consultants

Analysts sometimes offer unsatisfactory solutions to case problems by recommending either that some research be conducted to uncover problems or that a consultant be hired to do so. Although engaging in further research and hiring consultants may occasionally be useful recommendations as auxiliary steps in an analysis, it is still the analyst's job to identify the problems and decide how to solve them. When research or consultants are recommended in a case analysis, the rationale, costs, and potential benefits should be fully specified in the case report.

Rehashing Case Material

Analysts sometimes go to great lengths rewriting a history of an organization as presented in the case. This is unnecessary and wasteful: the instructor and other analysts are already familiar with this information. Similarly, student analysts sometimes copy case tables and figures and include them in a written report. This too is unnecessary. However, developing original graphs, pie charts, or other visual aids based on the case material is often a useful way to make a particular point.

Highlight 2 offers some further guidelines on approaching cases and gives an example of an effective student analysis.

HIGHLIGHT 2

ILLUSTRATIVE EXAMPLE ■ What Does Case "Analysis" Mean?

A common criticism of prepared cases goes something like this: "You repeated an awful lot of case material, but you really didn't analyze the case." And at the same time, it is difficult to verbalize exactly what "analysis" means: "I can't explain exactly what it is, but I know it when I see it!"

It is not surprising that confusion arises, because the term *analysis* has many definitions and means different things in different contexts. In terms of case analysis, analysis means going beyond simply describing the case information. It includes determining the implications of the case information for developing strategy. This may involve careful mathematical analysis of sales and profit data or thoughtful interpretation of the text of the case.

One way of approaching analysis involves taking a series of three steps: synthesis, generalizations, and implications. A brief example of this process follows.

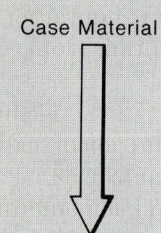

Case Material

The high growth rate of frozen pizza sales has attracted a number of large food processors, including Pillsbury (Totino's), Quaker Oats (Celeste), American Home Products (Chef Boy-ar-dee), Nestlé (Stouffer's), General Mills (Saluto), and H. J. Heinz (La Pizzeria). The major independents are Jeno's, Tony's, and John's. Jeno's and Totino's are the market leaders,

Not Thinking!

By far the worst mistake analysts make is not thinking. Often analysts mistakenly assume that, having simply organized the case material in a logical format, they have done a case analysis! And similarly, although analysts usually have some general knowledge of a firm or situation, they often ignore it when working on a case. For example, suppose a case involves a major automobile manufacturer. Although the case may say nothing about foreign imports, they may well have an important impact on the firm and should be considered. Analyzing cases *requires* that knowledge of management principles and sound logic from outside the case be applied.

Getting Discouraged

After attempting unsuccessfully to analyze the first case or two, analysts sometimes give up and assure themselves that they cannot do case analyses. Such a conclusion is almost always unwarranted and ignores the fact that performing case analyses is a *learned* skill. To be sure, some students master

A COMPREHENSIVE APPROACH TO ANALYZING STRATEGIC PROBLEMS AND CASES 583

> with market shares of about 19 percent each. Celeste and Tony's have about 8–9 percent each, and the others have about 5 percent or less. (Excerpted from "The Pillsbury Company—Totino's Pizza," in Philip Kotler, *Principles of Marketing* (Englewood Cliffs, N.J.: Prentice-Hall, Inc., 1980), pp. 192–195.
>
> **Synthesis**
>
> ⇩
>
> The frozen pizza market is a highly competitive and highly fragmented market.
>
> **Generalizations**
>
> ⇩
>
> In markets such as this, attempts to gain market share through lower consumer prices or heavy advertising are likely to be quickly copied by competitors and thus not be very effective.
>
> **Implications**
>
> Lowering consumer prices and spending more on advertising are likely to be poor strategies. Perhaps increasing freezer space in retail outlets could be effective; this objective might be obtained through trade discounts. Developing a superior product (such as better tasting pizza or microwave pizza) or increasing geographic coverage of the market might be better strategies for obtaining market share.
>
> Note that none of these three steps includes any repetition of the case material. Rather, they all involve extracting the meaning of the information and, by pairing it with strategic management principles, coming up with its strategic implications.

case analysis much more quickly than others. Yet most students can become skillful analysts of cases and problems if they continue working hard on the cases and learning from class discussions.

Highlight 3 is a handy summary of the steps to take in case analysis and of the use of the worksheets included in this chapter.

COMMUNICATION OF THE CASE ANALYSIS

The final task in case analysis that we will consider here is to communicate the results of the analysis. The most comprehensive and insightful analysis has little value if it is not communicated effectively. Communication includes not only organizing the information in a logical manner but also using proper grammar and spelling. In addition, the overall appearance of a written report and that of the presenters and visual aids in an oral report are often used by evaluators as an indication of the effort put into a project and of its overall quality.

HIGHLIGHT 3

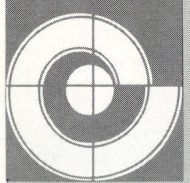

CHECKLIST ■ An Operational Approach to Case and Problem Analysis

☐ 1. Read the case quickly to get an overview of the situation.
☐ 2. Read the case again thoroughly, underlining relevant information and taking notes on potential areas of concern.
☐ 3. Reread and study the case until it is well understood.
☐ 4. Review outside sources of information that are relevant to the case, and record important information.
☐ 5. Complete the General Worksheet for Analyzing the Current Situation.
☐ 6. Review this worksheet in search of potential problems.
☐ 7. List all potential problems on the General Worksheet for Defining Problems and Their Core Elements.
☐ 8. Review this worksheet and list the major problems in order of priority.
☐ 9. Complete the Worksheet for Defining Problems and Their Core Elements.
☐ 10. Develop several feasible solutions for dealing with the major problems.
☐ 11. Complete the General Worksheet for Evaluating Alternative Courses of Action.
☐ 12. Review this worksheet and ensure that all relevant strengths and weaknesses have been considered.
☐ 13. Decide which alternative solves the problems most effectively.
☐ 14. Complete the General Worksheet for Implementing the Chosen Alternative.
☐ 15. Prepare a written or oral report based on the worksheets.

The Written Report

Good written reports usually start with an outline. We offer the framework given in Table 6 as one useful format. This outline is fully consistent with the approach suggested in this chapter and, with a few exceptions, involves writing out in prose form the information contained on the various worksheets.

Elements of a Written Report

TITLE PAGE. The title page includes the title of the case and the names of all persons who were involved in preparing the report. It is also useful to include the name and number of the course for which the case was prepared and the date the project was submitted.

A COMPREHENSIVE APPROACH TO ANALYZING STRATEGIC PROBLEMS AND CASES

TABLE 6 An Outline for Written Case Reports

1. Title page
2. Table of contents
3. Introduction
4. Environmental analysis
   A. General environment
   B. Operating environment
   C. Internal environment
   D. Assumptions
5. Problem definition
   A. Major problem 1 and evidence
   B. Major problem 2 (if applicable) and evidence
   C. Major problem 3 (if applicable) and evidence
6. Alternative courses of action
   A. Description of alternative 1
      a. Strengths
      b. Weaknesses
   B. Description of alternative 2
      a. Strengths
      b. Weaknesses
   C. Description of alternative 3
      a. Strengths
      b. Weaknesses
7. Chosen alternative and implementation
   A. Justification for alternative chosen
   B. Implementation specifics and justification
8. Summary of analysis
9. References
10. Technical appendices
    A. Financial analyses
    B. Other technical information

TABLE OF CONTENTS. The Table of Contents lists every heading in the report and the number of the page on which that particular section begins. If a variety of exhibits are included in a case report, it may be useful to include a Table of Exhibits listing every exhibit and the page number on which it is located.

INTRODUCTION. The introduction of a case analysis is not a summary of the case. It is a statement of the purpose of the report and a brief description of each of its major sections.

ENVIRONMENTAL ANALYSIS. In this section, the results of the analysis of each environmental component are reported. Subheadings should be used for each of the three major environments and for each relevant component or aspect listed in Table 2. Again, if any of the environments or categories has no relevance to a particular case, simply report that the analysis revealed nothing crucial for this particular situational element. Any assumptions made concerning the current situation should also be reported in this section.

PROBLEM DEFINITION. This section offers a concise statement of the major problems in the case and reviews the evidence that led to the conclusion that these are the major issues. Problems should be listed in order of their importance and should be accompanied by an account of the evidence.

ALTERNATIVE COURSES OF ACTION. This section describes each of the alternatives devised for solving the major problems in the case. The strengths and weaknesses of each alternative should be clearly delineated.

CHOSEN ALTERNATIVE AND IMPLEMENTATION. This section reveals which alternative has been selected and explains why it is the appropriate course of action. In addition, it should include a detailed description of how the alternative will be implemented and why this method of implementation is best.

SUMMARY OF ANALYSIS. This brief section simply restates what the report has been about. It describes what was done in preparing the report, the basic problems, and the alternative selected for solving them. It is also useful in this section to offer any additional information that supports the quality of the analysis and the value of the alternative chosen.

REFERENCES. Any outside materials used in the report should be listed alphabetically in an acceptable reference style, such as that used in articles in *The Academy of Management Journal*. (Such information should also be appropriately cited in footnotes throughout the report.)

TECHNICAL APPENDICES. Some cases require considerable financial analysis. Typically, key financial analysis is reported in the text of the report, but detailed analysis and calculations are placed here. Any other types of analysis that are too long or too detailed for the body of the report can also be placed here.

The Oral Presentation

Case analyses are often presented orally in class by individuals or teams of analysts. As is true for the written report, a good outline is critical, and it is often a good idea to provide each class member with a copy of the outline and a list of any assumptions that are made. Although there is no single best way to present a case or to divide responsibility among team members, simply reading a written report is unacceptable. (It encourages boredom and interferes with all-important class discussion.) It is important to emphasize the major points of the analysis and not get bogged down in unnecessary detail. If the instructor or a class member asks for more details on a specific point, of course, the presenter must supply them.

The use of visual aids can be very helpful in presenting case analyses in class. However, simply presenting financial statements or other detailed data contained in the case is a poor use of visual media. On the other hand, taking these statements or figures and recasting them in easy-to-understand pie charts or graphs can be very effective in making specific points. Remember that any type of visual aid should be large enough so that even people sitting in the rear of the classroom can see the information clearly.

Oral presentation of case analyses is particularly helpful to students who are learning the skill of speaking to a group, a common activity in many managerial positions. In particular, the ability to handle objections and disagreements without antagonizing others is a skill well worth developing.

SUMMARY

This chapter presented a framework for case analysis and offered some suggestions for developing and communicating high-quality case reports. Case analysis begins with analysis and recording of the current situation, including all relevant aspects of the environment, followed by analysis and recording of the problems or issues on which the case hinges. The next step is to formulate, evaluate, and record alternative courses of action in order to "narrow the field" to the best feasible alternatives. Then it is necessary to select one of the proposed courses of action, explain this choice, and describe how it is to be implemented.

We cautioned against several pitfalls that can plague the student (or the ill-prepared manager) engaged in case analysis, and we offered some guidelines for communicating case analyses in a written report and in an oral presentation.

Performing good case analyses takes a lot of time and effort. Analysts must be highly motivated and willing to get involved in the case and in class discussion if they expect to learn effectively and succeed in a course where cases are utilized. Analysts with only passive interest who perform "night before" analyses cheat themselves of valuable learning experiences that are critical in preparing for a successful management career.

APPENDIX[1]

Selected Sources of Secondary Information

Secondary sources of data are often useful in case analysis. They provide more thorough environmental analyses and can be used to support one's recommendations and conclusions. Many of the data sources listed below can be found in business libraries. Here they are grouped under five headings: General Business and Industry Sources, Basic U.S. Statistical Sources, Financial Information Sources, Marketing Information Sources, and Indexes and Abstracts.

GENERAL BUSINESS AND INDUSTRY SOURCES

Aerospace Facts and Figures. Aerospace Industries Association of America.

Annual Statistical Report. American Iron and Steel Institute.

Chemical Marketing Reporter. Schnell Publishing. Includes lengthy, continuing list of "Current Prices of Chemicals and Related Materials."

---

[1] Adapted from J. Paul Peter and James H. Donnelly, Jr., *Marketing Management: Knowledge and Skills*, 2nd ed. (Homewood, Ill: BPI/Irwin, 1989), pp. 907–919. Reprinted by permission.

APPENDIX

Computerworld. Computerworld, Inc. Last December issue includes "Review and Forecast," an analysis of computer industry's past year and the outlook for the next year.

Construction Review. Department of Commerce. Current statistics on construction put in place, costs, and employment.

Distribution Worldwide. Chilton Co. Special annual issue, *Distribution Guide,* compiles information on transportation methods and wage.

Drugs and Cosmetic Industry. Drug Markets, Inc. Separate publication in July, *Drug and Cosmetic Catalog,* provides list of manufacturers of drugs and cosmetics and their respective products.

Electrical World. January and February issues include two-part statistical report on expenditures, construction, and other categories by region; capacity; sales; and financial statistics for the electrical industry.

Encyclopedia of Business Information Sources. Paul Wasserman et al., eds., Gale Research Company. A detailed listing of primary subjects of interest to managerial personnel, with a record of sourcebooks, periodicals, organizations, directories, handbooks, bibliographies, and other sources of information on each topic. Two vols., nearly 17,000 entries in over 1,600 subject areas.

Forest Industries. Miller Freeman Publications. Inc. The March issue includes "Forest Industries Wood-Based Panel," a review of production and sales figures for selected wood products; extra issue in May includes a statistical review of the lumber industry.

Implement and Tractor. Intertec Publishing Corporation. January issue includes equipment specifications and operating data for farm and industrial equipment. November issue includes statistics and information on the farm industry.

Industry Surveys. Standard & Poor's Corp. Continuously revised analysis of leading industries (40 industries made up of 1,300 companies). Basic analysis features company ratio comparisons and balance sheet statistics.

Million Dollar Directory. Dun & Bradstreet. Lists U.S. companies with an indicated worth of $1 million or more, giving officers and directors, products, standard industrial classification, sales, and number of employees.

Middle Market Directory. Dun & Bradstreet. Inventories approximately 18,000 U.S. companies with an indicated worth of $500,000 to $999,999, giving officers, products, standard industrial classification, approximate sales, and number of employees.

Milutinovich, J. S. "Business Facts for Decision Makers: Where to Find Them." *Business Horizons,* March–April 1985, pp. 63–80.

Modern Brewery Age. Business Journals, Inc. February issue includes a review of sales and production figures for the brewery industry. A separate publication, *The Blue Book,* issued in May, compiles sales and consumption figures by state for the brewery industry.

National Petroleum News. McGraw-Hill, Inc. May issue includes statistics on sales and consumption of fuel oils, gasoline, and related products. Some figures are for 10 years, along with 10-year projections.

Operating Results of Department and Specialty Stores. National Retail Merchants Association.

Petroleum Facts and Figures. American Petroleum Institute.

Poor's Register of Corporations, Directors, and Executives of the United States and Canada. Standard & Poor's Corp. Divided into two sections. The first gives officers, products, sales range, and number of employees for about 30,000 corporations. The second gives brief information on executives and directors.

Quick-Frozen Foods. Harcourt Brace Jovanovich Publications. October issue includes "Frozen Food Almanac," providing statistics on the frozen food industry by product.

Statistical Sources. Paul Wasserman et al., eds. Gale Research Corp., 4th ed., 1974. A subject guide to industrial, business, social, educational, and financial data, and other related topics.

BASIC U.S. STATISTICAL SOURCES

Business Service Checklist. Department of Commerce. Weekly guide to Department of Commerce publications, plus key business indicators.

Business Statistics. Department of Commerce. (Supplement to *Survey of Current Business.*) History of the statistical series appearing in the *Survey*. Also included are source references and useful explanatory notes.

Census of Agriculture. Department of Commerce. Data by states and counties on livestock, farm characteristics, values.

Census of Manufacturers. Department of Commerce. Industry statistics, area statistics, subjects reports, location of plants, industry descriptions arranged in Standard Industrial Classification, and a variety of ratios.

Census of Mineral Industries. Department of Commerce. Similar to *Census of Manufacturers.* Also includes capital expenditures and employment and payrolls.

Census of Retail Trade. Department of Commerce. Compiles data for states, SMSAs, counties, and cities with populations of 2,500 or more by kind of business. Data include number of establishments, sales, payroll, and personnel.

Census of Selected Services. Department of Commerce. Includes data on hotels, motels, beauty parlors, barber shops, and other retail service organizations.

Census Tract Reports. Department of Commerce, Bureau of Census. Detailed information on both population and housing subjects.

Census of Transportation. Passenger Transportation Survey, Commodity Transportation Survey, Travel Inventory and Use Survey, Bus and Truck Carrier Survey.

Census of Wholesale Trade. Department of Commerce. Similar to *Census of Retail Trade*—except information is for wholesale establishment.

County and City Data Book. Department of Commerce. Summary statistics for small geographical areas.

Current Business Reports. Department of Commerce. Reports monthly department store sales of selected items.

Economic Report of the President. Transmitted to the Congress, January (each year), together with the *Annual Report* of the Council of Economic Advisers. Statistical tables relating to income, employment, and production.

Handbook of Basic Economic Statistics. Economic Statistics Bureau of Washington, D.C. Current and historical statistics on industry, commerce, labor, and agriculture.

Statistical Abstract of the United States. Department of Commerce. Summary statistics in industrial, social, political, and economic fields in the United States. It is augmented by the *Cities Supplement, The County Data Book,* and *Historical Statistics of the United States.*

Statistics of Income: Corporation Income Tax Returns. Internal Revenue Service. Balance sheet and income statement statistics derived from corporate tax returns.

Statistics of Income: U.S. Business Tax Returns. Internal Revenue Service. Summarizes financial and economic data for proprietorships, partnerships, and small business corporations.

Survey of Current Business. Department of Commerce. Facts on industrial and business activity in the United States and statistical summary of national income and product accounts. A weekly supplement provides an up to date summary of business.

FINANCIAL INFORMATION SOURCES

Blue Line Investment Survey. Quarterly ratings and reports on 1,000 stocks; analysis of 60 industries and special situations analysis (monthly); supplements on new developments and editorials on conditions affecting price trends.

Commercial and Financial Chronicle. Variety of articles and news reports on business, government, and finance. Monday's issue lists new securities, dividends, and called bonds. Thursday's issue is devoted to business articles.

Dun's Review. Dun & Bradstreet. This monthly includes very useful annual financial ratios for about 125 lines of business.

Fairchild's Financial Manual of Retail Stores. Information about officers and directors, products, subsidiaries, sales, and earnings for apparel stores, mail order firms, variety chains, and supermarkets.

Federal Reserve Bulletin. Board of Governors of the Federal Reserve System. The "Financial and Business Statistics" section of each issue of this monthly bulletin is the best single source for current U.S. banking and monetary statistics.

Financial World. Articles on business activities of interest to investors, including investment opportunities and pertinent data on firms, such as earnings and dividend records.

Moody's Bank and Finance Manual; Moody's Industrial Manual; Moody's Municipal & Government Manual; Moody's Public Utility Manual; Moody's Transportation Manual; Moody's Directors Service. Brief histories of companies and their operations, subsidiaries, officers and directors, products, and balance sheet and income statements over several years.

Moody's Bond Survey. Moody's Investors Service. Weekly data on stocks and bonds, including recommendations for purchases or sale and discussions of industry trends and developments.

Moody's Handbook of Widely Held Common Stocks. Moody's Investors Service. Weekly data on stocks and bonds, including recommendations for purchases or sale and discussions of industry trends and developments.

Security Owner's Stock Guide. Standard & Poor's Corp. Standard & Poor's rating, stock price range, and other helpful information for about 4,200 common and preferred stocks.

Security Price Index. Standard & Poor's Corp. Price indexes, bond prices, sales, yields, Dow Jones averages, etc.

Standard Corporation Records. Standard & Poor's Corp. Published in looseleaf form, offers information similar to Moody's manuals. Use of this extensive service facilitates buying securities for both the individual and the institutional investor.

MARKETING INFORMATION SOURCES [2]

Advertising Age. This important advertising weekly publishes a number of annual surveys or features of special interest related to U.S. national advertising statistics.

Audits and Surveys National Total-Market Index. Contains information on various

---

[2] Based in part on Gilbert A. Churchill, Jr., *Marketing Research: Methodological Foundations* (Hinsdale, Ill.: Dryden Press, 1987), pp. 188–201.

SELECTED SOURCES OF SECONDARY INFORMATION

product types including total market size, brand market shares, retail inventory, distribution coverage, and out of stock.

Commercial Atlas and Marketing Guide. Skokie, Ill.: Rand-McNally & Co. Statistics on population, principal cities, business centers, trading areas, sales and manufacturing units, transportation data, and so forth.

Current Sources of Marketing Information. Gunther, Edgar, and F. A. Goldstein. This is a bibliography of primary marketing. Subjects include basic sources of information, the national market, regional data on the economy, and advertising and promotion.

Dun & Bradstreet Market Identifiers. Relevant marketing information on over 4.3 million establishments for constructing sales prospect files, sales territories, and sales territory potentials and isolating potential new customers with particular characteristics.

Editor and Publisher "Market Guide." Market information for 1,500 American and Canadian cities. Data include population, household, gas meters, climate, retailing, and newspaper information.

Guide to Consumer Markets. New York: The Conference Board. This useful annual compilation of U.S. statistics on the consumer marketplace covers population, employment, income, expenditures, production, and prices.

Industrial Marketing. "Guide to Special Issues." This directory is included in each issue. Publications are listed within primary market classifications and are listed for up to three months prior to advertising closing date.

Marketing Communications (January 1968 to January 1972, formerly *Printer's Ink*, 1914–1967). Pertinent market information on regional and local consumer markets as well as international markets to January 1972.

Marketing Information Guide. Washington D.C.: Department of Commerce. Annotations of selected current publications and reports, with basic information and statistics on marketing and distribution.

National Purchase Diary Panel (NPD). Monthly purchase information based on the largest panel diary in the United States with detailed brand, frequency of purchase, characteristics of heavy buyers, and other market data.

Nielson Retail Index. Contains basic product turnover data, retail prices, store displays, promotional activity, and local advertising based on a national sample of supermarkets, drugstores, and mass merchandisers.

Nielson Television Index. Well-known index which provides estimates of the size and nature of the audience for individual television programs.

Population and Its Distribution: The United States Markets. J. Walter Thompson Co. New York: McGraw-Hill Book Co. A handbook of marketing facts selected from the U.S. *Census of Population* and the most recent census data on retail trade.

Sales and Marketing Management. (Formerly *Sales Management,* to October 1975.) This valuable semimonthly journal includes four useful annual statistical issues: *Survey of Buying Power* (July); *Survey of Buying Power, Part II* (October); *Survey of Industrial Purchasing Power* (April); *Survey of Selling Costs* (January). These are excellent references for buying income, buying power index, cash income, merchandise line, manufacturing line, and retail sales.

Selling Areas Marketing Inc. Reports on warehouse withdrawals of various food products in each of 42 major markets covering 80 percent of national food sales.

Simmons Media/Marketing Service. Provides cross referencing of product usage and media exposure for magazine, television, newspaper, and radio based on a strict national probability sample.

Standard Rate and Data. Nine volumes on major media which include a variety of information in addition to prices for media in selected markets.

Starch Advertising Readership Service. Measures the reading of advertisements in magazines and newspapers and provides information on overall readership percentages, readers per dollar, and rank when grouped by product category.

INDEXES AND ABSTRACTS

Accountants Digest. L. L. Briggs. A digest of articles appearing currently in accounting periodicals.

Accountants Index. American Institute of Certified Public Accountants. An index to books, pamphlets, and articles on accounting and finance.

Accounting Articles. Commerce Clearing House. Loose-leaf index to articles in accounting and business periodicals.

Advertising Age Editorial Index. Crain Communications, Inc. Index to articles in *Advertising Age.*

American Statistical Index. Congressional Information Service. A comprehensive two-part annual index to the statistical publications of the U.S. government.

Applied Science & Technology Index. H. W. Wilson Co. Reviews over 200 periodicals relevant to the applied sciences, many of which pertain to business.

Battelle Library Review. (Formerly *Battelle Technical Review* to 1962.) Battelle Memorial Institute. Annotated bibliography of books, reports, and articles on automation and automatic processes.

Bulletin of Public Affairs Information Service. Public Affairs Information Service, Inc. (Since 1915—annual index.) A selective list of the latest books, pamphlets, government publications, reports of public and private agencies, and periodicals related to economic conditions, public administration, and international relations.

Business Education Index. McGraw-Hill Book Co. (Since 1940—annual index.) Annual author and subject index of books, articles, and theses on business education.

Business Periodicals Index. H. W. Wilson Co. A subject index to the disciplines of accounting, advertising, banking, general business, insurance, labor, management, and marketing.

Catalog of United States Census Publication. Washington, D.C.: Dept. of Commerce, Bureau of Census. Indexes all available at Census Bureau Data. Main divisions are agriculture, business, construction, foreign trade, government, guide to locating U.S. census information.

Computer and Information Systems. (Formerly *Information Processing Journal* to 1969.) Cambridge Communications Corporation.

Cumulative Index of NICB Publications. The National Industrial Conferences Board. Annual index of NICB books, pamphlets, and articles in the area of management of personnel.

Funk and Scott Index International. Investment Index Company. Indexes articles on foreign companies and industries from over 1,000 foreign and domestic periodicals and documents.

Guide to U.S. Government Publications. McLean, Va., Documents Index. Annotated guide to publications of various U.S. government agencies.

International Abstracts in Operations Research. Operations Research Society of America.

International Journal of Abstracts of Statistical Methods in Industry. The Hague, Netherlands: International Statistical Institute.

Management Information Guides. Gale Research Company. Bibliographical references to information sources for various business subjects.

SELECTED SOURCES OF SECONDARY INFORMATION

Management Review.   American Management Association.

Monthly Catalog of U.S. Government Publications.   U.S. Government Printing Office. Continuing list of federal government publications.

Monthly Checklist of State Publications.   U.S. Library of Congress, Exchange and Gift Division. Record of state documents received by Library of Congress.

New York Times Index.   New York. Very detailed index of all articles in the *Times,* arranged alphabetically with many cross-references.

Psychological Abstracts.   American Psychological Association.

Public Affairs Information Service.   Public Affairs Information Service, Inc. A selective subject list of books, pamphlets, and government publications covering business, banking, and economics as well as subjects in the area of public affairs.

Reader's Guide to Periodical Literature.   H. W. Wilson Co. Index by author and subject to selected U.S. general and nontechnical periodicals.

Sociological Abstracts.   American Sociological Association.

The Wall Street Journal Index.   Dow Jones & Company, Inc. An index of all articles in *The WSJ* grouped in two sections: corporate news and general news.